# IF IT'S BROKE, FIX IT!

## DAN AND JUDY RAMSEY

*Founders of the Fix-It Club (www.FixItClub.com)*

A me                          Inc.

*To Heather, Aaron, Ashley, Rachelle, and Skylar, who bring great joy to us.*

**Publisher:** *Marie Butler-Knight*
**Product Manager:** *Phil Kitchel*
**Senior Managing Editor:** *Jennifer Chisholm*
**Senior Acquisitions Editor:** *Mike Sanders*
**Development Editor:** *Lynn Northrup*
**Production Editors:** *Billy Fields, Virginia Vasques*
**Copy Editor:** *Susan Aufheimer*
**Cover Designer:** *Doug Wilkins*
**Book Designer:** *Trina Wurst*
**Creative Director:** *Robin Lasek*
**Indexer:** *Tonya Heard*
**Layout/Proofreading:** *John Etchison, Becky Harmon, Trina Wurst*

# Contents

# Foreword

It's been my pleasure for 25 years to help America build and remodel its homes. My first TV show, *This Old House*, premiered in 1979 and I now host *Bob Vila's Home Again*. In addition, my work with Craftsman Tools, charities, and other opportunities keeps me very busy. So I don't always have the time to fix household things that break.

Yet, as a homeowner I know that even in the best-built homes things can go wrong and need fixing. Besides structural systems there are all those appliances and other household gadgets that quit working and get set aside until I have the time to fix them. Maybe the device only needs a new electrical cord or a simple switch. Maybe it needs a washer or some glue. I'll get to it one of these days.

So it's great to have Dan and Judy Ramsey's latest book, *If It's Broke, Fix It!*, in my home library. It's really easy to use! The Fix Everything Chart shows me exactly where to look for illustrated instructions to fix everything from an air conditioner to a yard trimmer and more than 500 common household things in between. This is the fix-it book *you* should have in your home library!

How can one book show you how to fix *everything?* It's all in the process. Just like there is a process for construction whether it is a house or a hotel, there is a process for finding out what's wrong with a broken household item and determining how best to fix it. It's called the Fix-It Process and Dan and Judy clearly know how it's done. The key is in knowing how the thing is *supposed* to work. That makes it much easier to find the problem. Then by the process of elimination you can quickly trace down the cause of the problem. A simple test or two and you're ready to fix it.

This book not only shows you how to fix *everything*, it also shows you how to fix specific things including common components like cords, fuses, and controls. For example, turn to the Fix-It Guide on *Faucet* and you'll see how it works; what typically can go wrong; how to quickly identify the problem; what parts, tools, and materials you'll need; then specific steps to making the most common repairs. Best of all, the Fix-It Guides are illustrated with photos and drawings to help you see what you're getting into.

What if there's just no way of fixing it? Dan and Judy show you how to recycle it! Maybe it can be reused by a charity to help others. Or maybe it can be turned into something else, reducing the cost to our environment. By fixing or recycling, you'll be doing your part to keep things out of the landfill. You'll also learn about warranties and how to get things fixed for free!

I hope you'll also visit Dan and Judy's excellent website, www.FixItClub.com, to get even more information on fixing things in your home. Learn the latest tips and tricks, find additional resources, and talk with experts who know how to get the job done right.

Bob Vila
Host of *Bob Vila's Home Again*
Author of *Bob Vila's Complete Guide to Remodeling Your Home*
Online at www.BobVila.com

# Introduction

Somewhere in your life there's probably a collection of things that are broken. It may be a list, box, pile, shelf, drawer, room, shed, or garage filled with gadgets, appliances, furniture, games, cameras, clocks, phones, TVs, toys, bikes, computers, and dozens of other things you'll get around to fixing—or tossing—someday.

Unfortunately, many things today are made to be replaced rather than repaired; it's often not cost effective to hire someone to fix them for you. Replacements are relatively cheap, so why not just toss it and get a new one?

Many reasons. First, the majority of household repairs are easy to do, taking just a few minutes—once you know how. Second, by extending its life, you are saving the environmental cost of making, shipping, and eventually dumping the device—not to mention the financial cost of buying a new one. Third, some things have sentimental value and cannot easily be replaced. Finally, learning to fix things can actually be fun, earning you bragging rights. "Yeah, I fixed it myself!" You've become the newest member of the Fix-It Club!

How can you fix it yourself? Figuring out what's wrong with something is *the most important step* to fixing it, followed by finding the right parts. Disassembly, installation of the new parts, and reassembly are relatively easy. Fortunately, it's the same process whether you're fixing a leaky faucet, a convection oven, a closet door, or a lawnmower. It's the Fix-It Process.

This book shows you how to determine quickly whether a specific household item in your life should be fixed, recycled, or tossed—and how to do it. It shows you how to repair, rebuild, adjust, recondition, restore, mend, fix, and maintain all the *things* in your life that make life easier. You'll also find out how to reuse or recycle *everything*. You'll learn how to make tossing things the *last* resort, not the *first*. You'll learn how to make sure everything you own has a long, productive life. And, because 50 to 75 percent of the cost of any repair by an expert is the cost of labor, you can put that money back in your pocket (along with the money you saved by not replacing the item) by fixing things yourself. You'll also save the cost of taking things to the dump. It's win-win!

Just as important, you'll find fixing things can actually be *fun*. Really! In a world of unsolvable problems, repairing something is an easy fix that offers the satisfaction of accomplishment. After working all week trying to solve problems that defy resolution, you can find enjoyment in fixing things in your spare time. You'll discover—or rediscover—some fascinating facts about physics, chemistry, electricity, and other laws of life. And you'll regain storage space previously occupied by broken things.

If it's broken, let's fix it!

## Finding Broken Stuff in Your Life

Why do things break so easily? Most things are built to sell at a competitive price while offering the retailer a specified profit. They're not built to last; they're built to be replaced in a couple of years. And they're designed for quick manufacturing, not easy repair. In fact, some gadgets are sealed against entry; you can't even get into them without breaking them! Fortunately, most things are repairable if you know how.

So what *should* you attempt to fix yourself? You're probably *not* going to disassemble and repair a microwave's magnetron! But you *can* replace the cord, fuse, or maybe the thermal cutout once you know how. You also can fix that broken door latch. You probably won't attempt to rebuild the lawnmower's engine, but you can replace the broken throttle, replace the blade, and do some maintenance to keep it from breaking. This book will show you how all these and hundreds of other things work, how to troubleshoot them, and how to tackle repairs to your level of comfort. Most important, it will encourage you to *extend* your level of repair comfort. There's nothing stopping you from advanced repairs except experience—which you'll develop from using this book.

You may not think you need to go *looking* for broken stuff, but you do. Besides the obviously broken (chipped dinnerware, the toaster that went on the fritz this morning), there are other broken things around you that need your attention. There's the broken-and-forlorn, such as the TV that quit one day and was relegated to the garage, or the necklace you put away after the clasp broke. And the biggest group of all is the about-to-break. It includes the faucet that's beginning to leak and the floor tile that's starting to lift at the corner. They're technically not broken *yet*, but will soon be added to your list of broken stuff. The repair will be easier, and you'll avoid additional damage, if you diagnose and repair now rather than later.

The first step to efficiently fixing things is figuring out what's broken or about to break. We strongly recommend that you start a notebook (a small spiral-bound notebook is about a buck at your favorite store). Take a look around your home and start a list of broken or about-to-break things. If you're really organized, describe the problem and list what parts you'll need. For your convenience, there's a *Fix-It Club Notebook* at the end of this book that you can write in or copy. It includes examples to get you thinking about fixing things. You also can cross-reference your list to pages in this book that offer step-by-step repair instructions.

## Using This Book

*If It's Broke, Fix It!* shows you how to use the Fix-It Process to repair everything in your household. The first section, **Fix Everything!,** covers proven fix-it methods and includes a comprehensive chart of more than 500 household items, cross-referenced to specific Fix-It Guides. The **Fix-It Guides** then offer clear, illustrated instructions for repairing common household items. They include hundreds of Fix-It Tips, Cautions, and other bits of information. The third section, **Fix-It Resources**, shows you where to get parts and additional help. Finally, there's the **Fix-It Club Notebook** that you can use or copy to help you get the most from your time and energy fixing things yourself.

Note that we have numerous cross-references to specific *Fix-It Guides* in this book. You'll see them identified in *italics* such as *Appliance Controls; Faucet;* and *Lawn Mower, Riding.* (We've grouped all three *Lawn Mower* Guides together and let you choose between *Reel, Riding,* and *Rotary.*)

There's one more resource. Please accept our personal invitation to be our guest at the next online meeting of our **Fix-It Club.** There are no dues and you'll find loads of supplementary information, tips, and resources at the Fix-It Club website (www.FixItClub.com). Visit us soon and say "I fixed it myself!"

—Dan and Judy Ramsey, founders of the Fix-It Club™

## Acknowledgments

This extensive book is the work of the authors, Dan and Judy Ramsey. However, we can't take all the credit. Many other people have served as resources as we developed and wrote this book. They include many of the resources listed in the *Fix-It Resources* as well as experts and visitors at our online resource, the Fix-It Club. Thanks for sharing your knowledge with our readers.

Thanks to Don Buchanan and the able staff at Coast Hardware of Willits, California, for their assistance and advice.

A special "thank you" goes to Heather Luedemann, who worked many hours helping us develop the extensive *Fix-It Resources* section of this book. She also helped develop the useful *Fix Everything Chart.* She has contributed to many of our book projects for more than 15 years. Thanks so much!

Thanks to Sheree Bykofsky for the idea of a new and more comprehensive book on fixing things, and for her efforts to make it a reality.

Once again, thanks to Mike Sanders, who saw the need for this project; as well as to Lynn Northrup, Susan Aufheimer, and Billy Fields, whose skills and attention to detail enhance this book.

Thanks also to our hero, Bob Vila, who graciously wrote this book's foreword. We are honored to have his participation and we invite readers to visit him online at www.BobVila.com, a house-full of useful DIY information and resources.

Most of all, we thank you, our readers, for supporting our efforts to share information that can enhance your life.

# Fix Everything!

What's *wrong* with it? That's the first big question in fixing broken things—*any* broken things! It doesn't matter whether it's a door chime, a barbecue grill, a child's toy, or a computer printer. Figuring out what's wrong with it is the most important task. Once you know what's wrong with it, you're well on the way to fixing it—or making an informed decision not to. Figuring out what's wrong with something may sound obvious, but it's often the step that keeps folks from fixing things easily.

Troubleshooting is a problem-solving process with the goal of returning an item to its as-designed state. The item doesn't work at all, doesn't work correctly, doesn't work efficiently, or doesn't stop working. But you can fix *anything* if you know how to troubleshoot it. And you can troubleshoot if you understand how an item works and how to figure out why it doesn't work. Here's the process:

- What does this thing *do?*
- How is it *supposed* to work?
- What *isn't* this thing doing that it *should* do?
- What's the possible cause(s) of the problem?
- What parts and tools will I need to fix it?
- What are the steps to fixing it?
- Once fixed, does it now work?

For example, a coffee maker, obviously, is an apparatus for brewing coffee. There are two types of coffee makers: drip and percolator. A drip coffee maker is designed to heat water, then pump it to drip through the coffee basket and into a carafe. Most drip coffee makers also keep the carafe of coffee warm. That's a drip coffee maker's as-designed state; that's what it's *supposed* to do.

What does it *not* do? In our example, the drip coffee maker doesn't keep the coffee hot, though everything else works. Knowing how a coffee maker is supposed to work, you will identify the problem to be within the warming element or controls. To check it, you need a multimeter (see "Multimeter" later in this section) for testing these components. Then, following the specific steps in the *Coffee Maker* guide, you disassemble, test, and, if needed, replace the part. Finally, you can brew yourself some coffee and know that it will stay warm. (Be sure to check out the *Fix-Everything Chart* of over 500 household things, cross-referenced to specific *Fix-It Guides*, found at the end of this section.)

## The Fix-It Process

So that's the Fix-It Process. You'll see it applied to hundreds of consumer items throughout this book. And you can apply it to thousands more—everything that's broken. That's because the Fix-It Process works for everything. It's a simplified version of a time-tested problem-solving system. If it's fixable, you can do it!

So let's take a look at some of the things that you can restore to working condition using the Fix-It Process. They include stationary, mechanical, electrical, and hybrid things. Every thing in your household falls into these categories.

## Stationary Things

Stationary things, of course, don't move, and include clothing, jewelry, furniture, walls, flooring, cabinets, fences, and a lot more. Even doors and windows are considered stationary; although they do open and close, you can't move them to another room. These are things that don't move on their own; they're stationary. You can move furniture or wear clothing, but part of their job description is to stay where they are put. In fact, if a stationary thing *doesn't* stay put, it's probably broken.

Troubleshooting stationary things is relatively easy because it can be done visually in most cases. You can see that the necklace clasp is broken, the cabinet drawer is stuck, the wall has a hole in it, or the fence is leaning.

Fixing stationary things, too, can be easy. In most cases the solution is to reattach something. The cabinet drawer may need the glide or a screw reattached or replaced. A shirt with a button missing simply needs a button reattached. A broken dish needs the broken part reattached. Most stationary things can be fixed with fasteners, either mechanical fasteners such as bolts and screws or chemical fasteners like adhesives.

## Mechanical Fasteners

There is a wide variety of mechanical fasteners available for do-it-yourself repair including nails, screws, bolts, and anchors. Your home has hundreds of fasteners in it, holding walls together, binding appliance components, keeping the floor from moving underfoot, and even fastening sleeves on to clothing. There is a wide variety of fasteners but they all have a single function—to hold two or more things together. When they don't, something's broken.

Fasteners include nails, screws, bolts, nuts, adhesives, and thread. Adhesives, such as glues, are chemicals that attach the surfaces of two or more components. Fasteners are easy to use and will help you fix hundreds of things around your home, so let's take a closer look at them.

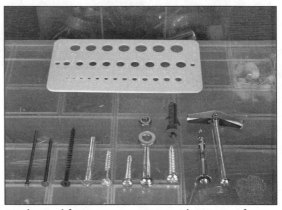

Mechanical fasteners come in a wide variety of shapes, sizes, and purposes.

*Nails* are thin, pointed, metal fasteners driven with a hammer to join two pieces of wood. There are dozens of varieties of nails, depending on the specific purpose. There are special nails for masonry, roofing, finishing, and other common applications. Nails are classified by the size of the shank and the shape of the head. Articles in this book will refer to specific types of nails needed. The most common type is called *common*, with large, flat heads for secure fastening. Next is *finish* nails with smaller heads that aren't so obvious if flush to or below the wood's surface. Nails are sized by length, indicated by a *d* or "penny." A 4d nail is 1½ inches long; an 8d nail is 2½ inches long.

*Screws* are pointed-tip, threaded fasteners installed with a screwdriver. The type of screwdriver used depends on the type of screw head: Round- and pan (flat)-head screws require a straight-tip screwdriver, Phillips-head screws require a Phillips screwdriver, and square-head screws require a square-drive screwdriver. Wood screws fasten wood, and sheet-metal screws fasten metal. Screws are sized by length. Screws are stronger than nails and easier to remove.

**COMMON WIRE NAILS**

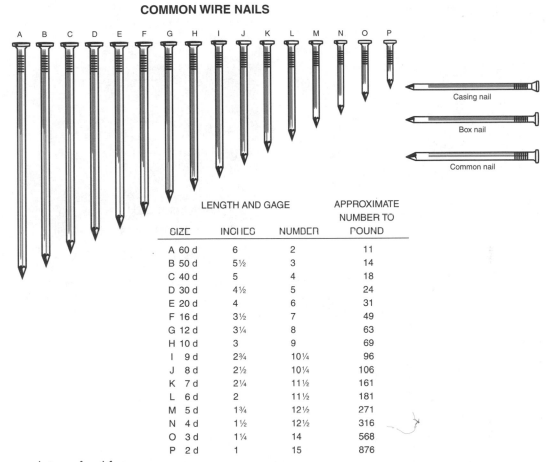

| SIZE | LENGTH AND GAGE | | APPROXIMATE NUMBER TO POUND |
|---|---|---|---|
| | INCHES | NUMBER | |
| A 60 d | 6 | 2 | 11 |
| B 50 d | 5½ | 3 | 14 |
| C 40 d | 5 | 4 | 18 |
| D 30 d | 4½ | 5 | 24 |
| E 20 d | 4 | 6 | 31 |
| F 16 d | 3½ | 7 | 49 |
| G 12 d | 3¼ | 8 | 63 |
| H 10 d | 3 | 9 | 69 |
| I  9 d | 2¾ | 10¼ | 96 |
| J  8 d | 2½ | 10¼ | 106 |
| K  7 d | 2¼ | 11½ | 161 |
| L  6 d | 2 | 11½ | 181 |
| M  5 d | 1¾ | 12½ | 271 |
| N  4 d | 1½ | 12½ | 316 |
| O  3 d | 1¼ | 14 | 568 |
| P  2 d | 1 | 15 | 876 |

Types and sizes of nail fasteners.

*Bolts* are flat-tipped, threaded fasteners that use a threaded nut to attach wood or metal together. A washer may be placed under the bolt head or the nut for a firmer fasten. Bolts are classified by the type of head. Stove bolts and machine screws (actually bolts) are turned with a screwdriver. Hexagon- and square-head bolts are held in place with a wrench while the nut is turned to tighten. A carriage bolt's head imbeds itself into the wood when the nut is turned. Bolts are sized by length and thread. Bolts are stronger than screws.

There are other handy fasteners. A *lag bolt* is a bolt head with a screw body. An *anchor* is an addition to a bolt or screw that helps anchor the fastener in a hollow wall or door.

*Thread* is a fastener for clothing and upholstered furniture. Thread is a long strand of fabric installed with a needle, either by hand or by a sewing machine. Thread is sold by fabric (cotton, nylon, polyester, etc.) and thickness (Tex or T). Cotton-wrap polyester is used for jeans, and poly-wrap polyester for a wide variety of clothing. T-18 thread is lightweight and T-50 is mediumweight. Thread needles are rated by the eye size, shaft length, and purpose.

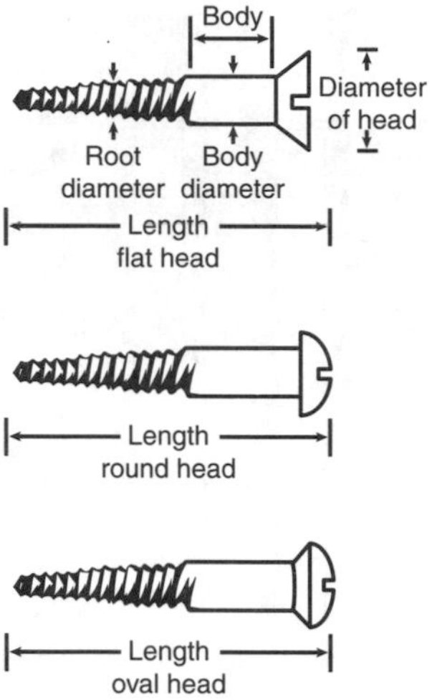


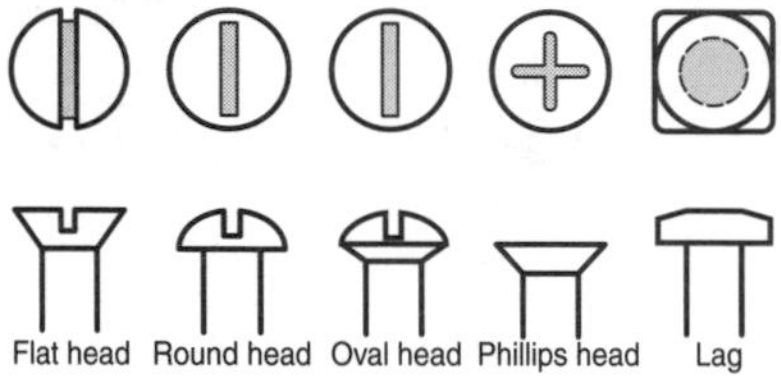


| Length (in.) | Size numbers | | | | | | | | | | | | | | | | | | | | | |
|---|---|---|---|---|---|---|---|---|---|---|---|---|---|---|---|---|---|---|---|---|---|---|
| | 0 | 1 | 2 | 3 | 4 | 5 | 6 | 7 | 8 | 9 | 10 | 11 | 12 | 13 | 14 | 15 | 16 | 17 | 18 | 20 | 22 | 24 |
| ¼ | x | x | x | x | | | | | | | | | | | | | | | | | | |
| ⅜ | x | x | x | x | x | x | x | x | x | x | | | | | | | | | | | | |
| ½ | | x | x | x | x | x | x | x | x | x | x | x | x | | | | | | | | | |
| ⅝ | | x | x | x | x | x | x | x | x | x | x | x | x | | x | | | | | | | |
| ¾ | | | x | x | x | x | x | x | x | x | x | x | x | | x | | x | | | | | |
| ⅞ | | | x | x | x | x | x | x | x | x | x | x | x | | x | | x | | | | | |
| 1 | | | | x | x | x | x | x | x | x | x | x | x | | x | | x | | x | x | | |
| 1¼ | | | | | x | x | x | x | x | x | x | x | x | | x | | x | | x | x | | x |
| 1½ | | | | | x | x | x | x | x | x | x | x | x | | x | | x | | x | x | | x |
| 1¾ | | | | | | x | x | x | x | x | x | x | x | | x | | x | | x | x | | x |
| 2 | | | | | | x | x | x | x | x | x | x | x | | x | | x | | x | x | | x |
| 2¼ | | | | | | x | x | x | x | x | x | x | x | | x | | x | | x | x | | x |
| 2½ | | | | | | x | x | x | x | x | x | x | x | | x | | x | | x | x | | x |
| 2¾ | | | | | | | x | x | x | x | x | x | x | | x | | x | | x | x | | x |
| 3 | | | | | | | x | x | x | x | x | x | x | | x | | x | | x | x | | x |
| 3½ | | | | | | | | | x | x | x | x | x | | x | | x | | x | x | | x |
| 4 | | | | | | | | | x | x | x | x | x | | x | | x | | x | x | | x |
| 4½ | | | | | | | | | | | | | x | | x | | x | | x | x | | x |
| 5 | | | | | | | | | | | | | x | | x | | x | | x | x | | x |
| 6 | | | | | | | | | | | | | | | x | | x | | x | x | | x |
| Threads per inch | 32 | 28 | 26 | 24 | 22 | 20 | 18 | 16 | 15 | 14 | 13 | 12 | 11 | | 10 | | 9 | | 8 | 8 | | 7 |
| Diameter of screw (in.) | .060 | .073 | .086 | .099 | .112 | .125 | .138 | .151 | .164 | .177 | .190 | .203 | .216 | | .242 | | .268 | | .294 | .320 | | .372 |

Types and sizes of screw fasteners.

bonding method. For example, cyanoacrylate (instant glue) is preferred for permanently bonding rigid plastic parts that don't face temperatures over 150 degrees. Some adhesives are waterproof while others are not; some need to be held together (clamped) while drying, and others don't. Read the instructions on the label for the appropriate application and use. You'll also see adhesives used in *Fix-It Guides*.

Common adhesive fasteners.

## Adhesives

Adhesives secure the surfaces of two materials together. There are many types of adhesives, most of them designed for use with specific materials and under specified conditions. Adhesives come in liquid, solid, or powder form, and some require a catalyst to activate them. Select adhesives based on their characteristics, strength, setting time and temperature, and

| Type | Use | Applicator | Strength | Set Time | Cure Time | Flex | Water-Resistance |
|---|---|---|---|---|---|---|---|
| Acrylic | Metal, glass, wood | Included (two-part) | Excellent | 5-10 minutes | 12-24 hours | None | Excellent |
| Contact | Plastic laminate, wood veneer | Brush, trowel, roller | Good | Short | 24-48 hours | Soft | Excellent |
| Cyanoacrylates (instant glue, super glue) | Plastic, rubber, metal, ceramic, glass, hardwood | Squeeze tube | Excellent | 1-4 minutes | 12-24 hours | None | Excellent |
| Epoxy | Any materials | Brush or wood stick | Excellent | 5-30 minutes | 1-12 hours | Medium to hard | Excellent |
| Hot melt | Fabric, leather, wood | Glue gun | Excellent | Contact | 5-10 minutes | Medium | Good |
| Latex glue | Fabric, carpet, paper | Brush or roller | Fair | Contact | 4-48 hours | Soft | Fair |
| Latex mastic (construction adhesive) | Floor and ceiling tiles, paneling | Trowel or caulk gun | Good | Contact | 1-4 days | Medium to hard | Good |
| Paste | Wallpaper, thin paper | Brush | Good | 30 minutes | 4-24 hours | Soft | Poor |
| Plastic | Wood, ceramic, glass, plastic, pottery | Brush | Fair | 5 minutes to 8 hours | 1-3 days | Medium to hard | Good |
| Polyvinyl resin | Wood, plywood, chipboard, paper | Brush or wood stick | Good | 1-4 hours | 24-36 hours | Medium | Poor |
| Resorcinol | Wood, plywood, hardboard, chipboard, paper | Brush or wood stick | Excellent | 4-12 hours | 24-36 hours | Firm | Excellent |
| Rosin mastic | Ceramic, plastic, wood | Trowel or caulk gun | Good | Contact | 1-4 days | Soft | Good |
| Rubber (styrene butadiene) | Wood, concrete, plastic, paper | Brush or spreader | Good | Contact | 24-72 hours | Soft | Good |
| Urea formaldehyde | Wood | Brush | Very Good | 15-30 minutes | 8-24 hours | Medium | Good |
| Urethane | Wood, metal, glass | Tube or caulk gun | Excellent | 15-30 minutes | 1-3 days | Soft | Excellent |
| White (PVA: polyvinyl acetate) | Wood, ceramics, paper | Brush | Good | 5-10 minutes | 8-12 hours | Medium | Fair |
| Yellow (aliphatic resin, carpenter) | Wood (indoors) | Brush | Very Good | 5-10 minutes | 1 hour | Medium | Fair |

**Adhesives Table**

Properties of popular household adhesives.

# Mechanical Things

Mechanical things *are* supposed to move. That's what they do. For example, a windup alarm clock is a mechanical thing. Other mechanical things include toys, tools, cars, zippers, etc. What do they all have in common? They technically are *machines*. That is, they convert one form of energy into another. A hand tool, for example, converts your energy into strength to turn a bolt or cut a board.

Troubleshooting mechanical things is a little more difficult than troubleshooting stationary things because you may have to take something apart. However, if you know what your broken item is *supposed* to do, you probably can figure out what needs fixing. For example, a windup alarm clock may run very slowly, not keeping the correct time—and making you late for work. Rather than toss it and get another one, carefully open it up and see if there's anything (a loose screw or dust) keeping a mechanism from turning as designed. Or the item just may need a small amount of lubricant to reduce resistance between moving parts.

## Lubricants

Lubricants decrease friction between moving parts, and are a vital part of fixing things. Many lubricants are petroleum-based. Thin lubricants are called *oils* and thicker lubricants are *greases*. Here are the most popular household lubricants and what they work best on:

- Machine or penetrating oil (such as WD-40) is a general lubricant for small moving parts.
- Silicon spray is a multipurpose product that lubricates, waterproofs, and reduces corrosion.

- Graphite powder or spray is a fine powder lubricant (sometimes in a base of light oil) for lubricating locks, bearings, and other very small parts.
- Penetrating oil lubricates as well as reduces and cleans corrosion from metal parts.
- Lithium grease is a petroleum-based grease with lithium powder in it to enhance lubrication of larger moving parts such as automotive gears.
- Silicone is an organic compound that is highly resistant to wear, heat, and water; it makes a great lubricant.

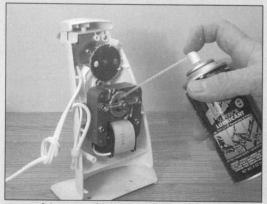

A careful spray of lubricant can extend the life of a small motor. Lubricate moving parts only—*never* electrical parts.

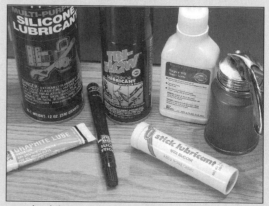

Popular lubricants.

# Electrical Things

Electrical things are devices that convert electricity into another form of energy. These include large and small appliances, computers, telephones, lighting, and a lot more. Electrical things convert electrical energy into movement, heat, cold, light, sound, images, and many other useful services.

Troubleshooting electrical things is surprisingly easy. Once you understand the device's as-designed state, you can define the problem and start looking for a solution. For example, a cord either delivers electricity to the device or it doesn't. An electrical switch is on, off, or in variable switches, at some value in between. A heating element either heats or it doesn't. By thinking of electrical devices as components that have specific jobs—pass electricity, stop electricity, produce heat, turn a blade, etc.— you can more easily figure out what's wrong and what to do about it.

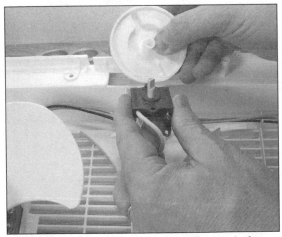

This variable-speed switch controls the speed of a fan. You can easily test and replace it.

Fortunately, there's a device that can help you test most electrical things. It's called a voltmeter, a volt-ohmmeter, a VOM, or a multimeter (because it takes more than one electrical measurement); they're all the same thing. A *multimeter* measures the amount of power (voltage) being applied, electricity (current) being used, and how much resistance it needs to overcome to do the job. Power is measured in volts (V), current is counted in amperes or amps (A), and resistance is calculated in ohms (Ω).

There's one more electrical term you've probably heard. Defining it will come in handy as you fix electrical devices. A *watt* is the amount of *power* consumed by an electrical device when it is running. A 750-watt toaster, for example, uses 750W (watts) of power when toasting your wheat, rye, sourdough, or other bread in the morning.

> **Fix-It Tip**
>
> If you don't know the wattage rating of an electrical appliance but you do know the amperage (current), multiply it by the voltage. The formula is: V × A = W. Since all plug-in appliances in your home are either 240V (electric stove or clothes dryer) or 120V (everything else), it's easy to figure wattage. A toaster that is rated at 7.75A (indicated by a label or plate on the toaster's bottom) uses 930W of electrical power (120 × 7.75 = 930).

Why is this all so important to troubleshooting electrical things? By checking the as-designed state against the actual state, you can determine whether something is working properly—and have the first clue toward fixing it. For example, if a switch is supposed to be *on* (little or no resistance to the flow of electrical current), but in checking the switch you find the resistance to be infinite (no electricity is passing through it), it's easy to decide that the switch is faulty. Remember: Know what it's supposed to do, then figure out what it's actually doing to decide whether it's working as designed. It's a simple rule that makes troubleshooting *any* electrical device easy.

### Electrical Cleaners

In many cases, electrical appliance and electronic gadgets need only a good cleaning to bring them back to life. Here are a couple of popular cleaners:

- Contact cleaners are special cleaners that dry on contact, and are used for fixing numerous electrical devices.

Electrical contact cleaner is useful for cleaning components in small and large appliances, following the manufacturer's recommendations.

- Canned (compressed) air is a useful cleaner for blowing off dust particles from electronics. Don't use high-pressure air from an air compressor on delicate parts.

Here's something else you should know about electrical devices: There are only a few types, making troubleshooting relatively easy. Small appliances, for example, either heat something, move something, or both. A toaster heats something (bread). A fan moves something (a blade). A hair dryer does both (heats and moves air). A refrigerator uses a motor to move coolant. Even computers and other sophisticated electrical devices have relatively simple functions. They pass, store, or display data.

## Continuity Tester

Electricity needs a continuous path or circuit in order to flow. It's like a two-lane road from point A to point B and back. If one or both lanes are blocked, traffic—in this case, electricity—stops. A *continuity tester* is useful for checking cords and wires to make sure they can conduct electricity.

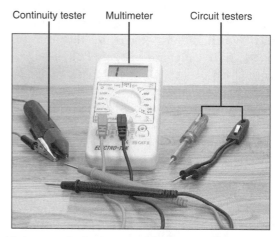

Various continuity testers, multimeters, and circuit testers are available at hardware and electrical parts stores.

A continuity tester can tell you whether electricity can flow through a cord.

To test for continuity, follow these steps:

1. Disconnect the cord from the power source (electrical receptacle). Make sure any switches on the device are turned on.

2. Attach the alligator clip to one prong of the cord.
3. Touch the tip of the continuity tester to the other prong. If there is continuity, the tester will light up. If not, it won't.

Here's how it works: The continuity tester sends electricity from an internal battery through one cord prong and down the wires. If the light gets electrical current from the other prong, it lights up, meaning that the path is good. Otherwise, something is stopping it. You can remove the cord from the appliance and test each of the two wires separately to see which one doesn't work. If both work, the short is in the appliance itself. You can buy a continuity tester for less than $5.

## Multimeter

A multimeter (also called a volt-ohmmeter or VOM) is another way of testing continuity. It also can measure the amount of alternating current (AC or household current) or direct current (DC or battery current) in a plugged-in or *live* circuit. It can check voltage, too. For example, a multimeter can verify that there are about 120 volts in an AC circuit or that a 9-volt battery is fully charged. In addition, a multimeter can check resistance. A continuity tester checks resistance, but answers *yes* or *no*. A multimeter checks resistance and reports how many ohms (the measurement of resistance) a circuit has.

**Fix-It Tip**

Troubleshooting some devices may not even require that you use a multimeter. Many major appliances have fault codes that you can read and decipher using the owner's manual. You press a button or two, read the resulting code, and look it up for repair instructions. And if you don't have the original owner's manual nearby, we'll show you where to find one later in this section, under "Plan Your Fix-It Project."

Multimeters are relatively inexpensive. The analog unit shown was $10 and the digital multimeter was $20, though you can pay $50 or more for more accurate models. The ones shown here are sufficient for most electrical tests called for in this book.

Multimeters are available in digital and analog models. Digital multimeters display readings in numbers. Analog multimeters indicate values with a needle over a scale.

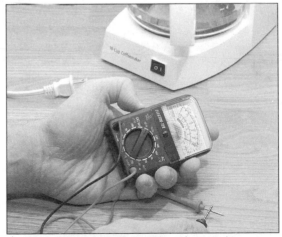

Analog multimeters measuring conductivity/resistance must first be adjusted for a zero reading. Check the instructions that come with a new multimeter.

You can use a multimeter to test motors, switches, controllers, and many other electrical gadgets. Specific instructions will come with the multimeter you purchase.

Here's how to use a multimeter to test an electric appliance:

1. Disconnect the cord from the power source, except when testing a live circuit.
2. Plug the test leads in to the multimeter.

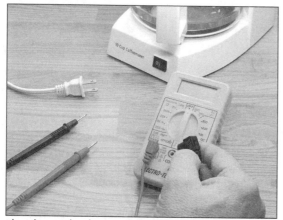

Plug the test leads in to the multimeter.

3. Select the function (ACV, DVC, resistance) and the range (maximum reading expected).

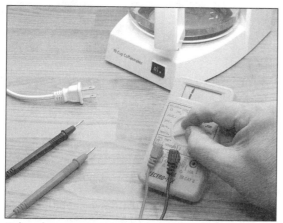

Select the appropriate function.

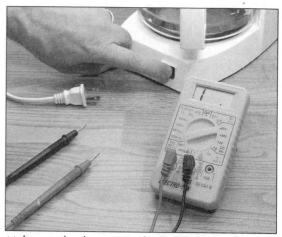

Make sure the device is unplugged and the switch is on.

4. Connect the probes to the cord or appliance component.

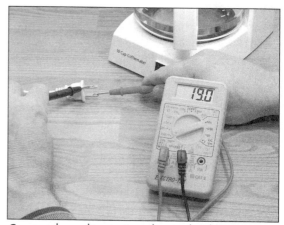

Connect the multimeter's probes to the device.

5. Interpret the reading. The *Fix-It Guides* and the device's owner's manual will tell you what to expect—and what to do about it.

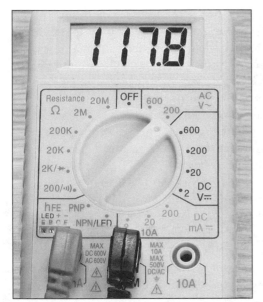

You can use a multimeter to check the voltage available at electrical receptacles in your home. Though electrical service is referred to as 120V or 240V, actual voltage can range as much as 10 percent up or down.

## Hybrid Things

The largest category of things is *hybrid*. That is, many things in our lives combine stationary (clothing) and mechanical (zipper), or mechanical (food mixer) and electrical (power). However, by looking at every thing by category you can more easily figure out what's wrong.

Troubleshooting hybrid things means simply looking at each job it does—or *doesn't* do—as a stationary, mechanical, or electrical function. For example, troubleshooting a lawnmower means looking at the handles and case as stationary; the wheels, engine, and blade as mechanical; and the starter and ignition system as electrical. You can break down any household *thing* to its systems, then components, to figure out what's wrong with it and how to fix it.

### Quick Test

Here's a *quick test* you can perform on any electrical device *without* disassembling it. Use a multimeter or continuity tester to check the appliance's continuity—ability to pass electricity from one plug prong to the other—when the switch is *on*. If it passes, the appliance is okay. If not, you'll need to disassemble it further to find the problem.

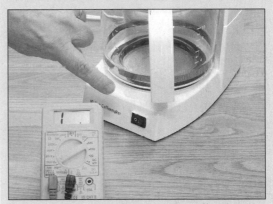

The reading with the device's switch off will show a reading of no conductivity (infinite resistance).

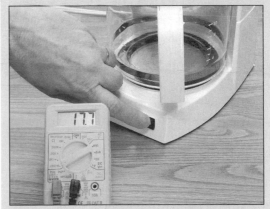

The reading with the device on will show some, but not infinite, resistance. If it shows infinite, the switch or other internal component is bad (the heating element, for example), and disassembly is required to fix the problem.

The same goes for *fixing* hybrid things. Think of everything as systems of components. Get the parts and tools needed for replacing the component. Fix it following the tips for the type of function (stationary, mechanical, electrical). Test it and adjust as needed. You're done.

What about all the new gadgets coming on the market every day? Most really aren't new; they are new-and-improved versions of things that have been around for many years. For example, the new DVD/CD players are simply combination gadgets; read the guides on fixing a *DVD Player* and fixing a *CD Player*.

## A Few Words About Warranties

Before tearing something open to fix it, consider whether it's really the manufacturer's problem or yours. Many consumer items carry a limited warranty that the item will function for at least the specified time after the consumer buys it new.

What *is* a warranty? A *warranty* is a guarantee by a seller or manufacturer to a buyer that the goods or services purchased will perform as promised, or a refund will be given, an exchange made, or a repair done at no charge. Warranties usually become effective when the manufacturer receives a warranty application from the buyer (not necessarily at the date of purchase) and are effective for a limited period of time. Warranties usually include limitations that exclude defects not caused by the manufacturer. Warranties are included in the price of the product.

*Extended warranties* are really not warranties at all. They are actually service contracts sold at an extra cost that is typically quite profitable for the retailer. That's why so many retailers ask if you'd like to purchase an extended warranty when you buy something. In some cases, the retailer makes more profit on the extended warranty than on the product it sold you.

Almost every purchase you make is covered by an *implied warranty*. The exceptions are items marked "as is" and sold in a state that allows "as is" sales. Implied warranties include *warranty of merchantability*, meaning the seller promises that the product will do what it is supposed to do. A *warranty of fitness* applies when the product package or the seller tells you that the product is suitable for the described purpose.

What is covered by a warranty? Warranties vary, but typically cover repair or replacement, though there may be a charge for labor (not parts) or shipping/freight costs. The manufacturer *or* the seller may be the one required to honor the warranty. The warranty term may be for 30 or 90 days or a year or more.

> **Fix-It Tip**
>
> As you shop for replacement things, open up the box and read the warranty card to find out how long the product or specific parts are covered for repairs or replacement.

Won't trying to repair something void the warranty? Maybe. Some warranties prohibit repairs not authorized or done by those authorized by the manufacturer. However, most things you buy will either not work as soon as you try to use them (they'll be repaired or replaced under warranty) or the day after the warranty expires (fixing is up to you).

What about recalls? More than 15,000 consumer items, including many things throughout a household, are subject to recalls by the Consumer Product Safety Commission (CPSC). A *recall* is an announcement from the CPSC that a specific product offers a significant risk to consumers. You should stop using the product and follow the instructions in the recall announcement. That may mean calling the manufacturer for a replacement or some other remedy. Each recall announcement is for a specific model of product, and the remedy is different for each product recalled. You can find out if products you've purchased have been recalled by contacting the CPSC at 1-800-638-2772 or online at www.cpsc.gov. You also can report unsafe products that you think should be recalled.

# Getting Parts and Materials to Fix It

Once you've figured out what's wrong with a household item, how are you going to get the parts to fix it? Fortunately, many parts are standardized and interchangeable. You may be able to pick up many of them at a nearby hardware store.

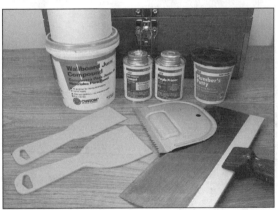

Many fix-it materials and tools can be purchased at your local hardware store or home center.

Standardized parts include screws, bolts, nuts, fuses, wires, cords, connectors, etc. Manufacturers use standardized parts not to make repairs easier for you, but to keep their manufacturing costs down. They can then buy millions of a specific screw at a fraction of a penny each.

Some parts are unique to the product. It may be because the manufacturer couldn't find a low-cost standardized part—or because the manufacturer wants to corner the market on replacement parts, as do some of the computer printer manufacturers. You must buy replacement ink cartridges from the manufacturer if you want to be sure you're getting one that fits. Coffee machines, too, often have replacement pots that are nearly as expensive as the new machine. Even car manufacturers know that the replacement parts market is profitable—if they use unique parts.

Some parts are relatively expensive, such as motors and controllers, costing half or more of the price of a new appliance. In some cases, the cost is high because the parts are unique and fit only a limited number of models. In most cases, however, they are expensive because they are complex—and necessary to operation. You won't find a replacement motor for your hair dryer at the hardware store. And if you do find one through the manufacturer's service department, it may cost nearly as much as a new hair dryer.

Some parts are designed *not* to be replaced. They are sealed or otherwise installed so you can't replace individual parts. That's okay for things like circuit boards because you're not going to replace components on them. You'll simply pull the errant circuit board and install the replacement. However, some gadgets, such as cellular telephones, are difficult to even open (except the battery compartment); internal parts are not intended to be replaced by the owner. But even on an item like a cell phone, you can do a few things to fix or at least extend the life of the item.

Where can you get parts when you need them? This book's *Fix-It Resources* includes hundreds of manufacturers, service centers, and parts retailers for many consumer items. In addition, it lists a wide variety of Internet resources. One, www.partsolver.com, says it offers *eight million* parts. By shopping around, you can cut the cost of replacement parts. These resources often offer diagrams that can help you in disassembling and reassembling things.

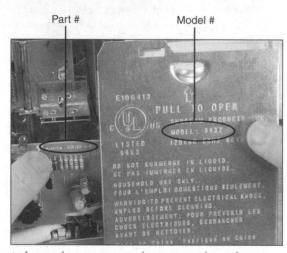

When ordering parts, make sure you have the model number and, if possible, the part number.

## Using the Right Tools

A *tool* is any mechanical implement that cuts, turns, grabs, attaches, or provides some other useful function. To fix things around your household, you'll need at least a few basic tools such as screwdrivers, wrenches, hammers, drills, and pliers. There are additional tools for specific jobs, such as a toilet plunger, level, clamp, paint brush, caulk gun, etc.

Which tools do you need in your fix-it toolbox? We recommend these basics:

- A good-quality 8- or 16-ounce curved-claw hammer for installing and removing nails
- An adjustable wrench (6, 8, or 10 inches long) for tightening and loosening bolts
- A set of screwdrivers or a combination screwdriver with assorted tips (standard and Phillips) for tightening and loosening screws

Basic tools include screwdrivers, pliers, adjustable wrench, utility knife, measuring tape, and a hammer—purchased for just $10 as a set. The tool box cost another $10.

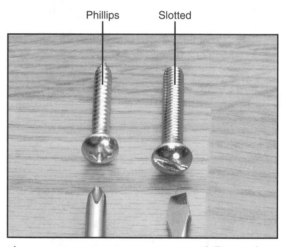

The two most common screw tips are Phillips and standard or slotted.

- Adjustable pliers (6, 8, 10, or 12 inches long) for holding or turning things
- A basic multimeter for testing electrical voltage, current, and resistance (see the "Multimeter" section previously).

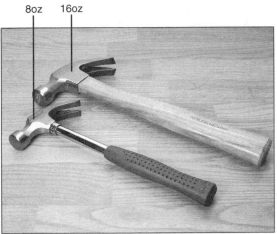

8oz  16oz

An 8-ounce hammer is good enough for many light household jobs. Select a 16-ounce hammer for driving 8d (8 penny) and larger nails. These medium-quality hammers were under $10 each.

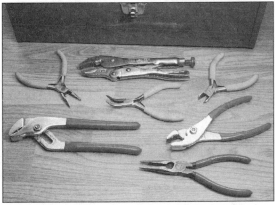

Pliers come in all sizes and shapes for special tasks. Buy them as you need them.

That's about it. For less than $25—including the cost of a small toolbox or tool apron to hold everything—you can have the basic tools you need to fix hundreds of things in your household. Just make sure you buy at least medium quality. A $3 hammer is hardly worth three bucks. A $10 hammer may last you many years. Besides, you'll probably save the cost of the tools on your *first* repair—and you get to keep the tools!

You also can expand your budget to upgrade any of the basic tools covered here. For example, you can invest a couple dollars more to get a better set of screwdrivers or even a power screwdriver with assorted tips. If you want to add on to this basic toolbox to make tasks easier—or to make even more repairs—you can get these:

- Hand or power drill with assorted bits for drilling holes in wood, metal, or plastic

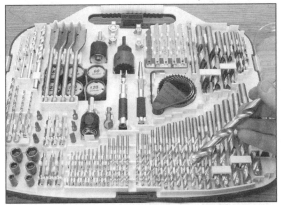

This set of medium-quality wood and metal bits and related drill components cost under $40—less than the cost of one repair.

- Wire stripper for cutting and removing the outer wrapper (insulation) from around wires

Wire strippers remove the plastic insulation from wires so the wires can be attached to electrical devices.

- Retractable-blade utility knife for cutting softer materials such as plastics
- Measuring tape for measuring the height, width, or depth of various materials
- Hand, hack, or power saw for cutting wood, plastic, or metal (depending on the blade used)
- Set of wrenches (open- and closed-end) with standard (inches) and metric (millimeter) sizes for bolts and nuts
- Socket wrench set with standard (U.S.) and metric sizes using ¼-, ⅜-, or ½-inch ratchet drives for bolts and nuts
- Allen wrench set for tightening and loosening Allen-head screws and bolts

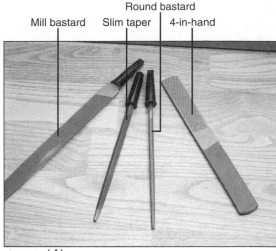

Assorted files.

Eventually you can purchase open- and closed-end wrenches, a socket wrench set or two, Allen wrenches, and some specialty wrenches that save time and frustration.

- Files are useful for removing excess metal, plastic, and wood.

In addition to common screws and screwdrivers, you may run into spanner and Torx fasteners. A spanner bit has a notch in the middle (sometimes found on coffee makers). Torx fasteners have six points. In addition, Torx tamper-resistant screws have a post in the center to make them even more difficult to open (found on some microwaves). If required, you can purchase these special tools at larger hardware stores or auto parts centers.

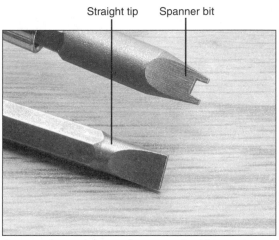

Spanner bit and a straight or standard bit.

A basic tool kit for painting projects will include these items:

- Paint brushes or paint pads for applying paint and other finishes to smaller surfaces (better brushes will cost more, but will last a lot longer and spread paint more easily and evenly)
- Paint roller (frame and cover) and tray for applying paint and other finishes to larger surfaces (a better-quality roller cover will last for years and apply paint more easily and evenly)

Torx tamper-resistant bit and screw. Notice the post in the middle of the six-pointed star screw.

- Cartridge gun for applying caulking and other sealers
- Scrapers and sandpaper for removing paint and other finishes from wood, metal, or plastic
- A-frame ladder or sturdy stepstool for reaching higher locations

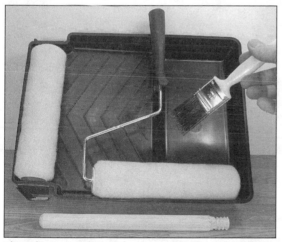

These basic painting tools (tray, roller, cover, handle, and brush) are all you need for touch-up painting jobs.

One of the keys to quick repairs is having a convenient place to work. Tools, standard parts, and good lighting are all together in one place. And it's a place where you can leave things spread out if needed without complaints or lost parts.

Like where? To start, a corner of the dining room or a spare room will work. Parts and tools can be in a small tool chest or even a cardboard box—nothing fancy, just efficient. Or you can use a small desk in an extra room or in your garage. A used student desk can be purchased for less than the cost of a repair and will give you working surface plus storage for tools and parts. Someday you may have a fix-it bench in the garage (as we do), or even a separate shop, with all the tools you've purchased with the money you've saved by fixing things yourself.

## Sewing

Many household sewing repairs can be completed with a few stitches, either by hand or on a sewing machine. Clothing, blankets, towels, dolls, upholstered furniture, and other items made with fabric occasionally need fixing. Seams and hems come unstitched. Tears and holes happen. You'll need needles, pins, thread, and scissors. If you use a machine, follow the manufacturer's instructions.

First, match the thread to the project. Use poly-wrap polyester for most fabrics, but cotton-wrap polyester works well for jeans. If you're not sure what thread or needle to use, ask at your fabric shop.

The *back stitch* is the hand alternative of the sewing machine straight stitch. It can be used to repair a seam. Insert a threaded needle (be sure to knot the thread) from below the fabric layers ⅛ inch to the left of where your stitching should begin. Pull the thread through the fabric until the knot is snug against the fabric. Then insert the needle ⅛ inch behind where the thread emerges. Then bring the thread up ¼ inch beyond this insertion and pull the thread up snug. Bring the needle up ¼ inch beyond the latest insertion and pull through. Continue stitching as far as needed.

A *slip stitch* can be used to repair a seam from the top. Push a threaded needle (be sure to knot the thread) through the material on one side of the opening, and then on the other. Continue until the seam is closed.

An *overhand stitch* is useful for reattaching fabric parts, such as an ear or limb of a stuffed animal. Begin by pushing the needle diagonally from the back edge of the opening to the front. Then insert the needle behind the first stitch and bring it out a stitch length away. Continue until the repair is completed.

The *cross stitch* will hold patches securely in place. Begin by sewing a series of angled stitches across the edge of the patch. When you reach the end of the seam or the outline of the patch, reverse direction and sew back over each of the angled stitches.

**Back Stitch**

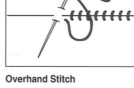
**Overhand Stitch**

**Slip Stitch**

**Cross Stitch**

The four most common types of sewing stitches for fixing things.

# Solder

Soldering is simply attaching two objects together with a metal alloy, called solder, that melts at relatively low temperature, then hardens into a metal joint. The type of solder used depends on the job: joining copper pipe, electronic parts, or other components. Some solders require a cleaning agent first, called a flux. Other solders have the flux combined with the solder.

Choose a soldering tool (iron or gun), solder, flux, and other tools based on the job you want to do. Follow the instructions that come with the soldering tool. Typically that means heating the work (pipe, electrical connection, etc.) with the soldering tool, then touching the solder wire to the *work* (not the soldering tool) until the solder melts to form a union.

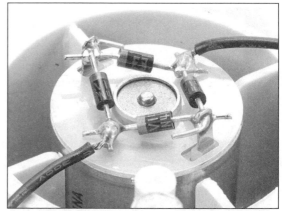
Some small appliances have diodes and other electronic components that can be purchased at an electronics store and soldered in as replacements.

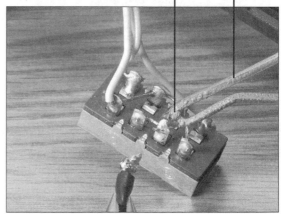
Joint    Soldering gun

To desolder, heat the joint until the components can be pulled apart. Clean up the joint, then install the components and solder them in place.

# Tips on Fixing Stuff

After you get everything you need and you start repairing household things, you'll learn some tricks and shortcuts. To save you some time we'll share some tricks and shortcuts with you—after we give a crash course in safety.

## Safety First!

Safety is a very important part of fixing anything. In one infamous example, technicians decided to find out what would happen if they tried to run the system with the various safety mechanisms defeated—at the Chernobyl Nuclear Power Plant. Fixing your toaster won't start a mushroom cloud of nuclear waste, but it can hurt you if you don't apply some common-sense safety rules:

> **Caution**
>
> Houses built before 1978 may contain lead paint. Before disturbing any surface, get a lab analysis of paint chips from it (about $5 per sample). Contact your public health department for information on how to collect samples and where to send them.

- Make sure the power source is disconnected before working on any electrical or gas system.
- Turn the water off ahead of the fixture before working on plumbing.
- Wear gloves if using caustic chemicals.
- Wear safety glasses if using a saw blade or any tool that can throw debris.
- Wear a breathing mask if working around dust or strong chemicals.
- Never place a body part where it can get hurt.
- Don't use a tool for any task but its intended purpose.

- Don't stand on something that won't support you.
- Don't try to fix anything when your thinking is impaired by lack of sleep, emotional stress, alcohol, medications, or illness.
- Plan it before you do it (we'll cover this in a moment).

Aluminum wiring was used in home construction during the 1960s and early 1970s—until it was discovered that its interaction with copper and brass electrical terminals was causing some house fires! The metals expand and contract at different rates and the aluminum wire was pulling away from the copper terminals. How can you tell if your house has aluminum wiring instead of copper? Aluminum wire is dull gray or silver; copper wire is dull orange. "AL" may be imprinted on the wire sheathing (covering). What can you do about it? You may want an electrician to upgrade your home's wiring with new aluminum-compatible connectors or by adding copper pigtail wires to the end of all electrical connections. You may be able to do it yourself, but do so under the direction of a licensed electrician.

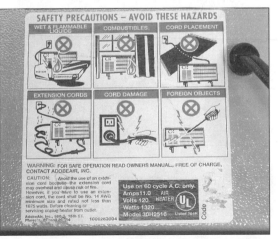

Many electrical appliances have warnings on their outside cases to tell you of potential dangers to safety.

Some electrical devices have labels telling you of potential danger due to high voltage inside. Heed them.

If the electrical device you're working on doesn't unplug, make sure the power is turned off to the circuit you're working on.

Should you worry about asbestos? Asbestos is a fireproof, nonconducting mineral that was used in building materials for many decades—until OSHA (Occupational Safety and Health Administration) determined that asbestos fibers are a health hazard. Tiny asbestos fibers can readily break away from building materials, and the fine dust can be inhaled or swallowed. And asbestos was used in many types of materials that are still in homes today. Should you worry? To be a health hazard the fibers must be friable or loose in the air. Disturbing asbestos insulation or breaking up products that have loose asbestos fibers is a health hazard and requires an asbestos-removal expert. However, products like roofing that has asbestos impregnated in it (because it's fireproof) aren't a significant health risk.

## Plan Your Fix-It Project

No matter what you're fixing, you can save time by spending some time on planning. Once you've figured out what's wrong with the item, gathered the parts and tools, and planned when and where you'll fix it, the repair is more than half done. The actual repair is relatively easy. So use your *Fix-It Club Notebook* (found at the end of this book) to analyze the job and collect everything you need; then once you have a few spare moments, you can get it done.

How will you know what parts you need? Many consumer products, especially electronics, have owner's manuals. However, even unassembled furniture, toys, and vehicles have manuals available for them either through the manufacturer or through a publisher. Check the *Fix-It Resources* section of this book. You often can get a copy of an owner's manual for newer products online.

Nearly every household product you purchase has an owner's manual with it. Save it! Write the date of purchase on it and file it somewhere you can easily find when you need it.

Why do you need the manual? Not only do product manuals typically include a troubleshooting chart, some also have a drawing of the product with specific information about parts, including numbers and where to get them. Drawings typically are exploded views that show how the item is assembled—quite handy for taking it apart and putting it back together.

Better owner's manuals include exploded views of the device, parts lists, and troubleshooting charts that make fixing the device much easier.

Many consumer products include information about the model and serial number. The *model* number indicates which design it is; the *serial* number is unique to each item. For example, a video camera model number may be CCD-TRV87 and the serial number 74596. The manufacturer, Sony in this case, probably made at least 74,000 of these units numbered from 00001 to whatever. (It could have started numbering anywhere, actually.) Though the model number is the same for all of them, the manufacturer may have made a slight modification in parts at, say, the fifty-thousandth unit, so the serial number is important.

Knowing model and serial numbers is also important to finding replacement parts that fit. These numbers typically are included on a plate or stamping on an underside of the product. Ovens often have them on a plate attached to the inside of a door jamb. In addition, major components, such as a motor, typically include a model and probably a serial number that can be used to find a replacement. It's helpful to take the part you need to replace to the parts store with you.

You will dramatically reduce the time needed to fix things if you have a handy place and a set of tools to do the job. Even if it's just a cardboard box with a few tools in it, having a regular work space will simplify the repair.

## Disassembling Things

Another important part of repair is disassembling things so that they can be reassembled in the same way whether it's done today, tomorrow, or once you've found some parts a month from now. Here are tips for smart disassembly:

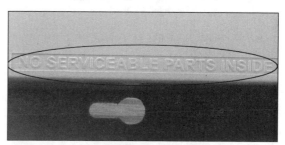

Some appliances specifically state "Do Not Service Parts Inside." That typically means that even if you get it open, there won't be anything in there to replace, so reconsider fixing it.

- Find a place where you can leave everything out for an hour or a day, in case you need to stop and get additional parts.
- Make notes on disassembly in your *Fix-It Club Notebook*.
- For tougher repairs or when you know it will be a while before you can get replacement parts, use a film or digital camera to take photos of the disassembly process.
- If you know you will be reassembling everything within the next couple of hours, lay the parts in a line as they come off, left to right, and reassemble right to left.
- Use old muffin pans, empty frozen dinner dishes, clean coffee cans, or other containers to collect parts as they are removed.

Some fasteners are hidden behind trim.

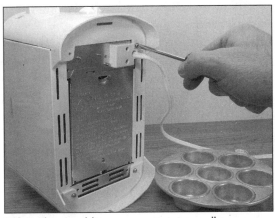

When disassembling, put parts in a small tray or container in the order of their removal. It makes reassembly much easier. (The mini-muffin pan pictured here costs less than $1.)

Intimidated by what you see when you open up something to fix it? Don't be. Most things are made of components—more than one part. And each of these components is replaceable. It's just a matter of figuring out how the thing works, which parts or components don't work, and replacing the problem part(s). Many *Fix-It Guides* in this book include photos or drawings that let you see what's inside the device or object—you'll know what you're getting in to.

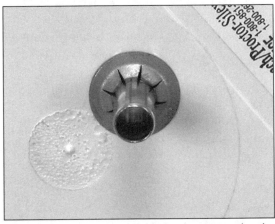

Some fasteners are not intended to be removed without damaging them. Fortunately, once removed, you can find a replacement at larger hardware stores.

Most parts either twist on or plug in. For example, disassembling an appliance requires untwisting (unscrewing) fasteners that hold the outside body together. Once inside, you may need to unscrew or unplug other parts. Many components are plugged together, especially electrical parts. For example, a couple of wires enter one side of a plastic plug and other wires run out the other side. To disconnect the part, find a tab on the connector and lift it or apply pressure to it and carefully pull the connector apart. Install the replacement component by plugging the two halves of the connector together. Most connectors go together only one way, so it's relatively easy.

You'll find that many consumer items are assembled using screws, clips, or both. In fact, if you *don't* find a screw or clip, the manufacturer is probably telling you there's nothing inside that the consumer can fix. You may be able to replace the entire component, however.

Some parts may be hard to remove because they are friction-fit (fit snugly) to a shaft. Don't force friction-fit parts; they may break. Instead, use a wide-blade screwdriver under the coupling to carefully twist and lift the coupling upward. If that doesn't work, try heating the coupling slightly (try a hair dryer) to expand the part enough to pull it from the shaft. Or slip a pair of thin wood wedges under the coupling. Then push the wedges toward each other and lift. If none of these succeeds in separating the friction-fit part from the shaft, you may have to take the appliance to a professional.

Some manufacturers use a pressure clip to hold a product's case together. To disassemble, look for a notch along the seam and insert the tip of a straight screwdriver to push and turn the clip, opening the case. Make sure you unclip all of the notches and remove all screws before disassembling the body, or you could break one of the small clips.

Many smaller consumer components can be disassembled by carefully prying the case apart.

## Finding Time to Fix It

When are you ever going to find the time to fix anything? Actually, you'll be surprised. By making the Fix-It Process easy to apply, and by having the parts and tools ready when you are, you'll find that many repairs can be done in minutes. Longer ones can be broken into stages that you can wedge between other things in your life. Where to find the time?

- If you're looking for a rewarding part-time hobby
- When your favorite TV show is a rerun
- When you need to do something that will most probably succeed
- When you have to get it repaired today so you can use it tomorrow
- When you want to make sure your day off is profitable
- When it's an heirloom that you don't want anyone else to work on
- When you want to have fun teaching a child how to fix things

You can pick up your *Fix-It Club Notebook* in a spare moment and troubleshoot something broken, then buy the needed parts on your next trip to the hardware store, and finally fix it that evening, on your next day off, or even on a once-a-month Fix-It Day. Whatever works.

# Finding an Expert Fixer

When should you consider hiring someone to fix something for you?

- When it's something you shouldn't be messing with, such as a microwave's magnetron or a freezer's refrigerant (you'll learn what *not* to mess with later in this book)
- When you can't find replacement parts, but think maybe a repair pro may know how to make it work

• When it's quite valuable and you don't want to take the chance of perhaps damaging it during repair
• When you just can't figure out what the heck's wrong with it, but want it fixed

Who can you get to fix it? Depending on what it is, the *Fix-It Resources* section includes contact information for manufacturers and service centers. Alternately, check area telephone books for appropriate listings such as *Appliances, Major*, or *Appliances, Parts & Supplies*, and *Automobile Repairing & Service*. Retailers from which you purchased merchandise may be able to direct you to local or regional repair centers. Also, ask among friends and neighbors because they can give you value judgments on whether specific repair services are customer friendly.

As we mentioned earlier, first check to determine if repair is covered under the manufacturer's warranty. Even if it isn't, ask the manufacturer to recommend a repair service. You'll find many manufacturers have websites that include parts and repair information as well as referrals.

You can make sure you select the best repair service for the job by asking a few questions:

• What experience do you have repairing this item?
• What training or certification do you have?
• Do you charge a flat rate or an hourly shop rate? What is that rate?
• Do you have a minimum charge?
• Is there a charge if you can't fix it?
• May I see your shop? (You'll see how your item will be treated.)

Remember to read anything you sign because verbal agreements *are not* binding. If the repair service says "$29.95" and the service contract you sign says "whatever we want to charge," you may wind up with a $300 repair on a $100 item. Most repair agreements include space for a do-not-exceed price; if not, write it in. And make sure the estimate includes both parts and labor. Ask what could happen to make the estimate go up. Ask if final bills usually come in under or over the estimate. Leave no room for surprises.

What should you tell the repair person? Indicate the symptoms and list the things you've done to attempt to alleviate them. For example, "The unit won't turn on. I've checked the electrical cord and it works, but I haven't found any fuses." Any information you can provide means less time the technician needs for diagnosing and should mean a smaller final bill.

Finding and checking a fuse can save you an expensive trip to a repair shop.

The fuse inside this blender is sealed, but can be accessed by removing the base.

Should you bring the unit in assembled or unassembled? That depends on whether you feel comfortable assembling the unit once it is fixed. Also, will the unit need assembly before the repair person can test it to make sure it's fixed? The best advice is: Bring it in assembled. A pro may actually charge more if it comes in unassembled. You can also call the shop and ask which is more efficient.

## How to Recycle *Everything*

Okay, there will be some things that you just can't fix—or don't want to pay to have fixed, or that will cost too much to fix. For example, if the repair on a small appliance approaches 50 percent of the cost of a replacement appliance, consider purchasing a new replacement item weighed against the environmental impact of throwing the old item in the trash.

Because recycling is subject to local interpretation and budgets, you may find that recycling things and parts may be quite easy or relatively difficult depending on where you live. The best place to learn about recycling is to call whatever company picks up your trash. If your area is rural and you must take trash and recycling to a landfill, transfer station, or recycle center, contact the company to find out what it can use and what it can't, and whether there is a charge.

For example, many communities have curbside pickup for trash and recycling. The recycled things may be collected in a single bin or need to be sorted by type: metals, plastics, papers, and yard waste. Some communities have curbside recycling for small and major appliances while others don't. And in some towns, there are private recyclers that will pick up just about any recyclable materials you put at the curb on a specified day.

Most major appliances are about 75 percent steel—and about a third of that is recycled steel. Other metals in appliances include copper, aluminum, and zinc—all recyclable.

Refrigerators, freezers, ranges, ovens, cook tops, clothes washers, dryers, dishwashers, dehumidifiers, room air conditioners, and trash compactors are all potentially recyclable.

Refrigeration appliances may require specialized recyclers to remove the Freon gas before recycling. That's why some recyclers and landfills charge a fee for accepting these appliances. Others charge a fee for any large objects that they accept.

You also can find local recyclers in your local telephone book under headings like *Recycle Centers* and *Scrap Metals*. Many will pay you for aluminum cans, clear glass, PET plastics, and nonferrous (non-iron) metals. PET stands for **p**ol**y**ethylene **t**erephthalate, a plastic resin used in many products—and easily recycled into new products.

### What Can You Recycle?

Recycling rules are localized. Your curbside recycling collector will probably accept many recyclables. Check with your local trash collector and/or recycler and any local recycling center for more information. However, many recyclers and communities use these guidelines:

- **Glass:** Unbroken glass containers (not tableware, ceramics, Pyrex, windows, light bulbs, mirrors, or broken glass). Clear glass is valuable, mixed color glass is nearly worthless, and broken glass is hard to sort. Don't bother removing labels.
- **Paper:** Newspapers and inserts (not dirty, not rubber bands, plastic bags, product samples, dirt, or mold). Some locations don't recycle cardboard, others do. Not waxed milk or juice cartons. Some recyclers require that magazines be recycled separately from newspapers.

## Reuse It—or Give It to Someone Who Will!

There are many things around your home that you can reuse instead of recycling or tossing. Think creatively before you banish something from your household. For example:

- Unrepairable clothing can become fix-it shop rags or quilting squares.
- Broken or discarded kitchen cabinets can be used as work cabinets in your fix-it shop.
- Extra drawers from a broken dresser can become under-bed storage containers.
- Ugly but usable hairdryers can be put to work thawing frozen pipes or making small patches of paint dry faster.
- Old tires can be nailed to walls in tight garages to reduce car scrapes or used in the yard as landscaping material or as play equipment.
- Polystyrene packing (peanuts) and other packing materials can be used to pack around breakable gifts or any package you need to mail or ship.

If you can't reuse something that's still in usable condition, give it to someone who can use it:

- Donate old eyeglasses to your local Lions Club.
- Some charities will accept operating computers and appliances.
- Old cell phones can be donated to groups that help homeless and/or low-income people to be used for emergency-only calls.
- Local charities may also accept diskettes, video tapes, polystyrene packing, compact discs, and holiday greeting cards.
- A senior center or homeless shelter may appreciate your old books and magazines.
- Packing peanuts and other packing materials are appreciated by your local mailbox/shipping store.
- Animal shelters gladly take donations of clean blankets and towels.

- **Metal:** Empty metal cans, caps, lids, bands, foil (not full cans, spray cans, or cans with paint or hazardous waste). Many recyclers don't even require that you remove labels.
- **Aluminum:** Lawn chairs, window frames, and pots (not metal parts attracted to magnets, nonmetal parts). Sometimes tin is recycled with aluminum.
- **Motor oil:** Call your garbage company or auto lube center. (Each year do-it-yourselfers *improperly dump* more oil than the *Exxon Valdez* spilled!)
- **Batteries** Take automotive batteries to a parts retailer; throw alkalines and rechargeables, such as those used in cordless phones, camcorders, razors, portable appliances, and computers in the trash unless prohibited; and recycle nickel-cadmiums.
- **Ink cartridges:** Send to a recycler or refiller. Your local office supply store may accept them.
- **Household toxins** (paints, oils, solvents, pesticides, cleaners): Call your garbage collector for advice. *Do not* dump them down storm drains.
- **Plastic:** Virtually everything made of plastic should be marked with a recycle code, but not all types can actually be recycled. You may be able to recycle plastic grocery bags at the grocery store; other plastic bags may have to be trashed. Any product made of a single plastic type should be marked and might be recyclable; those with mixed plastic types can't be recycled.
- **Things requiring specialized recyclers:** Major appliances with Freon (chlorinated fluorocarbon CFC) require trained technicians to remove; other items that require special recycling include antifreeze, asphalt shingles, car batteries, computers, ink and toner cartridges, rugs, smoke detectors, and single-use cameras.

| | |
|---|---|
| **1 PETE** | **Polyethylene Terephalate Ethylene**<br><br>PETE goes into soft drink, juice, water, detergent, and cleaner bottles. Also used for cooking and peanut butter jars. |
| **2 HDPE** | **High Density Polyethylene**<br>High Density Polyethylene HDPE goes into milk and water jugs, bleach bottles, detergent bottles, shampoo bottles, plastic bags and grocery sacks, motor oil bottles, household cleaners, and butter tubs. |
| **3 PVC** | **Polyvinyl Cloride**<br><br>PVC goes into window cleaner, cooking oils, and detergent bottles. Also used for peanut butter jars and water jugs. |
| **4 LDPE** | **Low Density Polyethylene**<br><br>LDPE goes into plastic bags and grocery sacks, dry cleaning bags, flexible film packaging, and some bottles. |
| **5 PP** | **Polypropylene**<br><br>PP goes into caps, disks, syrup bottles, yogurt tubs, straws, and film packaging. |
| **6 PS** | **Polystyrene**<br><br>PS goes into meat trays, egg cartons, plates, cutlery, carry-out containers, and clear trays. |
| **7 OTHER** | **Other**<br><br>Includes resins not mentioned above or combinations of plastics. |

Recycle symbols for common plastic packaging materials.

## Other Recycling Options

What if the recycler won't take it? Who will? In years past, organizations like the Salvation Army, Goodwill, and St. Vincent de Paul took non-working items as donations for rehabilitation. The items were rehabilitated along with the people who fixed them. Broken things created jobs. However, the labor market has absorbed these workers into the mainstream, providing jobs in restaurants, retail stores, and factories. So today, most of these organizations don't accept non-working items (except computers). In fact, such "donations" actually cost the group money because they have to dispose of the items. Goodwill Industries, for example, asks that donations be of "things you would give to a friend."

Another option is to recycle broken things at repair shops. For example, small appliance repair shops may accept nonworking items and reuse the parts. Or they may refurbish and resell items. Most won't pay you anything for the broken things—there's just not enough profit in it—but they may bring it back to working condition and save someone some money. And you won't have to pay to put it in the landfill.

If you learn to enjoy fixing things, donate something that breaks to your education. That is, put it on the workbench for a rainy day and disassemble it to figure out how it works. You may even be able to salvage and reuse an otherwise good motor, heat element, or switch. You'll be a member in good standing of the Fix-It Club!

## Fix Everything Chart

You can fix *everything*—if you know how something works. Here are more than 500 common household things cross-referenced to specific *Fix-It Guides* that help you understand, trouble-shoot, and fix them. Welcome to the Fix-It Club!

| Household Item | See Fix-It Guide(s) | Household Item | See Fix-It Guide(s) |
|---|---|---|---|
| Air conditioner | *Air Conditioner, Central*<br>*Air Conditioner, Room*<br>*Forced-Air Distribution* | Bathroom shower | *Faucet*<br>*Pipe*<br>*Tile*<br>*Drain System* |
| Air mattress | *Fix Everything: Adhesives*<br>*Toy* | Bathroom sink | *Faucet*<br>*Pipe*<br>*Drain System* |
| Air purifier | *Air Purifier* | | |
| Alarm clock | *Clock, Electric*<br>*Clock, Mechanical* | Bathtub | *Faucet*<br>*Pipe*<br>*Drain System* |
| All-terrain vehicle (ATV) | *Small Engine* | | |
| Aluminum siding | *Exterior Siding* | Battery | *Battery, Household*<br>*Battery, Button*<br>*Battery, Car*<br>*Battery Recharger* |
| Aluminum window screens | *Screen* | | |
| Answering machine | *Telephone Answering*<br>*Machine* | Battery-operated toothbrush | *Battery, Household*<br>*Electric Toothbrush* |
| Appliance controls | *Appliance Controls* | Battery recharger | *Battery Recharger* |
| Appliance heating element | *Heating Element* | Beard trimmer | *Hair Clipper* |
| Aquarium | *Fix Everything: Adhesives* | Bed | *Furniture, Wood*<br>*Furniture, Upholstery* |
| Asphalt | *Asphalt* | | |
| Audio amplifier | *Amplifier* | Bedding | *Fix Everything: Sewing* |
| Audio cassette | *Cassette Deck* | Bedroom furniture | *Furniture, Wood*<br>*Furniture, Upholstered* |
| Audio speaker | *Speaker* | | |
| Auto interior | *Furniture, Upholstered* | Bedroom lighting | *Lighting, Incandescent*<br>*Lighting, Fluorescent* |
| Automotive battery | *Battery, Car* | | |
| Baby monitor | *Security System* | Bicycle | *Bicycle* |
| Backpack | *Fix Everything: Sewing* | Bidet | *Toilet* |
| Ball | *Toy* | Bird bath | *Fix Everything: Adhesives* |
| Barbecue | *Gas Grill* | Black light | *Lighting, Fluorescent* |
| Basement | *Concrete*<br>*Drywall*<br>*Paneling*<br>*Paint*<br>*Pipe*<br>*Drain System* | Blender | *Blender* |
| | | Board game | *Fix Everything: Adhesives* |
| | | Boiler | *Boiler, Hot-Water*<br>*Boiler, Steam* |
| | | Bookcase | *Furniture, Wood* |
| Basketball | *Toy* | Box fan | *Fan* |
| Bassinet | *Fix Everything: Adhesives*<br>*Fix Everything: Sewing* | Bracelet | *Jewelry* |
| | | Bread maker | *Appliance Controls*<br>*Fan*<br>*Motor* |
| Bathroom exhaust fan | *Fan* | | |

| Household Item | See Fix-It Guide(s) |
|---|---|
| Breaker box | *Electrical Service Panel* |
| Brooch | *Jewelry* |
| Buffet | *Furniture, Wood* |
| Burglar alarm | *Security System* |
| Button battery | *Battery, Button* |
| Cabinets | *Furniture, Wood* |
| Camera | *Camera, Digital*<br>*Camera, Film*<br>*Camera, Video* |
| Camping equipment | *Fix Everything: Sewing*<br>*Fishing Reel* |
| Can opener | *Electric Can Opener* |
| Car battery | *Battery, Car* |
| Car radio | *Radio, Car* |
| Car seat | *Fix Everything: Sewing* |
| Carbon monoxide detector | *Smoke Detector* |
| Carpet | *Carpet* |
| Carpet cleaner | *Cooking Appliance*<br>*Electrical Cord*<br>*Motor*<br>*Appliance Controls*<br>*Vacuum Cleaner, Corded* |
| Carport | *Roof*<br>*Paint* |
| Cassette | *Cassette Deck*<br>*Video Cassette Recorder* |
| Cassette deck | *Cassette Deck*<br>*Remote Control*<br>*Speaker* |
| CB radio | *Radio, CB* |
| CD | *CD Player* |
| CD burner | *Computer*<br>*CD Player* |
| CD player | *CD Player*<br>*Remote Control*<br>*Speaker* |

| Household Item | See Fix-It Guide(s) |
|---|---|
| Ceiling | *Drywall*<br>*Plaster*<br>*Paint*<br>*Framing System* |
| Ceiling fan | *Fan* |
| Ceiling fan light | *Fan*<br>*Lighting, Incandescent* |
| Ceiling tile | *Tile* |
| Cellular telephone | *Telephone, Cellular* |
| Central air conditioner | *Air Conditioner, Central*<br>*Forced-Air Distribution* |
| Central vacuum | *Vacuum Cleaner, Corded* |
| Chain saw | *Small Engine* |
| Chair | *Furniture, Wood*<br>*Furniture, Upholstered* |
| Chandeliers | *Lighting, Incandescent*<br>*Fix Everything: Adhesives*<br>*Electrical Cord* |
| Changing table | *Furniture, Wood* |
| Chest of drawers | *Furniture, Wood* |
| Chimney | *Masonry*<br>*Fireplace/Stove* |
| Chipper | *Small Engine* |
| Christmas lights | *Holiday Decorations* |
| Circuit breaker | *Electrical Service Panel* |
| Clock | *Clock, Electric*<br>*Clock, Mechanical* |
| Clothes dryer | *Dryer, Clothes* |
| Clothes washer | *Washer, Clothes* |
| Clothing | *Clothing* |
| Coat | *Jacket* |
| Coffee grinder | *Coffee Grinder* |
| Coffee maker | *Coffee Maker* |
| Collectible | *Fix Everything: Adhesives*<br>*Fix Everything: Sewing* |
| Comfort controls | *Comfort Controls* |

| Household Item | See Fix-It Guide(s) |
|---|---|
| Compact disk (CD) | *CD Player* |
| Compact disk player | *CD Player* |
| Computer | *Computer* <br> *Computer Monitor* <br> *Computer Printer* <br> *Speaker* |
| Computer desk | *Furniture, Wood* |
| Computer monitor | *Computer Monitor* |
| Computer printer | *Computer Printer* |
| Computer scanner | *Camera, Digital* |
| Computer speaker | *Speaker* |
| Concrete | *Concrete* |
| Convection oven | *Oven, Convection* |
| Cook stove | *Cooktop, Electric* <br> *Cooktop, Gas* |
| Cooking appliance | *Cooking Appliance* |
| Cooktop | *Cooktop, Electric* <br> *Cooktop, Gas* |
| Cord | *Electrical Cord* |
| Cordless telephone | *Telephone, Cordless* |
| Cordless tool | *Battery Recharger* |
| Cordless vacuum cleaner | *Vacuum Cleaner, Cordless* |
| Cork flooring | *Flooring, Resilient* |
| Counter tile | *Tile* |
| Crib | *Furniture, Wood* |
| Cupboard | *Furniture, Wood* |
| Curling iron | *Hair Curler* |
| Curtains | *Window Curtain and Drape* |
| Deck | *Deck* <br> *Stairs* |
| Decorative lights | *Holiday Decorations* |
| Deep fryer | *Cooking Appliance* <br> *Appliance Controls* <br> *Heating Element* <br> *Electrical Cord* |
| Dehumidifier | *Forced-Air Distribution* |

| Household Item | See Fix-It Guide(s) |
|---|---|
| Desk | *Furniture, Wood* |
| Digital answering machine | *Telephone Answering Machine* |
| Digital camera | *Camera, Digital* |
| Digital clock | *Clock, Electric* |
| Digital video device player | *DVD Player* |
| Dimmer control | *Electrical Switch* |
| Dining chair | *Furniture, Wood* |
| Dining table | *Furniture, Wood* |
| Dirt bike | *Small Engine* |
| Discman | *CD Player* |
| Dishwasher | *Dishwasher* |
| Dog house | *Outdoor Structures* |
| Dog run | *Fence* |
| Doll | *Doll* |
| Door | *Door* |
| Door hardware | *Door Hardware* |
| Doorbell | *Doorbell* |
| Downspout | *Gutter* |
| Drain system | *Drain System* <br> *Septic System* |
| Drain waste vent system | *Drain System* |
| Drapes | *Window Curtain and Drape* |
| Dresser | *Furniture, Wood* |
| Driveway | *Asphalt* <br> *Concrete* |
| Dryer | *Dryer, Clothes* <br> *Dryer, Hair* |
| Drywall | *Drywall* |
| DVD | *DVD Player* <br> *Speaker* |
| DVD player | *DVD Player* <br> *Speaker* |
| Earring | *Jewelry* |
| Edger | *Yard Trimmer* |

| Household Item | See Fix-It Guide(s) | Household Item | See Fix-It Guide(s) |
|---|---|---|---|
| Electric blanket | *Electrical Cord*<br>*Heating Element*<br>*Appliance Controls* | Electrical switch | *Electrical Switch* |
| | | Electrical system | *Electrical System* |
| | | Electricity | *Electrical System* |
| Electric broom | *Electrical Cord*<br>*Motor*<br>*Appliance Controls*<br>*Vacuum Cleaner, Corded* | Espresso maker | *Espresso Maker*<br>*Coffee Maker* |
| | | Exercise equipment | *Exercise Equipment* |
| Electric can opener | *Electric Can Opener* | Exterior door | *Door*<br>*Door Hardware* |
| Electric clock | *Clock, Electric* | | |
| Electric cooktop | *Cooktop, Electric* | Exterior siding | *Exterior Siding*<br>*Masonry* |
| Electric drill | *Electrical Cord*<br>*Motor*<br>*Appliance Controls*<br>*Fuse* | Eyeglasses | *Jewelry* |
| | | Fan | *Fan* |
| | | Faucet | *Faucet* |
| Electric frying pan | *Cooking Appliance* | Fax machine | *Facsimile Machine* |
| Electric furnace | *Furnace, Electric*<br>*Forced-Air Distribution* | Fence | *Fence*<br>*Masonry*<br>*Concrete* |
| Electric heater | *Heater, Electric* | | |
| Electric iron | *Electric Iron* | File cabinet | *Furniture, Wood* |
| Electric knife | *Electric Knife* | Film camera | *Camera, Film* |
| Electric mixer | *Food Mixer* | Fine china | *Fix Everything: Adhesives* |
| Electric oven | *Oven, Electric* | Firebox | *Fireplace/Stove* |
| Electric pencil sharpener | *Electric Pencil Sharpener* | Fire extinguisher | *Fire Extinguisher* |
| Electric range | *Oven, Electric*<br>*Cooktop, Electric* | Fireplace | *Fireplace/Stove*<br>*Masonry* |
| Electric saw | *Electrical Cord*<br>*Motor*<br>*Appliance Controls*<br>*Fuse* | Fireplace insert | *Fireplace* |
| | | Fishing reel | *Fishing Reel* |
| | | Floor polisher | *Electrical Cord*<br>*Motor*<br>*Appliance Controls* |
| Electric shaver | *Electric Shaver* | | |
| Electric skillet | *Cooking Appliance* | Floor scrubber | *Electrical Cord*<br>*Motor*<br>*Appliance Controls* |
| Electric toothbrush | *Electric Toothbrush* | | |
| Electric water heater | *Water Heater, Electric* | | |
| Electric wok | *Cooking Appliance* | Floor tile | *Tile* |
| Electrical cord | *Electrical Cord* | Flooring | *Flooring, Resilient*<br>*Flooring, Wood* |
| Electrical outlet | *Electrical Receptacle* | | |
| Electrical receptacle | *Electrical Receptacle* | Floppy drive | *Computer* |
| Electrical service panel | *Electrical Service Panel* | Fluorescent lighting | *Lighting, Fluorescent* |

| Household Item | See Fix-It Guide(s) | Household Item | See Fix-It Guide(s) |
|---|---|---|---|
| Fondue pot | Cooking Appliance<br>Electrical Cord<br>Heating Element<br>Appliance Controls | Fuse | Fuse<br>Electrical Service Panel<br>Electrical System |
| Food blender | Blender | Fuse box | Electrical Service Panel |
| Food grinder | Electrical Cord<br>Motor<br>Appliance Controls<br>Fuse | Game system | Computer<br>Television |
| | | Game table | Furniture, Wood |
| | | Garage door opener | Garage Door Opener |
| Food mixer | Food Mixer | Garbage disposer | Garbage Disposer |
| Food processor | Food Processor | Garden cart | Garden Tool |
| Food sealer | Electrical Cord<br>Heating Element<br>Appliance Controls<br>Fuse | Garden equipment | Small Engine<br>Garden Tool |
| | | Garden hoe | Garden Tool |
| | | Garden tool | Garden Tool |
| Food slicer | Food Slicer | Gas cooktop | Cooktop, Gas |
| Food steamer | Steamer/Rice Cooker | Gas furnace | Furnace, Gas<br>Forced-Air Distribution |
| Football | Toy | | |
| Forced-air distribution | Forced-Air Distribution | Gas grill | Gas Grill |
| Formal dinnerware | Fix Everything: Adhesives | Gas oven | Oven, Gas |
| Foundation | Concrete | Gas range | Oven, Gas<br>Cooktop, Gas |
| Frame | Fix Everything: Adhesives<br>Fix Everything: Fasteners | | |
| | | Gas water heater | Water Heater, Gas |
| Freezer | Refrigerator | Gate | Fence |
| Fresh water system | Pipe<br>Faucet<br>Drain System | Gazebo | Deck<br>Outdoor Structures |
| | | Generator | Small Engine |
| Frying pan | Cooking Appliance | Glass pane | Window |
| Furnace | Furnace, Electric<br>Furnace, Gas<br>Furnace, Oil<br>Boiler, Hot-Water<br>Boiler, Steam<br>Forced-Air Distribution | Glassware | Fix Everything: Adhesives |
| | | Grandfather clock | Furniture, Wood<br>Clock, Mechanical<br>Clock, Electric |
| | | Grass shears | Garden Tool |
| Furnace blower | Forced-Air Distribution | Greenhouse | Outdoor Structures |
| Furniture | Furniture, Wood<br>Furniture, Upholstered | Griddle | Cooking Appliance |
| | | Grill | Gas Grill |
| Furniture drawer | Furniture, Wood | Gutter | Gutter |

| Household Item | See Fix-It Guide(s) | Household Item | See Fix-It Guide(s) |
|---|---|---|---|
| Gypsum wallboard | *Drywall* | Home theater | *Television* |
| Hair clipper | *Hair Clipper* | | *Amplifier* |
| Hair curler | *Hair Curler* | | *Speaker* |
| Hair dryer | *Dryer, Hair* | | *CD Player* |
| Hair straightener | *Hair Curler* | | *DVD Player* |
| | *Dryer, Hair* | Hot plate | *Hot Plate* |
| Hair trimmer | *Hair Clipper* | Hot tub | *Whirlpool* |
| Ham radio | *Radio, CB* | Hot water boiler | *Boiler, Hot Water* |
| Handbag | *Fix Everything: Adhesives* | Hot water system | *Water Heater, Gas* |
| | *Fix Everything: Sewing* | | *Water Heater, Electric* |
| Handheld vacuum | *Vacuum Cleaner, Cordless* | | *Pipe* |
| Hardwood flooring | *Flooring, Wood* | Household battery | *Battery, Household* |
| Hats | *Fix Everything: Sewing* | | *Battery Recharger* |
| | *Fix Everything: Adhesives* | Household radio | *Radio, Household* |
| Headphone | *Speakers* | Humidifier | *Humidifier* |
| Heat pump | *Heat Pump* | Hutch | *Furniture, Wood* |
| Heat systems | *Furnace, Electric* | Ice-cream maker | *Ice-Cream Maker* |
| | *Furnace, Gas* | Icemaker | *Icemaker* |
| | *Boiler, Steam* | Incandescent lighting | *Lighting, Incandescent* |
| | *Boiler, Hot Water* | Inflatable toy | *Toy* |
| | *Forced-Air Distribution* | Instant camera | *Camera, Film* |
| Heater | *Heater, Electric* | Intercom system | *Security System* |
| | *Heater, Kerosene* | Interior door | *Door* |
| Heating element | *Heating Element* | | *Door Hardware* |
| Heating pad | *Heating Pad* | Iron | *Electric Iron* |
| Hedge trimmer | *Small Engine* | Jacket | *Jacket* |
| | *Electrical Cord* | Jewelry | *Jewelry* |
| | *Motor* | Juice maker | *Juicer/Juice Extractor* |
| | *Fuse* | Juicer | *Juicer/Juice Extractor* |
| Highchair | *Furniture, Wood* | Kerosene heater | *Heater, Kerosene* |
| Hinge | *Door Hardware* | Kitchen sink | *Faucet* |
| | *Furniture, Wood* | | *Pipe* |
| Hinged door | *Door Hardware* | Knife | *Electric Knife* |
| | *Furniture, Wood* | Laminate flooring | *Flooring, Wood* |
| Hobby model | *Fix Everything: Adhesives* | Lamp | *Lighting, Incandescent* |
| Holiday decorations | *Holiday Decorations* | | *Lighting, Fluorescent* |
| Holiday lights | *Holiday Decorations* | Laptop computer | *Computer* |

| Household Item | See Fix-It Guide(s) | Household Item | See Fix-It Guide(s) |
|---|---|---|---|
| Lawn mower | Lawn Mower, Reel <br> Lawn Mower, Rotary <br> Lawn Mower, Riding | Outdoor furniture | Furniture, Wood <br> Furniture, Upholstered |
| Leaf blower | Electrical Cord <br> Motor <br> Small Engine | Outdoor lighting | Lighting, Incandescent <br> Lighting, Fluorescent |
| | | Outdoor structure | Outdoor Structures |
| Light fixture | Lighting, Incandescent <br> Lighting, Fluorescent | Outdoor tool | Garden Tool |
| | | Outside faucet | Faucet |
| Light switch | Electrical Switch | Oven | Oven, Electric <br> Oven, Gas <br> Oven, Microwave <br> Oven, Convection <br> Oven, Toaster |
| Lighting | Lighting, Incandescent <br> Lighting, Fluorescent | | |
| Linoleum | Flooring, Resilient | | |
| Lock | Door Hardware | Paint | Paint |
| Masonry | Masonry | Palmtop computer | Computer |
| Masonry fence | Masonry | Paneling | Paneling |
| Masonry siding | Masonry | Paper shredder | Electrical Cord <br> Appliance Controls <br> Motor <br> Fuse |
| Masonry wall | Masonry | | |
| Mattress | Fix Everything: Sewing <br> Furniture, Upholstered | | |
| | | Parquet flooring | Flooring, Wood |
| Meat grinder | Electrical Cord <br> Motor <br> Appliance Controls <br> Fuse | Pasta maker | Appliance Controls <br> Motor <br> Electrical Cord <br> Fuse |
| Mechanical clock | Clock, Mechanical | Pellet stove | Fireplace/Stove |
| Microwave oven | Oven, Microwave | Pencil sharpener | Electric Pencil Sharpener |
| Motor | Motor | Personal stereo | Portable Stereo |
| Motorboat | Small Engine <br> Battery, Car | Pet groomer | Hair Clipper |
| | | Pickaxe | Garden Tool |
| Motorcycle | Small Engine | Picnic table | Furniture, Wood |
| Necklace | Jewelry | Picture frame | Fix Everything: Adhesives <br> Fix Everything: Fasteners |
| Oil furnace | Furnace, Oil <br> Forced-Air Distribution | | |
| | | Pin | Jewelry |
| On-off switch | Appliance Controls <br> Electrical Switch | Ping pong table | Furniture, Wood |
| | | Pipe | Pipe <br> Plumbing System <br> Drain System |
| Oscillating fan | Fan | | |
| Outboard motor | Small Engine | | |
| Outdoor deck | Deck | Pitchfork | Garden Tool |

| Household Item | See Fix-It Guide(s) | Household Item | See Fix-It Guide(s) |
|---|---|---|---|
| Pizza oven | Cooking Appliance<br>Electrical Cord<br>Heating Element<br>Appliance Controls<br>Fuse | Radio | Radio, Household<br>Radio, Car<br>Radio, CB |
| Plaster | Plaster | Range | Cooktop, Electric<br>Cooktop, Gas<br>Oven, Electric<br>Oven, Gas |
| Playhouse | Outdoor Structures | | |
| Plumbing pipe | Pipe | Range hood | Fan<br>Appliance Controls |
| Plumbing system | Plumbing System | Receptacle | Electrical Receptacle |
| Police scanner | Radio, CB | Recessed lighting | Lighting, Incandescent<br>Lighting, Fluorescent |
| Polyurethane flooring | Flooring, Resilient | | |
| Pool table | Furniture, Wood | Rechargeable battery | Battery, Household<br>Battery Recharger |
| Popcorn popper | Popcorn Popper | | |
| Porch | Deck<br>Roof<br>Gutter<br>Paint<br>Siding<br>Masonry | Recliner | Furniture, Upholstered |
| | | Reel lawn mower | Lawn Mower, Reel |
| | | Refrigerator | Refrigerator |
| | | Remote control | Remote Control |
| Portable dishwasher | Dishwasher | Remote control toys | Toy<br>Remote Control |
| Portable stereo | Portable Stereo<br>Remote Control | Resilient flooring | Flooring, Resilient |
| | | Retaining wall | Masonry<br>Concrete |
| Pots and pans | Fix Everything: Adhesives<br>Fix Everything: Fasteners | Rheostat | Appliance Controls |
| Pottery | Fix Everything: Adhesives | Rice cooker | Steamer/Rice Cooker |
| Power tool | Electrical Cord<br>Motor<br>Fan<br>Fuse<br>Appliance Controls | Riding lawn mower | Lawn Mower, Riding |
| | | Roasting oven | Cooking Appliance<br>Electrical Cord<br>Heating Element<br>Appliance Controls<br>Fuse |
| Power toothbrush | Electric Toothbrush | | |
| Pressure washer | Small Engine<br>Garden Tool | Rocking chair | Furniture, Wood<br>Furniture, Upholstered |
| Printer | Computer Printer | Roll-top desk | Furniture, Wood |
| Propane stove | Cooktop, Gas | Roof | Roof |
| Pruner | Garden Tool | Room air conditioner | Air Conditioner, Room |
| Pump house | Outdoor Structure | Rotary lawn mower | Lawn Mower, Rotary |
| Purse | Fix Everything: Adhesives<br>Fix Everything: Sewing | Rotisserie | Rotisserie |
| | | Rubber flooring | Flooring, Resilient |

| Household Item | See Fix-It Guide(s) | Household Item | See Fix-It Guide(s) |
|---|---|---|---|
| Rug | Rug | Sliding doors | Door |
| Sander | Appliance Cord | Slow cooker | Slow Cooker |
| | Appliance Controls | Small appliance | Appliance Controls |
| | Motor | | Heating Element |
| | Fan | | Fan |
| Sandwich maker | Cooking Appliance | | Motor |
| Satellite system | Satellite System | | Fuse |
| Screen door | Screen | Small engine | Small Engine |
| | Door | Smoke detector | Smoke Detector |
| | Door Hardware | Snow apparel | Clothing |
| Screens | Screen | Snow blower | Small Engine |
| Sectional couch | Furniture, Upholstered | Snowmobile | Small Engine |
| Security sensor | Security System | Sofa | Furniture, Upholstered |
| Security system | Security System | Solar lighting | Battery Recharger |
| Septic system | Septic System | Spa | Whirlpool |
| Sewing machine | Sewing Machine | Space heater | Heater, Electric |
| Shaver | Electric Shaver | | Heater, Kerosene |
| Shed | Outdoor Structures | Speaker | Speaker |
| Shelf | Furniture, Wood | Sports equipment | Toy |
| Shovel | Garden Tool | | Fishing Reel |
| Shower head | Faucet | Sprinkler system | Pipe |
| Sidewalk | Asphalt | Stairs | Stairs |
| | Concrete | Stationary bike | Exercise Equipment |
| Siding | Exterior Siding | | Bicycle |
| | Masonry | Steam boiler | Boiler, Steam |
| Sink | Faucet | Steam cooker | Steamer/Rice Cooker |
| | Pipe | Stereo amplifier | Amplifier |
| | Drain System | Stereo speaker | Speaker |
| Sink drain | Drain System | Storage building | Outdoor Structures |
| Skylight | Window | Storage cabinet | Furniture, Wood |
| | Roof | Storm door | Door |
| | Framing System | | Door Hardware |
| Sleeping bag | Fix Everything: Sewing | | Screen |
| | Jacket (Zipper) | Storm window | Window |
| Slide projector | Appliance Cord | | Screen |
| | Appliance Controls | Stuffed toy | Stuffed Toy |
| | Lighting, Incandescent | | Doll |
| | Fan | | Fix Everything: Sewing |
| | Motor | | |

| Household Item | *See Fix-It Guide(s)* | Household Item | *See Fix-It Guide(s)* |
|---|---|---|---|
| Subfloor | *Subfloor*<br>*Framing System* | Track lighting | *Lighting, Incandescent* |
| | | Trash compactor | *Trash Compactor* |
| Sump pump | *Electrical Cord*<br>*Motor*<br>*Fuse*<br>*Appliance Controls* | Treadmill | *Exercise Equipment* |
| | | Tricycle | *Bicycle* |
| | | Trimmer | *Hair Clipper*<br>*Yard Trimmer* |
| Swimming pool | *Swimming Pool* | | |
| Swing set | *Fix Everything: Fasteners* | Trowel | *Garden Tool* |
| Switch | *Electrical Switch*<br>*Comfort Controls*<br>*Appliance Controls* | TV | *Television*<br>*Remote Control* |
| | | Upholstered furniture | *Furniture, Upholstered* |
| Table | *Furniture, Wood* | Upright vacuum | *Vacuum Cleaner, Corded* |
| Tape recorder | *Cassette Deck* | Vacuum cleaner | *Vacuum Cleaner, Corded*<br>*Vacuum Cleaner, Cordless* |
| Tea pot | *Fix Everything: Adhesives* | | |
| Telephone | *Telephone System*<br>*Telephone, Cordless*<br>*Telephone, Cellular* | VCR | *Videocassette Recorder*<br>*Remote Control* |
| | | Video camera | *Camera, Video* |
| Telephone answering<br>machine | *Telephone Answering*<br>*Machine* | Videocassette | *Videocassette Recorder* |
| | | Videocassette recorder | *Videocassette Recorder*<br>*Remote Control* |
| Telephone system | *Telephone System* | | |
| Television | *Television*<br>*Remote Control* | Vinyl fabric | *Furniture, Upholstered*<br>*Fix Everything: Sewing* |
| Tent | *Fix Everything: Sewing*<br>*Fix Everything: Adhesives* | Vinyl flooring | *Flooring, Resilient* |
| | | Vinyl siding | *Exterior Siding* |
| Thermal fuse | *Appliance Controls*<br>*Fuse* | Vinyl tile | *Flooring, Resilient* |
| | | Volleyball | *Toy* |
| Thermostat | *Comfort Controls*<br>*Appliance Controls* | Volleyball net | *Fix Everything: Sewing* |
| | | Waffle maker | *Cooking Appliance* |
| Tile | *Tile* | Wagon | *Toy* |
| Tiller | *Small Engine* | Walkie-talkie | *Radio, CB* |
| Timer | *Appliance Controls* | Walking path | *Asphalt*<br>*Concrete* |
| Timer motor | *Appliance Controls* | | |
| Toaster | *Toaster* | Walkman | *Portable Stereo* |
| Toaster oven | *Oven, Toaster* | Wall | *Drywall*<br>*Plaster*<br>*Paneling*<br>*Paint*<br>*Framing System* |
| Toilet | *Toilet* | | |
| Toothbrush | *Electric Toothbrush* | | |
| Toy | *Toy*<br>*Remote Control* | | |

| Household Item | See Fix-It Guide(s) |
|---|---|
| Wallboard | *Drywall* |
| Wall framing | *Framing System* |
| Wall outlet | *Electrical Receptacle* |
| Wall plaster | *Plaster* |
| Wallpaper | *Wallpaper* |
| Washer | *Washer, Clothes* |
| Washing machine | *Washer, Clothes* |
| Wastewater system | *Drain System* <br> *Pipe* <br> *Septic System* |
| Watch | *Jewelry* |
| Watch battery | *Battery, Button* |
| Waterbed | *Fix Everything: Adhesives* |
| Water heater | *Water Heater, Electric* <br> *Water Heater, Gas* |
| Water purifier | *Water Softener* |
| Water softener | *Water Softener* |
| Webcam | *Camera, Video* |
| Weedeater | *Yard Trimmer* |
| Weight bench | *Exercise Equipment* |
| Whirlpool | *Whirlpool* |

| Household Item | See Fix-It Guide(s) |
|---|---|
| Window | *Window* |
| Window blind | *Window Blind* |
| Window casing | *Window* |
| Window curtain | *Window Curtain and Drape* |
| Window drape | *Window Curtain and Drape* |
| Window fan | *Fan* |
| Window screen | *Screen* |
| Window shade | *Window Shade* |
| Wine rack | *Furniture, Wood* <br> *Fix Everything: Adhesives* |
| Wiring | *Electrical System* |
| Wok | *Cooking Appliance* |
| Wood-burning insert | *Fireplace/Stove* |
| Wood flooring | *Flooring, Wood* |
| Wood shed | *Outdoor Structures* |
| Wood siding | *Exterior Siding* |
| Wood stove | *Fireplace/Stove* |
| Wooden window screens | *Screen* |
| Yard trimmer | *Yard Trimmer* |
| Zipper | *Jacket* |

For additional information, be sure to visit us online at www.FixItClub.com.

# Air Conditioner, Central

Ah, central air conditioning. In many parts of the United States, it's practically a necessity. What did people ever do before it? And what can they do if it quits working on a hot day? Let's see.

## How Does It Work?

A central air conditioner is a large appliance system that cools an entire residence. It has two separate components: the condenser and the evaporator. The condenser unit typically is located outside the house. The evaporator coil is mounted with or near the heating furnace so the furnace blower can circulate the cool air throughout the house. Coolant lines run from the condenser to the evaporator, taking heat from the house and moving it outside.

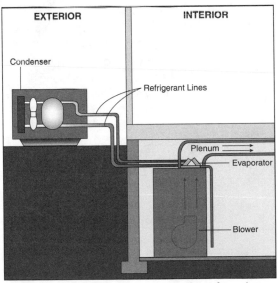

Centralized cooling systems remove heat from the house to cool it. Major components include the condenser and the evaporator.

## What Can Go Wrong?

Air conditioners are complex, and repairing them requires specialized training. Even so, you can handle routine maintenance and some minor repairs yourself. If not, you can more clearly explain to the technician what's wrong, saving the technician some expensive time.

> **Fix-It Tip**
>
> You can reduce repair costs by having your central air conditioning system checked and tuned up once a year—maybe during the fall when air conditioning technicians aren't as busy. They will test the refrigerant and other components as well as clean the unit. You can save a few bucks by cleaning it up and replacing filters yourself before the technician arrives.

## How Can I Identify the Problem?

If the system does not run, check the *Electrical Service Panel* for a tripped breaker or blown fuse. Also make sure the thermostat is set correctly.

If the system runs but does not cool, check for a clogged filter or malfunctioning blower. Inspect the condensing unit for blockages. If it still doesn't cool, call a technician to recharge the refrigerant. Note that some systems include a location for visually inspecting for low refrigerant.

If the system cycles too often, check the condensing unit's airflow, then the filter and blower; check the thermostat (see *Appliance Controls*).

If the outdoor unit is noisy, check the fan for obstruction. Tighten loose fan blades (see below) or loose screws in the housing.

If water drips from the bottom of the evaporator when the air conditioner is running, clear the evaporator drain (see the following steps).

If some rooms are too cool and others too warm, the distribution system may require balancing; see *Forced-Air Distribution*.

> **Fix-It Tip**
>
> Once a year, lubricate the fan motor with lightweight nondetergent oil if the owner's manual has instructions for doing so. If you don't have the manual, ask the technician how you can do this task yourself.

## What Parts, Materials, and Tools Do I Need?

There are very few parts you will be able to replace on a central air conditioner, except for filters. You can purchase filters at larger hardware stores and home centers or through the manufacturer or aftermarket supplier (see *Fix-It Resources*). The tools you may need for basic service include:

- Screwdrivers
- Wrenches
- Garden hose

## What Are the Steps to Fixing It?

Replace a filter:

1. Locate the filter(s) in the unit. Some are located on the condenser, while others are at the evaporator.
2. Remove the housing as needed to access and remove the filter.

3. Take the filter to a hardware store or home center for an exact replacement. If you need it, a part number may be on the filter or in the owner's manual. If a part number is not available, write down the central air conditioner's model number and take it with you for cross-referencing.
4. Reinstall the filter, making sure that the area around the filter also is clear of debris.

Clear the evaporator drain:

1. Remove the trap from the elbow.
2. Flush the trap with a garden hose, then pour 1 tablespoon of chlorine bleach through the trap to clean it.
3. Reattach the trap to the elbow.

Tighten loose fan blades:

1. Visually inspect the setscrews on the fan's hub for obvious damage or a loose screw.
2. If they are loose, tighten the setscrews with a wrench or screwdriver.
3. Check the fan's rotation to make sure it is smooth.

> **Fix-It Tip**
>
> Before restarting your central air conditioner in the spring (or after any long shutdown), turn power to the unit on for 24 hours before actually using it. This produces the heat needed to separate the oil from the refrigerant in the compressor.

# Air Conditioner, Room

Not all homes have—or need—a central air conditioner system. Necessity or economics may dictate that you install smaller air conditioners in a bedroom, nursery, or other living area for cooling during the hottest days. Of course, the "hottest day" is when it decides to quit working! Here's how to fix it. If you do have central air conditioning, see *Air Conditioner, Central*.

## How Does It Work?

A room air conditioner is an encased cooling unit for mounting in a window, through a wall, or as a console. It is designed for delivery of cool air to an enclosed space without ducts.

Here's how it works: Pressurized refrigerant flows through a room air conditioner, alternately in gas and liquid form. When the unit is on, the condenser pulls in refrigerant gas and pressurizes it, raising its temperature. The heated high-pressure gas travels to the condenser coils outdoors, where the fins distribute heat to the surrounding cooler air. The gas condenses into a liquid that travels indoors to the evaporator coils where, under reduced pressure, it vaporizes into a gas, absorbing heat from the room. The blower pulls room air through the air filter and across the evaporator coils, where it is cooled, then blown back into the room. It makes the room cooler by pulling the heat out of the air. The operation of the unit is controlled by a thermostat.

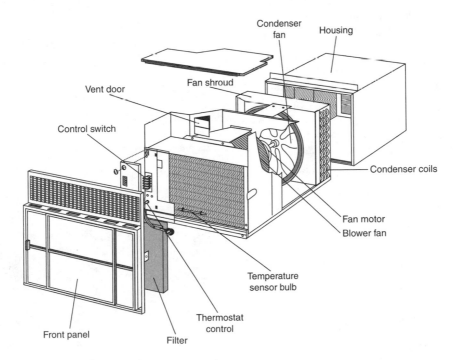

Components of a typical room air conditioner.

## What Can Go Wrong?

With a little maintenance, a room air conditioner should function satisfactorily for many years. The electrical cord might fail. The filter might need to be replaced. The coils might be dirty and the fins bent. The unit might be noisy and it might drip water inside. Routine maintenance includes cleaning or replacing the filter monthly during the cooling season and a yearly lubrication of the fan motor (unless the motor is permanently sealed).

## How Can I Identify the Problem?

If the unit does not run at all, check the *Electrical Service Panel* for a blown fuse or tripped circuit breaker. Test the *Electrical Cord*. Clean or replace the filter (see below).

If the unit repeatedly trips a circuit breaker or blows a fuse, clean the coils and straighten the fins (see below). If the problem continues, the unit may require professional service.

If the air conditioner turns on and off repeatedly, check for and remove any obstruction in the condenser, clean the coils, and if necessary, straighten the cooling fins (see below).

If the unit does not cool sufficiently, lower the thermostat and clean or replace the filter.

If the unit is noisy when running, tighten the housing screws and make sure clips are in place. Next, lubricate the fan *Motor* bearings (see below).

If the air conditioner drips water inside the room, check and flush the drain system (see below). Some condensation may be normal in high-humidity areas.

**Fix-It Tip**

During periods of high humidity, water dripping from the drip pan is normal.

## What Parts, Materials, and Tools Do I Need?

Replacement parts are available from the manufacturer and aftermarket suppliers (see *Fix-It Resources*) as well as from local hardware stores, electrical suppliers, and home centers. The tools you will need to fix a room air conditioner include these:

- Screwdrivers
- Wrenches
- Shop vacuum
- Fin comb
- Light (SAE 10) oil
- Garden hose

## What Are the Steps to Fixing It?

Maintain the filter and unit case:

1. Unplug the unit and remove the front cover.
2. Remove any clips holding the filter in place and remove the filter. It typically either is located in front of the evaporator coils or is attached to the back of the front panel.

The filter is usually located under the front panel and is easy to remove.

3. If the filter is not washable, or is damaged, replace it with an identical filter. If the filter is washable, vacuum off the heavy dirt and place the filter in a solution of light detergent and water. Squeeze out dirty water and rinse it with warm water. Squeeze out as much water as possible and let it dry before reinstalling it.

4. Use a shop vacuum with a brush attachment to loosen dirt from the cover and grilles. Spray the cover with a detergent-water solution and rinse it with clean water.

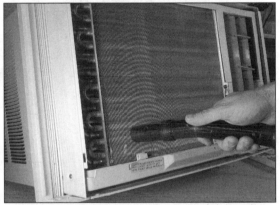

Use a shop vacuum to clean the grills of debris that can reduce the unit's efficiency.

5. Wipe the surface clean with a damp cloth.
6. Reattach the cover.

Clean the cooling coils:

1. Unplug the air conditioner, and remove it from the window if it is window-mounted.
2. Remove the housing as needed to access the cooling coils. Most units secure the back panel to the chassis with bolts or sheet-metal screws.
3. Vacuum the coils and evaporator fins with the brush attachment of a shop vacuum.
4. Make sure all components are clean and dry before reinstalling them.

**Fix-It Tip**

Room air conditioners can be very heavy to move. If you can't easily remove a window unit for winter, cover it with plastic sheeting and seal it with duct tape to protect it from the cold.

Straighten the coil fins.

Note: To avoid damage to the coil, use only an air conditioner coil fin comb (available at appliance parts stores) to straighten bent fins.

1. Unplug the unit from the electrical receptacle. If the unit is wired into the electrical system, turn off the circuit breaker or remove the circuit fuse in the *Electrical Service Panel.*
2. Remove any debris with a small brush before continuing.
3. Match up the fin comb to the fins to make sure that they fit properly and won't damage the fins.
4. Carefully fit the comb teeth between the coil fins in an undamaged section above the area to be straightened. Pull the fin comb down, sliding it through the damaged area.

Lubricate the fan motor:

1. Unplug the unit and remove it from the window or wall.
2. Remove the unit's cabinet or cover.
3. Find the oil ports on the *Motor* housing. If you can't find any, your motor might be permanently sealed and might not need lubrication.
4. Remove the caps from the oil ports. Insert a few drops of light (SAE-10) nondetergent oil into each port. Don't allow oil to contact electrical components.
5. Insert a drop or two of light (SAE 10) oil along the motor shaft where it meets the motor housing and the fan.

6. Rotate the fan by hand to work the oil into the motor.

7. Reassemble and reinstall the unit.

Check and flush the drain system:

1. Unplug the unit and remove the front cover. Take the unit out of the window or wall.

2. If the unit has an evaporator drain pan and a condenser drain pan, locate the drain tube connecting them. Pull out the tube from under the compressor base and run a thin wire through it to loosen any obstruction.

3. Flush the tube with 1 cup of a solution of chlorine bleach and water to prevent algae formation. If the unit does not have a drain tube, use a cloth to wipe clean the drain channels molded into the drain pan.

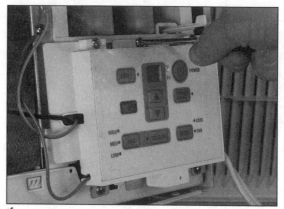

If necessary, you can remove, test, and replace the control panel, though this is really a job for a technician.

**Fix-It Tip**

Wait five minutes before restarting an air conditioner to lessen strain on the compressor.

# Air Purifier

It's a dirty world out there. And sometimes the dirt, pollutants, and pet hair come inside where people live and breathe. That's when you should consider an air purifier. Unfortunately, an air purifier, like just about everything else, eventually stops running or isn't as efficient as it used to be. That's when it's time for a special meeting of the Fix-It Club!

## How Does It Work?

An air purifier is a small appliance designed to filter airborne pollutants from indoor spaces. Although dust is most noticeable where it settles and collects, the average home has about three million dust particles suspended in every cubic foot of air. Scary, isn't it?

There are two types of air purifiers: the mechanical type and the electronic type. Both come in small-room and whole-house models. In a typical mechanical air purifier, a blade fan or a squirrel-cage fan draws air through a series of filters, including a prefilter (to remove the largest particles), one or more activated carbon or charcoal filters (to remove smaller odor-causing particles), and maybe a type of HEPA (**h**igh-**e**fficiency **p**articulate-**a**rresting) filter. Some mechanical units also include an ion generator to charge remaining dirt particles, causing them to adhere to room surfaces.

The most effective kind of air purifier uses an electrostatic precipitator to remove very fine particles, such as cigarette smoke and pollen, from the air in a room. The precipitator gives air particles a positive charge and then traps them with a negatively charged grid. The purifier also may contain filters to remove dust and

odors, as well as an ionizer to add negative ions to the clean air. The ionizer supplies a strong negative charge to one or more parts called needles. An intense electric field is developed at the point of a needle, and it creates ions in the atoms in the air. Positive ions are attracted to the needle, while negative ions flow outward. (Don't worry, there won't be a quiz.)

Electronic air purifiers are simple in design and typically require only periodic maintenance following instructions in the owner's manual.

## What Can Go Wrong?

Lots of things can go wrong with air purifiers. Fortunately, most of them are common problems that you can easily fix. The electrical cord might fail, the motor might fail, the switch might be faulty, the fan might be loose, or the motor shaft might be frozen. In addition, the precipitating cell might become dirty, motor bearings might be dry, filters and air intakes might be clogged or dirty, collector plates might be bent, and ionizer wires might be broken. You probably can fix any of these problems yourself.

## How Can I Identify the Problem?

The first step in solving a problem is defining it. If the unit does not run or runs sluggishly, make sure power is on at the outlet and test and replace the *Electrical Cord* if faulty. Test the *Motor* and replace or service it if needed. Make sure filters are installed according to manufacturer's directions. Inspect and service the switch as suggested in *Appliance Controls*. Check for a broken fan hub or loose setscrew on the fan (either one would allow the fan blades to spin freely on the motor shaft); replace a fan with a broken hub and tighten the setscrew. Try to turn the fan blades by hand; if the motor shaft sticks, lubricate the motor bearings.

If an electronic air purifier hisses, crackles, or pops excessively, remove and clean the cell following the manufacturer's directions.

If the unit is noisy in other ways, lubricate the *Motor* bearings, tighten the fan on the motor shaft, and remove any obstructions that might be hitting the blades.

If the air purifier fails to clean air, first check the owner's manual for air purifier capacity and compare it with your room size; replace the purifier if necessary. Check and clean or replace filters (below), position inlet and outflow sides of the unit away from obstructions like walls, drapes, and large furniture, vacuum dust and lint from filter covers and air passages. Remove the precipitating cell (electronic filters only) and examine the plates, they should be flat and uniformly spaced. If necessary, have the plates

repaired professionally or install a new cell. Test the precipitating cell (electronic purifiers only) and replace it if necessary. Locate and replace broken ionizer wires (electronic purifiers only).

If there is an ozone odor in the room (electronic purifiers only), look for a defective collector plate or ionizer wire. If the unit is new, however, a slight odor may be noticed for the first few weeks.

## What Parts, Materials, and Tools Do I Need?

You can get replacement parts from the manufacturer or aftermarket supplier listed in *Fix-It Resources*, and you can get common parts at your local hardware store. In addition, you'll need the following tools:

- Screwdrivers
- Pliers
- Multimeter
- Vacuum cleaner

## What Are the Steps to Fixing It?

Disassemble a mechanical air purifier:

1. Turn off the unit and unplug it. Press the release buttons to remove the intake grilles containing foam prefilters; then remove the filters.
2. Remove any screws holding the filter housing in place. To access the fan, remove the long screws holding the main housing together, and separate the halves.

3. Remove the fan by prying or twisting the locking ring from the end of the motor shaft (you probably should wear safety goggles for this step). Be careful not to bend the ring as you remove it.

4. Remove the screws holding the switch and the motor housing together. Then pull the housing apart to expose the motor. The switch module will now slide out from the channels in the housing.

Clean a foam filter:

1. Remove the intake grill from the air purifier.

2. Gently vacuum the filter through the grill.

Replace ionizer wires:

1. Unplug the air purifier and pull out the precipitating cell.

2. Use needle-nose pliers to unhook the wire spring from the connector at each end of the cell. If necessary, depress the connector with a screwdriver to free the wire.

3. Reverse the procedure to install the new wire.

Test the precipitating cell:

1. Remove the precipitating cell from the air purifier.

2. Set the multimeter (see *Fix Everything: Multimeter*) on R×1 (resistance times 1) to test resistance.

3. Clip one tester probe to the cell frame and touch the other probe first to the ionizer terminal, then, in turn, to each of the two outer collector terminals. A reading of 1 (infinity) indicates that the cell is okay. A lower ohms reading indicates a short circuit; replace the unit.

**Fix-It Tip**

Here are some cleaning tips to help you breathe easier and cut down on the times you have to fix your air purifier:

- Clean the prefilter in all purifiers and the precipitating cell in electronic purifiers frequently.

- Clean ion-emitter needles approximately every other month by gently wiping with a cotton swab dipped in rubbing alcohol.

- Replace the activated charcoal filter every three to six months, or according to the manufacturer's instructions.

- Replace HEPA filters at least once a year.

- Vacuum the inside of the purifier cabinet or wipe it gently with a damp cloth to remove dust each time you replace or clean any filters.

# Amplifier

What would you do without your music? Hopefully, you won't find out, because fixing an amplifier is a little more complicated than most things in your home. Fortunately, there are many things you can do to make your amplifier work without taking it to a repair person.

## How Does It Work?

An amplifier is an electronic device that magnifies and controls audio signal sources from a built-in AM-FM receiver as well as an external CD player, tape player, or other audio home-entertainment device. The output signal is fed to audio speakers.

## What Can Go Wrong?

Many things can go wrong with amplifiers, the most common being operator error. That is, if everything lights up but there is no sound, the speaker wires might not be connected or the speaker button might not be selected. Otherwise, the cord might be damaged or an internal fuse might be blown.

One of the most common causes of receiver problems is oxidation of electrical contacts and jacks. A jack is the connector used to mate a wire or plug to a circuit. A jack or plug that has gunk on it won't conduct electricity, so the next device in line doesn't get the signal.

Often, the problem is not in the amplifier but in one of the connections between it and either a source or the speakers. Use a continuity tester (see *Fix Everything: Continuity Tester*) or a multimeter (see *Fix Everything: Multimeter*) to check continuity of audio cords going in and out of the amplifier before attempting to open the unit up and look further.

## How Can I Identify the Problem?

Identifying the problem in an amplifier is easy: no power, no sound, or bad sound. Finding the source of the problem is a little more difficult. In some cases, the problem will actually be in an audio unit that feeds into the amplifier such as a *CD Player*, *Cassette Deck*, *DVD Player*, or *Speaker*.

> **Fix-It Tip**
>
> One of the first things you can try is to remove all other audio sources from the amplifier and use only the internal receiver to determine whether the unit is getting power or good sound.

## What Parts, Materials, and Tools Do I Need?

If you need to open up the amplifier for cleaning or to replace a *Fuse* or *Electrical Cord*, here's what you'll need:

- Phillips screwdrivers
- Soldering iron and solder
- Electrical contact cleaner spray or can of compressed air

## What Are the Steps to Fixing It?

Amplifiers are made up of many of the same components as other appliances, so fixing basic things is similar. For example, cords might not consistently deliver electricity, switches and controllers can cause problems, and fuses might need to be replaced. Frequently, what the amplifier needs most is a good cleaning.

The first step in fixing internal parts in an amplifier is to open it up. Most have a two-piece housing—top-front and bottom-back.

Disassemble an amplifier:

1. Make sure that the electrical cord is unplugged from the wall receptacle.
2. Remove screws on the side, back, or bottom to separate the cover from the chassis.

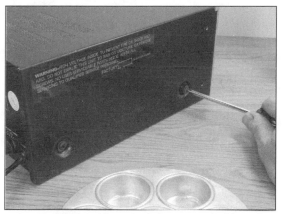

To open most amplifiers, look for screws holding the cover to the chassis.

3. Slide the two halves apart to expose the internal components mounted on the chassis (lower frame).

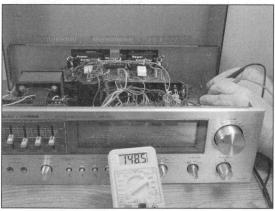

Once the chassis is open, look for obvious damage such as loose or burned wires.

4. Inspect the internal end of the electrical cord for looseness or damage caused by being pulled (a common problem) and replace as needed following the directions in *Electrical Cord*.
5. If there is no power, but the cord works, look for an internal fuse. Test the *Fuse* and replace as needed.

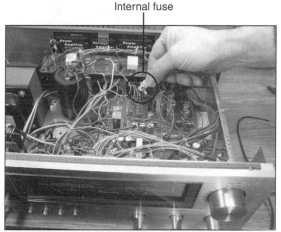

Besides fuses accessed from the back of the cabinet, many amplifiers include one or more internal fuses.

Use a multimeter to test all fuses.

6. Use a can of compressed air to carefully blow away dust that is attracted to electronic components. If excessive, use a vacuum cleaner with a plastic tip (so delicate parts won't receive static electricity) to clean the inside of the unit.

7. Use electrical contact cleaner to clean the input jacks and speaker terminals. If one of the input jacks is disconnected from the wires, either reconnect or resolder it (see *Fix Everything: Solder*).

If none of these measures solves the problem, seek professional help. Modern audio equipment is built using delicate components that cannot be repaired; instead, they are replaced. Your audio professional will know which ones to replace, where to get them, and how to do the job.

**Fix-It Tip**

Use a clean pencil eraser to clean cable pins on a regular basis. Use a quick shot of compressed air to remove eraser debris.

# Appliance Controls

Actually, appliance controls aren't household things—they are *parts* of things. Because they are parts of *dozens* of things in your home, knowing how to fix them is vital to fixing many things you own. For example, nearly all small and large household devices—from table lamps to heating furnaces—include switches. A few appliances with thermostats include the heating pad, hair dryer, toaster oven, and crock pot. You'll find timers in the coffee maker, washer, dryer, dishwasher, and microwave, just to name a few. Knowing how appliance controls work and how to fix them earns accolades in the Fix-It Club.

## How Does It Work?

Appliance controls are the devices that turn things on and off, regulate temperature, speed, and duration, and otherwise control appliance functions. Appliance controls include switches, thermostats, rheostats, and timing mechanisms. Some appliances, such as toasters, use mechanical controls while others, like microwave ovens, use digital controls. Knowing how they work will help you fix just about any of them.

Appliance *switches* vary in complexity and functions. Switches operate by making contact with the conductor of an electrical circuit. When an appliance is plugged in, it's connected to an electrical circuit in your home. Power runs through the wires of the circuit to the appliance. When the appliance's on-off switch is turned on, electricity flows through the switch to operate the appliance. There are several common types of switches: push-button, toggle, rocker, slide, and throw switch.

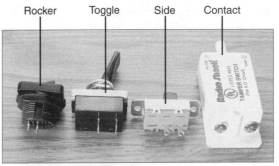

Rocker  Toggle  Side  Contact

Common appliance switches.

Variable-speed switch from a food mixer.

The back side of a toggle switch inside a food blender.

Other appliance controls are also switches. Rheostats, thermostats, solenoids, and timers, for example, are all types of switches. These components operate inside appliances to turn on motors, open and close valves, control heating elements, and turn on different parts of the appliance during different cycles, such as the rinse and spin cycles of a washing machine. Let's take a closer look at them.

A *thermostat* is a switch that controls temperature in a heating element or a cooling device. It opens and closes a circuit to furnish current based on temperature. Thermostats used in appliances may use a bimetal strip, bimetal thermodiscs, or a gas-filled bellows chamber to control the electrical contact. If faulty, they should be replaced rather than repaired.

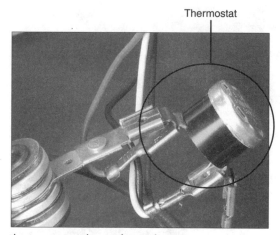

Thermostat

Thermostat inside an electric heater.

A *rheostat* is a variable controller that directs the amount of current flowing to many older appliance components. A blender with a dial control that can be turned to increase or decrease motor speed uses a rheostat to do so. Because rheostats can be damaged by moisture, they can easily malfunction.

A *timing mechanism* controls current flow based on a mechanical or digital timing device similar to a clock. Timing mechanisms on small appliances usually turn the appliances on

or off. Timers on major appliances—washing machine, dishwasher, dryer, frost-free refrigerator, or oven, for example—control the various cycles. Mechanical timers on large appliances consist of a shaft, gears, and a series of notched cams, one for each circuit or cycle. The timer is powered by a small timer motor. Digital timers are much simpler, using low-voltage electricity to control various functions such as turning on or off a device. While some timing mechanisms can be adjusted, those that are faulty should be replaced rather than repaired.

Many of these mechanical controls have been replaced, or at least are assisted, by digital controls. The good news is that digital controls are relatively trouble-free, going many years without service. The bad news is that when they do go out, there's no repair to do; you simply buy another unit and plug it in exactly as the old one. Of course, make sure you've solved any other electrical problems first so the digital controller won't be damaged on installation.

## What Can Go Wrong?

What can go wrong with appliance controls? They can quit controlling! Switches won't turn on and off, thermostats don't properly regulate heat, rheostats don't provide smooth control, and timers quit timing. In many cases, all that's needed is a good cleaning or reconnecting the wires. Otherwise, the controller should be replaced rather than repaired.

| Fix-It Tip | Sometimes the only problem with a controller is that an electrical connection to or from it has become loose. With the appliance unplugged, carefully wiggle the connection to make sure that it fits snugly. If there is corrosion at the terminal, remove the connection and clean the terminal with a small brush. |
| --- | --- |

## How Can I Identify the Problem?

If the appliance won't operate at all, test the on-off switch (see below) and replace if faulty. Also check the thermal *Fuse*.

You can purchase a replacement thermal fuse at Radio Shack or other electronic parts stores.

If the appliance doesn't heat, test the thermostat (see below) or rheostat (see below) and replace if faulty.

If the appliance doesn't come on at the set time, or if the machine doesn't change functions as designed, test the timer (see below) and replace it if it is faulty. It's usually more efficient to replace a faulty appliance control than to attempt repair. Some devices, such as heating pads, require replacement of the entire unit.

## What Parts, Materials, and Tools Do I Need?

Appliance controls typically are replaced, not repaired. In some cases, they may just need a careful cleaning of contacts. Otherwise, get replacement parts from the manufacturer or aftermarket supplier (see *Fix-It Resources*). Here's what you'll need:

- Multimeter
- Screwdrivers
- Small file for cleaning contacts
- Electrical contact cleaner

## What Are the Steps to Fixing It?

Test and service a switch:

1. Unplug the appliance and disassemble enough to access the switch. Disconnect one lead from the switch.

2. Set the multimeter on R×1 (resistance times 1) scale (see *Fix Everything: Multimeter*). Clip probes to the switch terminals or leads. Turn the switch on (for multispeed switches, press one switch at a time and note each reading). Zero ohms means the switch is okay. High or fluctuating ohms means the switch is broken or dirty.

3. Clean any switch contacts with a small file or with electrical contact cleaner. Contacts should make firm connection when the switch is on. If they don't, replace the switch rather than repair it.

4. Use electrical contact cleaner to clean less accessible switch contacts. In order to work cleaner into the switch, operate the control buttons as you spray the cleaner into apertures. Don't overspray.

Test and service a large-appliance thermostat:

1. Unplug and disassemble the appliance enough to access the thermostat.

2. Hook the clip of the multimeter (see *Fix Everything: Multimeter*) to one lead of the thermostat and touch the probe to the other. Or you can touch one probe of the multimeter to each terminal. The reading should be zero.

3. Turn down the temperature control dial; you'll see the contact points open at the thermostat. The meter should stop buzzing when the contacts open.

4. If the thermostat is faulty, replace it with a new one, following the manufacturer's instructions.

Test and service a small-appliance thermostat:

1. Unplug and disassemble the appliance enough to access the thermostat.

2. Set the multimeter (see *Fix Everything: Multimeter*) on R×1 (resistance times 1) scale. Place one probe of the multimeter on the output side and one probe on the input side. The reading should be zero.

3. Replace the thermostat if faulty.

Test a rheostat:

1. Unplug the appliance and disassemble enough to access the rheostat.

2. Set the multimeter (see *Fix Everything: Multimeter*) on R×1 (resistance times 1) scale. Clip the probes to the rheostat terminals or leads. Zero ohms means the rheostat is okay. As the probes are moved along the rheostat wire, the reading should change incrementally.

3. If necessary, use canned (compressed) air to clean around a rheostat wire.

Test a timing mechanism:

1. Unplug the appliance and access the timing mechanism.

2. Set the multimeter (see *Fix Everything: Multimeter*) to R×1 (resistance times 1) scale. Make a sketch of the timer wires for future reference, then disconnect all timer wires from their terminals. Make sure you'll be able to reconnect the wires exactly the same way when you're done.

3. Touch or clip one probe of the meter to the common terminal. Touch the other probe to each cycle terminal in turn. Rotate the timer control knob as you work. The multimeter should read zero ohms, meaning there's no resistance to the flow of electricity.

4. If one or more circuits do not give these results, the timer is faulty and should be replaced.

5. To replace a timer, disconnect its wires one at a time, connecting the corresponding wires of the new timer as you progress in order to avoid the chance of misconnection.

Test a timer *Motor:*

1. Unplug and disassemble the appliance enough to access the timer *Motor.*

2. Set the multimeter (see *Fix Everything: Multimeter*) on the R×10 scale and connect the leads to the two motor wires. A good motor should give a relatively high reading (usually 2,000 to 3,000 ohms), but not infinite (meaning no electricity will flow through it).

3. If the reading is infinity, replace the motor or the entire timer mechanism, as available.

Test and service electronic touch-pad controls:

1. If the entire pad does not work, check the circuit board or pad wiring on the rear of the pad for incomplete connections.

2. If a single button does not work, clean its contacts by rubbing them gently with a pencil eraser and then wiping away any residue with a foam swab dipped in alcohol.

3. If the pad still does not work, replace the entire assembly.

**Fix-It Tip**

Many digital control systems include error codes that can tell you what the problem is. The appliance's owner's manual or a helpful parts supplier can help you find and interpret the codes.

# Asphalt

Potholes breed. In no time at all, potholes on the street outside your home can breed smaller potholes in your driveway or even a walkway. Fortunately, you don't have to wait for the road crew to get an asphalt surface repaired. *You* can fix it. Here's how.

## How Does It Work?

Asphalt is a dark brown or black tarlike substance found in petroleum deposits. Heated up and mixed with crushed rock or other materials, asphalt becomes a relatively hard, smooth surface to support cars and people. In addition to being used on public roads, asphalt is popular for paving residential and commercial driveways, walkways, and paths.

> **Caution**
> Don't be taken in by unscrupulous workers who come to your door and offer to repair your driveway for a small fee. All they might do is spread used motor oil over the driveway. The repairs they perform may not last any longer than it takes for them to leave town.

## What Can Go Wrong?

Asphalt can crack, especially in cold areas where freeze/thaw cycles are common. Small cracks let in water that will freeze and expand, causing existing minor damage to become major. Periodic sealing will help keep cracks from starting, but won't prevent damage caused by settling of the ground or improper installation of the asphalt.

## How Can I Identify the Problem?

If an asphalt driveway, road, path, or sidewalk develops a small crack, you can fill it with asphalt-based caulk (see below).

If the asphalt has already developed a hole, you can patch it with asphalt patch (see below).

If you want to keep asphalt in good condition, you can periodically clean and seal it (see below).

## What Parts, Materials, and Tools Do I Need?

Replacement parts are available from local home improvement outlets. The tools you will need to fix asphalt include these:

* Shop vacuum
* Putty knife
* Hammer
* Chisel
* Caulking gun
* Asphalt-based caulk or sealer
* Rubber gloves
* Wire brush
* Asphalt patching compound
* Trowel
* 2 × 4 piece of lumber
* Thick (¾ to 1 inch) plywood
* Garden hose with sprayer or pressure washer
* Squeegee or push broom
* Sand
* Household cleaner

## What Are the Steps to Fixing It?

Fill a minor crack:

1. Sweep out loose material or vacuum it up with a shop vacuum.

2. If the crack is deep, fill it with sand, and compact it to within ½ inch of the surface.

3. Use a caulk gun to apply a continuous bead of asphalt-based caulk. Follow the instructions for drying time (usually about 10 minutes).

4. Compact and smooth the surface with a putty knife, being careful not to spread caulk too widely.

Fill a small hole:

1. Brush out any loose material or vacuum it up with a shop vacuum.

2. Clear away loose chunks and break off any unsupported edges of the old asphalt.

3. Spread asphalt patching compound in the hole using a trowel until the compound is mounded slightly higher than the driveway.

4. Use the end of a piece of lumber to tamp the patch down, level with the driveway surface.

Fill a larger hole:

1. Remove any loose debris and smooth jagged edges around the hole with a hammer and chisel. If the hole is deep, you can place and pack solid debris (rocks, etc.) in the hole as a foundation for the asphalt patch.

Fill the hole with rocks and other solid debris to form a base to reduce the amount of asphalt patch needed.

2. Fill the hole about halfway to the top with asphalt patch and tamp it down with the end of a piece of lumber.

Pour the asphalt patch into the hole.

3. Fill the hole to slightly above the surrounding asphalt.

4. Place a piece of thick plywood over the patch.

5. Drive a car slowly over the plywood to compact the patch.

Clean and seal an asphalt surface:

**Fix-It Tip**
Does your asphalt driveway need resurfacing? To find out, pour water on it on a hot day and watch to see if it runs off quickly, which it should do, or if it seeps in, meaning it needs resurfacing.

1. Use a pressure washer or a hose with a pressure nozzle to wash the asphalt surface.

2. Apply full-strength household cleaner on any remaining stains.

3. Spread on a thin coat of sealer with a squeegee or old broom.

4. Allow the sealer to dry for 24 to 36 hours before applying a second coat as needed.

**Fix-It Tip**
How much asphalt sealer do you need? Five gallons will cover a typical 10-feet by 25-feet driveway, depending on how porous the surface is. Check the sealer label for coverage estimates.

# Battery Recharger

Batteries offer portable power. Dozens of things in everyone's home run on batteries. Some household batteries (see *Battery, Household*) are use-and-toss, while others use a recharger to replenish their stored electricity. They include household battery rechargers (AA, AAA, C, D batteries) as well as all the new shop tools (drills, saws, vacuums, etc.) that run on special rechargeable batteries. Let's visit the Fix-It Club to find out how to keep all those batteries charging.

## How Does It Work?

Batteries produce electric current from the chemical reaction between two electrodes and an electrolyte. Battery rechargers convert 120V alternating current (AC) into small-voltage direct current (DC). The voltage ranges from 1.2V to 24V or more, depending on the battery and the charger.

Many cordless appliances are powered by a rechargeable nickel-cadmium (nicad) battery or battery pack consisting of as many as 20 cells. Each cell provides direct current at about 1.2 volts. Battery packs slip directly into the appliance or tool or have snap-on terminals. Some battery packs have built-in batteries that cannot be removed; they must be charged in the unit.

## What Can Go Wrong?

Lots of things can happen to rechargeable batteries, none of them unsolvable. Rechargeable batteries lose their power. Electrical contacts might not be making full contact. The charger may be defective. Batteries wear out or become defective.

## How Can I Identify the Problem?

If a cordless device (with built-in rechargeable battery) doesn't work, lacks power, or does not run long enough, make sure power is on at the outlet and the outlet is not wired into a wall switch that has been turned off. Also check the *Electrical Cord* and replace it if it is defective. Test the recharger unit (see below) and replace as necessary.

If a cordless device or rechargeable batteries run for shorter and shorter periods between rechargings, the nicad batteries are probably worn out. Inspect them for damage or leaks and replace as needed. Test the recharger unit (see below) and replace if not working.

If there is no leakage visible, test the battery pack and replace if necessary.

## What Parts, Materials, and Tools Do I Need?

There really aren't any replacement parts available for battery rechargers—except the rechargeable batteries themselves. You can open up the rechargers and check for obvious damage, such as a disconnected *Electrical Cord*, and clean internal contacts, but that's about all. Here are the tools you'll need:

- Screwdrivers
- Small file
- Electrical contact cleaner
- Multimeter

Household battery chargers include a transformer and a circuit board—not much to work on unless you're an electrical technician.

## What Are the Steps to Fixing It?

Restore full electrical contact:

1. Unplug the recharger from the electrical receptacle.
2. Use a small file, emery paper, or electrical contact cleaner to clean the contacts between the power handle and the charger.
3. Move the power unit in and out of the charger several times to be sure it makes full contact.

Test a DC output charger:

1. Set a multimeter (see *Fix Everything: Multimeter*) to the 25 DCV (direct current volts) scale.

2. Plug in the recharger to the electrical receptacle (outlet).
3. Touch the two multimeter probes to the appropriate charger contacts (+ and –). If the meter reads zero volts, reverse the probes.
4. The DCV output should be at or slightly above the charger's rated output. That is, a 9 VDC charger should give a reading of about 10 VDC.

Test an AC output charger:

1. Set a multimeter (see *Fix Everything: Multimeter*) to the 25 ACV scale.
2. Touch the two multimeter probes to the two charger contacts. If there is no reading, the transformer is faulty. Check an electrical supplier for a transformer of the same rating and size.

Test a battery pack:

1. Completely charge the battery pack.
2. Set a multimeter (see *Fix Everything: Multimeter*) on the DCV scale larger than the battery pack's rated output.
3. Touch the red multimeter probe to the pack's [+] terminal and the black probe to the – terminal.
4. Replace the battery pack if the reading is more than 1 volt below the rated output (8 VDC for a 9 VDC pack).

**Fix-It Tip**

Need to get rid of some old rechargeable batteries? Call your local solid waste management service for specifics, because some locations don't allow rechargeable batteries to be included with household trash. The store from which you purchase the replacement batteries *may* know about local regulations. Check www.rbrc.org/consumer to find out who in your area will accept old batteries.

# Battery, Button

Many small gadgets are powered by miniature batteries, often called button batteries because they are as small as a shirt button. They power watches, calculators, toys, palm computers, electronic notebooks, computer clocks, some cell phones, and many other household items. They are everywhere. Lucky for us, they are easy to check and replace.

## How Does It Work?

A battery stores and delivers electric current. All batteries contain two electrodes and an electrolyte, which produces the chemical reaction with the electrodes resulting in a current. In "dry" batteries, the electrolyte is a paste of powdered chemicals. A battery's voltage depends on the metals that are used in its electrodes and the number of cells.

A button battery contains powdered zinc and mercury oxide with an alkaline electrolyte. The zinc loses electrons as it becomes zinc oxide, while the mercury atoms gain electrons as the mercury oxide changes to mercury. Button batteries typically produce 1.35 volts. One side of the battery is marked with a [+], the positive side, and the other is the negative side. Button batteries are round, but come in various heights and widths.

## What Can Go Wrong?

Like other consumer batteries, they either work or they don't. They aren't rechargeable, so fixing one means replacing it. In addition, button batteries can corrode, losing their electrical connection. In extreme cases they can leak, damaging adjacent components.

**Caution** When replacing a button battery in a device, *always* replace it with the same size and type, indicated by the battery model number, typically etched on the top side.

## How Can I Identify the Problem?

If the device stops doing what it is supposed to do or is no longer accurate, inspect the battery for corrosion or leakage. A discolored, corroded, or leaking battery should be discarded. You also can test the battery to see if it has lost its power (see below) and replace it if it is faulty. To test a button battery, make sure you use the lowest DCV (direct current volts) scale on the multimeter (see *Fix Everything: Multimeter*), because voltage is very low.

## What Parts, Materials, and Tools Do I Need?

The only part you'll need to fix a button battery is another button battery. Tools, however, depend on what the battery is installed in, because you have to gain access to it to visually and electrically check it. Typical disassembly and testing tools for smaller electrical devices are these:

- Screwdrivers
- Pliers
- Wrenches
- Emery cloth for cleaning
- Multimeter

## What Are the Steps to Fixing It?

Test a button battery:

1. Look on the battery to determine the battery voltage.

Remove the button battery from the device and read the front to determine what the voltage should be; in this example it is 3V.

2. Set the multimeter (see *Fix Everything: Multimeter*) to the DCV scale.

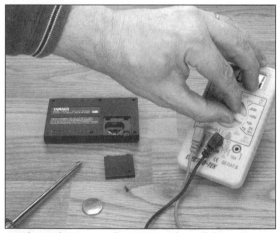

Set the multimeter to the DCV scale and the range that's higher than 3V.

3. Touch the red multimeter probe to the battery's [+] side and the black probe to the – side. If the reading is more than 10 percent below the rated output (2.7 volts for a 3V battery), the battery is bad and should be replaced.

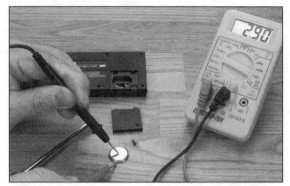

The bottom of many button batteries is –, and the top and edge are [+] so you can touch the probes to these locations to get a voltage reading.

**Fix-It Tip**

Check your other button battery–powered devices to determine if they use the same model, and purchase batteries in multiple packs to save money.

# Battery, Car

Click-click-click! That's not the sound you wanted to hear when you turned the ignition key, but there it is. It's a good thing that modern car batteries are *nearly* maintenance-free. But things can still go wrong with them—or they get too tired to do the job. In any case, it's an easy fix.

## How Does It Work?

A car battery produces an electric current when its terminals are connected to each other to form a circuit. All batteries contain two electrodes ([+] and –) and an electrolyte, which produces the chemical reaction that generates a current from the electrodes. "Wet" batteries, like those in cars, contain a liquid electrolyte. Modern car batteries are 12V.

A car battery is designed to produce the strong current needed to turn the starter motor. It does this by using a number of cells linked together. When running, the engine turns an alternator, which feeds current back into the battery to recharge it. A car battery contains plates of lead oxide and lead metal, immersed in a sulfuric acid electrolyte. As the battery produces current, both kinds of plate change to lead sulfate. Feeding a current into the battery reverses the chemical reaction.

Car batteries are rated by cold-crank amps (CCA), the minimum electric current (in amps) that a charged 12-volt battery can deliver for 30 seconds at 0°F (brrrrr) without falling below 7.2 volts. The higher the CCA number, the more power it can give you. Of course, you might not need to pay for all that extra power if you live in a warmer climate.

Marine and RV (recreational vehicle) batteries are similar to car batteries except that they can power things longer. They are called deep-cycle batteries. Deep-cycle batteries are designed for prolonged discharges at lower current and not for the high-current discharges that car starters need. Other than that, "fixing" either battery is about the same.

## What Can Go Wrong?

Car batteries either work or they don't—or they are just about ready *not* to work. What can happen? A battery can become discharged (little or no electric current), leak fluids, or fail to keep a charge. In a related and more common situation, the battery connections may not be working properly. Fortunately, these problems are fixable.

Many auto parts stores offer curbside battery service. Parts salespeople will come out to your car in their parking lot, check the battery, and even replace it and recycle your old one for you. The better ones will tighten connections rather than try to sell you a battery you don't need.

## How Can I Identify the Problem?

In many cases, the battery tells you when it's going out by not doing what it's supposed to do. Because the most power it uses is to turn the starter motor, that's typically when it tells you it's tired or sick. Click-click-click.

To identify the cause of the problem (battery, cables, starter), use the process of elimination to identify the cause. If your car doesn't even make a noise when you try to start it, check and clean the battery connections (see below). If the starter turns over but won't start and sounds weaker and weaker, test the battery (see below). If the lights have been left on and the car won't start, turn the lights off, wait a few minutes, and try again. If the car still will not start, you may need to jump-start the car and run it for a while to recharge the battery (see below). If the battery shows any signs of leakage, replace it immediately.

> **Caution**
>
> Work carefully around a battery. Battery acid is caustic. Leaking battery acid can harm skin, eyes, and car parts, so always wear gloves and eye protection.

## What Parts, Materials, and Tools Do I Need?

You may need a new battery. If you do, replace the old one with a new or rebuilt battery of the same group (size) and at least as much power (CCAs). You can usually recycle your old battery where you purchase your new one. Testing, cleaning, and installing a battery requires various tools and parts available from a local auto parts store:

- Battery terminal cleaner tool
- Wrench
- Battery charger
- Jumper cables
- Multimeter (for testing voltage)
- Hydrometer (for testing electrolyte in nonsealed batteries)

## What Are the Steps to Fixing It?

As you'll see, there are many things you can do yourself before you ever have to open your wallet for a new battery.

First, note that most maintenance-free (sealed) batteries have a built-in hydrometer that indicates the state of charge by the color displayed in a small window on the top. Normally, a bright-colored hydrometer indicates a full charge and a dark hydrometer indicates the battery needs charging. Some maintenance-free batteries have a spot of light on top of the battery to tell you whether the battery is charged; no light means no charge. Most such batteries have a label on them to tell you how to interpret what you see. If the battery

has a sealed top and no built-in hydrometer, you can hook up a multimeter (see *Fix Everything: Multimeter*) across the battery terminals to check the charge. A fully charged battery should read 12.6 volts or higher.

> **Caution**
>
> Before you disconnect that battery, make sure you know the code for your car's antitheft device. If your car is equipped with one, you'll have to enter the code into the car radio (see *Radio, Car*) before you can operate it again. You also may lose information stored in your car's computer about fuel consumption and other data.

Clean the battery and terminals:

1. Identify the terminals. One has a [+] (positive) symbol on or near it and one has a – (negative) symbol. The cable on one of these two terminals is attached to the engine (ground terminal, *usually* the negative terminal) and the other goes to the starter.
2. Remove the plastic terminal caps, if there are any, and carefully brush away any white powder (corrosion). If the battery cables attach to the battery with a nut, remove the nut and clean the terminal and cable with a wire brush, and then skip to step 6. If the battery uses terminal posts, follow steps 3 through 5.
3. Use a wrench to loosen the bolts at the end of the battery cable where it wraps around the ground terminal. Carefully wiggle the cable end up and down until it comes off the terminal; if the end doesn't come off the terminal easily, buy and use a battery terminal puller from the parts store. Then loosen and remove the cable on the other terminal.

> **Caution**
>
> Striking a terminal or cable end with a hammer to loosen it can loosen the terminal inside, ruining the battery.

4. Place the end of the terminal-cleaning tool over each terminal and rotate it a few times. The wire brush inside the tool will clean the terminal post.

Use a terminal-cleaning tool to clean the battery terminals.

5. Twist and open the terminal-cleaning tool to expose the round wire brush inside. Insert this brush into the cable ends and rotate the tool to clean the inside of the ends. If the cable ends are broken or the wire is frayed, replace the cable with one of the same length.

6. Use an old paint brush to dust away dirt and corrosion from the top and sides of the battery. Make sure the debris doesn't fall on other components or on the car's paint. If the battery is very dirty, remove it from the car and carefully clean it with a solution of a pint of water and a teaspoon of baking soda. Just make sure the solution doesn't get inside the battery.

7. Reattach the terminal cables.

Charge a battery with a charger:

1. Remove all the battery cell caps (if the battery is not maintenance-free) and cover the holes with a clean cloth to prevent spattering electrolyte.

2. Disconnect the negative battery cable and hook the battery charger cable clamps to the battery posts (positive to positive, negative to negative), then set the charger to 12V if it has a selector and plug in the charger.

3. Turn on the charger and check it regularly for the first couple of hours.

4. Continue to monitor a higher-amp (faster) charger. Let a trickle charger run for several hours or overnight. A full charge on a trickle charger could take 8 to 16 hours.

5. If the battery has removable cell caps, measure the specific gravity with a hydrometer every hour during the last few hours of the charging cycle (follow the instructions on the hydrometer). Consider the battery charged when there's no change in the specific gravity reading for two hours and the electrolyte in the cells is bubbling freely. The specific gravity reading of each cell should be nearly the same; if not the battery probably has one or more bad cells.

Jump-start a dead battery using another vehicle's battery:

1. Use a jumper cable to connect the dead battery's positive [+] terminal to the donor car's positive [+] terminal.

2. Connect the donor car's negative – terminal to the head of an engine bolt on the patient car's engine.

3. Start the donor car's engine, and then start the patient car's engine.

4. After the car that had the dead battery starts, remove the jumper cable in the reverse order of how it was installed.

**Fix-It Tip**

A trickle charger is best for charging your car's battery. It is safest and puts the least strain on the battery.

# Battery, Household

Batteries not included. Many things we buy today don't come with a source of power, batteries. And most batteries have the useful life of a two-year-old's attention span. So they are continually being replaced. But should they? The Fix-It Club knows!

## How Does It Work?

A household battery stores electric current that can be tapped when its terminals are connected to each other to form a circuit. All batteries contain two electrodes and an electrolyte; together they produce a chemical reaction that results in a current of electricity.

Small household batteries (AA, AAA, C, D) are also called "dry" batteries because the electrolyte is a paste of powdered chemicals. Alkaline batteries use an alkaline electrolyte. A battery's voltage depends on the metals that are used in its electrodes and the number of cells. Household batteries produce 1.5 or 9 volts of direct current (DC) electricity, depending on the model.

See also *Battery, Button* for information on the smaller batteries that power watches, calculators, toys, palm computers, electronic notebooks, computer clocks, some cell phones, and many other household items.

## What Can Go Wrong?

Household batteries work, work weakly, or don't work at all. They quit working because they corrode, leak, and lose their power.

| Fix-It Tip |
|---|
| Because batteries can corrode and leak and harm the very thing they are intended to power, remove batteries from items that are not used frequently. |

## How Can I Identify the Problem?

If a device powered by a household battery won't work, make sure the batteries are properly inserted, positive to positive and negative to negative. Clean the battery.

If a battery looks off-color or shows any sign of flaking or corroding, replace it with a new battery.

If a battery looks okay, gently polish both ends of the battery and all of the contacts inside the battery holder with a silver-polishing cloth, pencil eraser, emery board, or fine sandpaper; don't touch the cleaned areas.

If the device still won't work or works sluggishly, test the batteries with a multimeter, as below (see *Fix Everything: Multimeter* for more information on using a multimeter), or with the self-tester on the battery. Replace any batteries that test low. If the device still won't work, the problem is more serious than batteries.

| Caution |
|---|
| *Do not* recharge household batteries except those that specifically say "rechargeable." And recharge them only in battery recharging units. See *Battery Recharger.* |

## What Parts, Materials, and Tools Do I Need?

Here's what you need to test, clean, and replace batteries, all available at hardware stores and home centers:

- Multimeter
- Silver-polish cloth
- Pencil eraser
- Emery board
- Replacement batteries

## What Are the Steps to Fixing It?

Test a household battery:

1. Check the side of the battery to determine its DC voltage. Commonly, AA, AAA, C, and D are 1.5V, and rectangular batteries are 9V.
2. Set the multimeter to the VDC (volts of direct current) scale (see *Fix Everything: Multimeter*).
3. Touch the red multimeter probe to the battery's [+] terminal and the black probe to the – terminal. If the reading is more than 10 percent below the rated output (1.35V or 8.1V), the battery is bad and should be replaced.

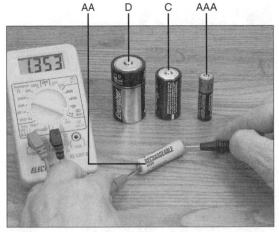

Make sure the battery voltage is at least 90 percent of the full-charge rate.

# Bicycle

Bicycles are simple transportation, but they, too, can need repair. Single- and three-speed bikes are relatively easy to repair, but those with more speed gears require more repair knowledge and finesse. It's a good thing that the Fix-It Club knows how to keep bikes in top condition.

## How Does It Work?

A bicycle is a vehicle with two inline wheels, a steering handle, an uncomfortable seat, and pedals. The pedals are used to turn the chain assembly that turns the rear wheel for forward motion.

There is a wide variety of bicycles from single-speed bicycles with pedal-controlled coaster brakes to multispeed bikes equipped with a sophisticated system of derailleurs, freewheels, chain rings, and pressure brakes. The extra components allow the bike to run easily through a range of gear combinations at the touch of a precision index shifter—and help you stop the bike.

| Caution | When parking a bicycle, use the kickstand to keep it from falling over. If you must lay the bike down on its side, lay it on the left side so as not to damage the freewheel, chain rings, and derailleurs. |
|---|---|

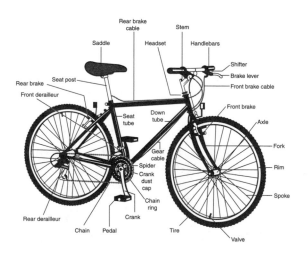

Components of the typical multispeed bicycle.

## What Can Go Wrong?

The list is short: Lubricated parts dry out. Tires go flat. Brakes get out of adjustment. Chains wear out.

Once you're done with a ride, make sure you clean dirt and debris off the tires, wipe moisture off components, and clean the chain of debris. If you wipe the chain, lightly lubricate it to replace the oil removed.

## How Can I Identify the Problem?

If the fork binds as you steer, clean and lubricate the headset (see below). Regular lubrication of other parts will keep a bike operating at its best (see below).

If a tire goes flat, you can repair it (see below).

If brakes do not stop the bike smoothly, you can adjust them (see below).

If a chain slips or comes off, you can repair or replace it (see below).

If the derailleur does not operate smoothly or causes the chain to jump gears, see your owner's manual for specific instructions on adjusting this sensitive mechanism.

## What Parts, Materials, and Tools Do I Need?

Replacement parts are available from bicycle shops, some hardware and toy stores, and other large retailers. The tools you will need to fix a bicycle include these:

- Screwdrivers
- Wrenches
- Hammer
- Pliers
- Wood block
- Spoons or tire levers
- Bicycle grease (available at bike shops)

- Lightweight (5–10 weight) oil
- Bicycle tire pump
- Chain tool
- Inner tube repair kit
- Air pressure gauge

## What Are the Steps to Fixing It?

Lubricate the headset (handlebar holder):

1. Remove the brake cable from the stop. Loosen the stem bolt with a wrench and remove the stem.
2. Remove the handlebars.
3. Loosen and remove the headset locknut at the top of the headset. Remove other components as needed.
4. Inspect all parts (especially bearings) for wear and replace as needed.
5. Remove the head tube to access the bottom bearings.
6. Clean any metal parts with solvent.
7. Lubricate the lower cup with bicycle grease and reinstall the head tube.
8. Lubricate the top cup with bicycle grease and reinstall the bearings.
9. Install other components in reverse order of disassembly.

Lubricate other parts:

1. Remove the brake and gear cables from their housings.
2. Lubricate the cables with bicycle grease and reinstall them in their housings.
3. Lubricate the brake pivot points with bicycle grease.
4. Lubricate all moving parts of both the front and rear derailleurs with bicycle grease.
5. Lubricate the chain with lightweight oil and wipe off the excess.

Fix a flat tire:

1. Check the tire's valve by submerging it in water and checking for air leaks.
2. Inspect the tire surface for cuts and holes, marking them with chalk to find them more easily later.
3. Use pliers to remove nails or glass.
4. Remove the wheel from the bicycle, following the instructions in your owner's manual.
5. Deflate and remove the tire from the rim.
6. Inflate the tube and run your hand around it to find the air leak. Mark the leak with chalk. Check the corresponding place on the tire for nails, glass, thorns, or other sharp objects and remove them.
7. Deflate the tube and use a tube patch kit to repair the damage, following instructions included with the kit.

Adjust cantilever brakes:

1. Loosen the anchor bolt that holds the brake cable.
2. Use a clamp to hold the brake pads in place on the tire rims.
3. Pull the cable taut and tighten the anchor bolt.
4. Remove the clamp and test the brake. If too tight, readjust.

Adjust side-pull brakes:

1. Turn the adjuster screw clockwise to adjust. If needed, loosen the anchor bolt for additional adjustment.
2. Use a clamp to hold the brakes firmly on the tire rim.
3. Use pliers to pull the lower end of the cable taut through the anchor bolt, then tighten.
4. Release the clamp. If the brake pads remain closed, slightly loosen the cable tension.
5. Locate the adjusted brake over the center of the wheel and tighten.

Replace a chain:

1. Shift gears until the chain is on the smallest freewheel cog and smallest chain ring.
2. Find the removable link in the chain and disassemble it with a chain tool. Remove the chain, remembering its path.
3. Install the new chain through the rear derailleur following same path as the old chain.
4. Install the new chain on the smallest freewheel cog and the largest chain ring.
5. Add or remove links in the chain for a proper fit.
6. Use the chain tool to install and fasten the chain link.
7. Lubricate the chain with lightweight oil and test the chain.

# Blender

Blenders are handy electrical gadgets that make chopping and mixing food easier—when they work. Otherwise, they are another thing that sits on a shelf waiting for the day you can get around to fixing it. Today is the day!

## How Does It Work?

A food blender is a motorized small appliance that blends, chops, and grates food. A blade inside a jar is connected to a motor shaft inside the unit. The blade's speed is controlled by varying electric current to the motor using one or more switches. Blenders come in countertop and handheld models.

> **Fix-It Tip**
>
> When purchasing a blender, look for one with the strongest motor, measured in watts (W). The wattage should be noted on the underside of the unit. A better blender has at least 250W.

## What Can Go Wrong?

Because blenders are simple motorized small appliances, the things that can go wrong also are simple. The electrical cord, motor, switches, or fuse may fail. Parts may become loose or worn and seals may leak. (To avoid spills, don't fill the blender jar more than two thirds full when in use.)

## How Can I Identify the Problem?

If the blender doesn't work at all, make sure power is on at the outlet. Check the *Electrical Cord*. Test the *Fuse* with a multimeter (see *Fix Everything: Multimeter*). Test the multispeed switch (see *Appliance Controls*). If all this fails, you'll need to test the universal *Motor*.

If the blender runs intermittently, check wire connections and replace any that are faulty; check the motor and replace if needed.

If the blender doesn't run at *some* speeds, check the multispeed switch (see *Appliance Controls*) and clean or replace it if it is faulty; check wire connections and repair any that are faulty.

If the motor runs but the blade doesn't turn, check the drive stud and tighten or replace as necessary. Also, check the blade and clean and lubricate or replace it if damaged.

If the jar leaks (a common blender problem), check the base and tighten if needed. Check the seal and replace the seal, blade assembly, or jar as needed.

> **Fix-It Tip**
>
> To wash a blender jar in a dishwasher, first disassemble it and remove the rubber seals. If it is too difficult to disassemble the jar, you can wash it by hand. Fill the jar half-full with warm water and add a drop of liquid detergent. Cover and blend the mixture at low speed for five seconds. Run the blender with clean water to rinse, then run it empty to dry the blades. Finally, remove the blades and wipe them with a cloth to get rid of any residue.

## What Parts, Materials, and Tools Do I Need?

Replacement parts are available from the manufacturer or aftermarket suppliers (see *Fix-It Resources*). These are the tools you'll need for disassembly and repair:

- Screwdrivers
- Pliers

## What Are the Steps to Fixing It?

Disassembly steps depend on what model blender you own. The following steps work for most standard blenders.

Disassemble a blender:

1. Unplug the blender and remove the jar. Undo the screws securing the baseplate. Separate the baseplate and attached motor collar from the base housing.

Turn the blender over to access screws holding the baseplate.

2. To remove the switch housing, remove the decorative facing to get at the top screws. Remove the lower screws from inside the blender base.

3. Hold the fan to keep the motor shaft from turning as you unscrew the drive stud. Remove the shield and any washers. Unscrew the fan nut to remove the fan.

Wear a leather glove to hold the fan in place as you disconnect it from the motor shaft.

You now can access and remove the motor and other components as needed.

4. Disengage the strain-relief fitting from the housing. Remove the wire connector joining the power cord and the lead to the brush housing.

5. Label and disconnect the lead wires from the switch block. Remove the motor mounting bolts and lift out the *Motor* if necessary.

6. To free the brushes, remove the leads attached to the brush housing. Use a screwdriver to press lead terminal through the slot in housing. The brush spring may pop out (don't lose it!).

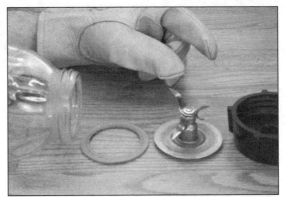

Wear a leather glove to get a grip on and loosen the blender's base.

Tighten a blender's drive stud:

1. Remove the base and turn the blender over to expose the motor's drive shaft.
2. Grip the drive shaft with a wrench or pliers, then turn the blender on its side to attach a wrench to the drive stud.
3. Hold the drive shaft steady as you turn the drive stud clockwise.

If the drive stud is too worn to tighten, simply reverse the instructions for tightening the stud, install the new part, and tighten it.

If the drive stud turns but the blade assembly doesn't, inspect the assembly socket into which the drive stud fits. It may be worn and require replacement. This is a common problem on blenders with metal drive studs and plastic blade-assembly sockets.

To service a blade assembly, tighten the base. If this doesn't solve the problem, inspect and, if necessary, replace the gasket.

# Boiler, Hot-Water

Many homes and apartments use hot-water boilers to keep comfortable in winter. They are relatively efficient, but not always easy to fix. Fortunately, understanding how they work and maintaining them can make them trouble-free longer. Also see *Boiler, Steam*. For water heaters, see *Water Heater, Electric*; and *Water Heater, Gas*.

## How Does It Work?

A hot-water heating system consists of a boiler to heat (but *not* boil) water, a network of pipes that distributes the water, and radiators that heat various rooms. A hot-water heating system uses the same type of boiler that a steam heating system uses (see *Boiler, Steam*). Controls include a combination gauge (or altitude gauge) that lets you check water temperature and pressure and lets you know when the boiler needs water or is malfunctioning. In some systems, a pressure-reducing valve takes care of the water automatically. The typical system also has an expansion tank that must be properly charged with air to prevent the water from boiling. Newer systems usually locate the expansion tank on the basement ceiling near the boiler; they also include a purge valve to release water and let in air as needed. Older systems sometimes have the expansion tank in the attic and include a gauge glass similar to that on a steam boiler.

## What Can Go Wrong?

Because they have few mechanical parts, hot-water heating systems usually perform reliably for many years. The most common problems are with the expansion tank or a circulator rather than the boiler. Here are some symptoms of problems: A hot-water system might produce no heat or poor heat and leaks can occur. Some radiators might not heat while others do. Pipes might make a clanging noise.

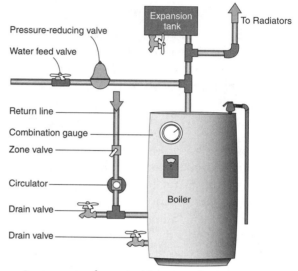

Components of a typical hot-water boiler.

**Fix-It Tip**

Place a pan of water on top of a radiator to add humidity to the air during the winter, if needed.

## How Can I Identify the Problem?

If the unit produces no heat, raise the thermostat, and check switches (see *Appliance Controls*), fuses, circuit breakers (see *Electrical Service Panel*), and the water level. Also check the burner's safety controls (see below).

If the unit doesn't produce enough heat, check the combination gauge, then the expansion tank (see below). Next, flush the boiler (see below). If water leaks from a heating system pipe, try repairing it yourself (see *Pipe*).

If only some radiators in the system heat up, bleed air from the cool units (see below). If you suspect that the circulator requires repair, call an experienced serviceperson.

If the pipes suddenly start clanging, the circulator may need professional service or replacement.

If there is a chronic banging noise, check the slope of all return lines; they must slope *toward* the boiler to work correctly.

If a single radiator warms only slightly, but evenly, water may be trapped inside. Make sure it slopes toward the return; if it does not, insert a wooden shim under the end opposite the return.

**Fix-It Tip**

Water pressure in a hot-water boiler is automatically maintained by a pressure-reducing valve. Periodically check the combination gauge and call an experienced serviceperson if the valve needs repair or replacement. If your system has no pressure-reducing valve, you can manually feed the boiler by opening the water feed valve and closing it again when pressure reaches 12 pounds per square inch. High water consumption is caused by a leak in the supply or return piping or in the boiler itself.

## What Parts, Materials, and Tools Do I Need?

Most components of a hot-water boiler system are available through larger plumbing supply houses. Check your local telephone book. For basic tests and repairs, you'll need these tools:

- Screwdrivers
- Pipe wrenches

## What Are the Steps to Fixing It?

Troubleshoot an expansion tank:

1. Check the pressure-relief valve. If water is spurting from it, there is too much water and not enough air in the tank.

**Reading a Combination Gauge**

The moving pointer shows actual pressure. The fixed pointer indicates the minimum pressure. If the moving pointer drops below the minimum, the system needs water. The lower temperature gauge shows water temperature. Maximum boiler water temperature is set by moving a pointer along the sliding scale of an aquastat. Don't try to adjust the aquastat.

2. Touch the side of the tank; the bottom half should feel hotter than the top. If the top is nearly as hot or as hot as the bottom, the tank is filled with water and requires bleeding. Once the system is cool, attach a hose to the tank's purge valve and drain 5 to 10 gallons of water from the system.
3. Return all valves to normal settings and start the boiler. Check the system's pressure on the combination gauge. If it is not within normal operating range, call for service.

Flush a boiler of rusty water:

1. Shut off power and open the drain cock and the air vents on the highest radiation units.
2. If the boiler has a manual feed, open it.
3. When the water runs clear, close the drain and vents and wait until pressure reaches 20 pounds per square inch (psi) of pressure.
4. Bleed each radiator until the pressure reaches 20 psi, then drain off the water. If the pressure falls below 12 psi, add more water.

Bleed a hot-water radiator:

1. Open the vent with a screwdriver or special tool supplied with the radiator.
2. When water (instead of air) comes out, close the vent.

# Boiler, Steam

Steam boilers are the heart of many efficient home and apartment heating systems. Because they have few moving parts, there is little to go wrong with them. Hopefully, you'll spend more time enjoying them than fixing them. The first step is understanding how they work so you can easily maintain them. Also see *Boiler, Hot-Water*.

## How Does It Work?

A steam heating system consists of a boiler to heat steam, a network of pipes that distribute the steam, and radiators that heat various rooms. A gas or oil burner heats water to the boiling point and sends hot steam to radiators in the residence. Modern boilers circulate water around the heat source through a series of passages or tubes. Boiler operation is regulated by a pressure gauge, regulator, pressure-relief valve, and low-water cutoff monitor. Most steam boilers include an automatic feed that supplies more water when it's needed.

## What Can Go Wrong?

Regular maintenance will help keep repairs to a minimum. The system might produce no heat or poor heat, water might be chronically low, the glass gauge might be clouded, and pipes might be noisy.

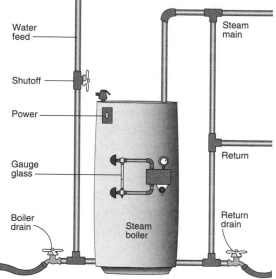

Components of a typical steam boiler.

## How Can I Identify the Problem?

If your system is running smoothly, a few regular maintenance measures will keep the system doing so (see below).

If there is no heat, check the thermostat, switches, fuses or breakers, and water level. A boiler burner is very similar to a gas or oil furnace (see *Furnace, Gas;* and *Furnace, Oil*).

If there is not enough heat, the boiler may need to be flushed (see below).

If the water level is frequently low, look for leaks in the return lines or the boiler itself. In either case, have a plumber or boiler service professional take a look.

If pipes are noisy, check the pitch of all returns; they must slope back toward the boiler. Adjust the slant, if necessary, with new pipe hangers.

> **Fix-It Tip**
>
> For safety and efficiency, make sure that there is a clear path around each radiator to allow air to circulate freely.

If a room radiator inlet valve leaks, tighten the packing nut. If necessary, repack the valve as you would a *Faucet.*

If a radiator won't heat, clean the air vent orifice with a fine wire. If the vent is permanently plugged, replace the vent.

> **Fix-It Tip**
>
> Most modern steam boilers have an owner's manual that describes operation, maintenance, and troubleshooting. If you can't find one for your unit, contact the manufacturer; the name will be somewhere on or near the controls.

## What Parts, Materials, and Tools Do I Need?

Replacement parts for a steam boiler should come from the manufacturer or an aftermarket supplier such as a local plumbing and heating supply retailer. Basic tools for maintaining and repairing your steam boiler include these:

- Screwdrivers
- Wrenches
- Hoses
- Fine wire

## What Are the Steps to Fixing It?

Monthly maintenance for a smooth running system:

1. Verify gauge accuracy by comparing the actual water level with the reading on the gauge. The owner's manual will have more specific instructions on how to make this comparison.
2. Test the relief valve by carefully lifting the lever to check operation while the boiler is running. The valve should release steam, then stop. If it continues to release steam, have the relief valve replaced.

3. Check the pressure gauge to make sure that steam pressure doesn't exceed the gauge's limit mark. If it does, contact a professional steam boiler service.
4. Open the low-water cutoff valve to flush sediment, allowing the water to run until it is clear. *Caution:* The water will be hot!

Flush a boiler:

1. Shut off the power and the automatic feed.
2. Attach hoses to the boiler drain and return drain.
3. Open the boiler drain and return drain to allow water to run out into a household drain.
4. Once the tank is empty, shut the drains.
5. Refill the boiler, and drain it again.
6. Repeat the flushing process until the water in the gauge is clear.

> **Fix-It Tip**
>
> If the gauge glass is dirty, you can clean it. First turn off the boiler and let it cool down; then drain the system to below the gauge level. Loosen fasteners holding the glass in place and remove it. Clean the glass, replace it, refill as needed, and turn the boiler back on.

# Camera, Digital

Digital cameras have become increasingly popular because of the quality of digital photography—and the lowering costs of the cameras. You can find a good-quality digital camera for less than the cost of a comparable film camera. And, like film cameras, the digital version is virtually trouble-free. In fact, most problems are really photography issues—poor exposure, inadequate lighting, thumb over the lens—rather than something you need to repair. Even so, knowing how they work and what can go wrong will keep your digital camera producing great photos longer with less trouble.

## How Does It Work?

A digital camera takes photographs that are electronic rather than on film. Digital photography blends the technologies of photography and computers. The digital camera uses a computer chip to record an image focused on it by a lens. The electrical charges are read and turned into digital information or data. The data for the image is then transferred to a removable and reusable memory card in the camera. The resulting images can be stored, viewed, enhanced, altered, and printed from a computer. You can buy a consumer-level digital camera for about $200, a semipro version for $800, or a professional model for $2,000 and up.

## What Can Go Wrong?

In most cases, the problems you might have with a digital camera can be resolved by referring to its owner's manual. It's amazing what digital cameras can do—and what settings are available to you if you know how to use them. So spend time with the manual. Unlike film cameras, it doesn't cost you anything to try things and see the resulting image.

As you can see, digital cameras have no parts that are easily replaced by the consumer. However, you can open it up to clean it or dry it if necessary.

What mechanical problems can occur with your digital camera? The camera might refuse to turn on or off. The image quality might be poor, the camera can use batteries too quickly, the camera might not connect with a computer, the flash might not work, the camera might not take pictures, or the screen might keep turning off.

> **Fix-It Tip**
>
> Digital cameras can rapidly go through batteries, especially if you use the lens zoom, a built-in flash, and the LCD. So keep a supply of fresh batteries on hand, preferably in the case in which they were purchased so the tips don't touch each other.

## How Can I Identify the Problem?

Again, you can identify and resolve many of the problems with digital cameras by referring to the owner's manual. Here are some general tips.

If the image quality is poor, check the lens to make sure it's clean.

If the camera won't turn on, check the batteries, or connect the camera to an AC adapter. If that doesn't work, remove all batteries, disconnect the AC adapter, wait a minute, reinsert batteries, and reconnect the adapter.

If the flash doesn't work, the camera won't take pictures, or the screen keeps turning off, check that the batteries are strong.

If the camera got wet, turn off the camera and remove all batteries and storage media. Let the camera dry completely for at least 24 hours before reinstalling the batteries and media. A can of compressed air will help dry it out more quickly.

If the camera uses batteries too quickly, use the viewfinder more and the LCD less. You also can replace the batteries with heavy-duty batteries suited to digital cameras (the ones that came with the camera probably are barely adequate). Use the power adapter whenever downloading images to a computer. You also can reduce battery drain by using a card reader to transfer images to the computer.

If the camera won't connect with your computer, make sure you have the latest version of the needed software drivers (in your digital camera package or online from the manufacturer). Check your computer for conflicts (two devices trying to use the same port); you may need technical assistance for this one. In some cases you can get things working again by connecting the digital camera, then turning off the computer and turning it back on.

**Fix-It Tip**

If you are unfamiliar with digital cameras, buy yours from a store that offers good advice and service. You may spend a little more than if you purchase from a discount store, but you will have a resource to use for questions and problems—a valuable asset.

## What Parts, Materials, and Tools Do I Need?

Don't try to take your digital camera apart! Follow the directions in the owner's manual on replacing batteries and troubleshooting your camera, but don't go beyond that. If it doesn't work, maybe it's under warranty. If not, hire a professional camera repair service with digital camera experience.

## What Are the Steps to Fixing It?

Know your camera. Perform regular maintenance on it as needed (clean the lens, keep fresh batteries in it). Keep your camera away from adverse environments (hot, cold, or wet places). Other than that, take it to a professional for service.

**Fix-It Tip**

If you are unfamiliar with digital cameras and computers, but still want to try one, ask among friends for some instruction. Most folks *love* to share their knowledge and advice.

# Camera, Film

Life is full of Kodak moments. Hopefully, you have a camera handy when they happen. And hopefully, the camera works. It's exasperating to take some great pictures only to learn a few days later that they didn't come out. Fortunately, there are many things you can do to keep that from happening and keep your film camera ready for good pictures.

## How Does It Work?

A camera holds light-sensitive film that is momentarily exposed to the light from an image. The film then is developed or processed into photographic prints outside of the camera. So-called instant cameras actually process and print the photo inside the camera. (Also see *Camera, Digital.*)

Popular film cameras fall into three main categories: 35 mm point-and-shoot, 35 mm SLR (single-lens reflex), and instant. The cameras differ in how the image is viewed (through the taking lens or through a separate viewer), how the lens is focused (automatically or manually), and how the image reaches the film. What they all have in common is a lens and a method of holding and moving photosensitive film. Some have built-in flashes or attachments for holding flashes (called the shoe). Others have various add-on accessories such as replaceable lenses, filters, lens covers or caps, and straps.

## What Can Go Wrong?

The most common problem with cameras is operator error. Sorry. Even point-and-shoot cameras won't work if a thumb is hiding the lens or if the batteries have insufficient power to operate the flash. And, in most cases, the problems are resolved by reading the owner's manual that comes with the camera and periodically replacing batteries. Unfortunately, some manuals suffer during translation or from poor writing—or both. Fortunately, you typically can find a friendly camera store clerk who will show you how to operate your camera if you don't have or just don't understand the owner's manual.

**Fix-It Tip**

Purchase a lens-cleaner brush or chemical from your local camera store and keep it with your camera. Or you can use canned air. Also make sure the camera has some type of lens cap or automatic cover to protect the lens from dust and scratches. Once damaged, the lens should be replaced or it will include marks in every photo you take thereafter.

## How Can I Identify the Problem?

Most camera problems will show up on a photo that doesn't look quite right, such as a consistent streak across all photos. The flash may not sufficiently illuminate the subjects. Or the lens motor doesn't allow it to zoom.

## What Parts, Materials, and Tools Do I Need?

Keeping your camera clean and in fresh batteries is relatively easy. All you'll need are a lens-cleaner brush or chemical, some batteries (see *Battery, Button;* and *Battery, Household*), and maybe a small Phillips screwdriver.

## What Are the Steps to Fixing It?

Beyond keeping your film camera in fresh batteries and the lens cleaned, there's actually little you can do to repair it. Any problems beyond these should be taken to a camera repair service once you've determined that the camera is no longer under warranty (see *Fix Everything: Warranties*). Plan to spend at least $50. Or you can replace the camera, donating the old one to a curious child.

**Fix-It Tip**

Put new batteries in, but the camera still doesn't work? Check to make sure that the batteries have full power (see below) and that they are installed correctly. The battery cover or holder typically will have a diagram showing how the batteries should be installed.

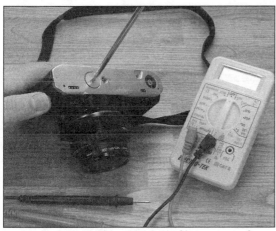

To test the battery in a typical SLR film camera, first open the battery compartment.

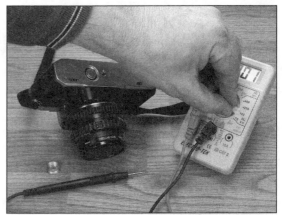

Set the multimeter to the appropriate function (DCV) and range.

Button battery

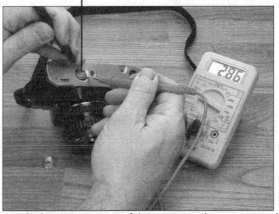

Test the battery in or out of the camera, placing one probe on the back (negative) and one on the edge (positive).

Carefully use canned air to clean the mirror and lens.

# Camera, Video

Video cameras, once a luxury, are relatively commonplace—especially at youth sporting events. Your authors have countless hours of long-forgotten high school baseball, football, track, cross-country, swimming, and other events packed away somewhere. We've had a few problems with video cameras over the years, so we know how to do some basic repairs—and how to maintain them to avoid having to fix them.

## How Does It Work?

A video camera, also called a camcorder, is a portable television camera combined with a video recorder. The camera section has a lens and special charge-coupled device or CCD (a microchip with thousands of tiny light-sensitive elements containing photodiodes). The CCD separates the picture into three color images using red, green, and blue color filters over adjacent light-sensitive elements. In the recorder section, the video signal from the CCD and the sound signal from the video camera's microphone are recorded on tape in the same way that a video recorder records sound. The signal is either analog (older) or digital (newer). The tape format may be VHS, VHS-C, or 8 millimeter, but otherwise video cameras are very similar in function, maintenance, and repair.

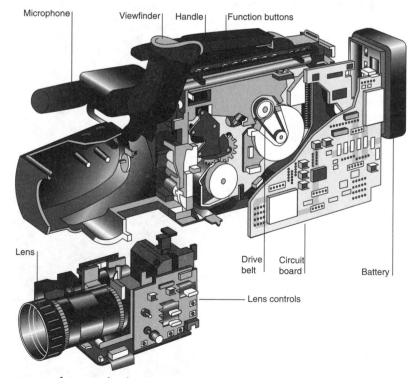

Microphone | Viewfinder | Handle | Function buttons

Lens

Drive belt | Circuit board | Battery

Lens controls

Components of a typical video camera.

## What Can Go Wrong?

Many problems with a video camera are actually caused by incorrect operation, so check your owner's manual thoroughly before attempting any repairs. However, contacts may be dirty, batteries may fail, fuses may fail, heads become dirty or worn, and the pinch roller or capstan may be dirty. The tape-loading belt may be broken or damaged, the audio heads may be dirty, or the microphone may be damaged or defective.

## How Can I Identify the Problem?

If the video camera doesn't work, make sure the battery is charged (see *Battery Recharger*) or replace a battery that won't hold a charge. Make sure the AC adapter is connected properly. Clean any dirty contacts on the battery, charger, and AC adapter with a cotton swab dipped in denatured alcohol. Remove corrosion with a clean pencil eraser, then wipe the area with an artist's brush to remove any debris. Find and test the *Fuse*, if any.

If the power goes off soon after starting, recharge a low battery. Also, turn the video camera power off, then turn it back on and eject the tape. If the problem persists, check the *Fuse*.

If the battery won't charge, clean the contacts and fully discharge the battery, then recharge it. If the problem persists, replace the battery (see *Battery Recharger*).

If the video camera works intermittently, remove and reseat the *Fuse* to establish good contact. If necessary replace the fuse.

If the picture quality is poor, clean the video heads with a head-cleaning tape. If the problem persists, have the video camera professionally serviced.

If the tape doesn't run, clean the camera with a head-cleaning tape or wipe areas that touch the tape with a lint-free cloth (available from electronics stores) moistened with denatured alcohol.

If the tape won't load or eject, inspect and replace a broken or damaged belt (see below). If the belt is not faulty, the tape transport system may be damaged and need professional service.

If there is no audio, clean the heads with a head-cleaning tape. If the problem persists, have the video camera professionally serviced.

If the video camera damages tapes, remove the carriage door and use tweezers and canned air to remove any debris from the tape transport area. Clean the area with a head-cleaning tape. Replace a broken or worn capstan belt (see below).

If the picture pulls to the right in playback mode, remove the tape carriage door and remove any debris blocking the brake. If the brake is broken, replace it or have it replaced professionally.

## What Parts, Materials, and Tools Do I Need?

Replacement parts are available from the manufacturer and aftermarket suppliers (see *Fix-It Resources*). Cleaning aids and some replacement parts may be available from local electronics stores. The tools you will need to fix a video camera include these:

- Cotton swabs
- Denatured alcohol
- Pencil eraser
- Artist's brush
- Head-cleaning tape
- Screwdrivers
- Tweezers
- Canned air

## What Are the Steps to Fixing It?

Disassemble a video camera:

1. Disconnect the power source.
2. Remove the tape carriage door by first removing any screws securing the door cover. Slide the cover upward, then pull it off.
3. Turn over the unit. Remove all screws holding the housing together, then lift off the housing. If wires link the housing to the rest of the video camera, disconnect and mark them for easier reassembly.
4. Remove any screws securing the main circuit board, then carefully remove the circuit board.

Replace a band brake:

1. Disconnect the power source.
2. Remove the tape carriage door and release the carriage.
3. Remove clips or screws to free the brake and belt. If they are otherwise secured, have the unit serviced.

4. Install a new brake with the felt side around the supply spool.
5. Reassemble in reverse order.

Replace a belt:

1. Disconnect the power source.
2. Turn over the unit. Remove all screws holding the housing together, then lift off the housing. If wires link the housing to the rest of the video camera, disconnect and mark them for easier reassembly.
3. Remove the belt if it is either worn or damaged.
4. Wipe the new belt with denatured alcohol to remove any protective coating; let the belt dry.
5. Thread the belt around the pulleys.
6. Reassemble in reverse order.

Release a stuck tape:

1. Disconnect the power source.
2. If the eject button fails, remove the housing and the main circuit board (see above).
3. Remove screws or unclip retainer clips securing the small circuit board and lift it out.
4. Press the tape-carriage release lever near the top of the camera with a screwdriver and carefully remove the tape from the carriage.
5. Use tweezers and an artist's brush or canned air to remove any debris.
6. Reassemble the video camera.

**Fix-It Tip**

For every few tapes you run through the video camera, use a head-cleaning tape to remove build-up on the record and playback heads. You can purchase a head-cleaning tape at an electronics store or wherever video cameras and video tapes are sold.

# Carpet

Carpet is one of the most popular floor coverings in homes and apartments. It's relatively inexpensive and easy to install, it's easy to care for—just run a vacuum over it—and it looks good. However, like everything else, carpet gets damaged or needs repair. It needs a visit from the Fix-It Club.

## How Does It Work?

Carpet is a floor covering made of heavy woven or felted fabric. It is stretched over a subfloor and secured at a room's edge using tack strips. Rooms with dimensions greater than 12 feet. typically require a seam to connect two pieces of carpet. Most carpet flooring has a pad underneath to soften the texture and, in some installations, to protect the carpet backing from moisture.

Fabrics used in carpet include wool, nylon, polyester, acrylic, polypropylene olefin, or (more commonly) a blend of two or more materials. In addition, most carpet materials are treated with a stain fighter to reduce absorption by staining fluids. Carpet pad materials include polyurethane foam, bonded polyurethane, rubber, and natural or synthetic fiber. Pads are graded by their density or weight.

## What Can Go Wrong?

Because carpets are always underfoot, they are subject to food spills, pet damage, and even burns. In addition, seams between carpet pieces can separate over time and need fixing.

**Fix-It Tip**

The most important thing you can do to extend the life of your carpet is to vacuum it regularly. Dirt and grit not only look bad, they can wear down the carpet fabric as they are ground in by foot traffic.

## How Can I Identify the Problem?

If chewing gum gets stuck in the carpet, use ice to get it out (see below).

If you have other spills or stains on your carpet (including pet accidents), try one of the new oxygen cleaners and follow the label directions.

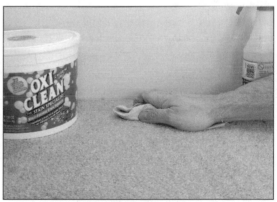

To clean spots from a carpet, first blot away excess liquid, being careful not to spread the stain.

Most stains can be removed from carpet using an oxygen cleaner.

If a section of pile is flattened, use a metal pet brush to lift the nap.

If loops on a shag or Berber carpet become loose, either carefully cut them off or reinsert them into the backing with an awl.

If your carpet has a minor burn, carefully snip off the tops of singed fibers with cuticle scissors.

If the carpet can't otherwise be cleaned, make a patch from a remnant left over from the carpet installation or from a closet corner (see below).

If a seam separates or a tear occurs in the carpet, you can stitch it back together (see below) or repair it with seam adhesive (see below).

**Fix-It Tip**

If you have new carpet installed, ask for a copy of the fabric label. It will include information on the fabric materials as well as care instructions. Keep any scraps of both carpet and padding to use for patching and for matching colors or deciding how much wear the carpet has taken later.

## What Parts, Materials, and Tools Do I Need?

To fix carpet you need only basic cleaning and repair tools. Some you already have and others you can buy at a flooring or building material store:

- Vacuum cleaner
- Mild detergent
- Ice
- Spatula
- Dry-cleaning fluid
- Cleaning rags
- Carpet patch tool
- Carpet cutter
- Scissors
- Hammer
- Nails or tacks
- Pliers
- Upholstery needle
- Monofilament thread (clear fishing line)
- Double-sided tape
- Latex seam adhesive

## What Are the Steps to Fixing It?

Remove chewing gum from a carpet:

1. Scrape away as much of the gum as you can with a spatula, then vacuum away any loose pieces.
2. Rub any remaining gum with a plastic bag filled with ice until the gum is frozen.
3. Use the spatula again to chip away the frozen gum.
4. Carefully apply a small amount of dry-cleaning fluid to dissolve any remaining traces of the gum. Blot up the dry-cleaning fluid.
5. Blot the area with a solution of ¼ tsp. of mild dishwashing liquid and 1 cup of warm water.

6. Rinse the area thoroughly, but don't soak it.

7. If necessary, use scissors to trim out any fabric that still has gum on it.

Patch a carpet:

1. Use a circular carpet patch tool (available through a flooring retailer) to remove a small section around a deep stain, burn, or tear.

2. Peel the cover tape from a piece of double-faced adhesive patch tape. Cut it larger than the hole, and fold it to insert it into the hole in the carpet.

3. Use the carpet cutter or utility knife to cut a patch piece from a carpet remnant, then press the patch firmly over the adhesive.

You can patch a small tear in a carpet using an adhesive.

Patch a larger carpet area:

1. Cover the area to be removed with a piece of trimmed scrap carpet.

2. Temporarily nail or tack the existing carpet around the edge of the patch piece so the carpet maintains tension when the bad part is removed.

3. Use the patch as a guide to cut through the bottom layer of the damaged carpet.

4. Remove the damaged section and install double-faced seam tape on the subfloor or padding around all sides of the hole.

5. Position the patch and press it firmly onto the tape.

6. Remove the temporary nails or tacks to release the tension.

Repair a seam or tear in carpet:

1. Pull the sides of the carpet together until they meet.

2. Temporarily nail or tack the carpet in place on either side of the tear.

3. Use a curved upholstery needle and light-weight monofilament thread to stitch the carpet. If necessary, use needle-nose pliers to pull the needle through the carpet backing.

4. Once the tear is sewn, secure the seam with a final stitch.

**Fix-It Tip**

You also can use carpet adhesive (available through flooring retailers or home centers) to mend the seam or tear, following directions on the adhesive container.

# Cassette Deck

Cassette decks are alive and well—or at least alive. Compact disc (CD) players have become more popular than cassette decks, but there still are millions of decks in use—though many of them are overdue for a meeting of the Fix-It Club. The repair process is relatively easy and replacement parts are readily available, so let's have at it.

## How Does It Work?

A cassette deck is a motor-driven electronic device that records and plays audio signals stored on a magnetic tape. The tape is encased in a housing called a cassette.

More specifically, the cassette deck player passes the cassette tape over magnetic heads that record or read the information already stored on the tape. The tape wheels are turned by a small belt connected to a motor. Newer cassette decks feature reliable electronic circuitry, which means most problems that occur are mechanical. Cleaning, lubrication, and replacement of broken belts will add years of useful life to a cassette deck. Most electronic problems require professional service, but there still are many things you can do to fix your cassette deck.

## What Can Go Wrong?

Many things can go wrong with cassette decks because they have numerous electrical and moving parts. The electrical power cord can be faulty. The drive belt can break or be damaged. The read and record heads can be misaligned, worn, or dirty. The pinch roller that pulls the tape past the heads can be glazed. The tape motion sensor may be faulty or dirty. Switches can fail and connections may be dirty. In many cases, the problem is with the cassette itself. However, if the problem is electronic, take the deck to a professional repair person.

> **Fix-It Tip**
>
> You can fix a bad cassette tape by carefully removing the screws that hold the cassette together, then rewinding the tape on the two spools and across the pad between them. If you're working on a treasured tape you don't want to toss, buy a new tape that looks just like it, then take it apart to see how things should look. You may even be able to borrow a part or two from the new cassette to fix the old one.

## How Can I Identify the Problem?

What are the symptoms? Let's take a look at some common symptoms to help you identify the problem.

If the deck won't work at all, make sure that power is on at the outlet and check the *Electrical Cord*.

If the tape hisses, the sound is weak, or there are no high tones, the heads may be dirty or misaligned. You can clean (see below) and demagnetize the heads, but head misalignment is best left to a professional.

If the tape spills out of the cassette, the tape itself may be faulty, the belt may be broken, or the pinch roller may need cleaning.

If the sound is garbled, the heads may be dirty or the belts may be dirty, stretched, or slipping, or the cassette may be faulty.

If the deck won't rewind or fast forward, the problem could be a broken belt or a faulty idler. Take it to a repair shop for service.

If the deck stops unexpectedly or won't stop at the end of a tape, the cassette may be dirty or the tape may be misaligned. Inspect the hubs and clean off any dirt. Gently drop the cassette flat on a table so that the tape lies evenly on the reels. The problem also could be with the pinch roller. Remove the deck and unscrew it from the front panel. Lift the roller assembly off the shaft for replacement. Alternately, the tape motion sensor may be faulty or dirty, which requires professional servicing.

If the deck won't record, the record/playback switch may be faulty, requiring professional service.

If the sound is distorted or intermittent, clean the external jacks, cables, and plugs. If that doesn't help, the heads may be faulty, requiring professional service.

## What Parts, Materials, and Tools Do I Need?

You can get replacement parts from the manufacturer or aftermarket supplier (see *Fix-It Resources*). You also may need these tools:

- Cleaning tape and solution
- Cotton swabs
- Denatured alcohol or head-cleaning fluid
- Degausser (demagnetizer)
- Tape-splicing kit

## What Are the Steps to Fixing It?

As noted earlier, there are many things you can do yourself to fix a problematic cassette deck. Here are the most common fixes.

Clean the heads using a cleaning tape:

Over time oxides come loose from the cassette tape and collect on the tape guides, capstans, and pinch rollers and can push the tape off the path. Even a little dirt on the head will affect the sound. Clean the heads after 10 to 20 hours of use, using a cleaning tape. Follow the instructions from the manufacturer.

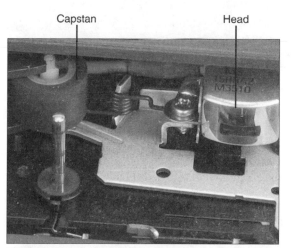

Capstan      Head

The head reads the signals off the tape. The capstan roller pulls the tape across the head.

To clean heads without a cleaning tape:

1. Open the cassette door and wipe the heads with a cotton swab moistened with denatured alcohol or head-cleaning fluid.
2. Turn the player on and hold a swab against each capstan and pinch roller as it turns.

Demagnetize tape heads:

Purchase a demagnetizer (degausser) from an electronic parts and supply store and follow manufacturer's recommendations.

Repair a cassette tape:

If a valuable tape breaks, you can splice it using a repair kit so that you can make a new copy of it. Avoid opening the housing whenever possible. If the end of the broken tape is visible, fish for it with double-stick tape wrapped over a toothpick. But if you must open the cassette, remove the screws or pry a bonded housing open, taking care not to let the tape unwind or fall out. Splice the tape following the repair kit instructions. Reinstall the repaired tape.

| Fix-It Tip | Before spending too much money on repairs, visit a store to determine how much a replacement cassette deck will cost. |

# CD Player

The compact disc or CD player was the first major entertainment appliance that used digital technology. It revolutionized the music industry, offering sound clarity unavailable on magnetic tapes—even the best. So when prices came down, the CD player became one of the most popular entertainment devices, now found in most homes and many cars.

## How Does It Work?

A CD player is an electronic device powered by a universal motor that rotates a flat plastic disc that has been stamped with a digital code representing specific sounds. As the player rotates the CD at high speed, the sound track—less than the width of a human hair—is read by a laser beam used to produce an electric stereo sound signal. This signal goes to an amplifier and speakers or earphones to reproduce the music represented on the CD.

## What Can Go Wrong?

CD players either work or they don't. The third option is that they work, but the sound skips—which typically is caused by a dirty or damaged disc rather than the player. CD players have few moving parts and are mostly trouble-free. In fact, there is little you can do besides clean the CDs, clean the machine, or replace cords. Just about everything else should be turned over to an electronics technician.

**Fix-It Tip**

You can use a CD repair kit, available where CDs are sold, to polish out scratches on the underside of the disc.

## How Can I Identify the Problem?

CD player problems are usually obvious, though the solutions may not be. If the player does not work at all, make sure the power supply is on at the outlet. Check the *Electrical Cord* and replace it if necessary; remove the housing and test the *Fuse;* test the on-off switch and replace it if needed (see *Appliance Controls*).

If the player works but produces no sound, check the connections to the stereo system, and clean the clear plastic reading lens.

If the player skips, check to be sure the CD itself is not scratched or dirty.

If the tray won't open or close properly, check the belt for dirt or wear; and check the tray for misalignment (remove, clean, lubricate, and reinstall).

If the sound is distorted, check and clean dirty output jacks.

**Fix-It Tip**

CD players and other electronic devices are dust magnets. Every month, carefully clean the interior of these devices with canned air or a vacuum.

## What Parts, Materials, and Tools Do I Need?

You can find CD cleaners, canned air, and other tools and parts at electronic stores, such as Radio Shack, or even at larger discount stores such as Wal-Mart. Replacement parts need to come from the manufacturer or after-market supplier (see *Fix-It Resources*). Here are some of the tools and materials you may need:

- Screwdrivers
- Multimeter
- Canned air or soft brush
- Foam swab or camera-lens tissue
- Lens cleaner fluid
- Clean, dust-free cloth
- White lithium grease
- Tweezers
- Cotton gloves
- CD cleaning fluid or denatured alcohol

## What Are the Steps to Fixing It?

The four primary fixes you can do to a CD player include cleaning a CD, cleaning the lens, cleaning the tray, and replacing the tray motor. Let's take a look at each:

Clean a CD:

1. Hold the disc by its hub and outside edges. (The music data is located on the back or bottom side of the disc.)
2. Blow dust from the bottom surface with a can of compressed air.
3. Clean dirt and fingerprints with a lint-free cloth dampened with CD-cleaning fluid or denatured alcohol, all available at electronics stores. Wipe from the center outward (not a circular motion).

Clean the lens:

1. To access the lens in a single-play unit, remove the housing and carefully lift up the hold-down clamp to expose the lens. To remove the lens in a carousel player, remove the player housing and unscrew the bracket secured to the top of carousel, then lift off the bracket.

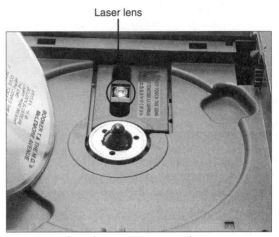

Laser lens

A compact disc player uses a central motor to rotate the disc while the lens reads digital information imprinted on the bottom of the disc.

2. Remove dust with canned air or a soft brush. If needed, use a foam swab or camera-lens tissue (not eyeglass tissue) dampened with lens fluid.

Service the disc tray and belt of a single-play unit:

1. Open the housing by removing the screws on the outside of the housing, and remove anything blocking the tray. Press the open-close control to extend the tray, and unplug the unit. To remove the clip-on tray front, brace the tray and slide the panel to one side.

2. Unplug any cables connecting the front panel to the interior. Remove the screws securing the front panel and gently tilt it off. If the panel won't move, check beneath it for clips or additional screws.

3. Lift off the hold-down clamp, screw, or spring on top of the disc tray. Gently pull the tray out of the player. Clean the travel rail and guides with a swab dampened with denatured alcohol. Lubricate the tray sparingly with white lithium grease.

4. Remove the belt to inspect for dirt, water, or damage. Avoid touching the belt with your fingers. Use tweezers or wear cotton gloves. Clean the belt with a lint-free cloth moistened with denatured alcohol. Replace the belt if it is damaged.

Service the tray motor:

1. Unplug the player and test the *Motor*.

2. A dirty motor plug can make the tray work intermittently. To clean the motor plug, unplug it and spray it with electrical contact cleaner. Then repeatedly plug and unplug the unit to verify contact.

3. To remove the motor, depress the end of each clip or bale with a finger and lift it up.

4. To replace the motor, carefully remove the drive belt with tweezers or gloved hand, then lift the motor out of its mount.

**Caution**

Most CD players are built with thin plastics—especially the tray or cover—that can be damaged. Be careful to not force them.

# Clock, Electric

Clocks are an integral part of our society. Clocks measure our waking hours, our working hours, and even our leisure hours. They offer a standardized measurement for time, one of our most valuable commodities. And when clocks don't work, we're late for something. Here's how to keep them running on time.

## How Does It Work?

A clock is an instrument for measuring time. Electric clocks rely on the 60-cycle-per-second alternations of household current (AC) to ensure accurate timekeeping.

A synchronous motor inside an analog clock drives a gear train, which in turn moves the clock's hands. Older clocks may have metal gears, but the gears of new clocks are generally made of plastic to reduce operating noise—and manufacturing costs.

When an alarm is set on an analog clock, a cam gear presses against a lever, which in turn holds a vibrator arm above a frame. At the preset time, the cam gear moves outward, allowing the vibrator arm to repeatedly contact, or buzz, the frame.

Digital clocks rely on electronic circuitry instead of gears and levers. If a component fails, however, the clock will probably have to be replaced, because most are difficult to repair.

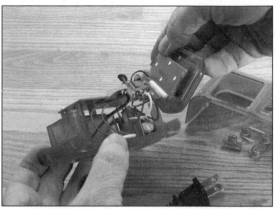

Digital electric clocks are made primarily of circuit boards that can't be repaired by the typical consumer.

## What Can Go Wrong?

So why won't your electric clock work? On analog clocks, hands can work loose, gear teeth can wear down or break, the clock might not run at all or might keep time poorly, or the clock can be noisy. On digital clocks, the cord or battery might not deliver power to the motor.

**Fix-It Tip**

With an inexpensive clock, it might not be worth your time to attempt repair. But before tossing the entire clock, check a local craft or electronic shop for a replacement digital clock mechanism.

## How Can I Identify the Problem?

If you're late for work, maybe you can blame—
and fix—the clock. Here are some typical problems:

If the hands work loose, use pliers to
squeeze the hands tighter to the central shaft.

If the clock does not run, make sure that the
power is on at the outlet and test the *Electrical
Cord*.

If the clock still does not run or keeps time
poorly, disassemble the clock (see below) and
remove any dirt or lint obstructing the *Motor*
or gears. Also, use a multimeter (see *Fix
Everything: Multimeter*) to test the field coil
inside the clock. Check the gears for wear;
replace the clock if the gears are damaged or
worn beyond use.

If the clock is noisy, check for loose parts or a
dry shaft. Secure a rattling crystal with a drop of
clear silicone adhesive. Tighten *Motor* mounting
screws. Apply a drop of light oil at the point
where the motor shaft exits the housing.

**Caution**

Always remember to unplug the clock
before disassembling and working on it.

## What Parts, Materials, and Tools Do I Need?

You can find replacement parts from the manufacturer or through aftermarket suppliers (see
*Fix-It Resources*). In addition, you can find digital clock units at larger craft stores. The tools
you'll need to fix an electric clock include
these:

- Screwdrivers
- Pliers
- Knife
- Electric contact cleaner
- Multimeter

## What Are the Steps to Fixing It?

Disassemble an electric clock:

1. Unplug the clock from the electrical outlet.
2. Carefully pry off the face cover with a
   knife blade.
3. Remove the screws from the case and slide
   the motor and gears out.
4. If necessary, desolder (see *Fix Everything:
   Solder*) the power cord leads from the field
   coil terminals to remove the cord.

Repair an analog alarm mechanism that
sounds at the wrong time:

1. Pull the alarm lever out and turn the clock
   hands until the alarm goes off.
2. Unplug the clock and pry off the crystal.
3. Move the alarm hand until it agrees with
   the time the alarm sounds.

Repair an analog alarm mechanism that
doesn't ring at all:

1. Access the alarm mechanism.
2. Spray the alarm mechanism with electrical
   contact cleaner.
3. Clean the vibrator arm.
4. Carefully bend the vibrator arm to adjust
   the gap between the arm and frame as
   needed.

**Fix-It Tip**

If you have an older clock that you like
but can't repair, consider replacing the
mechanism with an inexpensive digital
clock mechanism

# Clock, Mechanical

We've all come to rely on the accuracy of digital electric clocks—but many of us still have a mechanical clock or two around the house. It's a windup wall clock, a weight-driven cuckoo clock, or a travel alarm. Because it is mechanical rather than electrical, it is more subject to wear. That's where regular maintenance can make a real difference. See *Clock, Electric* for help in repairing an electric clock.

## How Does It Work?

A clock is an instrument for measuring and displaying time. Mechanical clocks are driven by spur gears that are powered by either a falling weight or an unwinding spring that turns the hands at a precise rate. The main shaft then turns the hour, minute, and sometimes second hands around the clock face to indicate current time.

## What Can Go Wrong?

Clocks can fall or be knocked over and damaged—sometimes beyond repair. However, most clock servicing is done because the mechanical clock isn't telling accurate time anymore. It's slowing down or has stopped. This is a preventable condition.

## How Can I Identify the Problem?

Most mechanical clocks will run for many years before needing professional service such as replacing worn gears or springs. You can lengthen the time between professional servicing and even the life of your timepiece by keeping it lubricated (see below). Just make sure you don't overlubricate it. You also can clean it (see below).

## What Parts, Materials, and Tools Do I Need?

Some replacement parts for mechanical clocks are available from the manufacturer and after-market suppliers (see *Fix-It Resources*). In addition, you can find mechanical clock faces, hands, weights, keys, and other components at larger craft stores and some hardware stores. The tools you will need to fix your clock include these:

- Small screwdrivers
- Small wrenches or nut drivers
- Turpentine or paint thinner
- Small brush
- Empty coffee can
- Lightweight household (sewing machine) oil

## What Are the Steps to Fixing It?

To clean a mechanical clock:

1. Carefully remove the clock mechanism from the case.

If the clock has a pendulum, remove it before disassembling the clock.

2. Pour a cup or two of turpentine or paint thinner in an empty coffee can or similar metal container.

3. Place a small-mesh screen or cheese cloth over the top of the coffee can and, if necessary, secure it to the can with a rubber band around the can's perimeter.

4. Set the clock mechanism securely on top of the can so the chemical vapors reach the internal parts.

5. Allow the vapors to work on the clock mechanism for at least 12 hours before removing. Carefully use a small brush to remove any debris.

6. Lubricate the clock (see below).

To lubricate a mechanical clock:

1. Carefully remove the clock's back cover to access the interior of the clock. Some models require that the clock mechanism be removed from the case.

Remove the back from the clock to access the mechanism.

2. Visually locate the working gears in the clock. If possible, wind the clock and watch it run for a few minutes to determine which are moving parts.

Inspect the mechanism for damage, then apply light-weight lubricant as needed.

3. Use lightweight oil to lubricate gear shafts sparingly. Wipe away excess oil.

4. Replace the clock back or the mechanism in the case.

# Clothing

What would we do without clothing? Besides attract a lot of attention, we'd probably spend at least part of the year shivering. Clothing is our outer layer that we can add to or remove as weather and fashion dictate.

## How Does It Work?

Unless you've been living in a nudist colony all your life, you know that clothing refers to articles of dress or wearing apparel made from cloth and other pliable materials. Clothing includes shirts, blouses, dresses, socks, sweaters, jackets, undergarments, and other apparel that serve both practical and aesthetic functions. Natural (cotton, silk) and man-made (polyester) materials are woven into fabric, then cut and sewn together into articles of clothing.

## What Can Go Wrong?

Clothing isn't made to last forever. However, the most common clothing problem that needs fixing is stains, a discoloration caused by food and drink, powders, oils, or dyes. Buttons occasionally need to be replaced. Infrequently, seams (joints between cloth components) fail and tears (within the fabric of cloth components) happen. Additionally, zippers can stick or break. Fortunately, many of these problems can be solved easily and the article of clothing can be returned to service at minimal cost.

**Fix-It Tip**

Here are some practical tips on dealing with stains:

- Treat stains immediately. Soak any washable garment with a stain in cold water before laundering or applying a stain remover. Some stains, such as blood, coffee, and wine, can set in warm water, making them more difficult to remove.
- Sponge a stain, don't rub it. Rubbing only spreads the stain and may damage the fabric.
- Read and follow clothing-label care directions before applying stain treatments. If it says no bleach, don't even use *color-safe* bleach on it.
- Test your stain solution on an inconspicuous area of the fabric.
- Check that a stain is completely gone before drying the garment, because heat can make stains permanent.

## How Can I Identify the Problem?

Laundry day is a good time to check all clothing before it goes into the washer. Look for discolorations, missing buttons, and tears. Sort problem clothing by the solution: stain removal or sewing. Treat any stains immediately. If possible, set aside any clothing that needs sewing for a time when you can do a few pieces at the same time (see *Fix Everything: Sewing*). It's much more efficient to do all your sewing once a week or once every couple of weeks, depending on your schedule and how important the items are. A favorite shirt may need a new button tonight (see below). If a zipper won't zip properly, see *Jacket*. If there is a tear or separated seam, see *Fix Everything: Sewing*.

## What Parts, Materials, and Tools Do I Need?

Stain-fighting products include these:

- Oxygen cleaner
- Enzyme-containing laundry detergent
- Bleach or color-safe bleach

Sewing repairs will require these:

- Assorted needles
- Assorted thread
- Assorted buttons

Don't know how to sew? See *Fix Everything: Sewing*.

As with so many fix-its, the job is easier if you're organized. Keep your stain removal aids near the washer and your sewing materials somewhere handy, such as in a basket near your favorite TV chair.

## What Are the Steps to Fixing It?

Remove spots and stains from washable garments:

1. Following the product's directions, apply an oxygen cleaner directly to the spot or stain and let the garment sit for several minutes.

2. Launder in the hottest water safe for the fabric, using detergent and color-safe bleach (unless the care label says not to). For bleach amounts, follow the instructions on the container. Wash delicates by hand or use the delicate cycle of your machine.

3. Repeat if necessary, letting the garment soak for a longer time.

Replace a button:

1. Match the replacement button to those on the garment, or replace all the buttons to give the garment a new look.

2. Button the other buttons and align the garment to locate button placement.

3. Insert a threaded needle through the garment from the back side and take one or two small stitches to mark button placement.

4. Sew the button on, using the stitching pattern as seen on other buttons on the garment. Sew loosely enough to leave space to button the garment when finished.

5. From the wrong side of the garment, insert the needle under the button stitches and pull the thread partially through, forming a loop. Insert the needle through the loop, and pull the thread snugly to form a knot. Trim the thread close to the knot with scissors.

Once the button is sewn on, remember to tie the thread in a knot so it won't come off again soon.

# Coffee Grinder

Ah, fresh-ground coffee! But maybe you wake up to a coffee grinder that sounds like Armageddon. Can you fix it? Or must you toss it?

## How Does It Work?

A coffee grinder is a small electric appliance that chops coffee beans with a spinning blade. A small universal motor spins a shaft in the center of the coffee grinder. The shaft rotates a blade that cuts coffee beans into small pieces. The size of the pieces, called grounds, depends on the amount of time the grinder runs as well as the sharpness of the blade.

## What Can Go Wrong?

Coffee grinders are relatively simple. The most common problem is that they get clogged up with grounds, which slows down the motor. In addition, the electrical cord can short out, the thermal limiter can burn out, or the motor shaft can stop rotating. In addition, the switch can malfunction and the blade can bend or become dull.

| Fix-It Tip | Keep your coffee grinder clean. Wipe the blade and bowl with a small rag after each use. Be careful, because the blade is sharp. Whatever you do, don't immerse the grinder in water because you'll ruin the motor. |
|---|---|

## How Can I Identify the Problem?

Besides producing the sound of Armageddon, your coffee grinder can do more to tell you that it's having problems—its symptoms can suggest possible solutions.

If the grinder does not run when turned on, make sure power is on to the outlet, then check the *Electrical Cord*.

If the grinder runs intermittently or doesn't stop, the switch may be clogged or damaged. Unplug the grinder and brush any grounds from the switch with a fine brush. Depress the switch several times with a toothpick. If the problem persists, disassemble the grinder to clean it and inspect the switch (see *Appliance Controls*) for breaks that you can fix.

If the grinder does not run, the *Motor* shaft may be frozen. Disassemble the grinder, clean the shaft and lubricate each bearing point with one or two drops of lightweight machine oil. Rotate the shaft to evenly distribute the oil.

If the grinder still does not operate, the thermal limiter may be burned out. If you can't readily find a replacement thermal limiter, it may be more cost effective to replace the grinder.

If the grinder vibrates, the blade may be bent. Inspect the blade and replace if it is damaged or dull. Another cause of vibration could be a worn motor bearing. Unplug the grinder and remove the access plate. The bearing is bad if the motor shaft moves when pushed back and forth; replace the grinder.

| Caution | Never run a coffee grinder when the bowl is empty because the blade may spin too fast and damage the motor. Also, don't operate a grinder for more than 30 seconds at a time or the motor may overheat. |
|---|---|

## What Parts, Materials, and Tools Do I Need?

Finding replacement parts for coffee grinders can be challenging, especially for off-brands, because you first have to figure out who actually made the unit. Check *Fix-It Resources* to find manufacturer or aftermarket parts. The tools you'll need for disassembly and cleaning include these:

- Screwdrivers
- Small pliers
- Brush or canned air

## What Are the Steps to Fixing It?

Fixing a coffee grinder requires disassembling and checking components as well as cleaning it.

Disassemble a coffee grinder:

1. Unplug the grinder. Remove screws underneath the unit to free the baseplate. Remove the blade by gripping it with a thick towel while turning the other end of the motor shaft counterclockwise with a screwdriver or small pliers.

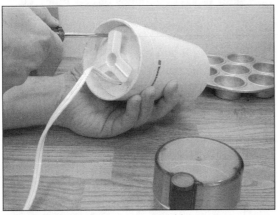

Most coffee grinders are accessed by removing fasteners on the base of the device.

2. If necessary, remove the *Motor* for testing. The motor will be held in place by a linking arm, screws, or a clip.

Motor

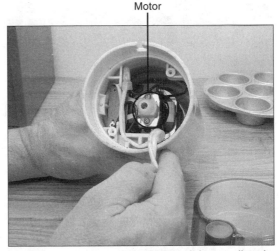

You can sometimes test the *Motor* while it's still in the device. You also can test the *Electrical Cord*.

**Fix-It Tip**

For better coffee and to keep the motor from overheating, use a pulsating action to grind the beans. To pulse, release the control switch every few seconds and press again immediately.

# Coffee Maker

Coffee is America's favorite noncarbonated beverage. It became increasingly so when electric coffee makers started coming home—probably right after electricity was invented. Today's household coffee makers have evolved to where they are simple in design, nearly problem-free, and inexpensive to replace. Even so, things can go wrong—and you can fix them!

## How Does It Work?

A coffee maker, also known as a coffee pot, is a small heating appliance designed for brewing coffee from ground beans. The two types of electric coffee makers are drip and percolator. Drip coffee makers heat water and pump it to drip through the coffee basket and into a carafe. Percolator coffee makers heat water into steam that pushes the hot water up a tube where it falls through the coffee basket and into the main compartment. Coffee makers use switches to turn on and regulate electricity for heating water, and controllers for warming elements in the base that maintain heat in the coffee. Quite simple.

## What Can Go Wrong?

Electric cords, switches, timers, thermostats, and heating elements can become inoperable or cause an electric short that damages components. Some coffee makers have fuses that will blow before damage can be done.

## How Can I Identify the Problem?

If the coffee maker doesn't work at all, make sure power is on at the outlet, check the *Electrical Cord*, the internal *Fuse* or thermostat (see *Appliance Controls*) and replace as needed.

If the coffee maker brews slowly, check the hot water tube for minerals or debris and clean it (see below).

If the coffee doesn't stay hot, test the *Heating Element* and the *Appliance Controls*.

If the coffee maker leaks, check the seals or gaskets and replace as needed (see below).

The cost of replacing a major component, such as an element, is about half the cost of a new coffee maker—if you can find one. If these components fail, seriously consider replacing the appliance.

## What Parts, Materials, and Tools Do I Need?

You can find replacement parts through the manufacturer or aftermarket supplier (see *Fix-It Resources*). The tools you'll need for disassembly and testing include these:

- Screwdrivers
- Wrenches or nut drivers
- Multimeter

## What Are the Steps to Fixing It?

Disassemble and test a drip coffee maker:

1. Unplug the unit from the electrical receptacle.
2. Remove the pot and basket. Remove or tape closed the water reservoir lid.
3. Turn the appliance over and remove all screws that secure the case halves. Lift off the case to expose the heating element and controls.

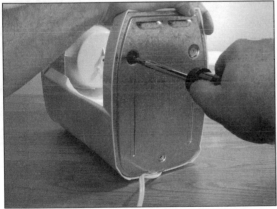

Some coffee makers use special fasteners that require unique screwdrivers.

4. Inspect the control cavity to determine if the solution is simple: disconnected wire, debris, etc. If so, fix, reassemble, and test. Otherwise, continue with the next step.

Heating and warming elements

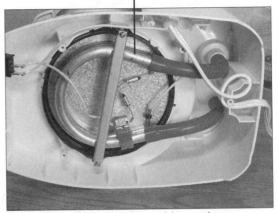

You may be able to see the problem without testing anything.

5. Use a Multimeter (see *Fix Everything: Multimeter*) to test the warming and heating elements (see *Heating Element*), and the switch, thermostat, and timer (see *Appliance Controls*).

Thermal fuse

Testing a thermal fuse in the heating element.

On/Off switch

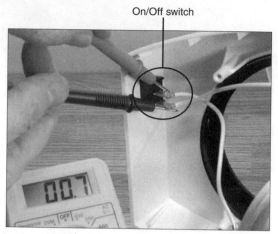

Testing a switch with a multimeter. The switch should get a reading of infinite when *off* and little or no resistance when *on*.

6. Replace any defective parts or decide to replace the appliance, as appropriate.
7. Reassemble the appliance and reinstall the pot and basket.
8. Fill the water reservoir approximately half-full, then plug in and turn on the coffee maker to test its operation.

Disassemble and test a percolator coffee maker:

1. Unplug the unit from the *Electrical Receptacle*.
2. Remove the basket, stem, and lid.
3. Turn the appliance over and remove all screws that secure the base. Lift off the base to expose the heating element and controls.

4. Inspect the control cavity to determine if the solution is simple: bad seals, disconnected wire, debris, etc. If you find a problem, fix, reassemble, and test. Otherwise, continue with the next step.
5. Use a Multimeter (see *Fix Everything: Multimeter*) to test the warming and heating elements (see *Heating Element*), and the switch, thermostat, and timer (see *Appliance Controls*).
6. Replace any defective parts or decide to replace the appliance, as appropriate.
7. Reassemble the appliance and reinstall the stem, basket, and lid.
8. Fill the coffee maker to approximately half-full, then plug in and turn it on to test its operation.

**Fix-It Tip**

If replacing a thermostat requires unriveting or desoldering it, consider taking the coffee maker to an appliance repair shop or recycling it.

# Comfort Controls

Your home has a comfort system of some type (see *Air Conditioner, Central; Furnace, Electric; Furnace, Gas; Furnace, Oil; Heat Pump; Boiler, Hot Water;* or *Boiler, Steam;* for example). What they have in common is that they all require controls to measure and regulate temperature and, in some cases, humidity. Because controls can go awry—and because they are relatively easy to check and fix—let's take a look at comfort controls as a component.

## How Does It Work?

The main comfort controller is a thermostat, which is basically a switch that turns a furnace or central air conditioner on or off at a preset temperature. Comfort controls may also include a humidistat, which is a device that senses changes in the moisture of your home.

A thermostat controls the temperature by sensing a temperature change at its location and turning the furnace on or off to maintain the preset temperature. Your comfort system's thermostat may be either mechanical or electronic. An automatic thermostat can be set to lower or raise the temperature in the home during preset times by using microprocessors and thermistor sensors.

A humidistat can change the humidity in your home by controlling a humidifier or dehumidifier in your comfort system.

## What Can Go Wrong?

Thermostats usually work without any problem for many years, but they eventually may become inaccurate or fail. You can clean, adjust, and replace a mechanical thermostat. An electronic thermostat, beyond replacing the backup battery (see *Battery, Household*), will require either replacement of the entire unit or repair by a professional technician.

If a mechanical thermostat is acting up, consider replacing it with a programmable digital thermostat. They've become inexpensive and can help you save energy costs because of their efficiency.

The location of your thermostat can greatly affect the efficiency of the comfort system. Make sure your home's thermostat is not placed in direct sunlight, in a draft, or near an exterior door or window. If it is you can move it, or, if it is located within a wall, you can pack insulation behind it.

## How Can I Identify the Problem?

If your comfort (heating and/or cooling) system fails to come on, first check your *Electrical Service Panel* for a blown fuse or tripped circuit breaker. Next, try cleaning the thermostat. If that fails, test the thermostat and replace if faulty. (See below.)

If the comfort system short-cycles, that is, it turns on and off repeatedly, clean the thermostat contacts.

If the comfort system does not turn off, clean the thermostat. If that fails to resolve the problem, test the thermostat and replace it if it is faulty.

If the humidifier does not turn on, check the *Electrical Service Panel* for a blown fuse or tripped circuit breaker; test the humidistat; replace a faulty humidistat.

**Fix-It Tip**

Save money with a programmable thermostat—it pays for itself in energy savings within just a few seasons. For example, if you lower the temperature in your home from 70° to 60° for an eight-hour period every night, you'll save about 9 percent of your energy use.

First, remove the control's cover.

## What Parts, Materials, and Tools Do I Need?

Replacement parts typically are not available for temperature and humidity sensors. However, many other components within comfort controls may be available through the manufacturer or dealer. Electronic comfort controls typically are replaced as a unit. The tools you'll need to access and check a comfort controller include these:

- Screwdrivers
- Level
- Small brush
- Coarse paper (such as a paper grocery bag)
- Room thermometer
- Insulated jumper wires

## What Are the Steps to Fixing It?

Clean and adjust a mechanical thermostat:

1. Remove the comfort control's cover by unscrewing or pulling on it.

2. Verify that the wall plate is absolutely level. If it is not, loosen the mounting screws and level the unit.

3. Use canned air or a small brush to clean all the parts.

4. Insert coarse paper (grocery bag or other heavy, rough paper) under each lever and clean by moving the lever and sliding the paper around.

5. If the furnace turns off and on too often or too seldom, move the anticipator pointer slightly toward or away from the longer setting.

6. To determine if the thermostat is accurate, hold an accurate room thermometer nearby while adjusting the thermometer coil.

This digital comfort control requires household battery power to remember settings. There is little a consumer can do with a printed circuit board except replace it.

Test a thermostat:

1. Remove the thermostat body.
2. Clip an insulated jumper wire to the R (red) and W (white) terminals on the baseplate. If the furnace goes on, the thermostat is faulty; if the furnace doesn't go on, the problem is with the furnace, its relay, or the transformer.

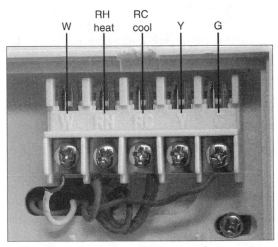

Find and connect the R and W terminals.

3. If you're testing a mechanical thermostat, clean and retest it. Replace it if necessary. If you're testing an electronic thermostat, replace it.

Test and replace a humidistat:

1. Set the humidistat higher than the humidity in the room. You may need a humidimeter for this task.
2. Turn off power to the comfort system at the electrical service panel.
3. Open the humidistat body.
4. Attach a jumper wire clip to the two terminal screws with wires on them.
5. Turn on power to the comfort system. If the humidistat drum operates, the humidistat is faulty.
6. To replace the humidistat, first turn off power at the *Electrical Service Panel*. Then disconnect the humidistat from the wiring and install a replacement unit.

---

**Fix-It Tip**

If you're replacing an older thermostat with a new programmable unit, get one that allows at least two daily cycles. Select one that allows you to vary the settings for the weekend or daily requirements.

# Computer

Computers seem to be both our friends and our enemies. They save us countless hours balancing the checkbook and keeping track of information. They also help us waste time surfing the Internet. But things can go wrong with computers and they definitely become our enemies—at least until we figure out what's wrong and fix them. Fortunately, you don't need to be a certified computer technician to regain your friendship with it.

## How Does It Work?

A personal computer (PC) is actually a system of electronic devices and cables, called hardware, controlled by programs, called software. Data enters the computer from the keyboard, mouse, modem, microphone, scanner, and other devices and is stored on either memory chips or the hard drive. The computer's brain is the central processing unit (CPU). The data is sent to output devices such as the *Computer Printer*, modem, sound card, and diskette drive to perform specific tasks. Computers are electronic machines.

## What Can Go Wrong?

Lots of things can go wrong with a PC. Most of them are software related. Software is the instructions that a programmer wrote to tell your computer what to do in various circumstances. Because of poor programming or disagreements between the hardware and the software, things sometimes don't happen as you expect them to. The best resolution is to refer to the software program's manual for troubleshooting tips. There are thousands of software programs out there. Quite often the problem is a disagreement between the program (such as

Quicken) and the computer's basic set of instructions, called the operating system (such as Windows XP). Start troubleshooting with the program, then move to the operating system. There are thick books available on each, so help is available. If all else fails, or if you're just not comfortable with or knowledgeable about computers, you may need to hire a computer technician to help you figure out what the conflict is and resolve it.

So let's move on to fixing hardware, the electrical components. What can go wrong? The *Electrical Cord* can fail. Connections may need to be tightened. An expansion card may be loose or faulty. Memory chips may be faulty. The monitor may fail. The keyboard or mouse may be dirty or damaged. The hard drive may fail. The power supply or its fan may get clogged and fail. As you can see, many of these problems occur because things get dirty or loose. So keeping your computer clean and well adjusted is a vital step in keeping it friendly. In addition, most modern computers come with an owner's manual that includes a troubleshooting chart specific to the model you purchased. Don't let your computer scare you.

> **Caution**
>
> To reduce the risk of damage caused by an electrical spike, plug your computer system into a UL-rated surge protector. Turn it off and unplug it entirely when a thunderstorm is brewing. If you come home after a storm and the power is still out, turn your computer off and unplug it so it isn't damaged if power comes back on with a surge.

## How Can I Identify the Problem?

What can you do about fixing your computer? First, learn how to open it up (see below). Next, consider the possible symptoms and the potential solutions (see below).

If the computer does not start, be sure that power is on at the outlet, then check the *Electrical Cord*. Test the power supply and replace it if it's faulty (see below).

If the computer starts but then freezes, reseat or replace memory expansion cards as needed (see below) or add new memory cards as needed.

If the disk drive or other device does not work or works intermittently, check cable connections (see below) and replace the cable if needed.

If the monitor does not work, see *Computer Monitor*.

If the keyboard does not work properly, disassemble and clean the keyboard tray (see below) and check the cable for obvious damage.

If you hear a loud, continuous noise inside the computer, lubricate the fan bearing with spray silicone lubricant (see below). If the fan continues to be noisy, replace it or the entire power supply (see below). The loud sound also could signal a hard disk about to quit or "crash." Back up all data on your computer and call for professional service.

If the hard drive won't read or write data, the drive may be faulty and need replacing. Call a local computer shop for service.

If the diskette (3.5 inch) drive won't read or write, clean the read/write head or replace the unit (see below).

If the mouse or trackball doesn't work smoothly, disassemble and clean it (see below). If cleaning fails to solve the problem, replace the mouse.

**Fix-It Tip**

To avoid problems caused by magnetism and static electricity when servicing a computer, use nonmagnetic tools and touch grounded metal or wear an anti-static wrist strap before touching any components.

## What Parts, Materials, and Tools Do I Need?

Fortunately, replacement parts for personal computers are interchangeable and readily available. In fact, if you buy a new hard drive, for example, installation instructions will come with it. Other hardware parts will include a telephone number you can call for assistance. Also refer to the list of manufacturers and aftermarket suppliers in *Fix-It Resources*. Here are the tools you'll need, most of them available at electronics stores such as Radio Shack:

- Screwdrivers
- Tweezers or chip removal tools
- Cotton swabs
- Denatured alcohol
- Multimeter
- Electrical contact cleaner
- Compressed air
- Lint-free cloth

## What Are the Steps to Fixing It?

Disassemble your computer:

1. Disconnect the power cord and external cables from the computer.
2. Loosen screws on the rear of the computer case.

Most personal computers (PCs) are relatively easy to open. At least every few months, open yours and use canned air to carefully remove any dust. Electronic devices are notorious dust collectors.

3. Lift or slide the case from the frame.
4. Reinstall by reversing the procedure, making sure the housing doesn't pinch any cables.

When any part of a computer system fails, first check the cable connecting that part of the computer.

Check external cables:

1. Verify that the cable isn't loose, defective, or plugged into the wrong socket.
2. Unplug and reconnect the cable several times, making sure that all pins and holes match up. If you see corrosion, use an electronic contact cleaner following instructions on the can.
3. Test the cable for continuity with a multimeter (see *Fix Everything: Multimeter*).
4. Hand-tighten any connection screws or wires that hold the cable to the computer.
5. If the cable still doesn't work, take it to a repair shop for testing and, if needed, replacement.

Diskette (erroneously known as "floppy") drives are so inexpensive that many people opt to replace them rather than repair them. If you're planning to replace it anyway, consider repairing it yourself; it might work or it might not. Diskette drives include two small motors, a read/write head, and probably a drive belt. If the drive can format a new diskette but can't read it, the problem is probably a dirty or misaligned head.

Clean a drive head:

1. Follow the instructions for disassembling the computer to access the diskette drive.
2. Disconnect the power cable. Remove screws from the drive housing, located on the sides or underneath the chassis.
3. Pry up the mounting tab with a finger. Slide the drive housing forward and disconnect the power and data cables. Carefully label the data cable (ribbon) so that you can reinstall it in the same manner when you are finished. Most have a stripe near one edge. Remove the drive from the housing.
4. Spray dust away from the bottom and interior of the drive with canned air. If there is a drive belt, carefully clean it with a foam swab moistened in alcohol. Carefully lift the load arm and clean it and the read/write head with a swab and alcohol. Reassemble the diskette drive.
5. If the diskette drive still doesn't work, replace it with a new drive, following the above steps and the instructions that come with the drive.

Service the power supply:

1. Before disassembly, use canned air and/or a small vacuum to clean around the fan and inside the power supply.
2. If necessary, follow the instructions for disassembling the computer to access the power supply, typically located on the back of the computer case.
3. Test the power supply for continuity using a multimeter (see *Fix Everything: Multimeter*). A reading of zero or infinity indicates the power supply is faulty.
4. To replace the power supply, remove the unit from the computer chassis by removing screws or bending metal tabs as needed.

Service a keyboard:

1. Disconnect the keyboard from the computer and turn it upside down. Remove the assembly screws and pry apart the top and bottom housings.
2. Carefully lift off the top housing and either shake out or blow out debris with canned air. Use an electrical contact cleaner to remove any residue or corrosion.
3. If the keyboard still doesn't operate properly, replace it.

Service a mouse or a trackball:

1. Unplug the mouse and turn it upside down. To remove the trackball, press the ball-cage housing cover clockwise or forward, depending on the model. (Most mice have instructions and arrows on the bottom.)
2. Remove the trackball and clean it with a lint-free cloth dampened with denatured alcohol. Allow to air dry.

3. Scrape any plaque from rollers on the inside of the ball cage and swab them with denatured alcohol. Use compressed air to blow out dust and debris from the interior.
4. Reassemble the mouse.

Expansion cards are controllers for add-ons such as modems, sound cards, memory cards, and printers. Expansion cards fit into slots on the computer's main control board, called the motherboard. Memory expansion cards also can be cleaned or replaced in the same manner.

Correct expansion card problems:

1. Remove the screw that attaches the expansion card to the computer chassis (on some models).
2. Grasp the expansion card with both hands and gently rock it back and forth while lifting to remove it from the motherboard. Be careful not to touch components on the card or nearby expansion cards without wearing an antistatic wrist strap.
3. Clean the card pins and the motherboard socket with a swab dampened in denatured alcohol.
4. Replace the card by lowering one end into place, then the other. Once in the slot, press the card down firmly.
5. Replace the attachment screw, if necessary.

**Fix-It Tip**

Many computer problems are with software rather than with hardware. Try reinstalling a program that is giving you trouble.

# Computer Monitor

Computers are useless without a monitor. You can't surf the Net or see what you typed on the keyboard. It's a good thing that computer monitors are virtually trouble-free. Besides checking to see if it's plugged in and making a few adjustments, there's little you can do to fix it without specialized help. Even so, let's take a look at how it works and how to tackle something you *can* fix, the monitor fuse.

## How Does It Work?

A computer monitor, sister to the *Television* monitor, displays information from a computer on a screen. The monitor uses digital values sent by a computer processor to create a stream of electrons that light up phosphors on the inside of the screen. The signals are in each of the three primary colors, combined into various color signals that seem to move

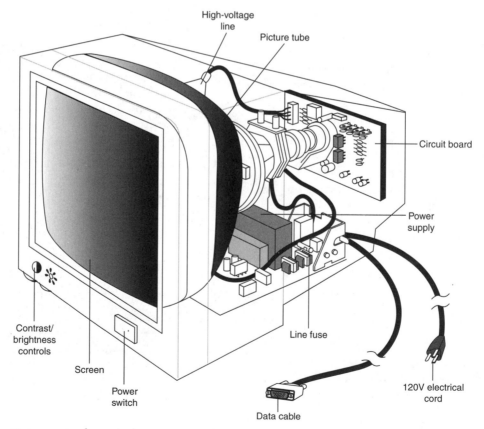

Components of a typical computer monitor.

across the screen. Portable computers use a screen made up of liquid crystal display (LCD) cells instead of phosphors. Computer monitors receive their signal from a monitor cable from the computer and their power from a separate *Electrical Cord.*

## What Can Go Wrong?

Computer monitor problems are not always problems with the monitor. Testing of the monitor must be done with the *Computer.* The monitor might not come on. The image on the screen might not be clear and bright.

## How Can I Identify the Problem?

If the monitor does not come on, make sure there is power to the *Electrical Receptacle.* Check the *Electrical Cord.* Check the connections between the monitor and the *Computer* and make sure the computer is on. Test the line *Fuse* (see below).

If the image on the screen is not clear and bright, check your owner's manual for instructions on adjusting the monitor. Typically there are adjustment buttons on the monitor face below the screen.

## What Parts, Materials, and Tools Do I Need?

Replacement cables and fuses are available from the manufacturer (see *Fix-It Resources*) as well as from local computer shops. Tools you may need to access, test, and fix a computer monitor include these:

- Screwdrivers
- Multimeter

## What Are the Steps to Fixing It?

Test and replace a monitor fuse:

1. Disconnect the monitor from the *Electrical Receptacle* and from the computer processor.
2. Lay the monitor on a padded surface and remove the housing screws (some may be under pop-out tabs).
3. Slide the rear housing off.

**Fix-It Tip**

A computer monitor gets its instructions from a video controller card in the computer. The card may be an add-on expansion card or it may be built into the main circuit board, called the motherboard. If it is a separate card, you may need to open the *Computer* and make sure the card is firmly connected. Also check the flat data cable that runs between the video card and the motherboard, if so equipped.

Power supply

Interior of a computer monitor. Identify but don't touch the power supply.

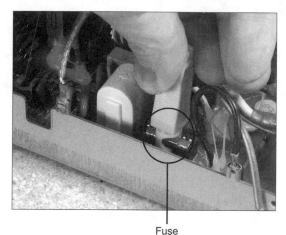

Fuse

Locate, remove, and test the line fuse, typically located near the power cord entry.

4. Locate the line *Fuse*, typically near the power cord entrance. Remove the fuse from its holder and test it with a multimeter (see *Fix Everything: Multimeter*). Replace the fuse if it is faulty.

# Computer Printer

Computer printers, like many of technologies' children, are relatively trouble-free. Change an ink or laser cartridge as needed and you'll have relatively few problems that need fixing. However, printers often break down just when you need them the most, so you should know how to perform some basic fixes to computer printers.

## How Does It Work?

A computer printer is an electronic component that gets data from a computer through a cable and converts the data into a series of small dots that form letters or images on paper.

There are three types of computer printers used by consumers: the older dot-matrix and the newer ink-jet and laser printers. Each prints differently. The dot matrix printer uses a printhead with pins that strike the paper through a replaceable inked ribbon. The ink-jet printer, also known as a bubble-jet printer, contains a printhead that moves back and forth across the sheet of paper, then moves the paper up after each pass. The print head fires tiny jets of ink onto the paper to produce rows of dots that build up into images and characters. In laser printers, a laser or light-emitting diode (LED) flashes rows of lights on and off toward the printing drum to make images.

## What Can Go Wrong?

Many printer problems can be solved easily. If a printer doesn't work, check for a loose connection or a paper jam. Jammed paper can usually be pulled out from under the roller, called a platen, once you've unplugged the printer. Many problems can be solved by checking the software configurations (including printer drivers), by restarting or rebooting, or by cleaning and lubricating. If you suspect a motor problem, however, you must have the printer serviced by a technician.

**Fix-It Tip**

Keep your printer covered when not in use to shield it from dust and debris. Electronic gadgets seem to attract things that aren't good for them.

## How Can I Identify the Problem?

If the printer does not turn on, make sure power is on at the outlet, then check to be sure that all cable connections are secure. Check the *Electrical Cord*. Also make sure that the cover is closed properly.

If the printer turns on but does not print, or print is distorted, check software configurations. Then turn the printer off, wait a few seconds to clear the memory, and turn it back on. If necessary, reboot the computer.

If the unit still doesn't print or print is distorted, check for a loose belt (dot-matrix only) and tighten, and remove and clean the printhead (dot-matrix and ink-jet printers only). If necessary, install a new factory-authorized head.

You also can run a self-test following instructions in the printer's owner's manual. If the test fails to identify the problem, contact a service center.

If the print on the page is smeared or streaked, clean all rollers, platen, and rails (dot-matrix or ink-jet printers) or clean the printhead or print cartridge and the corona wire of a laser printer. If the wire is broken, you'll need to have it replaced by a professional.

**Fix-It Tip**

Keep any software that comes with your printer, because it will include drivers as well as diagnostic tools. Alternately, most manufacturers offer software tools online.

## What Parts, Materials, and Tools Do I Need?

Many components on computer printers snap together, making disassembly relatively easy. For cleaning and repair, you may also need screwdrivers and some of the following supplies:

- Denatured alcohol
- Cotton swab
- Canned air or vacuum cleaner
- Clean cloth
- Household lubricating oil
- Silicone spray

## What Are the Steps to Fixing It?

Replace an ink-jet cartridge:

1. Release the ink cartridge by pressing down on it, then tipping it backward (or forward) and out.
2. To replace the cartridge, do the reverse, snapping the new cartridge into the cradle.

Clean an ink-jet head:

1. Remove the ink-jet head or cartridge following the above instructions.
2. Use a dry or alcohol-dampened swab to wipe away ink from each nozzle.
3. Reinstall the cartridge head.

Clean and maintain a dot-matrix or ink-jet printer:

1. Clean the interior of the printer by blowing out dust with a can of compressed air or by vacuuming with a small vacuum cleaner.
2. Clean guide rails with a soft lint-free cloth dampened with isopropyl alcohol, then relubricate the rails.
3. Lubricate rails with a drop of lightweight household oil. Slide the printhead to distribute the lubricant. Carefully spray silicone on cleaned gears.
4. Clean the platen and the rollers by turning the platen while holding a cloth dampened with alcohol against each roller.

Accessing cartridges and the head typically requires removing paper trays and component covers.

The controls and other mechanisms in many computer printers can also be accessed from the back and sides.

Clean a laser printer:

1. Let the printer cool completely, because it gets hot.
2. Blow out dust from around the drum and the corona wire.
3. Lightly rub a cotton swab along the corona wire to clean off built-up toner and dust.

Service a dot-matrix printer:

1. Unplug the printer and slide the printhead to the middle of the platen. Unfasten the head retainer clips and lift the head off the support pins.
2. Clean the pins with a dry swab. Replace the head if any pins are missing or if cleaning fails.
3. To adjust tension on the printer carriage belt, loosen (do not remove) screws on the gear mounting plate. Rotate the plate to adjust belt tension, then tighten the screws.

# Concrete

We have a love-hate relationship with concrete. By nature, it's flat and bland. But that's really what we should love about it. It does its job without calling attention to itself—until it breaks up. Then it's time to call a meeting of the Fix-It Club.

### Concrete Paves the Way

Less than a hundred years ago it was a long, long road trip from coast to coast, taking more than a month. The first national highway, the Lincoln Highway, had only a few miles of concrete. The rest was dirt or mud, by season. Then concrete became a popular road material and, by the mid-1920s, the cross-country trip took about a week. With today's cars and mostly asphalt-paved roads, it takes half that time or less.

## How Does It Work?

Concrete is a composite material made up of a binder (Portland cement), aggregates (small rock chips), and water. Once mixed, it's spread into an area with perimeter forms, then allowed to dry solid. Once dry, it is as hard and strong as stone. Concrete is used for building foundations and slabs, garage floors, driveways, sidewalks, fences, and many other uses. It is also the major component in concrete building blocks.

## What Can Go Wrong?

Concrete can crack, chip, erode, and break. Most damage is caused by water and weather—though earthquakes can also have an adverse effect.

## How Can I Identify the Problem?

If a concrete block is chipped, you can patch it (see below).

If a concrete block is damaged beyond repair, you can replace it (see below).

If a concrete-block basement wall leaks, you can seal it (see below).

If a concrete driveway, sidewalk, garage floor, wall, or other concrete surface is cracked, you can fill the crack (see below).

> **Fix-It Tip**
>
> Oil, if left standing, can chemically damage and weaken the concrete. Use sand to soak up patches of oil on concrete. Then clean the area with mineral spirits or a degreasing solution.

## What Parts, Materials, and Tools Do I Need?

Replacement parts are available from local building material suppliers and hardware stores. The tools you will need to fix concrete include these:

- Cold chisel
- Mason's trowel
- Small sledgehammer
- Wire brush
- Work gloves
- Cement patch
- Jointing tool
- Striking tool
- Mortar box
- Mortar
- Power drill with masonry bit

- Hammer
- Safety goggles
- Vacuum cleaner
- Hydraulic cement patch
- Small broom (whisk broom)
- Paint brush
- Concrete repair caulk
- Masking tape
- Bonding adhesive
- Vinyl-reinforced patching compound

## What Are the Steps to Fixing It?

Fill a small crack in concrete:

1. Clean out dirt and debris with a small broom.
2. Apply concrete repair caulk as a temporary repair until you can make a better repair with concrete patch.

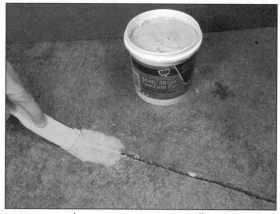

You can purchase concrete repair caulk at most hardware stores and home centers. Follow directions on the label.

**Fix-It Tip**

Repair concrete cracks as soon as you find them so they don't continue to enlarge.

Fill a larger crack in concrete:

1. Clear out loose debris with a metal chisel.
2. As needed, attach a board to contain the new concrete. Also use a board or masking tape to protect adjacent surfaces as needed.
3. Apply a thin layer of bonding adhesive.
4. Fill the area with cement patch in thin layers as directed by the manufacturer.

Patching a concrete block:

1. Remove loose material from the block with a chisel and a wire brush.
2. Spread the cement patch into the hole in layers using a trowel.
3. Smooth the surface of the patching material with a mason's trowel and allow to dry.

Replace a concrete block:

1. Use a chisel or a power drill with a masonry bit to remove the block beginning at the center.
2. Use a chisel and hammer to break up and remove remaining mortar.
3. Spread a bed of mortar in the lowest portion of the hole.
4. Spread mortar on the other three sides of the block.
5. Insert the new block in position in the hole, carefully aligning it to be flush at the front edge.
6. Use a striking tool to make the mortar conform to neighboring blocks.

Fix a water leak in a concrete-block basement wall:

1. Remove loose mortar and dirt from the wall using a wire brush and shop vacuum.
2. Remove loose concrete around cracks and small holes.
3. Apply hydraulic cement patch to the damaged area following the manufacturer's directions.
4. Use a mason's trowel or a jointing tool to finish installing the patch, and allow it to dry.

# Cooking Appliance

Many kitchens are equipped with a variety of small cooking appliances including grills, sandwich makers, waffle irons, frying pans, skillets, and electric woks that may need fixing. Some have controls built into the appliance, while others have them built into the detachable cord. We'll take a look at how to fix both types here, because they all work similarly.

## How Does It Work?

Cooking appliances are designed to cook food at changeable temperatures. In some units, the temperature control is permanently attached to the appliance; the unit *cannot* be immersed in water for cleaning. Those with removable controls often can be immersed with the controls detached. Some units with built-in controls have removable electric cords and some have built-in nonremovable cords.

Small cooking grills have one element and no thermostat to regulate temperature. Sandwich makers and waffle irons have two cooking surfaces with internal heating elements; cooking temperature is regulated by a built-in thermostat. In some cases the elements are exposed (you can actually see them turn red hot) or covered (you can't see the element, but you can feel the heat).

## What Can Go Wrong?

Many things can go wrong with these cooking appliances. Fortunately, most of the units are relatively simple in design and simple to fix. For example, the electrical cord may malfunction. The heating element may be broken. The terminal pins on detachable cords may be faulty. The thermostat may malfunction. Internal

wiring may have a short circuit. Other internal parts may be damaged or not working properly.

**Caution**

Make sure you read the cooking appliance owner's manual before trying to clean it. Some can be immersed in water (though typically not put in a dishwasher) while others have nonstick surfaces that only require wiping with a damp cloth. *Don't* immerse any part of the unit in water unless the manufacturer says it's okay.

## How Can I Identify the Problem?

In most cases, the problem is obvious. The *cause* of the problem may be a little more difficult to identify. If the appliance does not heat, make sure that power is on at the outlet and test the *Electrical Cord*, replacing it if needed. If this doesn't work, disassemble the unit and test the *Heating Element*.

On appliances that have removable power cords, inspect the terminal pins (see below). Test the thermostat (see *Appliance Controls*); if it doesn't work properly, carefully use contact cleaner and a brush to remove any food residue.

If the appliance heats on one side only, test each *Heating Element* and replace it if it is defective. While you have the unit open, check the internal wiring (see below).

If the appliance does not heat to the proper temperature, check the thermostat contacts (see *Appliance Controls*). Some cooking appliances have an adjustment to reset the temperature ranges; you'll need the owner's manual to do this job.

**Fix-It Tip**

The majority of problems with cooking appliances are caused by food. Pancake batter is especially tough on controls, seeping into crevices, then cooking into a hard mass.

## What Parts, Materials, and Tools Do I Need?

With basic tools and a multimeter, you can test and replace many components on cooking appliances. Replacement parts can be purchased from the appliance manufacturer or various aftermarket suppliers listed in *Fix-It Resources*. These are the tools you'll need:

- Screwdrivers
- Multimeter
- Small file
- Fine sandpaper
- Brass brush
- Contact cleaner

## What Are the Steps to Fixing It?

Disassemble and test cooking appliances:

1. Unplug the unit from the electrical outlet.
2. For appliances with a removable cord, use contact cleaner, fine sandpaper, a small file or emery board, or a brass brush to carefully clean the terminal pins located where the cord connects to the appliance.
3. Remove screws and/or clips to access controls on the unit or the removable cord. Clean the controls with contact cleaner, sandpaper, or file, being careful not to damage them or loosen parts.
4. Remove screws and/or clips to access the *Heating Element*. Use a multimeter (see *Fix Everything: Multimeter*) to test for continuity and replace any faulty element.

Remove screws to access the *Heating Element* and other internal components.

Use a multimeter to test the heating elements.

5. To adjust the heat control, follow the steps below.
6. To service the heat control, follow the steps below.

Adjust the heat control:

1. Use a candy thermometer to verify the appliance's actual heat against its indicated heat. If the cooking appliance cooks with liquids (fry pan, wok, etc.), add water to the half-full mark to test.
2. Adjust the heat indicator on the control or adjust the temperature-adjustment screw (if available) to match the unit's actual heat.
3. Recheck the actual temperature against the indicated temperature and readjust as needed.

Service the heat control:

1. Unplug the control and open the housing. Set a multimeter (see *Fix Everything: Multimeter*) on R×1 (resistance times 1) and touch the thermostat terminals with the probes. In the *on* position, the meter should read near zero ohms.
2. Clean any contacts to remove food or corrosion, then polish with fine sandpaper or steel wool. If the contacts have only a little debris, use contact cleaner.
3. If the heat control still doesn't work correctly, replace it with an exact replacement part.

**Fix-It Tip**

Use colored nail polish to mark small appliances and their respective detachable cords. Otherwise you might wind up with a drawer of cords and not be sure which plug-in cord goes with which small cooking appliance.

# Cooktop, Electric

In the "old" days, a stove was a stove. It included an oven or two and a few burners on top, all in a single unit. Today's major cooking appliance may have the cooktop separate from the oven(s). In addition, the fuel source may be different in the various units, gas or electric. Or a kitchen may have a cooktop and not an oven, or vise versa. That's why we'll look at electric cooktops separately from other components. See also *Cooktop, Gas; Oven, Electric;* and *Oven, Gas.*

## How Does It Work?

An electric cooktop is a cooking appliance that uses surface heating elements powered by electricity. The heating elements are controlled by switches that regulate the electric current reaching the heating elements. An electric cooktop operates on a 240/120-volt circuit— 240 volts for the heating elements and 120 volts for the clock, light, and other accessories. An electric cooktop may be part of a large appliance called an electric range or stove that also includes an electric oven. The control system for an electric cooktop may include a motorized timer and lots of dials, or it may be all digital.

Refer to *Oven, Electric* for an illustration of a typical electric cooktop and components.

## What Can Go Wrong?

Electric cooktops last a long time, but they can eventually fail. Elements can burn out. Switches and burner receptacles can fail. The control panel fuse, timer/clock, and *Electrical Receptacle* can fail.

## How Can I Identify the Problem?

If nothing on the range comes on, check the *Electrical Service Panel* and test the *Electrical Cord.*

If a surface element does not heat, first disconnect power to the range, then push the terminals of the element securely into the receptacle. If that does not cure the problem, check the element and test the switch (see below).

If accessories on the control panel fail, you can replace them (see below).

| Caution | Don't use foil to line the drip pans under the burners, because it can short out electrical connections. Nor should you use burners without drip pans, because cooking grease can damage wiring. |
| --- | --- |

## What Parts, Materials, and Tools Do I Need?

Replacement parts are available from the manufacturer and aftermarket suppliers (see *Fix-It Resources*) and from major appliance parts stores. The tools you will need to fix an electric cooktop include these:

- Screwdrivers
- Wire caps
- Multimeter

## What Are the Steps to Fixing It?

Check a plug-in burner element:

1. Unplug the range or disconnect power at the *Electrical Service Panel*.
2. Remove the heating element from its receptacle. Inspect it for burns or holes in the element and replace it if it appears damaged. Clean corroded terminals with fine steel wool.
3. Test the element by plugging it into a working receptacle on the range. Turn power back on. If the element still does not heat, replace it.
4. If the element heated in a different receptacle, you will need to test the nonworking element.
5. Disconnect power to the range before continuing.
6. Trace the wires from the burner's receptacle to the two corresponding terminals on the burner switch.
7. Set a multimeter (see *Fix Everything: Multimeter*) to R×1 (resistance times 1) and clip one probe to one of the corresponding terminals on the burner switch.
8. Unscrew the receptacle and touch the other probe to each of the receptacle contacts in turn. Only one contact should show continuity.
9. Repeat the test with a probe clipped on the second switch terminal. The other receptacle contact should show continuity.

**Fix-It Tip**

An ounce of prevention is worth a pound of problems. Keeping a cooktop clean is an effective way of preventing problems.

Replace a receptacle that fails either test. Simply cut the wires to the receptacle and splice the new receptacle's leads to the wires using a porcelain wire cap.

Check and replace a wired electric burner:

1. Unplug the range or disconnect power at the *Electrical Service Panel*.
2. Remove the drip pan and unscrew the element and the ceramic block from the range.
3. Remove the clips that join the two halves of the ceramic block. Tighten any loose connections and test the element. Replace the element if the terminals are burned or corroded.
4. Label and detach the wires from the element.
5. Set a multimeter (see *Fix Everything: Multimeter*) to R×1 (resistance times 1) and touch one probe to each terminal or terminal group. The meter should show continuity.
6. Test for proper grounding by clipping one probe to the sheathing and touching each terminal. The multimeter needle should not move. Replace the element if it fails any test.

Test an electric burner switch:

1. Unplug the range or disconnect power at the *Electrical Service Panel*.
2. Remove the screws or spring clips at each end of the control panel, located on the front or back of the cooktop. Move the panel to expose the controls and wiring.
3. Disconnect one wire from each pair of terminals corresponding to the suspect burner. Turn the switch for the suspect burner to the *on* position.
4. Set a multimeter (see *Fix Everything: Multimeter*) to R×1 (resistance times 1) and test for continuity. Replace the switch if there is no continuity.

Change an accessory fuse:

1. Unplug the range disconnect power at the *Electrical Service Panel*.
2. Raise the cooktop, unscrew the fuse, and screw in a same-amp replacement.

Replace a malfunctioning clock/timer:

1. Unplug the range or disconnect power at the *Electrical Service Panel*.
2. Remove the screws or spring clips at each end of the control panel, located on the front or back of the cooktop. Move the panel to expose the controls and wiring.
3. Remove leads and unscrew the timer from the panel, then remove the timer.
4. Install a new timer by reattaching leads in the same way they came off the old timer.

Test and replace a faulty control panel receptacle:

1. Unplug the range or disconnect power at the *Electrical Service Panel*.
2. Test the *Electrical Receptacle* with a multimeter (see *Fix Everything: Multimeter*). If the receptacle is faulty, continue with step 3.
3. Remove the cover from the control panel (see above), pull the receptacle through the front of the panel, and remove the leads.
4. Install an exact replacement receptacle, connecting the leads in the same way they came off the old receptacle.

# Cooktop, Gas

Now you're cookin' with gas! In many parts of the United States and Canada, gas is the least expensive fuel for cooking. It's also relatively efficient, giving nearly instant heat to whatever is set on the cooktop. Because there are no moving parts to speak of, a gas cooktop is virtually trouble-free. However, things still can go wrong, and that's where your developed fix-it skills come in handy.

## How Does It Work?

A gas cooktop is a cooking appliance that uses surface elements heated by natural gas or propane. A gas cooktop is often part of a large appliance called a gas range or stove that also includes a gas oven; if the oven is giving you trouble, see *Oven, Gas.* Some gas cooktops have a pilot light that stays lit all the time, waiting for a burner control knob to be turned on. Newer models have spark igniters that ignite the gas when needed. Air shutters control the mix of air and gas that flows to the burners.

Refer to *Oven, Gas* for an illustration of a typical gas cooktop and components.

## What Can Go Wrong?

A pilot light can go out. An internal range plug can malfunction. An ignition module can fail. Burner ports may need cleaning. An air shutter may need adjusting. Any repairs to a gas cooktop that involve the gas supply lines should be handled by a professional service technician.

## How Can I Identify the Problem?

If you smell gas, turn off the burner controls, ventilate the room, and relight the pilot (see below).

If you smell gas with all the pilots lit or with electric ignition, turn off the gas, ventilate the room, and call the gas company immediately.

If a surface burner doesn't light, check that the cooktop is plugged in and inspect the igniter and ignition (see below). Relight or adjust the pilot (see below). Clean the burner ports and clean the surface burner (see below). Adjust the air shutter (see below).

If the surface burner pilot doesn't stay lit or the flame is uneven or low, clean the pilot opening (see below) and adjust the pilot (see below). Finally, adjust the air shutter.

If the surface burner flame is too high, noisy, or blowing, reduce air to the flame by adjusting the air shutter (see below).

If the surface burner flame is yellow or sooty, increase air to the flame by adjusting the air shutter (see below).

If the clock, lights, or igniters don't work, check the internal range plug (see below).

## What Parts, Materials, and Tools Do I Need?

Replacement parts are available from the manufacturer and aftermarket suppliers (see *Fix-It Resources*) and from local appliance parts stores. The tools you will need to fix the cooktop include these:

- Screwdrivers
- Wrenches
- Sewing needle

## What Are the Steps to Fixing It?

> **Caution**
>
> Make sure you know how to shut off the gas to your cooktop for repairs and in case of emergency.

Disassemble a gas cooktop:

1. If the cooktop has electric components (clocks, lights, and spark igniters), unplug the unit for safety.
2. Remove the burner grates and set them aside.
3. Lift the front edge of the cooktop and prop it up with the support rod to access the inside of the cooktop.
4. As needed, remove fasteners holding the cooktop in the cabinet to remove the cooktop.

Relight a gas pilot light:

1. Turn off all cooktop controls and prop open the cooktop.
2. Place a lighted match near the opening of the pilot, located midway between the two burners.
3. If the pilot light doesn't stay lit, clean or adjust the pilot (see below).

Clean a pilot light:

1. Remove the metal shield covering the pilot light, held in place either by tabs or fasteners. (This might not be necessary on all models to gain access to the pilot opening.)
2. Insert a sewing needle in the pilot opening and move it up and down to remove any obstructions.

Adjust the pilot height:

1. Turn off all burner controls and prop open the cooktop (see above).
2. Locate the pilot adjustment screw on the side of the pilot, on the pilot gas line, or behind the burner control knob.
3. Turn the screw counterclockwise to increase the size of the pilot. The flame should be a sharp, blue cone, about ¼ to ⅜ inch high.

Check and replace igniters:

1. Turn on the other burner served by the same igniter. If the igniter sparks, the first burner control is faulty. Clean the tip and retest. If it is still faulty, continue with step 2.
2. Trace the igniter cable to a terminal on the ignition control module at the back of the range.
3. Remove the cover and disconnect the igniter cable.
4. Replace the igniter with a duplicate.

Clean burner ports:

1. Verify that the flash tube lines up with the burner ports and with the pilot or spark igniter. Adjust as needed.
2. Use a sewing needle to clean the burner ports opposite the flash tube.

**Fix-It Tip**

Don't clean burners with steel wool pads. Steel wool leaves behind small particles of metal that can short out the spark from an electronic ignition and prevent ignition of a burner. Instead use an abrasive cleaner and a nonmetal scouring pad.

Adjust a burner's air shutter:

1. Turn off all controls and raise the cooktop (see above).
2. Locate and loosen the air shutter.
3. Turn the burner to its highest setting.
4. Open or close the shutter until the flame has a sharp, blue cone, about ¼ to ⅜ inch high, then tighten the adjustment screw.
5. Turn off the burner, retighten the shutter screw, and replace the cooktop.

Check and replace the internal range plug:

1. Turn off all controls and raise the cooktop (see above).
2. Disconnect the internal range plug, often located at the rear of the cooktop.
3. Inspect the plug terminals and straighten bent terminals as needed.
4. Replace the internal range plug if the terminals are burned or otherwise damaged.

# Deck

A deck is an extension of your home's living space. It offers extra room for dining, entertaining, and relaxing in the sun (or shade). Decks need little maintenance and few repairs to keep them in good condition. Here's how to take good care of your home's deck.

## How Does It Work?

A deck is a flat structure adjoining a house. It consists of a floor, horizontal joists, horizontal beams, and vertical posts. In addition, a deck typically has perimeter railings and stairs. Decks are constructed of decay-resistant wood (redwood, cedar), pressure-treated wood, or newer plastic materials, and are held together with fasteners.

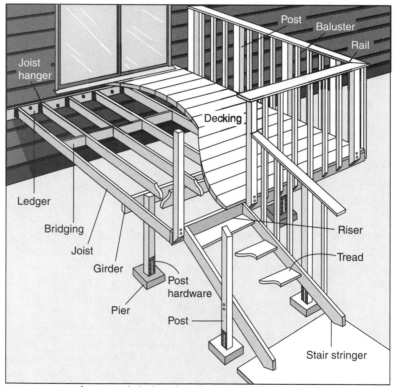

Components of a typical deck with rails and stairs.

## What Can Go Wrong?

From exposure to the weather, a deck's protective finish will deteriorate and need renewing. Boards warp and sometimes are damaged. The edges of deck boards may become rough and unsightly. Steps may be damaged. Parts can become loose.

## How Can I Identify the Problem?

If a deck's surface has turned gray, you can renew its look and protect it by refinishing the surface (see below).

If a board has cupped up, just remove the board, flip it over, and renail it.

If a board is damaged, replace it with a new board that has weathered at the lumber yard. Alternatively, you can age lumber by washing it with a solution of bleach and water and allowing it to dry.

If a step is damaged, you can replace it (see below).

If the deck bounces up and down, or sways, you can reinforce it (see below).

If a baluster or post is damaged, you can replace it (see below; also see *Stairs*).

## What Parts, Materials, and Tools Do I Need?

Deck repair materials are available from local hardware, lumber, and paint stores or home improvement centers. The tools and materials you will need to fix it might include these:

- Screwdrivers
- Electric sander
- Sandpaper block
- Wood plane
- Electric drill
- Pressure washer
- Hammer
- Wrenches
- Paint brushes
- Circular saw
- Crosscut saw
- Combination square
- Pry bar
- Bleach
- Broom
- Galvanized screws and nails
- Measuring tape
- Level
- Lumber
- Stain
- Wood preservative
- Wood sealer

## What Are the Steps to Fixing It?

Refinish a deck:

1. Use a hammer to refasten protruding nails.

Refasten protruding nails.

2. Trim raised edges with a sandpaper block, electric sander, or plane.
3. As needed, clean gray or dirty wood with a solution of 1 cup bleach in a gallon of water. Apply with a brush or broom.
4. Use a pressure washer to clean the deck, being careful not to damage the wood with excessive pressure.
5. Apply stain or wood preservative following the manufacturer's instructions.

6. Apply wood sealer following manufacturer's instructions.

Replace a deck step:

1. Use a hammer and pry bar to remove the damaged step.
2. Cut new stair treads to fit, using a combination square to cut the ends square.

3. Place the new stair treads on the stringers.
4. Drill pilot holes in the treads where the fasteners will go so that they don't split the treads.
5. Nail or screw the treads to the stringers.

Add support to deck joists:

1. Cut lumber to duplicate the size and length of the existing joist, using a combination square to cut the ends square.
2. Install the new joist against the old one and nail the ends in place.
3. Fasten additional nails, in pairs, every 18 to 24 inches through the joists.
4. Finish the repair by staining or painting to match the deck.

Add bracing to posts:

1. Measure diagonally from post to post and cut the first brace.
2. Set the brace in place and nail the higher end to one end post.
3. Fasten the other end of the brace to the opposite end post.
4. Nail the brace firmly to all posts.
5. If necessary, add a cross-brace between the posts to form an X.
6. Trim off excess wood at the ends.
7. Finish the repair by staining or painting to match the deck.

Replace a baluster:

1. Remove the damaged baluster by removing the screws or nails that hold it in place.
2. Measure and cut a replacement baluster.
3. Install the new baluster and use a level to make sure it is plumb (vertically straight).
4. Fasten the baluster with nails or screws as needed.
5. Apply wood preservative or finish that matches the deck.

Replace a post:

1. Remove all components (handrail, baluster) attached to the post.
2. Measure and cut a new post to the same length as the old one, using pressure-treated or decay-resistant wood.
3. Install the new post, fastening it to the footing as needed.
4. Install the handrail and side rails on the new post.
5. As needed, apply wood preservative, stain, and sealer.

# Dishwasher

Ah, the good old days when dishes were washed and dried by hand. Yeah, right! Next to the TV and the microwave, the dishwasher is probably the most used modern appliance there is. And, as with these other contraptions, the day it breaks down is memorable. So let's call a meeting of the Fix-It Club to figure out what dishwashers do—and how to keep them doing it.

## How Does It Work?

A dishwasher is a major appliance designed to clean dishes, silverware, pots and pans, and other kitchenware. It delivers water through the water inlet into the tub while the detergent dispenser releases detergent in stages to clean the dishes. The heating element warms the solution and a pump channels the water to spray arms that spray and clean the dishes.

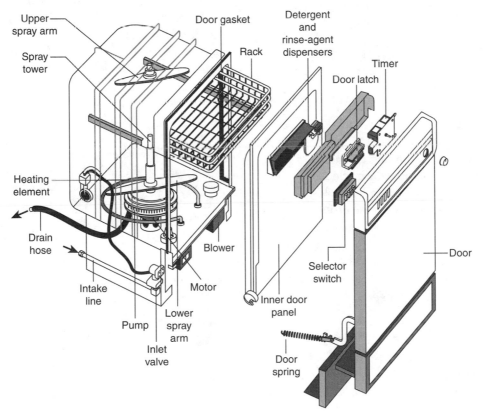

Components of a typical dishwasher.

When the wash cycle is complete, clean water is sprayed to rinse off the detergent. The heating element is also used to dry dishes. Some dishwashers have upper and lower spraying arms while others have a single arm. Also, some dishwashers have a dispenser that adds a rinsing agent to the rinse water.

Built-in dishwashers are installed under countertops with permanent wiring and plumbing connections. Portable models have a flexible coupler that connects to the sink faucet and a drain tube that runs through the sink drain. Power is supplied through a 120-volt plug.

> **Fix-It Tip**
>
> Help your dishwasher do its best job. Check the owner's manual to make sure you are loading the machine correctly. If your water is high in minerals, use a little extra detergent. Make sure the dishwasher is getting sufficient water from the supply line.

## What Can Go Wrong?

With all that water running through it, a dishwasher on the fritz can damage flooring and cabinets, so maintenance and troubleshooting is a good idea. What can cause problems? Switches and motors can fail. Dispensers and spray arms may become dirty and clogged. The heating element may malfunction. The door latch may be out of adjustment. Drain valve parts may need replacing. The drain hose may be clogged.

## How Can I Identify the Problem?

If the dishes are dirty or spotted, check your owner's manual for loading recommendations; test the selector switch (see *Appliance Controls*) and the timer *Motor*. Inspect the dispensers (see below), clean the spray arm (see below), and test the water temperature (see *Test a dishwasher heating element*, below).

If the dishwasher drains during the fill cycle, check the water supply line. Check the door latch and door switch (see below), inspect and clean the spray arm, inspect the float and float switch, and test the inlet valve solenoid (see below).

If the motor doesn't run, make sure there is power to the *Electrical Receptacle* and that there is not a blown fuse or tripped breaker at the *Electrical Service Panel*. Test the timer *Motor*; resistance should be about 3,300 ohms. Inspect the float and float switch (see below) and service the water inlet valve (see below).

If the motor hums, but doesn't run, test the timer *Motor*. Also check the door latch and door switch (see below) and test the *Motor*.

If you have poor water drainage, test the timer motor (see below), inspect the drain hose and spray arm (see below), and test the drain valve solenoid (see below).

If the dishwasher leaks around the door, adjust the door latch (see below), service the door springs (see below), or replace the door gasket (see below).

If the dishwasher leaks from the bottom, inspect the drain hose and spray arm (see below), then check the water inlet connection (see below).

If the water doesn't shut off, test the drain valve (see below).

> **Fix-It Tip**
>
> Most of the key components of a built-in dishwasher are accessible through the front panels. That means you probably won't have to remove it from the cabinet to figure out—and fix—what's wrong with it.

## What Parts, Materials, and Tools Do I Need?

The first place to start looking for replacement parts is your local appliance parts supplier. You also can check with the manufacturer and after-market suppliers (see *Fix-It Resources*). The tools you may need to fix a dishwasher include these:

- Screwdrivers
- Multimeter
- Wrenches
- Pliers
- Nut driver
- Thermometer

## What Are the Steps to Fixing It?

**Caution**

Before working on a dishwasher, always turn off power to the machine. Built-in models are plugged in under the sink. If you can't easily access the plug, turn off the appropriate breaker in the *Electrical Service Panel*. Also remember to locate the water supply shutoff and turn the water off before beginning repairs.

Access dishwasher controls:

1. Unplug the dishwasher or turn off power at the *Electrical Service Panel*.
2. Remove retaining screws on the interior door and on the front of the control panel, then remove the interior door panel.
3. Remove the control panel cover by removing the clips that secure the cover to the door.
4. As needed, also remove retaining screws to remove the lower front panel and expose the controls.

Check dishwasher dispensers:

1. Remove caked-on soap around the dispensers, check the covers, and replace any gaskets that are damaged.
2. Remove the interior door panel (see above).
3. As needed, remove the rinse agent dispenser held in place by tabs or other fasteners. Check the dispenser for stuck or broken parts and replace any damaged parts.
4. To test an electrically operated dispenser for continuity, first unplug or otherwise disconnect the dishwasher from the power source. Then use a multimeter (see *Fix Everything: Multimeter*) set on R×1 (resistance times 1) to test the unit, replacing it if the reading is infinite.

Clean the spray arm(s):

1. Either unplug the dishwasher or turn off power at the *Electrical Service Panel*.
2. Slide out the lower dish rack.
3. Rotate all spray arms and lift the spray tower to make sure that they move freely. If they don't, or if the arms wobble excessively, tighten or replace them.
4. To replace a spray arm, unscrew the spray tower *clockwise* by hand and remove it along with any fasteners and washers.
5. If the spray arm is *not* replaced, clean the holes in the existing spray arm and tighten.

Test a dishwasher heating element:

1. During the unit's first cycle, open the door and measure the water temperature with a meat or candy thermometer. If it is below 140°F, test the element.
2. Before working on the heating element, unplug the dishwasher or turn off power at the *Electrical Service Panel*.

3. Use a multimeter (see *Fix Everything: Multimeter*) set to R×1 (resistance times 1) to test the *Heating Element*. Look for a reading other than infinity. Also place one probe on a terminal and the other on the element's metal sheath to check for continuity to ground (not good!). Replace any element that fails either test.

Test and replace the door latch and switch:

1. To adjust the door latch, loosen the retaining bolts with a nut driver, slide the latch in or out, and tighten the bolts.
2. If the door latch closes securely and the machine will not run, test the switch.
3. Before continuing, unplug the dishwasher or turn off power at the *Electrical Service Panel*.
4. Set a multimeter (see *Fix Everything: Multimeter*) to R×1 (resistance times 1) and test the switch (see *Appliance Controls*) for continuity. The meter should indicate continuity with the switch button pushed in, and an open circuit when it's out. Replace the switch if your test results are different.
5. To replace the switch, remove the door switch retaining bolts (see step 1) and remove the switch assembly. Install a new door switch and reconnect the switch wires.

Test the water inlet valve:

1. Remove the lower front panel (see above). Make sure the incoming water line and the hose that connects the inlet valve to the tub are securely fastened.
2. Remove the wires from the inlet valve terminals.
3. Set a multimeter (see *Fix Everything: Multimeter*) to R×1 (resistance times 1). Touch a probe to each terminal. A good valve will show some, but not infinite, resistance.

Test the drain valve mechanism and solenoid (if so equipped):

1. Unplug the dishwasher or turn off power at the *Electrical Service Panel*.
2. Remove the lower front panel (see above) to inspect the *Motor*. If it has four wires, the motor is reversible and has no drain valve to service. Otherwise, continue with step 3.
3. Inspect the gate arm mechanism for free movement. Inspect the springs and replace them if they are missing or broken.
4. Disconnect the wires from the drain valve solenoid. Set a multimeter (see *Fix Everything: Multimeter*) to R×1 (resistance times 1). Clip a probe to each terminal on the solenoid and check for some, but not infinite, resistance (open circuit).
5. If replacing the solenoid, detach and label wires, springs, and screws, then install an exact replacement unit.

Inspect the dishwasher float and float switch:

1. Unplug the dishwasher or turn off power at the *Electrical Service Panel*.
2. Remove the lower front panel (see above). Make sure the clamp is secure and remove any kinks in the hose by hand.
3. If necessary, replace a broken or badly kinked hose using pliers to squeeze the spring clamp, and pull off the hose.
4. Disconnect the other end of the hose (under the sink); cut and install a new hose of the same length and size.

Test the dishwasher pump and motor assembly:

1. Unplug the dishwasher or shut off power at the *Electrical Service Panel.*
2. Remove the lower front panel (above) and manually turn the motor fan blades. If they don't move freely, look for obstructions or call for service.
3. Disconnect the *Motor* wires from their terminals.
4. Set a multimeter (see *Fix Everything: Multimeter*) to R×1 (resistance times 1) and attach a probe to each motor wire terminal. The motor should show little resistance.
5. Check the ground connection by placing one probe on the bare metal housing of the motor and the other probe on each terminal in turn. There should be no reading. If the motor fails either test (in steps 4 and 5), call for professional service.

Service dishwasher door springs and cables:

1. Unplug the dishwasher or shut off power at the *Electrical Service Panel.*
2. Remove the lower front panel (see above). Inspect the cables and springs. Replace damaged springs and cables in pairs to ensure proper tension.
3. Remove a damaged cable or spring and replace it following the manufacturer's instructions.

Replace door gaskets:

1. Open the dishwasher door and remove the dish racks.
2. Inspect the gasket for damage or brittleness and replace as needed.
3. Remove the gasket with a screwdriver or putty knife and install one of the same type, diameter, and length. The unit owner's manual may include a part number to help in tracking down a replacement gasket.

# Doll

Dolls can become lifelong treasures. Helping children learn about caring for human-looking toys, dolls offer an outlet for nurturing instincts. They've also become quite collectible by adults. Boys may prefer a teddy bear or a hand puppet, but they all function as imaginary friends that sometimes need to go to the doll hospital.

## How Does It Work?

A doll is a small-scale figure of a human being used especially as a child's plaything. Dolls are also keepsakes, collectibles, and sometimes valuable antiques. Repair of valuable antique dolls and porcelain dolls should be left to a professional or a "doll hospital."

Common play dolls come in three types. Soft dolls (or rag dolls) are made of durable fabric, usually with hair made of yarn. Cloth-body dolls have torsos made of cloth, heads and limbs that are plastic or vinyl, and hair that is either rooted or a glued wig. Some plastic or vinyl dolls are held together by flanged limbs or elastic. (Also see *Stuffed Toy*.)

## What Can Go Wrong?

Unlike children, dolls suffer in silence. They may get torn or lose an arm or leg without complaint. After years of use or storage, their stuffing may go flat, or they may need a gentle cleaning to revive them.

**Fix-It Tip**

Wash dolls with a mild detergent and a damp rag, then dry with a clean rag. If the doll's hair is rooted (fed through the scalp), you can shampoo it. Don't shampoo dolls with wigs, because water may damage the glue.

## How Can I Identify the Problem?

In most cases, the problem is evident, as is the solution. For example, if a cloth-body doll's body is severely damaged, replace it (see below).

If the head, arm, or leg comes off a doll with push-in limbs, use a hairdryer to make the plastic pliable, then reinsert the part into the body.

If the elastic inside the doll that holds the limbs or head on breaks, replace it (see below).

If a soft doll loses its shape, open a central seam and add fresh polyester stuffing available from a craft store.

If a wig comes loose, glue it back on with a white glue or super glue. If rooted hair is damaged beyond repair, cut it off close to the scalp and glue a wig over it—or find a doll hat that fits.

**Fix-It Tip**

Larger craft stores will have extensive doll-making and repair supplies including fabrics, stuffing, glues, and even parts. Take the doll in for a match and some advice.

## What Parts, Materials, and Tools Do I Need?

You can find most replacement doll parts in a local craft store or on the Internet (see *Fix-It Resources*). In addition, you may need these:

- Needles
- Thread
- Wire-cutting pliers
- White glue
- Scissors
- Elastic material
- Wire coat hanger

## What Are the Steps to Fixing It?

Replace a cloth-body doll's torso:

1. Undo the stitching holding the head and limbs to the torso. Then unstitch the body and use the fabric as a pattern (adding about ¾ inch all the way around for the seam) for the new body. Add about 1 inch of fabric to the limb and neck openings.

2. Sew the torso inside out, leaving the rear seam open. To attach plastic or vinyl pieces, turn up about 1 inch of fabric and sew through the holes located at the base of each piece.

3. Turn the torso right side out and stuff the doll with polyester filling.

4. Stitch up the rear seam with small, tight overhand stitches (see *Fix Everything: Sewing*).

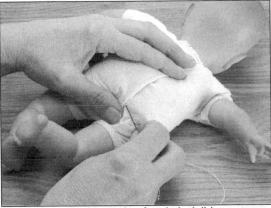

You can access the inside of a cloth doll by cutting a slit in its back, then closing it up when done.

Restring a plastic or vinyl doll:

1. Make two elastic stringing loops: one for the legs and head, and a shorter one for the arms. Loop sizes depend on the material's elasticity and the doll size. The elastic should hold the head and limbs securely while allowing smooth movement. Make tight knots in the end of the elastic to bind it.

2. If the head is attached with an internal hook that's broken or missing, make a new one from a wire coat hanger. Cut off a section with wire-cutting pliers and bend it into shape. Attach the hook to the head bar. Then secure the larger elastic stringing loop to the hook and push the loop down through the neck cavity and into the doll's torso. Position the doll head on top of the body.

3. To attach a leg, make a stringing hook to reach into the torso and grasp the loop hanging from the head. Pull the loop down through the leg hole and secure it to the hook inside the leg. Pull out the stringing hook and repeat the process for the other leg.

4. To attach an arm, hook one end of your stringing loop to the arm and feed the loop through the armhole. Use the stringing hook to pull the loop through the opposite armhole. Attach the loop to the hook on the arm, then remove the stringing hook.

**Fix-It Tip**

If you really enjoy repairing dolls, try one of the books or videos available on the subject. You can find them through your local book or craft store, or online. And some larger craft stores offer periodic classes in doll making and repair.

# Door

"Close the door!" "I can't!"

We often take doors for granted—until something goes wrong. Fortunately, doors are simple in construction and operation, meaning you can easily fix them if you know how they work and what to do when they don't. The Fix-It Club knows!

## How Does It Work?

A door is a moveable barrier that allows entry or exit into a defined space. Some doors swing on hinges, while others slide on tracks. Exterior doors typically are made of solid wood, while many interior doors have hollow cores. Fire doors are often made of or covered with metal. Some doors are made of glass with a metal frame rather than wood. Others are made of vinyl or even fiberglass. Yet they all operate and are repaired approximately the same way.

Doors include the door itself as well as the jambs (surrounding frame) and casing or trim. Doors also have locks, latches, knobs, and hinges, covered under *Door Hardware*.

Jamb

Trim

Door

Prehung doors are installed in an opening as a unit.

## What Can Go Wrong?

The most common problem with a door is that it sticks or binds. A door might not close properly. It might rattle. A sliding door might be jammed or not slide smoothly. An exterior door might let in a draft from outside.

**Caution**

Before removing a door from its hinges, make sure you have somewhere safe and solid to lean it. Doors can be heavy and, if they fall, can hurt someone or something.

## How Can I Identify the Problem?

If a door sticks or binds, remove excess wood or other material with a plane (see below). In humid climates, wood can expand and make a door stick to the jamb. Humidity control (see *Humidifier*) may solve the problem.

If a top-hung sliding closet door does not operate smoothly, adjust and lubricate it (see below).

If a sliding glass exterior door does not glide, clean and lubricate the tracks (see below).

If an exterior door lets in a draft, add weatherstripping (see below).

**Fix-It Tip**

As you vacuum your home, use a crevice tool to remove dirt and debris from the track of any sliding doors. Periodically use a brush or broom to loosen caked-on dirt that can make sliding doors stick and cause bigger problems.

## What Parts, Materials, and Tools Do I Need?

Hardware stores and home improvement centers are full of replacement parts, materials, and tools for fixing doors. The tools you'll need include these:

- Screwdrivers
- Hammer
- Pry bar
- Saw
- Utility knife
- Awl
- Nail set
- Wood plane
- Wood filler
- Tape measure
- Weatherstripping

## What Are the Steps to Fixing It?

Remove a door:

1. Open the door to expose the door hinges.
2. Tap the lowest hinge's pin *up* using a nail set (or an old flat screwdriver) and a hammer.
3. Pull the hinge pin up until about the top half of it is exposed. Repeat for the one or two other hinges, moving from the bottom of the door to the top.
4. Place a piece of wood under the center of the door to support the weight, then pull each of the pins out of the hinges, from the bottom of the door to the top.
5. Remove the door and place it somewhere safe.

Plane a door:

1. With the door hung, mark the location where material needs to be removed from the door.
2. If necessary, remove the door (see above) to easily access the area that needs planing.
3. Adjust the plane's blade to remove small increments of material.
4. Use the plane to remove material so the edge won't catch on the jamb as the door is closed.

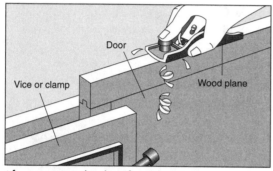

After removing the door from the hinges, use a wood plane to remove wood from the bottom or side of a door.

Service a sliding closet door:

1. Swing the door out and up to remove it from the track.
2. If the track is damaged, remove and replace it before continuing.
3. Inspect the rollers, tracks, and slots for obviously loose or damaged components. Replace and adjust as needed.
4. If the door is not level, adjust the pivots on the top and bottom of the door.
5. If there is a gap above the door, check for adjustable roller brackets and adjust as needed.

Repair a sliding glass door:

1. Lift the panel up and away from the door frame to remove the panel.
2. Inspect the wheels and replace them if they are worn or broken.
3. Clean the track and repair any damaged track runners before continuing.
4. Find and test the adjustment screws on either end of the panel to make sure that they are clean and work properly.
5. Replace the door in the frame and on the track. If necessary, use the adjustment screws to adjust the height of the door.

Weatherstrip a door:

1. Purchase a weatherstripping kit for the door or measure the door and take the dimensions to a hardware store for materials.
2. Install the weatherstripping on the hinge, top, and latch sides of the door opening, in that order (unless the weatherstripping manufacturer suggests otherwise). Weatherstripping is installed by nailing it in place with small brads, positioning it so the compressible surface is facing the door's perimeter. Closing the door will compress the weatherstripping to reduce air leaks.
3. Install a door sweep on the inside bottom of the door. Use a hacksaw or utility knife to cut the unit to length if necessary. Mark and drill the screw holes.

**Fix-It Tip**

Weatherstripping exterior doors may earn financial assistance from your local power company. Contact the company to find out more.

# Door Hardware

Fixing a *Door* and related weatherstripping is covered in a separate guide. Here we'll cover fixing the lock, latch, doorknob, and hinges—door hardware.

## How Does It Work?

A lock is a door fastener that is operated by a key or knob. A latch is a device that holds the door closed. A doorknob releases a door latch. A hinge allows an attached door to swing. Together these devices open, close, and secure doors.

Exterior doors often have both a key-in-knob lock and a deadbolt or rim lock. Interior doors usually require only a doorknob and latch. Both slide the latch into a strike plate mounted on the door jamb.

## What Can Go Wrong?

Door accessories are relatively trouble-free, but are used frequently, so problems can occur. Locks stick and work slowly. The key might break or might not open the door. The cylinder might move when the key turns. The key might turn but the bolt doesn't move. The bolt might not extend. Hinges might squeak, become loose or damaged. Keeping the door hardware clean and lubricated solves many potential problems.

## How Can I Identify the Problem?

If the key will not go into the lock on a very cold day, thaw the lock with a hair dryer or a deicing spray.

If a key breaks off in a lock, lift up the broken end with a straightened paper clip, then remove the stub with small pliers.

If a key won't easily slip in and out of the lock, have a new key made from one that isn't as worn. You also can lubricate the keyway with penetrating oil designed for locks or with graphite (never both).

If a key is difficult to turn and the key does not seem to be at fault, clean the lock and latch (see below). Also make sure the cylinder is properly aligned (see below).

If the cylinder moves when the key turns, tighten the screws that hold the cylinder in place.

If the key turns but the bolt doesn't move, follow the steps for fixing the bolt (see below).

If the bolt doesn't extend, check the alignment of the strike plate (see below).

If a push-button privacy lock gets activated, you typically can unlock it with a straightened paper clip pushed into the small hole in the center of the knob.

If a door rubs all along the length of its latch edge, tighten any loose hinge screws.

If a door sticks or binds, check the hinges (see below).

If the hinges squeak, remove, clean, oil, and replace the hinge pins.

## What Parts, Materials, and Tools Do I Need?

Replacement hardware for household doors is available at hardware stores and home improvement centers. In fact, you'll probably find an entire section of door hardware. These are tools you'll need to fix or replace door hardware:

- Screwdrivers
- Wrenches
- Cleaning solvent
- Canned air
- Penetrating oil or graphite powder
- Small file

## What Are the Steps to Fixing It?

Clean a lock assembly:

1. Remove the lock assembly from the door.

Use a screwdriver to loosen the lock assembly, then remove it by hand.

2. Soak the assembly with cleaning solvent, scrub it with a small brush, and dry it thoroughly with canned air.
3. Lubricate the components with penetrating oil.
4. Reassemble the lock assembly into the latch and reinstall it in the door.

Align a cylinder:

1. Loosen the mounting screws that hold the cylinder on the door.
2. Insert the key in the cylinder, then move the cylinder so that the key's teeth face upward.
3. Retighten the mounting plate screws and remove the key.

To fix a bolt that doesn't move:

1. Make sure that the cylinder is aligned (see above).
2. Remove any debris or paint around the bolt and lubricate it with lightweight oil.
3. If necessary, disassemble the cylinder and bolt to check for loose or broken parts and repair or replace any problem pieces.

Realign a strike plate:

1. Unscrew the strike plate screws and remove the plate.
2. Trim the hole in the jamb as needed so the bolt enters the jamb hole.
3. Temporarily place the strike plate over the jamb hole and close the door to make sure the strike plate fits in the hole. Adjust as needed.
4. Hold the strike plate in place while closing the door to verify that the bolt fits through the strike plate and into the jamb hole.
5. Continue holding the strike plate in position and open the door. Mark and drill the strike plate holes, then install screws to hold it in place.

Tighten hinge screws:

1. Open the door and use a screwdriver to tighten the hinge screws.
2. If screws spin in place, use longer screws.
3. If longer screws still don't firmly attach the hinge, remove the hinge and fill the holes with wood filler or wood slivers. Allow filler to dry. Then reinstall the hinges with long screws.

Adjust the height of a hinge:

1. Remove the hinge from the jamb and/or door.
2. If the hinge is too shallow, use a chisel to remove excess wood. If the hinge is too deep, cut and insert a piece of solid (not corrugated) cardboard in the hinge mounting area.
3. Reinstall the hinge.

**Fix-It Tip**

Once a year, carefully remove hinge pins from door hinges and lubricate them with silicone grease or lubricating oil. Removing and reinstalling hinge pins will go much easier if you have a second person help you hold the door.

# Doorbell

"Hey, your doorbell doesn't work!" "I know. I know. I was going to fix it this weekend." No more excuses! Here's how to test and repair a doorbell.

## How Does It Work?

A doorbell is a small electric device that signals residents inside when someone outside the door pushes a button. When the button is pushed, it completes a circuit with a transformer, letting electricity through to sound the bell or chime. Some doorbells use a small radio transmitter or a remote controller to activate the bell without wires.

Bell ⌐ Junction box    Transformer (behind)

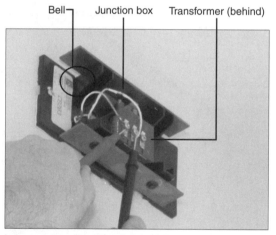

Components of a typical doorbell.

## What Can Go Wrong?

Loose wiring and faulty buttons are the most common doorbell problem. Power to the circuit may fail. Connection terminals may be corroded. The chime or transformer may fail. The sounding mechanism may be dirty or the grommets (mechanical chimes only) may deteriorate. The hammer arm may be bent (bells only). The unit may short circuit.

## How Can I Identify the Problem?

If there is no sound when the button is pushed, check the *Electrical Service Panel* for a tripped breaker or blown fuse. Tighten all wire connections behind the button, inside the signaling unit, and at the transformer. Look for damaged wires and splice any breaks by stripping both ends of the wire and joining them with a wire connector. Remove the button plate and look for corrosion around the terminals; clean with electrical contact cleaner or remove the wires from the screws and sand off any corrosion with fine sandpaper. Remove the plate and test the push button (see below). Test the sounding device (see below). Test the transformer (see below).

If the bell or chime sounds continuously, remove the button plate and look for touching or pinched wires. Tighten the screws and make sure all the wires are separated.

If the signal sounds muffled or faint, clean the sounding mechanism with a cotton swab or old toothbrush dampened with isopropyl alcohol (do not lubricate the mechanism). On mechanical chimes, inspect for old or deteriorated grommets that support the metal chime plates. Replace grommets if they are worn. Gently reshape a bent hammer arm on a bell using pliers.

## What Parts, Materials, and Tools Do I Need?

Exact replacement parts are available from local home improvement stores, electrical supply outlets, and hardware stores. The tools you will need to fix a doorbell may include these:

- Screwdrivers
- Wire strippers
- Wire connectors
- Electrical contact cleaner
- Fine sandpaper
- Multimeter
- Isopropyl alcohol
- Cotton swab or old toothbrush
- Pliers

## What Are the Steps to Fixing It?

Test the doorbell push button:

1. Loosen the screws that secure the push-button plate. If the plate has clips rather than screws holding it in place, carefully use a flat screwdriver to pry it up.
2. To test the button, hold the blade of a screwdriver across the terminals. If the sounding device sounds, the button is defective and needs to be replaced (continue with step 3). If there is no sound, test the other components.
3. Turn off power at the *Electrical Service Panel*, and disconnect the wires from the switch terminals.
4. Install the replacement switch by looping the end of each wire clockwise around its terminal screw and tightening the screw. Press the button to test.

**Fix-It Tip**

The first thing to check with a faulty doorbell is the button, especially one that is exposed to the elements. If needed, clean it with alcohol and a cotton swab.

Test and replace a doorbell sounding device:

1. Remove the transformer from its terminal in the unit.
2. Set a multimeter (see *Fix Everything: Multimeter*) on R×100 (resistance times 100). Probe the transformer terminal and each button terminal in turn. A reading of infinity or zero ohms means the sounding device is defective and should be replaced.
3. Turn off power to the doorbell at the *Electrical Service Panel*.
4. Loosen the terminal screws, remove the wires, and unscrew the sounding device from the wall.
5. Insert the wires through the back of the new chime assembly and attach the chime to the wall.
6. Attach each wire by looping the end clockwise around its terminal screw and tightening the screws.
7. Install the chime cover, restore power at the *Electrical Service Panel*, and test the new unit.

Test the doorbell transformer:

1. With power to the doorbell on, set a multimeter (see *Fix Everything: Multimeter*) on ACV, 50-volt range.
2. Attach the tester probes to the terminal screws holding the signaling system wires. If the reading is less than 6 volts or over 24 volts, the transformer should be replaced with one of equal voltage.
3. To replace the transformer, first shut off power to the circuit at the *Electrical Service Panel*.
4. Disconnect the signaling system and the house cable wires from the transformer. Install the new transformer leads through the hole in the panel and reattach all wires.

# Drain System

Thank goodness for the household drain system. It removes wastewater from sinks, tubs, showers, and even a wet basement, dumping it into the sewer or drainage system exiting your home. But what do you do when the drain system doesn't drain? You call a meeting of the Fix-It Club—pronto!

## How Does It Work?

A household drain system consists of the drain assembly at the sink, tub, shower, or floor and the pipes that conduct it out of the house. Most drains include a trap (a U-shaped pipe) below the fixture to trap sediment and to create a barrier that prevents drainage odors from traveling back up the pipe, through the drain, and into the room. Household drain systems also include a ventilation system to allow gases and odors to escape through a home's roof.

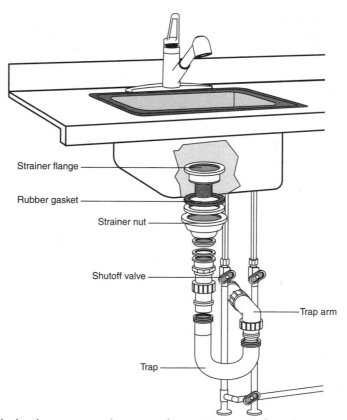

Strainer flange

Rubber gasket

Strainer nut

Shutoff valve

Trap arm

Trap

Sink drain systems include the drain, trap, and trap arm that removes waste from the sink in a kitchen or bathroom.

## What Can Go Wrong?

By far the most common problem with a drainage system is clogs. Fortunately, most clogs occur in the trap. In fact, that's the intent of the trap, to give household drains a place to collect sediment in a location that's easily accessed and cleaned. Less frequently, sink stoppers can get out of adjustment and pipes under the sink or in a wall can leak.

**Fix-It Tip**

The most common cause of clogged drains in bathtubs and showers is hair and soap sludge. Periodically use a drain cleaning product to dissolve these impediments and send them down the drain where they belong. Make sure you carefully follow instructions on the product's container.

## How Can I Identify the Problem?

Household drains will tell you when they have a problem doing their job. Solutions are relatively easy to apply. Ongoing maintenance will keep them from becoming damaging problems.

If a drain becomes clogged, first try to clear the drain with a plunger (see below).

If a sink stopper doesn't stop water from draining or doesn't open all the way, adjust the stopper (see below).

If the problem is at the main drain, use a plumbing auger or expansion nozzle to clear the line (see below).

If pipes under a sink leak, tighten connections or replace the drain flange (see below).

**Caution**

If the drain is completely stopped up, *don't* use chemical drain cleaners, as they can release noxious fumes and burn unprotected skin. You'll be left with a sink or tub full of caustic chemicals. Also, never use chemical drain cleaners with a plunger as the pumping action can splash the chemicals on you.

## What Parts, Materials, and Tools Do I Need?

You'll find replacement parts for household drain systems at your local hardware or plumbing supply store, along with tools to do the job right:

- Plunger
- Pipe wrench
- Screwdrivers
- Auger or wire coat hanger
- Expansion nozzle
- Garden hose
- Adjustable pliers
- Bucket and rags
- Plumber's putty
- Vinegar
- Bottle brush

## What Are the Steps to Fixing It?

Clear a clogged (not stopped) sink or bathtub with a plunger:

1. If you have a dishwasher, pinch off the rubber dishwasher drain hose that leads to the garbage disposer using a clamp or locking pliers. If clearing a bathtub, remove the drain stopper and cover the overflow opening with a wet rag.
2. Remove the sink basket or tub stopper and clean any debris from the drain opening.
3. Fill the sink or tub with sufficient water to cover the plunger cup, usually about 2 inches. If you are working on a double sink, seal the other sink with a stopper so the plunger can create a vacuum.
4. Set the plunger on the drain opening and repeatedly pump it up and down, then pull away sharply to dislodge debris. Repeat if necessary.
5. Turn on warm or hot water to flush loosened debris from the drain.
6. If the clog remains, use an auger (see below) or an expansion nozzle (see below) to clear the drain.

Clear a clog using an auger:

1. Remove the stopper or strainer. If unable to do so, disassemble the drain trap (see below) and feed the auger directly through the pipe. Make sure you have a pail and rags nearby in case of a water spill.
2. Release the setscrew on the auger and begin feeding the cable into the open drain.
3. Once the auger tip hits the clog, set the screw and crank the auger clockwise to break up the clog.

4. Continue breaking up the clog and moving it down the drain line with the auger. Once there is no more resistance to the forward motion of the auger, stop and carefully remove the auger.
5. If the clog can't be moved, continue twisting the auger to possibly snag and retract the clog.
6. Once the clog is cleared, flush the drain with boiling water.

Clear a clogged drain using an expansion nozzle:

1. Attach the expansion nozzle to a garden hose and attach the hose to a faucet.
2. Seal off all nearby drains so you can build water pressure in the line with the expansion nozzle.
3. Insert the nozzle as far into the open drain as possible.
4. Turn the water slowly to full force, inflating the nozzle to seal the drain and to apply water pressure for 15 to 30 seconds to clear the clog.
5. Once done, detach the hose from the faucet to let the nozzle deflate before removing it.

Clear a clog by removing the trap:

1. Place a pan or pail under the trap to catch water and debris.
2. Loosen the slip nuts on each end of the trap with adjustable pliers.
3. Remove the trap and pour out any water and debris. If the trap is blocked, use a straightened coat hanger to clear it.
4. If there is no clog in the trap, the blockage may be in the wall pipes. Use an auger or the coat hanger to clear the drain line on each side of the trap. Reinstall or replace the trap.

Adjust a bathroom sink stopper:

1. Remove the stopper from the drain. On some models, twist the stopper to free it from the pivot rod or unscrew the retaining nut on the back of the drainpipe and pull out the pivot rod.
2. Clean the stopper and replace the O-ring, if used.
3. Reinsert the stopper, reconnect the pivot rod, and tighten the retaining nut. To test, add water to the basin and watch to see if the stopper holds water; if it does not, continue with step 4.
4. Adjust the metal spring clip, sliding it up or down the pivot rod as needed to seat the stopper.

Stop leaks around the drain flange:

1. Remove the stopper and drainpipe, and disconnect the lift rod to remove the drainpipe from the sink.
2. Apply plumbers' putty or silicone caulk under the lip of the drain flange.
3. Reinstall the parts and wipe away any excess putty or caulk around the flange.

Service a bathtub drain assembly:

1. Remove the stopper and clean the drain.
2. Remove the overflow plate screws and remove the lift assembly. Clean debris from the pipe.
3. If necessary, purchase and install a replacement bathtub drain assembly following the manufacturer's directions.

Replace a drain flange:

1. Remove the pop-up stopper or strainer.
2. Remove the overflow plate and lift assembly.
3. Disconnect the lift rod and reinstall the overflow plate.
4. Use pliers to unscrew the drain flange.
5. Apply plumbers' putty or silicone caulk under the lip of the drain flange.
6. Screw the flange into the drain opening and thread the metal stopper into the cross piece.

**Fix-It Tip**

Most clogs can be avoided. Place strainer baskets in drain openings. Pour grease and coffee grounds into the trash instead of down the drain. Occasionally pour boiling water down each drain to keep it from getting clogged.

# Dryer, Clothes

"Is my shirt dry yet? I'm gonna be late!" The clothes dryer is one of the most used—and abused—devices in the typical household. It dries clothing, shoes, billfolds, loose change, discarded chewing gum, and who knows what else. The lint trap is stuffed with lint and bits of paper. The exhaust hose is stuffed with lint. The dryer takes twice as long to dry as it did a month ago. It's time to call the Fix-It Club!

## How Does It Work?

A clothes dryer is a large appliance for drying clothing, bedding, towels, and other linens.

Moisture is removed from clothing with a combination of air, heat, and motion. Gas and electric dyers differ mainly in the heat source. Both gas and electric models use a motor to turn a drive belt. The drive belt revolves the drum which holds the clothing. A blower directs air past the heat source and into the drum, where it draws lint and moisture from the fabrics through a lint screen and out an exhaust duct. Appliance controls regulate the options, such as temperature and drying time. Some machines use mechanical timers, while others rely on digital electronics.

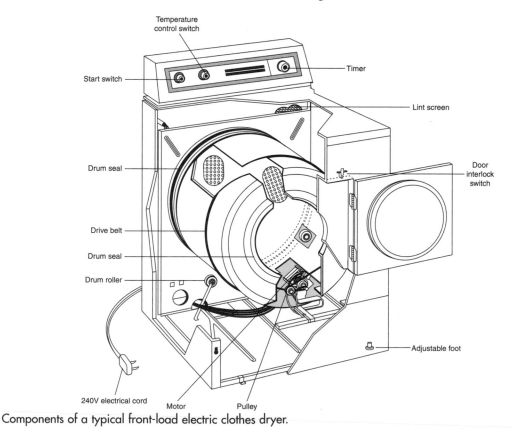

Components of a typical front-load electric clothes dryer.

## What Can Go Wrong?

A dryer is a sturdy machine that will usually last for many years. The most common problem is also the easiest to fix: a buildup of lint. In addition, the *Electrical Cord* can fail. Switches, the timer and the timer motor, thermostats, and the heating element can all fail. The drive belt and idler can malfunction. Many of these problems you can resolve yourself without calling a costly service person.

**Fix-It Tip**

Newer dryers use digital rather than mechanical timers and other controls. Many of these offer diagnostics that can be activated to report problems in the form of codes. Check your machine's owner's manual for information on how to activate and interpret diagnostic codes. They can save you hundreds of dollars in unnecessary repairs.

## How Can I Identify the Problem?

If your dryer doesn't run at all, check the *Electrical Service Panel* for a tripped circuit breaker or blown fuse and test the *Electrical Cord*. Test the door switch and the start switch for continuity (see *Appliance Controls*). Test the timer (see *Appliance Controls* or consult a professional who can read a wiring diagram) and test the timer *Motor*. If necessary, call a professional for service on the dryer *Motor*.

If the dryer takes a long time to dry, clean the lint screen and clean or unkink the exhaust duct and vent. Make sure you aren't drying too many articles at once.

If the motor runs but the dryer doesn't heat, test the temperature selector switch, the thermostats, the centrifugal switch (see *Appliance Controls*), the timer, the timer *Motor*, and the electric *Heating Element*. Or you can call a professional to service a gas element.

If the motor runs but the drum doesn't turn, check the drive belt and the idler (see below). Call for professional service on the drum.

If the dryer runs when the door is open, test the door switch (see *Appliance Controls*).

If the dryer will not turn off, make sure the room is not too cool for the dryer to operate properly; test the timer (see *Appliance Controls*) and the timer *Motor*; test the *Heating Element*, and test the thermostats (see *Appliance Controls*).

If the drying temperature is too hot, clean the lint screen, clean or unkink the exhaust duct and vent, test the thermostats (see *Appliance Controls*), and test and replace, if necessary, the *Heating Element*.

If the dryer is excessively noisy, level the dryer with the adjustable feet, and tighten any loose screws on the housing and rear panel. Also check the drive belt and idler (see below).

**Fix-It Tip**

No one likes to be overworked. Drying too many clothes at a time can slow drying time significantly. Remember to load the machine loosely, following the manufacturer's recommendations, for best results—and a happier dryer.

## What Parts, Materials, and Tools Do I Need?

Replacement parts are available from the manufacturer and aftermarket suppliers (see *Fix-It Resources*) and from local gas and electric appliance suppliers, larger hardware stores, and home centers. The tools you will need to fix a gas or electric clothes dryer include these:

- Screwdrivers
- Nut Driver
- Putty knife
- Blocks of scrap wood
- Multimeter

# What Are the Steps to Fixing It?

Disassemble a dryer:

1. Unplug the dryer or turn off power at the *Electrical Service Panel.*

> **Caution**
>
> Gas dryers typically have a shutoff valve on the gas line coming into the dryer. Make sure it is securely turned off before working on a gas dryer. Electric dryers are powered by 240V AC, so be extra cautious of loose or exposed wires. If you're in doubt about the safety of what you're doing, call your gas service or an electrician as appropriate.

2. Unscrew the control console at each end. Fasteners will be at the bottom front, top, or sides.

3. Place the console face down on a soft towel or other cushion on top of the dryer for further disassembly and testing.

4. Remove the console's rear panel to access the start switch, temperature selector, circuit diagram, and timer.

5. As needed, access the drum by removing a top-mounted lint screen (on some models), and pushing the blade of a putty knife between the dryer's top and body to disengage attachment clips.

6. As needed, remove the dryer's rear panel by moving the dryer away from the wall and removing any screws around the panel edges.

7. As needed, remove the toe panel by inserting a putty knife under the center top of the toe panel to catch the clip, then removing the panel.

8. As needed, remove the front panel by loosening screws at the panel corners to access the drum and motor.

9. Once inside the dryer, disconnect and label any wires attached to components you need to remove.

You now can service the drive belt and idler pulley (below) or test the *Motor, Heating Element,* and other components using a multimeter (see *Fix Everything: Multimeter*).

Service the drive belt and idler pulley:

1. Remove the top panel or raise the top and remove the front panel (see above).

2. Support the dryer drum on a block of scrap wood.

3. Push the idler pulley toward the motor pulley to slacken the drive belt, then disengage the belt.

4. Inspect the idler bracket, pulley, and spring, and adjust or replace as needed. Some idler pulleys are held in place by belt tension and others by spring tension.

> **Caution**
>
> Clothes dryers cause many fires that could be avoidable. Make it a habit to clean out the lint trap on your dryer after every load. And occasionally detach the vent hose and clean out any lint or other built-up material. At the same time, vacuum around the back of the dryer.

Some call it the most indispensable gadget invented by mankind. Others call it a curse. Most of us are somewhere in between; it's handy—when it works. If it doesn't, bring it to a meeting of the Fix-It Club.

## How Does It Work?

An electric hair dryer produces an instant blast of hot air, yet many are light enough to be held in one hand so the air can be directed. The dryer contains a very long coil of thin wire that develops heat. A jet of air blown by a fan behind the heating element carries away this heat. If the air flow is obstructed and the air becomes too hot, a thermostat cuts off the power.

The typical hair dryer includes an on-off switch, a fan-speed switch, a fan and motor, and a heat switch. Larger hood-type dryers work on the same principles with the same key parts, so the same repair instructions apply. Heated styling brushes are essentially the same in function, parts, and repair.

## What Can Go Wrong?

Because hair dryers are simple small appliances, few things can go wrong. The *Electrical Cord* might be faulty, the appliance might not heat, and the fan might not operate. That's about it.

> **Fix-It Tip**
>
> Hair dryers will overheat and the thermostat will turn it off if the vent becomes clogged with hair or dust. Periodically brush or vacuum the grille and filter screen. Also tighten screws occasionally so hair and moisture don't enter the housing.

## How Can I Identify the Problem?

Here's where to start looking if your hair dryer fails:

If the appliance doesn't work at all, make sure the power is on at the outlet and check the *Electrical Cord.*

If it still doesn't run, disassemble it to check the thermal cutout and service if necessary. Also test the *Motor,* switches (see *Appliance Controls*), and *Heating Element* with a multimeter (see *Fix Everything: Multimeter*).

If the fan doesn't work on every setting, check the fan switch (see *Appliance Controls*) and service if faulty.

If the dryer doesn't heat on every setting, check the heat switch (see *Appliance Controls*) and service if necessary.

If the fan works but the heat doesn't, check the heat switch (see *Appliance Controls* and *Heating Element*) and service if needed.

If the heat works but the fan doesn't, check the fan-speed switch (see *Appliance Controls*) and the fan *Motor* and service if faulty.

> **Fix-It Tip**
>
> The heating elements inside a hair dryer (and toasters, as well) are very fine wires. Treat them with special care to ensure that they aren't damaged as you are repairing other components. Also, inspect them for breaks and repair or replace any that look worn or broken.

## What Parts, Materials, and Tools Do I Need?

You can buy some replacement parts for hair dryers at small appliance parts stores and larger hardware stores. Or you can contact the manufacturer or online aftermarket parts dealers for replacement parts (see *Fix-It Resources*). The tools you may need to work on a hair dryer include these:

- Screwdrivers
- Wrenches
- Multimeter

## What Are the Steps to Fixing It?

Disassemble a typical hair dryer:

1. Unplug the dryer.
2. Remove the hair dryer nozzle and filter. On some models they are held on by tension, while on others by a small screw where the nozzle or filter meets the main body.
3. If the unit has an intake filter screen, remove and clean it.

Remove and clean the hair dryer filter screen.

4. Remove the screws that hold the housing together and remove the housing.

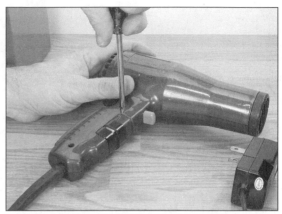

Remove the fasteners holding the housing halves together. Pull the halves apart carefully, because some switches will fall out.

Make sure you lay out the components so they are easier to reassemble once you've fixed the hair dryer.

5. Locate any switches (see *Appliance Controls*), the fan, and the *Motor*, then test them. In some cases you can see obvious damage or problems that can be repaired quickly. Or you may need to find and install replacement parts.

Heating element    Fan motor    Controls

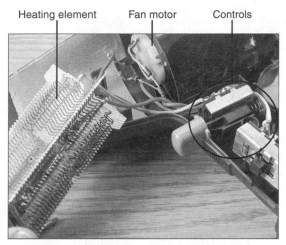

Components of a hair dryer: heating element, fan motor, and controls.

Service a thermal cutout:

1. Open the housing as above to open the *Heating Element* assembly.
2. Inspect the thermal cutout for damage or discoloration. The thermal cutout will be connected to one of the two wires leading from the *Electrical Cord* and inside the housing.
3. Carefully use canned air to clean internal components of dust, hair, and other debris. Be careful not to damage the sensitive element wires in the heating unit.

**Caution**

For safety, remember to let a hair dryer cool down before storing it.

# Drywall

Chances are drywall is all around you. It's the material that covers the walls in most homes built in the last 40 years. It replaced lathe-and-plaster wall material because drywall is easier—and faster—to install. It's also relatively easy to repair. You can do this!

## How Does It Work?

Drywall is a manufactured panel made out of gypsum plaster and encased in heavy paper. Drywall is also known as gypsum wallboard (GWB), plaster board, or Sheetrock. A drywall panel typically is 4 × 8 feet or 4 × 12 feet in size and ¼ to ⅝ inches thick. The panels are nailed or screwed onto the wall framing and the joints are covered with a special tape and joint compound. The wall or ceiling is then primed and painted. Sometimes texturing is added as a decorative element.

## What Can Go Wrong?

Drywall problems are relatively easy to spot. Nails sometimes pop out slightly from the drywall. Corners where walls meet get bumped and scraped and can be damaged. Tape can split. Dents, gouges, and holes appear. All are relatively easy to fix.

**Fix-It Tip**

You can buy handy drywall patching kits at larger hardware stores and home centers. Use them to patch holes in drywall walls and ceilings; the instructions are included. Note that a wall kit doesn't work on a ceiling because the ceiling requires a stiffer mesh to support the plaster patch material.

## How Can I Identify the Problem?

If a nail shows, you can hide it (see below).

If a piece of drywall tape splits, you can repair it with joint compound (see below).

If a dent, gouge, or hole appears, you can fill or patch it (see below).

If a corner has been damaged, you can restore its appearance (see below).

**Fix-It Tip**

Drywall patch and joint compound serve two different purposes. Drywall patch is used to fill a hole, so it is thick. Joint compound is used to fill a small crack, therefore it's thinner than drywall patch so it can seep in.

## What Parts, Materials, and Tools Do I Need?

You can pick up the tools and materials needed to fix drywall at most hardware stores and home centers. Depending on the job, these are the tools you'll need:

- Screwdrivers
- Hammer
- Drywall screws or ring-shank nails
- Drywall patch kit
- Keyhole saw
- Utility knife
- Files
- Drywall tape
- Drywall taping knife
- Sponge
- Primer and paint

## What Are the Steps to Fixing It?

Hide a popped nail:

1. Use a hammer or screwdriver to drive a ring-shank nail, or a screwdriver to fasten a drywall screw, about 2 inches above and below the popped nail. Make sure the heads are below the surface of the drywall without breaking the paper. This is called dimpling.
2. Carefully dimple the popped nail.
3. Cover dimples with plaster patch and allow them to dry as recommended by the manufacturer. Apply a second coat, if needed, and allow it to dry.
4. Sand the area with fine-grit sandpaper, then wipe the surface clean.
5. Prime and *Paint* the area, blending in with the paint on the rest of the wall.

Restore a wall corner:

1. Use a hammer and drywall screws to reform and tightly fasten a damaged metal corner bead. If necessary, use a metal file to smooth the corner.
2. Apply plaster patch to the corner as needed to fill in and smooth the corner edges.
3. Remove excess patch and let the repair dry thoroughly before continuing.
4. Sand the area with fine-grit sandpaper, then wipe the surface clean.
5. Prime and *Paint* the area, feathering it into the paint on the rest of the wall.

Repair split drywall tape:

1. Cleanly cut the edges of the split tape and pull away loose tape.
2. Use a drywall taping knife to spread joint compound over the seam.

Spread joint compound over the seam.

3. Cut and apply new drywall tape (don't use masking or duct tape).

Place the tape along the joint.

4. Spread additional compound over the tape and allow it to dry. If necessary, add a second layer of compound.

Spread joint compound over the tape.

5. Sand, prime, and *Paint* the area.

Repair a dent or gouge in drywall:

1. Trim away loose or frayed paper from the gouge with a utility knife.
2. Roughen the inside edges of the gouge with sandpaper so the plaster patch will adhere. Clean away any plaster dust.
3. Carefully dampen the damaged area with a wet sponge to prevent the plaster patch from shrinking.
4. Spread plaster patch in the dent or gouge and smooth with a drywall knife. If the patch shrinks after drying, repeat the process.
5. Sand, prime, and *Paint* the area.

Repair a small hole in drywall:

1. Remove loose drywall plaster and cut away torn paper with a utility knife.
2. Roughen the edges of the hole with coarse sandpaper, then wipe dust away from the hole.
3. Cut a piece of wire screening slightly larger than the hole—or use a drywall patch screen—and cover the hole with it. You may need a coat of fresh compound or a string to keep the screen in place.

4. Cover the screen with plaster patch, then let it dry before continuing.
5. Once dry, sand, prime, and *Paint*.

Patch a larger drywall hole:

1. Mark out a rectangle around the hole with a straightedge or carpenter's rule.
2. Cut through the paper surface on the marked lines using a utility knife or key-hole saw.
3. Cut a piece of drywall 2 inches each direction larger than the hole. Remove the 2-inch perimeter, but leave the facing paper.
4. Spread plaster patch around the outside edges of the hole and along its inside edges.
5. Place the patch in position and hold it in place for several minutes while it begins to adhere. Spread more patch as needed with a drywall knife.
6. Once dry, sand, prime, and *Paint*.

Repairing holes larger than about 8 inches square requires support from behind. Cut out the drywall to the centers of the adjoining studs, nail 2 × 2 inch supports to the top and bottom, nail or screw in the patch, tape it, and smooth it. Sand, prime, and *Paint*.

**Fix-It Tip**

Filling a drywall hole may require two coats of patching material. For best results, apply the first coat and let it dry before finishing with a second coat. Always follow instructions on the patch container.

# DVD Player

Over the past few years, DVD players have dropped in price by 90 percent or more. Once costing over $1,000, you can now buy one for about $100. Or you can buy a combination DVD/CD player for less than the two units separately. And you can get a DVD player installed in the latest computers. But what do you do if your DVD player needs fixing? Let's take a look inside.

## How Does It Work?

A DVD player is an electronic **d**igital **v**ideo **d**evice. A small motor rotates a flat plastic disc that has been stamped with a digital code representing video and audio data. The data is sent to and translated by a television. A DVD player operates similarly to a *CD Player*.

## What Can Go Wrong?

Like CD players, DVD players are relatively trouble-free. You can clean the machine, replace cords, and replace faulty motors, belts, and trays. More often, problems with DVD players are caused by faulty DVD discs, either damaged or dirty.

**Fix-It Tip**

A good investment is a CD/DVD repair kit for polishing out surface scratches, available at larger stores where CDs and DVDs are sold.

## How Can I Identify the Problem?

What's the problem? If the player does not work at all, make sure the power supply is on at the outlet. Check the *Electrical Cord* and replace if necessary, remove the housing and test the *Fuse*, and test the on-off switch (see *Appliance Controls*) and replace if needed.

If the player works but produces no picture or sound, check the connections to the television. If it still doesn't work, check and clean the objective lens.

If the player skips, make sure that the DVD disc is not dirty or scratched.

If the tray won't open or close properly, check the belt for dirt or wear. Then check the tray for misalignment. If needed, remove, clean, lubricate, and reinstall the tray following the instructions in the owner's manual.

**Fix-It Tip**

Before attempting any repairs to your DVD player, refer to the troubleshooting section of the unit's owner's manual. If the unit is under warranty, the manual will tell you whom to contact.

## What Parts, Materials, and Tools Do I Need?

You can find replacement parts through the DVD manufacturer or through an aftermarket supplier such as an electronics store. Check the owner's manual or the *Fix-It Resources* section of this book. Tools and materials you may need include these:

- Screwdrivers
- Canned air or soft brush
- Foam swab or camera-lens tissue
- White lithium grease
- Lens cleaner fluid
- Clean cloth
- DVD/CD cleaning fluid or denatured alcohol
- Multimeter

## What Are the Steps to Fixing It?

Clean a DVD disc:

1. Hold the disc by its central hub and outside edge.
2. Blow dust from the bottom surface with a can of compressed air.
3. Clean dirt and fingerprints from the bottom surface with a lint-free cloth dampened with CD/DVD-cleaning fluid or denatured alcohol, wiping from the center outward.

Service a DVD player disc tray:

1. Open the housing by removing mounting screws and anything blocking the tray. Press the open/close control to the extend tray, then unplug the unit. To remove a clip-on tray front, brace the tray and slide the panel to one side.

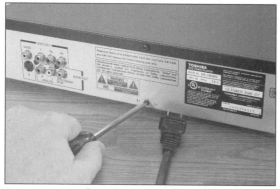

Remove screws from the rear of the case to remove the top and access internal components.

2. Unplug cables between the front panel and the interior. Remove any screws securing the front panel and remove the panel. If it won't move, check beneath it for clips or additional screws.
3. Remove the hold-down on top of the disc tray and gently pull the tray out of the player. Clean the travel rail and guides with a swab dampened with denatured alcohol. Lubricate lightly with white lithium grease.

4. Remove the drive belt (using gloves or tweezers) to inspect for dirt, water, or damage. Clean with a lint-free cloth moistened with denatured alcohol. If the belt is damaged, replace it.

DVD tray

Once inside a DVD player, you'll see that it's mostly made up of circuit boards. Not much to work on—except testing a fuse and maybe replacing the tray motor.

Service a DVD tray motor:

1. Unplug the player and test the *Motor* with a multimeter (see *Fix Everything: Multimeter*).
2. Unplug the motor plug and spray it with electrical contact cleaner, then plug it back in.
3. To remove the motor, unscrew or depress the end of each bale and lift out the motor. Replace the motor if necessary.

Clean the objective lens:

1. Remove the housing and lift the hold-down clamp to expose the lens.
2. Remove dust with canned air or soft brush. If needed, use a foam swab or a camera-lens tissue dampened with lens fluid.

# Electric Can Opener

Electric can openers aren't a necessity of life; they are a convenience. You *could* dig into the back of the collect-all drawer and find the manual can opener if necessary. However, it's typically easy to fix an electric can opener that's gone awry, so let's see how it's done.

## How Does It Work?

An electric can opener is a motorized small appliance. Electric can openers come in countertop, under-cabinet, and cordless models. On most models, clamping the cutting blade to the edge of the can also activates the motor and the feed gear that turns the can. Once the lid is cut all around, on some models, a switch automatically shuts off the motor.

## What Can Go Wrong?

As with other small appliances, most problems are either electrical or mechanical. Electric cords and switches can become inoperable. Motors can be defective. Motors, wheels, or grinding wheels can become jammed. The cutting wheel can become worn. The feed gear can become worn or dirty. The feed gear may be damaged or filled with debris (labels, food, metallic bits.)

**Fix-It Tip**

Regular maintenance can dramatically increase the functional life of an electric can opener. Occasionally detach the cutter and its shaft and clean in hot, sudsy water using a clean rag or brush to make sure you don't get cut by the blade.

## How Can I Identify the Problem?

If the can opener won't run at all, make sure the power is on to the outlet and that the *Electrical Cord* is not faulty.

If the motor stops after extended use, or if it won't start again after it has started, the motor's internal overload protector may be tripped. Wait 10 minutes for the motor to cool, then try using it again.

If the cutting wheel rotates but does not cut properly, replace it.

If the feed gear rotates but doesn't turn the can, clean residue from the gear teeth with a knife or stiff brush. Replace the feed gear if necessary.

If the *Motor* runs but the feed gear does not turn, disassemble the unit and check for worn gears inside. If either gear is defective, replace both.

**Fix-It Tip**

Larger cans may cause an electric can opener to slow down or to stall. Rather than burn out the electric can opener's motor, use a mechanical can opener.

## What Parts, Materials, and Tools Do I Need?

Replacement parts are relatively standard between various models and manufacturers of electric can openers. If you need replacement parts, try the manufacturer, aftermarket appliance parts suppliers (see *Fix-It Resources*), and larger hardware stores in your area or online. Here are the tools you may need:

- Screwdrivers
- Wrenches
- Pliers
- Sandpaper
- Electric contact cleaner
- White lubricant
- Multimeter

## What Are the Steps to Fixing It?

Disassemble an electric can opener:

1. Unplug the power cord. Lift or slide off the cutter assembly depending on the model.

Cutter assembly

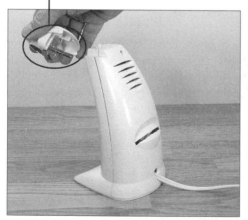

Remove the cutter assembly if detachable.

2. Unscrew the housing screws and remove the housing from the back plate.

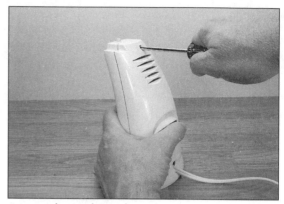

Remove the appliance housing.

3. Use a screwdriver or socket wrench to remove the motor screws, then carefully lift the motor out of the housing.

Gears    Motor

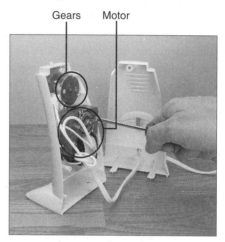

Unscrew the motor from the mounting.

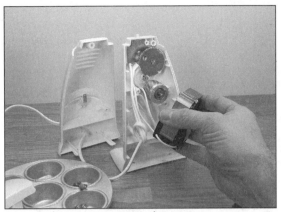

Remove the motor to access the gears.

4. Unscrew or unclip internal gears (see *Motor*) and replace as needed.

Service the on-off switch:

1. Unplug the power cord and remove the housing.
2. Unscrew the switch cover, if any. Clean the switch contacts with an emery board or fine sandpaper, then remove sanding residue with electrical contact cleaner.
3. As needed, use pliers to bend the switch contacts to ensure firm contact between leaves only when the switch is pressed.

Service the gears:

1. Unplug the power cord. Inspect the feed gear and clean or replace as needed.
2. Check internal gears (see *Motor*) by opening the appliance case and carefully removing the gears. Teeth may be missing, they may be warped, or they may require lubrication with white lithium grease.
3. If the gears need to be replaced, make sure that they match in every measure, including circumference, width, and number of teeth.

**Caution** Never immerse the can opener in water, because you will damage the electrical components.

# Electric Iron

Electric irons are simple small appliances that require only routine maintenance to keep them ironing for years. And if they do need fixing, they are relatively easy to troubleshoot and repair.

## How Does It Work?

Whether it's a basic no-frills iron, a cordless model, a compact travel iron, or an electronic iron loaded with features, all steam irons work in the same way. They press out wrinkles in fabric using moisture, pressure, and heat. When the steam valve is closed, the iron operates dry. When the steam valve is open, water drips into a heated steam chamber, where it exits as steam through vents in the soleplate. The iron's working surface, the soleplate, may be plain metal or coated with an easy-to-clean nonstick material.

## What Can Go Wrong?

Fortunately, there is very little inside a well-made iron that can go wrong. Most repairs are for faulty cords, damaged handles, and mineral deposits that hamper steam irons. Problems with an iron's electronic complements should be dealt with by an authorized service center. It typically is more cost effective to replace rather than repair an iron with internal problems. Check the owner's manual for your iron to learn the manufacturer's suggestions for cleaning, what water to use, and storage tips.

**Fix-It Tip**

Soft-water systems add minerals that can harm an electric steam iron and your clothes, so don't fill the iron with softened water. Instead, use filtered or distilled water.

## How Can I Identify the Problem?

As with many small appliances, regular maintenance makes a dramatic difference in how trouble-free your electric iron will be. Even so, things can happen.

If the iron doesn't heat, make sure power is on to the outlet, check the *Electrical Cord*, and check the thermostat (see *Appliance Controls*) and replace if necessary.

If the iron heats but steams improperly, inspect the soleplate and clean the vents (see below) and flush sediment out of the steam chamber (see below).

If the iron produces too much or too little heat, test the *Electrical Cord*. Also test and, if needed, adjust calibration of the thermostat (see *Appliance Controls*).

If the iron does not spray properly, inspect and clean the nozzle (see below).

If the iron leaks or spits, clean the steam vents, nozzle, and tank.

If the iron sticks to fabric, clean or repair the soleplate. If the iron stains fabric, clean the soleplate, clean the tank with a commercial cleaner, and use distilled or filtered water.

**Caution**

Iron carefully around buttons, zippers, and other attachments or decorations that can scratch the soleplate.

## What Parts, Materials, and Tools Do I Need?

Larger hardware stores may have replacement parts for popular-brand electric irons. Also, you can get them from the manufacturer or an aftermarket supplier (see *Fix-It Resources*). Maintenance and repair tools you'll need to fix an electric iron include these:

- Screwdrivers
- Toothpicks or pipe cleaners
- Sewing needle
- Commercial electric iron cleaning solution or vinegar and water
- Commercial soleplate cleaner or baking soda and water
- Oven thermostat
- Steel wool
- Emery cloth
- Metal cooking pot

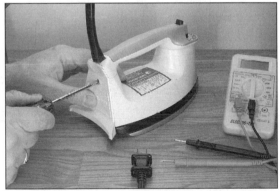

Access the internal parts of an electric iron by removing the rear cover panel. Some irons have unique fasteners to keep you from opening them. Check with your local hardware store for an appropriate screwdriver.

## What Are the Steps to Fixing It?

Clean an iron:

1. Unplug the iron and make sure it is cool before cleaning.

2. Use a toothpick or pipe cleaner to remove buildup in the steam vents, making sure the debris doesn't fall into the vents.
3. Use a fine sewing needle to carefully clean the spray nozzle of mineral deposits.
4. To flush sediment from a steam iron, pour ½ cup water and ½ cup vinegar into the water tank. Place the iron on a rack over a broiling pan and set the iron to steam until the tank runs dry. Repeat if necessary, or follow the instructions for using a commercial iron cleaner.

Service the steam and spray mechanism:

1. Unplug the iron.
2. Use a fine sewing needle to unclog the steam valve assembly. Also, check the valve spring and replace it if it is broken or has lost tension.
3. If the spray pump is accessible, remove it and check for leaks by placing the spray tube in water and squirting the pump. Clean or replace as needed.

Clean a metal soleplate:

1. Unplug the iron.
2. Use a sponge and commercial soleplate cleaner or baking soda and water to remove dirt buildup on the soleplate. Rinse well with water and dry. Don't use harsh abrasives or immerse an electric iron in water.
3. Use very fine steel wool (0000) or an emery cloth to remove scratches and burns on the soleplate, then clean the soleplate.

**Fix-It Tip**

Unless the instructions with your iron say it's okay, don't let water stand in your steam iron between uses. Drain all water from the iron, wrap the cord loosely around the handle, and store the iron in an upright position.

# Electric Knife

An electric knife can dramatically "cut" food preparation time—*if* it's working properly. And one that *isn't* working properly can cause injury. So let's call a quick meeting of the Fix-It Club and make sure your electric knife makes the cut.

## How Does It Work?

An electric knife is a hand-held, motor-driven appliance for cutting food. It's simple in operation: A gear assembly converts a motor's rotary motion into a reciprocating (back-and-forth) action. The driver arm moves a pair of serrated blades, pushing one forward as it pulls the other one back.

## What Can Go Wrong?

Most electric knife problems are the result of dull or unclean blades. The blades can be misaligned or the rivet that holds the two blades together can be worn. In addition, the electric cord can be faulty, internal wiring can be damaged, switches can be dirty or faulty, and bearings can be dry.

**Fix-It Tip**

Let the knife's motor do the work. Don't force the knife blade down hard while cutting or you could wear out the motor.

## How Can I Identify the Problem?

If the knife won't work at all, make sure power is on at the outlet; check the *Electrical Cord*. If possible, check for loose wires and reconnect them. Test the switch (see *Appliance Controls*). Clean the switch by spraying with electrical contact cleaner. Lubricate the *Motor* with one or two drops of light machine oil on each motor bearing.

If the knife slices poorly, check the blade alignment.

If a blade is bent, carefully press it against a flat surface. If that doesn't work, replace both blades.

If the electric knife is noisy, the drive gears may need to be replaced (see *Motor*).

**Fix-It Tip**

The owner's manual that came with the electric knife when new probably will have additional troubleshooting suggestions as well as parts information and resources.

## What Parts, Materials, and Tools Do I Need?

Replacement parts are available from the manufacturer or aftermarket parts suppliers (see *Fix-It Resources*). Tools and materials you may need include:

- Screwdrivers
- Light machine oil
- Light silicon or other grease

## What Are the Steps to Fixing It?

Service the driver assembly:

1. Unplug the electric knife and carefully remove the blades.
2. Remove the screws at the back of the housing and pull the housing apart. Be careful: The blade retainers will be loose and fall out as you open the housing.

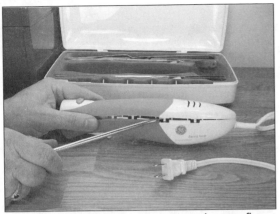

Once the retaining screws are removed, use a flat screwdriver or a putty knife to gently pry the housing apart.

3. Remove all screws holding the driver assembly and motor to the housing. Lift the motor and driver assembly from the housing.

Motor

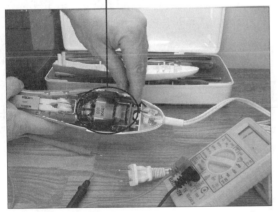

As needed, test the *Motor* in place or remove it for testing and replacement.

4. Inspect mechanical parts for wear. If the fan doesn't turn smoothly by hand, clean and lubricate the driver assembly with lightweight grease. Add a drop of light machine oil to each bearing before re-assembling parts.

**Fix-It Tip**

If you decide you can't fix that electric knife, but the problem isn't the *Motor*, save the motor in your Fix-It Toolbox because you may be able to use it for another repair.

# Electric Pencil Sharpener

The electric pencil sharpener is still a popular gadget. Inexpensive and handy, it's found in homes where kids do homework and parents struggle with Form 1040. Quite often, however, it's in the pile of things ready for the Fix-It Club.

## How Does It Work?

An electric pencil sharpener is a small motorized appliance for sharpening or refreshing the points on lead pencils. Inside the hole, a small electric motor turns a blade assembly at high speed. The blades shave wood and lead from the pencil's end, bringing it to a point. Most electric pencil sharpeners are powered through a 120V electrical cord, though some are battery operated.

## What Can Go Wrong?

The most common problem with electric pencil sharpeners is clogs from wood and lead shavings. In addition, the *Electrical Cord* can fail, the blade can become dull, and the motor can malfunction. Preventive maintenance (cleaning and lubricating) can dramatically extend the life of an electric pencil sharpener.

**Fix-It Tip**

Enclosed pencil sharpeners have a shavings tray where wood and lead shavings collect. Be sure to empty the tray often.

## How Can I Identify the Problem?

If the unit does not operate when a pencil is inserted into the hole, make sure power is on at the outlet, then test the *Electrical Cord* and replace if faulty.

If the unit still does not operate, the problem could be in the motor. Test the *Motor* and replace it or the device.

If the unit operates but does not cut a sharp point or seems very sluggish, the shavings tray may be overfilled and the unit plugged up in other areas. Disassemble the unit (see below) and use canned air to clean it out.

If the unit still operates sluggishly or does not sharpen well, the blade may be dull. You can try disassembling it and using a small file to sharpen the blades—or you can replace the unit.

**Fix-It Tip**

At least once a year, unplug, disassemble, and lubricate the electric pencil sharpener's *Motor* or shaft—unless it has sealed bearings. Check the owner's manual.

## What Parts, Materials, and Tools Do I Need?

It's difficult to find replacement parts for electric pencil sharpeners, because the devices themselves are so inexpensive. However, once you've disassembled the device you can clean out debris and even test the motor. Here's what you'll need.

- Screwdrivers
- Needle-nose pliers
- Canned air
- Multimeter

## What Are the Steps to Fixing It?

Disassemble an electric pencil sharpener:

1. Unplug the device from the *Electrical Receptacle*.
2. Remove the shavings tray and empty it.
3. If screws on the bottom attach the top and bottom covers, remove them with a screwdriver. If clips hold the covers together, use needle-nose pliers to unclip them.

Remove fasteners to access the inside of the electric pencil sharpener.

4. Remove the covers and use canned air to blow away any debris from around the motor and blades.

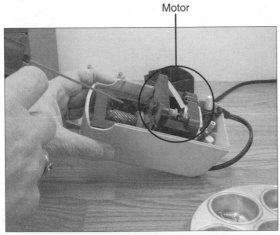

Motor

Use canned compressed air to remove debris. Wear safety goggles to keep debris from getting in your eyes.

**Caution**

Whenever you use canned air to remove debris, make sure your eyes are shielded by safety goggles. If you don't have them, aim the air nozzle, close your eyes, then spray, opening your eyes again after 5 to 10 seconds when the debris settles. It's not optimum, but it works.

5. As needed, use a multimeter (see *Fix Everything: Multimeter*) to test the *Electrical Cord* and *Motor*.
6. Reassemble components, covers, and tray.

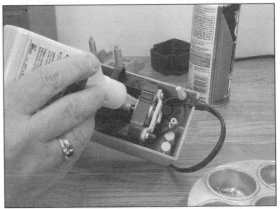

Sparingly apply lightweight lubricant to the motor shaft (not the electrical components).

# Electric Shaver

Electric shavers are increasingly popular with both men and women—especially shavers that can be used in the shower. But, like everything else, electric shavers can break down. Here's how to fix them *before* you get nicked.

## How Does It Work?

An electric shaver is a motorized small appliance for cutting body hair. A motor inside the shaver moves miniature blades. A fine screen holds the hairs that protrude through the screen so that the cutting blades can slice through them. The shaver is powered by either household current through an electric cord or internal rechargeable batteries.

The two most popular types of electric shavers are foil-head and rotary-head. A foil-head shaver moves rows of blades back and forth using an oscillator. A rotary-head shaver's motor rotates three blades in unison, each with its own gear, blade, and screen.

## What Can Go Wrong?

Many repairs to an electric shaver can be avoided by cleaning the appliance after every use and following the manufacturer's maintenance guide. In addition, the *Electrical Cord* may need replacing, the recharger may need service, or the motor may be faulty. The head can become clogged and the cutting edges can be damaged. Fortunately, you can make many repairs yourself.

**Fix-It Tip**

The best way to avoid problems with your electric shaver is to regularly inspect and maintain it. Review the owner's manual for specific requirements of your model.

## How Can I Identify the Problem?

Most electric shaver problems are easily identified and resolved. If the shaver doesn't work at all, make sure power is on at the outlet, check the battery and recharge it if it is low (see *Battery, Household* and *Battery Recharger*), and check the *Electrical Cord*. If necessary, test the *Motor* and switches (see *Appliance Controls*).

If the shaver operates sluggishly, clean and lubricate the heads. For rechargeable units, check the battery and recharge if needed (see *Battery, Household* and *Battery Recharger*). If the shaver is noisy or cuts poorly, clean and lubricate the shaver. Also check the *Motor*. On foil-head shavers, check the oscillator.

If the shaver pinches skin, check the screen for corrosion or damage and service the head.

**Fix-It Tip**

You can find replacement-part kits for popular brands and models of shavers at large retail chains. The kits include new screens, blades, and other replaceable components. Shaver cleaning kits include special brushes and lubricants.

## What Parts, Materials, and Tools Do I Need?

Replacement parts for electric shavers are available through retail stores or online, from the manufacturer or from aftermarket suppliers. Basic repair tools include:

- Screwdrivers
- Shaver lubricant
- Small brush

## What Are the Steps to Fixing It?

Service a foil-head shaver:

1. Unplug the appliance. Remove the head assembly held on by screws, clips, or a pressure button.
2. Remove the screen from the head and carefully clean it. If the screen is damaged or corroded, replace it.
3. Remove the blade assembly from the oscillator assembly. Inspect and clean the blade assembly with canned air.
4. If your foil-head shaver requires lubrication, follow the manufacturer's instructions for doing so.

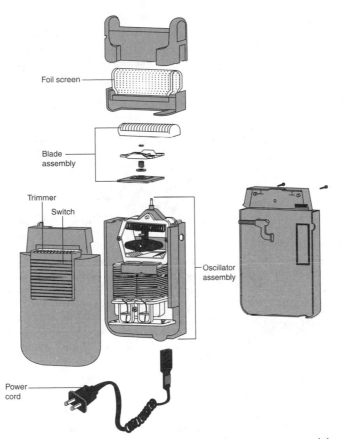

A foil shaver is relatively easy to disassemble and service. Your model may vary from this illustration, but the components are the same.

Service a rotary-head shaver:

1. Unplug the appliance. Remove the head assembly from the housing.
2. Remove the shaver head from the blade assembly and place the assembly on a flat surface.

3. Remove the screens and the blade unit. Clean the screens with a small brush and inspect the blades. If the screen is damaged or corroded, replace it.
4. If your rotary-head shaver requires lubrication, follow the manufacturer's instructions for doing so.

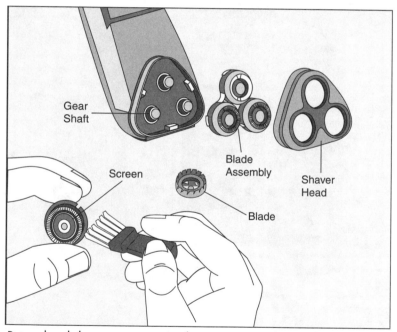

Gear Shaft

Screen

Blade Assembly

Blade

Shaver Head

Rotary-head shavers, too, are simple to maintain with periodic cleaning and lubrication.

# Electric Toothbrush

Electric toothbrushes give kids—and adults—one less excuse not to brush after meals. Unless the toothbrush is broken. Luckily, electric toothbrushes are relatively easy to fix and inexpensive to replace.

## How Does It Work?

An electric toothbrush uses a small DC (direct current) motor to move the toothbrush shaft from side to side or back and forth, depending on the model. Most models are cordless, using a charger to replenish power. Less-expensive models operate on batteries.

## What Can Go Wrong?

Problems usually involve either the brush heads, which are easily replaced if worn or faulty, or the charger. The power handle is typically sealed to prevent shock, so internal repairs should be left to a professional.

Who can repair your sealed electric toothbrush? Because they are small motorized electric appliances, nearly any small appliance repair shop can do it. Make sure you clean the unit well before delivering it to the repair person. Also be sure it's worth the cost of repairs. It might be more cost effective to just buy a new one.

## How Can I Identify the Problem?

If the appliance doesn't work at all, make sure the power is on at the outlet, then test the *Electrical Cord* and charger (see *Battery Recharger*) with a multimeter (see *Fix Everything: Multimeter*), and replace the cord or charger if needed.

If the unit still doesn't work, clean the charger post. If the charger shocks the user, have it professionally serviced or replace it.

> **Fix-It Tip**
>
> Even a poorly running electric toothbrush is good for something. You can recycle it for use as a grout scrubber, or use it to clean hard-to-reach areas around sinks.

## What Parts, Materials, and Tools Do I Need?

Replacement parts for electric toothbrushes—including new brush heads—are available from the manufacturer and aftermarket suppliers (see *Fix-It Resources*), and are typically sold through drug and discount stores. If you do need to work on an electric toothbrush, about the only tools you'll need are a screwdriver and maybe a multimeter.

## What Are the Steps to Fixing It?

Clean a charger post:

1. Unplug the charger from the outlet.
2. Use a fine emery cloth to clean the charger post.
3. Spray the charger post with electrical contact cleaner, then wipe excess cleaner away.

Clean a brush head:

1. Remove the brush head from the toothbrush driver.
2. Run the brush head under warm water for a minute to loosen debris and sanitize the head.
3. Reinstall the brush head.

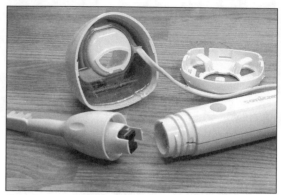

Components inside an electric toothbrush charger typically are sealed from entry, so if it goes bad you must replace the entire unit.

**Fix-It Tip**

Depending on use, replace the brush head every three to six months unless directed otherwise by the manufacturer.

# Electrical Cord

One of the most common things in your home—and one of the most common to need fixing—is the electrical cord. That list includes cords on large and small appliances, electric tools, electric clocks, computers and printers, anything that gets its power through an electrical outlet in the wall. That means knowing how to fix electrical cords is important to knowing how to fix a lot of things in your home.

## How Does It Work?

A cord is a small, flexible, insulated electrical cable with a plug at one or both ends that connects an electrical device with a source of electricity. There is a wide variety of cords, each with wires and plugs designed to carry a specific electrical load.

## What Can Go Wrong?

Cords and plugs can break. Through repeated use, they can develop shorts and stop delivering electricity to the item that needs power. Fortunately, they are relatively easy to test and repair or replace.

### Cord Wires

Most small appliances use two-wire 14- or 16-gauge cords with two-prong plugs. Heating appliances (iron, toaster, space heater) use heavy insulated wires. Grounded appliances use three-wire 12- or 14-gauge cord with three-prong plugs. Large appliances (range, air conditioner, clothes dryer) use three-wire 6- or 8-gauge cord with special three-prong plugs. As you can see, the *lower* the wire gauge number, the *greater* the electrical current it can carry.

## How Can I Identify the Problem?

Frequently, problems with appliances, tools, and other electrical devices can be traced to the cord or plug. Test it for continuity (see below) and replace if faulty (see below) before completely disassembling and testing the device itself.

If the plug of an electrical device shows obvious damage, you can replace it without replacing the entire cord (see below)—just be sure that replacement cords and plugs are of the same type and rating.

Because the function of an electrical cord is to deliver electricity to the device, you'll be testing it for this trait, called *continuity*.

### Plugs

Lamps and smaller appliances use flat-cord plugs. Plugs on electrical devices typically are manufactured with and sealed to the cord. Quick-connect replacement plugs are easy to install but won't stand up to repeated plugging and unplugging because they are not sealed to the cord. Medium and larger appliances and devices typically use round-cord plugs, often with a third prong for grounding the circuit. Some heating appliances use detachable cords. If you replace a detachable cord, make sure the new cord is of the same power rating and prong configuration.

## What Parts, Materials, and Tools Do I Need?

You can buy replacement cords, cord wire, and various prongs at larger hardware stores. The tools you need to test and replace electrical cords include these:

- Multimeter or continuity tester
- Screwdrivers
- Wire stripper
- Wire connectors

## What Are the Steps to Fixing It?

Test an attached 120-volt power cord:

1. Unplug the appliance or device.
2. Disassemble the device to access the cord terminals. Unclip, unscrew, or desolder the cord's connectors from the device. If there is a loop or strain-relief fitting, remove it.
3. Set your multimeter (see *Fix Everything: Multimeter*) ohmmeter on R×1 (resistance times 1) scale. Or you can use a continuity tester (see *Fix Everything: Continuity Tester*).

Using a continuity tester to check an attached power cord. Make sure the appliance's switch is on.

Using a continuity tester to check a power cord that's removed from the appliance.

4. Clip a jumper wire across the cord leads (or twist the two wires together). Clip or touch the meter's probes to the plug prongs. The meter should read zero ohms.
5. Bend and pull on the entire cord. A steady zero-ohms reading means the cord is okay. A high or fluctuating reading means the cord is faulty and should be replaced with an exact duplicate.

Test a removable cord for continuity:

1. Unplug the appliance.
2. Set the multimeter (see *Fix Everything: Multimeter*) on the R×1 (resistance times 1) scale. Or you can use a continuity tester (see *Fix Everything: Continuity Tester*).

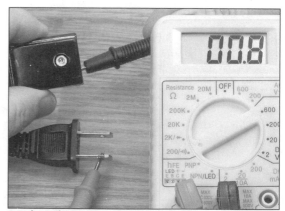

Touch probes to the plug prong and one of the female plug ends to determine if there is continuity.

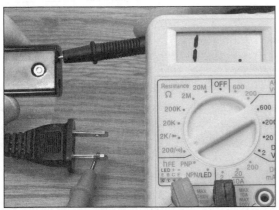

An infinite reading on the multimeter indicates that there is a break in the cord—or that you're not testing both ends of the same cord wire.

3. Clip a jumper wire across the male plug and insert the test probes into the female plug.

4. Bend and pull the cord along its entire length. If the meter reads zero ohms (no resistance to the flow of electricity), the cord is good. A high or fluctuating reading means there is an open circuit. Replace the cord and/or the plug.

Test a 240-volt power cord:

1. Unplug the appliance.

2. Unscrew and remove the terminal block cover plate, found where the cord enters the electrical device. If there are any signs of damage, replace the block. If the block is okay, test the power cord.

3. Set your multimeter (see *Fix Everything: Multimeter*) on the R×1 (resistance times 1) scale.

4. Clip the meter probes to the plug's outer prongs.

5. Clip the jumper wire across the outer cord terminals.

6. Bend and pull the cord. Replace the cord if the multimeter reads above zero ohms or fluctuates.

7. Clip the jumper across the middle and one outer terminal, then clip the multimeter to the corresponding plug prongs. Look for steady zero-ohms readings. If readings fluctuate, replace the cord and/or plug.

Replace a power cord:

1. Unplug the appliance.

2. Remove the old cord.

3. Remove insulation from the new cord if necessary (see below).

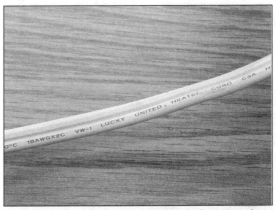

Some power cords are imprinted with their specifications. This one says "18AWGX2C" meaning there are two 18-gauge wires.

4. Connect the new cord leads to the appliance leads or terminals.

Strip a cord or other electrical wire:

1. Insert ¼ inch of the tip of wire into the corresponding hole in the jaws of an electrical wire stripper tool.

2. Close the tool to cut and remove insulation from the end of the wire.

3. Verify that the insulation is cleanly cut and removed from the wire. If not, repeat the process using a larger or smaller gauge hole in the stripper tool.

Replace a flat-cord plug:

1. Unplug the electrical appliance or device.
2. Use a wire stripper or wire cutting tool to remove the old plug from the cord.
3. Unscrew or otherwise open the new plug to expose the contacts or terminal screws within the plug.
4. Feed the cord's wires into the new plug, and tie a knot in the wires to ensure that pulling on the cord in use will not pull the wires from the plug terminals.
5. Remove (strip) insulation from the cord's ends and attach them to the plug's terminals, following the replacement plug manufacturer's instructions.
6. Reassemble the plug and test for continuity before use (see *Fix Everything: Multimeter* or *Fix Everything: Continuity Tester*).

Replace a quick-connect plug:

1. Unplug the electrical appliance or device.
2. Cut the old plug from the cord. Do not separate or strip wire ends.
3. Pinch the prongs of the new plug and pull out the plug core.
4. Feed the cord through the rear of the shell. Spread the prongs apart and insert the cord into the plug core.
5. Squeeze the prongs together to pierce the cord's wires. Then slide the plug's core back into its shell.

Easy grip plug          Trim fit plug          Flat handle plug

You can purchase various replacement plugs at hardware stores and electrical suppliers.

# Electrical Receptacle

They are all around us. Also known as outlets and wall plugs, electrical receptacles are convenient resources for tapping into the power of electricity. They are relatively simple in operation, so there is little to go wrong. However, when you've tested and replaced everything else except the electrical receptacle, it's time to give it a quick check. Luckily, it's a relatively easy task.

## How Does It Work?

An electrical receptacle or outlet is a socket into which the wiring for portable lamps, appliances, and other electrical devices can be plugged. It provides the connection between the building's electrical circuit and the corded appliance or other device that requires electricity to operate. Receptacles in older homes have two holes, hot and neutral, while newer homes add a third hole for a grounding connection for safety.

## What Can Go Wrong?

Receptacles crack and develop shorts. They may not hold plugs in place securely. They can be the wrong color or paint-splattered after you paint. Receptacles are inexpensive and easy to test and replace.

It's a good idea to invest in an electrical receptacle analyzer. Why? Because it's cheaper than repairing the damage caused by a bad receptacle. For example, before plugging your expensive stereo or other device into an outlet in your new home, test it to make sure that it is properly wired and grounded. A combination of glowing lights will tell you what is happening with your receptacle.

## How Can I Identify the Problem?

If something you plug into a receptacle doesn't work, first test that item in another receptacle. Make sure the power is on if the receptacle is controlled by a switch.

If the receptacle still seems at fault, test it (see below) and replace it if faulty (see below).

**Fix-It Tip**

If you have an older home, invest in a circuit tracer. You can plug it into any electrical receptacle in your home and, with a companion tester, identify which circuit breaker or fuse in your electrical service box controls it. Then mark the box as appropriate. In an emergency you can quickly turn off a problem circuit without shutting down the whole system.

## What Parts, Materials, and Tools Do I Need?

You'll be surprised at how easy most electrical receptacles are to replace—and how little they cost. Hardware stores sell basic electrical receptacles for about a dollar each. And you can replace one in just a few minutes. Here are the tools you may need:

- Electrical continuity or circuit tester
- Receptacle analyzer
- Screwdrivers
- Pliers
- Electrical tape
- Wire stripper
- Wire nuts

## What Are the Steps to Fixing It?

Test an electrical receptacle:

1. Turn off power to the circuit and verify that it actually is off before continuing.

2. Insert one probe of a continuity tester (see *Fix Everything: Continuity Tester*) into each slot of the receptacle. If the tester glows, the receptacle is working. Test both plugs of a duplex (two-plug) receptacle.

3. If the receptacle fails the test, remove the cover plate, disconnect the screws holding the receptacle in the box, and pull the receptacle out.

4. Restore power at the electrical service box. Carefully touch one probe of the continuity tester to a brass screw terminal and the other to a silver-colored terminal. The tester light will glow if power is coming to the receptacle.

5. If the receptacle fails the test, check power across the hot and neutral (not the bare ground) wires coming into the wall box. If the tester glows, power is coming to the wires, but not through the receptacle. Replace the receptacle (see below).

Replace an electrical receptacle:

1. Shut off power to the box at the *Electrical Service Panel* and confirm that the circuit is off using a circuit tester.

2. Remove the cover plate and unscrew the mounting screws. Without touching wires or terminals, pull out the receptacle.

3. Hold a new and identical receptacle near the old one to see how the wires should be installed on the replacement. Some use terminal screws on the side while others have slots on the back for inserting bare wires. Many replacement receptacles have both.

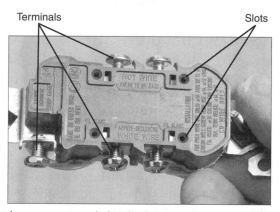

This new receptacle has both terminal screws (sides) and wire slots (back).

4. Unscrew the terminals and carefully pull away the wires. Make sure the wire ends are clean and free from insulation. If needed, use a wire stripper to remove insulation from the last ¼ inch of the wire.

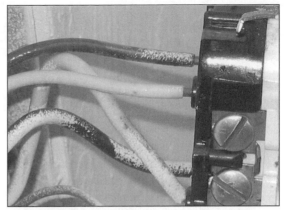

Make sure all wires are correctly installed before inserting the new receptacle into the box.

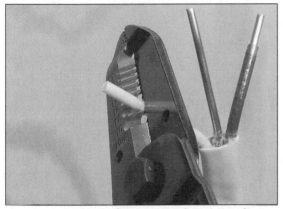

If necessary, strip the last ¼ inch of insulation from the ends of the wires.

5. Attach each wire to the new receptacle in the same way it was attached to the old receptacle. The white wire typically is connected to a silver terminal and the black or color wire is connected to a brass terminal. Use electrical tape as needed to cover all terminals and bare wires.

6. Gently push the outlet into the box. Tighten the mounting screws, and check that the receptacle is straight.

7. Replace the cover plate, restore power, and test with a receptacle analyzer.

# Electrical Service Panel

Power to the people! Fixing electrical things around your home sometimes means going to the source: the electrical power source. That's the electrical service panel where utility wires deliver electricity for distribution to the many circuits in your home. If you've checked the electrical device and the *Electrical Receptacle*, but haven't found the problem yet, maybe it's in the service panel, sometimes known as the main. Let's look.

## How Does It Work?

The electrical service panel is the main panel or cabinet through which electricity is brought into the building and then distributed to various branch circuits. Power from the utility company (or your solar power system!) enters the panel through three large wires—two hot and one neutral. The main neutral wire connects to a neutral bus or common bar, and the two hot mains connect to the main power shutoff, either a large circuit breaker or a pull-out fuse.

Each of the two bars carries 120 volts. All circuit breakers or fuses in the service panel are connected to one or both of these bars. Fuses and breakers rated at 120 volts are attached to a single hot bar; 240-volt breakers or fuses are attached to both hot bars.

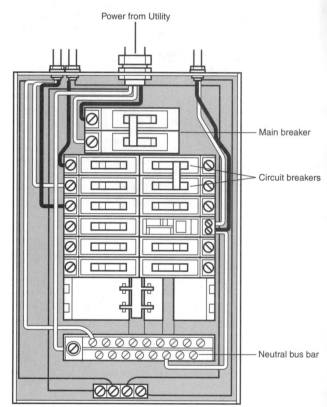

Power from Utility

Main breaker

Circuit breakers

Neutral bus bar

The electrical service panel receives power from the utility company and distributes it to your home through safety circuit breakers.

Each 120-volt circuit has a black or color wire connected to a circuit breaker or fuse; the white wire is connected to the neutral bus bar. Ground wires also lead to a neutral bar. Power runs through each fuse or breaker and then out of the panel via a hot wire to whatever receptacles, lights, or appliances are on the circuit. White neutral wires bring power back to a neutral bus bar in the service panel, completing the loop, also known as an electrical circuit.

## What Can Go Wrong?

Electrical service panels have components inside them that are designed to fail: fuses or circuit breakers. They form the first line of defense for your home, protecting you and your family from electrical fire and shock. An overloaded circuit blows the circuit breaker or fuse—the weakest link—in the circuit. It's fixable or replaceable.

 **Caution** *Never touch the bus bar inside an electrical service panel unless the main breaker has been turned off or the main fuse removed.*

## How Can I Identify the Problem?

Electrical service panels are not locked boxes. You can open them, look at them, and replace a fuse or restart a circuit breaker without hurting anything. Think of it as the electrical *safety* panel.

If an appliance or light won't turn on, try switching on another light or appliance on the same circuit. If that doesn't work either, check the service panel for a tripped circuit breaker (see below) or blown fuse (see below).

If a circuit breaker keeps tripping for no apparent reason, test the circuit breaker and replace it if it is faulty (see below).

**Fix-It Tip** If you're not sure exactly how safe your electrical service panel is, hire an electrician to take a look at it—*before* there's a problem.

## What Parts, Materials, and Tools Do I Need?

You can find replacement fuses, circuit breakers, and even electrical service panels at larger hardware stores and home improvement centers. Besides these, about all you may need are:

- Screwdrivers (for removing the cover, *not* for touching electrical wires!)
- Fuse puller (if the box includes fuses)
- Multimeter

## What Are the Steps to Fixing It?

Reset a tripped circuit breaker:

1. Inspect the ends of each circuit breaker in the service panel, looking for one that has its switch leaning toward the *off* side rather than *on*. Some circuit breakers instead have a red button that can pop out if tripped.
2. Once you find a tripped breaker, check the circuit index on the inside of the panel to determine what circuit the breaker controls and make sure everything inside the home that's on this circuit is *off* or unplugged.
3. Reset the circuit breaker switch or button. If it immediately trips, the problem is probably in the circuit's wiring; you'll need an electrician.

## Mapping Your Household Circuits

When making a repair, knowing which circuit controls which outlet speeds the job and makes working safer. That's why modern electrical codes require service panels to have an index telling which receptacles, lights, and appliances are on which circuit. If your panel has no index, creating one takes a couple of hours and a helper. Here are the steps:

1. Draw a rough floor plan of your house, noting the location of every receptacle, switch, light, and appliance. On the service panel, place a numbered piece of tape next to each breaker or switch.

2. Turn on all the lights in the house. Plug a light, fan, or radio into as many receptacles as possible, and switch them all on. Turn on the dishwasher and open the door of the microwave.

3. To communicate with your helper, use a pair of walkie-talkies or two cellular phones. Start at the top of the panel. Switch off the circuit and have your helper identify the room without power. On the map, jot down the number of the circuit next to each outlet that is turned off. Repeat these steps for each circuit.

4. Write an index that accounts for all the fixtures, receptacles, and hardwired appliances in your home. Attach the index to the inside door of the electrical service panel. Some circuits may wander through several rooms. This can be confusing, but it is not dangerous.

Find the tripped circuit breaker and move it to the *on* position.

4. Replug any appliances or other electrical devices or turn on lights in the problem circuit to see if they trip the circuit breaker again. If so, the problem is in the device. If not, everything is probably okay.

Replace a screw-in fuse:

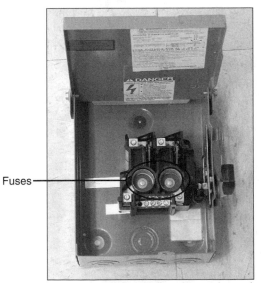

Fuses

Some subpanels (smaller electrical panels for branch circuits) use screw-in fuses. Older homes might, too.

1. Examine the fuse for tell-tale damage. Screw-in fuses typically have a glass that allows you to inspect the metal strip inside; a damaged strip means the fuse is blown and requires replacement. If the metal strip is broken completely, the circuit was overloaded. If the fuse window is blackened, the cause is a short circuit—meaning that somewhere wires are touching each other or a wire is making contact with metal.

2. If you find a fuse that is blown, remove the fuse and replace it with one of the exact amperage (15- 20- or 30-amp).

Replace a cartridge fuse:

1. Turn off the power. Use a fuse puller to remove the cartridge fuse.

2. Test the cartridge fuse by touching both ends with the probes of a multimeter (see *Fix Everything: Multimeter*) set to measure resistance. If the fuse tests for low resistance, called continuity, it is good. If not, it has blown.

3. Replace the fuse with an exact replacement.

Test a circuit breaker:

1. Touch the prongs of a multimeter (see *Fix Everything: Multimeter*) to the breaker's terminal screw and a ground. If there is no power, the breaker is faulty and requires replacement.

2. Shut off the *main* circuit breaker or switch and remove the cover to the electrical service or circuit breaker panel.

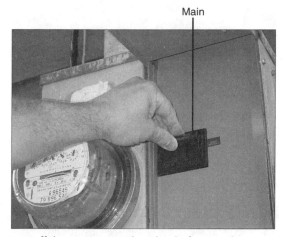

Main

Turn off the *main* circuit breaker before working on the electrical service panel.

3. Loosen the screws holding the damaged breaker and pull it from the panel. Identify and remove the wires connected to the circuit breaker.

4. Replace the circuit breaker with one of the exact amperage (15- 20- or 30-amp), attaching the wires into the new breaker. Mount and fasten the replacement circuit breaker. (Some circuit breakers snap into place in the panel, while others require screw fasteners.)

5. Restore power and test the circuit.

**Caution**

When working around an electrical service panel, wear rubber-soled shoes so that you don't conduct electricity. If the floor by the panel is wet, lay down some boards and lay a rubber mat on top of the boards before continuing. Water is a great conductor of electricity—and your body is mostly water!

# Electrical Switch

We take electrical switches for granted. Flick a wall switch and something is supposed to happen, typically a light or fan goes on. So what do we do if the light or fan *doesn't* come on? We call a meeting of the Fix-It Club!

## How Does It Work?

An electrical switch is a device designed to break the flow of electric current. When turned *on*, a switch completes the electrical circuit and current flows to the light or other device the switch controls. When the switch is *off*, the electrical circuit is not complete, denying power to whatever the switch controls.

The most common household switch is a two-way (sometimes called a single-pole) switch, which is a toggle switch marked *on* and *off*. Other household switches include the three-way switch for controlling a light from two switches, and the dimmer switch for varying the amount of electricity that goes to the light or other apparatus.

## What Can Go Wrong?

Switches, by design, are relatively simple, so typically either they work or they don't. The other option is that they don't work *safely*, meaning the electricity arcs or sparks in the switch—a potential fire hazard.

Most electrical switches wear out from use in 5 to 20 years, depending on quality and frequency of use. Additionally, wires can become loose and not make connection, caused by poor installation or other factors.

> **Fix-It Tip**
>
> If you're buying a new switch that will get lots of use, spend a little more and buy one that is labeled "commercial" or "spec-rated." Internal parts are sturdier and will stand up to use longer—and safer.

## How Can I Identify the Problem?

An electrical switch can have one or more of these common symptoms: The light fixture (or other device) doesn't turn on even with a new bulb, the switch pops when you turn it on, the switch wiggles when you flick it. In each of these cases, replace the switch. Fortunately, switches are inexpensive and you can replace one without having to test it.

> **Fix-It Tip**
>
> Only one electrical switch in a group of three-way switches can be a dimmer switch. The remaining switch must be a standard three-way.

## What Parts, Materials, and Tools Do I Need?

You can find replacement electrical switches at most hardware stores and home improvement centers. Specialized switches may require that you visit an electrical or lighting supply store. In addition, you may need some of these tools:

- Screwdrivers
- Continuity tester or multimeter
- Wire stripper
- Pliers
- Electrician's tape
- Masking tape

## What Are the Steps to Fixing It?

Test an electrical switch:

1. Turn off power to the switch's circuit at the *Electrical Service Panel.* This requires identifying the correct circuit breaker and turning it *off,* or finding the appropriate fuse and unscrewing it from the panel.
2. Remove the cover plate and use a tester to make sure power is off before proceeding.
3. Disconnect the old switch by removing the top and bottom screws holding the switch to the electrical box that is mounted in the wall.

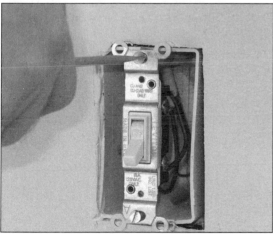

Once the power is off, remove the switch from the electrical box.

4. Pull the switch toward you to expose the wires on the side and rear. If a wire is loose or broken, you've probably found the problem.

5. Unscrew the terminal screws on the switch about ¼ inch and remove the wires. Some switches instead have wires inserted into holes in the rear of the switch; if this is the case, insert a small thin screwdriver in the slot below the wire to release it.
6. Use a continuity tester (see *Fix Everything: Continuity Tester*) to test the switch. Clip one probe to each of the two terminals, then flip the switch on and off. The tester should light only when the switch is on. You also can use a multimeter (see *Fix Everything: Multimeter*) set to resistance in ohms for this test. If the switch is faulty, replace it.

Replace an electrical switch:

1. If any wires from the box are damaged, remove the damaged portion, making sure you have sufficient length to reach the terminal box.
2. If necessary, use a wire stripper to remove insulation from the last ¾ inch of the ends of the wires.
3. Use the strippers or pliers to bend the end of the wire in a semicircle so it can wrap around the terminal screw. If there are no terminal screws on the switch, insert the straight wires into the appropriate holes on the back of the switch.

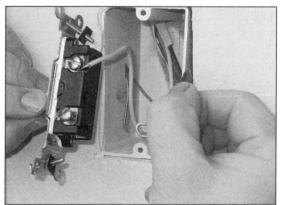

Remove the wires from the old switch and attach them to the new unit.

4. Attach the wires to the terminals and tighten them.

5. Replace and screw the switch into the terminal box, making sure the switch is plumb—straight up and down.

6. Replace the cover plate, restore power, and try the switch.

Replace a three-way switch:

Follow the above steps for replacing a two-way or single-pole switch. The primary difference is the number of terminals; three-way switches have an additional or common terminal. Make sure you mark the terminal and wire locations as you remove the old switch and install the new switch in the same way.

Replace a dimmer switch:

1. Shut off power at the *Electrical Service Panel.* Pull off the rotary knob of the switch with firm outward pressure. Underneath is a standard switch cover plate. Remove the cover plate. Remove the mounting screws and carefully pull out the switch body.

2. A dimmer has wire leads instead of terminals. Remove the wire nuts and test for power by touching the probes of the tester to both wires, or to either wire and the metal box, or to one wire and the ground wire. If power is detected, shut off the correct circuit in the service panel.

3. With the probes of a continuity tester (see *Fix Everything: Continuity Tester*) touching the terminal on each side, the tester should show continuity with the switch *on* and no continuity with the switch *off.* If you get different results, replace the switch.

4. As needed, replace the switch by connecting the dimmer wires to the power wires with electrical nuts.

**Fix-It Tip**

If three switches control a single light or group of lights, they are actually *four-way* switches. Count the number of switches and add one. Make sure you get the correct replacement switch type for the job.

# Electrical System

A home electrical system is the wiring in a house, the *Electrical Service Panel* where electricity enters the house, and every *Electrical Switch*, *Electrical Receptacle*, and other device that allows use of the electrical power provided. The electrical system supplies power for lighting, heating, and operation of electrical equipment and appliances. When it doesn't work, chances are that you can fix it!

## How Does It Work?

How does electricity do its job? Electrical current flows to the electrical device through a hot (usually black) wire. The current flows back to its source over the neutral or ground wire. Current is the flow of electrons in a wire, measured in amperes or amps. Volts are the pressure that moves the electrons along the wires. Ohms measure the resistance to the flow of an electric current.

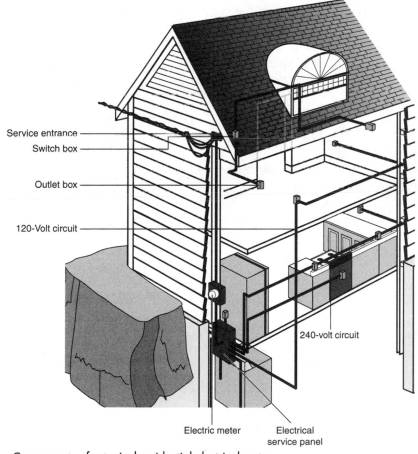

Service entrance

Switch box

Outlet box

120-Volt circuit

240-volt circuit

Electric meter

Electrical service panel

Components of a typical residential electrical system.

Power for most homes comes from a regional power company. Wires bring the electricity to an electrical meter where household usage is measured, then to the electrical service panel, which distributes the power to individual circuits. Household circuits are either 120-volt or 240-volt. The 120-volt circuits power most of a home from lighting to blenders to refrigerators. A few large appliances, such as electric kitchen stoves, dryers, central air conditioners, and water heaters, run on 240-volt circuits.

**Fix-It Tip**

Be sure any light, appliance, switch, receptacle, or other electrical device you use has an approval label by Underwriters Laboratory. The label means the device meets safety standards.

## What Can Go Wrong?

The power source coming into your home can fail. Wires within your home can short out or fail. Circuit breakers can trip and fuses can burn out. Electrical receptacles and electrical switches can malfunction.

## How Can I Identify the Problem?

If *all* your home's lights and electric gadgets suddenly quit working, check the *Electrical Service Panel* to see if the main breaker or fuse has tripped. Also check to see if your neighbors have power. If in doubt, call the power company.

If an individual circuit breaker trips or a fuse burns out, check the *Electrical Service Panel*.

If an electrical appliance or device quits working, refer to the specific *Fix-It Guide* for testing instructions.

If an *Electrical Receptacle* or *Electrical Switch* malfunctions, test and replace if necessary.

If you suspect a short or wire failure in your house electrical system, call a licensed electrician.

## What Parts, Materials, and Tools Do I Need?

Replacement parts for electrical systems are available from local hardware stores, home centers, and electrical suppliers. The tools you will need to fix electrical system components include these:

- Multimeter
- Screwdrivers
- Wrenches

## What Are the Steps to Fixing It?

Refer to the specific *Fix-It Guide* in this section of the book for instructions on fixing the component or device.

**Fix-It Tip**

Call an electrician if you have any doubts about working on your electrical system or any doubts about your system's safety.

# Espresso Maker

Need an espresso-jolt of caffeine to get your motor started in the morning? Enjoy a cappuccino or latte during the day? You can enjoy these beverages in your own home—if your espresso maker works! Here's what you can do if it doesn't.

## How Does It Work?

A home espresso maker is a small appliance for brewing coffee beans using steam rather than hot water. An electric steam-pressure espresso maker heats water, forcing the resulting steam through a filter basket filled with finely ground dark-roast coffee beans. Higher-quality espresso makers also have pumps. In addition to espresso, many units can make cappuccino (espresso topped with steam-frothed milk) and latte (espresso mixed with steam-heated milk) beverages.

## What Can Go Wrong?

A simple espresso maker is similar in operation to a *Coffee Maker*; many of the same things can go wrong with it. Electrical cords, switches, the heating element, thermostat, and fuse can all fail. In addition, the pressure gasket can be damaged or the safety plug may have opened, and the steam tube or frother can become clogged.

## How Can I Identify the Problem?

If the appliance does not work, make sure power is on at the outlet and test the *Electrical Cord*. Also test the switch, the thermostat (see *Appliance Controls*), the *Fuse*, and the *Heating Element*, servicing or replacing as needed.

If no espresso drips from the filter cup, the grounds may be too fine or tamped too hard.

If the espresso comes out too quickly and is weak, make sure you use the proper grind and the correct amount of water, usually recommended as ¼ cup per 2 tablespoons of coffee.

If the espresso spurts from around the filter cup, inspect and clean the filter cup. Make sure that the filter basket assembly seats completely. Also verify that you are using the correct ratio of coffee and water. Remove and replace the gasket as needed.

If the espresso is not hot, test the *Heating Element* and thermostat (see *Appliance Controls*).

If the unit makes little or no steam, turn the unit off and let it cool, then disassemble and clean the frother and the steam tube.

> **Fix-It Tip**
>
> Mineral deposits can easily build up and block passages in espresso makers. Use distilled or filtered water if possible. Also clean the espresso maker periodically, following the manufacturer's recommendations.

## What Parts, Materials, and Tools Do I Need?

You can find replacement parts for your espresso maker from the manufacturer or through aftermarket suppliers (see *Fix-It Resources*). In addition, some larger stores that sell these appliances will have replacement parts available. Here are basic tools you may need for fixing an espresso maker:

- Screwdrivers
- Pliers or wrenches
- Multimeter

## What Are the Steps to Fixing It?

Service the pressure cap:

1. Carefully remove the pressure cap gasket.
2. Remove any screws holding the pressure ring in place and remove the ring.
3. Inspect the pressure cap for cracks and replace as needed.

Service the hot-water dispenser head:

1. Remove the locking ring with a screwdriver.
2. Carefully remove the filter screen and gasket.
3. Clean all parts with soapy water and replace the gasket if necessary.

Service the frother assembly:

1. Unscrew the frother from the steam tube and remove the vent ring.
2. Check the rotor and replace it if it is damaged.
3. Wash all parts of the frother assembly with warm soapy water.
4. Dry and reassemble the frother assembly.

Electrical parts, such as the power cord, on-off switch, boiler, and hot water coil, can be tested with a multimeter (see *Fix Everything: Multimeter*).

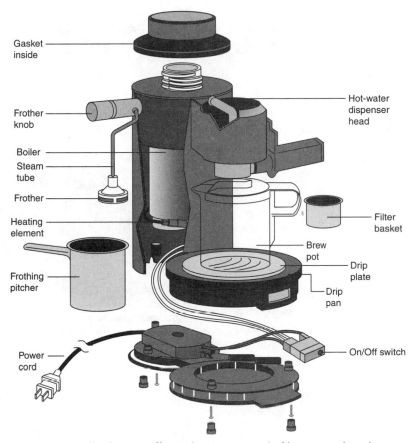

Gasket inside

Frother knob

Boiler

Steam tube

Frother

Heating element

Frothing pitcher

Power cord

Hot-water dispenser head

Filter basket

Brew pot

Drip plate

Drip pan

On/Off switch

An espresso maker brews coffee with steam instead of hot water, though many units can do both.

# Exercise Equipment

Huff ... Puff ... Won't this exercise equipment *ever* break down? You wish! Actually, most exercise equipment is designed to take rough treatment with minimal problems. The biggest problem is lack of maintenance, lubricating moving parts, and keeping batteries fresh. Even so, sometimes a stationary bike, treadmill, or other exercise equipment quits. What to do? Burn calories fixing it!

## How Does It Work?

The stationary bike and the powered treadmill remain the most popular home exercise machines. The bike is a belt-flywheel machine that simulates riding a standard bicycle. The treadmill is a motor-driven machine that simulates taking a walk or a jog. In addition, many people have free weights and weight machines in their exercise room, but most don't break or need much maintenance.

## What Can Go Wrong?

The stationary bike uses a flywheel that is driven by a chain and belt that are powered by pedaling the bike. So the chain or belt can break or fall off, stopping the flywheel.

Treadmills rely on an internal *Motor* to move the running belt positioned over a running platform. The motor can burn out or, more likely, the belt can break or require adjustment. And controls can fail.

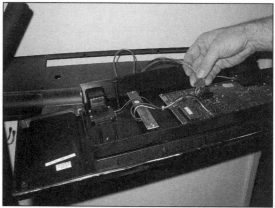

Treadmills use electronic circuit boards to control electric motors. There is little you can do on a circuit board except replace any fuses and make sure the board is plugged in.

**Fix-It Tip**

As basic maintenance, wipe down your exercise equipment with a soft dry rag after each use to keep perspiration from corroding metal parts. Once every few months, clean surfaces with mild household cleaner and water.

## How Can I Identify the Problem?

With a little routine maintenance (see below), there's little to go wrong with a stationary bike or a treadmill. The belt may occasionally need adjustment; the belt is correctly tensioned if it gives about ½ inch when you try to lift it off the flywheel with a screwdriver. If the belt tension knob no longer works, check the belt adjustment clasp. If the chain is too loose, replace it as you would the chain on a regular *Bicycle*. Belt and chain adjustments may require removal of the flywheel case.

Some electronic monitors are powered by internal batteries located near the controls. Check and replace them every few months depending on use.

## What Parts, Materials, and Tools Do I Need?

You can find many replacement parts for exercise equipment through the manufacturer or aftermarket supplier (see *Fix-It Resources*). Basic fasteners (screws, bolts) and lubricants are available at hardware stores. Here are the tools you may need:

- Screwdrivers
- Wrenches
- Multimeter

## What Are the Steps to Fixing It?

Remove a flywheel case from a stationary bike (to replace a belt or chain):

1. Locate and remove side and bottom screws from the case.
2. Use a socket wrench to loosen and remove all bolts holding the crank and pedal to the bike.
3. Remove the pedal, crank, and case side.

Adjust a stationary bike's belt:

1. Set the flywheel tension knob to its lowest setting.
2. Unhook the belt adjustment clasp and adjust the belt.
3. Rehook the clasp when proper tension is achieved.

Tighten a treadmill belt:

1. Unplug the treadmill.
2. Turn the rear positioning bolt(s) one-quarter turn clockwise.
3. Check the treadmill belt tension; repeat as needed.

Center the treadmill belt:

1. Set the controls to run the treadmill at 2 MPH.
2. Identify the adjustment bolt on the side where the belt is loose and turn it clockwise one-quarter turn.
3. Watch the treadmill belt for 60 seconds and readjust it if needed.

**Fix-It Tip**

To minimize repairs, periodically lubricate an exercise machine's moving parts following the manufacturer's recommendations.

# Exterior Siding

Siding is your home's skin. If your residence looks like it needs a house call from a dermatologist, maybe there are some things you can do first. You don't want to be the cause of a neighborhood infection.

## How Does It Work?

Siding is the wall covering of boards fastened to an exterior building frame or sheathing. Siding can be made of numerous natural and man-made materials, including wood, vinyl, and aluminum. Most are either overlapping or interlocking, depending on their design, to keep moisture from easily penetrating the wall sheathing. Brick, stone, and stucco are also used as siding material (see *Masonry*).

## What Can Go Wrong?

Siding boards can bow. Shingles can be damaged. Nails in vertical panels can pop out. Pieces of clapboard siding can split. Vinyl siding can be punctured or torn. Aluminum siding can suffer dents.

**Fix-It Tip**

> Maintaining vinyl and aluminum siding is relatively easy. Simply wash it once a year with a mild soap solution. Remember that harsh cleaners can damage nearby plants.

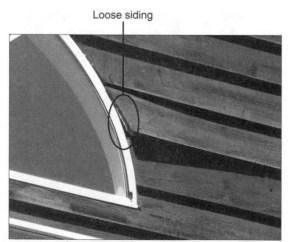

Loose siding

Exterior siding can easily work loose, especially around window and door openings.

## How Can I Identify the Problem?

If a siding board bows out from the house, you can reattach it to flatten it (see below).

If shingle siding is damaged, you can easily replace the damaged pieces (see below).

If nails in vertical panels pop out, you can replace the nails with screws for a solid repair (see below).

If a piece of clapboard siding is split, you can close up the split (see below).

If a piece of vinyl siding is damaged, you can patch it (see below).

If aluminum siding is dented, you can repair it (see below).

## What Parts, Materials, and Tools Do I Need?

Replacement parts are available from local home improvement outlets. The tools you will need to fix exterior siding include these:

- Screwdrivers
- Drill
- Caulking gun and weatherproofing caulk
- Galvanized nails
- Galvanized screws
- Wood stain
- Hammer
- Nail set
- Exterior paint
- Paint brush or pad
- Wood chisel
- Wood adhesive
- Mini-hacksaw blade
- Pry bar
- Safety goggles
- Work gloves
- Zip tool
- Metal snips
- Utility knife
- Sandpaper
- Metal primer
- Wedges
- Automotive body filler
- Sheet metal screws

## What Are the Steps to Fixing It?

Fix bowed wood siding:

1. Drill pilot holes through the siding and into underlying wall studs to avoid splitting the wood.
2. Install long galvanized screws through the siding and into the studs.
3. Recess the screw heads and cover them with weatherproofing caulk.

Replace damaged wood siding:

1. Insert wedges under the course directly above the damaged shingle.
2. Remove the damaged shingle with a nail puller or other tool, or by cutting it into pieces with a chisel.
3. Drive in or remove nail heads that will be in the way of installing the new siding.
4. Install the new shingle, cutting as needed to make sure that it fits snugly.
5. Use galvanized nails or screws to fasten the new shingle firmly in place.
6. Recess the screw heads and cover them with weatherproofing caulk.

Repair popped nails:

1. Identify which nails are above the surface and look for a probable cause. If replacement or repair to the siding is needed, see above.
2. Use a nail puller or pry bar to remove the popped nails.
3. Replace the nails with longer galvanized nails or screws of the same or slightly wider shanks.
4. Recess the screw heads and cover them with weatherproofing caulk.

Repair clapboard siding:

1. If clapboard siding is cracked, insert a putty knife or pry bar into the crack to widen it, then inject exterior (waterproof) wood adhesive.
2. As possible, nail each side of the split so the crack will close around the adhesive.
3. Recess the nail heads and cover them with weatherproofing caulk.
4. Touch up the repair with matching exterior *Paint* or wood stain.

**Fix-It Tip**

Paint and stain aren't just makeup, they're foundation. Make sure that siding is protected from moisture and pests by keeping it well painted to seal it.

Fix vinyl siding:

1. Use an installer's zip tool to unlock siding above the damaged piece. These tools are available at larger hardware and building material stores.
2. Pry down and slide the tool along the edge to free it.
3. Insert temporary wedges under the loose siding course.
4. Remove nails above the damaged section with a nail puller or claw hammer.
5. Remove the damaged area with snips or a utility knife.
6. Cut a replacement section 2 inches larger than the damaged piece.
7. Install the replacement through the top flange, centering it in the opening.
8. Relock the siding edges with the zip tool.

Fix dented aluminum siding:

1. Drill a small hole at the center of the dent.
2. Install a screw partially into the siding to give you something to grip.
3. Use pliers to pull on the sheet metal screw and pop out the dent.
4. Remove the screw.
5. As needed, sandpaper the dent, clean, and fill with automotive body filler.
6. Once the filler is dry, apply a metal primer.
7. Paint the surface with two coats of a similar color in an area significantly wider than the dent.

**Fix-It Tip**

Wood siding's worst enemies are moisture and wood-boring pests. You can minimize damage by making sure that *Gutters* are keeping water from the surface, and that nearby plants aren't giving moisture and bugs a clear path to the siding. A once-a-year walk-around inspection of wood siding is a good idea.

# Facsimile Machine

Facsimile or fax machines, once only used by big businesses, are found in millions of homes and home offices. They are inexpensive (under $100) and most can double as a telephone. And they are relatively trouble-free. When one does decide to act up, threaten to fix it!

## How Does It Work?

A fax machine is an electronic device that scans a paper image and transmits it by modem to another fax machine.

A document fed into a fax machine passes over a device containing a single row of light detectors. The device scans the page, producing an electrical signal of varying voltage that represents the dark and light parts of the page. The pattern is sent along a telephone line to the receiving fax machine, which decodes the signal and translates it into an exact image, a facsimile.

The two types of fax machines, plain paper and thermal, are distinguished by the paper they use. A thermal fax machine contains a thermal printer with heating elements that prints rows of dots on a roll of heat-sensitive paper. A newer plain-paper fax machine contains an ink-jet or laser printer to print a copy of a document being sent to it.

## What Can Go Wrong?

Either type of fax machine contains few serviceable parts. Routine maintenance, however, will help avoid most problems. The best course of action is to use quality supplies and periodically clean the machine.

## How Can I Identify the Problem?

Symptoms will help you determine the cause. If the unit won't work, make sure the power is on at the outlet and test the *Electrical Cord*.

If the fax can't send or receive documents, make sure that the phone line is connected and not damaged. Check to be sure the line is plugged into the correct fax port. Test the wall jack and replace it if it is faulty (see *Telephone System*).

If the fax can send but not receive (or vice versa), check the phone line as above and replace the lamp if burned out.

If the fax still will not function properly, take the unit to a service center or replace the unit.

If there are marks or blank spots on incoming documents, open the cover and clean the glass with a clean lint-free cloth dampened with denatured alcohol.

If a plain-paper fax leaves marks or blank spots on documents, open the cover and wipe up any spilled toner. Clean corona wires if dirty, or replace the drum if damaged, following the manufacturer's instructions for replacement.

If a thermal fax won't print, locate the thermal head and clean it by wiping it with a clean lint-free cloth dampened with denatured alcohol. Make sure that the paper is installed correctly, because the printer will print on only the coated side.

## What Parts, Materials, and Tools Do I Need?

There are so many models of fax machines that replacement parts are best found through the original manufacturer or authorized parts supplier (see *Fix-It Resources*). To disassemble and check a fax, you'll need some tools:

- Screwdrivers
- Denatured alcohol
- Canned air
- Lint-free cloth
- Small brush

## What Are the Steps to Fixing It?

To service a plain-paper fax, refer to *Computer Printer.*

Service a thermal fax:

1. Unplug the unit from the power source and the incoming telephone line.
2. Open the unit and wipe the platen using a cloth dampened with denatured alcohol.
3. Allow the platen to dry thoroughly before use.
4. Use a small brush or canned air to remove dirt and dust from the paper trough.

Canned air is useful for cleaning dust and paper particles from a fax machine.

5. If accessible, wipe the exposure lens and mirrors with a lint-free cloth.

Replace the exposure lens in a thermal fax:

1. Unplug the unit from the power source and the incoming telephone line.
2. Turn the unit over and remove the bottom housing.
3. Once the bulb is cool, twist it out and pull it from the socket.
4. Replace the bulb with an identical model, avoiding touching it.

# Fan

You'll find electric fans in many places throughout your home. Besides ceiling and portable fans, they are in air conditioners, range hoods, computer power supplies, and bathroom vents. They are in just about every room of your home. If they decide to not work, here's what you can do about it.

## How Does It Work?

A fan is a device that produces a current of air. There are many kinds of fans—freestanding, oscillating, box, ceiling, and more—but they all function in the same way. An electric fan uses a motor to rotate a blade assembly. The blades are angled and shaped to move and direct air currents. The fan will have one or more control switches to turn it on and off as well as to control its speed. The fan may also have a gear assembly to move the fan from side to side, or oscillate, for greater air movement.

## What Can Go Wrong?

Simple in operation, fans are easy to troubleshoot. The electrical cord may need replacing. Switches can be dirty or faulty. The motor may fail. The clutch knob and gear assembly may be faulty. Blades may be unbalanced, loose, or need lubricating.

| Fix-It Tip |
| --- |
| A multispeed fan can quit working on one or more speeds. If so, you either can repair it (see *Appliance Controls*) or live with it, using the other speeds. |

## How Can I Identify the Problem?

If the fan doesn't work at all, make sure power is on at the outlet, then test the *Electrical Cord*. Test the *Motor* and replace it if it is faulty. Clean and test the speed-control switch and service it if it is faulty (see *Appliance Controls*).

If the fan works on only some speeds, clean and test the speed-control switch (see *Appliance Controls*).

If an oscillating fan doesn't move from side to side, check the clutch knob, then the gear assembly. If it is faulty, service the gear assembly.

If the fan blades turn slowly, check the blades for a loose hub and tighten if needed. If the fan shaft is noisy or dry, lubricate it.

## What Parts, Materials, and Tools Do I Need?

Replacement parts for fans can be purchased from the manufacturer or an aftermarket supplier (see *Fix-It Resources*). Some parts can be purchased through larger hardware stores and home centers. Here are the tools you'll need to make most repairs:

- Screwdrivers
- Multimeter
- Small washers
- Electrical tape

## What Are the Steps to Fixing It?

An oscillating fan uses a set of gears, called a gear assembly, to move the fan head from side to side. When an oscillating fan doesn't move, the cause is typically a loose or worn gear or clutch knob. If the oscillating gears are worn and you don't want to replace them, simply reassemble the gear assembly and lock it in a stationary position.

Service fan blades:

1. Unplug the fan.
2. Remove the front blade guard or grill.

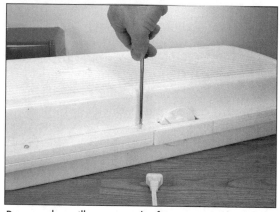

Remove the grill to access the fan motor and controls.

3. Remove the spinner, nut, or cotter pin that attaches the blade assembly to the motor shaft, then remove the blade assembly.

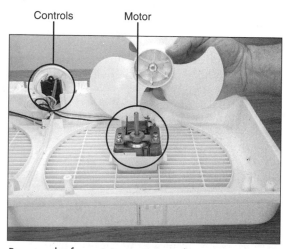

Controls          Motor

Remove the fan spinner to access the motor.

4. Remove the back blade guard to inspect and clean the motor housing and shaft.
5. Inspect the blade assembly for wear and damage. A damaged blade can unbalance the fan and wear out the blade-assembly shaft. Tighten the setscrew if needed.

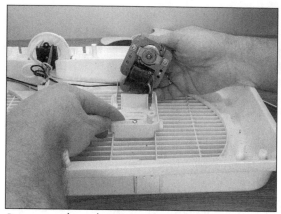

Remove and test the *Motor* as needed.

Wobbling blades can be noisy and reduce the fan's efficiency. You can purchase a balancing kit for some ceiling fan units or you can tape small washers on the blades to balance them.

Balance fan blades:

1. Unplug the fan.
2. Remove the fan blades and inspect them for nicks, damage, and debris that would make them unbalanced. Replace the blades in other locations on the fan to see if that resolves the balance problem.
3. Tape small washers to the top side of a blade and run the fan at various speeds to test it for balance. Once the best location is found, attach the washers with tape or glue.

Service a fan's gear assembly:

1. Remove the clutch knob from the *Motor* housing.
2. Remove the motor housing screws and housing to expose the gear assembly.
3. Check the gear assembly for alignment and wear. Tighten or replace as needed.

**Caution**

Some fan motors have a built-in capacitor, a device that stores electricity. Think of it as a small, yet powerful battery—and stay away from it.

# Faucet

Dripping faucets can be nerve-wracking—and costly. Lucky for you there's a special meeting of the Fix-It Club being called on faucets right now.

## How Does It Work?

A faucet is a plumbing fixture for drawing water from a pipe. Household faucets use simple valves that control the flow of water. There are several types of valves—compression (sometimes called stem-and-seat), disk, ball, and cartridge are the most common. Outdoor faucets typically are compression or a long-stem compression design called a freezeless sillcock. Faucets also use different configurations of levers and handles to open and close the valves. That's why they look different.

Faucets are fed from below by hot- and cold-water supply lines. Shutoff valves in the lines can be turned off while you're working on a faucet.

To repair a faucet, you first need to know what kind of valve is inside. Start by identifying the brand and, if possible, the model. You can then take this information (or the removed faucet) to a plumbing supply store or home center for repair parts or kits. If you've kept the owner's manual for the faucet from the last time it was replaced, you'll have brand, model, and even parts information you need.

## What Can Go Wrong?

Many new faucets are nearly maintenance free. The most common complaint about faucets is that that they drip or leak. Repair kits are available for most home faucets and they are relatively easy to install.

## How Can I Identify the Problem?

If a faucet leaks, replace seals and gaskets (see below).

If a shower head leaks, create a better seal or replace seals (see below).

If a sillcock wears out, replace the washers (see below).

If a compression faucet drips from the spout, replace the washer and/or the seat (see below).

If a faucet leaks from the handle, replace O-ring(s), replace the packing washer, tighten the packing nut, or replace worn packing, depending on the valve type (see below).

If a ball or cartridge faucet leaks from the collar, replace worn O-rings (see below).

If a disk faucet leaks around the base or has reduced flow, replace cracked or pitted disk assembly or worn inlet seals (see below).

If there is water under the sink, tighten the faucet-set locknuts under the sink. You also can replace putty or a gasket, replace a worn faucet, or replace leaky supply tubes (see below).

If the aerator leaks around the edge, replace the washer in the aerator (see below).

If the spray hose leaks or has reduced flow, replace the O-ring on the diverter valve, replace a worn washer at the base of the spray head, or clean the diverter valve and spray head (see below).

## What Parts, Materials, and Tools Do I Need?

Just about all the parts and tools needed to fix faucets are available through larger hardware and plumbing stores or home improvement centers. The tools you'll need include these:

- Screwdrivers
- Adjustable wrench
- Plumbing or pipe wrench
- Valve seat wrench
- Plumber's grease
- Plumber's putty
- Plumber's tape
- Vinegar
- Small brush

## What Are the Steps to Fixing It?

Service a compression faucet:

1. Turn off the water supply and open the faucet handle to relieve water pressure.
2. Carefully pry off the trim cap with a small screwdriver or putty knife.
3. Remove the locknut with an adjustable wrench, then lift the spindle out of the faucet.

4. As needed, remove and replace the O-ring. Before reinstalling, coat the stem lightly with plumber's grease.
5. As needed, remove the retaining screw and pry out the washer. Install an exact-replacement washer and tighten it.
6. As needed, inspect the seat and replace if damaged.
7. Install the valve and tighten, then reinstall the handle and test.

Repair a reverse-compression faucet:

1. Turn off the water supply and open the faucet handle to relieve water pressure.
2. Carefully pry off the trim cap with a small screwdriver and remove the handle screw. Unscrew the packing nut and lift out the stem assembly.
3. As needed, pry out the washer under the packing nut and replace it.
4. As needed, remove the seat washer and replace it with one that fits exactly. Rethread the spindle and washer back onto the stem, and reassemble the faucet.

Change the packing in an older compression faucet:

1. Turn off the water supply and open the faucet handle to relieve water pressure.
2. Remove the handle and any trim.
3. Remove the packing washer or string and clean the area of debris.
4. Insert a new packing washer into the packing nut, replace the stem, reassemble the handle, and test.

Service a cartridge faucet:

1. Turn off the water supply and open the faucet handle to relieve water pressure.
2. Remove the handle (often held on by a hex screw) and any trim.

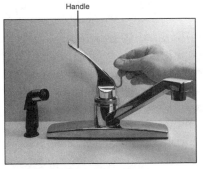

Remove the faucet handle.

3. Unscrew the retainer nut by hand or with adjustable pliers and lift it off the faucet.

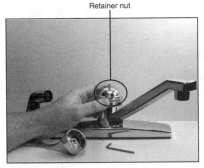

Remove the retainer nut to access the cartridge.

4. Remove the retainer clip, if any, that holds the cartridge in the faucet body.
5. Remove the cartridge stem and lift it out of the faucet body.

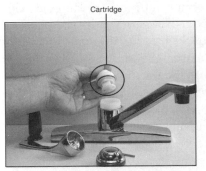

Remove and, if needed, replace the cartridge with an exact replacement.

6. If the cartridge is worn or damaged, replace it. If the O-rings are damaged, replace the rings only.

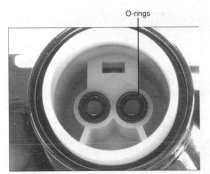

Below the cartridge are two O-rings that seal the water from entering the faucet when it isn't supposed to (dripping).

7. Reassemble and test the faucet.

Service rotating-ball faucets:

1. Turn off the water supply and open the faucet handle to relieve water pressure.
2. Remove the handle by loosening the setscrew under the handle.

3. Carefully turn the adjusting ring clockwise so the ball moves easily without the handle attached; do not overtighten.
4. Reinstall the handle, aligning the setscrew with the flat spot on the ball lever, and test the faucet.
5. If additional service is needed, refer to the faucet owner's manual or a rotating-ball faucet repair kit.

**Fix-It Tip**

When working on a faucet still attached to the sink, make sure you close the drain to prevent losing any small parts.

Service a disk faucet:

1. Turn off the water supply and open the faucet handle to relieve water pressure.
2. Remove the trim cap with a small screwdriver, then remove the handle screw and pull off the handle.
3. Use an adjustable wrench to unscrew the locknut, then lift the disk assembly from the faucet body.
4. Inspect the assembly. If it is damaged, replace it with a new unit.
5. As needed, purchase and install a spring-and-seat repair kit made for the make and model of faucet.
6. Tighten the locknut, reinstall the handle, and test the faucet.

Replace a faucet:

1. Turn off the water supply and open the faucet handle to relieve water pressure.
2. Carefully loosen the coupling nuts at the shutoff valves and at the base of the faucet.
3. Carefully remove the supply tubes.
4. Remove the locknuts that hold the faucet to the sink and lift the faucet out.

5. Clean the area where the old faucet sat.
6. As needed, install the new spray hose and supply tubes, if any, through their holes in the sink.
7. Set the rubber gasket that came with the faucet on the sink where it will be mounted. If no gasket is supplied, apply plumber's putty.
8. Set the faucet into position and center it.
9. From under the sink, attach the faucet locknuts to hold it to the sink.
10. Reinstall the supply lines, then turn them on and test the faucet. Turn it on carefully because the line and faucet have air in them.

Repair or replace a leaking shower head:

1. Remove the shower head from the pipe.
2. Clean the arm threads and wrap them with plumbers' joint tape.
3. Screw the head back on and hand-tighten it. Remove any excess compound or tape.
4. Test and retighten as needed.

Repair a shower head that leaks at the swivel:

1. Unscrew the shower-head body from the swivel-ball ring.
2. Find the O-ring or a similar seal inside. Replace it and screw the shower head back into place.

Repair an outdoor sillcock faucet:

1. Shut off the water at the plumbing branch or meter.
2. Loosen and open the faucet top.
3. Remove the stem.
4. Replace the washer, apply plumber's grease, and replace the stem.
5. Turn on water at the branch shutoff or the meter.

To attach a new spray hose, follow instructions on the replacement spray hose.

Clean an aerator (the mesh filter at the end of a faucet spout):

1. Unscrew the aerator from the spout.
2. Disassemble the aerator, noting the order that parts are removed. Replace the washer if it is worn or cracked.
3. Clean the screen and aerator disks with vinegar and a small brush.
4. Reassemble the aerator and thread the assembly back onto the spout.

Service a diverter valve:

1. Turn off the water supply to the faucet and remove the spout (see above).
2. Remove the diverter valve, typically located on the faucet body for a single-lever faucet and under the spout nut on a double-handle faucet.

3. As needed, clean or replace the diverter valve. If the O-ring needs replacement, do so.
4. Reassemble and test the diverter valve.

Clean a spray head:

1. Remove the screw cover from the nozzle with a small screwdriver.
2. Remove the disk, seat, and sleeve, inspecting each for condition. Replace as needed.
3. Reassemble and test.

**Caution**

To avoid damage to plated plumbing fittings, wrap wrench jaws with masking tape, rubber, or a soft rag.

# Fence

Good fences make good neighbors. That's why you want to keep your fence in good condition. It's relatively easy to take a few minutes once a month to check your fence line and make sure it's in good repair. If it isn't, here's what you can do.

## How Does It Work?

A fence is a property enclosure made of pickets, boards, rails, chain-link fabric, or other materials.

Wood is the most popular fencing material and one that takes on many forms, including privacy, rail, and picket. Wood is also the easiest fencing material to work with. See *Masonry* for repairs to masonry fences and walls, including brick and stone, and see *Concrete* for repairs to concrete fences and walls. Chain-link fencing, if installed correctly, is virtually maintenance-free.

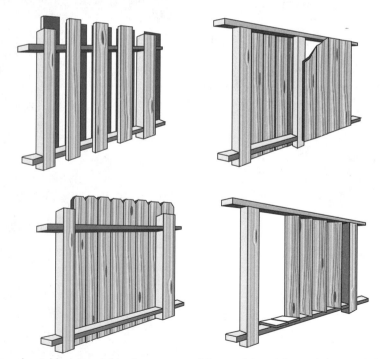

Good neighbor (top left), alternate panel (top right), solid panel (bottom left), and louvered (bottom right) are popular types of wood privacy fencing.

## What Can Go Wrong?

Being outdoors all the time, fences take all the abuse that the elements can deliver. Posts come loose and wobble. Rails and boards deteriorate. Gates sag.

## How Can I Identify the Problem?

If a post wobbles, you can reinforce it (see below).

If a post leans, you can straighten it with a turnbuckle (see below).

If a gate or fence sags, you can reinforce it (see below).

If individual pickets, boards, or chain links deteriorate, you can carefully remove them from the fence and replace them with duplicates.

> **Fix-It Tip**
>
> A wooden fence will last longer if you keep dirt away from fence boards. Also paint or finish the wood to protect it from the elements.

## What Parts, Materials, and Tools Do I Need?

Replacement parts are available from local home improvement outlets. The tools you will need to fix a fence include these:

- Screwdrivers
- Hammer
- Drill
- Garden trowel
- Shovel
- Sledgehammer
- Handsaw
- Wrenches
- Concrete
- Wheelbarrow
- Eye screws
- Turnbuckle

## What Are the Steps to Fixing It?

Replace a wooden fence post:

1. Check for wooden post rot by removing dirt around the bottom with a trowel and using an old screwdriver to probe the wood. Replace if the wood is soft.
2. Brace the post to keep it in position while you remove the rotten post.
3. Disconnect the rails and siding from the post.
4. Dig out the old post and any concrete holding it in place.
5. Prepare the post hole for the new post by lining it with gravel and, as needed, preparing concrete.
6. Install the replacement post, using a level to make sure the post is plumb on two adjoining sides. Fill the post hole with gravel or cement as needed.
7. Once the post is firm (concrete is dry), attach the rails and siding to the new post.

Straighten a leaning post or sagging gate:

1. Install an eye screw at the highest point on the leaning post or the gate frame.
2. Install another eye screw diagonally from the first.
3. Install a turnbuckle between the two eyes and tighten it until the post is plumb or the gate frame is square.

Reinforce a sagging fence or gate frame:

1. Identify the best location for installing a metal support, typically on corners.
2. Select a galvanized metal support bracket for installation on the fence or gate frame. Many sizes and shapes are available at hardware stores.
3. Brace the fence or gate in the position you want it to stay, then install the metal support using screws or nails.

Mend a chain-link fence:

1. Identify the area that needs to be replaced.
2. Stretch a rope from one side of the damaged area to the other and pull it taut to relieve pressure on the fabric.
3. Undo the fabric twist at the top of either side of the damaged fabric.
4. Remove the damaged chain-link fabric.
5. Install replacement fabric of the same size and width.
6. Use pliers to tighten the twists at the top of the fabric.
7. Carefully remove pressure on the fabric.

**Fix-It Tip**

Chain-link fences are made of galvanized metal fabric of various sizes. Make sure you get the right size fabric to mend your fence.

# Fire Extinguisher

Fire extinguishers are useless—until the moment when they are vital. To make sure they are ready when you are, periodically check your home's fire extinguisher(s) and perform any maintenance needed. Here's how.

## How Does It Work?

A fire extinguisher is an apparatus, usually containing chemicals, for putting out a fire. It extinguishes a fire by excluding oxygen so that combustion can no longer continue. The extinguisher must deliver a powerful spray of water, foam, or powder to smother the whole fire as quickly as possible, so its contents are pressurized. Some extinguishers produce a jet of carbon dioxide, a heavy gas that prevents burning.

## What Can Go Wrong?

Fire extinguishers are relatively simple in function and operation, so little can go wrong with them. The primary problem with them is that they eventually leak pressure so they cannot deliver the extinguishing ingredient to the fire when needed. Make sure you check the charge meter every few months and replace the unit if it falls below the *full* range.

### Fire Extinguisher Classes

*Class A* extinguishers are designed to fight blazes in wood, paper, rubber, and most plastics. Install one near fireplaces and in the living areas and bedrooms.

*Class B* extinguishers contain dry chemicals that smother fires fueled by oil, solvents, grease, gasoline, kerosene, and other flammable liquids. Install them in kitchens, workshops, and garages.

*Class C* extinguishers also contain dry chemicals to smother fires in electrical equipment. Use them in workshop areas and near electrical service panels.

Most household fire extinguishers are multipurpose class A-B-C. They are effective against all of the common fires in homes and so are most popular.

Make sure you read and understand the instructions on your fire extinguisher *before* you need it.

## How Can I Identify the Problem?

Pressurized fire extinguishers include a pressure meter that indicates the state of the internal pressure, typically *full* or *refill*. If the meter does not indicate *full*, refill or replace following instructions on the unit. Check the fire extinguisher's pressure meter once a month.

Most household fire extinguishers have a gauge to indicate whether the unit is *full* and what to do if it isn't *(refill, discard)*.

### Using a Fire Extinguisher

Here's how to use the most common type of household fire extinguishers:

1. Pull the pin near the top of the extinguisher.
2. Approximately 6 feet away from the fire, aim the nozzle at the base of the fire.
3. Press the trigger and move the spray from side to side to smother the entire fire.
4. Continue spraying until the fire is completely out. Use a second fire extinguisher if necessary.
5. Don't reuse without recharging the extinguisher following the manufacturer's instructions, or replacing the unit.

# Fireplace/Stove

Many homes use a wood, gas, or electric stove or fireplace for primary or secondary heat. Others use them for ambiance. Fireplaces and stoves are relatively trouble-free and many are efficient heat sources. Here's how the Fix-It Club takes care of fireplaces.

## How Does It Work?

An open wood fireplace consists of a hearth where wood is burned for heat and a chimney flue for expelling the smoke. Because heat can be lost with the smoke, a fireplace insert is often installed to increase heat retention. A freestanding wood stove, pellet stove, and gas stove also decorates and warms a home and requires some of the same maintenance and repair as a fireplace. (The terms "stove" and "fireplace" typically are used interchangeably.)

All fireplaces have the same two requirements: regulated air to feed the fire and a means of expelling smoke and fumes. A shuttered damper in the chimney provides an exit for smoke as well as creates an updraft that draws fresh air to the fire. Many new fireplace designs also use outside air intake vents under the fireplace so as not to draw warm air from the room. Gas fireplaces often have an inlet/outlet vent that expels fumes through a duct in an outside wall while drawing in fresh air.

Pellet stoves burn pellets made from sawdust and mill shavings; the pellets are loaded into a hopper at the top or front of the stove and delivered to the combustion chamber at a controlled rate by a motorized auger. Combustion air, blown into the chamber, develops superheated air. Room air is drawn across the heat exchanger by a fan, heated, and then returned to the room. Residual combustion gasses are vented outside, normally through a 3-inch flue that exits out the unit's back or top.

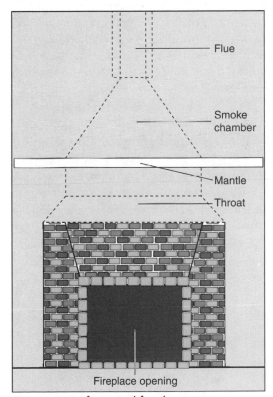

Components of a typical fireplace.

## What Can Go Wrong?

A chimney will need cleaning. A fire may burn poorly and send smoke back into the room. A stove's door gasket may wear out or come loose. A stove connector may corrode. Bricks or mortar may be damaged. The igniter of a gas stove may fail.

**Fix-It Tip**

Make a bed for a better fire. Keep a ½-inch bed of ash in the fireplace after cleaning as an insulator to prevent heat from being absorbed into the hearth.

## How Can I Identify the Problem?

If a fire burns poorly and sends smoke back into the room, make sure the damper is fully open. Verify that the chimney is clean and free of obstructions (see below). In addition, you can have a wind cap or chimney cap installed or you can install air vents in the floor on either side of the fireplace (see below).

If a stove connector is corroded, you can replace it (see below).

If fireplace bricks or mortar are damaged, you can repair them using a 1-to-3 mix of fire-clay cement and sand (see *Masonry*).

If a gas stove will not ignite, you can replace the igniter (see below) and adjust the pilot (see below).

If a pellet stove will not feed pellets, check the controls (see *Appliance Controls*) and the *Motor*.

**Caution**

Install a carbon monoxide detector in a room with a fireplace to alert you to a buildup of carbon monoxide that might be caused by a downdraft or a plugged-up chimney.

## What Parts, Materials, and Tools Do I Need?

Replacement parts are available from the manufacturer (see *Fix-It Resources*) as well as from local fireplace shops and suppliers. The tools you will need to fix one of the various types of fireplaces include these:

- Screwdriver
- High-temperature sealant
- Measuring tape
- Jigsaw
- Electric drill
- Pliers
- Wrenches
- Metal snips
- Crimping tool
- Chimney brushes
- Shop (not household) vacuum cleaner
- Duct tape
- Sewing needle
- Self-tapping sheet-metal screws
- Dropcloth or other heavy cloth

## What Are the Steps to Fixing It?

Sweep a chimney:

1. Remove all loose items from the fire surround and the hearth.
2. Cover the fireplace opening with a heavy fabric cover and seal it with duct tape. Also cover nearby flooring and furniture with a dropcloth.
3. From atop the roof, push a chimney brush from the chimney top down toward the fireplace below, moving the brush up and down to loosen debris.

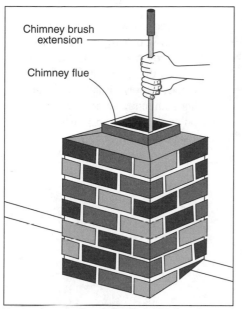

Chimney brush extension

Chimney flue

Use a chimney brush to clean the fireplace chimney, adding extension rods to move the brush farther down the flue.

4. Continue pushing the brush down the chimney by adding extension canes and moving the brush to loosen debris.

5. When the brush reaches the bottom of the chimney, withdraw the brush.

6. Allow the dust to settle for at least one hour before removing the cover over the fireplace opening.

7. Use a shop vacuum cleaner to remove debris from the fireplace floor and the smoke shelf.

Install air vents in a wood floor or subfloor:

1. Visit a fireplace shop or department of a large building materials store for advice on what vents should be installed and where.

2. Measure the opening needed for the vents you have chosen, and mark it with a pencil.

3. Drill a hole in one corner of the opening.

4. Use a jigsaw to cut the perimeter of the hole.

5. Install the vent following the manufacturer's recommendations. Many vents are held in place by their own weight and don't require fasteners.

Replace a corroded stove connector:

1. Inspect and measure the pipe and connector to be replaced. Use these measurements to purchase replacement stovepipe, connectors, and other needed materials.

2. Remove fasteners holding the stovepipe, collar, joints, and flue connection.

3. Disassemble the connector, being careful not to disturb soot that can become airborne.

4. Reassemble the connector, using replacement components as needed.

5. As needed, secure all joints with self-tapping ¼-inch sheet-metal screws.

Replace a stove door gasket:

1. Remove the old gasket from the door, starting at the seam.

2. Clean the gasket channel of old sealant using a screwdriver.

3. Apply high-temperature sealant around the gasket channel.

4. Press the new gasket firmly into the sealant bed and trim the end of the gasket to fit tightly.

5. Close and tightly latch the door for 24 to 48 hours or as recommended by the sealant manufacturer to allow for complete drying.

Check and replace igniters on a gas fireplace or stove:

1. Turn off the gas shutoff valve.

2. Trace the igniter cable to a terminal on the ignition control module at the back of the stove.

3. Remove the cover and disconnect the igniter cable.

4. Replace the igniter with a duplicate.

Clean a gas pilot light:

1. Turn off the gas shutoff valve to the gas fireplace or stove.
2. Remove the metal shield covering the pilot light.
3. Use a sewing needle to carefully remove debris in the pilot opening, blowing away any loose debris.
4. Turn the gas shutoff valve on and test the gas pilot light.

Adjust the pilot height:

1. Turn off the gas shutoff valve to the gas stove.
2. Locate the pilot adjustment screw on the side of the pilot, on the pilot gas line, or behind the control knob.
3. Turn the screw counterclockwise to increase the size of the pilot. The flame should be a sharp, blue cone, about ¼ to ⅜ inch high.

**Fix-It Tip**

Depending on what type and how much fuel you burn in a fireplace, have the chimney and flue inspected regularly by a professional. The CSIA (Chimney Safety Institute of America) certifies chimney sweeps who can clean a chimney and perform a general structural inspection.

# Fishing Reel

"I got a bite!" *Keeping* the bite on the line depends on more than skill. It also depends on your fishing tackle being in top shape so it can rewind the line with the proper speed and tension. When you've got a fish on the line, it's too late to fix a broken reel. So checking and fixing your fishing reel is a good thing to do before you set out to catch the big one.

## How Does It Work?

A fishing reel is a small winch mounted on a fishing rod to retract a fishing line. The four most common types of fishing reels are fly reels, open-face spinning reels, closed-face spinning reels, and bait-casting reels. If you're a fisher-person, you already know which to use when. Here's how to troubleshoot and repair them.

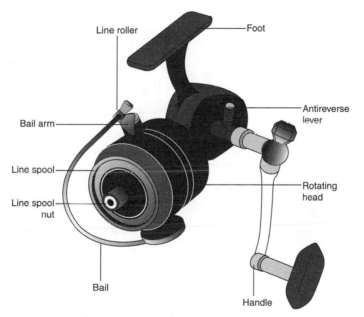

Components of a typical open-face spinning reel.

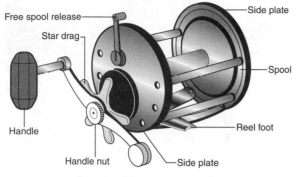

Free spool release

Side plate

Star drag

Spool

Handle

Reel foot

Handle nut

Side plate

Components of a typical bait-casting reel.

## What Can Go Wrong?

Keeping a fishing reel clean and lubricated will avoid many problems. Parts do, however, wear out and break. The spring on a fly reel spool can become fatigued, causing the spool to loosen. The spring-and-pawl mechanism that keeps the spool from turning on its own in the frame may wear out or break. The bail of an open-face spinning reel may break. Bait-casting reel drag washers and springs may wear or break.

**Fix-It Tip**

Fly reels last longer if cleaned with a small amount of alcohol or kerosene after every use. Also apply lightweight oil on other moving parts of the reel before storage. The same advice goes for spinning and bait-casting reels. A little preventive maintenance can add years to your fishing enjoyment.

## How Can I Identify the Problem?

If a fly reel is not working properly, you can replace a broken spool catch spring (see below).

If the bail of an open-face spinning reel breaks, you can replace it with a new one (see below).

If the bail springs of an open-face spinning reel don't make the bail snap over and catch the line properly, you can replace them (see below).

If a bait-casting reel does not operate properly, you can replace the drag washers and springs (see below).

**Fix-It Tip**

If you fish saltwater, you know that fishing tackle can be damaged by the salt if not rinsed thoroughly in fresh water. In addition, you should carefully lubricate moving parts *except* the fishing line, which can be damaged by lubricants.

## What Parts, Materials, and Tools Do I Need?

Replacement parts for fishing reels are available at sporting goods stores, fishing tackle stores, and from the manufacturer (see *Fix-It Resources*). The tools you will need to fix a fishing reel include these:

- Screwdrivers
- Pliers
- Wrenches
- Lubricants

## What Are the Steps to Fixing It?

Install a bail and spring on an open-face spinning reel:

1. Unscrew the nut that fastens the line spool to the reel.

Remove the line spool nut.

2. Unscrew the bail and remove the locknut securing the bail arm.
3. Remove the bail spool.

Bail    Spool

Nut

Remove the bail spool.

4. Inspect the bail and roller, replacing if damaged or corroded.
5. Install the new bail through the bail arm.
6. Remove the old spring using pliers.
7. Inspect and, if necessary, replace the spring. If okay, reinstall the spring.
8. Attach the roller on the bail and bail arm.
9. Tighten the bail locknut.

Inspect and lubricate or replace internal components as needed.

Replace drag washers and springs on a baitcasting reel:

1. Unscrew the handle nut and remove the handle, making sure you don't lose the drag washer or star drag.
2. Remove the plate screws, then the plate and spool.
3. Remove the bridge screws from the plate.
4. Remove the bridge, main gear, spring, and ratchet.
5. Remove, clean, and lubricate the drag washers and spring.
6. Replace any worn parts as needed.
7. Reassemble the reel components in reverse order.

Replace a spool catch spring on a fly reel:

1. Remove the axle cover and old spool catch V-spring.
2. Install the new V-spring against the catch.
3. Align the cover and spool screw holes, fastening the axle cover.

# Flooring, Resilient

Resilient flooring is tough. It stands up to traffic, food spills, and moving furniture for many years before starting to show its age. Lucky for you, resilient flooring problems are relatively easy to fix. Here's how.

## How Does It Work?

Resilient flooring is a big family of finished flooring products that includes vinyl, polyurethane, linoleum, cork, and rubber materials. Resilient flooring comes in sheets of 6 to 12 feet wide and in small tiles, typically 12 inches square. Both types are laid in solvent- or water-base adhesive on concrete, plywood, or hardboard. Some tiles have the adhesive already applied to the back, called self-adhesive tiles. Resilient floors are easy to maintain, and they resist moisture and stains.

## What Can Go Wrong?

Stains do sometimes happen. Tile edges come loose and curl. Bubbles lift the tile. Holes and gouges appear. All are fixable.

**Fix-It Tip**

To avoid stains setting in your resilient flooring, wipe up all spills immediately. The worst stain is mustard, especially on lower-grade resilient flooring that has a thin wear layer.

## How Can I Identify the Problem?

If your resilient floor has a stain that detergent won't banish, you can try several other products (see below).

If a tile has a loose edge, you can reglue it (see below).

If a bubble pops up, you can flatten it (see below).

If a small hole or gouge appears, you can fill it (see below).

If a tile is damaged further, you can replace it (see below).

If a small spot of a resilient sheet floor is damaged, you can patch it (see below).

**Fix-It Tip**

Small holes in vinyl flooring can be patched with a seam-welding product offered by the flooring's manufacturer or from flooring stores.

## What Parts, Materials, and Tools Do I Need?

You can purchase replacement tile, materials, and tools at flooring stores and home centers. However, the best source of replacement tile is the partial box of extra tiles left from the installation—if you have them. The materials and tools you'll need include these:

- Replacement tile
- Tile adhesive
- Notched adhesive spreader
- Putty knife
- Utility knife

- Framing square
- Towel
- Tile filler or clear nail polish
- Steel wool
- Electric iron
- Brush

## What Are the Steps to Fixing It?

Before using any cleaner, test it on an inconspicuous area. Try, in order, the following cleaners:

- Denatured alcohol
- Chlorine bleach (don't use on cork)
- Turpentine (don't use on rubber)
- Nail polish remover (don't use on vinyl or rubber)
- Lighter fluid (don't use on vinyl)

Remove stains from a resilient floor:

1. Apply the cleaner with a clean cloth and allow the surface to dry before continuing.
2. Rinse with water and let the floor dry again.
3. Apply polish or wax if recommended by the flooring manufacturer.

Reglue a loose tile:

1. Soften the adhesive under the tile by placing a clean towel under a warm electric iron on the tile surface.
2. Carefully lift the loosened tile with a putty knife, then remove adhesive from under the tile.
3. Use a notched spreader to apply a water-base adhesive under the tile.
4. Press the tile down firmly and place a weight on the tile overnight.

Remove a bubble under resilient flooring:

1. Soften the adhesive under the tile by placing a clean towel under a warm electric iron on the tile surface.
2. Use a utility knife to carefully slit the bubble from one edge to the other.
3. Use the utility knife's blade to hold the slit open while you insert a syringe of water-base adhesive (see *Fix Everything: Adhesives*) under the tile. You can buy adhesive in syringes at most hardware stores.
4. Press down firmly and place a weight on the tile overnight.

Repair a small hole or groove in a resilient floor:

1. Use a utility knife to scrape the damaged flooring surface until you reach the layer under the wear layer.
2. Apply a resilient tile filler product available from a flooring store. Alternately, you can use clear nail polish.
3. Allow the area to dry and buff with fine-grade steel wool.

Replace a single resilient tile:

1. Soften the adhesive under the tile by placing a clean towel under a warm electric iron on the tile surface.
2. Carefully lift the loosened tile with a putty knife and lift the tile out. Alternatively, you can cut the tile with a utility knife and remove it.

Cut the problem tile with a utility knife.

Remove the old tile and clean off excess adhesive from the surface where the new tile will go.

3. Remove old adhesive with a putty knife, making sure the surface where the new tile will go is flat and clean.

4. Test the size and location of the tile, trimming it as needed.

5. Apply new water-base adhesive using a notched adhesive spreader or brush, following instructions on the adhesive. If you are reinstalling a self-adhesive tile, remove the backing sheet.

Remove the backing sheet on a self-adhesive tile.

6. Heat the new tile by placing a clean towel under a warm electric iron on the tile surface.

7. Carefully place the new tile into the prepared spot.

Place the tile in the prepared spot.

8. Press down firmly and place a weight on the tile for 24 hours or as directed by the adhesive manufacturer. Some manufacturers suggest using a joint sealer between tiles.

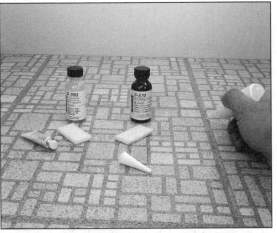

Install a joint sealer following the manufacturer's directions. Some need to be premixed.

Patch a resilient sheet floor:

1. Mark and cut around the damaged flooring area using a framing square and a utility knife.
2. Cut a new piece of flooring, using the old one as a guide. If the floor has a pattern, match it up exactly.
3. Use a putty knife and solvent to remove old adhesive from the subfloor or underlayment where the patch will be installed.
4. Test the size and location of the tile, trimming it as needed.
5. Apply adhesive to the patch using a notched adhesive spreader.
6. Place the patch in the prepared space.
7. Press down firmly and place a weight on the tile for 24 hours or as directed by the adhesive manufacturer. As soon as possible, wipe away any excess adhesive.

# Flooring, Wood

The beauty of wood flooring is hard to beat. It can also be hard to maintain. Dropped objects can dent it. Spills can damage the finish. Moving furniture can scratch it. What can you do about it? Fix it!

## How Does It Work?

Wood flooring comes in solid and laminate versions. Most solid wood flooring is ⅜ to ¾ inch thick, sanded and finished to stand up to abuse. The wood may be hardwood such as oak, walnut, cherry, or mahogany, or softwood such as pine or spruce. Laminate flooring material is made of layers with wood typically the main ingredient. The top layer may be either real wood or a photograph of real wood, covered by a polyurethane wear layer.

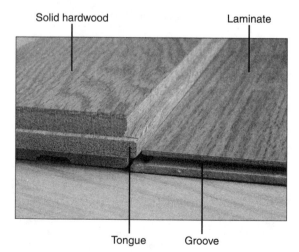

Solid hardwood      Laminate

Tongue      Groove

Wood flooring can range from ³⁄₁₆ to ¾ inch in height.

## What Can Go Wrong?

The most common problem with a wood floor is damage to the finish. The damage may be water marks, burns, scratches, or gouges. If the wood floor is one of the newer prefinished varieties, check with the manufacturer before attempting to repair the finish. Repairs to all wood floors depend on the finish that protects the wood. You may have to experiment a bit to find what works. Be sure to follow the manufacturer's directions when using any stripping or finishing products.

### Know Your Flooring

If you know the brand of the flooring finish installed in your home, you're halfway to fixing any problems. For example, if you find out it's Minwax spar urethane, you can read the side of a can to find out how to repair it. The same goes for Danish oil or any other finish. If your flooring is prefinished or a laminate, check with the manufacturer to find out what products are needed to repair the surface.

## How Can I Identify the Problem?

If there are water marks on a solid wood floor, you may be able to wax or steel wool them away (see below).

If there is a minor surface burn on a solid wood floor, sand it lightly and wipe it clean, then finish as desired.

If the burn is deeper, scrape out the burned wood with a sharp knife, and apply scratch hider, a putty stick, or stick shellac.

If the wear layer of a laminate floor is damaged, cover it with a polyurethane finish for protection.

If there is a shallow scratch, try scratch stick. For deeper scratches, fill with matching wood putty, putty stick, or stick shellac and let dry.

## What Parts, Materials, and Tools Do I Need?

Most of the materials and tools you'll need for fixing a wood floor are available at the local hardware store. They include these:

- Paste wax or solvent-base liquid floor wax
- Soft cloth
- Fine-grade (0000) steel wool
- Mineral spirits
- Putty stick
- Shellac stick
- Finish products

## What Are the Steps to Fixing It?

Eliminate water marks from solid wood flooring:

1. Rub the water marks with fine-grade steel wool and a little paste wax or a solvent-base liquid floor wax.
2. If the marks remain, wipe the wax with a soft cloth and rub again with steel wool and mineral spirits.
3. Wipe clean.

Periodically clean wood flooring with a product made for the type of finish the flooring has: stained, oiled, or polyurethane.

# Food Mixer

Food mixers are relatively simple appliances. Even so, they can have problems. When they do, here's how to take care of them.

## How Does It Work?

A food mixer is a motorized small appliance that blends recipe ingredients in a mixing bowl. A small motor rotates detachable beaters in opposite directions. A speed controller varies the electrical current delivered to the motor, thus controlling the beaters' speed.

There are two types of food mixers: portable (or hand) mixers and stationary (or stand) mixers. Portable mixers are lightweight, with small motors for easier mixing and blending jobs. Stand mixers use larger motors and components to manage bigger jobs, such as kneading dough or mixing large batches of ingredients. They both work about the same and can be fixed the same way, too.

## What Can Go Wrong?

As with other simple small appliances, problems typically involve the parts you use the most. The *Electrical Cord* may be faulty. Switches, the motor or motor fuse, and the speed control can all fail. Beaters can be bent or worn and gears can be misaligned.

> **Fix-It Tip**
>
> Mixer speed controls have numerous wires and contacts. If the contacts become corroded or need cleaning, use a small piece of emery paper. Of course, make sure you don't remove excessive amounts of the contact, or it will not close.

## How Can I Identify the Problem?

If the mixer doesn't work at all, make sure the power is on to the electrical outlet and check the *Electrical Cord*. Next, test the switch (see *Appliance Controls*), and check the *Fuse* and replace if defective.

If the mixer doesn't function on all speeds, test the speed control switch and replace it if faulty (see *Appliance Controls*).

If the motor hums but the beaters don't turn, test the *Motor* and replace it if it is seized.

If the mixer vibrates, check to see if the beater shafts are bent or worn and replace if needed. Also check internal gears for misalignment and service if needed (see *Motor*). Finally, examine the *Motor* and replace it if the shaft is bent or the motor is sparking.

> **Fix-It Tip**
>
> As you disassemble a food mixer, list the components on a piece of paper as they are removed. Note any special information, such as "black wire fastens to upper terminal." Then simply reverse the list to reassemble the appliance.

## What Parts, Materials, and Tools Do I Need?

Replacement parts for specific-model food mixers are available through the manufacturer or aftermarket parts suppliers (see *Fix-It Resources*). The tools you'll need to dismantle and repair a food mixer include these:

- Screwdrivers
- Small wrenches
- Multimeter

## What Are the Steps to Fixing It?

Disassembling, testing, and fixing a food mixer is similar to disassembling, testing, and fixing other small appliances. Refer to *Electrical Cord, Appliance Controls, Motor, Fuse,* and *Fix Everything: Multimeter* for repair guidelines.

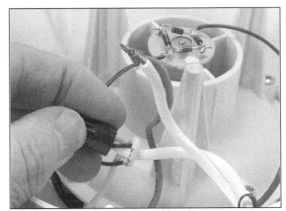

You can test the electrical cord by disconnecting it from the motor and using a multimeter.

Remove fasteners on the food mixer's base to access internal parts.

**Fix-It Tip**

Modern food mixers typically contain circuit boards. Do not attempt to repair them. If one tests defective or you suspect that it is so, remove and replace it with an identical circuit board from a parts supplier.

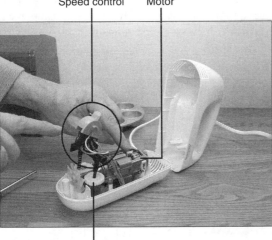

Speed control    Motor

Gears

A food mixer is simply a motor with gears and speed controls.

# Food Processor

Food processors are food mixers on steroids. They have more power and do more tasks than mixers. That means they also have more things that may need fixing. If your food processor isn't working as well as it should—or at all—let's take it to the Fix-It Club.

## How Does It Work?

A food processor is an appliance that mixes dough and chops, slices, dices, and liquefies food. It has a larger capacity and a larger motor than either a blender or a mixer, and can replace both smaller appliances.

There are two types of food processors: direct drive and belt drive. A direct-drive food processor is similar to a food blender, with the motor underneath the food bowl. A belt-drive food processor places the bowl and motor side by side, connecting the two with a drive belt and wheels.

## What Can Go Wrong?

Because they can do more, food processors may require more repair than other small kitchen appliances. Even so, there are many similarities. The *Electrical Cord, Motor,* motor *Fuse,* and switches may fail. The blade can become dirty or damaged. The gear or drive belt can become worn or broken. Seals can fail. One of the most common problems is a belt that needs adjusting or replacing.

**Fix-It Tip**

Every time you wash a food processor's bowl and blades, take time to inspect them for obvious cracks or damage.

## How Can I Identify the Problem?

If the food processor won't run at all, be sure power is on at the outlet and check the *Electrical Cord.* Check the *Motor* and the *Fuse.*

If the unit runs intermittently, check the wire connections and repair any that are faulty. Also check the *Motor* and, on belt-drive models, check the belt for condition and correct tension. Replace or adjust as needed.

If the unit doesn't run at some speeds, check the multispeed switch (see *Appliance Controls*) and the wire connections using a multimeter (see *Fix Everything: Multimeter*).

If the motor turns but the blades don't, clean and lubricate the blade and repair or replace if damaged. On direct-drive models, check gears for wear and replace if worn or broken. On belt-drive models, check the drive belt and replace it if it is broken, or adjust tension if needed.

If the bowl leaks, make sure the bowl is tightened onto the base; check the seal and replace it if it is damaged.

**Fix-It Tip**

About once a year, apply a small amount of white lubricant paste (available in tubes) on gears, bearings, or other moving parts to reduce friction. Make sure the lubricant doesn't touch or rub off on electrical components, where it can conduct electricity.

## What Parts, Materials, and Tools Do I Need?

Motors, drives, gears, and belts should be replaced with parts from the manufacturer or an authorized aftermarket supplier (see *Fix-It Resources*). Common tools for disassembling and repairing food processors include these:

- Screwdrivers
- Pliers
- Wrenches
- Lubricant
- Multimeter

## What Are the Steps to Fixing It?

Disassemble a food processor:

1. Remove the control knob and remove any screws that hold the body together.
2. Remove plugs as needed to disconnect the circuit board from the electrical source. Remove other components that restrict access to the internal parts.
3. Turn the processor upside down and remove the base. In some cases you'll first need to pry off some feet.
4. Remove the drive belt and/or the drive gear.
5. Remove the *Motor*. Typically, this means disconnecting the cord and removing any motor mounting screws.

Service a gear:

1. Remove the processor's housing and components as needed to access the gears (see *Motor*).
2. Clean the gears with a toothbrush and inspect them for wear or damage.
3. Replace any damaged gears. If the gears are in good condition, lubricate them and reassemble.

Adjust or replace a food processor's drive belt:

1. Remove the housing as needed to access the drive belt.
2. Move the drive belt by hand to determine whether the belt is too loose or too snug.
3. Loosen the adjustment wheel setscrew or nut and adjust the belt tension as needed.
4. If necessary, replace the belt with one of the exact same dimensions.
5. Make sure the adjustment screw or nut is tightened so it does not work loose.

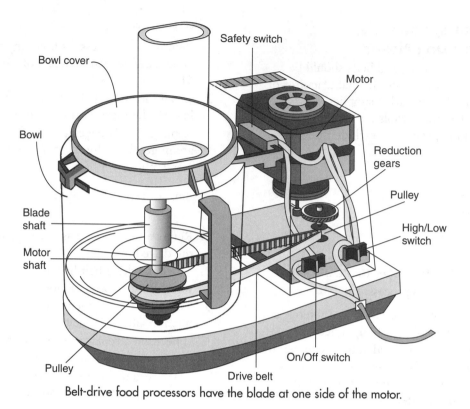

Bowl cover

Safety switch

Motor

Reduction gears

Pulley

High/Low switch

Bowl

Blade shaft

Motor shaft

Pulley

Drive belt

On/Off switch

Belt-drive food processors have the blade at one side of the motor.

Service a food processor's drive shaft:

1. Disassemble the unit to expose the drive shaft.
2. Turn the drive shaft by hand; if it turns easily, it is probably worn and requires replacement.

3. Remove the drive shaft following instructions in the owner's manual. Some units pry off, while others are held in place with standard fasteners.
4. Inspect the old drive shaft for the cause of the problem. Repair or replace as needed.

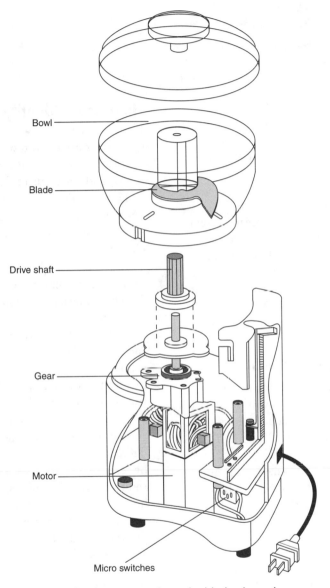

Bowl

Blade

Drive shaft

Gear

Motor

Micro switches

Direct-drive food processors have the blade above the motor.

# Food Slicer

Not all cooks have a food slicer in their kitchen, but those who do wouldn't be without it. It does only one job, but it does it well—unless it needs to be fixed. Here's how to fix it.

## How Does It Work?

A food slicer is a small appliance for quick, accurate cutting of meat, cheese, bread, vegetables, and other foods. It uses a motor to spin a serrated circular blade. Food held in a sliding tray is cut as it is pushed past the spinning blade. The stainless-steel blade is removable for cleaning, but it cannot be sharpened. You'll need to replace it if it becomes dull or is damaged.

## What Can Go Wrong?

Because a food slicer is just a blade and a motor, few things can go wrong with it. A dull blade or a buildup of food residue is usually the culprit behind slicer problems. Blades and gears can be damaged. The power cord, switch, or motor can be faulty. The thickness guide and tray guides can be dirty. The slicer can become jammed. The blade can be clogged with food, or be loose or dull. The thickness guide may need adjustment.

**Fix-It Tip**

To reduce stress on gears, let the motor warm up for a few seconds before slicing, especially denser foods.

## How Can I Identify the Problem?

If the slicer doesn't work, make sure power is on at the outlet and test the *Electrical Cord*. Test the switch (see *Appliance Controls*) and the *Motor*, and repair or replace if faulty.

If the slicer slips during use, clean the rubber feet and any suction cups that hold the slicer in place with denatured alcohol or glass cleaner.

If the slicer makes excessive noise, access the gears and examine for wear or damage (see *Motor*); replace any missing feet to prevent rocking.

If the food tray doesn't slide smoothly, clean the tray guides with a clean sponge dipped in soapy water and lubricate with a few drops of salad oil; remove any food residue around the tray and blade and clean both with soapy water.

If excessive pressure is required for slicing, remove the blade and clean it with soapy water. Tighten the blade retaining screw with a coin or screwdriver. Replace a dull blade. Also try removing the thickness guide and washing it in hot soapy water or in the top rack of the dishwasher, then lubricate it as needed. Adjust the thickness guide to cut thinner pieces and remove any pieces of food jammed in the guide.

**Fix-It Tip**

You can make slicing thin steaks and fish easier by chilling the meat first in the refrigerator. Don't freeze it.

## What Parts, Materials, and Tools Do I Need?

Replacement parts for a food slicer should come from the original manufacturer or an aftermarket supplier (see *Fix-It Resources*). Tools you'll need for disassembly and repair of a food slicer include these:

- Screwdrivers
- Denatured alcohol or glass cleaner
- Petroleum jelly

## What Are the Steps to Fixing It?

Disassemble a food slicer:

1. Unplug the slicer's *Electrical Cord* for safety.
2. Loosen the retaining screw and tap the slicing blade lightly from behind to loosen it. Remove the screw and carefully lift the blade away.
3. Remove the tray by tipping the slicer over onto its motor and gently prying the tray guide off the rails.

4. Support the motor with one hand and loosen the motor retaining screw, then slide the motor away from the slicer head.
5. Remove screws as needed to separate the halves of the motor housing, exposing the pinion gear, *Motor*, and on-off switch (see *Appliance Controls*) for inspection, repair, or replacement.

Service the thickness guide:

1. Loosen the control knob and remove the thickness guide's threaded shaft.
2. Remove, wash, and dry all parts of the thickness guide.
3. Lubricate the guide shaft with petroleum jelly, then reinstall the guide.

> **Fix-It Tip**
>
> For fewest repairs, take a moment after using a slicer to clean it, especially the blade. Of course, make sure it is unplugged first.

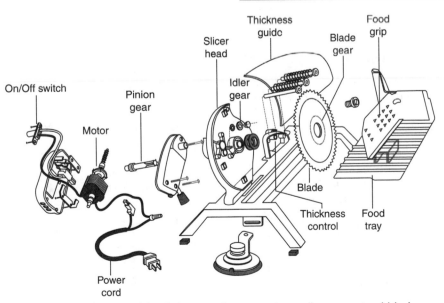

Exploded view of a typical food slicer appliance; it's basically a motorized blade.

# Forced-Air Distribution

Many home heating and cooling systems move air throughout the home using a forced-air distribution system. A gas furnace, oil furnace, and electric furnace all do this, as does a central air conditioner. (See *Furnace, Gas; Furnace, Oil; Furnace, Electric;* and *Air Conditioner, Central.*) Rather than repeat this information in each of the system guides, let's take a look at how air—no matter how it's made hot or cool—can be distributed efficiently.

## How Does It Work?

A forced-air distribution system simply picks up air from the heating or cooling source, typically a large furnace or air conditioner, and moves it through the house in large pipes called heating ducts. The return system brings cooler air to the heating device. An encased electric fan, called a blower, moves the air through the system as needed.

## What Can Go Wrong?

If the air isn't being distributed, first check the *Comfort Controls* to make sure they are working properly. Also make sure that distribution isn't stopped by a blocked filter. Clean or replace filters as needed. Also clean the blower blades.

If the blower is running, but not distributing air, check the blower belt or direct drive (see below); replace a faulty belt (see below).

If the blower motor does not work, test the *Motor* and replace it if it proves faulty (see below).

If the blower is working, but air distribution isn't even throughout the house, balance the system (see below).

## What Parts, Materials, and Tools Do I Need?

Replacement parts for forced-air systems are available through larger hardware stores, heating system supply houses, and the blower manufacturer (see *Fix-It Resources*). Leaks in ducts are relatively easy to seal using duct tape. Tools and parts you might need include these:

- Screwdrivers
- Wrenches
- Lubricant
- Replacement filter
- Multimeter

## What Are the Steps to Fixing It?

Replace a filter:

1. Turn off power to the furnace at the *Electrical Service Panel*.
2. Find the filter. It is typically near or above the blower motor.

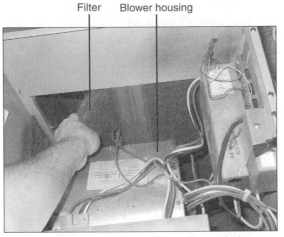

Filter    Blower housing

This forced-air system filter is located on a ledge above the blower. Others are accessed through a narrow door in the blower chamber.

3. Wearing breathing protection, carefully remove the filter. Clean or replace it as needed. Some filters can be washed, while others require replacement. Check the owner's manual for specific information and model number.

4. Reinstall the access panel and restore power to the furnace.

Adjust blower-belt tension:

1. Turn off power to the furnace at the *Electrical Service Panel.*

2. Remove the access panel to the blower and inspect the belt for any cracks or signs of wear.

3. Check for slack in the blower belt by depressing it midway between the pulleys. If there is more than about 1 inch slack, tighten the belt adjustment; if less, loosen the adjustment. Typically, there is an adjustment bolt on or near the pulleys.

4. Reinstall the access panel and restore power to the furnace.

Test and replace a direct-drive blower *Motor:*

1. Turn off power at the *Electrical Service Panel* or the unit-disconnect switch.

2. Remove access panels to the blower.

Blower motor                Controls

The blower motor has numerous electrical leads to and from it. Look for an electrical diagram near the blower for connection information, or check the owner's manual.

3. Remove the motor wire leads, marking them for later reinstallation.

4. Carefully discharge and disconnect the capacitor following the blower manufacturer's instructions. Remember that a capacitor acts like a high-voltage battery that can shock you even when it is disconnected.

5. Remove the retaining bolts on the mounting bracket.

6. Test the motor following instructions in the *Motor* guide. Replace the motor with one of the exact size, model, and rating if needed.

Balance the distribution system:

1. Open all registers throughout the house.
2. Find and open all dampers within the forced-air ducting system. They may be under the floor (in a basement or crawl space) or in a ceiling (in an attic or access area).
3. Place identical thermometers 3 feet from major ducts for 30 to 60 minutes and note temperature differences. To verify, rotate thermometer locations and retest.
4. Adjust the dampers as needed to produce even heat through each room of the house.
5. Once the system is balanced, mark the position of each damper for future reference. If you also have an air conditioning system that uses the forced-air distribution system, turn the furnace off and the AC on to rerun the test. Adjust and mark the dampers for balance during the cooling season.

# Framing System

A home's framing system is its skeleton. The system includes the floor frame, wall frames, and the roof frame. More than 90 percent of U.S. homes are framed with wood, but steel is an increasingly popular framing material. Though you may not directly do any fixing to your home's framing system, you need to know how it's built because the framing system supports the *Electrical System, Plumbing System, Drywall,* and many other components of your home.

## How Does It Work?

The floor frame sits on a house's foundation and consists of posts, beams, sill plates, joists, and the subfloor. Wall frames include horizontal plates and the vertical studs. Extra supports, called headers, are added above windows and doors. The roof frame is made of rafters and is usually supported by ceiling joists. Once the frame is built, plumbing, electrical, HVAC, and other systems are installed.

### Finding Studs

Need to find a stud in a wall? You can purchase a stud finder at any hardware store; directions are included. Alternatively, you can tap on a wall and listen for the hollow space between studs. In addition, electrical receptacles and switches typically are nailed to one side of a stud; remove the face plate to check location. In most homes, studs are spaced 16 inches o.c. (on center), so once you find one stud you typically can find the next with a measuring tape.

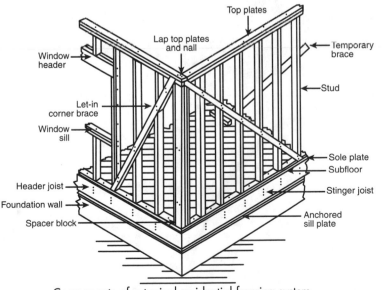

Components of a typical residential framing system.

## What Can Go Wrong?

A home's framing is generally quite sturdy and should last for many years, even several generations. Most problems that occur are actually in the coverings attached to the framing—the roof, the ceiling, the walls, and the floors. Framing can be damaged by water leaks and pest infestations. Roofs, ceilings, walls, and floors can be water damaged and can suffer dents, holes, gouges, and other hurts.

## How Can I Identify the Problem?

If you find damage to the framing of your home, you probably will need professional assistance, maybe including an exterminator.

If there is damage to the roof, ceilings, walls, or floors of your home, consult the appropriate guide in this section for repair details and a list of needed tools.

# Furnace, Electric

There are numerous ways to heat your home. One of the most popular in many regions—where electricity is less expensive than other fuels—is with an electric furnace. Other ways of heating homes include gas and oil furnaces, steam boilers, and wall or freestanding electric heaters. (See *Furnace, Gas; Furnace, Oil; Boiler, Steam;* and *Heater, Electric.*)

## How Does It Work?

An electric furnace uses electrical energy to warm air for distribution throughout the home. An electric forced-air heating (EFA) system includes a *Heating Element, Comfort Controls,* and *Forced-Air Distribution* systems, each covered in other guides. The source of power, electricity, runs through the *Electrical Service Panel.*

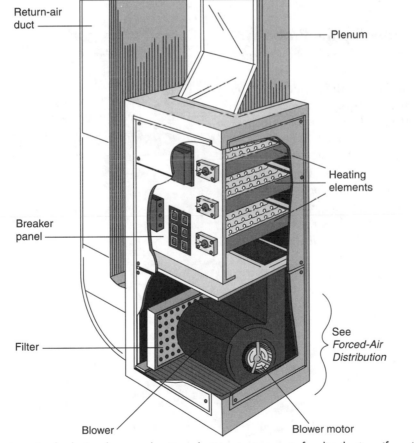

Return-air duct

Plenum

Heating elements

Breaker panel

Filter

See *Forced-Air Distribution*

Blower

Blower motor

An electric furnace is a simple device that uses heating elements to warm air for distribution. If you're not getting heat, first check the unit's breaker or fuse panel.

## What Can Go Wrong?

The furnace may not come on. The system may not produce enough heat. The furnace may short cycle (turn on and off repeatedly). The blower may run continuously. The furnace may be noisy.

> **Fix-It Tip**
>
> Don't try to repair electric furnace heating elements or other major electrical components. Refer to *Heating Element* and other guides for troubleshooting information and call a professional HVAC (heat-ventilation-air conditioning) technician for service.

## How Can I Identify the Problem?

If the furnace won't run, check the *Electrical Service Panel* for a blown fuse or tripped breaker. Also make sure the power switch on or near the furnace is turned on. Check the unit for a reset button and try it. Some units have a built-in breaker or fuse panel.

If there is not enough heat, raise the thermostat setting five degrees to see if it turns the unit on. If the unit still does not generate enough heat, check the *Comfort Controls*. Clean or replace a dirty filter, clean the blower assembly (see *Forced-Air Distribution*), and make sure that all registers are open and not blocked.

If the furnace turns on and off repeatedly (cycles), clean or replace the filter and clean the blower assembly (see *Forced-Air Distribution*).

If the furnace is noisy, make sure access panels are mounted and fastened securely; spray squeaking belts with fan-belt dressing and replace worn or damaged belts; adjust the blower belt; lubricate *Motor* and blower oil ports.

If the element does not heat, refer to *Heating Element* for guidance.

If some rooms are too cool and others too warm, the distribution system may require balancing. Refer to the guide on *Forced-Air Distribution*.

> **Fix-It Tip**
>
> If resetting circuit breakers or replacing damaged fuses in the furnace and the *Electrical Service Panel* doesn't restore power to the furnace, call an HVAC technician or an electrical contractor with electric furnace training and experience.

# Furnace, Gas

Many people totally ignore the home heating system—until it quits. That's when you pull out this book and quickly read up on fixing heating systems. If your system is powered by natural or propane gas, keep reading. Otherwise, check the guides on *Furnace, Electric; Furnace, Oil; Boiler, Steam;* or *Boiler, Hot Water.* If you suspect problems in the *Forced-Air Distribution* system or the *Comfort Controls,* check those guides as well. Then meet back here!

## How Does It Work?

Natural or propane gas from an outside source is piped to the furnace where it is burned to produce heat. Usually a fan-driven forced-air distribution system blows the warmed air through ducts that vent into the various rooms of the house. Older gas furnaces use a standing-pilot ignition. Maintenance involves turning off the pilot each spring and relighting it each fall. Newer, more efficient gas furnaces use an electric spark to light the gas as necessary.

## What Can Go Wrong?

Most gas furnaces are quite reliable. What are the symptoms of problems? The furnace may not produce heat or may not produce enough heat. The pilot light may go out repeatedly or refuse to light. The thermocouple may be faulty. The pilot may light but not ignite the burner. The furnace may be noisy. There are some maintenance and a few minor repairs that you can make. However, major service should be left to a trained technician.

**Fix-It Tip**

To minimize problems with your gas furnace, take time each month to check the air filter and clean or replace it if necessary. Once a year, clean the blower blades, lubricate the blower motor, and inspect the belt.

## How Can I Identify the Problem?

If there is no heat, check the *Electrical Service Panel* for a burned fuse or tripped breaker. Relight the pilot light (see below).

If there is not enough heat, adjust the burner air shutter (see below); and clean the burner ports (see below).

If the pilot light does not light or does not stay lit, clean the pilot orifice carefully with a toothpick, test the thermocouple and replace it if it is faulty (see below).

If the flame flickers, adjust the pilot (see below).

If there is an exploding sound when the burner ignites, adjust the pilot to a higher setting and clean the pilot orifice and the burner ports.

If the burner takes more than a few seconds to ignite, clean the pilot orifice and adjust the pilot light.

If the burner flame is uneven, clean the burner ports. If the burner flame is very yellow, clean the burner; open vents in the furnace room to provide more air; adjust the burner air shutter.

If the furnace makes a rumbling noise when the burners are off, clean the burner and adjust the burner air shutter.

If the air is too dry, wash or replace the evaporator pad if you have a humidifier; test the humidistat (see *Comfort Controls*); and adjust the water-level float to raise the water level.

If some rooms are too cool and others too warm, the distribution system may require balancing. Refer to the guide on *Forced-Air Distribution*.

> **Fix-It Tip**
>
> Be sure your filter is the right size for your furnace.

## What Parts, Materials, and Tools Do I Need?

Some replacement parts for gas furnaces are interchangeable (filters, fasteners) and available at your local hardware store. Others, such as burners and controls, must be purchased from the manufacturer or aftermarket supplier (see *Fix-It Resources*) through a heating equipment supplier listed in your local telephone book.

The primary tools you will need for fixing a gas furnace include these:

- Screwdrivers
- Wrenches
- Pliers
- Wire brush
- Multimeter

## What Are the Steps to Fixing It?

To light the pilot on a standing-pilot (always on) ignition system, follow the lighting instructions located near the control. Otherwise, try these steps:

Light the pilot:

1. Set the control knob to the *pilot* position. Hold a long match under the pilot gas port.
2. Press the control knob; the pilot should light. Hold the control knob down until the flame is burning brightly (about 30 seconds). Release pressure on the knob, and turn it to the *on* position.

Press and hold the pilot control knob to start the pilot.

3. If the pilot goes out when you release the control knob, try relighting, holding the control knob down longer. If the pilot again goes out, check the thermocouple (below).

Adjust the pilot:

1. Remove any cap covering the pilot adjusting screw on a combination control.
2. Turn the adjusting screw counterclockwise to increase the flame or clockwise to decrease it. It is correctly adjusted when the flame envelops the thermocouple bulb by ½ inch and appears dark blue with a small yellow tip.

Test and replace a thermocouple:

1. Hold the control knob to *pilot* and light the pilot as above.
2. Unscrew the thermocouple fitting with an open-ended wrench.
3. Set a multimeter (see *Fix Everything: Multimeter*) to the DVC (lowest voltage) scale.
4. Clip one multimeter lead to the end of the thermocouple tube nearest the pilot, and the other lead to the fitting on the other end of the tube.
5. If the multimeter shows a reading besides zero, the thermocouple is functioning. Replace the thermocouple tube.
6. If there is no reading, you will need to clean or replace the thermocouple following steps 7 through 11.
7. Release the control knob and shut off the main gas valve on the gas-supply pipe that leads into the burner. Shut off power to the burner at the *Electrical Service Panel*.
8. Remove the thermocouple from its mounting bracket.
9. Wipe the combination control clean and install a new thermocouple, tightening it by hand, then give it a one-quarter turn with a wrench.
10. Insert the thermocouple into the pilot bracket, being careful not to crimp the tubing.
11. Turn on power to the furnace and relight the pilot (above).

Adjust an adjustable burner air shutter:

1. Set the thermostat to its highest setting to keep the burner running. Once the furnace has heated up, remove the burner access panel and loosen the locking screw.
2. Open the shutter by turning it to the right until the blue base of the flame appears to lift slightly from the burner port surface. Then close the shutter until the flame reseats itself on the surface.

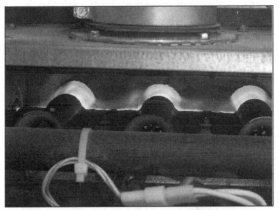

Make sure the flame is well-formed and blue.

Clean removable burner tubes and ports:

1. Shut off gas and power to the furnace.
2. Unscrew or loosen and remove the tubes from the supporting bracket.
3. Carefully clean the tubes with a brush or vacuum, making sure not to damage the burner ports.
4. Use a stiff wire to clear any debris from clogged ports.

# Furnace, Oil

In many regions of the country, oil is king. It's the most popular (read: least expensive) fuel for heating homes and other structures. Even if oil isn't as cheap today, it was when the furnace was purchased. It may be too expensive to convert to another fuel source. Other popular heating systems include the *Furnace, Gas; Furnace, Electric; Boiler, Steam;* and *Boiler, Hot Water.* Fortunately, an oil furnace is simple in operation and relatively trouble-free. When it's not, it's time to fix it—or call someone who can.

## How Does It Work?

An oil furnace uses a low-grade petroleum derivative as fuel to heat air, hot water, or steam. An oil forced-air system (OFA) includes the blower and ducting to distribute the heated air throughout the house. Modern home oil systems use pressure burners. Oil is sprayed into a combustion chamber at high pressure, propelled by a blower, and ignited by an electric spark. The oil burns as the mist is sprayed. These units are more efficient than older models.

## What Can Go Wrong?

Oil burners are generally quite reliable. Routine maintenance is the key to avoiding expensive repairs. And there are several things you can do before calling for repair service. The burner may not run, or may run but not fire. The burner may cycle too often or it may smoke or squeal. The chimney may smoke.

## How Can I Identify the Problem?

If the burner doesn't run, set the thermostat a few degrees higher than normal to see if it comes on. If it still doesn't come on, check switches (see *Appliance Controls*), and breakers and fuses (see *Electrical Service Panel*). If the unit has a reset button, press it. Also oil the *Motor* at any oil ports (see below).

If the unit doesn't want to start and run, first check the *Electrical Service Panel* to make sure that the ignition is getting power. If there is power, check the built-in safety controls (see below) that may turn the system off if they perceive problems.

If the burner cycles too often, replace the filter (see below). Also, oil and adjust the blower (see *Forced-Air Distribution*).

If the burner runs but won't fire, make sure the oil valves are open and that there's oil in the tank. Check the tank level with a clean stick.

If the burner smokes or squeals, shut off the unit, let it cool, and fill the oil cups. Recheck them after the motor has run for an hour.

If the chimney smokes even after the flue has warmed up, the unit is wasting fuel; call for professional repair.

**Safety Controls**

Oil furnaces and other heating systems include safety devices that monitor operation and turn off the unit if something goes wrong. In some cases, the safety device can be the problem.

If you encounter an operating problem with an oil furnace, first reset the safety and try again.

If the burner kicks off again, shut off all power at the *Electrical Service Panel*; the burner motor and ignition may be protected by separate fuses or breakers.

If the sensor has a photocell, wipe it with a clean rag or tissue and see if the furnace starts.

If the safety is a stack switch mounted on the flue, remove the screw holding the unit to the stack, slide it out, and wipe off the sensor.

If the furnace won't start after three tries, seek professional assistance. Unburned oil can accumulate in the combustion chamber and "flash back."

> **Fix-It Tip**
>
> At the beginning of the heating season and every month or two during it, inspect the oil heating system for filter condition and clean as needed. In addition, older furnaces require the burner *Motor* to be lubricated periodically. Newer units have permanent lubrication. You can tell which your system has by looking for *oil* ports where the lubricant, a few drops of light non-detergent oil, is added.

## What Parts, Materials, and Tools Do I Need?

Some replacement parts for oil furnaces can be found at larger hardware stores, and others are available through your fuel dealer or its supplier. Ask. The tools you'll need for fixing an oil furnace include these:

- Screwdrivers
- Wrenches
- Replacement filter
- Lightweight lubricating oil
- Vacuum cleaner

> **Fix-It Tip**
>
> Just before the heating season starts, make sure you inspect the chimney and flue for air leaks and pests (animal and bird nests). Repair any cracks. Test for air leaks by using a burning candle.

## What Are the Steps to Fixing It?

Clean or replace a filter:

1. Open or remove the blower access door, typically located on the front or side of the furnace housing.
2. Remove the filter; some slide out, while others are pressed into place.
3. Use a vacuum cleaner to remove dirt and dust from the area around the filter. Some units have a dry-foam filter that also needs periodic vacuuming.
4. Replace the filter with one of the same dimensions and density, preferably the model suggested by the manufacturer.
5. Close or reinstall the blower door, making sure that any interlocks are in the correct position to operate.

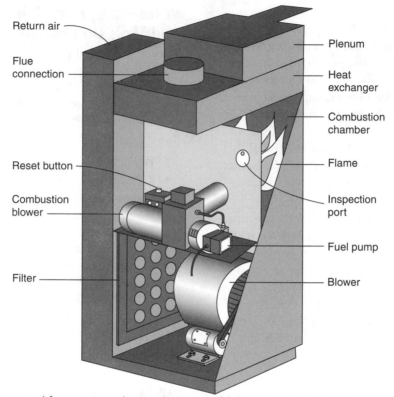

Return air

Flue connection

Reset button

Combustion blower

Filter

Plenum

Heat exchanger

Combustion chamber

Flame

Inspection port

Fuel pump

Blower

An oil furnace is similar to other types of furnaces. The main difference is that heating oil fuels the burner that heats the air.

# Furniture, Upholstered

Few things offer more comfort than an over-stuffed chair. However, being so popular means that chair gets lots of wear and tear. The same goes for sofas and other padded furniture. It's a good thing that the Fix-It Club knows what to do when upholstered furniture loses its comfort.

## How Does It Work?

Upholstered furniture is padded furniture that is covered with fabric, leather, or vinyl. A frame provides support and sets the shape of upholstered furniture. Cotton or foam padding gives the furniture lightweight mass, making it soft.

## What Can Go Wrong?

Upholstered furniture can get dirty. The upholstery can be torn or burned. A seam can fail.

## How Can I Identify the Problem?

If your upholstered furniture is dirty, you can clean it with commercial upholstery cleaner. Make sure it is a cleaner intended for the specific type of upholstery you need to clean and follow the manufacturer's instructions carefully. Or try a powerful new oxygen cleaner. Whatever you use, test-clean an inconspicuous area first.

If cleaning isn't sufficient and the upholstery is solid color, you can try spray-on coloring agents to give it a covering color.

If the upholstery suffers a tear or torn seam, you may be able to sew it (see *Fix Everything: Sewing*) or glue it (see *Fix Everything: Adhesives*).

If the tear or seam cannot be sewn without showing, or there is a small hole, you may be able to patch it (see below).

If tacks come out of upholstered furniture, you can replace them.

If the frame is damaged, see *Furniture, Wood* for tips on repairing wood components.

## What Parts, Materials, and Tools Do I Need?

You can get upholstery materials and fabrics from an upholstery supply store, some fabric stores, and on the Internet. Adhesives are available at many retail stores. The tools you will need to fix upholstered furniture include these:

- Upholstery needles
- Sewing needles
- Upholstery thread
- Fabric adhesive
- Spray-on color
- Iron-on patches
- Upholstery tacks
- Small hammer
- Electric iron

## What Are the Steps to Fixing It?

Patch a tear in fabric or vinyl upholstery:

1. Insert an iron-on patch through the tear so that the adhesive side contacts the backside of the torn fabric.
2. Iron one side of the tear until the patch sticks firmly to the back of the cloth on that side.
3. Adjust the torn spot for smoothness over the other side of the patch.
4. Iron the second half of the patch, moving it toward the tear.
5. If necessary, apply fabric adhesive to the tear for a stronger bond.

Patch a hole in fabric or vinyl upholstery:

1. Locate and remove excess material from a hidden area of the upholstered furniture sufficiently large to cover the hole.
2. Trim the upholstery to match the hole and surrounding pattern.
3. Apply an iron-on patch (see above) or apply adhesive to a backing cloth to the back of the damaged area.

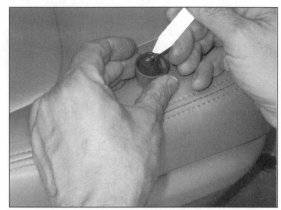

You can purchase vinyl repair kits at larger hardware and automotive stores to repair a tear in vinyl upholstery.

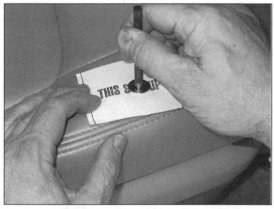

Vinyl repair kits typically include a texture pad to duplicate the fabric's texture for a seamless repair.

**Fix-It Tip**

Which adhesive will work best in repairing upholstered furniture? Check the information under *Fix Everything: Adhesives* for specific guidance, or take the fabric sample to an upholstery fabric or sewing supply store for assistance.

4. Use fabric adhesive or a small iron-on patch to install the material patch in the hole.
5. Allow the adhesive to fully dry before use.

# Furniture, Wood

Without furniture we'd be sitting on the floor, surrounded by food, dishes, and an assortment of appliances and utensils. Wood furniture holds the *things* in our lives. Fortunately, furniture doesn't just fall apart; it gives warnings. And most furniture can easily be repaired—if you know how.

## How Does It Work?

Wood furniture is a broad category of living equipment around your home. It includes chairs, tables, beds, desks, and free-standing cabinets. Because built-in cabinets are similar in design and repair, we'll cover them here, too. Sofas and upholstered chairs are covered under *Furniture, Upholstered*.

The components of wood furniture and cabinets include doors, shelves, drawers, frame, and finish. A furniture door is a swinging or sliding barrier that opens or closes to offer access; doors are attached with hinges, and some use hardware to make opening them easier. A shelf is a thin, flat component fastened at intervals within the cabinet. A drawer is a sliding box or receptacle opened by pulling out and closed by pushing in; it uses runners or tracks on the bottom or side to allow movement. The furniture frame is functional, holding components together, and the finish is decorative and protective.

## What Can Go Wrong?

Doors sag, stick, or refuse to close properly. Glass panels in doors get broken. Sliding cabinet and furniture doors stick and bind. Shelves sag. Drawers stick due to humidity or damage, or because glides need fixing. Furniture joints become loose. Cracks and splits appear. Wood surfaces get burned, scratched, gouged, and damaged by moisture. Veneer blisters and separates.

### Humidity and Wood

Humidity—moist air—is the enemy of wood, especially fitted wood. Wood absorbs moisture and expands or dries out and contracts. As it does so, furniture doors, drawers, and other surfaces either don't fit snugly or they fit too snugly. The solution is to live in an area of moderate humidity, to equip your sealed home with humidifiers and dehumidifiers, or to buy plastic furniture. Alternatively, you can select furniture that doesn't have precise fits and uses metal glides, and make sure the surface is well-sealed against moisture.

## How Can I Identify the Problem?

If a cabinet or furniture door sags, sticks, or refuses to close properly, first suspect the hinges (see below).

If the door still sticks, try the steps for unsticking a door (see below).

If the door itself is warped, try to straighten it (see below).

If a hinge is recessed too deeply, you may be able to correct it with a shim (see below).

If a glass panel is broken, you can replace it (see below).

If a sliding door binds or sticks, you can widen its channel; if it wobbles in its track, you can shim the channel (see below).

If a shelf sags, reinforce it (see below).

If a drawer bottom is warped, turn the drawer bottom upside down or replace the bottom (see below).

If you suspect a drawer is out of square, you can resquare it (see below).

If a drawer seems to stick in a particular spot, it may need lubricating; try running a bar of soap along the cleats and runners.

If lubrication does not work, try lightly sanding the runners, testing the drawer often. Or you may need to realign the guide or tracks (see below).

If a wood runner is damaged, you can repair it (see below).

If a furniture joint becomes loose (for example, a leg wobbles), you can reinforce it with glue (see below), or you can add a couple of nails or screws angled into the joint, then cover the holes with wood fill.

If a split appears, such as in a wood chair seat, you can repair it (see below).

If the wood surface of a piece of furniture is burned, you can minimize the damage (see below).

If a piece of wood furniture has a scratch or minor gouge, you may be able to camouflage it with a furniture touch-up stick, or you can repair it (see below).

If veneer blisters or separates, you can repair it (see below).

## What Parts, Materials, and Tools Do I Need?

Furniture repair is a big business. It's also a big hobby. You'll find hundreds of replacement parts, materials, and tools for fixing furniture and cabinets available at hardware stores and home improvement centers. If you enjoy fixing furniture, refer to *Fix-It Resources* for books and suppliers that can show you how to do even more.

The tools you will need to fix furniture and cabinets include these:

- Screwdrivers
- Clamps
- Awl
- Nails, brads, screws
- Hacksaw
- Nail puller
- Plane
- Hammer
- Sandpaper
- Pry bar
- Putty knife
- Carpenter's square
- Chalk
- Wood wedges
- Wood filler
- Wood glue
- Measuring tape
- Metal braces
- Steel wool
- Furniture polish or wax
- Mineral spirits
- Touch-up stick

**Fix-It Tip**

What can you do if a drawer sticks so bad that you can't remove it from the furniture or cabinet? Try removing the drawer below and pressing upward on the bottom of the stuck drawer to slide it forward. You may also be able to grasp the back of the stuck drawer and carefully push it forward.

A touch-up stick is useful for filling in small gouges.

- Utility knife
- Heat lamp or high-wattage hair dryer
- Wax paper

## What Are the Steps to Fixing It?

Repair a gouge in wood furniture:

Apply wood filler or putty to fill in a gouge or deep scratch on furniture.

1. Using a putty knife, fill gouges or deep scratches with wood filler, slightly overfilling so you can sand down to a flat surface. Let the filler dry thoroughly.
2. Using coarse sandpaper, sand the area nearly flush to the furniture surface. Finish sanding with fine-grit sandpaper.
3. Clean away any dust with a tack cloth or clean rag.
4. Paint or restain the repair as needed.

Repair a blistered or separated veneer:

1. Place a damp cloth over the blister and apply a hot iron to steam-heat the veneer. Smaller blisters typically are removed by this process. If the blister remains, continue with the next step.
2. Use a utility knife to carefully slit the veneer.
3. Insert wood glue under the edges of the slit veneer, slightly overfilling.
4. Use a small roller to force out excess glue and to flatten the area. Clean away any excess glue. Don't use a weight, because it could stick to the veneer.
5. Allow the glue to fully dry before reusing the furniture.

Reinforce a furniture joint:

1. Disassemble the loose joint.
2. Clean both parts of the joint of old glue or wood.
3. Reglue the joint and clamp in place, following the glue manufacturer's recommendations. If the fitting is loose, add a small wedge of wood for additional support.

Repair a split in wood furniture:

1. Carefully pry apart the split and use a small wedge of wood to keep it open while you work.
2. Clean out any old glue from the opening to make sure that the new glue adheres well.
3. Apply ample wood glue to both surfaces using a small brush or toothpick. You can wipe excess glue off once you're done.
4. Remove the wedges.
5. Clamp the repair and remove the excess glue. Allow the glue to dry fully (see instructions) before reusing the furniture.

Minimize a minor burn on wood furniture:

1. Carefully buff the area with fine steel wool moistened with mineral spirits; the scorch should disappear.
2. Wipe the area clean of debris and mineral spirits.
3. Polish the surface to renew its sheen and to provide protection.

Repair a scratch or spot on wood furniture:

1. Carefully clean the marred area with mineral spirits and a clean rag.
2. Use very fine steel wool and high-quality furniture oil to gently rub the marred area, rubbing with the grain.
3. Once the damage disappears, remove any residue with a rag or tack cloth.

Service loose, bent, or worn door hinges:

1. Tighten the hinge screws. Replace the hinges if they are bent or worn.
2. If the door still does not work properly, remove the door.
3. Fill the screw holes with wood putty.
4. Once the putty is dry, replace the screws.

Unstick a door:

1. Open and close the door to determine where it is sticking. To make the sticking point visible, coat the door's edges with powdered chalk, then close and open the door a few times. The lack of chalk will tell you where the door is sticking.
2. Use a plane carefully to remove material where the door sticks. You may also need to remove material from the frame that surrounds the closed door.
3. Repeat as needed until the door opens and closes easily.

Straighten a warped door:

1. Remove the door from the furniture or cabinet.
2. Wet the concave (bulging) side of the warp with wet cloths or sponges.
3. Heat the opposite side of the warp with a heat lamp or high-wattage hair dryer.
4. Apply clamps and scrap wood as needed to force the door straight.

Replace a glass panel in a door:

1. Carefully remove any loose glass from the door panel.
2. Use a putty knife carefully to pry out the molding or other components holding the glass in place. Some glass panels are held in place by screws or brackets.
3. Remove the remaining glass and carefully vacuum out the grooves.
4. Place a new pane of glass, the same size as the old one, in the door.
5. Install new molding or reattach the old molding (depending on condition), being careful not to break the glass.

Modify a sliding door channel:

1. If the channel is too narrow, use medium-grit sandpaper to sand the channel, then vacuum to remove any dust and debris.
2. If the channel is too wide, remove the door and add a bead of wood glue or filler to the channel as needed.

Shim a door hinge:

1. Open the door to expose the hinge.
2. Unscrew the hinge from the frame.
3. Place a piece of solid (not corrugated) cardboard behind the hinge to be shimmed.
4. Mark and cut the cardboard to fit under the hinge.
5. Install the trimmed cardboard under the hinge and reinstall the hinge.
6. Open and close the door several times to test the hinge.

Reinforce a sagging shelf:

1. Remove the shelf and reinstall it upside down.
2. Install metal braces or glue blocks at the rear center below the shelf.
3. Once the shelf is level, fasten screws through the back of the cabinet and into the shelf to help support it.

Replace a drawer bottom:

1. Remove the drawer from the furniture or cabinet.
2. Carefully remove the back of the drawer by removing nails or other fasteners. If this cannot be done easily, instead carefully pry the bottom from the drawer.
3. Turn the old bottom over and reinstall it *or* replace it with a new one of the same size and thickness.
4. Make sure the door is square (measure across to opposite corners; both diagonals should be equal) before fastening the bottom in place.

Realign a wood drawer guide:

1. Use a small square to check alignment of the guide; it should be perpendicular to the drawer front.
2. Use recessed screws and wood glue to secure the guide. If the screws spin in the holes, use wood filler in the hole before replacing the screw.

Realign a metal drawer track:

1. Remove the drawer from the furniture or cabinet.
2. Inspect the metal drawer track for adjustment screws.
3. Loosen, adjust, and tighten adjustment screws as needed to realign the track.

Repair a wood runner:

1. Remove the drawer from the furniture or cabinet.
2. Unscrew or cut out the runner.
3. Remove excess glue or wood before installing the replacement runner.
4. Install the new runner using wood glue and screws as needed.

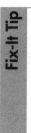

**Fix-It Tip**

If you are using glue, make sure you select the best type for the project. See *Fix Everything: Adhesives*. Also read the label on the glue bottle to know how long it will take to dry and whether clamping or pressure is needed.

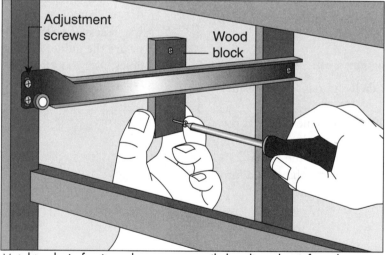

Metal tracks in furniture drawers can easily be aligned, reinforced, or replaced.

# Fuse

Fuses are all through your house—and rightly so. They are the weakest link in the chain for good reason. They keep electricity surges from damaging appliances and circuits. Fortunately, they are also easy to test and to replace. Here's how the Fix-It Club fixes fuses. (Refer to *Electrical Service Panel* for household electrical circuit fuses and circuit breakers.)

## How Does It Work?

An appliance fuse is an electrical safety device with a metal strip that melts and interrupts the appliance's electrical circuit when the circuit is overloaded or the appliance overheats. Electrical fuses protect electrical devices from electrical overloads. Thermal fuses protect them from overheating.

Electrical fuses are mounted on the outside of the unit in a screw-out receptacle marked "Fuse," or inside the unit near the cord and/or a power supply. Thermal fuses typically are installed inside an appliance on or near one of the electrical cord wires. Fuses are clipped, screwed, or soldered into place. Most fuses open a few seconds after a substantial overload begins. Slow-blow fuses are designed to protect equipment where heavy, periodic demands for current would blow a common fuse even though the apparatus is operating normally. Quick-blow fuses open at even a momentary overload; they are used to protect delicate or sensitive components.

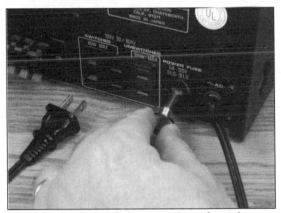

Many appliances and electronics have fuses that are accessed without opening the housing.

## What Can Go Wrong?

A fuse can blow, meaning the metal within the fuse casing (usually glass) melts and interrupts the electrical circuit. An appliance or a portion of an appliance will not operate once a fuse has blown. The purpose of a fuse is to stop operation of the appliance or electronic component before the unit is damaged.

> **Fix-It Tip**
>
> Learn to read fuses. A blown fuse that appears smoked or bubbled may indicate a short in the equipment. A clear and otherwise undamaged fuse typically is just worn out and doesn't point to any other electrical problems in the device.

## How Can I Identify the Problem?

If an appliance or piece of electronic equipment will not operate, or a portion of it will not operate, you can test the fuse (see below) and replace it if needed.

If you replace a fuse and the unit still will not work or very quickly blows the fuse again, you will need to check further to find the problem (see the *Fix-It Guide* for the appropriate item).

## What Parts, Materials, and Tools Do I Need?

Many replacement fuses are available from hardware and electronics stores. Special fuses may be available from the manufacturer and aftermarket suppliers (see *Fix-It Resources*). The tools you will need to test and replace fuses include these:

- Multimeter or continuity tester
- Soldering gun and solder

## What Are the Steps to Fixing It?

Test a fuse:

1. Touch each end of the fuse with a probe of the multimeter set at R×1 (resistance times 1) or with a continuity tester (see *Fix Everything: Multimeter* or *Fix Everything: Continuity Tester*).
2. The fuse should show continuity, the passage of electricity through the fuse. Replace a fuse that does not.

> **Caution**
>
> *Never* replace a fuse with anything except the type and rating indicated by the device's manufacturer. Don't install a 10-amp fuse in a device designed for a 5-amp fuse. Also, don't install a slow-burn fuse or even a common fuse in a device designed for a quick-blow fuse.

3. If the appliance or electronic component still does not work, or if the fuse blows again, you will have to look further for the solution. Refer to the appropriate *Fix-It Guide* in this book.

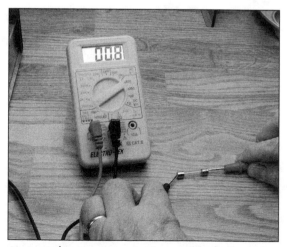

Use a multimeter or continuity tester to check an appliance fuse.

# Garage Door Opener

"Open sesame!" Garage door openers are the unsung heroes of modern life. Without them we would have to actually get out of the car to open the door. With them we simply push a button and drive right in—unless the opener doesn't work (or the garage is full of broken stuff). It's a good thing that garage door openers are relatively low maintenance and easy to fix.

## How Does It Work?

A garage door opener is an electric motor appliance that opens a garage door at the push of a button. The button can be one that's wired into the household electrical circuit or one that's on a battery-powered remote-control unit usually carried in a car. Most garage door systems have both. The button sends an infrared or radio signal to the control unit that, in turn, activates an electric motor with a track-and-pulley system that moves the door. Most garage door opener units also have a light that goes on automatically and shuts off after a pre-set interval.

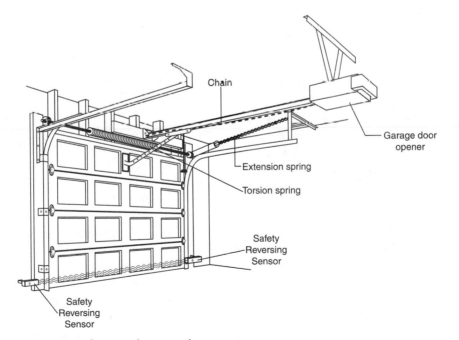

Components of a typical garage door opening system.

## What Can Go Wrong?

The opener may not respond when the remote or wall button is pushed. The opener may raise the door but not close it. The opener may run but not open the door. The opener may operate without a command. The door may not open or close completely. The door may reverse when closing. The opener may have to work too hard. Because garage door openers are little more than a motor and electronic controls, most of the service you can perform includes replacing batteries, testing the motor or controls, or lubricating and aligning mechanisms.

**Fix-It Tip**

At least once a year, test and replace batteries in the remote controllers.

## How Can I Identify the Problem?

If the door opener doesn't respond, make sure the cord is securely plugged into a properly operating *Electrical Receptacle*. Wait 15 minutes for a motor overheated by a binding door and try to open it again. As needed, test the *Motor*.

An electrical receptacle is typically installed near the garage door opener.

If the door raises but won't close, make sure the beam sensor is plugged in and properly aligned according to the owner's manual directions.

**Fix-It Tip**

Don't take your garage door opener for granted. Once a season, test the unit to make sure it opens and closes smoothly and that safety features (automatic reversing) work as described in the owner's manual. At the same time, inspect the door, tracks, and opener chain or drive to make sure grime or debris won't soon stop operation. A 10-minute inspection can give you confidence—and reduce potential problems.

If the opener operates by remote, but won't operate by the hardwired button, look for loose connections or damaged wires. Test for continuity or a short (see *Fix Everything: Multimeter*) or call for an electrician.

If the remote control does not work, check its battery (see *Battery, Household* or *Battery, Button*) for sufficient power. Also make sure the antenna is outside the opener housing.

If the opener runs but doesn't open the door, look for wear of the worm gear or chain-drive sprocket; if needed, have it professionally serviced. Pull the disengage cord to reset the catch and reactivate the opener. Replace a broken chain or worn gears.

If the opener operates by itself, look for a stuck button on the remote control. If this fails, have a faulty circuit board checked and, if needed, replaced.

If your garage door opener opens a neighbor's garage door as well—or vice versa—check the owner's manual to learn if the frequency can be reset and how.

If the door doesn't open or close completely, look for and remove any obstructions and inspect the door for misaligned tracks, loose hardware, or uneven spring tension. Make sure the open and close limits and sensitivity are set correctly according to the owner's manual.

If the door reverses while closing, look for an obstruction and remove it. Make sure nothing (even a spider web) is blocking the electric eye. Make sure the close limit is set according to the owner's manual.

If the opener works too hard, increase spring tension or replace a bad spring. Have the door serviced to repair a worn chain sprocket or worm gear.

Maintaining the door itself will lessen the need for opener repairs (see below).

## What Parts, Materials, and Tools Do I Need?

Replacement parts are available from larger hardware stores and specialty garage door opener retailers. The tools you will need to fix a garage door opener include these:

- Screwdrivers
- Wrenches
- Degreaser
- Mallet

## What Are the Steps to Fixing It?

Garage door maintenance:

1. Inspect and, if necessary, remove and clean dirty hinge rollers with degreaser or kerosene, replacing each assembly before removing the next.

2. Twice a year, lubricate the roller bearings and roller shaft with lightweight oil. Also remove any debris from the track.
3. Check and adjust the door lock bar. To adjust, loosen the screws and move the lock-bar guide bracket up or down as needed. Make sure that all screws are tight.

If the power goes out, you still can open your garage door by pulling the release rope and manually lifting the door.

4. Inspect the door operation for smooth, uniform movement.
5. As needed, loosen mounting screws and use a mallet to straighten a misaligned track.

Most garage door opener systems have easily accessed adjustments.

# Garbage Disposer

A garbage disposer, also known as a disposal, is often treated like a mechanized goat. Feed it anything. Unfortunately, a garbage disposer doesn't have the intestinal fortitude of a goat—so it can break. That's when you can step up and fix it.

## How Does It Work?

A garbage disposer is a motorized appliance that grinds waste from food preparation into liquid for washing down the drain.

The disposer motor turns a flywheel to which impellers are attached. Food waste within the chamber is repeatedly hit and cut by these rotating impellers, grinding it into small particles that can be flushed through the drain pipe and into the septic or sewer system. If a dishwasher is nearby, a line from the dishwasher attaches to the garbage disposer so debris from the dishwater can be caught by the disposer. The entire disposer unit is attached to the bottom of the sink using a flange, ring, and mounting bolts. It is plugged into an under-sink electrical outlet for power.

With minimal maintenance, a garbage disposer can outlive a goat. Simple maintenance includes ensuring that a disposer's enemies—grease, large items, hard items, and fibrous foods—be eliminated from its diet.

## What Can Go Wrong?

How can you tell when something your garbage disposer ate disagrees with it? The unit will either become clogged or make extraneous noise. What causes these problems? The flywheel may be jammed. Hoses and seals can leak. The impeller can become worn. The motor can fail. Fortunately, they all can be fixed.

**Fix-It Tip**

If the disposer won't start after unjamming, wait at least 10 minutes for the motor to cool fully, then press the reset button, if there is one, on the underside of the unit and try again.

## How Can I Identify the Problem?

Not sure where to start looking? If the unit doesn't work at all, make sure power is on to the outlet and test the *Electrical Cord*. Test the *Motor* with a multimeter (see *Fix Everything: Multimeter*) and service or replace it if it is faulty.

If the unit does not turn, check the flywheel for jamming and service if needed (see below).

If the disposer leaks water, check and service or repair loose or worn hoses and seals (see below).

If the disposer turns but doesn't grind up waste, check the impellers for wear and replace if needed (see below).

## What Parts, Materials, and Tools Do I Need?

Though there are motor and impeller replacement kits for most popular garbage disposers, you'll probably need to get them from the manufacturer or aftermarket supplier (see *Fix-It Resources*). Here are some tools for removing and repairing garbage disposers:

- Hex wrench (check for one in a pouch attached to or near the disposer)
- Screwdrivers
- Multimeter (for testing the motor)

## What Are the Steps to Fixing It?

Before working on the disposer, unplug it under the sink, or, if it is wired directly into the house, trip the circuit breaker or remove the fuse at the main electrical box (see *Electrical Service Panel*).

Service the flywheel:

1. Inspect the bottom of the disposer for a six-sided (hex) hole.
2. If it has one, look for a hex wrench in a pouch on or near the disposer. The hex wrench is used to rotate the motor shaft and flywheel without having to access the inside of the garbage disposer. If you don't find one, check your toolbox or purchase one. Don't use a screwdriver or other tool because it can damage the hex hole.
3. To free the flywheel, insert the hex wrench in the hex hole and rotate it in a circle in both directions.

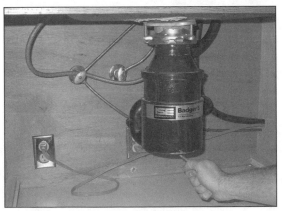

Insert the hex wrench on the bottom and turn to rotate the flywheel.

Stop leaks in hoses and seals:

1. Place a hand at various locations around the disposer to identify the source of the leak.
2. As needed, tighten fittings to eliminate the leak.
3. If the leakage is from underneath the garbage disposer, it is probably leaking through the flywheel seal and into the *Motor*. Remove the garbage disposer from the drain system, disassemble the unit and replace the seal, or take the unit in for service.

Service worn impellers:

1. Unplug the garbage disposer from the electric receptacle or turn it off at the circuit breaker box.
2. Remove all hose fittings connected to the disposer. Some garbage disposers can then be removed by twisting to free them from the support ring. Others require that the unit be unscrewed from the ring.
3. Carefully remove the garbage disposer from under the sink, being aware that it is heavy.
4. To service worn impellers on many models, dismantle the unit and remove the flywheel lock nut and flywheel.
5. Remove the impellers or sharpen them in place, depending on the model. If the impellers cannot be sharpened, the flywheel assembly will need to be replaced as a unit.

### Buying a Replacement

If you are buying a replacement garbage disposer because the last one couldn't stand up to its diet, consider buying a heavy-duty model. Better units can handle more types of waste, because they usually have stainless-steel grind/impeller assemblies, as well as heavy-duty motors. There are safety differences as well. Heavy-duty models usually have a jamming-prevention system to reverse the grinding direction, or they use some other mechanism to clean obstructions.

# Garden Tool

After spring has sprung is not the time to discover that your garden tools have, too. Spend a little time each fall checking your garden tools for things to fix and things to recycle (some tools are too inexpensive to bother repairing). You'll then have the entire winter to fix them.

## How Does It Work?

Garden tools are all those implements that make it easier to grow flowers, vegetables, trees, and lawns. Garden tools include shovels, hoes, hoses, shears, and clippers. They help us dig and refill holes, eliminate weeds, water roses and radishes, prune trees and shrubs, trim grass, and much more.

## What Can Go Wrong?

Handles break on shovels, hoes, and other tools. Hoses leak. Cutting and digging edges become dull. Tools get rusty. Handle grips become loose.

## How Can I Identify the Problem?

If a garden tool's handle breaks, you can replace it (see below).

If an otherwise good hose springs a leak, you can stop that leak (see below).

If a cutting or digging edge becomes dull, you can sharpen it (see below).

If a tool is rusty, you can renew it (see below).

If the wooden handle grips of a tool are loose, you can tighten them (see below).

**Fix-It Tip**

To prevent rust, clean your garden tools thoroughly after every use and coat them lightly with lightweight oil such as WD-40 or mineral oil.

## What Parts, Materials, and Tools Do I Need?

Replacement parts are available from local hardware stores, home improvement centers, and garden centers. The tools you will need to fix your garden tools include these:

- Bench vise
- Electric drill
- Hammer
- Wood file
- Galvanized wood screws
- Sharp knife
- Penetrating oil or kerosene
- Steel wool, emery paper, or a wire brush
- Epoxy adhesive
- Mallet

## What Are the Steps to Fixing It?

Replace a tool handle:

**Caution**

Don't try to repair a broken tool handle, because a repaired handle will be weak. Replace the handle instead.

1. Clamp the tool blade in a bench vise.
2. Remove the handle from the hasp using a drill, hammer, or other tools as needed.
3. Insert the new handle into the hasp.

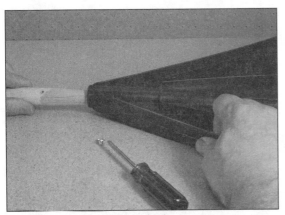

Insert the new handle into the hasp.

4. Tighten the handle in the hasp using fasteners.

Use a screw and screwdriver to firmly attach the handle to the tool head.

Fix a leaky hose:

1. Cut through the hose on either side of the bad section using a sharp knife.
2. Attach male and female hose couplings to the cut ends, following the directions that come with the couplings. If the new hose fittings don't slide in easily, try softening the ends of the hose in hot water or lubricating them with soap or cooking oil.

Sharpen a garden tool:

1. If possible, remove the cutting edge from the handle.
2. Place the tool head in a bench vice or otherwise secure it against movement.
3. Use a file to sharpen the edge, following the original bevel. Remove any burrs or rough spots.

Remove rust from a tool:

1. Place the tool in a bench vise with the blade pointing down.
2. Coat the blade with kerosene or penetrating oil.
3. Brush downward, using steel wool, emery paper, or a wire brush.
4. Wipe away the rust residue with a soft brush or cloth.
5. Wash the blade in warm, soapy water and allow it to dry thoroughly.
6. Sharpen the blade (see above).

Tighten a loose wooden handle grip:

1. Remove the handle from the tool head (see above).
2. Remove excess or uneven wood from the end of the handle so that it will smoothly fit back into the tool head.
3. Spread epoxy adhesive in the tool hasp (where the handle fits).
4. Insert the wood handle and apply pressure or use a mallet to ensure a tight fit.

# Gas Grill

In most areas of this country, gas grills hibernate through the winter. But when the first nice day of springlike weather arrives, millions of them are dragged out from the garage and immediately put back to work. Hopefully, they work. If yours doesn't, keep reading.

## How Does It Work?

A gas grill is an outdoor cooking appliance, fueled by propane or natural gas, for grilling or barbecuing a variety of foods outdoors. A controlled amount of gas passes from the metal tank or household gas lines through fittings and a hose to the burners, where the gas is slowly consumed, creating heat for cooking on the grill top. Gas grills have become more popular than charcoal grills thanks to their ease of use.

## What Can Go Wrong?

Because they are simple in operation, it's relatively easy to determine what's wrong with a problematic gas grill. Gas can leak from fittings or from the hose itself. The igniter may not spark.

> **Caution**
>
> Always transport a propane gas tank *upright* with the valve completely closed and the safety plug screwed in tightly.

## How Can I Identify the Problem?

At the beginning of each barbecue season and after filling and reattaching the propane tank, you should test the unit for gas leaks. Follow instructions below and/or purchase a gas leak check kit at a hardware store or propane tank supplier.

> **Fix-It Tip**
>
> You can clean soiled stone briquettes by burning them soiled-side down for at least 30 minutes.

## What Parts, Materials, and Tools Do I Need?

Because most working components within gas grills are made by a small number of manufacturers, many parts are interchangeable and readily available. First check the gas grill department of a larger home improvement center or hardware store. If you don't find the part you need, contact the grill's manufacturer or an aftermarket supplier (see *Fix-It Resources*).

Replacement parts for gas grills are available through larger hardware stores.

To disassemble and repair your gas grill, you'll need the following tools and materials:

- Wrenches
- Small paint brush
- Soapy water

## What Are the Steps to Fixing It?

Test the propane tank valve for leaks:

1. Turn the grill control knobs on the front (and, on some models, the side) of the barbecue to the *off* position.
2. Turn the propane tank valve fully counterclockwise to close it.
3. Mix a test solution of equal parts of dishwashing liquid and water in a small container.
4. To test for leaks, apply the test solution liberally to the connection between the regulator fitting and the tank valve using a small paint brush. Apply the test solution to the valve handle and threads, the length of the hose, and the connection between the hose and the regulator. If bubbles appear at any point, there is a gas leak.

5. Tighten the connections and retest.
6. If you still see bubbles at any of the tested connections, close the tank valve and replace the leaking component.

Test the hose fittings for leaks:

1. With the tank valve open, brush the test solution on the fitting at the other end of the hose, located under the control knobs.
2. Turn the control knob to *high* and test the hose and fittings leading from the control knob to the grill. Turn the right control knob to *off*. Repeat the process for the other control knobs.
3. If you see any bubbles during any of these tests, close the tank valve and contact your propane dealer or your local gas utility. Do not use the barbecue until the leak is corrected.

**Fix-It Tip**

If your grill uses a home gas line, periodically inspect the connections for corrosion. If you find a problem, contact your gas supplier for repairs.

# Gutter

Gutters are usually taken for granted—until it rains! Then fixing gutter problems may be immediately added to your job jar. Too late? Maybe not. Let's see how you can fix gutters, rain or shine.

## How Does It Work?

A gutter is a shallow channel or conduit installed along the eaves of a house to catch and carry off rainwater. A downspout is the pipe that carries rainwater from the roof gutters to the ground or the storm sewer system. To work properly, water needs a clear and smooth path into the gutters and down through the downspouts. Gutters should be leakproof and free of debris. Most gutter and downspout systems today are made of galvanized steel, aluminum, vinyl, fiberglass, or wood.

## What Can Go Wrong?

The most common problem with gutters and downspouts is clogs. In addition, gutters can sag, and gutters and downspouts can leak.

## How Can I Identify the Problem?

If water sits in the gutter, drains slowly, or overflows, clean the gutters and downspouts (see below), then install screens (see below).

If water runs behind the gutter and down the fascia or siding, install a drip edge (see below).

If water pools below the downspout, reposition or install a splashblock and replace a damaged section of downspout (see below).

If a metal gutter leaks, you can patch it (see below).

If a downspout leaks, you can replace a section (see below).

If a gutter sags, you can install gutter hangers (see below).

If a section of gutter is damaged beyond repair or ice builds up along a cleaned gutter, call for professional evaluation.

**Fix-It Tip**

When shopping for a replacement part, bring along a piece of your system to be sure you get a part that fits exactly.

## What Parts, Materials, and Tools Do I Need?

Replacement parts for a gutter system are usually found in hardware stores and home centers. The tools you will need to fix gutter systems include these:

- Screwdrivers
- Ladder

**Caution**

Some gutters are strong enough that you can lean a ladder against them. But many are easily damaged. To be safe, use a ladder stabilizer or place a 2x4 inside the gutter to keep it stable.

- Drill
- Rubber gloves
- Safety goggles
- 2×4 lumber
- Small broom (whisk broom)
- Putty knife
- Garden hose with power nozzle
- Gutter cleaning wand
- Leaf guards
- Scissors
- Drip edge
- Metal snips
- Flat file
- Hammer
- Sheet-metal screws
- Coarse sandpaper
- Clean rags
- Fiberglass mesh
- Roofing cement
- Spikes and ferrules
- Strap hangers
- Level
- Auger
- Hacksaw
- Roofing (or building) paper
- Roofing nails

## What Are the Steps to Fixing It?

Clean a gutter:

1. Remove debris at the edge of the roof, in leaf guards, in open gutters, and in leaf strainers, beginning at the location farthest from the downspout.

2. Use a garden hose with a power nozzle to wash dirt and grit off the gutter, brushing debris toward the downspout with a whisk broom. If needed, use a small putty knife to dislodge material that adheres to the gutter.

**Fix-It Tip**

Wear good-quality rubber gloves to remove debris from gutters, making sure that sharp edges don't puncture the gloves. Also, wear eye protection that will keep flying debris (from water pressure) from hitting your eyes.

You can purchase a gutter cleaning wand that extends to 4+ feet at larger hardware stores and home centers.

The gutter wand head sprays water directly into the gutter to wash away debris.

Clean a downspout:

1. Wearing rubber gloves, reach down the drop outlet and pull out as much debris as possible.
2. Aim a hose into the drop outlet and flush debris through the elbow and out the bottom of the downspout.
3. As needed, use an auger to clear the downspout of debris.

Downspout    Gutter

The downspout takes water from the gutter. Inspect the gutter and downspout for telltale indicators of overflowing water or damaged downspouts.

Install a leaf guard:

1. Wearing rubber gloves, insert a leaf guard at the top of each downspout.
2. As needed, bend or trim the leaf guard to snugly fit the opening.

Install a gutter screen:

1. Lay the gutter screen along the roof edge near where it will be installed.
2. Fasten pieces together to make a continuous gutter screen along the length of the gutter.
3. Cut excess from the end of the gutter screen to fit the gutter.
4. Place the screen in the gutter, clipping or fastening it in place as needed for a secure fit.

Install a drip edge:

1. Cut the drip edge to the length of the gutter with metal snips.
2. Remove burrs from any cut metal edges and smooth rough spots on any cut vinyl edges with a flat file.
3. Install one side of the drip edge between the roofing material and the roofing paper along the roof edge.
4. Push the drip edge under the roofing until it overhangs it by at least 1 inch.
5. Attach the drip edge to the roof with roofing nails.

Replace a damaged downspout:

1. Cut a replacement section to length using a hacksaw and remove any burrs from the cut edges with a flat file.
2. Fit the replacement section into the downspout assembly.
3. Drill a hole through the overlap of the ends and drive in a sheet-metal screw.
4. Install additional support brackets as needed.

Patch a gutter:

1. Clean the gutter (see above), especially in the area that will be patched.
2. Use coarse sandpaper to remove rust or debris and smooth the surface, wiping it with a dry rag.
3. Cut a piece of fiberglass mesh larger than the hole, then use roofing cement to attach the patch to the inside of the gutter.
4. Spread additional roofing cement over the patch to securely fasten it to the gutter.

Install gutter hangers (straps):

1. Remove damaged hangers as needed.
2. Use a level to verify that the gutter slopes evenly.
3. Install strap hangers following the manufacturer's instructions. In most cases that means installing the lips onto the gutter edges, positioning the strap on or under the edge of the roofing material, adjusting it until the gutter is in position, and driving roofing nails into it.
4. Apply roofing cement over each nail head to keep out rain water.

Install gutter hangers (spike and ferrule):

1. Remove damaged spikes and ferrules (washers) using the claw of a hammer.
2. Use a level to see that the gutter slopes evenly.
3. Drill a hole in the gutter lip for the new spike.
4. For both new and replaced spikes, fit the ferrule inside the gutter and insert the spike through the gutter hole and through the ferrule. Then drive the spike into the fascia and rafter.

Install gutter hangers (brackets):

1. Remove damaged spikes and ferrules (washers) using the claw of a hammer.
2. Use a level to see that the gutter slopes evenly.
3. Nail a bracket into the fascia board and clip it into the gutter edge.

# Hair Clipper

Nobody admits to using an electric hair clipper anymore—but they still sell briskly. And, because they are relatively inexpensive (about the price of one or two haircuts) some models are subject to frequent problems. It's a good thing that hair clippers are relatively easy to fix.

## How Does It Work?

An electric hair clipper is a small motorized appliance that moves cutting blades across stationary blades to cut hair. An electric beard trimmer operates in the same way, except the motor and blades typically are smaller. Even electric dog grooming clippers operate similarly. The clipper is powered either by household current through an electrical cord or by a rechargeable battery.

## What Can Go Wrong?

Many repairs to hair clippers and beard trimmers can be avoided by cleaning the appliance after every use and following the manufacturer's maintenance guidelines. In addition, the electrical cord may need replacing, the recharger may need service, or the motor may be faulty. The cutting blades can become clogged and the cutting edges can be damaged. Fortunately, you can make many repairs yourself. Some new models actually clean themselves.

## How Can I Identify the Problem?

If the clipper doesn't work at all, make sure power is on at the *Electrical Receptacle*, check the battery and recharge it if it is low (see *Battery, Household* and *Battery Recharger*), and check the *Electrical Cord*. Unplug the unit, turn it over, and manually move the blades. If necessary, test the *Motor* and switches (see *Appliance Controls*).

If the hair clipper or beard trimmer operates slowly, clean and lubricate it as directed by the owner's manual. For rechargeable units, check the battery and recharge if needed (see *Battery, Household* and *Battery Recharger*).

If the unit is noisy or cuts poorly, clean and lubricate it. Also check the *Motor*.

## What Parts, Materials, and Tools Do I Need?

Replacement parts for electric hair clippers and beard trimmers are available through retail stores or online from the manufacturer or aftermarket suppliers. Basic repair tools include these:

- Screwdrivers
- Lightweight lubricant

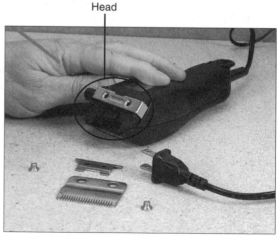

Remove the fasteners holding the hair clipper head in place.

Switch

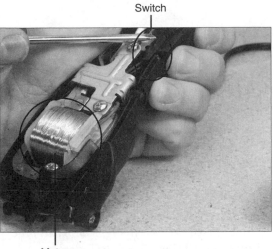

Motor

Remove the fasteners holding the two halves of the case in place to expose the motor and switch.

# Hair Curler

All those natural curls must come from somewhere. If yours are assisted by a hair curler or curling iron appliance, here's what you can do if it doesn't work.

## How Does It Work?

Hair curlers and curling irons are heating devices designed to curl human hair. Both hair curlers and curling irons contain heating elements controlled by a thermostat. In addition, a thermal cutoff or fuse prevents appliance burnouts due to overheating. In a set of curlers, a solid metal plate transfers heat from the element to the warming posts on which the rollers are placed. In contrast, the curling iron is heated by an element located inside the barrel. Both are simple heating appliances and relatively easy to repair—once you figure out what's wrong.

## What Can Go Wrong?

The most common problem with hair curlers and curling irons is a faulty power cord. In addition, internal wiring may be faulty, swivel contacts may be dirty or corroded, a heating element may fail, the thermal cutoff may be faulty, and the switch may be faulty.

**Fix-It Tip**

Hair curlers and curling irons are relatively inexpensive appliances and replacement parts may be difficult to find so it may be more cost-effective to replace rather than repair them. But give it a try anyway.

## How Can I Identify the Problem?

If the appliance does not heat, first make sure the power is on at the outlet, then test the *Electrical Cord.*

If the unit still does not work, disassemble it to look for wires disconnected from any terminals and reattach them. While the device is open, test (see *Fix Everything: Multimeter*) the on/off switch if there is one (see *Appliance Controls*) and replace as needed. Check the *Fuse.* Test the thermal cutoff (see below) and replace it if the part is available. Test the *Heating Element* using a multimeter. If you still can't find the problem, replace the appliance.

**Fix-It Tip**

Because hair curlers and curling irons typically require a lot of electricity to operate and because they frequently are plugged into a GFCI (ground fault circuit interrupter) receptacle in the bathroom, first check the receptacle by pressing the red button to reset it.

## What Parts, Materials, and Tools Do I Need?

Replacement parts may be available from the manufacturer's service centers (check the owner's manual for location) or through small appliance parts dealers. Here are the basic tools you'll need to test and fix a hair curler or curling iron:

- Screwdrivers
- Pliers
- Multimeter

## What Are the Steps to Fixing It?

Disassemble and test a curler set (depending on the model):

1. Unplug the curler and remove the cover and rollers.
2. Unscrew the base or pry open the access plate with a small screwdriver.
3. Slide the access plate forward and upward with your thumbs to expose the inner parts.
4. Remove the roller trays from the housing and remove the power cord.
5. Disconnect the connectors attaching the thermostat to the heating element and remove the thermostat, held on either by clips or screws.
6. Test the electrical components using a multimeter (see *Fix Everything: Multimeter*).

Thermal fuse

Hair curlers and other heating appliances typically have a thermal fuse or cutout that can be replaced with parts from an electronics store such as Radio Shack.

Disassemble and test a curling iron (depending on the model):

1. Unplug the curler and, if necessary to continue, remove the base.
2. Loosen screws joining the housing halves and gently separate them.
3. Disconnect the connectors attaching the thermostat to the *Heating Element* and remove the thermostat (see *Appliance Controls*).
4. Test the electrical components using a multimeter (see *Fix Everything: Multimeter*).

Test a thermal cutoff (a small electric component in a wire between one side of the power cord and the heating element):

1. Disassemble the hair curler or curling iron as described above.
2. Set the multimeter (see *Fix Everything: Multimeter*) to the R×1 (resistance times 1) scale and clip probes to each side of the thermal cutoff component. The multimeter scale should indicate zero ohms, meaning there is no resistance and it is working. If not, take the component to a service center for an exact-replacement part.

# Heat Pump

A heat pump has dual personalities. It warms in the winter and cools in the summer. Or at least that's how it's supposed to work. If it doesn't, call a meeting of the Fix-It Club. Here's the agenda.

## How Does It Work?

A heat pump is a heat exchanger that removes heat from indoor air to cool it and extracts heat from outside air and pumps it indoors to heat a home. It takes advantage of liquid's tendency to absorb heat as it expands.

A heat pump has an outdoor unit in which a fan moves air through a coil that absorbs heat. A compressor then superheats the vapor and sends it through refrigerant lines to a second coil in the interior distribution unit. A blower pushes return air through the coil, warming the air and forcing it into the ducts. Meanwhile, refrigerant travels back to the outdoor unit to begin another full cycle through the pump. An automatic reversing valve reverses these flows as needed to keep the home's interior comfortable.

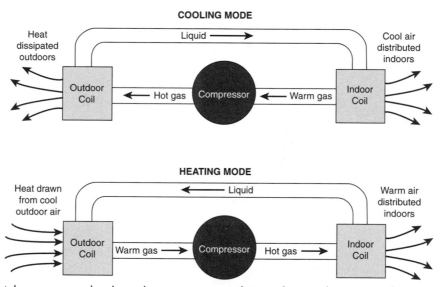

A heat pump cools a home by moving interior heat to the outside; it warms the home by moving exterior heat to the inside.

## What Can Go Wrong?

"Why is it cold [hot] in here?" Maybe the heat pump isn't working as it should. Common symptoms include: The pump may not run, the unit may short cycle, and the automatic defrost cycle may malfunction.

> **Fix-It Tip**
>
> Heat pumps work well down to about 15°F. Below that, most require a backup heating source, usually electric-resistance elements installed in the furnace, ducts, or pump cabinet. That's why heat pumps aren't as popular (or as efficient) in colder climates.

## How Can I Identify the Problem?

If the heat pump does not run, check fuses and breakers (see *Electrical Service Panel*). Also, check the unit to see if it has a *reset* switch on the outdoor unit.

If the unit short cycles, clear any debris around the outdoor coil. Also check the filter and blower unit (see below).

If the defrost cycles last more than 15 minutes or occur more than twice an hour, or ice accumulates on the outdoor unit, check the unit's owner's manual for specific instructions or contact an HVAC (heat-ventilation-air conditioning) technician.

If your heat pump is off for more than an hour at temperatures lower than 50°F, follow the steps below to restart a heat pump at low temperature.

If some rooms are too cool and others too warm, the distribution system may require balancing. Refer to the guide on *Forced-Air Distribution*.

> **Fix-It Tip**
>
> Outdoor heat pump units can be clogged with leaves or even pests such as squirrel nests. Before starting the system after a lengthy hibernation, make sure you remove the cover and clean out any debris.

## What Parts, Materials, and Tools Do I Need?

Replacement parts for your heat pump are available from the manufacturer or an aftermarket supplier such as an electrical or heating supply store (see *Fix-It Resources*). Here are the basic tools you'll need to access and maintain a typical heat pump:

- Screwdrivers
- Wrenches
- Light oil
- Vacuum cleaner

## What Are the Steps to Fixing It?

Clean or replace a filter:

1. Open the blower access door on the outdoor unit.
2. Remove the filter inside the unit by either sliding or unwrapping it. Clean the area with a vacuum or a damp cloth.
3. Clean a dry-foam filter or replace other types.
4. Install the cleaned or new filter and firmly close the blower access door.

Oil and adjust the blower unit:

1. Visually check the *Motor* and any pulleys for small lubrication ports or holes; they may have an arrow with the word *oil* nearby.
2. Lubricate oil ports with light (SAE-10) lubricating oil.
3. If the unit has a belt drive, adjust the belt to be slightly loose but not slipping. If the belt is worn or cracked, replace it. Tighten mounting bolts as needed.

Restart a heat pump at low temperature:

1. Turn the system selector switch to *emergency heat*.
2. Wait six hours, then return to the normal heat setting.

# Heater, Electric

Depending on where you live—and the cost of electricity—you may have one or more electric heaters in your home, built-in or portable. And they may need fixing. Fortunately, they are relatively simple in operation and as simple to troubleshoot and repair.

## How Does It Work?

Electric baseboard and wall heaters are room air-heating units. A baseboard heater has one or more horizontal heating elements and is controlled by a thermostat. Baseboard heaters are mounted at the base of a room wall. Air is drawn in through the bottom and heated by the electrical elements. The warm air then rises into the room. The electric elements are often shaped like metal fins, and some are filled with fluid to maximize their heat retention. Often several units are installed around the perimeter of a room.

An electric wall heater is a forced-air heating device. The wall heater fits into the wall and uses a fan to circulate air that has been warmed by an electric heating element. The fan and row of heating elements inside the unit are controlled by a thermostat. Wall heaters are often installed in bathrooms, laundry rooms, and other areas to provide supplemental or occasional heat.

A portable electric or "space" heater is designed to warm a small area. There are two types. In convective heaters, air heated by one or more heating elements is blown into the room by a fan. In radiant heaters, the elements heat a liquid that radiates heat into the room rather than blowing it in.

A ceramic heater, a type of convective heater, uses a larger ceramic element that allows the heater to be run at lower temperatures, making it somewhat safer than other convective heaters that rely on conventional elements.

Additional components in a typical electric heater include control switches, elements, and a motorized fan. Heaters also typically have a thermostat. For safety, portable heaters usually include a tip-over switch, which shuts off the heater if it's knocked over, and a thermal cutoff, which shuts off an overheating unit. Some cutoffs reset after the heater has cooled down, but others must be replaced if they trip.

## What Can Go Wrong?

Even though there are few parts to the typical electric heater, most of the parts can make the heater stop working. Heating elements burn out. The thermostat can fail. Power cords and switches can fail. The fan in a wall heater can fail. The most common problems are caused by switches, thermostats, and heating elements. In addition, higher-watt heaters can trip a circuit breaker or blow a fuse, stopping electricity to the circuit.

**Caution**
Make sure nothing flammable is on or near an electric heater.

## How Can I Identify the Problem?

Though they are relatively simple in operation, electric heaters have many things that can go wrong with them and stop them from heating.

If the heater does not come on, make sure power is on to the unit (see *Electrical Service Panel*). If the circuit is delivering electricity, test the *Electrical Cord*, the thermostat (see *Appliance Controls*), and the *Heating Element*.

If the heater comes on but does not produce sufficient heat, check the heating elements to see if they are glowing.

If a fan-equipped heater comes on but the fan does not operate, test the fan (see *Motor*). Also, use a vacuum cleaner to remove any dust or debris around the fan and elements.

Make sure the heater sits level on a hard surface so the tip-over switch will not prevent the heater from working. Remove the control housing and check for burned wires. Replace any that look damaged. Test the thermostat and replace it if needed (see *Appliance Controls*).

> **Caution**
> Dust and lint can ignite; blocked vents can cause the unit to overheat. Make sure you carefully vacuum or wipe away accumulated dust and debris.

## What Parts, Materials, and Tools Do I Need?

Most replacement parts for electric heaters need to come from the manufacturer or after-market supplier (see *Fix-It Resources*). Because there are so many brands and models, hardware and electrical stores don't carry very many. However, you can disassemble the heater, remove the problem component, and take it to a knowledgeable clerk for assistance in replacing it. Here are the tools you'll need:

- Screwdrivers
- Adjustable pliers
- Long-nose pliers
- Multimeter

## What Are the Steps to Fixing It?

Disassemble a radiant heater:

1. Unplug the heater and let it cool completely before disassembling it.
2. To access wiring, remove the screws holding the control housing in place at the edges and lift it away.

Unplug the heater, let it cool, then remove the housing.

3. To remove the thermostat, pull off the knob and remove the electrical leads, marking their location with tape. You may need to remove the retaining nut to free the thermostat.
4. To remove the power switch, label and disconnect the leads. Some switches are secured by clips on the top and the bottom; others are fastened by screws.

Controls

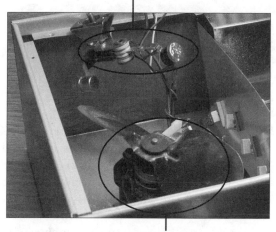

Fan motor

Primary components of a radiant heater include switches and controls, a motorized fan, and the radiant elements.

Disassemble a convective heater:

1. Unplug the heater and let it cool completely before disassembling it.
2. Remove the rear grille and the control knobs. Remove the front grille by unscrewing the fasteners on the back of the housing.
3. Remove the front grille by lifting the control housing and pulling the front grille toward you. The *Motor, Fan, and Heating Element* are now accessible for testing and repair (see *Fix Everything: Multimeter*).
4. Remove the thermostat from the control housing and disconnect the wires. Remove the heat control's mounting screws and clips to access and disconnect wires.

Service a ceramic heating element:

1. Inspect the unit for screws and hidden fasteners, removing them as needed.
2. Remove clips, fasteners, and other components to reveal the *Heating Element*.
3. Test each element using a multimeter (see *Fix Everything: Multimeter*) set on the R×1 (resistance times 1) scale. The reading should be approximately 10 ohms.
4. To replace a faulty ceramic *Heating Element*, disconnect the terminal lead on each side and lift the element out of its housing. Be sure to note the element's position, so it or a replacement can be reinstalled with the least effort.

# Heater, Kerosene

Kerosene heaters aren't the fire hazards they once were. In fact, safety laws have made them very safe for most household heating situations. These safety laws also have made them more complex and more difficult to fix. You can keep the home fires burning safely by doing basic maintenance and repairs yourself.

> **Caution**
>
> Check local laws concerning kerosene heaters. They have been banned in some areas and use is restricted in other areas. Be sure that your heater is legal in your area.

## How Does It Work?

A kerosene heater is a portable heating unit fueled by kerosene. Kerosene in the fuel tank or sump is absorbed by the wick skirt. At the wick's top, the kerosene is ignited for primary combustion by a battery-powered ignition plug. The kerosene continues to vaporize and burn in primary combustion. The burner controls the rate and volume of fresh air drawn through the base of the heater. It also reburns vapors in the burner's baffled chambers or chimneys, which is secondary combustion. Modern kerosene heaters are radiant (with reflector) or convection (air flow-through) types.

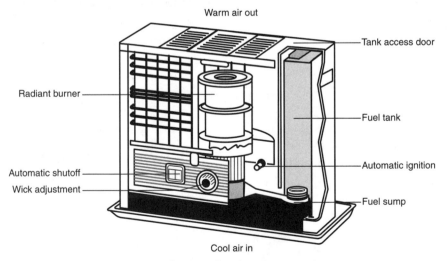

Components of a typical radiant kerosene heater.

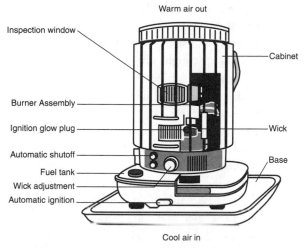

Warm air out
Inspection window
Cabinet
Burner Assembly
Ignition glow plug
Wick
Automatic shutoff
Base
Fuel tank
Wick adjustment
Automatic ignition
Cool air in

Components of a typical convection kerosene heater.

## What Can Go Wrong?

The wick may need replacing or reconditioning. The heater may not light. The flame may flicker or die. The flame may smoke or smell. The wick may burn too quickly. The wick adjuster may stick.

## How Can I Identify the Problem?

If the heater won't light, fill an empty fuel tank, eliminate impurities in the system (see below), check the igniter batteries, adjust the wick until the igniter contacts the top of the wick, and replace a faulty igniter (see below).

If the flame flickers or dies, remove any water in the system (see below), burn clean a wick covered with carbon or tar (see below), or trim away the dirty part of the wick.

If the flame smokes or causes odor, lower the wick to reduce the flame, move the heater out of direct drafts, make sure the chimney is

level, burn the wick clean of carbon or tar (see below), trim away the dirty part of the wick, or clean the system of impure kerosene (see below).

If the wick burns too quickly, clean the system of impure kerosene (see below).

If the wick adjuster sticks, clean the system of impure kerosene (see below) and burn the wick clean of carbon or tar (see below), or trim away the dirty part of the wick.

If the wick has worn out or become damaged, you can easily replace it by a series of quick and simple steps (see below).

## What Parts, Materials, and Tools Do I Need?

You can find common replacement parts for kerosene heaters at fireplace stores, larger hardware stores, and directly from the manufacturer (see *Fix-It Resources*). The tools you will need to fix a kerosene heater include these:

- Screwdrivers
- Drill and bit
- Old toothbrush
- Vacuum cleaner
- Rags
- Scissors

## What Are the Steps to Fixing It?

Eliminate impurities in kerosene:

1. Remove the wick and dry it on absorbent paper.
2. Drain the cartridge tank and the burner tank, wiping up any spilled kerosene.

**Fix-It Tip**

> Keep your owner's manual handy and refer to it often, because kerosene heater models differ and the owner's manual has the specific information on maintaining and repairing your heater.

3. Reinstall the wick.
4. Fill the tank with clean, pure K-1 low-sulfur kerosene or as recommended by the manufacturer. Recycle dirty fuel by calling your local hazardous waste recycler for instructions.

Burn off a carbonized wick to restore its softness:

1. Remove all the fuel from the tank or wait until the tank is empty.
2. Turn the wick to its highest position. Light it with a match if you cannot light it automatically. Be sure the chimney is properly centered.
3. Allow the wick to burn until the fire is completely out and no carbon remains on the wick.
4. Remove any remaining ash with an old toothbrush.
5. Vacuum away any residue or soot from the burner area.

Replace the wick on most kerosene heaters:

1. Drain or burn off all the fuel in the tank and allow the heater to cool completely.
2. Follow the manufacturer's recommendation for activating the automatic shutoff. For many models simply hit the heater body with your hand.
3. Remove the batteries.

4. Open the front grille and remove the chimney.
5. Remove the safety shutoff reset lever by pulling it straight out of the cabinet.
6. Remove the cabinet.
7. Slide the electrical wire connectors off the battery case.
8. Remove the screws at the side of the extinguisher assembly and lift it out.
9. Remove the wick adjuster mechanism by loosening the wing nuts until you can turn the retainers that hold it in place.
10. Fold the wick and slide it out.
11. To install the new wick, turn the wick adjuster counterclockwise as far as it will go.
12. Fold the new wick and slide it into the adjuster. The red line on the outside of the wick should match the bottom edge of the adjuster.
13. Turn the wick adjuster clockwise as far as it will go.
14. Check the height of the wick, then press it against the teeth inside the adjuster to obtain a firm grip.
15. Slide the rubber packing over the wick and allow the tails of the wick to drop down.
16. Replace the wick and adjuster mechanism in the fuel tank, making sure the wick fits evenly in place.
17. Position the adjuster knob to the front of the heater and tighten the wing nuts onto the retainers. Turn the knob clockwise and counterclockwise a few times to make sure the mechanism is functioning smoothly.
18. Recheck the height of the wick. If it has changed, readjust it.
19. Trim any ragged edges that appear at the top of the wick.

20. Replace the cabinet on the fuel tank and reattach.
21. Push the automatic shutoff reset lever into its slot. It will snap into place. Slide the lever fully to the left to reset the auto shut-off mechanism.
22. Replace the chimney and snap the grille shut.
23. Replace the batteries.
24. Make sure the top of the wick is even and level.
25. Wait about 20 minutes before lighting the heater to allow the fuel to saturate the wick. Don't cut, pull, or soil the new wick.

Replace a kerosene heater igniter:

1. Remove batteries from the case to avoid danger of shock or accidental ignition. Test the batteries because they can cause poor ignition or lack of ignition (see *Battery, Household*).
2. Let the heater cool completely.
3. Remove the guard and burner to gain access to the ignition mechanism.
4. Push down the ignition knob.
5. Remove the ignition coil by pushing in and turn it counterclockwise.
6. Install the new ignition coil.
7. Reinstall the burner, guard, and batteries.

**Caution**

Use only the fuel recommended by the manufacturer of your kerosene heater. Some models identify the fuel on the side of the heater. If not, check the owner's manual or contact the manufacturer and identify the model number.

# Heating Element

When a wire gets a lot of electricity running through it, the wire glows "red hot." If you can keep that wire from burning up, you can use the heat for lots of tasks around your house. You can toast bagels or dry clothes, for example. That's what a heating element does—and that's why you'll find heating elements in dozens of appliances and devices throughout your home. Here's how to keep them glowing.

## How Does It Work?

A heating element is an appliance component that consists of a metal wire heated by a *controlled* electric current. The resulting heat is then used to warm or heat something. Heating elements are found in dozens of everyday appliances and gadgets we rely upon (see *Coffee Maker*; *Electric Iron*; *Heater, Electric*; *Heating Pad*; *Popcorn Popper*; *Water Heater, Electric*; *Dryer, Hair*; and *Slow Cooker*, to name just a few).

Most heating elements are open ribbon, open coil, or enclosed coil and are made of a nickel and chrome alloy. The material responds to electric current by resisting its flow and heating up. It is converting electricity into heat. Its rating is determined by the length and diameter of the wire (resistance in ohms) as well as the electrical current it can carry and voltage it needs to push the current.

## What Can Go Wrong?

Heating elements are relatively simple. They either work or they don't; they are on or off. Heating elements can break and burn out, sag, and become misshapen. Most elements cannot be repaired, but they usually can be replaced. If you can't remove the heating element to replace it, you'll probably need to replace the entire appliance.

## How Can I Identify the Problem?

If an appliance that should produce heat does not, inspect the element for breaks or obvious damage. If you don't see any damage, test the element for continuity (see below).

> **Fix-It Tip**
>
> If you are replacing a heating element, make sure you know its part number, size, resistance (in ohms), current capacity (in amps or amperes), and how much voltage it requires (120V or 240V).

## What Parts, Materials, and Tools Do I Need?

Replacement heating elements are available from the appliance's manufacturer or one of many aftermarket suppliers included in *Fix-It Resources*. Tools you'll need to access and test heating elements include these:

- Screwdrivers
- Wrenches
- Multimeter

## What Are the Steps to Fixing It?

Test an element for continuity (ability to pass electricity from one end to the other) and replace it:

1. Turn off power to the appliance or device. If the unit is plugged in, unplug it from the electrical receptacle (outlet); if the device is wired into the circuit (such as an oven), turn off the circuit at the *Electrical Service Panel*.

2. Disassemble the appliance or device to access the heating element, following the guides in this book for your appliance. Some heating elements, such as plug-in units in electric ovens, are relatively easy to remove (see the guide for *Oven, Electric*).

Ribbon elements

The heating element in an electric heater is a wire ribbon.

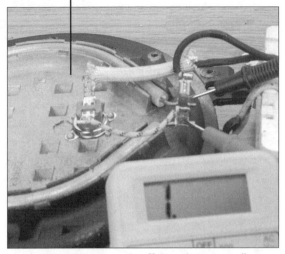

Sealed heating element

Cooking appliances and coffee makers typically have a sealed heating element that either works or doesn't.

3. Set the multimeter (see *Fix Everything: Multimeter*) to R×1 (resistance times 1).

4. Touch the multimeter probes to each end of the element.

5. High resistance (kilo-ohms or thousands of ohms) indicates the heating element is okay. A reading of infinite resistance indicates a broken element.

6. If a heating element is faulty, replace it with one of the exact size, shape, power rating, and resistance.

7. Reassemble the appliance or device and turn it on or plug it in to test it.

A toaster or hair dryer (see *Toaster* and *Dryer, Hair*) uses a very thin heating element that is wound around a nonconducting frame of mica or other material. The element is so thin that it easily can be damaged during dismantling or in installation, so be very careful when replacing the unit.

A toaster's heating element is very thin and can easily burn out.

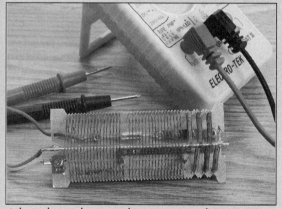

A hair dryer's heating element, too, is thin; it's typically wrapped around an insulated frame.

# Heating Pad

Ah! There's nothing like a heating pad to soothe away aches. Such a simple device. Yet, they sometimes quit for no apparent reason. Fortunately, they are relatively easy to troubleshoot and repair—or replace.

## How Does It Work?

A heating pad is a small electrical device with a continuous electrical wire encased in a plastic pad. Heating pads include a removable fabric cover; wet heating pads also have a spongelike liner that holds moisture to pass heat.

## What Can Go Wrong?

Most heating pads are relatively maintenance-free. But the electrical wire within the heating pad can be broken, causing the pad to heat intermittently or not at all. The thermostat can malfunction. Often, the best solution when a heating pad malfunctions is to replace the entire device. Before doing so, however, identify the cause of the problem. Maybe you can fix it yourself.

**Fix-It Tip**

Small appliance repair shops typically won't repair heating pads because they are so inexpensive to replace.

## How Can I Identify the Problem?

If the heating pad won't come on at all, make sure power is on at the outlet. You can test the *Electrical Cord*, but you still may not be able to determine if the problem is inside the pad itself.

If the unit goes on and off as you manipulate the pad, the problem is probably a broken wire within.

If the unit works on some settings and not others, the problem is probably in the thermostat; if you can open the thermostat, follow the instructions for repair in *Appliance Controls*.

**Fix-It Tip**

The most common fix to heating pads is cleaning out the control unit on the cord. Unplug the heating pad, then use a screwdriver to open up the control unit. If parts are loose, tighten them. Otherwise, you may need to invest in a new heating pad.

## What Parts, Materials, and Tools Do I Need?

Again, there are few parts to a heating pad so finding replacements may be difficult. You'll need instructions for testing the cord and thermostat, noted above, and a couple of tools to test the unit yourself:

- Screwdrivers
- Multimeter

Off

On

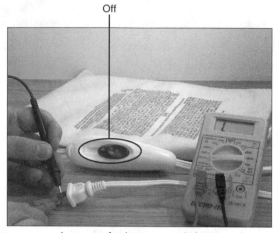

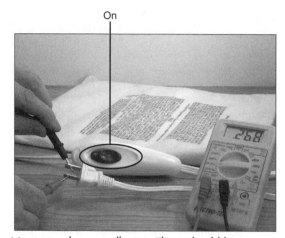

To test conductivity of a heating pad, first attach a multimeter (see *Fix Everything: Multimeter*) to the electrical cord prongs with the controller off. The reading should be infinite resistance (in ohms).

Next, turn the controller on. There should be some, but not infinite, resistance to electricity.

# Holiday Decorations

Christmas, Hanukkah, and other festivals of lights benefit from lots of decorations. Unfortunately, when everything is unpacked each year, lights may not work and other decorations could be broken. Fortunately, many can easily be fixed. Here's how.

## How Does It Work?

Holiday decorations are those strings of lights and other ornamentation that add color and festivity to holiday celebrations. Holiday lights are strings of low-wattage light bulbs that are designed to decorate an indoor holiday tree, the outside of a home, a fireplace mantle, a stairway, or anywhere else a homeowner wishes to add light and color. Other holiday decorations include ceramic, glass, plastic, and other figurines, animated figures, tree ornaments, stuffed toys, and a wide variety of other objects.

## What Can Go Wrong?

Holiday lights are relatively simple in operation, so the things that can go wrong typically are just as simple. Whole light strings may not glow and single bulbs may burn out. The same goes for other decorations. Figurines get chipped and broken. Ornaments fall and crack. Animated figures won't move. Stuffed toys get torn and lose their stuffing.

## How Can I Identify the Problem?

First, let's take a look at holiday lights. If a string of lights does not come on at all, make sure power is on at the outlet. Plug the set of lights into another outlet to verify that the outlet is not the problem. If the string still doesn't light, test the *Electrical Cord*.

If the lights are blinking and you don't want them to, look for clear bulbs with a red tip or a different-looking base (these are blinker bulbs), and replace any you find with clear bulbs.

If the outlet and plug test good and the lights still do not work, check the string of lights from end to end until the whole string of lights works properly (see below).

Many repairs of other holiday decorations can be accomplished with the proper type of adhesive. Determine what the decoration is made of and refer to *Fix Everything: Adhesives* to decide what adhesive will create the best bond for your decoration. Follow the directions for applying that adhesive to the material.

If stuffed holiday toys are injured, see *Stuffed Toy* for repair instructions.

> **Fix-It Tip**
>
> Bulb blown out? Don't throw away the bulb you think has caused a problem until you retest the string. The bulb may still be good.

> **Caution**
>
> You can be shocked handling a broken bulb or the bulb's socket. Once you've located the problem visually, unplug the string of lights before attempting to fix it.

## What Parts, Materials, and Tools Do I Need?

Replacement parts for holiday lights are available at most stores where holiday decorations are sold. And adhesives are widely available. To work on holiday decorations you may need these tools:

- Multimeter
- Appropriate adhesive
- Basic sewing supplies
- Fasteners (from a hardware store)

## What Are the Steps to Fixing It?

Locate the problem in a string of holiday lights:

1. Visually check each bulb in a string and replace any that are damaged or missing. Make sure that all screw-in bulbs are tight.
2. Plug the string into an electrical receptacle.
3. Gently tap each bulb to see if it flickers or causes the strand to flicker. If it flickers, unplug the strand and inspect the bulb and its base for obvious damage and replace if needed.
4. To locate and replace a bad bulb in a strand that won't light, use a bulb that you know works and, one at a time, substitute it for each of the bulbs on the string, replacing each bulb with the previous socket's bulb until the strand lights.

5. To locate the bad bulb in a strand that flickers, start at the end closest to the plug and touch each bulb until the flickering stops or starts. Replace the bulb and retest the string, because the problem may be in the wires.
6. To locate a blown fuse on a light string, plug a working light set into the one that doesn't work. If the test set doesn't light up, replace the fuse in the nonworking strand or replace the strand.

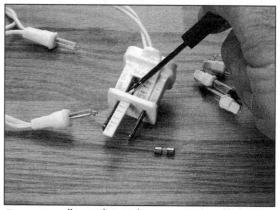

Fuses typically are located in or near the electrical cord plug.

# Hot Plate

Hot plates are yesterday's microwaves. They are still handy for heating up a pot or skillet of food when a stove isn't handy or necessary. Let's check in with the Fix-It Club for info on repairing a hot plate.

## How Does It Work?

A hot plate is a small electric appliance for cooking in a small space. The main parts of a hot plate are the heating element(s) and one or more devices to regulate the heat. Some hot plates have a calibrated thermostat, while others simply have an on/off switch.

## What Can Go Wrong?

A burned-out heating element is one of the most common problems with hot plates. The electrical cord or the thermostat may be faulty. Internal wiring can be damaged. Contacts may have become fused.

**Fix-It Tip**

If the cord is detachable, always plug one end firmly into the hot plate before plugging the other end into the wall outlet.

## How Can I Identify the Problem?

If the hot plate doesn't heat, make sure power is on at the outlet and test the *Electrical Cord*. You may need to examine internal wiring for damage or wear and replace any wiring or connections that look burned or otherwise faulty. Test the thermostat (see *Appliance Controls*) and the thermal *Fuse* (if the appliance has one) and replace as necessary. Test the *Heating Element* and replace it if it is faulty.

If the hot plate is not level or tips when used, check for damaged feet and repair or replace as needed. If the unit includes a leveling leg, adjust it with a screwdriver.

If the hot plate doesn't shut off or heats whenever it's plugged in, inspect the thermostat contacts and repair or replace the thermostat (see *Appliance Controls*).

**Fix-It Tip**

Food spills can dramatically reduce the life of your hot plate. Keep the burners and plugs clean.

## What Parts, Materials, and Tools Do I Need?

Replacement cords can be found at many larger hardware stores. If you need to buy a replacement part, check with the manufacturer or an aftermarket appliance supply source (see *Fix-It Resources*). The tools you'll need to disassemble and test a hot plate include these:

- Screwdrivers
- Wrenches
- Multimeter

## What Are the Steps to Fixing It?

Disassemble and test a hot plate:

1. Unplug the hot plate from the electrical receptacle.

2. Find the screws or bolts holding the hot plate together and carefully remove them, noting where they should be reinstalled.
3. Remove the housing to access the burner(s), internal wiring, and other components.
4. Use a multimeter (see *Fix Everything: Multimeter*) to test each electrical component; replace as needed.

> **Caution**
> Don't plug a hot plate into an extension cord; plug it directly into the electrical receptacle to reduce the chance of fire.

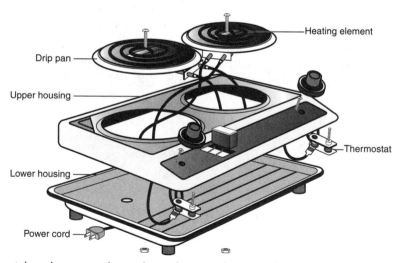

Drip pan
Upper housing
Lower housing
Power cord
Heating element
Thermostat

A hot plate is simply an electric heating element with temperature controls.

# Humidifier

It's not the heat, it's the humidity; it's not the cold, it's the dryness.

In many parts of the United States, comfort means putting water into the air, taking it out, or both. That's where a humidifier comes in handy. It puts moisture into the household air to increase comfort—unless it quits working. Here's what to do if it quits.

## How Does It Work?

A humidifier is an appliance designed on the principle of evaporation to increase moisture in the air. Water from a reservoir is added to an evaporation pad. A fan blows air through the pad. Fine droplets of water are placed in the air, thus increasing the humidity of the room. Both room and tabletop humidifiers work on this principle.

The two types of evaporative room humidifiers are drum and pump. A drum humidifier gathers water into an evaporation pad by immersing the pad, wrapped around a drum, into a reservoir of water. Water dripping from the rotating pad is absorbed by air current produced by a fan. A pump humidifier uses a pump to gather water from the reservoir and distribute it through the evaporation pad. Air from the fan blows through the pad and picks up the droplets to moisturize the air. Both types of humidifiers have operational controls, an evaporation pad, a fan, a water reservoir, and a humidistat. Some *Forced-Air Distribution* systems include an evaporative humidifier that works in the same way.

An ultrasonic humidifier works on completely different principles from standard room humidifiers. It's electronic. Beyond normal cleaning and testing of the *Electrical Cord* or switch (see *Appliance Controls*), service of an ultrasonic humidifier should be left to a service technician.

## What Can Go Wrong?

As you see, evaporative humidifiers are relatively simple appliances. Many humidifier problems result from dirty or damaged evaporative foam or filters. The electrical cord may malfunction. The humidistat, float control, and fan can be faulty.

The humidistat is sensitive to the level of moisture in the air. If humidity is lower than the control point set, the humidistat turns on the fan and pump (or pad rotator). See below for service instructions.

Many humidifiers have a hollow float inside that helps control water level, or tells the operator (that's you) when to refill the reservoir. In some cases, you'll need to adjust or replace the float (see below).

| Fix-It Tip | Humidifier water conditioners are available that can soften the water and reduce algae to make your unit last longer. Stay away from those with perfumes that can leave residue to clog the evaporator pad. Clean the unit with a disinfectant at least once a season. |
|---|---|

## How Can I Identify the Problem?

If the unit doesn't work, check the water level and fill if low. Make sure power is on at the outlet and test the *Electrical Cord*. Test and service the humidistat if it is faulty (see below). Also check the float control and service it if it's faulty (see below).

If the humidifier doesn't sufficiently increase humidity, check the evaporation pad and service it if it is dirty. Also check the humidistat and service it if it's faulty (see below).

If the humidifier is noisy, test the fan *Motor* and service it or replace it if it's faulty.

Motor

Test the fan motor using a multimeter.

If the humidifier smells bad, check the evaporation pad and clean or replace it; check the water reservoir and clean and refill it if it is dirty.

## What Parts, Materials, and Tools Do I Need?

The most important replacement part on most humidifiers is the evaporative pad. Fortunately, you can find replacements for most popular models at local hardware stores. If you can't find parts, refer to the unit's owner's manual for information on ordering replacement parts. *Fix-It Resources* contains contact information for many consumer appliance manufacturers.

You'll need a few tools to check and fix a humidifier:

- Screwdrivers
- Wrenches
- Multimeter

## What Are the Steps to Fixing It?

Service an evaporation pad on a pump humidifier:

1. Unplug the humidifier or otherwise make sure that power to the unit is *off*.

> **Caution**
>
> Humidifiers run on electricity with water, so it's vital that you unplug the humidifier before attempting to repair it. Safety first!

2. Lift the pad frame from the humidifier housing and hold it so excess moisture will drip back into the reservoir.
3. Remove the pad from the frame.

4. Rinse the pad with clean water or replace it. If you use soap or detergent, make sure the pad is completely rinsed of residue before reinstalling.

5. While the humidifier is open, clean the reservoir and inspect the inside of the appliance for any obvious problems.

Service the float control:

1. Remove the top cover and inspect the float. Make sure the float rod is straight and secure and that the float is clean. When cleaning the float, make sure you don't bend the rod.

2. Move the float manually to determine at what level the float switch is activated. If necessary, adjust the switch (see *Appliance Controls*) to make sure it activates at the appropriate level.

3. Check all electrical connections on the float switch to make sure they are tight.

Service the humidistat:

1. Mark and disconnect any wires attached to the humidistat.

2. Use a multimeter (see *Fix Everything: Multimeter*) to test the humidistat. It should conduct in the *on* position, but not in the *off* position.

3. If necessary, replace the humidistat with an exact replacement part.

**Fix-It Tip**

Remember to lubricate the humidifier *Fan* at least twice during each season it runs. Use a few drops of machine oil. See *Fix Everything: Lubricants*.

# Ice-Cream Maker

Mmmmm. Homemade ice cream! Okay, it's not hand cranked—it's turned by a motor—but the result is still delicious. Many of us have an ice-cream maker somewhere in the garage or storage that needs to be repaired—or at least dusted off—and put back to work. Soon!

## How Does It Work?

An electric ice-cream maker is a tabletop appliance for mixing and freezing ice cream at home. A small electric motor drives gears that turn the canister filled with the ingredients for ice cream. The canister is surrounded with ice and rock salt to freeze the contents. Alternately, a hand crank on top replaces the motor.

## What Can Go Wrong?

Although durable, ice-cream makers can require a few repairs. A common problem is damage to motors or gears from mixing too large batches of ice cream or from neglecting a jammed mixing paddle. The electrical cord can fail and motor bearings can dry out.

**Fix-It Tip**

Your ice-cream maker's owner's manual will tell you what and how much of each ingredient to put in the canister for a single batch. Putting too much in it can make it overflow and possibly damage the motor or gears.

## How Can I Identify the Problem?

If the motor doesn't work, make sure power is on at the outlet and test the *Electrical Cord*. Lubricate dry *Motor* bearings with lightweight machine oil (see *Fix Everything: Lubricants*). Test the *Motor* and replace if necessary.

If the ingredients don't mix properly, inspect the paddle for damage and replace if necessary. You also may need to replace worn or damaged gears (see *Motor*).

If the motor runs but the paddle doesn't turn, check and replace worn or damaged gears (see *Motor*).

If the appliance is unusually noisy, replace worn or damaged gears (see *Motor*). If the gears look okay, try lubricating the *Motor*.

**Fix-It Tip**

After each use, make sure the ice-cream maker is thoroughly cleaned. And, at least once an ice-cream season, disassemble the power unit and carefully lubricate the gears and motor shaft, wiping off excess oil.

## What Parts, Materials, and Tools Do I Need?

You can find a replacement motor or other parts through the manufacturer or an after-market parts supplier (see *Fix-It Resources*). Lubricants and fasteners are available through a local hardware store. Here are the tools you'll need for disassembly and testing:

- Screwdrivers
- Wrenches
- Multimeter for testing components

## What Are the Steps to Fixing It?

Disassemble an ice-cream maker:

1. Make sure the unit is unplugged from the electrical receptacle.
2. Remove the *Motor* unit, if easily detached. If it is on the side, remove the ice bucket or other components to access the motor and gear assembly.
3. Turn the motor unit upside down and remove the cover or baseplate to access the motor and gears.
4. Carefully remove gears and check for wear.
5. Clean any debris around the gears and motor, then remove the motor and test it with a multimeter (see *Fix Everything: Multimeter*).
6. Replace any worn or broken parts. Carefully lubricate (see *Fix Everything: Lubricants*) and reassemble.

**Fix-It Tip**

If you are buying a new or replacement ice-cream maker, look for one with durable metal rather than breakable plastic gears. How can you tell? If the box doesn't tell you, open it and check the owner's manual.

# Icemaker

"Need some more ice? No problem; we have an icemaker!" Because not every refrigerator freezer has an icemaker—it can be added later—it's considered a separate appliance. Fortunately, icemakers are relatively simple in operation and easy to fix when they don't work. Here's the Fix-It Process for icemakers.

## How Does It Work?

An icemaker is a small appliance that fits inside a refrigerator's freezer and makes ice cubes.

The water flows through a tube to an inlet valve on the back of the refrigerator. When water is needed, the valve lets the water flow into an ice cube mold, where it freezes. When a thermostat senses that the ice is cold enough, a heater melts the ice surface so that ejector blades can push the cubes into a bin. The cycle repeats until a shutoff arm stops it when the bin is full.

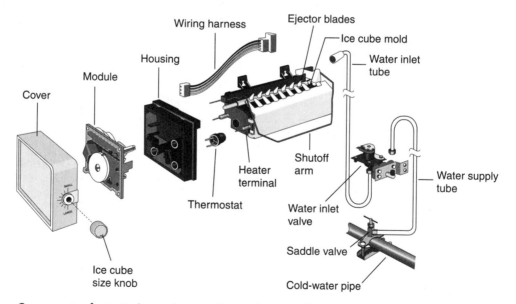

Components of a typical icemaker unit for a refrigerator freezer.

## What Can Go Wrong?

Simple as they are, things can go wrong with an icemaker. The unit can get too little or too much water. Modular or nonmodular controls (the unit's motor and switches) may malfunction. The thermostat may be faulty. The water inlet valve may need service.

## How Can I Identify the Problem?

If the ice cubes have watery or hollow centers, the icemaker is getting too little water. Alternatively, excess water or ice in the bin is caused by too much water. Turn the water supply screw to adjust. If adjustment does not remedy the problem, you may need to service the water inlet valve (see below).

If you suspect trouble with the *Motor* or switches (see *Appliance Controls*) in an icemaker, use a multimeter (see *Fix Everything: Multimeter*) to test the components. If the motor or switches test faulty, replace either the bad components or the entire module. If not, you may only need to replace the thermostat (see below)

**Fix-It Tip**

Maybe it's not cold enough for ice. A freezer must be 5°F or colder for an icemaker to work properly. Freezers typically operate between 0° and 8°F.

## What Parts, Materials, and Tools Do I Need?

Replacement parts are available from appliance parts stores or the manufacturer (see *Fix-It Resources*). The tools you will need to fix an icemaker include these:

- Screwdrivers
- Needle-nose pliers
- Nut driver
- Metallic putty
- Multimeter

## What Are the Steps to Fixing It?

Disassemble an icemaker:

1. Unplug the refrigerator.
2. Remove the icemaker's front cover by unscrewing or prying it off as needed (refer to the owner's manual for specifics).
3. Remove the ice bin, shelves, and vertical partition.
4. Remove remaining screws, disconnect the icemaker wires from the harness connector or socket, and remove the unit from the freezer.
5. Remove the back access panel (see *Refrigerator*) and any fasteners that hold the inlet valve to the refrigerator.

**Fix-It Tip**

To access the motor, switches, and thermostat in a nonmodular icemaker, first remove the front cover of the icemaker. The on-off switch is activated by the shutoff arm. The holding switch keeps power flowing to the ejector blades during the ice release phase. The water inlet valve switch controls the flow of water from the inlet valve. Use a multimeter (see *Fix Everything: Multimeter*) to test these *Appliance Controls*.

Replace a thermostat in a control module:

1. Unplug the refrigerator.
2. Remove the icemaker control module and its housing.
3. Remove the thermostat from the housing.
4. Replace the thermostat, using metallic putty where the thermostat touches the case.

Service the water inlet valve:

1. Turn off the water supply at the saddle valve on the pipe.
2. Disconnect the inlet valve from the refrigerator (see above).
3. Unscrew the tubes from the valve, letting excess water drain into a bowl.
4. Unplug the wires from the valve.
5. Use a multimeter on R×10 (resistance times 10) to probe both terminals on the valve solenoid. An infinite reading means the valve solenoid is bad; a reading of 1,000 ohms or less means it is probably good.
6. Remove the plate and filter screen from the water inlet. Wash a clogged screen with a toothbrush under running water. Replace the screen if it is rusted or damaged.

# Jacket

Don't forget your jacket! Jackets and other outerwear must stand up to the elements. But when they don't, they, too, can be taken to the Fix-It Club for repair.

## How Does It Work?

A jacket, of course, is worn over indoor clothes to insulate the wearer's body. The amount of protection offered depends on the type and fabric of the jacket.

## What Can Go Wrong?

Though they are simple in function, jackets have problems, too. Jackets get stained. Tears and holes happen. Buttons disappear. Zippers stick, separate, and lose teeth.

**Fix-It Tip**

To make a zipper work more smoothly, rub a candle over the zipper, then open and close the zipper. The candle's wax will serve as a lubricant and reduce friction.

## How Can I Identify the Problem?

If a jacket becomes stained, treat and wash it as soon as possible (see below). Promptly treating stains (and repairing damage) to a jacket often keeps the problem from becoming worse. If the jacket is not washable, take it to a dry cleaner or use a home dry-cleaning product.

If the jacket is torn, mend it as soon as possible to avoid further damage (see *Fix Everything: Sewing*).

If a button is missing, find a close replacement or replace all the buttons (see *Clothing*).

If the zipper sticks or has separated, you may be able to repair it (see below).

If a zipper cannot be repaired, either replace the garment or take it to a clothing alterations and repair service, depending on the garment's value.

**Fix-It Tip**

If the jacket is washable, launder it frequently to avoid ground-in dirt. Depending on the fabric of the jacket, you may be able to treat it with a stain-blocking spray available at larger grocery and variety stores.

## What Parts, Materials, and Tools Do I Need?

If you have basic sewing skills (see *Fix Everything: Sewing*) you can fix jackets and other outer garments with easy-to-find materials and tools:

- Thread and needle or sewing machine
- Oxygen-based cleaner
- Replacement buttons and zippers

## What Are the Steps to Fixing It?

To repair fabric, see *Fix Everything: Sewing*; to replace buttons, see *Clothing*.

Remove spots and stains from a washable jacket:

1. Apply an oxygen cleaner directly on the spot or stain. Let the jacket sit for several minutes.
2. Launder the jacket in the hottest water safe for the fabric, using detergent and color-safe bleach (unless the care label says "no bleach"). For bleach amounts, follow instructions on the container.
3. Repeat if necessary, letting the jacket soak for a longer time.

Repair a zipper with missing teeth:

1. Realign and close the zipper.
2. With heavyweight thread, stitch tightly over the zipper several times ¼ to ½ inch above the missing teeth. You've created a new stop above the damage.

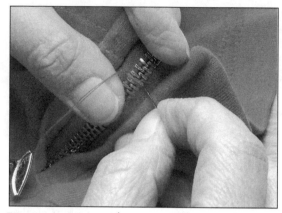

To repair a zipper with missing teeth, sew a new stop above the damage.

# Jewelry

One of the largest categories of things that need fixing in many homes is jewelry. That includes clasps, posts, rings, brooches, watchbands, and even eyeglasses. They all break—and they all need tiny tools and good eyesight to fix. So let's take a closer look at how to fix them.

## How Does It Work?

Of all the components—collectively known as *findings*—that make up most pieces of jewelry, the most vulnerable is the clasp. It's the clasp that holds the piece securely around the neck, wrist, or ankle of the wearer. Related are the pins and hinges that allow jewelry or eyeglasses to pivot or move.

## What Can Go Wrong?

Clasps can become loose and not hold the piece of jewelry securely. Jump rings can open. Posts can detach from pierced earrings. Clips on standard earrings can become bent and uncomfortable. Pin or brooch fasteners can become worn. Ring prongs or bezel settings can need repair. Watchstraps may need adjusting or replacing. Eyeglass screws can become loose or even lost. All are fixable.

## How Can I Identify the Problem?

It's relatively easy to identify the problem, but fixing it depends on identifying which component needs repair. Here are some common jewelry findings:

- A box snap has a V-shaped spring that slides into a boxlike sheath.
- A fold-over clasp has a curved arm that rotates on a hinge.
- A figure-eight fitting fits over a post to provide extra security for many types of clasps.
- A spring ring contains a spring that compresses when the nub is pulled back.
- A banger snap clasp has a V-shaped prong that widens as it slides into a sheath, securing the clasp.
- A lobster clasp pivots to open.
- A jump ring is a metal ring that can be pried open.

See below for instructions for repairing these and other jewelry components.

> **Caution**
>
> Don't try to repair wristwatches or expensive and keepsake jewelry. Take them to a professional jeweler or watch repair service.

> **Fix-It Tip**
>
> Inspection and maintenance are the best methods of keeping jewelry and eyeglasses functioning longer. Most important, clean jewelry regularly using jewelry cleaning products specific to the type of metal that's in them. Check and tighten eyeglass frames, especially reading glasses that are frequently put on and removed.

## What Parts, Materials, and Tools Do I Need?

You can purchase replacement parts from a jeweler, jewelry supply store, or department store. Some online resources are available as well (see *Fix-It Resources*). Here are some of the tools you may need:

- Small screwdrivers
- Small standard pliers
- Specialized jewelry pliers (flat-, round, needle-nose)
- Eyeglass repair kit (may contain helpful tools and supplies)
- Nail file
- Emery board
- Spring-bar tool

## What Are the Steps to Fixing It?

Repair a lobster clasp:

1. Realign the hook and latch of a bent clasp by carefully moving them with needle-nose pliers until the parts meet.
2. Close the gap between the ends by carefully squeezing the sides of the jump ring with pliers until the ends meet.

Repair a fold-over clasp:

1. Bend the tab back onto itself if the clasp doesn't snap closed. Test and repeat if needed.
2. Reshape the arm as needed with needle-nose pliers.

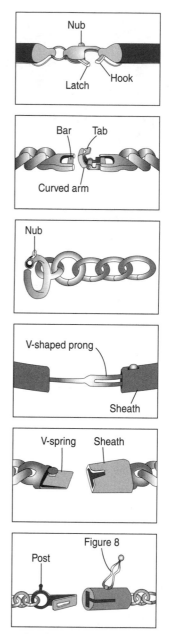

Common jewelry clasps, from top: lobster, fold-over, spring ring, banger snap, box snap, and figure eight.

Repair a spring-ring clasp:

1. Remove the ring by opening the loop holding the spring ring to the jewelry piece.
2. Position the replacement spring ring and close the gap between the ends by gently squeezing the sides of the ring with pliers until the ends meet.
3. Replace the entire ring if the spring breaks or the nub snaps off.

Repair a banger snap clasp:

1. Widen the V-shaped prong by inserting the blade of a small screwdriver and gently twisting.
2. Test and adjust the clasp until it snaps securely into place.

Repair a box snap clasp:

1. Pry open the leaves of the V with a nail file or other flat tool.
2. Reshape a bent sheath by manipulating it with flat-nose pliers.

Repair a figure-eight clasp:

1. Carefully squeeze the center of the eight with round-nose pliers.
2. Test and repeat until the eight fits snugly over the post.

Repair a jump ring:

1. Grip each end with needle-nose pliers and carefully twist the ends in opposite directions. Stop once the gap is large enough to slip the jump ring over an adjacent ring or other fitting.
2. To close a jump ring, twist the ends in opposite directions with pliers until the ends meet.

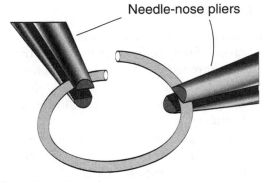
Needle-nose pliers

Repairing a jump ring.

Reattach a post setting:

1. Test the setting to verify that the post and prong sit firmly in the cup or disc. If they do not, replace the setting.
2. Remove old adhesive by carefully scraping the cup and stone with a pin or other pointed metal object.
3. Use a toothpick to place a spot of epoxy onto the cup, making sure you cover the prong with adhesive.
4. Slide the stone onto the prong and hold it in place for three to five minutes.
5. Allow the earring to completely dry before use.

Repair hoop earrings:

1. Grasp the wire or catch and carefully bend it back into shape with flat-nose pliers.
2. Use a fine emery cloth to buff out any marks caused by the pliers.

Repair a clip-on earring:

1. If the clip falls off, reinsert the clip into the holes.
2. Use pliers to carefully squeeze the flanges toward each other.
3. To adjust spring tension, gradually bend the neck forward or backward with pliers.
4. If this fails, remove the clip from the earring and bend the spring to increase or decrease tension.

Repair a pin or brooch:

1. Straighten a pin stem by holding the brooch firmly while carefully pulling the stem through the jaws of flat-nose pliers.
2. Straighten a bent tip by bending it, then filing the end to a point with a fine emery board.
3. Tighten a loose or wobbly pin stem by carefully squeezing the point flanges together with flat-nose pliers.
4. Tighten a ball clasp latch by positioning the latch so the nubs point up, then firmly squeezing both sides of clasp together with flat-nose pliers.

Replace a watchband or spring bar:

1. Use small pliers to grasp, depress, and remove the spring bar holding the band to the watch.
2. Remove the spring bar from the band. If it is damaged, replace the spring bar.
3. Install the spring bar in the loop of the new watchband and insert one end of bar into lug. Use small pliers to maneuver the spring bar into place.

Repair eyeglass frames:

1. Carefully check to see if the hinge is damaged (and needs replacement by an optometrist) or simply requires that the screw be tightened or replaced.
2. Use a small screwdriver to carefully tighten or replace the screw. Do not overtighten.
3. Once firmly in place, place a drop of instant glue on the screw to keep it in place. Be careful not to allow the glue to touch other parts.

**Fix-It Tip**

You probably can't repair a finger ring yourself, but you can clean it using jewelry cleaning products available at larger household and discount stores. Most jewelers will clean and inspect rings and other jewelry for free, especially if you purchased the ring there. They want to earn your future business.

# Juicer/Juice Extractor

Fresh-squeezed OJ in the morning! It's a good way to wake up. A *bad* way is to hear the grinding of a motor and gears carelessly ripping that orange beyond edibility! Because juicers and juice extractors are simply motor-driven blade appliances, fixing them can be relatively easy. Hey, it's worth a try.

## How Does It Work?

Juicers are small appliances designed to process citrus fruits into juice. Juice extractors are small appliances that shred various fruits and vegetables and separate the juice from the pulp. Typically, juice extractors are more powerful—and more expensive—than juicers.

Juicers use a motor and gear assembly to drive a spring-loaded shaft and reamer. The reamer activates an internal switch that starts the motor. The rotating reamer rubs against the fruit, releasing juice into a container.

Juice extractors typically use centrifugal force to extract juice through a filter, though some models compress the fruit to force out the juice.

## What Can Go Wrong?

Things that can go wrong with juicers and juice extractors are those common to other motorized small appliances. Electric cords, internal wiring, switches, brushes, and motors can fail. The spindle or reamer may be damaged and drive gears may be stripped. Fortunately, many of these things can be fixed.

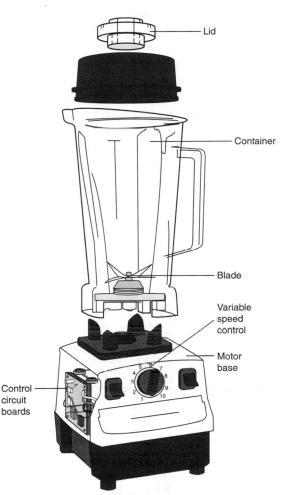

A juicer is similar to a blender except it has additional power and specialized blades.

**Fix-It Tip**

Make sure your juicer or juice extractor is clean before use. Not only is it more sanitary, it also will operate more easily, reducing the need to fix it.

## How Can I Identify the Problem?

If the juicer or extractor doesn't work, first make sure power is on at the outlet. Check the *Electrical Cord*; look for broken wires or corroded connections; test the *Motor*.

If the juicer still doesn't work, the brushes may need replacing. Either take the appliance to a repair center or replace it.

If the *Motor* stops or slows during use, an internal *Fuse* may have burned out (extractors only); if the extractor has an internal *Fuse*, press the reset button or let the motor cool for at least 10 minutes and start again; turn off the juicer and check for pulp buildup around the shaft (juicers only); if there is pulp around the shaft, remove the reamer and clear the pulp away with a moist sponge.

If the motor runs but the reamer does not turn (juicers only), disassemble the juicer (see below) and inspect the spindle and coupling. Replace any broken or cracked parts if possible; if the reamer is cracked or the portion that fits over the spindle is worn, replace it. Also inspect the gears (see below) for worn or damaged teeth and replace them as a set if needed (see *Motor*).

| | |
|---|---|
| **Fix-It Tip** | Juice extractors use a special filter basket that can be damaged or bent. If it is damaged, replace it before reusing the appliance. |

## What Parts, Materials, and Tools Do I Need?

Replacement parts for a juicer or juice extractor are available from the manufacturer or aftermarket sources (see *Fix-It Resources*). To disassemble and fix these small appliances, you'll need these tools:

- Screwdrivers
- Wrenches
- Sponge
- Paper towels
- Silicone lubricant
- Multimeter

## What Are the Steps to Fixing It?

Disassemble a juicer or a juice extractor (standard models):

1. Unplug the power cord.
2. Remove any parts that come off without tools.
3. Remove the base using screwdrivers or wrenches.
4. Remove the *Electrical Cord*.
5. Remove screws holding the *Motor* and switch (see *Appliance Controls*) to the housing and carefully remove the motor from the housing.
6. Remove the gears.
7. Inspect, test with a multimeter (see *Fix Everything: Multimeter*), and replace worn or damaged parts as needed. Refer to the owner's manual for part numbers and resources.

Service a drive system:

1. Disassemble, as above, to access the gear assembly.
2. Remove the gears and spindle.
3. Clean and inspect the gears (see *Motor*), checking for worn teeth or other components.
4. Replace parts as needed, referring to the owner's manual.
5. Reassemble the unit, applying silicon lubricant to the gear teeth.

| | |
|---|---|
| **Caution** | When applying lubricant, make sure you don't get any on electrical components. Lubricants can conduct electricity and cause problems. |

# Lawn Mower, Reel

Yes, reel lawn mowers are still around. Human-powered ones are the best choice for small lawns, enclosed lawns, and for people who don't mind the exercise. Besides being more ecologically friendly than gas mowers, they are relatively inexpensive to buy and to maintain. Tuneups are not required and maintenance is relatively easy. Here's how to fix and keep your reel lawn mower cutting. If your reel lawn mower is driven by a small engine, also see *Lawn Mower, Rotary* and *Small Engine*.

**Fix-It Tip**

Preventive maintenance includes washing down the reel mower after every use, then spraying metal surfaces that may rust with a lightweight oil or penetrating oil for protection.

## How Does It Work?

A reel lawn mower is a machine for cutting grass. It's either human-powered or small-engine powered. Cutting blades attached to the reel spin and cut grass as the mower is rolled across the lawn. It's that simple.

## What Can Go Wrong?

The mower may cut unevenly or tear grass rather than cut it. A blade can be bent. An engine-driven reel mower may have the same problems that any gas-driven machinery may have.

## How Can I Identify the Problem?

If the blades do not cut well, you can sharpen them following the instructions in your owner's manual or the general guidelines below.

If a blade is bent, you may be able to reshape it by lightly tapping it into alignment by hammering it near the edge. If the blade is badly bent, you can replace it.

If the mower does not cut evenly, you can adjust the rollers (see below).

If the reel mower has small-engine problems, see *Small Engine*. If it has problems with the clutch, belt, or pulleys, see *Lawn Mower, Rotary*.

## What Parts, Materials, and Tools Do I Need?

Replacement parts are available from the manufacturer and aftermarket suppliers (see *Fix-It Resources*) and from mower shops, local hardware stores, and home improvement centers. The tools you will need to fix a reel lawn mower include these:

- Screwdrivers
- Flat file or flat sharpening stone
- Grinding paste
- Locking pliers
- Lightweight oil
- Newspaper

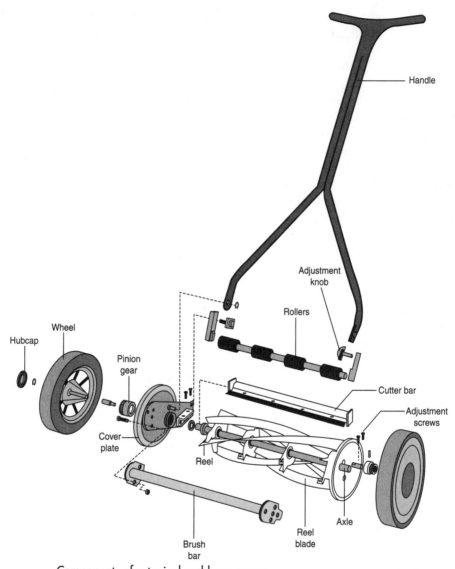

Components of a typical reel lawn mower.

## What Are the Steps to Fixing It?

Sharpen blades:

1. Put the mower on a workbench or other area where you can easily service it.
2. Use a fine flat file or a flat sharpening stone to remove any burrs from the blade and cutter bar.
3. Apply grinding paste to the blades' cutting edges.
4. Rotate the reel backward for 10 minutes to sharpen the cutter bar and the blades.

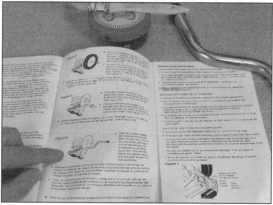

Sharpening kits containing tools, grinding paste, and instructions are available through larger hardware stores and home centers.

Some reel mowers require that you remove a wheel and secure the axle to rotate the wheel backward. Check the mower owner's manual for specific directions.

5. Remove excess grinding paste.
6. Test and adjust the mower (see below).
7. Place a piece of newspaper between the reel and cutter bar, then rotate the reel to make sure that the blade cuts smoothly. If not, adjust the mower (see below).

Adjust the mower:

1. Loosen and adjust each end of the roller shaft to the same height. Most units have an adjustment nut at the ends of the roller shaft.
2. Turn the reel, checking for contact with the cutter bar. As needed, adjust the reel to touch but not be stopped by the cutter bar.
3. Insert a strip of newspaper between the reel and the cutter bar, then rotate the reel to verify that it cuts evenly. Adjust as needed; adjustments typically are located at each end of the cutter bar.

Reel blades

Cutter bar

Adjust the cutter bar for even contact with the reel blades.

# Lawn Mower, Riding

It's fun to ride around the yard on the mower, watching scrubby grass (and weeds) turn into trimmed lawn. However, when the grass looks as bad after you mow as it did before, or the mower doesn't want to start, riding mowers aren't as much fun. That's when it's time to put on your Fix-It Club hat and have some more fun.

## How Does It Work?

A riding lawn mower is a gas-powered machine for cutting grass. The engine turns a rotating blade that cuts the top off the grass blades to a specified height. The operator sits atop the mower on a tractor-type seat with speed and height controls nearby. Riding mowers also can be used to pull small utility carts for other yard jobs. Other grass cutters include the reel lawn mower and the rotary lawn mower (see *Lawn Mower, Reel* and *Lawn Mower, Rotary*).

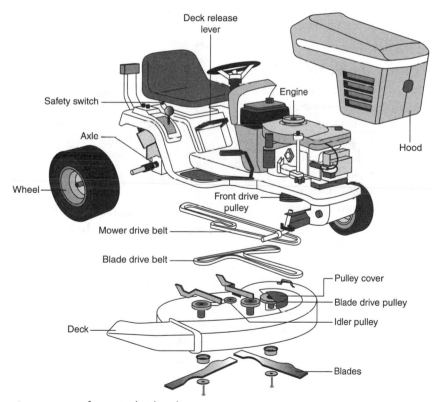

Components of a typical riding lawn mower.

## What Can Go Wrong?

The mower may cut poorly or unevenly. The V-belts may slip or come off during use. The belt may squeal or wear quickly. The mower may vibrate excessively when the clutch is engaged. The mower may be hard to shift or may not move when the clutch is engaged. The engine may not start, may lose power, or may die during use.

## How Can I Identify the Problem?

If grass is poorly or unevenly cut, try mowing at a slower speed and adjusting the engine speed with instructions in your owner's manual. Scrape away any dried grass and other debris caked under the mower deck. Sharpen or replace dull or bent blades (see *Lawn Mower, Rotary*). Check and replace a worn belt.

If the V-belt slips or comes off during use, clear any debris in the belt area, adjust the drive-belt tension (see below), or have the belt replaced. Adjust and tighten pulley fasteners or have a service center replace worn parts.

If the belt squeals or wears excessively, adjust the drive-belt tension (see below) and look for obstructions around the belt. If that doesn't work, take the mower in for professional service.

If the mower vibrates excessively when the clutch is engaged, scrape away any debris accumulated under the deck. Balance the blade (see *Lawn Mower, Rotary*) and replace the blade if needed. If that fails, adjust drive-belt tension (see below). If you find that the drive belt, pulley, or other belt-drive part is damaged, consider having it replaced by a professional.

If the mower is hard to shift or doesn't move when the clutch is engaged, adjust the drive-belt tension (see below). Also make sure the mower is lubricated according to the owner's manual specifications. As needed, have the mower serviced for damaged or maladjusted clutch/brake pedal linkage.

If the engine doesn't start, loses power, or dies during use, see *Small Engine* for additional suggestions.

## What Parts, Materials, and Tools Do I Need?

Replacement parts are available from lawn mower repair services or the manufacturer (see *Fix-It Resources*). Tools needed to fix a riding lawn mower include these:

- Screwdrivers
- Wrenches
- Scrap lumber
- Leather work gloves

## What Are the Steps to Fixing It?

Remove the mower deck:

1. Make sure that the parking brake is locked.
2. Place scrap lumber under the front and rear of the deck.
3. Use the deck lever to lower the deck.
4. Remove attachments from the deck.
5. Remove the blade drive belt from the front pulley.
6. Remove the front and rear deck fasteners, following instructions in your owner's manual.
7. Use the deck lever to raise the deck.
8. Remove the scrap lumber.
9. Remove the deck from under the mower.

> **Caution**
>
> Wear leather work gloves when working around sharp edges such as the mower blade(s) and deck to prevent injury. You can take them off for the delicate work, but you'll be glad you have them on when you handle sharp edges. And never put your hands, or anything else, under the mower while it's running.

Adjust the drive belt:

1. Remove the belt from the large idler pulley.
2. Remove the belt from the adjustable idler pulley.
3. Carefully remove the spring-loaded large idler pulley.
4. Loosen the adjustable idler pulley and move it slightly toward the rear of the mower to tighten it—or move it toward the front to loosen it—and retighten the pulley.
5. Replace the belt.
6. Check belt tension and readjust as needed.

# Lawn Mower, Rotary

Time to cut the lawn—again?! A rotary lawn mower makes the job easier, but it doesn't *cut* the grass without your help, so you'd better get started. Hopefully, it will start up quickly and be back resting in the shed soon. If it's reluctant to work or just plain stubborn, here's what you can do.

## How Does It Work?

A rotary lawn mower is a powered machine for cutting grass. Rotary mowers come in self-propelled or push types, powered by either a gasoline engine or an electric motor. It's called a rotary motor because a long thin blade is rotated from its center to cut grass evenly. Some rotary mowers have a mulching blade designed to lift grass clippings, then cut and recut them into finer pieces that serve as mulch for the lawn. See *Lawn Mower, Riding* for information on larger rotary motors.

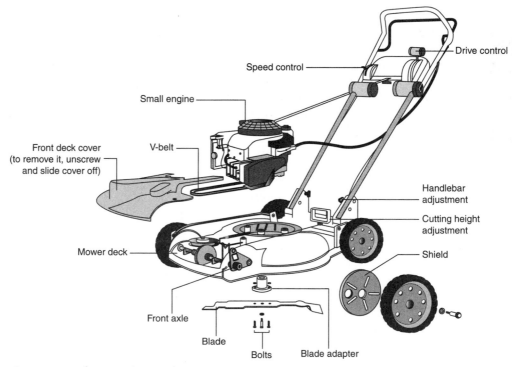

Components of a typical rotary lawn mower.

## What Can Go Wrong?

The mower may cut unevenly or tear grass rather than cut it. The mower may vibrate excessively or be noisy. The engine may not start, or may run poorly. The engine may run, but the mower won't move. The electric motor may not run.

## How Can I Identify the Problem?

If the mower cuts unevenly, first check and clean a dirty blade. If this fails, service or replace a dull, unbalanced, or bent blade (see below), and check the owner's manual to correctly adjust the wheel height.

If the mower vibrates excessively, you can balance or replace a blade (see below). Also, with the mower *not* running, clean clippings from under the mower deck and clear the discharge chute following the owner's manual instructions. Never work under the mower deck with the mower running!

If the engine won't start or runs poorly, see *Small Engine*.

If the engine runs, but the mower of a self-propelled machine doesn't move, check the drive system (see below).

If an electric mower won't start, test the *Electrical Cord*, *Motor*, and switches (see *Appliance Controls*).

| Fix-It Tip | One of the Fix-It Club's mantras is: "Save the owner's manual!" You'll discover why as you try to disassemble and fix a rotary lawn mower or practically any other household device you have. |
|---|---|

## What Parts, Materials, and Tools Do I Need?

You can find many replacement parts through local hardware stores and other aftermarket suppliers. Also check with the manufacturer (see *Fix-It Resources*). The tools you will need to fix a rotary lawn mower may include these:

- Screwdrivers
- Scrap lumber
- Work gloves
- Hammer
- Wrenches
- Multimeter
- Flat file

## What Are the Steps to Fixing It?

Service the mower blade:

1. Disconnect the spark plug cable for safety.

| Caution | Why do you need to disconnect the spark plug cable before beginning any repairs? Rotating the blade by hand can make the engine start—if there is spark. Think of those old movies where the pilot would start a plane by turning a switch ("Switch on!") and the helper would spin the propeller. Now imagine that the helper had his arm around the prop! |
|---|---|

2. Use scrap lumber to wedge the blade into a stationary position so it won't turn when you loosen it.

3. As needed, remove the blade with wrenches and a gloved hand (for protection). Use a pencil to mark the side of the blade that faces *down* for proper reinstallation.

4. Inspect the rotary blade for damage and replace as needed. Some blades have a metal bar called a stiffener that also should be checked. If necessary, replace the blade with one as recommended by the manufacturer.

5. Use a flat file to sharpen the blade, filing only in one direction. Follow the original contour of the blade edge.

6. Insert a screwdriver through the center hole and hold the screwdriver to determine if the blade is balanced. If it is not, use a file to trim metal from the heavier (lower) end until it is evenly balanced.

7. Reinstall the blade, making sure that the blade is installed as it was removed for proper operation.

8. Reconnect the spark plug.

Service control cables:

1. Disconnect the spark plug cable for safety.

2. Remove the controller cover and loosen the locknuts.

3. Remove all slack from the cable, reposition the locknuts as needed, and tighten the locknuts.

4. Test the controller by moving it through the various positions and making sure it responds appropriately. If it doesn't, readjust it.

5. Reconnect the spark plug.

Replace the wheel drive belt:

1. Disconnect the spark plug cable for safety.

2. Remove the cover over the wheel drive belt.

**Fix-It Tip**

Some rotary lawn mowers require that you remove the entire deck cover to access the drive belt. To remove the deck cover, unscrew the bolts and slide the cover off. The owner's manual probably will include more instructions.

3. Tilt the pulley toward the engine and remove the belt from the pulley.

4. Tilt the mower to remove the other end of the belt from around the blade pulley.

5. Install the new belt in the opposite order: around the blade pulley and then around the wheel pulley.

6. Tighten the wheel pulley adjustment so the belt moves ¼ inch when pushed halfway between the two pulleys. Readjust as needed.

7. Reconnect the spark plug.

# Lighting, Fluorescent

Fluorescent (tube) lighting is more efficient than incandescent (bulb) lighting, so it's popular in areas where you need lots of light but don't want a big electric bill. That includes places like the kitchen and garage or workshop. Because they are simple in operation, fluorescent lighting systems are also easy to fix. Here's what you need to know.

## How Does It Work?

A fluorescent lighting fixture converts electricity into light by making gas inside a phosphor-lined tube glow. The fluorescent fixture is either wired into the house electrical system or plugged into a nearby receptacle. Electrical voltage is delivered to the fluorescent tube by a component called the ballast. When the fixture is turned on, more electricity is needed than during normal operation, so a starter tells the ballast to boost the voltage. Once running, the starter turns off and the ballast maintains the voltage to a lower operating level.

Fluorescent lighting typically is easy to work on with the exception of smaller units that may not allow access to internal parts. If the bulb is okay but the unit still doesn't work, check the *Electrical Cord* and replace the unit as needed.

## What Can Go Wrong?

Any of the main components of a fluorescent lighting fixture can be the source of problems. That includes fluorescent tubes, starters, ballasts, and switches. Problems with fluorescent lighting systems are relatively easy to diagnose and solve.

> **Caution**
>
> Be especially careful when handling fluorescent lighting tubes. They are quite fragile and contain phosphor and inert gasses. *Don't* drop them or let them hit a hard surface!

## How Can I Identify the Problem?

If the lamp will not light at all, make sure power is on, then try replacing the tube. You can also test the *Electrical Cord*.

If the light still does not work, try replacing the starter (see below), then the ballast (see below).

If the lamp glows dimly, the cause is either a defective tube or starter.

If the ends of the tube light but the middle is dim or dark, the starter or the tube may be defective.

If the light flickers, the tube may be burning out, or the starter or ballast may be defective.

If the light repeatedly flashes on and off, the tube or the starter may be defective.

If the socket doesn't firmly hold the tube, first make sure that the pins are straight. If the pins are not straight, the socket may need replacing.

## What Parts, Materials, and Tools Do I Need?

Most replacement parts for fluorescent lighting fixtures are available at larger hardware and lighting stores. The tools you'll need to fix a fixture include these:

- Screwdrivers
- Wrenches
- Multimeter

## What Are the Steps to Fixing It?

Replace a starter:

1. Turn off power to the fixture.
2. Lift the fixture diffuser or cover (if installed) and tubes to access the starter, a round plug-in component attached near the larger ballast.
3. Twist out the old starter and replace it with one that has the identical part number and rating. A hardware clerk can help you select the proper replacement.

Replace a ballast:

1. Turn off power to the fixture.
2. Remove the diffuser, tubes, and cover plate.

3. Identify the ballast, a large heavy component often near the center of the fixture. Disconnect wires to the ballast and disconnect the ballast from the fixture. Test with a multimeter (see *Fix Everything: Multimeter*).
4. Replace the ballast with one of the same rating as the old unit. Mount the new ballast and reconnect wires in the same manner as they were disconnected.
5. Replace the cover plate, tubes, and diffuser.
6. Plug in or turn on the circuit to verify that the fixture is working.

Replace a socket:

1. Turn off power to the fixture.
2. Remove the diffuser, tubes, and cover plate.
3. Disconnect wires from the socket.
4. Disconnect and remove the socket.
5. Replace the socket with a duplicate unit.
6. Replace the cover plate, tubes, and diffuser.
7. Plug the light in or turn on the circuit to verify that the fixture is working.

# Lighting, Incandescent

Where were you when the lights went out? Chances are you were somewhere that needed lighting! In most cases, all that's needed is to replace a burned-out bulb. But sometimes it takes a little more work to fix incandescent (bulb) lighting systems. Here's what you can do about it.

## How Does It Work?

An incandescent lighting fixture is simply a system that requires an incandescent bulb, the oldest type of electrical lighting. Incandescent bulbs contain a tungsten wire filament that glows when electricity runs through it. These filaments are relatively fragile and don't last very long. Newer lighting systems use gas (see *Lighting, Fluorescent*) or gas and a filament (halogen) to produce light more efficiently. Because incandescent lighting is simple and the bulbs are inexpensive, they will be with us for a long time.

## What Can Go Wrong?

Of course, bulbs can burn out. But what can be wrong if you replace the bulb and the fixture still doesn't illuminate? Lighting fixtures can be cracked, wires can come loose, and sockets can fail. Fortunately, all are fixable by the do-it-yourselfer.

> **Caution**
>
> Incandescent lighting fixtures typically have a label to tell you the maximum power they can safely deliver to a bulb, measured in watts (W). For safety, don't install a 75W bulb in a 60W fixture.

## How Can I Identify the Problem?

If the light fails to glow when you turn on the switch, first try a new bulb of equal or lesser wattage. If the new bulb doesn't illuminate, but other electrical things on the same circuit still operate, you may need to replace the entire fixture or a component.

> **Fix-It Tip**
>
> Broke a bulb in the fixture and can't remove the base? Cut a potato in half and, with the light switch off, insert the potato over the broken base, then unscrew the base.

## What Parts, Materials, and Tools Do I Need?

You can easily find replacement parts for incandescent lighting fixtures at your local hardware store. The tools you may need include these:

- Screwdrivers
- Wire cutters
- Multimeter to test the electrical circuit

## What Are the Steps to Fixing It?

Replace an incandescent lighting fixture:

1. Turn the circuit off at the *Electrical Service Panel*.
2. Remove the light cover and unscrew the bulb(s). Some lighting fixtures are mounted on a short, threaded pipe called a nipple.

3. Disassemble any hardware holding the lighting fixture in place. You may need to remove trim to find hardware or fasteners.

4. Pull the fixture from the electrical box.

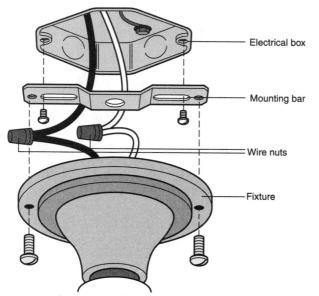

Electrical box

Mounting bar

Wire nuts

Fixture

An incandescent light fixture is relatively simple, requiring only a firm mounting and electrical power wires.

5. Disconnect the fixture wires from the circuit wires. They may be connected with electrical nuts or with electrical tape.

6. Take the fixture to an electrical or hardware store for a replacement. You will need to match wattage as well as make sure that the mounting holes correspond.

7. Follow the fixture manufacturer's instructions for preparing the fixture for installation. In most cases, remove insulation from the last ½ inch of the wire, connect like to like (black-to-black, white-to-white), and attach the wires with nuts or electrical tape.

8. Attach the new fixture to the electrical box using mounting screws, then tighten the screws.

9. Once the fixture is installed, turn the circuit on at the *Electrical Service Panel*.

# Masonry

Brick and stone make beautiful siding on a home, giving it a solid, permanent look. It's a good thing that little can go wrong with masonry siding. Some preventive maintenance and some minor repairs will keep masonry siding looking good for many years. Masonry walls, fences, and fireplaces also endure for many years.

## How Does It Work?

Masonry is brick, stone, and stucco that is often used as siding that is attached with an adhesive mortar or grout. For information about wood, vinyl or aluminum siding, see *Exterior Siding*. Many fireplaces, chimneys, fences, barbecues, walls, and other items are also made of masonry.

## What Can Go Wrong?

Mortar and stucco can crack and chip away. Bricks can erode.

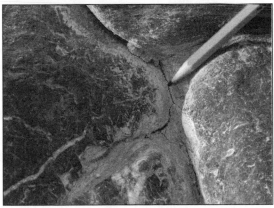

Cracks can show up in mortar between rocks or bricks in masonry fireplaces, walls, or siding.

**Fix-It Tip**

You can freshen the appearance of most masonry surfaces with a simple pressure washing. However, be careful not to remove mortar or other bonding.

## How Can I Identify the Problem?

If mortar or brick have deteriorated, you can replace them (see below).

If stucco has cracked or fallen away, you can patch the area (see below).

## What Parts, Materials, and Tools Do I Need?

The materials you'll need for fixing masonry siding are available at building material suppliers and larger home centers. The tools you will need to fix masonry siding include:

- Cold chisel
- Mason's hammer
- Trowels
- Mixing trough
- Safety goggles
- Sledgehammer
- Wire brush
- Work gloves
- Mortar mix
- Stucco
- Straightedge board
- Wire mesh
- Galvanized nails

# What Are the Steps to Fixing It?

**Fix-It Tip**

When chipping away at brick or mortar with a chisel, make sure you wear safety glasses. Safety gloves are also a good idea to protect your fingernails.

Replace brick and mortar:

1. Chip away at the damaged brick and the surrounding mortar with a cold chisel and mason's hammer.
2. Remove all mortar so that the new brick and mortar will fit easily.
3. Coat the replacement brick with mortar on the edges adjacent to other bricks, then install the brick.
4. Use a trowel to force additional mortar into the joints.
5. Use the trowel to remove excess mortar.

Repair stucco:

1. Remove loose material with a cold chisel and mason's hammer.
2. Inspect the underlying wire mesh. If it is damaged or missing, install a new piece on the wall with galvanized nails.
3. Prepare the stucco patch following the manufacturer's directions.
4. Fill the hole with stucco patch in layers until it is overflowing.
5. Use a straightedge to remove excess stucco so the surface is level.
6. Allow the stucco patch to dry before priming and painting.

**Fix-It Tip**

If your home has an exterior surface of synthetic stucco (exterior finish and insulation system, or EFIS), make sure you use the appropriate patch material. Ask your local home center. EFIS systems are especially susceptible to moisture damage and should be inspected for cracks at least once a year, and repaired as needed.

Coat the edges adjacent to the new brick before installation.

# Motor

Small and large appliances have a *Motor*, a *Heating Element*, or both. Motors are important components to hundreds of devices we use in daily life. This guide will show you how motors work and how to fix them when they don't.

## How Does It Work?

A motor turns electrical energy into motion. Actually, it uses electricity's magnetism to attract, then repel components to rotate a shaft. You can attach fan blades, knife blades, wheels, or a dozen other components to the shaft to make useful devices. To name a few: *Blender, Cassette Deck, CD Player, Coffee Grinder, Computer* fan, *Computer Printer* head, *DVD Player, Electric Can Opener* ... you get the idea. These and hundreds of other functional gadgets rely on electric motors to give them motion.

Smaller appliances typically use what's called a universal motor. It's simple, efficient, and relatively inexpensive. It's called "universal" because it can run on either alternating current (AC) or direct current (DC) power. The part that stands still is called the stator and the rotating part is the rotor. It's as simple as that.

Some small appliances use a variation called the shaded-pole motor. It works about the same as the universal motor, but is less expensive to manufacture so it typically goes into lower-cost, low-load, small appliances.

Larger appliances, as you can imagine, require more power. Many use a split-phase induction motor to develop more rotating power, called torque, than smaller motors can muster. Split-phase induction motors, too, have stators and rotors.

Smaller things such as battery-operated appliances and tools get their power from DC batteries, so they are made to run on direct current. They don't have much motion or torque, but they get the job done in a small space.

What's the difference? Usually it's cost. Most manufacturers use the least expensive motor that does the job. Fortunately, checking whether a motor runs or doesn't is about the same for any type of motor. Unless you're adventuresome, you probably won't dismantle a motor and replace components. If it works, you'll use it; if not, you'll recycle it.

Many motors include a drive mechanism of some type that transfers the shaft rotation to some other component. You can fix or replace drive mechanisms as well (see below).

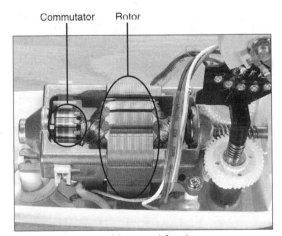

Motor inside a variable-speed food mixer.

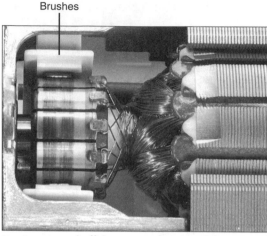

Brushes

Turning on and off the motor's brushes (left, top, and bottom) creates a magnetic field that makes the motor shaft rotate.

## What Can Go Wrong?

Though efficient, motors can work against themselves. A small problem can become a big one quickly, and soon the motor is damaged beyond repair. Fortunately, most motors will tell you—sometimes subtly, sometimes not—that they are having problems. Motors burn out and freeze up; they get noisy, overheat, and wobble.

**Fix-It Tip**

Hearing noises that may be a motor going out? Turn off the appliance immediately. It may be something rubbing against the moving parts or it may be a problem in the motor itself. In either case, the faster you catch it the easier it will be to troubleshoot and fix it.

## How Can I Identify the Problem?

If gears on the motor shaft wobble, the bearings may be worn out or some of the moving parts may be misaligned.

If you see sparks inside the motor, the rotor, stator, or brushes may be worn or damaged.

If you smell a mild odor of hot oil, metal, or plastic, the motor is overheating and may require lubrication.

If you smell a pungent, acrid odor, the motor's windings may be damaged.

If the motor is too hot to touch, something may be blocking ventilation around the motor.

If the motor makes a grinding noise, bearings may be worn out.

**Fix-It Tip**

Parts inside a motor rotate, so they require lubrication to minimize friction. Some motors have holes on them marked *oil* where drops of lightweight oil can be added. Other motors have hard plastic bearings that don't require lubrication but may eventually wear out after years of use. Check the owner's manual for your appliance to determine what regular service the motor requires.

## What Parts, Materials, and Tools Do I Need?

If you have electrical experience and some advanced tools, you may be able to repair a motor yourself. However, most consumers opt to test and, if necessary, replace the motor. You can buy one through the appliance's manufacturer or an aftermarket supplier (see *Fix-It Resources*).

Once you've disassembled the appliance (see the appropriate *Fix-It Guide*), here are the tools you'll need to test an electric motor:

• Screwdrivers
• Wrenches (standard and hex)
• Multimeter

## What Are the Steps to Fixing It?

Test an appliance motor:

1. Make sure that the power cord wires are disconnected from the motor. If it is easy to do, remove the motor from the appliance, though motors can be tested in place.

2. To test continuity (the flow of electricity) through the motor, set the multimeter (see *Fix Everything: Multimeter*) on the R×1 (resistance times 1) scale to measure resistance (in ohms). The multimeter's internal battery will send a small electrical current through the motor's wires.

This hair dryer motor and fan can be tested easily using a multimeter.

3. Attach one of the multimeter's probes to the motor's common lead, usually white.

4. Attach the other probe in turn to each of the other wires on the motor. The probe will check to see if it can measure the multimeter's input signal at the output. A low or moderate reading (in ohms) means the component is okay. A zero or infinite reading means the motor's windings or another component has a short.

5. If it tests faulty, replace the motor with one of the same type, power rating, and size.

Service a motor's drive mechanism:

1. Tighten the setscrew that attaches the pulley or collar to the shaft.

2. Adjust the drive belt so it is not so tight it wears out the shaft nor so loose that it doesn't rotate with the pulley. If the belt is worn or damaged, replace it.

3. Check and tighten or replace any reduction or worm gears on the shaft. Gears typically come in pairs and should be replaced as pairs.

Service gears:

1. Disassemble the appliance to access the motor's gears.

2. Remove and inspect gears for obvious damage or wear and replace as needed. Gears, especially, are susceptible to damage because many are made of plastic that can break or chip.

3. Reassemble and test.

Service fan blades:

1. Disassemble the appliance to access the motor's fan blade.

2. Remove, inspect, and repair the fan blades. If not repairable, damaged fan blades should be replaced because they can spin unbalanced and potentially damage the motor.

3. Reassemble and test.

**Fix-It Tip**

Install a new motor or reinstall the old motor in the exact same way as it was removed, making sure that all wires are connected as they were originally.

# Outdoor Structures

Outdoor structures are extensions of our homes. They are more living space, more storage space, and more things to fix. It's a good thing that most outdoor structures are relatively easy to fix. Here's how the Fix-It Club takes care of various outdoor structures.

## How Does It Work?

An outdoor structure is a building or add-on that is separate from your home while serving its occupants. It can be a storage building, woodshed, gazebo, playhouse, doghouse, pump house, or other building. Outdoor structures have many of the same features as a house, including flooring, roofing, framing, and others. Decks and gazebos are closely related, so if your gazebo needs repair, see *Deck*.

Outdoor structures include storage buildings and woodsheds. See other guides for *Deck* and *Fence* repairs.

## What Can Go Wrong?

Outdoor structures often don't receive the same maintenance that a home does, even though they may suffer more from weather extremes and other hardships. Roofs and gutters leak. Siding is damaged. Concrete floors crack. Windows get broken. Paint peels. A door can stick and its hardware can fail to work properly. Cabinets and drawers can stick or sag. Electrical receptacles and electrical switches can fail.

**Fix-It Tip**

Power wash your outdoor structures yearly when you power wash the outside of your house, deck, and driveway.

## How Can I Identify the Problem?

If a roof leaks, see *Roof*.

If a gutter or downspout leaks, see *Gutter*.

If siding is damaged, see *Masonry* and *Exterior Siding*.

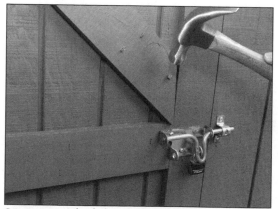

Once a year, check the condition of all outdoor structure hardware and renail any popped nail heads.

If a concrete floor cracks, see *Concrete*.

If a window is broken, see *Window*.

If interior or exterior paint is damaged, see *Paint*.

If a door or door hardware are damaged, see *Door* or *Door Hardware*.

If storage cabinets or drawers are damaged, see *Furniture, Wood*.

If a structure sags, see *Framing*.

Smaller outdoor structures use simple roof truss systems. Check periodically for damage.

If an outlet or switch fails, see *Electrical Receptacle* or *Electrical Switch*.

If there's a problem with plumbing, see *Drain System, Faucet, Toilet, Pipe*, or *Plumbing System*.

## What Parts, Materials, and Tools Do I Need?

Replacement parts are available from local hardware stores, home improvement centers, and lumberyards. The tools you will need to fix an outdoor structure may include:

- Screwdrivers
- Hammer
- Wrenches
- Electric drill
- Adhesives

# Oven, Convection

Microwaves weren't the first cook-it-fast devices. Convection ovens have been around for many years, offering the advantage over microwave ovens of browning foods. That's because convection ovens cook from the outside in rather than from the inside out as microwaves do. Meats, especially, look like they were cooked in a conventional oven, only faster—unless the oven doesn't work.

## How Does It Work?

A convection oven is an appliance for baking *and* roasting food. It works like a conventional oven but includes a fan that circulates hot air around the food, allowing it to cook faster than in a conventional oven and more evenly than in a microwave. Hybrid ovens combine the advantages of both a convection oven and a microwave oven in one unit.

Convection ovens use a motor-driven circulating fan that's mounted between the unit's inner and outer housings. A timer controls the fan and the heating element. Additional controls are located inside the front control panel. Convection ovens are sometimes combined with conventional or microwave ovens.

## What Can Go Wrong?

The electrical cord may need replacing. The timer, selector switch, temperature control shaded-pole motor, heating element, fan thermostat, or thermal cutoff may fail.

**Caution**

A convection oven uses lots of electrical current, so it should be on a household circuit dedicated to it—just as your refrigerator or stove should be. Otherwise, the convection oven may trip a circuit breaker or blow a fuse.

## How Can I Identify the Problem?

Because a convection oven is an electrical appliance, the best way to test its components is with a multimeter (see *Fix Everything: Multimeter*).

If the oven doesn't heat and the on-off light doesn't work, make sure the power is on at the outlet, then check the *Electrical Cord*. Next, test the *Appliance Controls*.

If the oven doesn't heat and the on-off light works, test the *Appliance Controls, Motor,* and *Heating Element.*

If the oven heats but the fan doesn't work, test the *Motor.* Check the fan for blockage.

If the oven burns food or overheats, test the thermostat and the thermal cutoff (see *Appliance Controls*).

If the oven won't shut off, test the temperature control (see *Appliance Controls*).

Each convection oven model is slightly different, so refer to your owner's manual for specific components, parts numbers, and troubleshooting guides. The instructions here are for typical convection ovens.

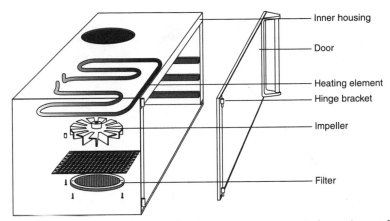

A convection oven is a standard oven with a circulation fan to bake and roast food.

## What Parts, Materials, and Tools Do I Need?

If the oven is out of warranty, you can purchase replacement parts from the manufacturer or buy aftermarket parts from one of the major appliance parts suppliers listed in *Fix-It Resources*. For basic repairs you'll need the following tools:

- Screwdrivers
- Adjustable wrench
- Multimeter

## What Are the Steps to Fixing It?

To access any of the components you'll need to first disassemble the convection oven.

Disassemble a convection oven:

1. Unplug the oven. Remove the door, shelves, and all control knobs. Remove screws behind the timer knob and around the edges of the front housing. Lift off the control-panel housing. Disconnect the light before completely removing the housing.

2. To remove the selector switch, loosen any screws and metal tabs holding the switch to the panel base.

3. To remove the timer, loosen any screws securing it.

4. To remove the temperature control, unscrew the locking ring around the temperature control spindle.
5. Slide the unit's base forward, then lift it over the control panel.
6. Remove any outer housing screws, then grasp the housing and remove it.
7. Test and replace internal components as needed, referring to the owner's manual or a parts diagram available from the manufacturer.

**Fix-It Tip**

Take care of your convection oven. Wash the fan filter often with grease-cutting cleaner. Clean the interior of the oven with nonabrasive spray cleaner and a damp sponge.

# Oven, Electric

Cooking ovens really haven't changed much over the years, except that the controls have become more sophisticated. You now can set controls to start and stop cooking at various times, even checking and regulating temperatures for you, so that dinner is ready when you are—if it works correctly. If not, here's how you can fix it.

## How Does It Work?

An electric oven is a baking chamber. It's either part of an electric range or a standalone appliance without the cooktop. It is a 240/120-volt circuit—240 volts for the heating elements and 120 volts for the accessories. A thermostat senses and regulates oven temperature. Time and temperature are regulated by an electric timer motor or by a digital controller. Most electric ovens have two heating elements, the main one on the bottom of the chamber and another one on the top, typically used for broiling. Also see *Cooktop, Electric; Oven, Gas;* and *Cooktop, Gas.*

## What Can Go Wrong?

One or both oven elements may burn out. The temperature control may malfunction. The oven selector switch may not work properly. The capillary tube (the tube attached to the oven wall that senses the temperature in the oven and activates the control that adjusts the temperature) may be out of adjustment. The temperature control may not be accurate. The door may not close properly.

**Caution** In self-cleaning ovens, the capillary tube contains a caustic fluid. Wear rubber gloves and handle it gently.

## How Can I Identify the Problem?

If the oven does not heat at all, make sure a fuse has not blown or a circuit breaker tripped at the *Electrical Service Panel* and test the *Electrical Cord.* Test the oven *Heating Element* (see below), test the temperature control (see below), and check the oven selector switch (see below). Also see *Appliance Controls.*

If the oven doesn't hold the selected temperature, check the capillary tube and test or recalibrate the temperature control (see *Calibrating oven temperature* below).

If the self-cleaning cycle doesn't work, reclose and relock the door, test the oven element (see below), test the temperature control (see below), and test the oven selector switch (see below).

If the oven door does not close properly, adjust the door or replace the springs (see below). If necessary, replace the door gasket (see below).

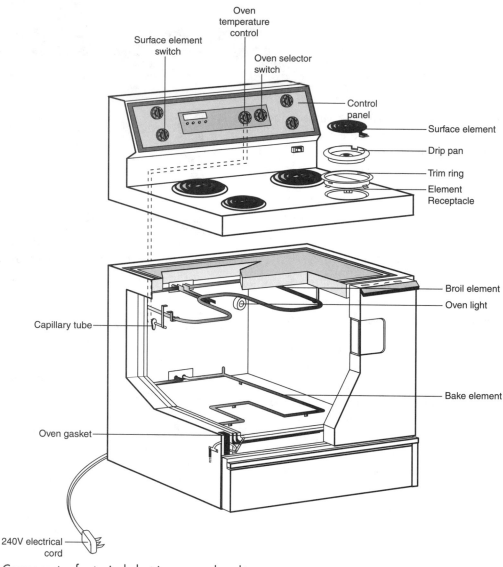

Surface element switch

Oven temperature control

Oven selector switch

Control panel

Surface element

Drip pan

Trim ring

Element Receptacle

Broil element

Oven light

Capillary tube

Bake element

Oven gasket

240V electrical cord

Components of a typical electric oven and cooktop.

## What Parts, Materials, and Tools Do I Need?

Replacement parts for an electric oven are available from the manufacturer and after-market suppliers (see *Fix-It Resources*) as well as from local appliance parts suppliers. The tools you will need to fix an electric oven include these:

- Screwdrivers
- Wrenches
- Nut driver
- Crimp-on terminals
- Oven thermometer
- Safety goggles
- Plastic scraper
- Rubber gloves
- Multimeter

## What Are the Steps to Fixing It?

Test and replace an oven element:

1. Unplug the oven or turn off power at the *Electrical Service Panel*.
2. Remove the screws or nuts that fasten the element to the back of the oven.

Heating Element

Remove fasteners attaching the element to the oven.

3. Unscrew any support brackets and pull the element forward to expose the wiring.
4. Remove the wires from the element terminals, being careful not to bend the terminals or let the wires fall back through the opening.
5. Carefully remove the element from the oven.
6. Inspect the wire terminals for burns or damage and replace if needed.
7. Set a multimeter (see *Fix Everything: Multimeter*) to R×1 (resistance times 1) and touch probes to each of the terminals. The meter should show continuity. If it doesn't, the element should be replaced
8. Use the same R×1 range to test for continuity to ground with one probe on a terminal and the other on the element. If the needle moves, there is a grounding problem and the element should be replaced.
9. If you replace the element, make sure it is of the same size, shape, and resistance as recommended by the manufacturer. Reinstall in reverse order.

Test and replace the temperature control:

1. Unplug the oven or turn off power at the *Electrical Service Panel*.

2. Open the oven control panel by removing fasteners or clips around the perimeter. If any of the terminals appear discolored or burned, replace the temperature control (steps 7 through 9 below).

3. If the control has more than two terminals, identify which terminals to test, using the diagram located on the rear panel, inside the storage drawer or control panel, or in the owner's manual.

4. Set a multimeter (see *Fix Everything: Multimeter*) to R×1 (resistance times 1). Disconnect one wire from the terminals being tested, and clip on the tester probes. Set the oven temperature dial to 300°F.

5. If the multimeter doesn't indicate continuity, replace the control following steps 7 through 9 below.

6. Remove the capillary tube from its supports in the oven and push it through the rear wall. Then, from the back of the range, pull the tube out of the oven.

7. Unscrew the two temperature control screws in the front and remove the control from the back of the range.

8. Label and disconnect the wires, replace any burned wire connectors.

9. Connect the new control and screw it in place. Push the capillary tube through the back and into the oven, then clip it to its supports.

Test and replace the oven selector switch:

1. Unplug the oven or turn off power at the *Electrical Service Panel*.

2. Open the control panel (see above) and set a multimeter (see *Fix Everything: Multimeter*) to R×1 (resistance times 1). Disconnect one wire from each pair of terminals being tested, and check for continuity in each position.

3. To replace the switch, remove any screws from the front of the control panel and pull the switch out the back. Label and disconnect the wires.

4. Replace the switch with an exact replacement part.

Calibrating oven temperature:

1. Test oven temperature with an oven thermometer in the oven and by setting the temperature control to 350°F. Wait 20 minutes, then check the temperature every 10 minutes for the next 40 minutes and calculate the average.

2. If the result is off by less than 25°F, the control is normal. If it is off by 25° to 50°, recalibrate the temperature control with the following two steps. If the temperature is off by 50° or more, replace the control.

**Fix-It Tip**

Some ovens have a calibration ring on the back of the temperature-control knob. On others, temperature adjustments are made with a screw inside the control-knob shaft. If the capillary tube touches the oven wall, reposition it on its support clips. If the capillary tube is damaged, replace it and the temperature control switch with exact-replacement parts.

3. Remove the oven control knob.

4. If the knob has a ring with marks indicating *decrease* and *increase*, loosen the screws and turn the knob to move the ring in the appropriate direction, then retighten the screws.

5. If there is no ring, hold the control shaft still with adjustable pliers. Insert a thin screwdriver, and chip away the factory seal. Then turn the inside screw clockwise to raise the temperature or counterclockwise to lower it. A one-eighth turn should adjust the temperature about 25°.

Service an oven door:

1. To fix a cocked door, open the door and loosen the screws securing the inner panel. Hold the door at the top and twist it from side to side to seat it securely on its hinges.

2. Partially tighten the door screws; do not overtighten screws on a porcelain door because the surface may chip.

3. Test the seal by inserting a piece of paper between the seal and the top corners of the oven. The seal should tightly grip the paper.

4. To replace cabinet-mounted springs, remove the storage drawer and the oven door. Unhook and replace the springs. Replace both springs even if only one is broken.

Replace oven gaskets:

1. Unplug the oven or shut off power at the *Electrical Service Panel* and pull the oven away from the wall.

2. Remove the gaskets by unscrewing or unclipping any retainers.

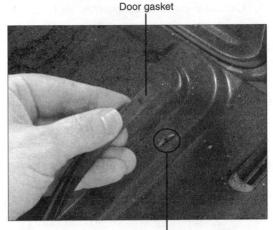

Door gasket

Clip

Some oven door gaskets are clipped in place with a special fastener.

3. Locate and loosen the oven liner bolts from the back of the unit.

4. Partially remove the oven liner by rocking it back and forth. Disconnect the gasket from between the liner and the cabinet.

5. Place the new gasket behind the oven liner rim.

6. Reinstall the oven liner and reattach it to the back of the oven.

Replace door-mounted gaskets:

**Fix-It Tip**

On self-cleaning ovens, the gasket is held between the panels of the oven door and can be replaced only by taking the door apart.

1. Unscrew the door hinge arms and remove the door.
2. Remove inner panel and edge screws as needed. You may need to carefully bend tabs to remove the cover.
3. Remove any screws holding the window assembly to the panel.
4. Remove the window assembly to reveal the gasket attachment.
5. Remove the gasket between the window assembly and the inner door panel.
6. Install the new gasket in reverse order or by following the manufacturer's instructions.

**Fix-It Tip**

To adjust a loose-fitting gasket, use your fingers or the tip of a plastic scraper to wedge the excess between the door panel and the window assembly. Starting at the top of the door, push the gasket in, tightening the screws as you go.

# Oven, Gas

Gas ovens are relatively simple in operation and require little maintenance. That's good news because it means you probably won't have many fix-it jobs on your gas oven. But if you do, here's how to do it.

## How Does It Work?

A gas oven is the baking chamber fueled by natural or propane gas. Some gas ovens have a pilot light that stays lit all the time, igniting the burners as needed. Newer models have spark igniters or an electrically heated coil, called a glow bar or glow plug to ignite the gas on demand. Igniters are wired to an ignition module that produces the high voltage required for sparking. A thermostat controls oven temperature by regulating the gas supply to the oven. If you're having trouble with the cooktop attached to your gas oven, see *Cooktop, Gas*.

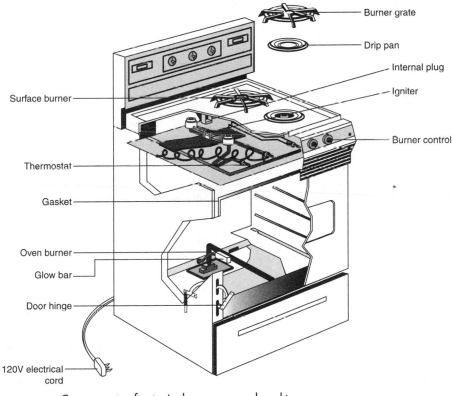

Components of a typical gas oven and cooktop.

## What Can Go Wrong?

The pilot light may go out. The burner ports may need clearing. The igniter and ignition module can malfunction. The fuse and glow bar (if equipped) can fail. The door may need adjusting and gaskets may need replacing. The thermostat or capillary tube may be faulty. The pilot may need adjusting. The burner flame may need adjusting.

> **Caution**
> Make sure you know how to shut off the gas to your oven for repairs and in case of emergency.

## How Can I Identify the Problem?

If the oven burner doesn't light and it has an electric igniter, make sure that the range is plugged in and that there is power from the *Electrical Service Panel*. Relight or adjust the pilot (see below), clear the burner ports (see below), and inspect the igniter and ignition module on ovens with electric igniters (see below). Also test the *Fuse* (below the oven bottom and baffle, next to the safety valve) and glow bar on ovens with glow bar igniters (see below).

If the oven burner pilot doesn't stay lit, clear the pilot opening (see below) and adjust the pilot (see below).

If the oven doesn't work at the set temperature or the oven bakes unevenly, check the door (see below) and gasket (see below); clear the burner ports (see below); or call for service on a thermostat or capillary tube.

If the self-cleaning cycle of an oven doesn't work, check the owner's manual for instructions. Then check the door (see below) and gaskets (see below), or call for service on a thermostat or capillary tube, as needed.

> **Caution**
> Self-cleaning ovens often have a capillary tube that contains a caustic fluid. Wear rubber gloves and handle it gently.

Newer gas ovens may have digital controls that aren't serviceable by the consumer. Check the owner's manual for troubleshooting tips and how to get plug-in replacement parts as needed. Some units also have diagnostic tests and error codes that tell you what's wrong with the unit.

## What Parts, Materials, and Tools Do I Need?

Replacement parts are available from local appliance parts stores, the manufacturer, and aftermarket suppliers (see *Fix-It Resources*). The tools you might need to fix a gas oven include these:

- Screwdrivers
- Wrenches
- Nut driver
- Sewing needle
- Multimeter

## What Are the Steps to Fixing It?

Relight an oven pilot:

1. Turn all controls *off*, open the doors, and allow gas to dissipate.
2. Hold a lighted match near the tip of the pilot on the burner assembly. If a burner does not light within two minutes, adjust the pilot, step 3.
3. Turn the pilot adjustment screw (located near the pilot or the thermostat) in small increments and retest until the pilot has a blue flame.

Clean an oven burner:

1. Turn all the appliance controls to *off*.
2. Remove the oven bottom (typically held in place by tabs or fasteners).
3. Remove the baffle beneath the oven bottom.
4. Turn on the oven and watch the burner. If the flame is not continuous along the length of the burner, some flame ports may be clogged. Turn off the oven and let the burner cool, then clear each port in the burner with a sewing needle.

Adjust an oven flame:

1. Turn all of the appliance controls to *off*. Open the door and remove the oven bottom and baffle (see above).
2. Turn on the oven and inspect the flame.

3. Identify the air shutter that will be adjusted. It may be at the base of the oven burner, just above the safety valve, or somewhere along the gas delivery tube.

4. Loosen the setscrew that locks the shutter or plate, and adjust the opening to increase or decrease the amount of air mixing with the gas.
5. Turn the oven on again to verify the adjustment, repeating as needed.
6. Once the flame is correctly adjusted, turn off the oven and tighten the setscrew.

Check and replace an oven spark igniter:

1. Turn all of the appliance controls *off*.
2. Open the door and remove the oven bottom and the baffle (see above).
3. Unscrew the igniter from its mounting bracket and inspect it for cracks or other defects. Replace it if it is damaged.
4. To replace a faulty igniter, find the ignition control module, unscrew the cover, and disconnect the module. Install the replacement part and test.

Check and replace a glow bar:

1. Turn on the thermostat.
2. Turn off power to the appliance.
3. Unscrew the cover plate over the glow bar ring at the back of the range and disconnect the plugs, or find the glow bar beneath the oven baffle.
4. Set a multimeter (see *Fix Everything: Multimeter*) to R×1 (resistance times 1) and touch a probe to each glow bar terminal. Replace the glow bar if it does not show continuity. If the glow bar has continuity, the safety valve may be faulty, requiring professional service.
5. Replace a faulty glow bar by unscrewing it from the burner support bracket and the oven wall, then pulling the glow bar free of the terminal block.
6. Mount the replacement glow bar in the burner support bracket, reconnect its plugs, and replace the metal cover.

Service an oven door:

1. To fix a cocked door, open the door and loosen the screws securing the inner panel. Hold the door at the top and twist it from side to side to seat it securely on its hinges.

2. Partially tighten the door screws; do not overtighten screws on a porcelain door because you might chip the surface.

3. Test the seal by inserting a piece of paper between the seal and the top corners of the oven. The seal should tightly grip the paper.

4. To replace cabinet-mounted springs, remove the storage drawer and the door. Unhook and replace the springs. Replace both springs even if only one is broken.

Replace oven gaskets:

1. Unplug the oven or shut off power at the *Electrical Service Panel*, shut off gas to the oven, and pull the oven away from the wall.

2. Remove the gaskets by unscrewing or unclipping retainers.

3. Locate and loosen the oven liner bolts from the back of the unit.

4. Partially remove the oven liner by rocking it back and forth. Disconnect the gasket from between the liner and the cabinet.

5. Place the new gasket behind the oven liner rim.

6. Reinstall the oven liner and reattach it to the back of the oven.

**Fix-It Tip**

On self-cleaning ovens, the gasket is held between the panels of the oven door and can be replaced only by taking the door apart.

Replace door-mounted gaskets:

1. Unscrew the door hinge arms and remove the door.

2. Remove inner panel and edge screws as needed. You may need to carefully bend tabs to remove the cover.

3. Remove screws holding the window assembly to the panel.

4. Remove the window assembly to reveal the gasket attachment.

5. Remove the gasket between the window assembly and the inner door panel.

6. Install the new gasket in reverse order or by following the manufacturer's instructions.

# Oven, Microwave

The microwave oven was invented in (drum roll) 1945! And the first commercial microwave was sold nine years later. It was another 13 years, in 1967, before they were put on the market to households. And another dozen years before they started to become widely popular. Today, microwave ovens are in 90 percent of all U.S. homes. Fortunately, they are virtually trouble-free. When they are not, here are some things you can do about it.

## How Does It Work?

A microwave oven is an appliance for heating and cooking food more quickly than a conventional oven. A magnetron inside the oven produces a beam of electromagnetic waves, called microwaves. The beam is reflected throughout the microwave to heat the food from the inside out rather than the outside in as conventional ovens do. The magnetron is powered by a transformer, capacitor (dangerous!), and diode, which convert household AC power into the high-voltage DC power that the magnetron needs. Controls tell the magnetron how long to stay on and at what power setting.

## What Can Go Wrong?

Fortunately, microwave ovens are nearly trouble-free. Many of the problems can be fixed by the owner. For example, the power cord can be damaged, the interlock switch, thermal cutout, fan, turntable motor, temperature probe, or light bulb may need to be replaced, or the door may not close properly.

**Caution**

Never attempt to service the magnetron in a microwave oven. It is extremely dangerous.

## How Can I Identify the Problem?

If the microwave will not work at all, make sure power is on at the outlet and test the *Electrical Cord*. Test the *Fuse* and replace it if it is faulty. Also check the door to make sure it closes properly. Test and, if needed, replace the fan (see *Motor*).

If the oven doesn't cook or cooks only intermittently but the display is on, check the door interlock switch, the thermal cutout (see *Appliance Controls*), and the fan (see *Motor*), replacing parts that don't pass the test.

If the oven keeps blowing fuses, check for a faulty door interlock or monitor switch (see *Appliance Controls*).

If the carousel won't turn, inspect the plastic coupling beneath the tray. Check the roller assembly and make sure the tray is sitting level on the turning mechanism.

If you still have trouble with the microwave, take it to a repair center that works on microwave ovens.

Microwave cases typically are fastened together using Torx tamper-resistant screws. You'll need a special screwdriver or hex bit to remove these fasteners. Make sure you get the correct size, because there are at least seven sizes. Make an imprint of the screw with some clay and take it to a large hardware or auto parts store.

## What Parts, Materials, and Tools Do I Need?

You can find replacement parts from the manufacturer or from aftermarket suppliers (see *Fix-It Resources*). Tools you'll need to disassemble and test a microwave oven include these:

- Screwdrivers
- Wrenches
- Multimeter

## What Are the Steps to Fixing It?

Service a microwave oven door:

1. Inspect the door for obvious problems, such as broken components.
2. Inspect and clean the door seal along the inside front edge of the oven. Use a mild detergent in warm water; rinse and dry before use.
3. Inspect the door hinge to ensure that it isn't damaged.
4. Inspect the door latch on the outside and inside of the door to make sure it works smoothly and that it is not blocked by baked-on food.

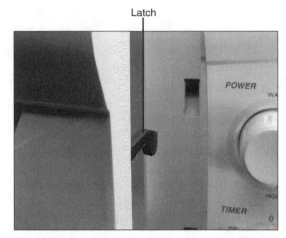

Latch

Check the door latch to make sure that it is tight and works freely.

Disassemble a microwave oven:

1. Unplug the microwave oven and remove all trays or carousels inside the oven cavity. If the unit is built-in, remove fasteners (typically on the underside of the cabinet) holding the unit in place and remove the microwave oven.
2. Turn the unit on its back or side and remove screws or bolts that hold the housing to the frame.
3. Carefully remove the housing and set it aside to access components within the microwave.
4. Identify the capacitor (see the owner's manual) and make sure you *don't touch it*. Capacitors hold an electrical charge after the appliance is unplugged.

Magnetron

The magnetron is the main component of a microwave; don't attempt to service it. Leave that job for a trained appliance technician.

Capacitor

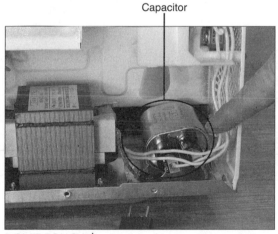

DON'T TOUCH the capacitor!

Fuse

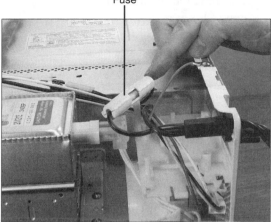

A microwave's fuse typically is located inside near the electrical cord. You can test and replace it.

5.  Inspect and, if needed, clean switches and other simple components. *Don't* disturb the magnetron (probably encased in a secondary housing).
6.  Use a multimeter (see *Fix Everything: Multimeter*) to test the *Electrical Cord*, fan (see *Motor*), *Fuse*, interlock, and other appliance components.
7.  Reassemble and test the microwave oven.

Test a temperature probe:

(Temperature probes have two ends: a sensor end that measures temperature and a connection end that delivers the results to the microwave.)

1. Place the temperature probe's sensor into a cup of hot water.
2. Set the multimeter (see *Fix Everything: Multimeter*) to measure resistance (R×1, or resistance times 1 scale).
3. Place the multimeter's test tips on each side of the temperature probe's connection end. The resistance (in ohms) should be more than zero but less than infinite. If infinite, the temperature probe isn't sending a signal to the microwave; replace the probe with an identical part.
4. If the temperature probe is okay, the control board inside the microwave may need to be replaced. Take the microwave oven to a service shop for repair.

**Fix-It Tip**

Microwave ovens are heating appliances of 500 to 1,500 watts. Make sure there is sufficient ventilation space around a microwave to keep it relatively cool. Manufacturers typically suggest at least 2 inches of clearance behind and beside the microwave oven. Check the unit's owner's manual for specifics.

# Oven, Toaster

Toaster ovens are handy, especially when you want to bake something but don't want to heat up the entire kitchen with a full-size oven. Or if you want only a small portion. Think of a toaster oven as a big toaster or a small oven. Here's how to fix one that needs repair.

## How Does It Work?

A toaster oven is a small heating appliance that toasts bread, waffles, etc., and may (depending on the wattage) also function as a miniature oven. Some allow you to bake and broil foods, offering precise temperature and function controls.

To operate a toaster oven, controls are set, the door is opened, food is placed on a shelf, and the door is closed. If set for toasting, the toaster thermostat operates the upper and lower heating elements as selected by the controller. If set for baking or broiling, the baking thermostat operates the heating elements as selected by the temperature controller and possibly by a timing mechanism.

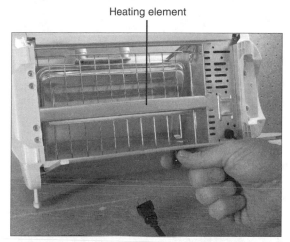

Heating element

You can access the heating element through the clean-out door on the underside.

The features of toaster ovens vary considerably from model to model. However, most operate in the same manner and can be diagnosed and repaired similarly.

## What Can Go Wrong?

The problems that toaster ovens may present are similar to those of other heating appliances. The electrical cord may need replacing. The main switch, the thermal fuse, and the solenoid may be faulty. The thermostat may be faulty or need recalibrating.

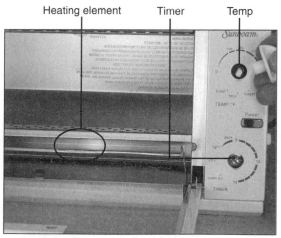

Heating element     Timer     Temp

Components of a typical toaster oven.

Thermal fuse

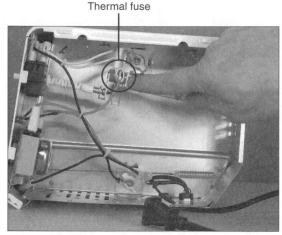

Location of the typical toaster oven's thermal fuse.

## How Can I Identify the Problem?

If the oven doesn't work at all, make sure the circuit breaker or fuse is on at the *Electrical Service Panel* and test the *Electrical Cord*.

If the oven doesn't work on its toaster and oven functions, test the main switch (see *Appliance Controls*). As needed, check the *Fuse*.

Most toaster oven controls can be accessed by removing the unit's side panel.

If the toaster function doesn't turn off unless the door is open, test the solenoid and the switch (see *Appliance Controls*). Then check the thermostat and replace it if inaccurate (see *Appliance Controls*).

If the toaster oven stays on when the door is opened, check the main switch (see *Appliance Controls*). If the oven doesn't heat, test the *Heating Element*.

**Fix-It Tip**

Need to replace the toaster oven? Consider spending a little more to purchase one that is heavier than other models. The components will typically be of better quality and will probably stand up to longer use.

## What Parts, Materials, and Tools Do I Need?

Replacement parts are available from the manufacturer and aftermarket suppliers (see *Fix-It Resources*) and from local appliance parts houses and larger home centers. Refer to the guides mentioned above (*Electrical Service Panel*, *Electrical Cord*, *Appliance Controls*, and *Heating Element*) for specific requirements and step-by-step procedures.

**Caution**

As you remove levers and knobs, mark each with a piece of masking tape or draw a diagram, because some parts are interchangeable. Remember to put screws and other small parts in a container rather than let them roll around on the table and get lost.

# Paint

Paint is practical as well as decorative. Not only does paint make the inside and outside of your home more attractive, it also protects material from the elements. And it's relatively easy to fix paint problems. Here's how.

## How Does It Work?

Paint is a mixture of pigment (color) in a liquid vehicle (latex, oil, or epoxy) that dries as an opaque solid film. Paint is applied to walls, ceilings, cabinets, floors, and even appliances inside a home, and to exterior walls, shutters, gutters, and fences, as well as many other surfaces both indoors and outdoors. Paint protects and decorates the surface it is applied to. Paint is versatile.

## What Can Go Wrong?

Paint can crack and peel, chip, and otherwise become less attractive and lose its protective ability.

## How Can I Identify the Problem?

If otherwise good paint on a wall, ceiling, floor, or cabinet in your home has a problem area, you may be able to delay the need for a full paint job either with a thorough cleaning or with a touch-up paint job (see below).

If an appliance is chipped or scratched, you can touch it up (see below).

If exterior paint looks dingy and/or has mildewed spots, you can clean it with a hose or power washer (see below) and save repainting for another day.

## What Parts, Materials, and Tools Do I Need?

Your best bet for finding materials and tools for painting is at a paint store. It typically can give you valuable advice and show you tools that will save time. You'll need these:

- Paint to match the existing surface
- Paint brushes
- Paint rollers

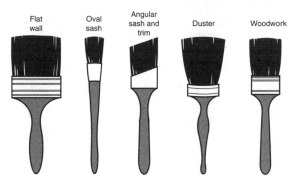

Flat wall    Oval sash    Angular sash and trim    Duster    Woodwork

There is a wide variety of paint brushes available at paint and hardware stores. In addition, most come in various sizes. Ask a clerk to help you select the best one for the job at hand.

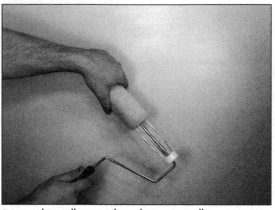

Buy and install a good-quality paint roller cover on the roller frame.

- Household (such as oxygen) cleaners
- Fine-grit sandpaper
- Garden sprayer
- Exterior paint cleaner
- Garden hose
- Pressure washer

## What Are the Steps to Fixing It?

Clean a painted interior surface:

1. Wash the surface with a sponge and mild detergent. If that fails, move to step 2.
2. Clean the surface with an oxygen cleaner, then rinse. If that doesn't remove problem stains, try step 3.
3. Carefully scrub the surface with an abrasive household cleaner, then rinse. If that doesn't work, move to step 4.
4. Repaint the problem area, making sure you perform any needed repairs (see *Drywall* or *Plaster*) first.

Touch up an interior wall:

1. If a wall is stained, use a paint roller to apply stain-killing primer over the stains. Allow the surface to dry thoroughly.
2. If a wall has been damaged and repaired, use a roller and brushes to apply paint over the repaired area, blending the edges into the surrounding area. Allow the surface to dry thoroughly.
3. Apply a second coat over the stained or repaired area to cover at least 6 square feet. Allow the surface to dry thoroughly before replacing furniture and pictures.

Clean exterior paint and kill mildew:

1. Fill a garden sprayer with exterior house cleaner, following the manufacturer's instructions.
2. Use a pressure washer or a garden hose with a power nozzle to rinse off the cleaner and surrounding area.

**Caution**

A pressure washer is a great tool. But use it carefully, because it puts the water under enough pressure to take off flaking or otherwise deteriorating paint, to damage aging wood, or other things the stream of water hits. Follow any instructions with the machine, and keep enough distance from the surface being washed to avoid damage. Be very careful using a power washer when you are standing on a ladder; the sudden pressure when you turn the washer on could upset your balance.

3. Let the surface dry thoroughly.
4. Apply touch-up primer and paint if needed, feathering the edges to blend with the old paint job.

Touch up a painted appliance:

1. Use fine-grit sandpaper to sand rust or other imperfections.
2. Clean the sanded and surrounding surface with paint thinner.
3. Apply a thin coat of rust-inhibiting metal primer. Allow the surface to dry thoroughly.
4. Carefully mask off an area wider than the primed area.
5. Spray enamel paint over the unmasked area in a single light coat. Allow to dry.
6. Gently sand the area and repaint as needed.

# Paneling

Paneling is a wall covering product that offers the beauty of wood or other natural surface at lower cost. In addition, paneling typically is sealed with a protective coating that makes it easier to clean than most wall surfaces. Also, paneling is relatively easy to fix.

## How Does It Work?

Paneling is decorative wood panels joined in a continuous surface, typically sold in 4 × 8 feet sheets that are ⅛ to ⅜ inches thick. Paneling is attached to *Drywall*, furring (thin wood) strips, or wall framing studs using nails, screws, or adhesive.

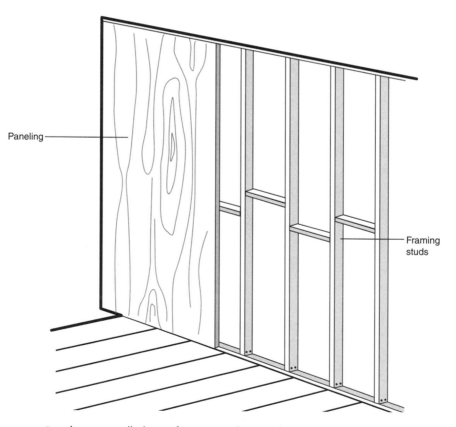

Paneling

Framing studs

Paneling is installed over framing studs (as shown here), drywall, or furring strips, depending on the application.

## What Can Go Wrong?

Paneling gets dirty. Marks and small scratches appear. Paneling buckles from moisture and edges become loose. Nails pop up. And sometimes deep gouges, scratches, and even holes happen. You can fix them.

## How Can I Identify the Problem?

If the paneling is dirty, try a thorough cleaning with a good household cleaner, such as an oxygen cleaner.

If marks and small scratches appear, make a cosmetic repair with a touch-up stick or paste wax.

If a panel has buckled from moisture, refasten it with more nails, or pull the panel loose and apply panel adhesive to the studs (see below).

If nails pop up, reset them with a hammer and nail set, then use a touch-up stick if needed.

If the panel is heavily damaged, you can replace the entire panel (see below).

**Fix-It Tip**

You can touch up scratches on wood paneling with touch-up sticks and pens available at hardware stores and home centers. Make sure you get a color approximately the same as that of the panel you're fixing.

## What Parts, Materials, and Tools Do I Need?

You can find replacement parts, materials, and tools for paneling fix-it projects at most hardware and building material stores. Here's a list:

- Replacement paneling
- Metal putty knife
- Pry bar
- Caulk gun
- Hammer
- Nail set
- Panel adhesive
- Pliers or nail puller
- Paneling nails or finish nails
- Touch-up stick
- Chisel or scraper

## What Are the Steps to Fixing It?

Refasten loose paneling:

1. Use a pry bar or metal putty knife to loosen the panel's edge.
2. Carefully remove nails from the loose edge using pliers or a nail puller.
3. Apply a bead of panel adhesive (see *Fix Everything: Adhesives*) along the exposed studs or furring strips with a caulk gun, and allow the adhesive to become tacky before pressing the panel back in place.
4. Nail the panel in place using paneling or finish nails of approximately the same color as the panel. If needed, use a touch-up stick to cover the nail heads.
5. Remove excess adhesive that has squeezed out between panels.

Replace a panel:

1. Use a pry bar or metal putty knife to loosen the panel's edge.
2. Carefully remove nails from the loose edge using pliers or a nail puller.
3. Remove the panel, starting at the bottom of the wall and working up.
4. Remove old nails and clean up the area behind the panel of old adhesive.
5. Apply a bead of panel adhesive (see *Fix Everything: Adhesives*) along the exposed studs or furring strips with a caulk gun, and allow the adhesive to become tacky.
6. Press the new panel into place and tap it against the studs, drywall, or furring strips.
7. Nail the edges of the panel with a hammer and nail set.
8. Cover nail heads with a touch-up stick as needed.

**Fix-It Tip**

If you're just plain tired of paneling, you can prime the surface and paint over it. Make sure you choose a primer and paint that are recommended by the manufacturer for application over coated paneling.

Household plumbing pipe seems invisible. You don't really see it—until it bursts in the basement or under a kitchen sink. Then you need to know something about pipe—and quickly! This guide tells you what you need to know about plumbing pipe. Refer to *Plumbing System, Drain System, Faucet, Garbage Disposer,* and other guides for information on other aspects of your home's plumbing.

## How Does It Work?

Household plumbing pipes are installed in walls and under floors during construction. They carry fresh water to kitchens, bathrooms, utility rooms, and so on. A separate system carries wastewater from a sink or toilet to the main drain and out of the house to the sewer or septic system.

Pipe is available in cast-iron, brass, copper, galvanized steel, and plastic. Fittings are connections between pipes that allow pipes to turn or attach to a fixture such as a faucet or water heater.

How the fittings are installed on pipe depends on the material. For example, copper pipes are soldered together or joined with compression or flare fittings. Plastic pipes are joined with plastic screw-on fittings or PVC cement. In addition, transition fittings can be used to join plastic and metal pipes.

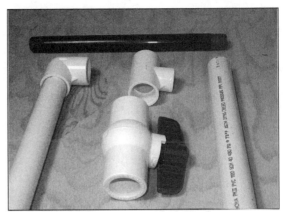

Plastic (PVC) pipe comes in a variety of types, sizes, and connections.

## What Can Go Wrong?

Pipe doesn't move, nor is it subject to wear. So the greatest cause of pipe problems is age (pipes become brittle or corrode, fittings fail) or damage from freezing.

> **Fix-It Tip**
>
> Plumbing in your home was installed to follow local plumbing codes at the time the house was constructed. Before doing more than repairing existing pipe, check with local building departments to find out whether permits and inspections are required.

## How Can I Identify the Problem?

If water leaks from a pipe, you can trace it to its source, then fix it. However, tracing it may require that you crawl around under the house, in an attic, or maybe even open up a wall.

## What Parts, Materials, and Tools Do I Need?

Parts for repairing pipe and fittings are available from a plumbing supply outlet, large hardware store, or plumbing department of a home center. Tools you'll need include these:

- Pipe repair kit (for emergencies)
- Pipe tape
- PVC primer
- PVC cement
- Pipe cutter or hacksaw
- Small wire brush
- Emery cloth
- Flaring tool and reamer
- Paste flux
- Solder
- Propane torch

## What Are the Steps to Fixing It?

Solder copper pipe:

1. Clean the inside of the fitting with a small wire brush or with an emery cloth until it begins to shine.
2. Clean the outside of the pipe in the same manner as the fitting. Avoid touching the cleaned surfaces.
3. Brush a thin coat of paste flux inside the fitting and outside the end of the pipe.
4. Insert the pipe end into the fitting. Then turn it to spread the flux. Wipe off excess flux.
5. Use a propane torch (on soft flame) to heat the pipe joint evenly until the pipe is hot enough to melt the solder.
6. Apply solder (see *Fix Everything: Solder*) around the entire joint rim. Carefully wipe off excess solder.

Connect a compression fitting on copper pipe:

1. Slide a nut and ring over the pipe.
2. Insert the pipe onto the connection.
3. Slide the compression ring and nut to the threads and tighten the nut with a wrench.

Connect a flare fitting on copper pipe:

1. Slide flare nuts over the pipe end.
2. Clamp one end of the pipe into the flaring tool and screw the ram into the pipe end to flare it.
3. Insert the flared end onto the connection, then screw the flare nuts onto the connection. Use two wrenches to tighten the nuts.

Cut rigid copper with a pipe cutter:

1. Slide the pipe cutter onto the copper pipe.
2. Tighten the cutting wheel until it lightly scores the surface.
3. Rotate the pipe cutter around the pipe once, then tighten the cutter slightly and repeat until the pipe is cut.

Join plastic pipe:

1. Cut the plastic pipe with a pipe cutter or hacksaw, bracing it so it doesn't bend or rotate.
2. Remove burrs from the end of the pipe with a utility knife or emery cloth.

3. Insert pipe into the fitting to make sure it fits correctly, called a dry fit.
4. Use a pencil to draw a line across the joint.
5. For PVC pipe, apply PVC primer to the pipe and fitting, following directions on the primer can.
6. For all plastic pipe, liberally apply cement to the outside of the pipe end and to the inside of the fitting.

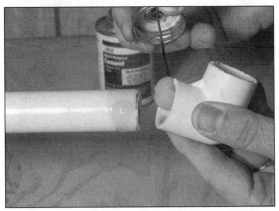

Use PVC primer followed by PVC cement to join plastic pipe.

7. Immediately install the fitting on the pipe, making sure that the pencil lines are aligned.
8. Remove excess PVC cement and let it dry for the amount of time specified on the PVC cement label.

Replace a leaking threaded iron or steel pipe:

1. Shut off water to pipe and drain it.
2. Cut through the damaged pipe with a hacksaw.
3. Unscrew the cut sections from the fittings.
4. Replace the old pipe with two nipples joined by a center union.
5. Apply pipe tape to the nipple threads.
6. Screw one nipple into the fitting and tighten with a wrench.

7. Slide the ring nut over the nipple, then screw the hubbed nut onto the nipple.
8. Screw the threaded nut onto the second nipple, then screw the nipple into the second fitting.
9. Tighten the nipple and nut.
10. Apply pipe tape to the threaded nut.
11. Slide the ring nut to the center of the union and screw it on.

Patch rigid copper pipe with plastic pipe:

1. Shut off the water supply to the damaged pipe and open a faucet to drain the pipe.
2. Cut out the damaged pipe section with a pipe cutter or hacksaw. Clean off the end of the copper pipe.
3. Measure the gap between the pipe ends.
4. Cut rigid plastic pipe of the same diameter as the copper pipe to fit the gap, allowing for transition fittings. Clean off the end of the plastic pipe.
5. Sweat solder (see *Fix Everything: Solder*) the copper section of the fitting to the end of the copper pipe.
6. Screw the brass and plastic sections of the fittings to the copper sections.
7. Dry-fit the plastic pipe patch to make sure it fits properly.
8. If you are using PVC, apply primer (see above). For all plastic pipes, apply solvent to the inside of the fittings and outside of the pipe ends.
9. Reinstall the plastic pipe patch.

**Fix-It Tip**

Need to connect pipes of two different materials, such as copper to plastic or plastic to steel? First visit a plumbing store and describe what you're trying to do to a knowledgeable clerk. There are special fittings made for various applications.

# Plaster

Millions of homes have plaster walls, the precursor to *Drywall*. In fact, many modern homes are still constructed with plaster, especially homes built with a retro look. Drywall isn't better, it's just cheaper to install and requires less skill than plaster. If you live in a home with plaster walls, here's how to fix them.

## How Does It Work?

Plaster is a pasty composition of lime, water, and sand that hardens when it dries. It's used for coating walls, ceilings, and partitions. Plaster is spread over masonry or lath (strips of wood, metal, or gypsum). In older homes, plaster was applied in one to three coats. All-purpose, one-coat plasters are now available to make plastering easier. There are numerous plaster-patch products available to make repair easy, too.

## What Can Go Wrong?

Plaster walls and ceilings can develop small to large cracks from drying or ground movement. Furniture, doorknobs, and other objects also can make holes in plaster. If it becomes wet, plaster can bulge or even disintegrate.

## How Can I Identify the Problem?

If a plaster wall or ceiling develops a crack, you can fill it in (see below).

If a plaster surface suffers a hole or bulge, you can also fill it (see below).

If there is a larger hole in a plaster ceiling, you can most easily repair it with a ceiling patch kit.

### Which Plaster?

You can patch a hole in plaster or drywall with joint compound, spackling compound, or patching plaster. Each has advantages and disadvantages. Joint compound applies smoothly and sands easily, but it takes 24 hours to dry and it shrinks. Spackling compound dries quickly and shrinks minimally, but is harder to sand smooth. Patching plaster dries in as little as two hours, doesn't shrink, and is durable, but it is difficult to sand.

**Fix-It Tip**

Patching plaster powder, when mixed with water, must be used quickly before it dries. If it begins to get too hard to use, add a little water to thin it out. If in doubt, throw it out.

## What Parts, Materials, and Tools Do I Need?

Plaster patching materials and tools are relatively easy to find at larger hardware stores and home centers. Here's what you'll need to patch plaster:

- Patching plaster
- Sandpaper
- Primer and paint
- Broadknife or putty knife
- Mister
- Latex bonder

- Small soft-bristle brush
- Masonry chisel
- Hammer
- Vacuum cleaner

## What Are the Steps to Fixing It?

Repair a small crack in plaster:

1. Widen the crack to about ⅛ inch using a chisel or pointed tool, then remove any loose plaster.
2. Fill the crack with patching plaster following directions on the container.
3. Once the plaster is dry, sand with progressively finer sandpaper.
4. Prime and *Paint*.

Patch a large crack in plaster:

1. Widen the surface of the crack using a hammer and chisel.
2. Remove debris with a small soft-bristle brush.
3. Thoroughly wet the crack so it will absorb the plaster patch.
4. Use a putty knife or broadknife to spread patching plaster (prepared according to package directions) in the hole.
5. Allow to dry for 24 hours or as directed by the patch manufacturer.
6. Apply a second coat of patching plaster and allow it to dry before continuing.
7. Sand the surface smooth, seal it with primer, then *Paint*.

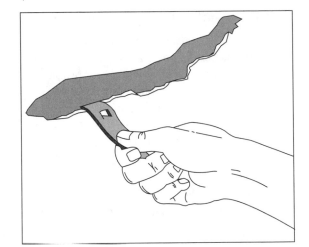

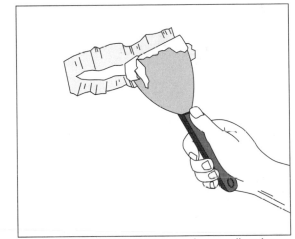

Widen the crack so that the new plaster will stick to the old plaster, then spread patching plaster over the area.

Repair a small hole or bulge in plaster:

1. Identify the cause of the hole. If the problem was behind the wall or ceiling (such as *Pipe*), first repair the underlying problem. If you can't determine the cause of the damage, consider hiring an experienced remodeler. Make sure you solve the problem, not just plaster over it.

2. Use a masonry chisel to dig back until you hit solid plaster. Vacuum or brush out debris.

3. Dampen the edges of the hole for better adhesion.

4. Apply patching plaster mixed according to package directions, starting from the edges of the hole and working toward the center.

5. Use a broadknife to smooth the surface of the patch, then let dry for 24 hours or as recommended by the plaster manufacturer.

6. Sand the surface, prime, and *Paint*.

**Fix-It Tip**

Instead of a second coat of plaster patch, apply a top coat of joint compound. It's easier to sand and finish.

# Plumbing System

Out of sight, out of mind. Most of us don't think about our home's plumbing system—hot and cold water, toilets, drains, etc.—until something goes wrong. Most of it is hidden in walls or under cabinets. Fortunately, the parts that need fixing are easier to get to. Let's take a closer look at your home's plumbing system.

## How Does It Work?

A household plumbing system is the series of pipes, faucets, drains, and their attached devices and fixtures that bring fresh water into a home and take wastewater out to a sewer or septic system. Whether the water comes from a municipal system or a private well, water comes into your home through a large pipe. If you purchase your water, a meter on the pipe records your usage. Near the meter is a shutoff valve for turning the water supply off before it enters the house.

> **Caution**
> Make sure you know where the shutoff valve is so you can minimize water damage in an emergency.

When the water comes into your home, one pipe branches off to the water heater to supply hot water to various fixtures. The rest of the (cold) water continues on to the fixtures and appliances. Water in those supply lines is under pressure (about 50 pounds per square inch (psi) so that it will flow rapidly when you open a faucet or turn on a dishwasher or clothes washer.

Other, larger pipes and related drains collect wastewater from those same fixtures and appliances and conduct it to a main sewer or septic system.

## What Can Go Wrong?

Pipes can leak or break. Fixtures and appliances can also leak. Drains sometimes don't drain or drain slowly. Fixtures and pipes also get clogged.

## How Can I Identify the Problem?

Most plumbing problems occur at a fixture or inside a pipe. The overall plumbing system, the pipes and fittings, seldom cause problems.

If a pipe leaks or breaks, turn off the water supply to that pipe or to the entire house, then repair the *Pipe*.

If a *Faucet* or appliance leaks, shut off the water supply to it, then repair it (see the guide in this section of the book for the specific fixture or appliance).

If a drain won't drain or drains slowly, see *Drain System*.

If a fixture or pipe gets clogged, see the guide in this section for the specific fixture or appliance.

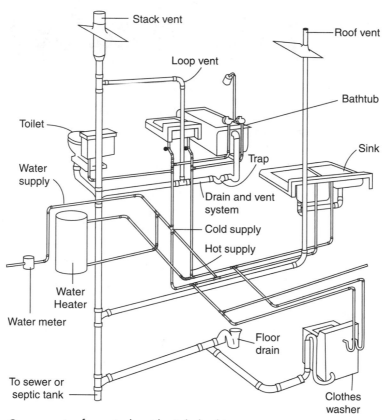

Components of a typical residential plumbing system.

Plumbing repairs may get messy, but most are fairly simple. Plumbing relies on just two basic principles: pressure and gravity. The pressure is created by the difference in height of the nearest water storage tower and the elevation where the water comes out of the system in your home. Gravity makes drains work.

## What Parts, Materials, and Tools Do I Need?

Replacement parts are available from local plumbing and hardware stores and home centers. Refer to specific *Fix-It Guides* for tool recommendations.

# Popcorn Popper

You don't need to have a home theater to enjoy popcorn and a movie. Or just popcorn. And you don't have to accept microwave popcorn. You can make the real thing with a popcorn popper—and you can fix the popper when it breaks from constant use.

## How Does It Work?

A popcorn popper is a small electric appliance designed for heating kernels of popcorn to the point where they pop into an edible form. Corn poppers come in two basic types, hot-air poppers and oil poppers. Hot-air poppers have a fanlike impeller that agitates the kernels with a turbulent stream of hot air in the popping chamber. Oil poppers use a rotating rod to stir the kernels in a small amount of heated cooking oil. The heat in both styles of popper is generated by a heating element in the base, activated by a simple on-off switch and controlled by a thermostat. Both types include a motor. The heating element can be either a horseshoe-shaped solid rod or a springlike resistance coil.

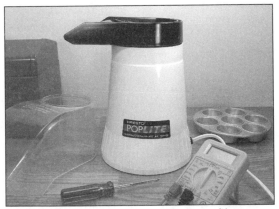

An electric popcorn popper is a motorized heating appliance.

## What Can Go Wrong?

A faulty thermostat or thermal cutoff is often the cause of common popcorn popper problems such as scorched or unpopped corn and excessive popping time. Motors and other components can be replaced, but it may be as economical to replace the entire unit. As with other small heating appliances, the electrical cord, the switch, the thermal cutoff, and the heating element or coil all could be faulty.

**Fix-It Tip**

Oil poppers can easily get dirty because excess oil splatters and cooks onto metal components. After every use, clean the popper with a sponge dampened in soapy water; then rinse with clear water. *Don't* immerse the unit in water unless the manufacturer says it's safe to do so.

## How Can I Identify the Problem?

If the unit does not work at all, make sure power is on at the *Electrical Receptacle* and test the *Electrical Cord*, replacing if necessary. Also test the switch and the thermal cutoff (see *Appliance Controls*), replacing as needed.

If the unit doesn't heat, test the *Heating Element* (oil popper) or inspect the element (hot-air popper). If the element is faulty, replace the popper.

If an oil popper's stir rod doesn't stir, test the *Motor* and replace it if it is faulty or replace the popper.

If a hot-air popper's fan doesn't work, disassemble the popper and clean any debris blocking the impeller.

## What Parts, Materials, and Tools Do I Need?

Replacement parts for popcorn poppers typically are available only from the manufacturer. Check the owner's manual for parts numbers and parts ordering instructions. To disassemble and test an oil or hot-air popper, you'll need these tools:

- Screwdrivers
- Wrenches
- Multimeter

## What Are the Steps to Fixing It?

Disassemble a hot-air popper:

1. Unplug the popper and turn it upside down.
2. Remove the screws holding the chute to the base and remove the chute.
3. Remove the screws or fittings to loosen the motor.
4. Remove screws holding the motor base and impeller housing. Separate the base and housing to expose the heating coil and circuitry.
5. Use a multimeter (see *Fix Everything: Multimeter*) to test the *Motor, Heating Element*, and *Appliance Controls*, replacing as needed.

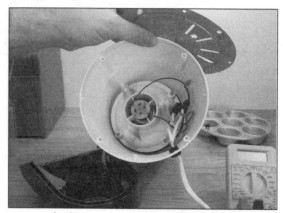

Remove the base cover to access the motor.

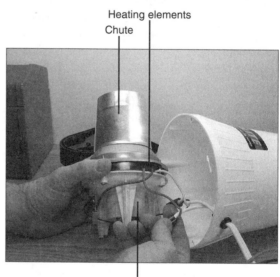

Heating elements
Chute
Fan motor

A hot-air popcorn popper consists of a chute, heating element, and fan motor. The element and fan can be tested with a multimeter.

Disassemble an oil popper:

1. Unplug the popper and turn it upside down.
2. Remove any screws securing the access plate. All serviceable components are beneath the plate.
3. Use a multimeter (see *Fix Everything: Multimeter*) to test the *Motor, Heating Element*, and *Appliance Controls*, replacing as needed.

# Portable Stereo

For some people, portable music devices—radio, cassette player, CD player, MP3 player—are the greatest invention since string cheese. "Gotta have my tunes!" But, like most everything else, they break and need fixing. Here's how to fix portable music devices without missing a beat.

## How Does It Work?

A portable stereo is a compact version of its full-size counterpart: an *Amplifier, Cassette Deck*, and/or *CD Player*. (The exception is the new MP3 player that typically comes in only a portable version.) What makes portable units different from the bigger versions is portability—they are smaller and are powered by batteries rather than through electrical cords. Some deliver sound to headphones while others use small built-in speakers.

## What Can Go Wrong?

A portable stereo is vulnerable to mechanical problems caused by dirt and moisture, so a system that is kept clean and dry will have far fewer problems. If the stereo uses rechargeable batteries, the problem might be in the charging system, especially plugs, contacts, and jacks.

The most common problem with portable stereos is low-power or dead batteries. When any problem occurs with a portable music device, first test the batteries and clean the contacts. Then examine the headphones for breaks in the cord and loose connections that can interfere with the sound quality. While some headphones can be repaired, most are so small and inexpensive that replacement may be more practical.

**Fix-It Tip**

Like their full-size counterpart, portable cassette players need their heads cleaned once in a while. The head is the surface that reads (hears) or writes (records) music signals off the tape. Use a cassette tape cleaner kit as recommended by the manufacturer.

## How Can I Identify the Problem?

All types of portable music devices:

If the unit doesn't work, check and replace batteries (see *Battery, Household*), clean corroded battery contacts with fine sandpaper, and carefully adjust battery contacts as needed to improve battery performance. Also spray electrical contact cleaner into the jack and wipe excess with a cotton swab. If that doesn't solve the problem, open the unit and inspect the jack for broken connections; resolder (see *Fix Everything: Solder*) connections as needed (see below).

If the sound is intermittent, look for corroded or bent contacts in the headphone plug or jack. Also check for a broken headphone wire and repair or replace the wire if you find one broken. Check for a loose or broken external antenna.

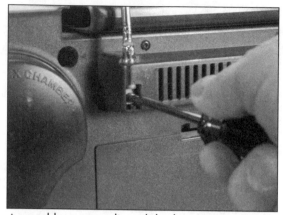

A portable stereo radio with bad reception may only need a new antenna—or the antenna tightened.

If the sound is fuzzy, try the headphones in another unit and replace the headphones if necessary.

If the function buttons don't work, clean any dirty button mechanisms with electrical contact cleaner, then carefully lubricate them with white lithium spray.

Cassette players/recorders:

If the cassette doesn't play high-frequency sounds, clean the head with a head-cleaning tape. If the heads look worn or damaged, have a professional technician replace them.

If the tape moves but there is no sound, check for dirty control mechanisms (push buttons) and clean any that are dirty with electrical contact cleaner.

If the unit damages tapes, disassemble and inspect the unit (see below). If the player is driven by belts, clean them with a cotton swab moistened in alcohol. Replace any broken, glazed, or cracked belts. If the player is driven by gears, replace any that have broken or worn teeth.

If the unit won't record, try a different tape in the unit.

If the record button won't engage, carefully clean the button mechanism with electrical contact cleaner, and lubricate with white lithium spray.

If the record unit does not erase, demagnetize the erase head (see *Cassette Deck*) or have the head professionally serviced or replaced.

CD player:

If a portable CD player distorts sound, clean the laser lens and the disc (see *CD Player*).

MP3 player:

Refer to "All types of portable musical devices" above.

**Fix-It Tip**

Hang on to the owner's manual. Set aside a specific drawer or file box where all owner's manuals go. They typically offer troubleshooting charts to make fixing things easier. They also have parts and service information you'll need.

## What Parts, Materials, and Tools Do I Need?

Replacement parts for most portable music devices are available from the manufacturer or from an aftermarket supplier (see *Fix-It Resources*). The tools and materials you'll need to disassemble, inspect, and clean portable music devices include these:

- Screwdrivers
- Pliers
- Electrical contact cleaner
- Cotton swabs
- Denatured alcohol
- Lens-cleaning disc
- Canned air
- Soldering iron and solder

## What Are the Steps to Fixing It?

Disassemble a portable music device:

1. Remove the batteries (see *Battery, Household*) from the unit. Battery compartment covers typically are located on the back or edge, held in place by a pressure clip or a small screw.
2. Remove all housing screws and unclip any tabs along the edges where the housing meets.
3. Once you've accessed the device's interior, inspect it for obvious problems or loose parts.
4. Don't remove the circuit board unless it is necessary to access additional components you think are broken and repairable (such as a built-in speaker). Handle components carefully—even fingerprints can damage intricate circuit boards.
5. Reassemble.

Resolder a headphone jack:

1. Open the device to access the internal components (see above). Find the jack and inspect all connections for looseness, cracks, or damage.
2. If the jack wires are loose, resolder them (see *Fix Everything: Solder*) following instructions that came with the soldering iron or gun. Avoid disturbing other connections on the board.

Replace a drive belt:

1. Open the device to access the internal components (see above). Find the drive belt(s). This may require carefully removing a circuit board. Inspect the belts for glazing, cracking, and other damage.
2. Purchase exact-replacement belts in sets. (If one is going out, any others probably will soon.)

3. Reinstall the belt(s) in the original configuration, being careful not to damage them.

Clean the laser on a portable CD player:

1. Remove batteries from the unit and disassemble (see above) as needed to access the laser lens. Some lenses are accessed without disassembly; just open the CD top and there it is.
2. Use canned air to blow dust out of the disc area.
3. Use lens-cleaning fluid and a cotton swab to clean the laser lens. Remove excess fluid with a dry swab.

**Fix-It Tip**

You can buy a cleaning kit for cassette decks and CD players at Radio Shack or other stores that carry electronic equipment. They are easy to use and come with full instructions.

# Radio, Car

Radios have been installed in cars since 1929. They have evolved, adding FM, eight-track tape players, cassette tape players, and now compact disc (CD) players. As they get more complex, however, there are fewer things that you, the car owner, can do to repair them. Even so, you still can fix a few things—and replace the radio with a new one if needed.

## How Does It Work?

A car radio receiver uses an antenna to gather audio signals, which it then amplifies and feeds to speakers for your enjoyment. The radio signals are amplitude modulated (AM) or frequency modulated (FM). The units often include other entertainment components, similar in design and repair to battery-operated miniature component systems, so refer to the *Portable Stereo* guide for more information on them.

## What Can Go Wrong?

As with other portable stereo devices, a car radio/tape/CD unit is vulnerable to mechanical problems caused by dirt and moisture. Keep the system clean and dry to minimize problems and repairs. The two most common problems are static noise and a faulty antenna.

**Caution**

Antitheft devices in modern cars require that a code, stored in memory, be automatically input before the radio will operate. Knowing this, a thief *might* not steal the radio because it won't operate without the code. That's the theory, anyway. Unfortunately, the code is stored only as long as your car's battery works. Once it dies or drops below operating level, the code is *gone!* So make sure you know the radio's code—just in case the battery goes dead or is disconnected for even a minute (to replace the battery). Write it on the car key or in an obscure location in the owner's manual, somewhere a thief wouldn't be able, or think, to look. Someday you'll thank us!

## How Can I Identify the Problem?

If the radio won't work, make sure the car battery is fully charged (see *Battery, Car*). Also look under the dashboard for any wires that may have become unplugged.

If the sound is fuzzy, disassemble the unit and locate the volume control; spray electrical contact cleaner into the control and rotate or slide the control several times to lubricate the mechanism. Replace a damaged or broken antenna (see below).

If the radio signal crackles, check the antenna for a tight connection. Check the battery ground connection to make sure it is tight. Also, find and replace the noise-suppression filter on or near the alternator. You'll need the car's owner's manual, a service manual, or a helpful auto parts clerk to find and replace it.

> **Fix-It Tip**
>
> Remember to clean your car's *Cassette Deck* and *CD Player* at least twice a year, depending on how much you use them. Use a cassette tape cleaner or CD cleaner kit as recommended by the manufacturer.

## What Parts, Materials, and Tools Do I Need?

Most modern radios are built on printed circuit boards that can't be repaired by anyone but trained technicians. However, there still are tests you can perform and parts you can replace. Check your local auto parts supplier or electronics supplier for parts and tools. Here's what you'll need:

- Screwdrivers
- Wrenches
- Electronic contact cleaner
- Denatured alcohol
- Soldering iron and solder

## What Are the Steps to Fixing It?

Diagnose a clicking noise on your car radio:

1. If the sound is a high-pitched whine that gets higher as the engine speeds up, the cause is probably a defective noise-suppression filter. Buy an exact-replacement unit from an auto parts store and make sure it has installation instructions included.

2. If the sound is a ticking that doesn't get higher pitched but does become more frequent as the engine speeds up, it's probably defective spark plug wires or a defective ignition coil capacitor. Purchase the replacement parts from an auto parts store that can advise you on installation.

Replace an external car antenna:

1. Loosen the antenna mounting nut on the car fender and remove the antenna. If there is no mounting nut, you may need to access it from the underside of the fender. In some cases, you will need a special tool to remove the nut.

2. Follow the manufacturer's instructions for installing the replacement antenna.

Replace a built-in antenna:

You can't. Many automotive antennas are built into the frame or body of the car. To determine if your car's antenna is replaceable, check the owner's manual or ask an auto parts clerk.

Remove a car radio:

There are many models and installations, so this is a general discussion. Car radios typically are held in place by brackets. A face plate is a decorative cover that hides the fasteners (screws and nuts) that hold the radio on the brackets. Once removed, the radio unit will slide toward you, allowing you to unplug electrical connections to the power, the speaker, and the antenna system. Fortunately, most modern car radios are interchangeable and include installation instructions.

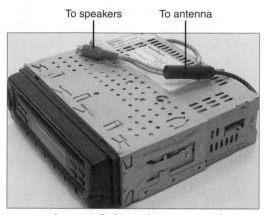

To speakers    To antenna

A car radio typically has only two external wires, one from the power source and one from the antenna.

Clean electronic components:

1.  Unplug the receiver and open the housing (see above).

2.  Use canned air to blow dust from components, including any power cords and speaker jacks.

3.  Use electrical contact cleaner or a cotton swab dipped in denatured alcohol to clean electronic components as needed.

4.  If you find broken components on a circuit board, replace the circuit board. You can use a soldering iron and electronic solder (see *Fix Everything: Solder*) to try to repair a component before you purchase a new circuit board.

# Radio, CB

CB radios have been quietly popular for 30 years. When they first came on the scene, CB radios were liberating. They gave housewives, bored commuters, and students of human nature a new language: CB. "Ten-four" became an abused term. After the wild interest moved on to the Internet chat rooms, CB continued to serve its initial purpose: two-way communication on a budget. Here's how to fix a CB, good buddy.

## How Does It Work?

A citizens band (CB) radio is both a receiver and a transmitter. A radio receiver is an electronic device that receives audio signals through an antenna, then amplifies and sends the sound to speakers. A transmitter does the opposite: it takes microphone (a reverse speaker) signals, converts them into electronic signals, and distributes them via an antenna. CB radios have 40 channels on which you can speak and/or listen. Some, such as channel 9, are set aside for special purposes (emergency assistance), but most are open to whatever you want to talk about. Mobile radios and mobile telephones work approximately the same way.

## What Can Go Wrong?

Mobile CB radios, those installed in cars and trucks, run on car battery power. Base stations are corded radio transmitters and receivers. A battery or cord may need replacing. Many CBs have fuses that can be replaced, often from the back of the unit. Contacts can be bent or corroded. Controls and switches may be dirty. Antennas can break or become disconnected.

Citizens band radios are miniature receivers and transmitters that fall under the jurisdiction of the Federal Communications Commission (FCC). Work on the transmitter components should be done only by an FCC radiotelephone-licensed service person.

Because CB radios transmit electronic signals, they come under the jurisdiction of the Federal Communications Commission. You'll need an FCC technician's license to work on a CB or mobile radio, other than a few tasks that can't impact transmission. Cleaning a CB is okay, as is replacing an antenna. And you can replace a *Fuse*.

## How Can I Identify the Problem?

If the CB radio won't work, make sure the battery is charged (see *Battery, Car*), or the *Electrical Cord* for a base unit tests okay and replace it if needed.

If the sound is fuzzy, disassemble the unit and locate the volume control. Spray electrical contact cleaner into the control and rotate or slide the control several times to lubricate the mechanism. Replace a damaged or broken antenna (see below).

If the sound is crackly or whines, check the car's noise-suppression filter and ignition coil capacitor (see below).

## What Parts, Materials, and Tools Do I Need?

CBs are digital wonders. That means there is little you can do to them without the help of an FCC-licensed technician. Even so, you can clean and maintain your unit. Here are some basic tools for the job:

- Screwdrivers
- Wrenches
- Canned air
- Electronic contact cleaner

## What Are the Steps to Fixing It?

Diagnose noise on your CB radio:

1. If the sound is a high-pitched whine that gets higher as the engine speeds up, the cause is probably a defective noise-suppression filter. Buy an exact-replacement unit from an auto parts store and make sure it has installation instructions included.
2. If the sound is a ticking that doesn't get higher pitched but does become more frequent as the engine speeds up, it's probably a defective spark plug wire or a defective ignition coil capacitor. Purchase the replacement parts from an auto parts store that can advise you on installation.

Replace a CB antenna:

1. Loosen the antenna mounting nut on the car fender and remove the antenna. Some CB antennas are temporarily mounted with a magnet base and run a wire between the antenna and the CB radio.
2. Follow the manufacturer's instructions for installing the replacement antenna. (There are entire books on selecting and mounting CB antennas!)

Clean electronic CB components:

1. Unplug the CB radio from power and from the antenna.
2. Remove the screws holding the case together, typically mounted on the bottom of the case.
3. Look for labels and other indications of the transmission circuitry. *Don't touch it.* You need to be an FCC-licensed technician to work on the transmitter.
4. Use canned air to blow dust from other components including any power cords and speaker jacks.
5. Use electrical contact cleaner or a cotton swab dipped in denatured alcohol to clean electronic components as needed.
6. Reassemble.

# Radio, Household

Radios are all around us. Inside the house we have the *Amplifier* with built-in stereo receiver, a *Portable Stereo* that runs on batteries, and a variety of corded household radios. This guide will cover how to fix small corded radios: clock radio, table radio, digital radio, kitchen radio, and others. (See the guides on *Radio, Car*; and *Radio, CB* for information on how to fix those types.)

## How Does It Work?

A radio receiver is an electronic device that receives audio signals through an antenna, then amplifies the resulting sound and delivers it to your ears through speakers. The signals are either amplitude modulated (AM) or frequency modulated (FM). Of course, it's a little more complicated than that, but the rest isn't important to the user.

The radio component of a portable stereo, clock radio, and table radio is basically the same in each type of device. As a result, these units share many of the same problems and repairs. The main difference in radios is whether the tuner is analog or digital. Most newer tuners are digital, but many older radios still in use have analog tuners. Digital radios have few easily serviceable parts. Digital radios are quite reliable, but if a part does fail, take the radio to an authorized repair center—or recycle it.

## What Can Go Wrong?

Household radios are corded radio receivers and amplifiers. That means power cords may need replacing. Contacts can be bent or corroded. A dial cord can be broken or the gears jammed. The station indicator pointer may be misaligned. Controls and switches may be dirty. Antennas break.

**Fix-It Tip**

Having problems getting up in the morning because your alarm radio doesn't work? Some units have a backup battery that saves your alarm settings if the power goes out. If the battery is dead, it doesn't remember them and you don't get up in time. Test and replace the battery (see *Battery, Household;* or *Battery, Button*), typically mounted in a small compartment accessed through a cover on the bottom or back of the radio.

## How Can I Identify the Problem?

If the radio won't work, make sure the power is on at the outlet and test the *Electrical Cord* and replace if needed.

If the station indicator won't move, check the pointer (see below). Less expensive household radios use a station frequency pointer mounted on a dial cord that's moved by a small wheel on the side of the radio. Better household radios use a digital frequency readout that cannot be adjusted.

If the sound is fuzzy, disassemble the unit and locate the volume control (see *Appliance Controls*); spray electrical contact cleaner into the control and rotate or slide the control several times to lubricate the mechanism. Replace a damaged or broken antenna (see below).

| Fix-It Tip |
|---|
| Don't throw away the owner's manual that came with your household radio. It not only tells you how to maintain it, it also tells you where to get parts. In addition, it probably includes warranty information to determine whether you need to fix it yourself or return it. |

## What Parts, Materials, and Tools Do I Need?

Most modern radios are built on printed circuit boards that can't be repaired by anyone but trained technicians. However, there still are tests you can perform and parts you can replace. Check your local Radio Shack or other electronics supplier for parts and tools. Here are a few tools you may need:

- Screwdrivers
- Wrenches
- Electronic contact cleaner
- Denatured alcohol
- Soldering iron and solder

## What Are the Steps to Fixing It?

Reset a dial pointer:

1. Turn on the radio and find a strong radio signal somewhere near the middle of the dial. Listen for the frequency (such as 740 AM or 96.5 FM).
2. Use a piece of tape or a grease pencil to mark the dial for where the pointer *should* be for that frequency.
3. Unplug the receiver and open the housing. Typically, there are two to four screws accessed from the underside of the radio.
4. Inspect the pointer mechanism for obvious problems, such as a cord that came off the end rollers or a break in the cord. If the cord is broken, replace or repair it.
5. Loosen the spring clips, then move the pointer along the dial cord until the station being received lines up with the tape or mark on the dial.
6. Tighten the clips on the cord, making sure you don't move the pointer.
7. Plug the radio in and verify that the dial pointer reads correctly.

Replace an external antenna:

1. Loosen the antenna screw on the radio's exterior and remove the antenna. (See *Portable Stereo* photo.) Replace it with an exact-replacement unit available through the manufacturer or an electronics store.
2. If there is no exterior screw, you will need to open the radio to access the antenna base (see below).

Replace an internal antenna:

1. Unplug the receiver and open the housing. Typically, there are two to four screws accessed from the underside of the radio.
2. Find and remove the internal antenna (or the internal base of the external antenna). Internal antennas typically are numerous wires wound around a flat piece, then sealed to minimize moisture and damage.
3. Inspect the wires wound around the antenna for obvious damage. Also make sure the antenna is firmly plugged into the main circuit board. If the antenna is damaged, replace it. If no replacement is available, attempt to repair the antenna, which is not easy because of all the fine wiring, or replace the radio as a unit.

Clean electronic components:

1. Unplug the receiver and open the housing (see above).
2. Use canned air to blow dust from components, including any power cords and speaker jacks.
3. Use electrical contact cleaner or a cotton swab dipped in denatured alcohol to clean electronic components as needed.
4. If you find broken components on a circuit board, replace the circuit board. As a last resort before purchasing a new circuit board, you can use a soldering iron and electronic solder (see *Fix Everything: Solder*) to attempt a repair.

**Fix-It Tip**

Soldering electronic components can be tricky. If you want to try it, buy a medium-quality (not cheap, not professional) soldering iron or gun from an electronics store and ask the clerk how to use it. Make sure instructions come with the tool, but it's useful to hear someone explain it.

# Refrigerator

No one wants to go back to using iceboxes to keep food fresh—except maybe the iceman. Instead, we'll keep paying the electric bill and enjoying cold leftovers. And we live in confidence that if it's broken, we can fix it.

## How Does It Work?

A refrigerator is a large appliance for chilling food. A motorized compressor forces refrigerant through two sets of metal coils. In one set, the refrigerant becomes a gas and absorbs heat. In the other set, the gas changes into a liquid and disperses that heat to the room air.

Most refrigerators today have a system for eliminating frost. A timer turns on a defrost heater about every 12 hours to warm the evaporator coils on the back of the refrigerator. Some freezers also include an automatic defroster while others must be defrosted manually. The melted frost from either system drains into a pan under the refrigerator and evaporates.

Also see *Icemaker*.

## What Can Go Wrong?

Refrigerator-freezer units are relatively trouble-free. Repairs to the sealed refrigeration system, the compressor, condenser coils, and evaporator coils are best left to a professional. But repairs to most other parts are relatively easy. Lint and dust clogging the condenser coils is one of the most common refrigerator problems. When airflow across the coils is blocked, the unit may run continuously or not run at all. Regular vacuuming of the coils will prolong the life of any refrigerator. The refrigerator may

stop operating. The unit may cycle too often. Food may not be kept cool enough or may be kept too cold. The defrost system may fail. The refrigerator may make too much noise. Door seals may fail.

## How Can I Identify the Problem?

If the refrigerator does not run at all, make sure power is on at the *Electrical Receptacle* and test the *Electrical Cord*. Check the thermostat and adjust. Test the thermostat (see *Appliance Controls*). Clean the condenser coils if needed.

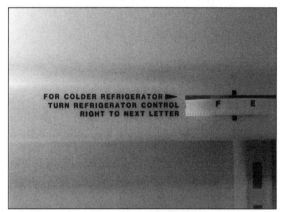

FOR COLDER REFRIGERATOR
TURN REFRIGERATOR CONTROL
RIGHT TO NEXT LETTER

Before taking anything apart, first make sure that the cause isn't misadjusted refrigerator or freezer controls, typically located inside and at the back of the refrigerator.

If the unit short cycles, clean dirty condenser coils. Next, test the fan *Motor* and replace it if necessary.

If food in the refrigerator is not kept cold enough, check the thermostat setting and test it if necessary (see *Appliance Controls*). Also make sure the condenser coils are clean, test the fan *Motor*, check the door gaskets, and replace them if needed (see below).

If food is too cold, check the thermostat setting and test the thermostat (see *Appliance Controls*).

If the refrigerator does not defrost as it should, the defrost heater may need replacing by a professional.

If the refrigerator makes too much noise, try leveling it with the adjusting feet.

If the unit makes a frequent metallic noise, test the fan *Motor*.

If the door seals fail, replace them (see below).

**Fix-It Tip**

To operate efficiently, a refrigerator must be level. To level a refrigerator, place a bubble-type level on the top of the unit and use a wrench to lengthen or shorten the front feet of the refrigerator. You may need to remove the front kick-cover to access the feet.

## What Parts, Materials, and Tools Do I Need?

Replacement parts are available from the manufacturer and aftermarket suppliers (see *Fix-It Resources*). More conveniently, you may be able to find replacement parts through the retailer that sold you the refrigerator or at an appliance parts store. The tools you'll need to fix a refrigerator-freezer unit include these:

- Screwdrivers
- Wrenches
- Multimeter

## What Are the Steps to Fixing It?

Test and replace door gaskets:

1. Test the door seal in several places by closing a piece of paper in the door, then pulling it out. There should be some resistance, indicating that the door is sealed.

**Fix-It Tip**

You can realign a warped door by loosening the gasket retaining screws slightly, then grasping the door and twisting it until the door fits flush against the frame when it is closed. Retighten the screws.

2. Remove the old gasket one section at a time. Some gaskets are held on by retaining strips, others by screws or even adhesive.
3. Install an identical gasket using the retaining strips or screws, or new adhesive.

**Fix-It Tip**

Refrigerator door hinges (located on the top- and bottom-front of the doors) can work themselves loose. You can tighten a loose door hinge using a screwdriver or nut driver. Some hinges have a plastic cover over them that must first be pried off.

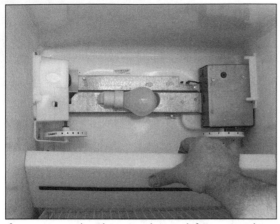

If you suspect that the controls are defective, unplug the refrigerator and remove the cover to the controls, typically at the back of the interior.

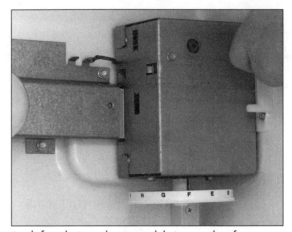

Look for obvious damage, debris, or other factors that may cause problems. If necessary, you can open the control panel and check for visible problems. Consider calling a refrigerator technician for anything more.

# Remote Control

Before the TV remote control was invented, we got much more exercise than we do now. Of course, we had fewer channels then. Mechanical TV tuners wouldn't be practical today in the world of 500+ channels. And remote controls also come with room air conditioners, heating systems, and even gas fireplaces. So let's get at least a little exercise by trying to understand and fix remote controls.

## How Does It Work?

A remote control is a handheld device for turning on or off, selecting features, and adjusting electronic equipment such as televisions, VCRs, DVDs, stereo equipment, and many other household devices including your garage door opener. When a button is pressed, the remote control unit sends out an infrared (invisible) signal that's read and interpreted by the device. A remote control is a battery-powered transmitter.

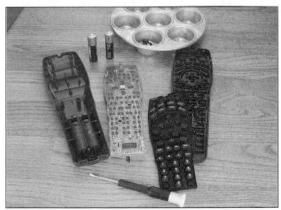

Remote controls typically consist of circuit boards, batteries, a touch pad, and case. Usually the problem is caused either by low batteries or damage from dropping or immersing the remote.

## What Can Go Wrong?

The very thing that makes remote controls so useful—their portability—makes them vulnerable to damage. Circuit boards can be cracked and soldered connections can fail. Water or other liquids can be spilled and leak into the case. Damage can sometimes be repaired, but a new remote is not that expensive so many people opt to replace rather than fix. Think of all the adventure they're missing!

## How Can I Identify the Problem?

If a remote control unit stops working, first check the battery compartment (see *Battery, Household*) to make sure the batteries are making good connections. Clean the tips if needed.

If the batteries are inserted correctly and the remote still does not work, replace the batteries.

If the remote still won't work, try gently cleaning the battery contact points with a pencil eraser or a dab of electronic contact cleaner.

If the device stops working after being dropped, disassemble it and check for a cracked circuit board.

If water spills on the remote, disassemble it and let it dry.

If soda or other beverages spill on the remote, disassemble and clean it out as well as possible (see below).

### Remote Codes

Don't remove the batteries unless you know the programmable remote code! Can't find the code for your programmable remote? Check your owner's manual for the code or instructions on how to make the remote search for the code. If you have Internet access, visit www.xdiv.com/remotes for a list of codes for various manufacturers.

## What Parts, Materials, and Tools Do I Need?

Many remote controls are difficult to open, except for the battery area, which is where most problems occur. Some control cases have screws while others use clips to keep the two halves together. Here are the tools you'll need:

- Screwdrivers
- Cotton swabs
- Old toothbrush
- Electrical contact cleaner

## What Are the Steps to Fixing It?

Service a remote control:

1. Open the battery compartment (see *Battery, Household*) and remove all batteries.
2. Remove any housing screws located in the battery compartment or on the bottom of the case.
3. Remove the case and inspect the circuit board for damage. If the board is dirty, spray it with electrical contact cleaner and use cotton swabs to dry it.
4. Remove the keypad and gently wipe the surface with mild soapy water and let it dry.
5. Use canned air to blow out dust and debris from the housing.
6. Once all components are dry, reassemble the unit and install fresh batteries. You may need to reprogram codes in the unit following instructions in the owner's manual.

# Roof

It's nice to have a roof over your head. It's also nice when that roof doesn't leak or blow away. Here are some things you can do to fix any roofing problems to save you hundreds of dollars—and thousands of raindrops.

## How Does It Work?

A roof is the outside top covering of a home or other structure. Typically, it's made up of lumber called rafters covered by plywood or planks, roofing felt, and roofing shingles. The roof rafters are supported by ceiling joists. The shingles are made of asphalt, fiberglass, wood, tile, or metal. Galvanized metal flashing is installed anywhere that water might seep through, such as at the edges or where two roofs meet, called valleys.

## What Can Go Wrong?

Roofs leak. It's their most common problem and can cause lots of damage to things under the roof, like ceilings and home contents. So if your roof leaks, repair it immediately. Even better, inspect your roof periodically and repair or replace damaged areas before leaks occur. Flashing can also develop holes, and joints can come open. If there's a problem with gutters or downspouts, see *Gutter*.

## How Can I Identify the Problem?

If an asphalt shingle roof leaks, you can repair a single tab (see below) or replace one or more damaged shingles (see below).

If a wood shingle or shake roof has damaged shingles or shakes, you can replace them (see below).

If a flat roof shows damage, you may be able to repair it rather than replace it (see below).

If a clay tile or concrete tile roof suffers damage, you can repair it (see below).

If a metal roof has a hole, you can patch it (see below).

If flashing joints are damaged, you can repair them (see below), and if there are small holes in the flashing itself, you can fill them (see below).

## What Parts, Materials, and Tools Do I Need?

Replacement roofing materials are available through building material suppliers, often sold in bundles. The tools you will need to fix a roof include these:

- Ladder
- Roofing cement
- Pry bar or nail ripper
- Hammer
- Caulking gun
- Silicone caulk
- Chisel
- Nail puller
- Galvanized roofing nails

Working on a ladder to check or repair roofing? Make sure you're working safely. Be sure the ladder is solid and that rungs (steps) aren't loose. Also make sure that you have a sufficient lean to an extension ladder, typically about one fourth the length. That is, move the base of a 12-foot ladder about 3 feet from the point directly below where the top of the ladder touches. And never climb above the third rung from the top.

- Flat spade
- Utility knife
- Roof patch
- Tile clips or masonry nails
- Scrap wood
- Saws
- Pliers
- Wire brush
- Medium-grit sandpaper
- Clean rags
- Trowel
- Safety glasses
- Metal shears
- Soldering gun
- Work gloves

## What Are the Steps to Fixing It?

Repair a roofing tab:

1. Carefully lift the tab to expose the damaged area.
2. Apply roofing cement on the bottom side of the tab to liberally cover the damaged area.
3. Firmly press the tab down with a weight to ensure a good bond.

4. As needed, apply roofing cement on the top of the tab over the damaged area, removing any excess cement.

Replace damaged shingles:

1. Remove all damaged shingles, being careful to not damage adjacent shingles.
2. Remove nails using a pry bar.
3. Fasten the new shingles in place from the bottom row to the row before the top.

### Shingles Gone Bad

How can you tell if asphalt shingles are going bad? Minute gravel in the gutters indicates that the surface gravel on shingles has been worn away by the elements—or the shingles were very cheap. Also look for obvious damage such as missing tabs or debris (pinecones, leaves) wedged under tabs. The worst condition is when old asphalt shingles dry up and begin to curl, lifting off the roof.

Higher course

Lower course

Remove the old shingles, replace the lower row, then replace higher row(s), carefully fastening them to the roof sheathing.

4. Spread roofing cement on the underside final row or course of shingles.
5. Carefully insert the final shingle into place, pressing down to make sure that the cement firmly sets.

Replace wood shakes:

1. Use a wood chisel to split and remove the damaged shake.
2. Remove nails using a pry bar or nail ripper.
3. Cut the replacement shake(s) to size.
4. Install the replacement shake(s) using galvanized roofing nails or screws.
5. Cover the exposed nail heads with roofing cement.

Repair a flat roof:

1. Remove surface gravel from the damaged area with a flat spade.
2. Cut away a rectangular piece around the damaged section of roofing with a utility knife.
3. Fill the area to be patched with roofing cement.
4. Lay the patch material (roofing or fiberglass mesh) in place over the patched area.
5. Spread additional roofing cement over the mesh with a trowel and smooth the surface.
6. By hand, spread fine gravel over the patch to protect the surface.

Repair a tile roof:

1. Wearing safety glasses, use a large hammer to break up the tile to be removed.
2. Remove nails using a pry bar or nail ripper.
3. Select the replacement tile and set it in place.
4. Attach the tile with tile clips or masonry nails, depending on how the other tiles were installed.

Patch a metal roof:

1. Measure and mark the location for the metal patch.
2. Use metal shears to cut a piece of metal identical to the roofing material (type, thickness, and shape). As needed, file the edges.

3. Place the patch in position, then use a soldering iron or gun and flux to seal the patch to the roof.

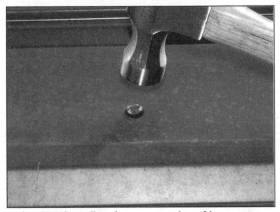

Make sure that all nails on a metal roof have a non-metal washer under them to minimize corrosion.

Seal flashing joints:

1. Remove old sealant with a putty knife and a wire brush.
2. Wipe the area with a clean cloth and, as needed, a cleaner to remove all debris.
3. Use a caulking gun to apply silicone caulk along the joint.
4. Use a putty knife to force the caulk into the joint.
5. Smooth the caulk line with an edge of the putty knife.

Repair flashing:

1. Remove loose rust, dirt, and old finish on the flashing with a wire brush, then clean the area with a rag.
2. Remove any remaining rust with medium-grit sandpaper and clean with a dry rag.
3. Fill any small holes in the flashing with roofing cement.
4. Cover any areas that may cause future problems with roofing cement.

# Rotisserie

You've seen them on late-night TV infomercials. Maybe you have one in the kitchen—or in storage until it's fixed. Fortunately, rotisseries are relatively easy to test and fix. Let's see how the Fix-It Club does it.

## How Does It Work?

A rotisserie is a small heating appliance with a rotating spit. An open rotisserie has a covered heating element, a wire grilling rack, and a roasting spit that is turned by a motor. The rotisserie allows air to circulate freely around food for consistent heat. Fat drains away into a removable tray for disposal. Because many rotisseries have separate power cords for the motor and element, you also can use the appliance as an electric grill. An enclosed rotisserie has two heating elements, one on top and one on the bottom of the cabinet, so it also can serve as a broiler oven.

## What Can Go Wrong?

A rotisserie is subject to the same problems as other small heating appliances. The power cord, the heating element, the timer, the motor, the thermostat, and the switch can all malfunction. They are relatively easy to diagnose and fix.

## How Can I Identify the Problem?

If the rotisserie doesn't heat, make sure power is on at the outlet and test the *Electrical Cord* and replace it if it is faulty. Test the *Heating Element* and replace it if it is faulty.

If the rotisserie has a timer, check for damaged leads and test the timer for continuity (see *Appliance Controls*).

If cleaning with electrical contact cleaner fails, replace the timer (see *Appliance Controls*).

If the rotisserie has a separate on-off switch, test the switch (see *Appliance Controls*) and replace it if it is faulty.

If the rotisserie is noisy, check the *Motor* gears and replace the motor if necessary.

If the rotisserie heats but the spit doesn't turn, test the *Motor* and replace it if it is faulty.

If the rotisserie heats poorly, test the timer (see *Appliance Controls*) and replace it if necessary. Test the thermostat (see *Appliance Controls*) and replace or repair it if it is faulty.

## What Parts, Materials, and Tools Do I Need?

You can find replacement parts for your rotisserie from the manufacturer or aftermarket suppliers such as small appliance parts houses. The tools you'll need to fix a rotisserie include these:

- Screwdrivers
- Wrenches
- Multimeter

## What Are the Steps to Fixing It?

Disassemble a rotisserie:

1. Make sure the appliance is unplugged and cool before you begin to disassemble it.

2. Use screwdrivers and wrenches as needed to remove the motor from its support, then remove and separate the motor case.

3. Remove the spit, supports, and grilling rack. Some components lift out or unplug while others require unfastening with screwdrivers and wrenches.

4. You now can use a multimeter (see *Fix Everything: Multimeter*) to test the *Motor*, *Heating Element*, and *Appliance Controls* as needed.

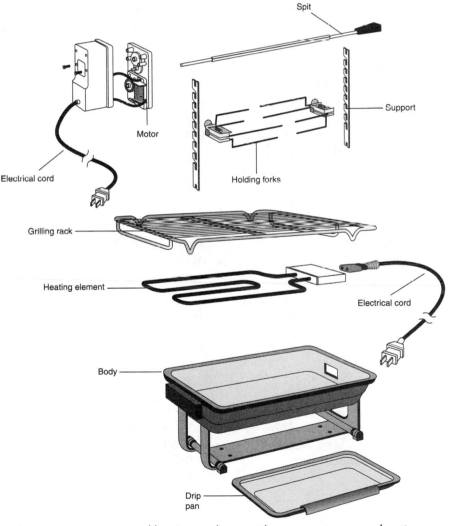

A rotisserie is a motorized heating appliance with a temperature control or timer.

# Rug

Rugs are both functional and aesthetic. They are also old in design. Rugs have been used to decorate homes and soften steps for thousands of years. Better-quality rugs wear very well and can outlive their original owners. Of course, they need periodic cleaning and fixing. Here's how it's done.

## How Does It Work?

A rug is a piece of thick heavy fabric, usually with a nap or pile, that is used as floor covering. Purists say that anything over 6 feet by 9 feet is a *Carpet*. However, most decorators say that the primary difference between a rug and a carpet is that carpet is attached to the subfloor while a rug typically is not. Rugs vary from spot or area rugs to room-size rugs. They include rag rugs, braided rugs, woven rugs, jute rugs, oriental rugs, and others.

## What Can Go Wrong?

The edges of rugs fray. Braided rugs come unbraided. Some rugs need binding. Rugs get spilled on and burned. You can do minor repairs to a rug, but if the rug is valuable or the repair is major, look into professional help available through better rug dealers.

**Fix-It Tip**

An *oriental rug* is handmade in Islamic countries (Turkey, Iran, Egypt) or in the Far East (India, China). If it looks like an oriental rug design but is machine-made or made elsewhere, it's an *oriental-design rug*.

## How Can I Identify the Problem?

If there is a cut or tear in the rug, patch the back side with tape (see below) or sew it together.

If the edges of a rug fray, you can sew the edge (see below).

If a braided rug is coming unbraided, you can rebraid and rebind it (see below).

If a jute rug begins to fray at the edges, you can trim and bind the edge (see below).

**Fix-It Tip**

A braided rug is made of three strips of fabric that are braided together. The braid is then coiled and stitched to itself using linen thread.

## What Parts, Materials, and Tools Do I Need?

You can find rug repair materials and tools at fabric stores and sewing centers as well as the sewing department of larger household stores. In addition, some specialized rug shops carry tools and materials for repairing rugs. Here's a starting list:

- Adhesive (duct) tape
- Curved upholstery needle
- Heavy-duty thread
- Linen thread or monofilament (for braided rugs)
- Cotton binding tape
- Putty knife
- Quality fabric scissors

## What Are the Steps to Fixing It?

Repair a cut in a rug:

1. Turn the rug over and use a putty knife to push fabric back through the tear.

Push the fabric back through the cut to the top layer of the rug.

2. With your hands, work the two edges of the tear together.
3. Seal the tear with tape.

Seal the cut with tape.

Sew the frayed edge of a rug:

1. Beginning about ¼ inch from the damage, sew over the edge with an upholstery needle and heavy-duty thread of a matching color.

2. Continue wrapping the thread around the frayed area until all the frayed area is covered.

Repair a braided rug:

1. Remove damaged stitches holding the coil together and unwind the rug as needed.
2. Remove any worn or damaged material and reattach as a continuous braid.
3. Recoil the braid.
4. Use an upholstery needle and linen thread to resew the coil with small, tight stitches.
5. Reinforce the outer edges by attaching a strip of cotton binding tape to the perimeter using small, tight stitches.

Trim and bind a jute rug:

1. Use heavy-duty shears to trim the frayed edge of the rug.
2. Cut a strip of cotton binding tape 2 inches longer than the raw edge of the rug.
3. Evenly fold the binding over the rug's edge and secure it in place with cross-stitches (see *Fix Everything: Sewing*) through the binding and rug.
4. Fold the opposite end of the binding under the rug and secure it with cross-stitches.

**Fix-It Tip**

You can clean your own rugs using household carpet and rug cleaner. However, if you are unsure of the material or outcome, consider having a commercial rug cleaner do the job.

# Satellite System

It's just 22 miles away, that satellite in the sky. Yet it's high enough, somewhere over Texas, to send line-of-sight signals to nearly any location in the continental United States. Only land obstructions—buildings, mountains, trees, snow—can keep it from beaming reruns of *I Love Lucy* simultaneously to every receiver.

## How Does It Work?

A satellite system consists of a dish antenna that captures radio waves, a cable that delivers the signal to a descrambler, and the descrambler that converts the signals into audio and video for your TV or computer. Of course, the descrambler first makes sure that you are a subscriber in good standing to the service. At the other end, a television station transmits the signal to the satellite. Cable TV companies, too, use satellite feeds, but the delivery is via a cable to each subscriber's home.

Older home satellite dishes are as large as 12 to 15 feet in diameter, while the newest models are just 18 inches in diameter and easy to install with the manufacturer's directions. You now can buy equipment and a subscription to download—or even upload—digital computer data such as Internet access.

## What Can Go Wrong?

If you experience a problem, first contact the programming service to be sure the signal is okay. If it is, the problem may be with the receiver or the descrambler. In either case, refer to the owner's manual for guidance or contact the manufacturer for repair. Don't attempt to repair a descrambler.

> **Fix-It Tip**
>
> Snow, ice, or heavy rain can interfere with a satellite dish's incoming signal. If you live in an area of heavy snowfalls, you can install a dish cover that will shield the equipment from snow or ice. Unfortunately, it doesn't stop interference from a heavy rain.

## How Can I Identify the Problem?

Fortunately, satellite systems include various diagnostic programs and relatively comprehensive owner's manuals that will walk you through most problems. In addition, the descrambler's manufacturer and the signal subscription service will both have online and telephone assistance.

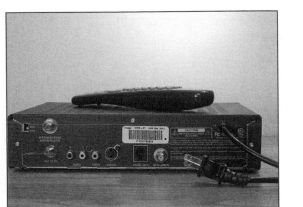

Most satellite descramblers cannot be worked on except by authorized service centers. The only exception is if the unit has a fuse inside, typically located near the power cord.

**Fix-It Tip**

Need assistance from your satellite network provider? Contact Dish TV at 888-438-3474 (getdish.com) or DirecTV at 800-347-3288 (directv.com). In addition, customer service phone numbers are included on your monthly bill. *Satellite Orbit* magazine (orbitmagazine.com) includes names and contact information for other subscription satellite services as well as listings of *all* satellite entertainment feeds.

# Screen

Screens are intended to keep bugs out while allowing breezes into living spaces. When they don't work as intended, you can fix them with simple tools, easy-to-find materials, and just a little time. Here's how.

## How Does It Work?

A screen is a woven mesh stretched and attached to a frame at a window or door opening to keep pests out of the house and small children and household pets in the house. The most common screening materials are vinyl-coated fiberglass and aluminum. Aluminum screens are less likely to tear or sag, but they dent easily and may corrode. Fiberglass won't dent or corrode, is less expensive than aluminum, and is available in a variety of mesh types, including very fine solar-screening mesh that reduces ultraviolet radiation.

## What Can Go Wrong?

Screen fabric can tear and sometimes develop holes. Fabric can pull away from the screen frame.

## How Can I Identify the Problem?

If a screen has a small tear or hole in it, you can repair it (see below).

If a screen pulls away from its frame, you can reattach it (see below).

If a screen suffers more than minor damage, you can replace it (see below).

## What Parts, Materials, and Tools Do I Need?

Replacement parts for door and window screens are available from local hardware and building supply stores. The tools you will need to fix screens include these:

- Screwdrivers
- Cotton swabs
- Toothpicks
- Nylon fishing line
- Model cement
- Scissors or tin snips
- Spline roller
- Pliers
- Adhesive
- Duct tape or other tape
- Paint
- Putty knife

## What Are the Steps to Fixing It?

Repair a small tear in a screen:

1. Use pliers and other tools to bend the torn strands of screen fabric back to their original positions.
2. Apply model cement to the tear, spreading the cement with a cotton swab.
3. Use a toothpick to open as many holes as possible before they seal over with cement.

Repair a larger tear in a screen:

1. Cut a patch of similar screening (aluminum, plastic, or fiberglass) to overlap the damaged area by ¼ inch.
2. Place the patch over the hole so that the ends of the strands fit into the mesh on the screening.
3. Attach the patch using a small sewing needle and nylon fishing line or an appropriate adhesive (see *Fix Everything: Adhesives*) to secure the patch.
4. Finish dressing the patch using a toothpick or other tool to align fibers and/or remove excess glue.

Replace a screen in a metal frame:

1. Place the screen face down on a work surface.
2. Use a straight screwdriver or other pointed object to remove the spline that holds the screen in place in the frame groove.
3. Cut fiberglass screen with scissors and aluminum screen with heavy-duty shears or tin snips as needed, making sure that the replacement is at least 1 inch larger than the screen opening.
4. Stretch the new screen evenly over the opening and use duct or other tape to temporarily hold it in place.
5. Starting in a corner, press the spline into the groove with the blade of a spline roller or a straight screwdriver.

Lay the screen material in place over the groove.

6. Continue pressing the spline into place around the perimeter of the screen.

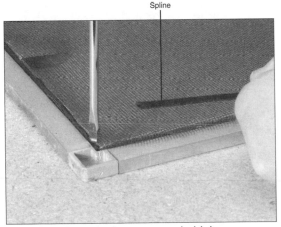

Press the spline into the groove to hold the screen edge in place.

7. Trim the end of the spline as needed.
8. Trim the edge of the fabric as needed.

Replace a screen in a wood frame:

1. Carefully pry off the molding with a putty knife.
2. Remove the old screen and all staples or tacks, repairing the frame as needed (see *Furniture, Wood*).
3. Cut new screen 4 inches wider and 8 inches longer than the opening.
4. Double the fabric at one edge and staple it to the frame.
5. Stretch the fabric across the opening, doubling the fabric at the edges and stapling them in place. Trim off excess fabric.
6. Reinstall the frame molding, then *Paint* as needed.

**Fix-It Tip**

If you are fixing one screen today, chances are you'll be fixing another one soon. Consider buying an entire roll of screening. It's less expensive by the roll and you'll have matching screening for future repairs.

# Security System

If you have a security system on your house, your neighbors probably already hate you. False alarms on most systems are much more prevalent than true ones. By keeping your security system in top operating condition, you'll not only sleep better, your neighbors will too.

## How Does It Work?

A security system is a set of sensors designed to trigger an alarm if someone unauthorized tries to gain entry into a home. Sensors placed at strategic locations throughout the house, or an automobile, check current status (okay, not okay) and report back to the central control unit. The control unit keeps track of all the sensors and their current status. If it decides there is a problem, it activates an audible alarm and/or an automatic telephone dialer that can summon help by phone.

The two primary types of security systems are wired and wireless. A wired system is connected by small, low-voltage wires routed discretely throughout the house. A wireless model uses tiny radio transmitters to signal the central control unit when activated. Control units typically have a battery backup activated if there is a power failure or if the wires are cut.

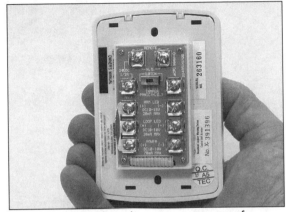

The central control unit has wire connections from each of the sensors.

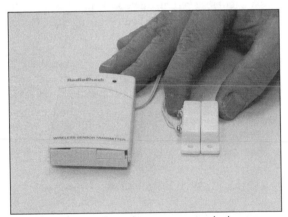

You also can install single sensor controls that manage security at a single location such as a specific door or window.

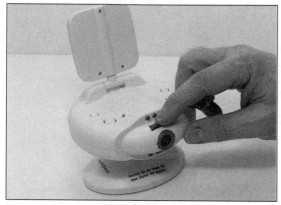

Some security systems include a video camera to monitor outside the front door or in a child's room.

## What Can Go Wrong?

False alarms happen more often than not. Some are due to user error, while others are caused by nonthreatening events such as high winds or a thunderstorm. Other than that, most security systems have self-diagnostics built in that can be used to determine the cause of a problem.

### Know the Code!

If your security system has an entry code (most home alarm systems do), make sure it's one you can easily remember, such as a birth date, Social Security number suffix, or keyboard pattern. And, of course, make sure it's easy for other members of your household to remember. There's no panic like standing at the system keypad trying to disarm an alarm when you're not sure of the code—at two in the morning!

## How Can I Identify the Problem?

If the system triggers frequent false alarms, verify the code and run a diagnostics test on the system (check the owner's manual). If the alarm rings again, check the wiring and sensors. Clean or tighten wire connections at sensors and the control unit. Replace a worn-out microwave sensor. Check the sensitivity of all vibration- or motion-detecting sensors. Trim any tree or shrub branches that may hit a window with a vibration sensor. Make sure the lens on a passive infrared motion sensor is clean.

If you can't arm the system, make sure that all doors and windows are closed and locked. Check for tripped sensors and replace any that are faulty.

### Fix-It Tip

The owner's manual for your security system is vital. Make sure you have it in a handy location and that at least one member of your household has read it thoroughly. If you purchase a system and have someone install it, ask questions while they work to learn what they don't tell you in the manual. If you lease the system or pay for supporting services, let the alarm company service the unit.

## What Parts, Materials, and Tools Do I Need?

The most common parts that fail are the sensors. Make sure replacements are exact substitutes for the ailing sensor. You can buy them from a security company or an electronics store. Here are some basic tools for fixing your security system:

- Screwdrivers
- Razor blade
- Multimeter

## What Are the Steps to Fixing It?

Test a wired sensor:

1. Disconnect one wire and activate the sensor.
2. Set the multimeter (see *Fix Everything: Multimeter*) on R×1 (resistance times 1) scale (resistance in ohms), touch the probe to the sensor's terminal screws, and note the reading.
3. Deactivate the sensor and run the test again. If the sensor is okay, one reading will be zero (no resistance) and the other infinity (no circuit). Replace the sensor if both readings are zero or infinity.

Replace a magnetic switch sensor:

1. Turn the alarm controller off and disconnect power to the security system.
2. Unscrew the magnet and switch, then detach the wires.
3. Attach the wires to contacts in the new switch and screw the switch onto the window frame.
4. With the window closed, align and install the magnet on the window sash.
5. Set the multimeter (see *Fix Everything: Multimeter*) on R×1 (resistance times 1) scale, touch the probe to the sensor's terminal screws and note the reading.
6. Activate the sensor and run the test again. If the sensor is okay, one reading will be zero (no resistance) and the other infinity (no circuit). Replace the sensor if both readings are zero or infinity.

Replace a plunger switch sensor:

1. Disarm and turn off power to the security system.
2. Unscrew the door frame switch and move it aside to access and remove contact screws.
3. Attach the wires to the contact screws on the new unit and install the new unit on the door frame along with the new plate.
4. Set the multimeter (see *Fix Everything: Multimeter*) on R×1 (resistance times 1) scale, touch the probe to the sensor's terminal screws and note the reading.
5. Activate the sensor and run the test again. If the sensor is okay, one reading will be zero (no resistance) and the other infinity (no circuit). Replace the sensor if both readings are zero or infinity.

Replace a vibration glass-break detector:

1. Disarm and turn off power to the security system.
2. Use a razor blade to remove the old unit.
3. Remove the sensor's wires and install them on the new sensor. Some are attached with screws, while others require soldering (see *Fix Everything: Solder*).
4. Adjust the sensor following the directions that accompany the unit.
5. Set the multimeter (see *Fix Everything: Multimeter*) on R×1 (resistance times 1) scale, touch the probe to the sensor's terminal screws, and note the reading.
6. Activate the sensor and run the test again. If the sensor is okay, one reading will be zero (no resistance) and the other infinity (no circuit). Replace the sensor if both readings are zero or infinity.

# Septic System

Uh-oh! Smells like trouble with the septic system! Of course, those who live in developed areas have a sewer system that sends waste to a sewer line under the street and on to a treatment plant. Those who have a septic system on their property have to manage the system themselves. And when they don't ...

## How Does It Work?

A septic system transfers liquid and solid household wastes to a holding tank for treatment.

A house's sewer line delivers the waste to a septic tank buried nearby. Solid wastes settle to the bottom of the tank where microorganisms digest them. Wastewater flows to distribution boxes that release it through drain pipes for dispersal in the drain field. The septic tank should be pumped of accumulated solids as needed. Some plumbing codes require that water from sinks and showers (called greywater) is distributed in a separate system that doesn't require a chemically active tank.

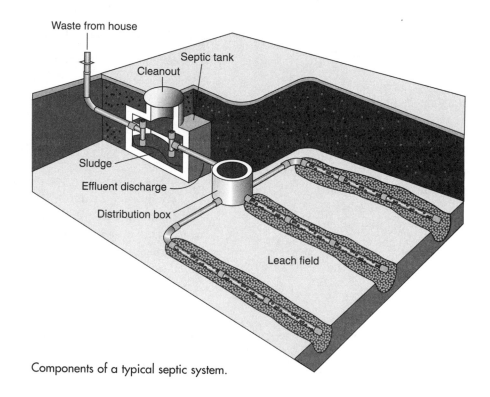

Components of a typical septic system.

How often should you have your septic tank pumped? It depends on the capacity of the tank and the number of people who live in the house. A household of two with a 1,000-gallon tank may need to have the tank pumped only about every six years. But a household of six with a tank of 2,000 gallons may need to have it pumped about every three years. You can call a septic pumping service for additional guidelines; some will come check the level of your tank once a year and advise you.

## What Can Go Wrong?

The main drain from the house to the septic system may become clogged. Pipes in the drain field may be broken. The septic tank may overflow. In many cases, the problem is caused by damage to the surrounding soil (heavy equipment) or the lack of periodic pumping.

**Caution**

If your home is on a septic system, don't dispose of any chemicals that may kill the bacteria, such as paint thinner or photographic chemicals, by putting them down the drain. Also avoid flushing anything that won't dissolve in water. At the least, it won't dissolve and you'll have to have it pumped out. At worst, it will clog the system and cause bigger problems. And make sure that your garbage disposer is rated for use with septic tanks; the owner's manual will tell you.

## How Can I Identify the Problem?

If all the drains in the house work sluggishly or don't drain at all, check and clear the main drain (see *Drain System*).

If you smell sewage around the septic tank or the drain field, or if you see black or gray water oozing up from the drain field, call for professional septic system service.

**Fix-It Tip**

When you purchase a home with a septic system, make sure you get a plot map that shows the location of the septic tank and drain field. In the future, don't plant any trees or large shrubs near the septic tank or on top of the field, because roots can interfere with the tank and pipes.

# Sewing Machine

A sewing machine can be your good friend—especially if you want to fix *Clothing*, a *Stuffed Toy*, a *Jacket*, or many other things around your household. To keep that friendship alive and thriving, make sure you perform regular maintenance and, if you see a problem, fix it.

## How Does It Work?

A sewing machine is a small appliance that unites or fastens things by stitching. All sewing machines produce a stitch by hooking the needle thread around a second or bobbin thread. Fabric is pulled through the machine using metal feet called feed dogs. Speed is controlled by a foot or knee pedal. Numerous other adjustments can be made to produce various stitches and patterns.

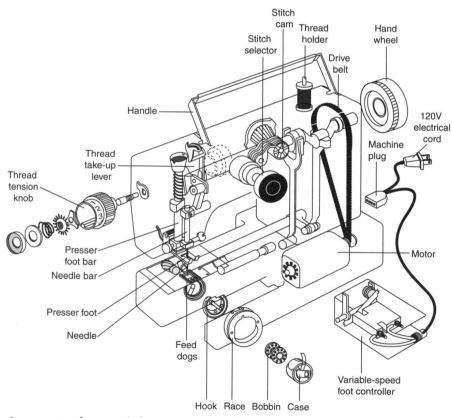

Components of a typical electric sewing machine.

## What Can Go Wrong?

Sewing machines are reliable appliances that can give many years of good service with minimal care. Routine lubrication is the key to a long sewing machine life (see below). The electrical cord and on-off switch can fail. The bobbin or take-up lever may be jammed. The drive belt may be faulty or loose. The bobbin, bobbin case, hook, and tension spring may be corroded or rough. The motor may be faulty.

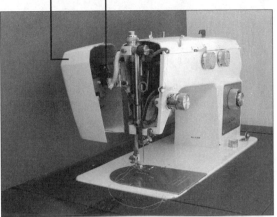

If your sewing machine has a working light but it isn't working, open the head, then remove and test the bulb. Check electrical connections as needed.

| Fix-It Tip |
| --- |
| The most common—and most easily fixed—problem with sewing machines is caused by a bent, broken, loose, or incorrect sewing needle. Always buy quality needles and check their condition before starting a sewing project. |

## How Can I Identify the Problem?

If the machine doesn't turn on, make sure power is on at the *Electrical Receptacle* and test the *Electrical Cord*. Test the on-off switch (see *Appliance Controls*).

If the machine runs or hums but doesn't sew, check the bobbin assembly for jammed thread (see below). Also lubricate a dry machine, tighten the clutch knob, and check the drive belt (see below).

If the needle or the bobbin thread breaks, see the sewing machine owner's manual for correct settings and check for jammed thread.

If the fabric feeds poorly, clean lint from the feed dogs.

Any other repairs to a sewing machine should be done by an experienced technician who has access to replacement parts.

## What Parts, Materials, and Tools Do I Need?

Replacement parts are available from the manufacturer and aftermarket suppliers (see *Fix-It Resources*) and from local sewing machine shops. The tools you will need to fix a sewing machine may include these:

- Screwdrivers
- Sewing machine oil
- Tweezers
- Emery cloth
- Small brush

## What Are the Steps to Fixing It?

Lubricate a sewing machine:

Carefully tip or lift the sewing machine from the cabinet to expose components for lubrication.

1. Unplug the sewing machine.
2. Apply one drop of high-quality sewing machine oil to any parts that move, being especially careful not to oil electrical parts.

**Fix-It Tip**

Sewing machine oil may seem expensive for just a few drops needed each year. However, sewing machine oil is a good lightweight oil for lubricating many other smaller household devices, motor shafts, and things that squeak.

Service mechanical parts:

1. Unplug the sewing machine.
2. Clean the thread tension assembly using tweezers to remove tangles of thread around the disks.
3. Use a fine emery cloth to sand off burrs or rust from the bobbin thread tension assembly. Replace any damaged parts.

The bobbin assembly is located under the needle plate.

4. As needed, adjust the presser bar screw until the foot is straight.
5. As needed, clean the feed assembly: Raise the presser foot, needle, and needle plate. Then unfasten and remove the feed assembly. Remove any obstructions such as thread and lint.

Service the drive belt:

1. Unplug the machine.
2. Remove the top cover and the hand wheel cover, held in place by screws or other fasteners.
3. Remove the belt and inspect it for damage and wear, replacing as needed.
4. Reinstall the belt and tighten the motor mounting bolts. Check the belt tension by pushing on the side of the belt.

# Slow Cooker

Slow cookers (sometimes known by the brand-name Crock Pot) are simple yet ingenious devices for people on the go. You just can't get slow-cooked flavor from a microwave. Slow cookers can be turned on in the morning and offer hot chili, Swiss steak, or another satisfying meal for dinner. Because they are so simple, there is little that can go wrong with them. Let's take a look inside.

## How Does It Work?

A slow cooker is a small appliance with a ceramic pot, a heating element, and a metal shell for slow-cooking foods in liquid. The wire element made of Nichrome encircles the metal liner that transfers heat to the crock. The tight lid and low, steady temperatures reduce evaporation and promote thorough cooking. Most slow cookers have a removable pot for easier cleaning—and easier access to internal parts.

## What Can Go Wrong?

Actually, little can go wrong with this simple appliance. The cord can need replacing. The thermostat, heating element, and switch can be faulty. And the crock can crack.

> **Fix-It Tip**
>
> Most slow cookers have a maximum power rating of less than 300 watts, making them relatively safe to leave on all day or overnight. However, make sure the unit is placed on a surface that can withstand spills—just in case contents boil over.

## How Can I Identify the Problem?

If the cooker doesn't heat, first make sure the power is on at the *Electrical Receptacle*. Check the *Electrical Cord*. Check the *Heating Element* and the *Appliance Controls*.

If the cooker has a thermostat, service it as you would a switch (see *Appliance Controls*). Test the *Heating Element* with a multimeter (see *Fix Everything: Multimeter*) and replace it if it is faulty.

If the cooker heats on one temperature only, test the switch and the thermostat (see *Appliance Controls*). Test the *Heating Element* and replace as needed.

If the cooker overheats, check the thermostat (see *Appliance Controls*) and replace if faulty.

If the cooker leaks, check the crock for cracks and replace the crock or cooker as needed.

> **Fix-It Tip**
>
> Slow cookers are inexpensive to replace compared to buying a replacement heating element or controls. If these components are faulty, try repairing them yourself before buying a new element or controls. If the element or controls are damaged beyond repair, it may be most cost-effective to buy a new slow cooker.

## What Parts, Materials, and Tools Do I Need?

Replacement parts are available through the manufacturer or a small appliance parts store. The tools you'll need for disassembly and testing include these:

- Screwdrivers
- Wrenches
- Multimeter

## What Are the Steps to Fixing It?

Disassemble and test a slow cooker:

1. Unplug the appliance from the electrical receptacle.
2. Remove the pot, inspect it for cracks, and replace the pot if necessary.
3. Turn the unit over and remove the base that is held on by screws, clips, or nuts.

This slow cooker has a friction washer on the bottom that will be damaged in removal and must be replaced.

This smaller slow cooker (actually a potpourri pot) has a removable nut on the bottom that allows access to internal parts.

4. With the base off, remove wire connectors and test the *Electrical Cord* with a multimeter (see *Fix Everything: Multimeter*).
5. Access and disconnect the electrical leads to the *Heating Element*(s) and test with a multimeter.

Cord       Wire

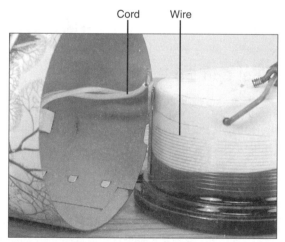

The heating element in this case is electrical wires wrapped around the ceramic pot and connected to the end of the electrical cord. Test for continuity with a multimeter.

6. Replace the electrical cord or heating elements as needed and reassemble.

# Small Engine

Small engines are all around us, powering lawn mowers, snow blowers, chain saws, generators, motorcycles, boats, snowmobiles, and many other handy tools and toys. So knowing how small engines work and what to do when they don't will put you in good standing in the Fix-It Club.

## How Does It Work?

A small engine is an internal combustion gasoline engine that produces less than 40 horsepower. To produce power, the engine ...

1. Mixes fuel and air.
2. Compresses the mixture.
3. Adds a spark to ignite it.
4. Exhausts the resulting fumes.

These four steps make up the power cycle. A two-stroke or two-cycle engine mixes and compresses in one rotation, then ignites and exhausts during the second rotation or stroke. A four-stroke or four-cycle engine requires a full rotation for each of the four steps. Most small engines are two-stroke—and larger ones, like that in your automobile—are four-stroke. Two-stroke engines aren't as powerful, but they're much cheaper to build. Small engines have one or maybe two cylinders or areas where the explosions occur.

Another important fact is how the engine is cooled. Car and other larger engines are cooled by circulating liquid through channels within them. Because small engines don't develop as much heat, they typically are cooled by the surrounding air.

## What Can Go Wrong?

Regular maintenance can keep repairs to a minimum. A starter rope may be broken or jammed. A recoil starter spring may be weak or broken. An electric starter battery may be low, connections may be loose or corroded, or a power cord may be damaged. Air filters get clogged. Fuel can become contaminated; a fuel cap breather hole may be blocked or a fuel filter clogged. A fuel line can be clogged or damaged. A choke may become sticky. A belt may slip.

## How Can I Identify the Problem?

If you want to keep repairs to a minimum, follow a regular maintenance program (see below). For further maintenance, consult your owner's manual and/or a technician.

If the starter doesn't make the engine turn over, check the starter rope (see below), then look for a weak or broken recoil starter spring (see below). Also check an electric starter's battery and connections and the *Electrical Cord*.

If the engine does not run smoothly or smokes, clean a clogged air filter (see below).

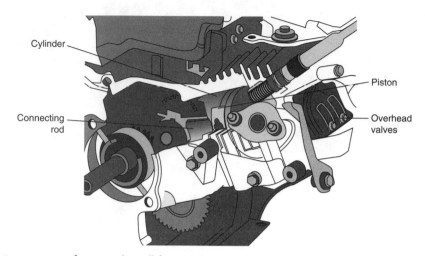

Components of a typical small four-stroke engine used to power lawn mowers, tillers, and other equipment. A two-stroke engine has most of the same components.

If the engine turns over but won't start, stalls, or dies during use, add fuel, clean a clogged fuel filter with solvent or replace it, clean a clogged fuel line (see below), and clean a sticky choke mechanism with solvent.

If the engine starts to stall at idle speed, check your owner's manual for adjustment to the idle speed.

If the engine dies during use, overheats, is very noisy, or runs unevenly, add oil to the oil tank if it is low and let the engine cool, then restart it.

If the engine runs, but the device doesn't, look for a slipping belt (see *Fix-It Guides* for specific machines).

## What Parts, Materials, and Tools Do I Need?

Replacement parts are available from the engine's manufacturer and aftermarket suppliers (see *Fix-It Resources*), as well as from small engine service shops and larger hardware stores. The tools you will need to fix a small engine may include these:

- Screwdrivers
- Stiff plastic-bristle brush
- Lightweight oil, lithium grease, or silicone lubricant
- Pliers
- Engine oil
- Gasoline

- Carburetor-cleaning solvent
- Petroleum solvent
- Dish detergent
- Soft cloth
- Pipe cleaner
- Needle or wire
- Scissors

## What Are the Steps to Fixing It?

Maintain a small engine:

Before each use:

1. Remove debris from the air intake screen, muffler, oil filter, and governor linkage areas with a stiff plastic-bristle brush.
2. Remove the air intake screen to clean the flywheel fins.
3. If you are working on a four-stroke engine, check the oil level and add oil as needed.

Twice a year (depending on use and manufacturer's recommendations):

1. For a four-stroke engine, change the oil. Drain the old oil into a container through the drain plug or pour it out through the filler hole and refill with new oil. (Two-stroke engines don't need this step because the oil is in the fuel.)

### Disposing of Fuel

How can you safely get rid of dirty fuel left over from cleaning an engine? The best way is to buy an approved fuel container and mark it "Recycle" for dumping fuel, oil, and other petroleum waste products. Once full, take it to a hazardous waste station in your area (call your recycler for details). Make sure the container is sealed and kept away from other combustibles and heat sources.

2. Apply a small amount of lightweight oil, lithium grease, or silicone lubricant to all exposed control cable and pivot points (clutch and throttle controls).
3. Clean or replace any air filter as needed.

Replace a recoil starter rope:

1. Disconnect the spark plug cable for safety.
2. Disengage the throttle cable from the housing and remove the housing as needed to access the starter.
3. Remove the handle from the rope, which is often held in place by a knot or retainer pin.
4. Unfasten the other end of the rope from the starter using pliers or a cutter as needed.
5. Knot the end of the replacement rope.
6. Tighten the pulley counterclockwise all the way, then back it off two turns and hold it firmly.
7. Thread the unknotted rope end through the pulley hole.
8. Thread the rope through the housing hole and pull it taut.
9. Slowly release the pulley, allowing the rope to wind around the pulley.
10. Attach the handle and reassemble as needed.
11. Reconnect the spark plug cable.

Replace a recoil starter spring:

1. Disconnect the spark plug cable for safety.
2. Remove the housing and the spring cover.
3. Carefully remove the rope from the pulley to release spring tension.
4. Remove and replace the spring as recommended by the manufacturer.
5. Reinstall the pulley, rope, and housing following the instructions above.
6. Reconnect the spark plug cable.

Clean a foam air filter:

1. Remove the cover and lift out the foam filter.
2. Clean dirt and grease from the housing interior with a soft cloth.
3. Wash the filter with dish detergent and hot water and rinse with clear water.
4. Allow the filter to fully dry before reinstalling.

Service fuel lines and tank:

1. Disconnect the spark plug cable for safety.
2. Use a needle or fine wire to unclog gas cap breather holes, then clean the cap with a carburetor-cleaning solvent.

3. Remove and inspect the fuel. If the fuel has sediment in it or smells like mothballs, it is contaminated and should be drained and replaced.
4. If there is a blockage in the fuel line(s), clear it with a pipe cleaner and petroleum solvent.
5. Replace the fuel filter.
6. As needed, flush the tank and fuel line with fresh fuel.
7. As needed, fill the fuel tank.

**Fix-It Tip**

For additional step-by-step service and repair instructions on small engines, refer to *Small Engine Repair Made Easy* by Dan Ramsey (see *Fix-It Resources*).

# Smoke Detector

Smoke detectors and smoke alarms are complex, specialized devices that are also relatively inexpensive, so when one starts acting up, the first thing to consider is throwing it out and buying a new one. However, there are many things you can do to save yourself some money, time, and trash. You can fix it!

## How Does It Work?

A smoke detector is a small device that sounds an alarm when it senses smoke or fire. There are two kinds of smoke detectors—photoelectric and ionization. Photoelectric units throw out a beam of light that, if broken by smoke, will trigger an audible alarm. Ionization units give nearby air an electrical charge and measure whether the charge stays constant; if not there probably is a fire present eating up the oxygen in the air, so the alarm goes off. Photoelectric detectors are better where smoldering fires might be, such as electrical fires in walls, making them a good choice for bedrooms and kitchens. Ionization units are better in areas where a controlled fire might get out of control, such as in a furnace room. Some models combine both types of detectors. Smoke detectors are either powered by an internal battery or household current backed up by an internal battery. Some smoke detectors are part of a home *Security System*.

## What Can Go Wrong?

A properly working smoke detector doubles the odds of surviving a home fire. The most common reason for a smoke detector not working is also the easiest to solve: a battery that needs to be replaced. Connections can loosen and sensors can be blocked. The alarm and sensors can malfunction.

## How Can I Identify the Problem?

If you hear a chirping sound from the unit, test and replace the battery (see *Battery, Household*), or tighten any loose connections on an alarm powered by the house current. You also can vacuum in and around the alarm to eliminate dust or dead insects clogging the sensors.

If the detector fails to sound after cleaning (see above), replace the unit.

If the alarm fails to sound when there is smoke, test and replace a bad battery (see *Battery, Household*).

If the alarm sounds when there is no smoke, relocate the alarm if it is within 20 feet of an oven or furnace or 10 feet of a bathroom or utility room. Also replace the battery. If these steps fail, check the owner's manual. If all else fails, replace the unit.

---

**Fix-It Tip**

Is someone in your house a sound sleeper or hard of hearing? Consider buying a smoke detector that has a loud alarm and flashing lights, then making sure the alarm is near enough to that person to do some good. Alternatively, make sure that someone in your house, when hearing the alarm, is responsible for awakening those with the "Do Not Disturb" sign.

---

## What Parts, Materials, and Tools Do I Need?

Replacement batteries and replacement smoke detectors are available from many local outlets. The tools you will need to test and fix a smoke detector include these:

- Screwdrivers
- Candle

## What Are the Steps to Fixing It?

Test a smoke detector:

1. Press the battery-test button on the unit to make sure the battery is properly connected.
2. If the unit has a battery that's more than a year old, replace the battery (see below).

3. Light a candle and hold it approximately 6 inches below the detector so that heated air will rise into the unit.
4. If the alarm doesn't sound within 20 seconds, blow out the candle and let the smoke rise into the unit.
5. If the alarm still doesn't sound, open the unit up and make sure it is clean and that all electrical connections are solid.
6. If, again, the alarm doesn't sound, replace the smoke detector.

Replace a smoke detector battery:

1. Remove the smoke detector cover, typically by carefully pulling down on the case's perimeter or by twisting the case counterclockwise.

First, carefully remove the smoke detector's cover.

2. Locate and remove the battery. Use a multimeter (see *Fix Everything: Multimeter*) to test battery voltage. As needed, replace it with a new one.

3. Close the case and test the smoke detector (see above).
4. Read the owner's manual for additional troubleshooting tips and possible adjustments.

Remove the sensor to access the battery and other components.

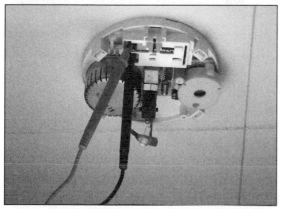

You can test the battery in place or remove the smoke detector to remove the battery.

**Fix-It Tip**

Buying a replacement smoke detector? Read the packages and check the price. By shopping around, you often can get a quality unit for the price of a cheapie.

# Speaker

Speakers are the last link in the process of hearing sound. The amplified signal from a stereo receiver, a CD player, or an electric guitar or other instrument is fed to the speaker system for conversion into audible sounds. Fortunately, speakers are relatively simple in design and can be fixed easily.

## How Does It Work?

Speakers for a home stereo or entire home entertainment system amplify the sound generated from another component of the system. The typical speaker is a collection of complementary parts. The typical enclosure (speaker case) has a 6- to 15-inch-diameter cone woofer for low frequencies, a 3- to 6-inch-diameter dome or cone midrange driver (commonly called a speaker), and a small tweeter for high frequencies. Audio signals move along speaker cables to a terminal block at the back of the enclosure. Once inside, a crossover network divides incoming frequencies into the appropriate ranges, sending each to the correct driver. Drivers then convert this input into mechanical movement of the cone which, in turn, moves the air in a way that is detected by your ears as sound.

## What Can Go Wrong?

Speakers are most likely to suffer from improper use. The enclosure can be damaged or come unglued. The speaker can blow an electrical or thermal fuse. Wiring can be faulty. The voice coil can be faulty, a speaker can be blown, a crossover network can be faulty, or a solder connection can be faulty. Cables and connections can be faulty; a driver cone can be damaged. Speakers may not be in phase. Level controls can be broken. All are repairable problems.

Oops! One loose speaker wire can stop all sound to the speaker.

## How Can I Identify the Problem?

If the speaker does not produce any sound, check other components for proper connection and adjustment. Disassemble the enclosure (see below) to check the electrical or thermal *Fuse*, and replace or reset as needed.

If no sound comes from all drivers in one speaker, check the *Fuse*, test speaker, and crossover network wiring and replace if necessary. Also test with another speaker and cable. If there is still no sound, the problem is with the receiver.

If no sound comes from one driver, test the driver (see below). Also lightly press the cone with a finger. If the voice coil does not move in and out freely, replace the driver.

If the sound is distorted or mushy, use your hand to flex the cable with a low-volume input. If sound varies, replace the cable and clean the connections. Also check polarity of the speakers (see below). Carefully press the cone in and out with your fingers to determine smooth action, and replace it if action is not smooth.

If the speaker is noisy, check the voice coil. Use rubber cement or a repair kit to repair any small holes in the cone. If the driver is badly damaged, have it reconed by a professional or replace the driver. You also can clean the volume control with an electronic contact cleaner.

If sound is intermittent, check the speaker cable and connections, test the thermal *Fuse*, and check the voice coil.

Should you replace the driver or have it reconed? The answer depends on the cost of a replacement and your budget. Common drivers for low-cost audio systems are relatively inexpensive to replace (so you can gamble and try to fix it yourself). Larger drivers for better audio equipment and musical instrument amplifiers are relatively expensive, costing $50 or more. Drivers for that classic Fender amp probably should go to a professional service person.

## What Parts, Materials, and Tools Do I Need?

You can buy replacement speakers, speaker repair kits, foam, wire, and other parts and materials at electronic and audio stores. These are other things you may need:

- Multimeter
- Rubber cement
- Kraft paper patch or repair kit

## What Are the Steps to Fixing It?

Disassemble a speaker unit:

1. Unplug the speaker cable. If the speaker is a powered unit, unplug it from the *Electrical Receptacle* (outlet).
2. Remove the speaker enclosure's front grille to access the drivers and the crossover network. Grilles are secured with snaps, Velcro, or screws.
3. Unfasten the drivers, as needed. Drivers on a bass reflex speaker are screwed in from the front. Some speakers are sealed in position and may require a sharp knife to break the seal. If so, replace the seal with sealer from an electronics store when the repair is finished.

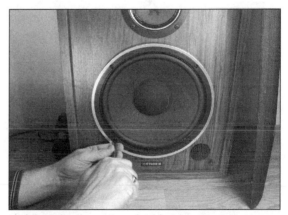

Unfasten the driver (speaker) by removing screws around the perimeter.

4. Lift the driver from the enclosure to gain access to the wire connectors that attach the terminal block to the driver. Use pliers to carefully remove the wires from the rear of the driver or the terminal block, or both locations. Note that some internal wires are soldered rather than clipped; see *Fix Everything: Solder*.

Check to make sure the wires from the terminal block at the rear of the speaker enclosure are connected to the back of the driver.

5. Remove the crossover network, as needed. Most are accessed from the front of the unit, though some are inside and are accessed once the main driver is removed.

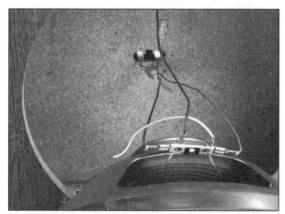

The crossover network typically is made up of small capacitors and resistors that may need to be replaced if the speakers aren't getting high or low frequencies.

6. Find the unit's *Fuse* and test it with a multimeter (see *Fix Everything: Multimeter*).
7. Use the multimeter to test resistance and continuity on the driver(s), crossover network, and/or the terminal block as needed. Most drivers will have their resistance indicated on the back side, such as 8 ohms.

8. Replace components as needed and reassemble.

Repair a damaged cone:

1. Identify the location of any small holes on the cone.
2. Apply rubber cement to the front and back side of any holes in the cone. If necessary, place a piece of thin kraft paper over the first layer of rubber cement to keep the cone from tearing.

If the cone is torn or has numerous large holes, have the driver reconed or replace it.

Obtain correct polarity (phasing):

1. Check the audio output device (stereo receiver, CD player, etc.) to make sure the speaker wires are correctly attached. The red terminal is [+] (positive) and the black one is – (negative). Better-quality speaker wire has a corresponding color code or some indication of polarity preference. If yours does not, attach the two wires in any manner, but make sure that the same wire that is [+] on the source is [+] on the back of the speaker enclosure.
2. Connect the wires up to the speaker enclosure in the same manner: [+] wire to [+] terminal, – wire to – terminal. The result will be richer bass tones.

**Fix-It Tip**

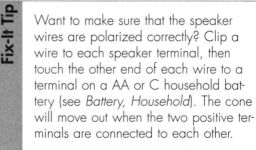

Want to make sure that the speaker wires are polarized correctly? Clip a wire to each speaker terminal, then touch the other end of each wire to a terminal on a AA or C household battery (see *Battery, Household*). The cone will move out when the two positive terminals are connected to each other.

# Stairs

Stairs are diagonal ladders that offer access to an area above or below the main floor. Imagine having to use a real ladder to go upstairs! If the stairs in your home are ready to be replaced by a ladder—or they just make too much noise or have other problems—here's what you can do about it.

## How Does It Work?

Stairs, or a stairway, is a series of steps leading from one level of a residence to another. A stairway is made up of several parts. The riser is the vertical board under the tread. The tread is the horizontal surface of the step that is actually walked on. The stringers are the inclined sides of the stairs that support the treads and risers. On some stairs, molding covers the joint between each riser and tread. Nosing covers the exposed front of each tread.

Open stairways also have handrails and related components, collectively called the balustrade. The newel post supports the handrail at the top and bottom of the stairway or at the turn on a landing. Balusters provide support for the handrail between the newel posts.

## What Can Go Wrong?

The most common problem with stairs is that they squeak; they can even move when you step on them. Newel posts, handrails, and balusters loosen over time. All are easily to fix.

## How Can I Identify the Problem?

If a stair squeaks and is open from behind, squirt a small amount of polyurethane foam sealant along the open space between the tread and the riser. Alternatively, insert glue-coated wedges between the tread and the riser with a hammer and driving block.

If the entire tread is loose and you can access it from the back, screw two or three metal angle brackets at the joint of the tread and the riser.

If a wood-finished stair squeaks, you can perform a temporary or permanent repair (see below).

If a newel post is loose, you can tighten it with a small angle bracket (see below) or with screws (see below).

If a baluster is loose, you can tighten it up (see below).

If a handrail is loose, drill a hole at an angle through each baluster into the handrail and screw the baluster to the rail.

## What Parts, Materials, and Tools Do I Need?

Basic stairway components, such as treads and risers, can be cut from wood available at a lumberyard. Decorative pieces may be found through larger supply houses or online (see *Fix-It Resources*). Here are the tools and materials you'll need for common stair fixes:

- Hammer
- Drill
- Screwdrivers
- Chisel
- Wood filler
- Wood glue
- Angle brackets
- Paint or stain
- Sandpaper
- Screws
- Saws
- Sealant
- Finish nails

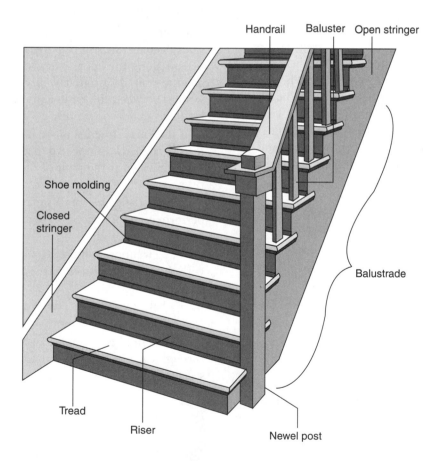

Components of a typical stairway system.

## What Are the Steps to Fixing It?

Quiet a wood stairway from squeaking:

1. For a temporary fix, squirt powdered graphite into the joint of the tread and the riser.
2. For a permanent fix, drill pilot holes into the wood of the squeaking stair, then drive ring-shank flooring nails in through the holes. Fill with wood filler, then sand, and paint or stain.

Tighten a newel post with angle brackets:

1. Screw a small angle bracket to the base of the newel post to support the joint.
2. Install a second angle bracket at another side of the post if necessary.

To hide the angle brackets, use a chisel to notch out grooves in the wood surfaces for the bracket, then fill with wood filler, then sand, and *Paint* or stain. Alternatively, you can mount them as above and paint the area to make them less conspicuous.

Tighten a newel post with screws:

1. Carefully drill pilot holes near the newel post's base and into the floor, then countersink the holes (drill a wider, shallow hole above the first so the screw head can be countersunk).
2. Apply wood glue between the post and the floor. Insert flat-head wood screws into the holes and tighten.
3. Fill the holes with wood filler, then sand and *Paint* or stain.

Tighten a baluster:

1. Pry off any molding with a putty knife.
2. Drill a pilot hole into the tread, then countersink the hole.
3. Apply wood glue around the hole.
4. Insert a wood screw and tighten.
5. Replace the molding.

**Fix-It Tip**

Having trouble finding replacement newel posts or balusters? You can remove the component and have a woodworking or cabinet shop make you a new one. Or you can check local salvage yards for similar components. You also may find replacement parts online (see *Fix-It Resources*).

# Steamer/Rice Cooker

If you enjoy steamed vegetables or rice, you probably already own a steamer/rice cooker. They are relatively inexpensive—because they are relatively simple in operation. Yet they, like other small appliances, may need some work at the Fix-It Club.

## How Does It Work?

A steamer is a small appliance designed to steam foods, primarily vegetables. A rice cooker is a steamer designed specifically for steaming rice, but many can be used to steam other foods as well. All steamers use enclosed heating elements. Some include a thermostat. Simple steamers have a rotary timer that turns off the elements after a set time. Other units have a sensor that knows when the water has boiled off in the pan and automatically switches to a lower heat setting.

## What Can Go Wrong?

The electrical cord may need replacing. The heating element or resistor may be faulty. Switch contacts or other appliance controls may become dirty.

## How Can I Identify the Problem?

If the steamer doesn't turn on, make sure the power is on at the *Electrical Receptacle*. Test the *Electrical Cord* with a multimeter (see *Fix Everything: Multimeter*).

If the *Heating Element* tests faulty, replace the appliance.

If the resistor tests faulty (see below), replace it or the appliance.

## What Parts, Materials, and Tools Do I Need?

Because steamers are simple in operation and inexpensive to replace, replacement parts may be difficult to find. First, try the manufacturer, then aftermarket suppliers (see *Fix-It Resources*). Larger hardware stores will have replacement cords and maybe some enclosed heating elements. Here are the tools you'll need to fix a steamer/rice cooker:

- Screwdrivers
- Wrenches
- Small file
- Electrical contact cleaner
- Multimeter

## What Are the Steps to Fixing It?

Disassemble and test the appliance:

1. Unplug the cooker from the *Electrical Receptacle*. If the appliance has a plug-in cord, remove it.
2. Remove the cover and the pan.
3. Turn the steamer over and remove the fasteners holding the base.
4. As needed, test the *Heating Element*, resistor, and service switch contacts (see below).

Test the heating element:

1. Disconnect the heating wire from one terminal.
2. Set the multimeter (see *Fix Everything: Multimeter*) at R×1 (resistance times 1) scale to measure resistance.
3. Touch the tester probes to the two terminals. The heating element is okay if the meter reads near zero ohms.

Test the resistor:

1. Remove the lead to the heating element.
2. Set the multimeter (see *Fix Everything: Multimeter*) at R×1 (resistance times 1) scale to measure resistance.
3. Touch the tester probes to the two terminals. The heating element is okay if the meter reads approximately 20 ohms.

To service switch contacts: Press down on the lever arm to verify that the switch contacts make full contact. If not, use a small file to file the contacts. As needed, spray the contacts with electrical contact cleaner.

Spray contacts as needed with electrical contact cleaner.

**Fix-It Tip**

The best preventive maintenance is thoroughly cleaning the appliance after every use. Food buildup can cause avoidable mechanical and electrical problems.

# Stuffed Toy

Most of us have had a cherished stuffed toy during our childhood—and maybe still have it in our adulthood. It's a wonder they survive the pulling, tugging, crushing, and other loving abuse given them. If they haven't survived intact or a child or grandchild's stuffed toy is ready for repair, take it to the Fix-It Club.

## How Does It Work?

A stuffed toy is a fabric caricature of a person, animal, or object. Modern stuffed toys are stuffed with polyfill or foam. Older toys may be stuffed with toxic foams or plastics. In addition, stuffed toys may have fabric or plastic limbs, eyes, ears, or other features that require repair. (Also see *Doll.*)

## What Can Go Wrong?

Ears, noses, eyes, and other pieces get torn off. Seams open. Sound boxes fail. Old stuffed toys lose their plumpness.

**Caution**

Some older toys may be stuffed with toxic plastic foam or polystyrene pellets. Remove and replace this stuffing with polyfill—or keep it somewhere away from children. You can buy bags of polyfill at craft and fabric stores.

## How Can I Identify the Problem?

If an ear, nose, eye, limb, or other part becomes detached, you can reattach it (see below).

If a seam comes open, you can stitch it closed (see *Fix Everything: Sewing*).

If a sound box fails, you can replace it (see below).

If the toy seems flat, you can restore its plumpness (see below).

**Fix-It Tip**

Does a valuable antique stuffed toy need new stuffing? Because it may be delicate and may lose value if damaged, consider hiring a professional who is skilled in doll restoration to do the job.

## What Parts, Materials, and Tools Do I Need?

Replacement parts (eyes, noses, hands, sound boxes) for stuffed toys are available from crafts stores or sewing centers. In addition, sewing and craft shops can supply the tools you'll need:

- Needles
- Thread
- Soft brush

## What Are the Steps to Fixing It?

Close an open seam:

1. Use slip stitches to stitch along the seam (see *Fix Everything: Sewing*), poking leaking stuffing back in as you sew.
2. If the toy has fur, use a soft brush to fluff it up over the completed stitches.

Reattach an ear or limb:

1. Pin the ear or limb to the head or body.
2. Sew it into place with overhand stitches (see *Fix Everything: Sewing*).
3. For added security, stitch along both sides of the ear or limb.

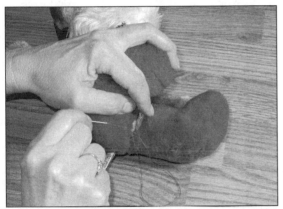

You can reattach a stuffed toy's limb with overhand stitches.

Replace a stitched nose and mouth:

1. Mark the outline of the nose.
2. Fill in the area with tight satin stitches of embroidery thread (see *Fix Everything: Sewing*).
3. Finish a nose with one horizontal stitch across the top.
4. Sew an inverted Y underneath the nose to create a mouth.

Replace a button eye:

1. Stitch through the head, if it is soft.
2. Pull the thread tightly and knot it securely at the back of the head.

 **Caution**

Don't replace a button eye on a stuffed toy that a child will use; they can come off and be swallowed. Instead, install a lock-in eye (see below).

Replace a lock-in eye:

1. Open the seam at the back or the side of the head and remove stuffing as needed.
2. Push the eye through the material.
3. Attach the washer from inside the head.
4. Stitch up the seam using slip stitches (see *Fix Everything: Sewing*).
5. If it is a furred creature, use a soft brush to fluff up the fur over the seam.

Replace a sound box:

1. Open the rear seam.
2. Remove the old sound box.
3. Insert a new sound box.
4. Press stuffing securely around the new sound box.
5. Stitch up the seam using slip stitches (see *Fix Everything: Sewing*).
6. If it is a furred creature, use a soft brush to fluff up the fur over the seam.

Restore plumpness:

1. Open a side seam or other accessible seam.
2. Insert fresh stuffing, making sure it is evenly distributed.
3. Stitch up the seam, using slip stitches (see *Fix Everything: Sewing*).

# Subfloor

"Gee, I wonder how my subfloor's holding up." No, it's probably not something you think about often. In fact, you might never consider your home's subfloor—until it begins squeaking or you have to replace the covering over it (see *Carpet; Flooring, Resilient;* or *Flooring, Wood*). It just does its job day after day: supporting the flooring you walk on. Let's call a quick meeting of the Fix-It Club to take a look at the subfloor.

## How Does It Work?

A subfloor is a floor laid on top of the floor joists, to which a finished, decorative floor is fastened. If your home's floor is of poured concrete, that's the subfloor. Plywood or planks also provide a solid platform to which tile, vinyl, hardwood, carpet, etc. can be fastened with nails or adhesives. To hold the finish flooring, the subfloor must be stable, relatively smooth, and waterproof.

## What Can Go Wrong?

The most common problem with a wood subfloor is annoying squeaks when someone walks across the floor. Squeaks occur when pieces of wood rub together. Concrete subfloors don't have this problem, but they can become water damaged and crack.

## How Can I Identify the Problem?

If a wood subfloor squeaks, first you must try to locate the squeak. If the floor joists can be seen from below the floor (as from a basement or crawlspace), watch from below while someone walks across the floor above. You may spot movement between joists and subfloor, or loose bridging between joists. Mark the location with chalk or another marker so you can find it again when you've gathered the needed tools and materials.

If you can get at the squeak from below through a basement or crawlspace, you can repair it with an angle iron, screws, a cleat, or a shim (see below).

> **Fix-It Tip**
>
> Wish you could lubricate a squeaky floor? Maybe you can! Wood flooring can be "lubricated" with talcum powder. Spread the powder over the boards in the problem area and work it in between the boards using your hand or a small brush. Then walk around the area to work the powder in. Repeat a few times and you may remove the squeak—without having to drive a nail.

If the squeaky subfloor is below a wood floor and there is no access to the subfloor from below, you can refasten the loose section of subfloor to the nearest joist through the finish floor (see below).

If the squeaky subfloor is beneath tile, vinyl, or carpet and there is no access from below, you can try to reset the loose boards from above (see below).

If the subfloor is concrete and shows damage, you will need to remove the flooring material and use a concrete patch product (available at hardware stores) to fix it, following the manufacturer's instructions (see *Concrete*).

## What Parts, Materials, and Tools Do I Need?

Replacement parts are available at building material retailers, hardware stores, and home centers. The tools you will need to fix a damaged subfloor include these:

- Hammer
- Screwdrivers
- Drill
- Angle iron
- Screws
- Nails and washers
- Cleats and wood blocks

## What Are the Steps to Fixing It?

Repair a squeaky floor from below with an angle iron:

1. Find and mark the location of the squeak from below the subfloor.

2. Install an angle iron on the joist so the top of it is about ¼ inch below the top of the joist.
3. Firmly screw the angle iron into the subfloor to pull it down onto the joist.

**Caution**

Make sure that the screws installed in the subfloor from below are not longer than the subfloor and flooring is thick, or they will come up through the flooring!

Repair a squeaky floor from below using screws:

1. Drill holes through the subfloor slightly smaller than the screw threads.
2. Install washers and wood screws ¼ inch shorter than the total floor thickness.

Repair a squeaky floor from below using a cleat:

1. Mount a cleat against a joist under the loose boards.
2. Prop and tap so the cleat is snug against the subfloor.
3. Nail to the joist.

Repair a squeaky floor from above (wood floors):

1. Use a stud finder to locate the joist.
2. Drill pairs of pilot holes angled toward each other
3. Drive 3-inch ring-shank nails or screws through the flooring, and the subfloor, and into joist.
4. Set the nailheads or countersink the screws, and cover them with wood putty that matches the color of the boards.

Repair a squeaky floor from above (not recommended for ceramic or other hard tile that may break):

1. Locate and mark the location of the squeak.
2. Using a hammer and a block of scrap wood as a buffer, pound the floor firmly over the squeaky boards in the area around the squeak to force loose nails back into place.

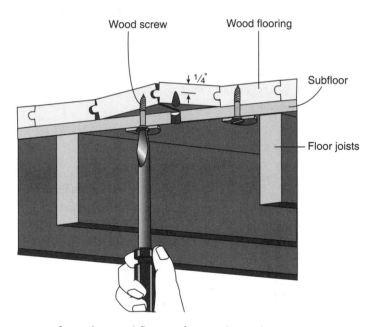

You can fasten loose subflooring from underneath using screws.

# Swimming Pool

Pool problems? Water level going down quickly? Icky stuff floating? Pump not pumping? Sounds like a job for … the Fix-It Club!

## How Does It Work?

A swimming pool is a tank for swimming and wading. There are wading pools that get dumped after every use or so. There are above-ground pools with a metal frame lined with vinyl. There are also in-ground pools lined with concrete, tile, or a vinyl liner. A pump circulates the water. A skimmer is the inlet to the pump that removes large debris. A filter takes out the smaller impurities. Chlorine and other chemicals purify the water before it gets pumped back into the pool.

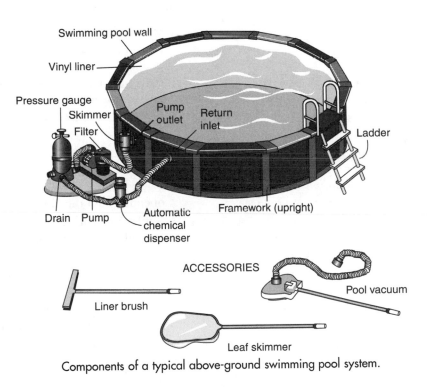

Components of a typical above-ground swimming pool system.

## What Can Go Wrong?

The biggest problem that most swimming pools face is properly balancing the water chemistry. In addition, vinyl liners may suffer tears or holes. Filters can become clogged. Pumps may malfunction.

## How Can I Identify the Problem?

If water chemistry is not balanced, you can correct it by following instructions included with a pool chemical test kit.

If the vinyl liner is torn or has a hole, you can patch it using a vinyl repair kit (follow the instructions included). You may be able to patch the liner without draining the pool (see below).

If the filter is clogged, you can clean it following the instructions in your owner's manual.

If the pump does not operate properly, you can replace the impeller and shaft seal (see below), and test and replace the *Motor*.

## What Parts, Materials, and Tools Do I Need?

Replacement parts are available from the manufacturer (see *Fix-It Resources*) and pool and spa retailers. The tools you will need to fix your swimming pool include these:

- Screwdrivers
- Pool chemistry test kit
- Goggles
- Vinyl patch kit
- Groove joint pliers
- Multimeter (for testing the *Motor*)

## What Are the Steps to Fixing It?

Patch a vinyl pool liner:

1. Locate the leak. (Of course, if you are patching the liner in an area that is wet, you'll need goggles.)
2. Cover the leaking area with a scrap of vinyl fabric. It will be held in place by suction until you can install a permanent patch, step 3.
3. Find the patch kit that came with the pool or purchase a patch kit for the pool liner.
4. Cut a patch about twice the size of the opening from the vinyl in the patch kit.
5. Apply vinyl adhesive from the patch kit to one side of the vinyl patch.
6. Fold the sticky side of the patch together to keep the adhesive dry and take it underwater to the leak.
7. Quickly remove the temporary patch, and unfold and apply the permanent patch.
8. Smooth out any bubbles with your hand or a flat tool to ensure full adhesion and to speed drying of the adhesive.

Replace a pump seal:

1. Turn off the pump motor and close the input and output valves.
2. Loosen the fasteners that secure the tube connecting the pump and motor.
3. Move the motor away from the pump housing.
4. Remove fasteners holding the diffuser to the backplate.
5. Inspect the diffuser and O-ring for wear, replacing as needed.
6. As needed, remove fasteners attaching the impeller to the shaft. Alternatively, the impeller may be screwed on to the end of the shaft.
7. Remove the impeller and seal from the shaft.
8. Inspect and replace the impeller and seal.
9. Reassemble the pump.

**Fix-It Tip**

Concrete in-ground pools are built in place. Heavy equipment digs the rough hole, workers finish by hand, reinforcement bar is installed in a mesh, then concrete is sprayed into the area and worked smooth by hand. To fix damage to concrete pools, check with local pool suppliers for supplies and contractors to get the job done.

# Telephone Answering Machine

"Wait for the beep." Remember when real, live people answered the telephone? That was before automated telemarketers. Today, it's a rarity when someone you're calling says "Hello?" instead of "You've reached …"—unless his or her telephone answering machine is broken! If that person is a member of the Fix-It Club, that answering machine can be running again—before a telemarketer calls!

## How Does It Work?

A telephone answering machine is a device designed to record audio telephone messages for later playback. Once the telephone rings a specified number of times, a telephone answering machine plays a recorded message to the caller and then records the caller's response. Cassette-type answering machines store outgoing and incoming messages on one or two audiotapes similar to those used in audiocassette players. Digital answering machines use a computer chip to announce and record the messages.

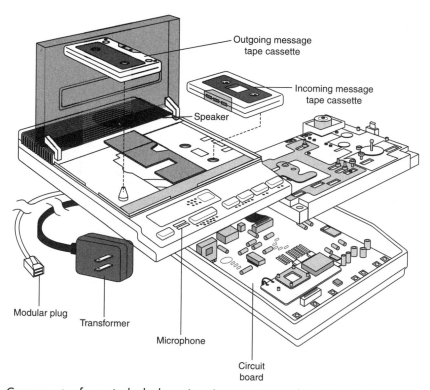

Components of a typical telephone (tape) answering machine. Digital phone answering machines have similar parts.

## What Can Go Wrong?

In most cases, problems with telephone answering devices are caused either by operator error (trying to figure out how it's supposed to work) or low batteries, if equipped. In addition, the power cord may be faulty, the belt may be loose or broken, the telephone cord or modular plug may be damaged, the play and record heads and the tape path may be dirty, and the play or record heads may be magnetized.

> **Fix-It Tip**
>
> If you suspect that the telephone line itself may be the problem, consider buying a phone line tester (about $5.00 at electronics stores). It will tell you if there is a signal or not and whether the internal lines are crossed. Also, replace the telephone cord with the shortest one you need.

## How Can I Identify the Problem?

If the unit doesn't take messages, first check the owner's manual for a troubleshooting chart or other diagnostics. Some include self-checks that will tell you what the problem is.

If the machine doesn't work at all, first make sure power is on at the *Electrical Receptacle* and test the *Electrical Cord*.

If the machine is digital, there is little you can do to replace individual components. Try cleaning the machine with canned air and electronic cleaner (see *Fix Everything: Electrical Cleaners*).

If the tape reels don't move, check the cassette and replace it if it is faulty. If that doesn't fix the problem, replace a loose or broken belt (see *Cassette Deck*).

If the machine doesn't respond to calls, try replacing the telephone cord or modular plug (see *Telephone System*).

If the tape jams, repair or replace a faulty tape cassette (see *Cassette Deck*). Also, clean the heads and the tape path (see *Cassette Deck*). If necessary, replace a broken or stretched belt (see *Cassette Deck*).

If the message quality is poor, clean dirty heads or repair or replace a faulty tape (see *Cassette Deck*).

> **Fix-It Tip**
>
> If your tape answering machine is plain worn out, consider replacing it with a digital unit. It's about the same price for the same features, and it has fewer moving parts to go wrong. However, there's little you can do with a digital unit once something *does* go wrong, so buy a unit with a good warranty.

## What Parts, Materials, and Tools Do I Need?

You may be able to find replacement parts and tools at an electronics supply store such as Radio Shack. Refer to the individual *Fix-It Guides* mentioned above for specific tools and procedures.

# Telephone System

Depending on whom you ask, the telephone is one of the world's greatest or worst inventions. Most people, however, agree that it is both. It can bring you the friendly voice of a loved one or that of a rude stranger at 2 A.M. It can deliver useful Web pages or annoying faxes. Sometimes you wish it *would* break—of course, then you would have to fix it!

## How Does It Work?

A telephone is a low-voltage transmitter and receiver for distributing and reproducing sounds over a distance. A call from a fixed telephone goes through a series of local and main exchanges that route it to the called telephone. The call may be transmitted over metal cables, radio links, fiber-optic cables, or a combination of these components. All together, it's called a telephone system. A cellular (mobile) portable telephone (see *Telephone, Cellular*) connects by radio signals to a nearby base station, then through telephone lines.

## What Can Go Wrong?

The telephone itself may be defective. The modular jack may be defective. The phone lines inside the house, which are your responsibility, may be defective; the lines outside the house, which are the telephone company's responsibility, may be defective.

**Fix-It Tip**

Check your telephone bill. You may or may not be paying a small monthly charge for wiring service. If so, the telephone company will service all wires in your home's telephone system, including those inside the walls and to the jack. If you're not paying for this service, the company's not responsible for inside wiring.

## How Can I Identify the Problem?

First, determine whether the problem is with an individual telephone or the telephone line. If a phone does not operate at all, unplug it and plug another phone into the jack. If the second phone works, the problem is probably in the first telephone. If the second phone doesn't work either, plug the first phone directly into the telephone network interface module located outside in the box where the telephone lines enter your home. (If the box where the phone lines enter your home does not have a plug for the telephone, use the phone jack nearest where the lines come into the house.) If the phone now works, the problem is inside the house. If the phone still does not work, the problem is in the telephone company's lines coming to the house. Contact your phone company for repairs.

If the phone does work when plugged into the telephone network interface module, the problem is between there and the module in the house. Use a screwdriver to remove the covers of both the network interface module and the modular jack, and disconnect the red and green wires. Telephone lines come with an extra pair of yellow and black wires, so substitute yellow for red and black for green at the telephone network interface module and at the modular jack. (If you have a second phone number for your house, the yellow and black lines may already be in use.)

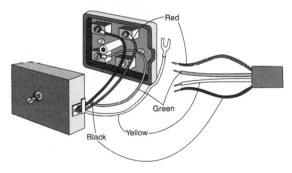

Wiring a modular telephone jack.

If you get a continuous dial tone, even when dialing, the red and green wires are probably reversed. Try the following options. If you have the same problem on all your telephones, remove the network interface module cover and switch the red and green wires leading to the phones. If the problem affects only one telephone, use a screwdriver to remove the cover of the modular jack serving that telephone and reverse the red and green wires leading from the jack to the telephone.

Other problems may occur within the telephone itself. Although many telephones can be replaced inexpensively, some problems can be resolved easily by checking connections and settings.

If there is no sound from a classic telephone headset, you may be able to remedy the problem (see below). Electronic phones are harder to service (sometimes impossible, because many new ones are sealed).

## What Parts, Materials, and Tools Do I Need?

Replacement parts are available at electronics and telephone supply stores and larger hardware stores. The tools you will need to fix a home telephone system include these:

- Telephone line tester

> **Fix-It Tip**
>
> If you have many problems with your telephone service, consider purchasing a telephone line tester through an electronics supply store. With it you can easily test the telephone signal at the phone box outside of your house as well as individual lines and jacks within it.

- Screwdrivers
- Denatured alcohol
- Emery cloth

## What Are the Steps to Fixing It?

Improve transmitter sound on a standard phone:

1. Unscrew the mouthpiece cover and lift out the transmitter.
2. Clean off dirt with a foam swab dipped in denatured alcohol.
3. Clean metal contacts beneath the transmitter.
4. Raise the metal contacts slightly with a screwdriver and clean with an emery cloth.
5. Reassemble the headset and make a call. If poor sound persists, have the phone serviced by a professional or replace it.

Improve receiver sound on a standard phone:

1. Unscrew the earpiece cover and lift out the receiver.
2. Loosen terminal screws and remove the wire leads.
3. Clean the leads and screws with an emery cloth.
4. Reconnect each wire terminal securely to its screw.
5. Reassemble the handset. If poor sound persists, have the phone serviced by a professional or replace it.

# Telephone, Cellular

Cellular phones have taken over communications. With them we conduct international business as well as call home to see what's for dinner—or what to pick up for dinner. Fortunately, they are virtually trouble-free. Even so, there are things you can do to keep them that way.

## How Does It Work?

A cellular phone (handheld mobile phone) is a small, portable telephone with a built-in antenna. The phone is recharged by plugging it into a household electrical outlet or from a car battery by connection through the cigarette lighter unit.

The mobile telephone (vehicle-mounted mobile phone) connects by radio signals to a nearby base station in what's called a cell. Each cell varies in size depending on the number of callers in the cell. As the mobile phone moves from one cell to another, it automatically connects to the base station in the next cell. Each base station then sends the call to a mobile exchange, which connects to a main exchange in the network.

**Fix-It Tip**

Cell phones can be recycled. If you decide to replace a working cell phone (perhaps to change providers), you may be able to donate your phone to be used as an emergency-only phone for a homeless or low-income individual or family. Ask your service provider.

## What Can Go Wrong?

Actually, there's not much that can go wrong with a cell phone—at least not much you can fix. Most cell phones are purchased or leased under contract with a cellular service provider, so needed repairs are done by the contractor, not the consumer. And with the cost of cell phones going down every day, it's often cheaper to replace the unit rather than repair it. In most cases, cell phone problems are caused by a low battery, a damaged charger, or by mishandling—such as dropping the phone out the window of a car.

**Caution**

The most important maintenance you can do is keep your cell phone dry because moisture can corrode electronic circuits very quickly. Cell phones are difficult to dry out. Don't take your cell in the pool.

## How Can I Identify the Problem?

In most cases, your cell phone will either work or it won't. It may be a problem of signal strength, easily tested by trying to call from another location. More often, it's a battery problem. If the battery will not hold a charge, try discharging the battery entirely by leaving it disconnected from the charger unit. If the phone still will not maintain a charge, the problem could be with either the phone or the charger unit, and professional service from your provider will be necessary. There is little else you can do to repair a cell phone.

First, check the cell phone owner's manual for troubleshooting tips.

Most cell phones have unusual fasteners to discourage you from opening up the case.

At least once a week, wipe your cell phone clean with a soft cloth slightly dampened in a mild household cleaner. Alternatively, carefully spray the unit with a disinfectant to reduce germs. Make sure you don't get the mouth or ear holes wet.

# Telephone, Cordless

At one time in ancient history, where you talked on the telephone was limited to the length of the cord. Mobile telephones didn't need cords, but they were expensive. Then, a couple of decades ago, someone figured out how to produce cordless telephones in the price range of standard corded telephones and the world began buying them by the millions. Today, more cordless phones are manufactured than corded units. And, just like their predecessors, they sometimes need fixing.

## How Does It Work?

A cordless telephone is a phone that has a base connected to a standard phone jack and an electrical wall outlet. The base receives the signal from the telephone line and translates it into radio waves that are transmitted to the cordless handset. The base also includes a recharger for the handset's batteries. Recharging takes place when the handset rests on the base.

## What Can Go Wrong?

Cordless telephones are nearly bulletproof, especially the newer models with integrated circuitry. In fact, some cordless phones are sealed and don't offer a way of getting into them without breaking them. Even so, there are things that can go wrong that you can fix. For example, a low battery can make communication difficult—and it's easily remedied. In addition, cordless phones can pick up noisy interference from outside sources such as power lines, motors, televisions, and other telephones. You can shield the phone or select an alternate channel to improve reception. You also can minimize future problems by keeping the phone clean, especially the recharging contacts on the base.

> **Fix-It Tip**
>
> Use a pencil eraser to clean the contacts on a cordless telephone's base, then use compressed air or contact cleaner to remove any residue and debris left by the eraser.

## How Can I Identify the Problem?

Most problems with cordless phones are easy to identify and resolve. If the phone doesn't work at all, make sure that the power is on at the electrical outlet. Then test the phone line by plugging another telephone into it. Check the low battery indicator and recharge the battery if needed. If the battery won't hold a charge, replace it with an exact replacement (size and voltage). Cordless phone batteries typically last a year with regular charging, but they can last for a longer or shorter time depending on use and maintenance.

If the phone is noisy, and the unit has a manual channel selector, switch to another channel. Even some automatic channel selectors have an override selector. If that doesn't work, plug the base into a different electrical outlet in a distant part of the house to see if the interference is through a specific electrical circuit or appliance in your home.

If the antenna is obviously damaged or broken, replace it (see below).

## What Parts, Materials, and Tools Do I Need?

You'll need only a few tools to perform most fixes on your cordless phone. These are the ones most frequently used:

- Screwdrivers
- Multimeter (for testing the battery)

## What Are the Steps to Fixing It?

Maintain proper charging:

1. Once a month, clean the charge contacts on both the base and the handset with a pencil eraser.
2. Once a month, leave the phone off the base until the battery completely discharges, then put it back on the base to recharge it (unless your owner's manual gives other instructions). If the battery does not recharge, replace it.

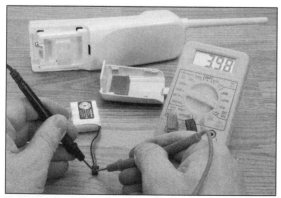

You can check the battery with a *Multimeter.*

Replace an antenna on a cordless telephone:

1. Inspect the antenna to determine how it is installed. If you are still not sure, take it to a retailer that sells replacement parts and ask a clerk. Antennas on newer cordless phones screw in. Older models may require that the unit be disassembled, the antenna desoldered, and the new one soldered into place (see *Fix Everything: Solder*).
2. If disassembly is required, remove the cover to the battery compartment and look for screws or clips that allow access to the antenna and other components.

Remove screws and pry apart the two halves of the case.

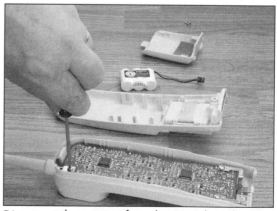

Disconnect the antenna from the circuit board, typically attached with a single screw.

Remove and replace the antenna with an exact-replacement part.

If the base unit requires service, first unplug the unit from the electrical outlet. Some cordless telephones have a battery in the base for backing up incoming and outgoing messages. Look for a battery cover, remove it, and test the battery (see *Battery, Household*) before disassembly. If necessary, disassemble the base unit by removing screws and/or clips from the underside to gain access. Test and replace components using a multimeter (see *Fix Everything: Multimeter*) and following the phone owner's manual.

# Television

TVs are our favorite time wasters. Fortunately, they are virtually trouble-free. When they are not, it's time to fix them. Before calling the TV repair service, there are many things you can do yourself to eliminate or reduce the cost of technical repair.

## How Does It Work?

A television receiver is an electronic device that receives audio and video signals from an antenna, cable/satellite, or a video player and converts those signals into visible light rays and audible sound. A television receiver displays a picture as horizontal lines on the screen. Each line contains a series of red, green, and blue stripes. At viewing distance, the lines and stripes merge and we see a sharp picture in full color. Modern televisions rely on solid-state electronic components that require servicing by a trained technician.

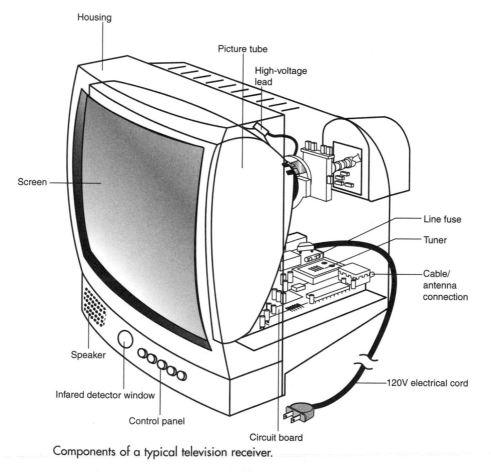

Components of a typical television receiver.

## What Can Go Wrong?

Most problems that you can fix are caused by loose connections or improperly set controls. TVs made since about 1990 are often adjusted with a handheld remote and on-screen commands. Finer adjustments can be made by a television service technician. Problems that appear suddenly indicate a failed component, especially if the set has recently been subjected to shock, vibration, or excessive heat. The picture and sound quality gradually deteriorate due to aging.

## How Can I Identify the Problem?

There are many things you can do before calling for service. First, switch to a different channel or wait a few hours to see if the trouble might be with the cable/satellite service or the broadcaster. Get out your owner's manual and make sure the controls are set properly. Make sure power is on to the *Electrical Receptacle* and test the *Electrical Cord*. In addition, check the *Remote Control*.

Most modern TVs have adjustments for brightness, color, and sound. Refer to the owner's manual for adjustment instructions.

If there are color blotches in the image, they are usually caused by magnetization of the TVs metal parts or picture tube. Most sets have a built-in device for demagnetizing. Turn the set on for one to two minutes, then turn it off. Repeat several times at half-hour intervals. If this fails, demagnetize the picture tube by running a degaussing coil (available with instructions at electronics parts stores) across the tube with the set turned off.

If bright areas of a picture look silvery and details are indistinct, the picture tube is defective. When brightness is turned to low level, the picture will appear normal but dull. With brightness up, detail in white areas is lost. The picture may improve after the set has been on for an hour or more, but you'll eventually have to replace the tube.

**Fix-It Tip**

How long should your television set last? TVs have an average life of three to eight years of moderate to heavy (eight or more hours per day) use. Most TVs typically last about five years. Before investing in costly repairs, check the price of a replacement set.

## What Parts, Materials, and Tools Do I Need?

Replacement parts are available from the manufacturer and aftermarket suppliers (see *Fix-It Resources*) and from local electronic stores. The tools you will need to fix a TV include:

- Screwdrivers
- Wrenches
- Tuner or electronic cleaner

## What Are the Steps to Fixing It?

Refer to *Fuse* and *Appliance Controls* for information on testing and replacing electronic components.

Service a mechanical tuner (solid-state tuners must be professionally serviced):

1. Remove the metal plate protecting the tuner, typically attached to the front of the cabinet.
2. To clean the contacts, carefully spray them with tuner or electronic cleaner, turning the channel selector to distribute the cleaner over the contacts.
3. If replacement is required, you may need to desolder the unit to remove it (see *Fix Everything: Solder*).

**Fix-It Tip**

Older TVs have vacuum tubes instead of solid-state components. You can purchase them through specialized parts suppliers (see *Fix-It Resources*) and larger electronics stores.

# Tile

Tile is tile. The installation, maintenance, and repair of tile flooring is just about the same as that on a counter or in a shower. That means this guide covers fixing tile around your home, wherever it is.

## How Does It Work?

Tile is molded clay that has been prepared for use as flooring or as countertop or wall covering; or it is natural stone that has been cut for the same purpose.

Ceramic and natural stone tiles are widely available. Several types of ceramic tile are in popular use. Glazed ceramic tile is baked, coated with glaze, and baked again, creating an extremely hard surface layer. Quarry tile is baked but left unglazed, leaving it porous. It is softer and thicker than glazed tile. Porcelain mosaic tile, made in units of less than 6 square inches, is made of porcelain or natural clay composition, either plain or with an abrasive mixture throughout. Natural-stone tile is simply cut from stone. Granite and marble tiles are usually polished and sealed after cutting, while slate tiles are cut along natural faults, leaving a textured appearance.

Tile flooring, walls, or countertops are installed over a solid base, creating extremely hard and durable surfaces that will serve for many years with little maintenance other than cleaning. Tile is installed with an adhesive, and space between the tiles is filled with grout, a sandy paste that hardens soon after application.

## What Can Go Wrong?

Grout can become dirty and stained. It can crack, chip, or even come out in chunks. A single tile or several tiles can also crack, chip, or break. As mentioned, whether the tile is on a floor, countertop, or wall, repairs are basically the same.

## How Can I Identify the Problem?

If grout is dirty or stained, you can make it sparkle again (see below).

If grout is chipped, cracked, or missing, you can replace it (see below).

If a tile is damaged, you can replace it (see below) without damaging the tiles around it.

## What Parts, Materials, and Tools Do I Need?

Replacement tiles and the materials and tools needed to fix them are available from retail tile stores and home centers. The tools you will need to fix tile include these:

- Replacement tile

**Fix-It Tip**

Whenever you install new tile on a floor, wall, or counter, set aside a few extra tiles for the day when you may need to replace a few. Wrap them up in clean paper, sealed with tape, and write the tile color and where it was installed. If you write it on the edge of the package, you'll be able to read it easier if it's stacked on a shelf.

- Electric drill
- Hammer
- Vacuum cleaner
- Cold chisel
- Pry bar
- Grout
- Grout sealer
- Tile adhesive
- Grout cleaner or bleach
- Household cleaner
- Sponge
- Clean white towel or paper towels
- Brushes
- Putty or grout knife
- Notched trowel

## What Are the Steps to Fixing It?

Clean grout:

1. Spray on a commercial grout cleaner or heavy-duty all-purpose bleach-based cleaning solution (use ¼ cup of chlorine bleach in 1 quart of warm water to eliminate mold and mildew). Let soak for several minutes.
2. Scrub with a stiff brush and rinse thoroughly.
3. Dry with a clean white towel or paper towels.
4. Apply grout sealer to keep the grout clean for up to a year.

Regrout tile:

1. Scrub the tile and grout thoroughly with a strong household cleaner. If there is any mildew, scrub the tile joints with a toothbrush dipped in bleach and rinse thoroughly.
2. Remove any damaged grout with a putty knife, grout knife, or other sharp tool. Vacuum up any mess.

Remove old grout and clean surfaces before applying new grout.

3. Scrub the area again, but leave it damp.
4. Mix sufficient tile grout according to the package instructions. Apply grout with a damp sponge, wiping firmly in areas that need grout. Smooth the new grout with a clean damp sponge. If needed, apply more grout and smooth again, until the tile joints are completely filled.
5. Let the grout dry for at least twelve hours. Scrub the tile firmly with a clean cloth to remove any grout on the tile.
6. Seal the grout with an appropriate grout sealer, following the manufacturer's instructions.

**Fix-It Tip**

Seal grout yearly to prolong its beauty and its effective life.

Replace a tile:

1. Drill a row of holes and score a line with a hammer and cold chisel. Or break up the tile with the hammer and cold chisel.
2. Along the chisel line, use a pry bar to pry up pieces of the tile. After the first broken piece of the tile comes out, the rest will come out easily.
3. Scrape out the old adhesive, if possible, with a putty knife.
4. Use a notched trowel to spread new adhesive.

5. Center a replacement tile in the patch area.
6. Place a block of wood over the new tile to protect its surface, and seat the tile evenly with the surrounding surface. You may have to tap it gently with a hammer.
7. Let the tile adhesive set according to package directions. Then mix a small batch of grout. Use a wet sponge or a trowel to force it into the seams, and wipe off the excess. Repeat as needed until the joint is filled.
8. Clean tile thoroughly of any excess grout.
9. Seal the grout with an appropriate grout sealer, following the manufacturer's instructions.

**Fix-It Tip**

If you don't have any leftover tile from the initial tile installation, check with local tile stores. They sometimes have open stock where you might find a replacement.

# Toaster

Toasters aren't just for toasting bread anymore. They also toast bagels, frozen waffles, breakfast strudel, and other breakfast and snack items. No wonder they break down! Fortunately, toasters are relatively easy to fix. If it's unfixable and you decide to toss it instead, you'll know what to look for in your next toaster.

## How Does It Work?

A toaster is an electric heating appliance with a timer, carriage, and latch. Most pop-up toasters work in the same manner. A slice of bread or other appropriate food item is placed through a slot in the top of the toaster and into the carriage. A lever lowers the carriage. When the carriage reaches the bottom of the chassis, it latches in position, an internal switch turns on the heating elements, and a timer starts. Once the timer finishes its cycle, it turns off the elements and a solenoid releases the spring-loaded carriage that pops up the toast. A toaster oven works differently to do the same thing on a wider variety of foods (see *Oven, Toaster*).

## What Can Go Wrong?

Toasters malfunction frequently for two major reasons. First, most toasters are built to be throwaway appliances. Second, malfunctions are frequently caused by particles of food that interfere with the operation of the toaster. Other problems with toasters include cords that malfunction, latch assemblies that are damaged or obstructed, or faulty elements and thermostats. Modern toasters use circuit boards within the controls that, if damaged, should be taken to an appliance repair center or tossed.

**Fix-It Tip**

Bread drops particles as it toasts, collecting on the bottom of the toaster appliance. Depending on how often you use your toaster, it's a good idea to clean out the crumb tray at least once a week. Some units slide out from the front, while others require that you unlatch a cover underneath the unit—preferably over the trash can. Also take a moment to look inside for loose food trapped behind element wires where it can short out an element.

## How Can I Identify the Problem?

If the toaster doesn't work at all, make sure power is on at the *Electrical Receptacle* and test the *Electrical Cord*.

If the carriage lowers but doesn't latch or latches stiffly, look inside for food debris that may be blocking the carriage. If the latch is damaged or obstructed, service the assembly (see below).

If the bread toasts only on one side, check the *Heating Element*(s) for damage and replace as needed; or replace the toaster.

If the carriage doesn't pop up and the toast burns, check the thermostat calibration and correct any inaccurate calibration (see below).

If the thermostat is faulty, replace the thermostat or the toaster. Check the solenoid switch and solenoid; if faulty, service (see below) or replace.

If the toast is too light or too dark, check thermostat calibration and correct if necessary (see below).

## What Parts, Materials, and Tools Do I Need?

You can purchase some replacement parts at appliance service centers. For others you may need to contact the toaster's manufacturer (see *Fix-It Resources*). Here are the tools you'll need:

- Screwdrivers
- Canned air
- Appliance lubricant
- Continuity tester or multimeter

## What Are the Steps to Fixing It?

Service the latch assembly:

1. Unplug the toaster from the electrical receptacle.
2. Remove or open the crumb tray and empty it. Turn the toaster over above a trash container and carefully empty out any crumbs before continuing.
3. Remove the toaster cover by removing levers, knobs, and fasteners (typically on the underside or underneath labels).

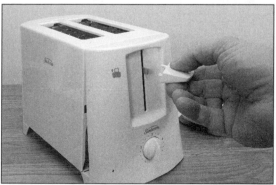

Remove the carriage lever and unfasten the cover panel.

4. Inspect the latch assembly for obvious damage or crumbs. Use canned air to clear debris from the latch assembly.

Controls (on circuit board)

Inspect the latch assembly and check the carriage for debris that may stop smooth operation.

5. Move the carriage lever up and down to check for smooth operation. If the carriage moves stiffly, sparingly apply an appliance lubricant on the latch rod.
6. Verify operation of the latch to ensure that it works smoothly. If necessary, carefully bend the latch to make sure it catches properly.
7. You also can inspect and test the *Heating Element*(s) while you have the toaster open.

Service a solenoid:

1. Remove the crumb tray cover to access the solenoid switch, typically located near the thermostat on the controller side of the toaster.
2. Use a continuity tester (see *Fix Everything: Continuity Tester*) or multimeter (see *Fix Everything: Multimeter*) to test the solenoid switch (see *Appliance Controls*). If faulty, remove and replace it.
3. To replace the solenoid, you may need to disassemble the toaster, as above. If the solenoid is installed with rivets, replace the chassis as a unit or the entire toaster.

Recalibrate a thermostat:

1. Disassemble the toaster, as above, to access the controls (see *Appliance Controls*) including the thermostat.

2. Identify the calibration knob, screw, or nut. It may be obvious because it is an adjustment on the controller, or you may need to refer to the toaster's owner's manual. Typically, moving the knob toward the solenoid switch shortens the toasting cycle (if toast is too dark) and moving it away lengthens the cycle (if toast is too light).

Calibration knob

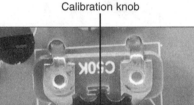

Identify and adjust the calibration knob, typically located behind the toasting selector knob.

3. Reassemble the toaster, plug it in, and use a piece of bread to test the adjustment. If adjusting the thermostat doesn't solve the problem, replace the thermostat or the toaster.

# Toilet

"Jiggle the handle!" It's a common phrase in many homes—even plumbers'. It seems like the toilet bowl flushing mechanism is one of the most common fix-it problems. Why else would there be rows of toilet fix-it parts at most hardware stores? So how can you take care of these and other toilet plumbing problems? Keep reading.

## How Does It Work?

A toilet is a bathroom fixture that usually consists of a water-flushed bowl and seat. Two mechanisms operate simultaneously when a toilet is flushed: a flush valve and a fill (ball cock) valve. Tripping the flush handle raises the flush valve, releasing water from the tank into the bowl. The rushing water creates a siphoning action in the bowl that forces wastewater down the drain. As the tank empties, the lowering water level lowers a float that's connected to the ball cock. As the float falls, it operates the fill valve inside the ball cock. Meanwhile, the flush valve closes itself after the water drains from the tank. With the fill valve open and the flush valve closed, the tank fills and the rising water lifts the float. When it reaches a preset level, the float closes the fill valve in the ball cock. At that point, the tank should be full and ready to flush again.

There are various versions of this mechanism, sometimes with their own brand name. However, they essentially all work about the same.

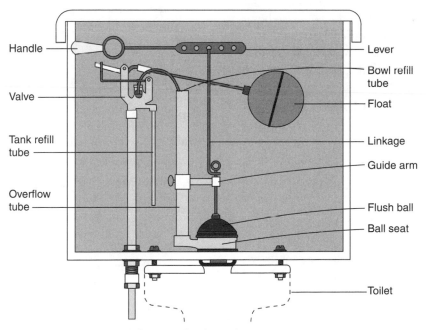

Components of a typical toilet tank.

## What Can Go Wrong?

A toilet can get plugged up and overflow or drain slowly. The handle can quit working effectively, and the flush mechanism or lift chain may need adjusting or replacing. The ball cock can malfunction. Leaks sometimes develop. A seat may need replacing. And a porcelain fixture can crack. All of these problems are fixable with basic tools and instructions.

## How Can I Identify the Problem?

If the toilet bowl overflows, use a plunger or auger (see below) to eliminate clogs.

If the toilet does not flush, tighten or replace the defective handle (see below), adjust or replace the lift chain (see below), or replace the flush mechanism (see below). Jiggling the handle forces the lift chain or rod to reseat the flush mechanism, telling you that something is awry.

If the bowl drains sluggishly, remove the clog with a plunger or auger, or raise the water level in the tank (see below).

If water runs continuously through the toilet, lower the water level in the tank (see below), adjust or replace a lift chain or wire (see below), repair or replace a worn flush valve (see below), clean or replace the valve seat assembly (see below).

If water appears under the tank, tighten the tank hold-down bolts (see below), lower the water level in the tank, replace the float valve (see below), replace a malfunctioning ball cock, or tighten nuts on the water supply line, replace leaking supply line (see below). As a last resort, reseat the toilet (see below).

If the seat is cracked or unsightly, replace it (see below).

If the bowl or tank is cracked or otherwise unacceptable, replace the entire toilet (see below).

## What Parts, Materials, and Tools Do I Need?

Replacement parts are available at just about any hardware store. Special models may require a trip to a plumbing supply store. In either case, make sure you have model numbers, typically imprinted on the inside or underside of the tank unit. The tools you will need to fix a toilet (depending on the job) include these:

- Plunger
- Auger
- Wrenches
- Hacksaw
- Penetrating oil
- Vinegar
- Rubber gloves
- Toothbrush
- Plastic container or bucket
- Rags
- Sponge
- Bristle brush
- Nylon scrubbing pad
- Pliers
- Screwdrivers
- Emery cloth
- Masking tape

## What Are the Steps to Fixing It?

Unclog a toilet using a plunger:

1. If the bowl is full or overflowing, put on rubber gloves and use a plastic container to bail out half the water. If the bowl is empty, add water to half full.
2. Place the plunger firmly over the larger drain opening and move it up and down rapidly several times. If the water goes down the drain, you probably removed the blockage.

Make sure you turn off the water to the toilet before disassembling anything. The water shutoff is located on the wall below the tank and behind the seat. If you can't find it, turn off the main water valve.

Don't get caught without a Plan B. Have plenty of rags, a sponge, and a pail nearby to catch water or clean up spills.

3. Use the plunger again to be sure the water is running freely. Then pour in a pail of water and plunge one more time before flushing the toilet to refill the bowl.

4. If the blockage remains after plunging, use an auger (see below).

Unclog a toilet using an auger:

1. Determine the direction in which to guide the auger. Some toilets are rear draining and others are front draining.

2. Feed the curved tip of the auger into the drain opening. Crank clockwise and push with moderate pressure until the auger tightens up, then crank in the other direction. When the auger tightens again, reverse the direction until the auger is as far in the drain as it will go.

3. Pull the handle up and out to remove the auger. If it jams, push gently, then pull again. You may have to turn the handle as you pull up.

4. Augering may either push the blockage through or pull gunk up into the bowl. After augering, remove any large pieces, wearing rubber gloves. Finish with a plunger to ensure that the drain runs freely.

Adjust or replace a flush handle:

1. Remove the cover from the toilet tank (the higher part at the back of the toilet). If the handle is loose, tighten the locknut with a wrench. If the nut won't budge, apply penetrating oil and let it set before removing.

2. Unhook the chain from the trip lever and slide the trip lever, with the handle attached, through the hole in the tank.

3. Soak the handle threads in vinegar for an hour or so to remove mineral deposits, then scrub clean with an old toothbrush.

4. Reinstall the assembly, tighten the locknut and adjust the lift chain (see below).

Adjust the lift chain:

1. If the handle must be held down while the toilet is flushing, the chain may be too long. Shorten it by hooking the upper end through a different trip lever, or use long-nose pliers to open and remove some chain links. Alternatively, replace the chain with a new one.

2. Some flush assemblies have a lift wire instead of a chain. If the wire binds against its guide, flushing is impaired. Loosen the guide with a screwdriver, then adjust it so that the flush valve falls freely onto its seat.

Clean the valve seat:

1. Turn off the water supply and flush the toilet to drain the tank. Wearing rubber gloves, use a large sponge to mop out most of the remaining water. Disconnect the refill tube and slide the flapper valve off the overflow pipe.

2. With emery cloth, gently scour inside the valve seat and along its rim, removing any debris. If the valve seat is badly pitted, replace it or install a rebuild kit that consists of a new flapper valve and valve seat, following the kit's instructions.

3. Reassemble the mechanism, then turn on the water supply and flush to check for leaks.

Replace the flapper valve:

1. Unhook the refill tube and lift chain, then remove the flapper valve (see above).

2. Purchase and install a replacement valve seat following the manufacturer's instructions. If you cannot find a flapper valve that fits the seat, or if the leak persists after replacing the flapper valve, install a rebuild kit (see above).

Replace the float ball:

Note: Some toilets use proprietary float systems that must be replaced as a unit following manufacturer's instructions.

1. Grasp the float arm with locking pliers, and unscrew the float ball. If it will not come off, use pliers or a wrench to remove the float arm from the ball cock.

2. Screw a new ball onto the float arm and screw the arm back onto the ball cock.

3. Flush the toilet and adjust the water level as necessary (see below).

Replace the flush mechanism:

1. Shut off the water supply and flush the toilet. Remove the tank cover and place a container on the floor beneath the tank to catch water runoff. Wearing rubber gloves, sponge up any water remaining in the tank.

2. With an adjustable wrench or adjustable pliers, unscrew the nut and disconnect the supply line where it enters the tank.

3. Attach locking pliers to the nut at the base of the ball cock and loosen the locknut under the ball cock with an adjustable wrench or adjustable pliers. Unscrew the nut, and lift the ball cock up from the tank.

4. Use a bristle brush or a nylon scrubbing pad to clean the opening in the tank where the ball cock was. Position the assembly in the tank with the cone-shaped washer of the new ball cock centered over the hole, and tighten the locknut snugly; do not overtighten, or it may crack.

5. Place the refill tube into the overflow pipe, reconnect the supply tube, and slowly turn on the water. Tighten the locknut slightly if the new hardware leaks.

6. Adjust the water level in the tank as necessary (see the following sidebar).

## Adjusting the Water Level

A toilet tank's water level should be ½ to 1 inch below the top of the overflow pipe. A low water level results in an incomplete flush. If the level is too high, the water will drain into the overflow pipe and the toilet will run continuously. Here's how to adjust the water level in the tank:

1. To lower the water level, gently lift the float arm and bend it down slightly to keep the water level 1/2 to 1 inch below the top of the overflow pipe.

2. To raise the water level, bend the float arm to raise the float ball, making sure that the ball does not rub the tank.

3. To raise or lower a plastic float arm, turn the knob at the ball cock.

Tighten leaky bolts or washers:

1. If water is leaking from the bottom of the tank, first try tightening the tank hold-down bolts. Shut off the water and drain the tank. Use locking pliers or a wrench to keep the nut under the tank from spinning, and turn the screw inside the tank with a screwdriver. Turn the water back on and test.

2. If that doesn't work, shut off the water again, flush the tank, and mop any remaining water from the tank. Disconnect the supply line, unscrew the hold-down bolts, and remove the tank. Replace the gaskets and rubber washers, and reassemble.

Replace a toilet seat:

1. Toilet seat bolts may be hidden under plastic caps. Pry open each cap. Hold each bolt with a screwdriver, and unscrew the nut with adjustable pliers. Some nuts have plastic "wings" that make pliers unnecessary.

2. If the bolts are corroded, apply penetrating oil and allow it to stand for four to six hours and try again. If the bolts still will not budge, apply masking tape to the toilet rim to protect it, and then cut through them with a hacksaw.

3. Replace the seat and bolts, then hand-tighten the nuts. Align the seat with the bowl and tighten the nuts one-quarter turn.

Reseat or replace a toilet:

1. If a toilet base leaks or you need to replace the toilet, shut off the water, drain the tank, disconnect the supply lines, and sponge water out of the bowl.

2. Grasp the tank bolts with pliers and unscrew them, then lift off the tank.

3. Remove the toilet seat.

4. Remove the floor bolt caps and unscrew the nuts with an adjustable wrench. Straddling the toilet, rock it from side to side and carefully lift it off the bolts. Call your local recycler for information on how to dispose of the old toilet.

5. Lay the toilet upside down on a protected surface; remove old wax, unless you're installing a new toilet.

6. Press a new wax ring over the opening of the old or new toilet, depending on which you will be installing.

7. Position the toilet over the bolts and press it into place. Tighten the nuts. Reinstall the tank and the seat.

**Fix-It Tip**

A flange-type plunger fits into the toilet drain and exerts more pressure than an old-style cup plunger.

# Toy

*'Twas the day after Christmas*
*and all through the house,*
*Not a toy was unbroken,*
*not even Mickey Mouse.*

Sound like your house? Toys get some rough treatment and, unfortunately, many of them don't stand up to it very well. That means someone (guess who) is going to have to fix the toy or toss it. Fixing it is really the better option, so let's take a look at how to fix all those things we collectively call "toys."

## How Does It Work?

A toy, of course, is an object for a child (or some adults) to play with. A visit to any toy store demonstrates the enormous variety of toys available for children. However, many of those toys have common elements and many can be repaired following a few simple principles. They roll, move, make noises, or include numerous parts.

## What Can Go Wrong?

Plastic toys and plastic parts of toys break. Battery-powered toys lose their power. The most common problem with rolling toys is losing their wheels, axle, or handle. All kinds of inflated balls deflate over time and occasionally leak.

## How Can I Identify the Problem?

If a battery-powered toy won't run, the problem is often with a battery (see *Battery, Household*) or the *Battery Recharger* (see below).

If a plastic toy or a plastic part of a toy breaks, you can bond it with adhesive (see below).

If a plastic part comes loose from a piece of wood or metal, drill holes through both surfaces and fasten them with bolts or rivets.

If a wheeled toy loses a wood or metal wheel, you can repair or replace it (see below).

If an axle is broken, you can replace it (see below).

If a ball deflates, reinflate it with a hand pump. If the ball doesn't retain air, you can repair and reinflate it (see below).

If a stuffed or other fabric toy is torn or has a seam come undone, see *Doll* and *Fix Everything: Sewing*.

## What Parts, Materials, and Tools Do I Need?

Replacement parts are available from the manufacturer and aftermarket suppliers (see *Fix-It Resources*), as well as from local hardware stores and craft shops. The tools you will need to fix various toys include these:

- Screwdrivers
- Pliers
- Mallet
- Hammer
- Electric drill
- Pump with inflating needle
- Bolts and other fasteners
- Sandpaper
- Elastic band, string, or tape
- Masking tape
- Adhesives

| Fix-It Tip | Keep a wide selection of glues and adhesives in your fix-it toolbox for emergency repairs. If the containers are small, also keep the packaging because it will have instructions in a *larger* typeface than that appearing on the adhesive container. |
|---|---|

- Dowels
- Steel rods

## What Are the Steps to Fixing It?

Bond a broken plastic toy:

1. Lightly roughen both edges of the break with sandpaper and wipe off any dust.
2. Apply adhesive (see *Fix Everything: Adhesives* to determine the best type of adhesive for the item) to both surfaces to be joined.

3. Clamp the pieces with an elastic band, string, or tape.
4. Let the repair dry well before releasing the clamp.

Apply adhesive to the broken toy following recommendations on the adhesive label.

Repower a battery-operated toy:

1. Test the batteries (see *Battery, Household*) and replace as needed.
2. Verify that the batteries are inserted all the way, touching the contacts. If the battery does not touch the contacts, use a screwdriver to gently pry up the contacts just enough to make good contact.

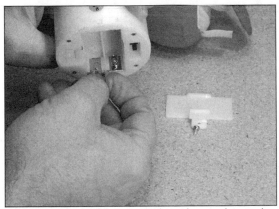

Make sure the battery terminals make an electrical connection with the toy's contacts.

3. Check for corrosion on the terminals and clean them if needed.

4. If the toy uses a rechargeable battery, examine the charger as well as the battery (see *Battery Recharger*).

Repair a split wood wheel:

1. Drill holes in each piece of the broken wheel for the dowels.

2. Add wood glue to the dowels (for more on glue, see *Fix Everything: Adhesives*).

3. Clamp the wheel together with masking tape.

Replace a broken axle:

1. With pliers, pry off the push nuts and unscrew the lock washers. Remove the wheels and flat washers, then slide out the axle.

2. Cut a new axle from a round steel rod. Install the axle, then slide flat washers and wheels on the ends of the axle. Place lock washers over the wheels.

3. Install a push nut over the ends of the axle and tap them into place with a hammer.

Mend a leak in a sport ball:

1. Submerge the ball in a tub of water and rotate it slowly, looking for escaping air bubbles that identify a hole. Dry the area, then mark the leak with a piece of masking tape.

2. Heat the blade of an old knife or screwdriver by moving it back and forth over a flame. Rub the hot blade over the leaky area until the vinyl melts. Let the vinyl harden for at least 5 minutes.

3. Reinflate the ball by pushing the inflator needle into the ball's valve hole. Use a hand pump to inflate the ball to the recommended pressure. Don't overinflate. You also can use a bicycle tire tube patch kit to repair leaking sports balls. Get one at bicycle shops, sporting goods stores, or large discount stores and follow the instructions provided.

Stop a leaking valve:

1. Clean the valve with a wet inflating needle inserted a few times to wash away dirt and debris.

2. If the problem persists, plug the valve by breaking off a toothpick in the hole.

**Fix-It Tip**

Can't fix that toy? Don't throw it away! You may be able to use wheels, motors, axles, and other parts to fix future toy breaks.

# Trash Compactor

There's a lot of air in trash. Empty cans, milk cartons, and other containers were once filled with product and now they're empty. It's a sin to send them to the dump like that where they take up landfill space. Better to compact trash and recyclables using a trash compactor. Of course, it's one more gadget that sometimes needs fixing, but if you're a member of the Fix-It Club, you're not worried.

## How Does It Work?

A trash compactor is a device that compresses trash and recyclables into small, tight bundles for easy disposal. Items are placed in the compactor, the drawer is closed, and the switch turned on. Inside, an electric or hydraulic ram inside the unit moves downward until it forces the air out of the trash, compacting it. The ram then reverses direction so you can remove the bundle for disposal. Internal switches turn the ram on and off as needed.

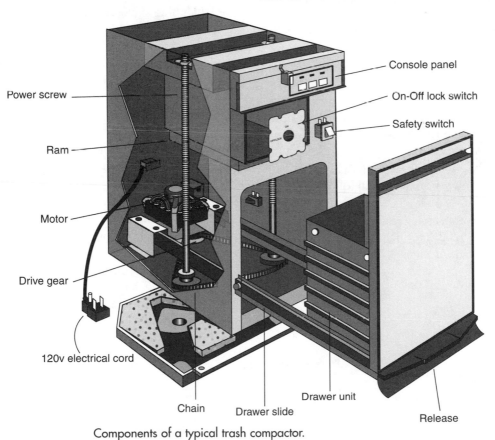

Power screw

Ram

Motor

Drive gear

120v electrical cord

Chain

Drawer slide

Drawer unit

Console panel

On-Off lock switch

Safety switch

Release

Components of a typical trash compactor.

## What Can Go Wrong?

Most common trash compactor problems include failed switches and worn sprockets, chain, roller bearings, and power nuts. The motor can burn out. Debris can become stuck inside and limit movement.

> **Caution**
>
> *Never put aerosol cans or flammable items in the trash compactor!*

## How Can I Identify the Problem?

If the compactor doesn't come on, check power at the *Electrical Receptacle* and test the *Electrical Cord*. Make sure the drawer is completely closed. Look for and reconnect loose terminal wires. Test the drawer safety and on-off switches (see *Appliance Controls*). If all else fails, test the *Motor*.

If the compactor starts, then stops, test the top-limit switch (see *Appliance Controls*) and the *Motor*.

If the motor runs but the ram doesn't move, check for a damaged chain (see below) or a faulty drive gear (see *Motor*).

If the compactor makes unusual noises, check the owner's manual and follow instructions for lubrication.

If the compactor starts but doesn't compact completely, check for debris in the power screw threads or nuts.

## What Parts, Materials, and Tools Do I Need?

Replacement parts are available from the manufacturer and aftermarket suppliers (see *Fix-It Resources*) as well as from local plumbing supply stores and appliance parts stores. The tools you might need to fix a trash compactor include these:

- Screwdrivers
- Wrenches
- Nut driver
- Multimeter

## What Are the Steps to Fixing It?

Disassemble a trash compactor:

1. Unplug the electrical cord, or turn off the breaker or remove the fuse from the *Electrical Service Panel*.
2. Unfasten the brackets or screws around the compactor to remove it from the cabinet for easier repair.
3. Remove the top and side cover panels with wrenches or nut drivers.
4. Lay out a protective pad where you will work, then remove the bottom panel, being careful of debris that may fall out.
5. Remove the cover panels to access the motor, chain, and switches.
6. As needed, remove fasteners holding the control panel in place. Test the *Electrical Cord*, *Motor*, switches and other controls (see *Appliance Controls*) using a multimeter (see *Fix Everything: Multimeter*) and replace as needed.

### Read the Owner's Manual

Refer to the trash compactor owner's manual for specific information on and sources of replacement parts. Make sure you specify the model and serial number, typically found near the door, when ordering replacement parts. You'll also want to read the manual for instructions on lubricating and maintaining your trash compactor. An hour once or twice a year can extend the compactor's life by many years.

Replace or adjust a chain:

1. Unplug the electrical cord, or turn off the breaker or remove the fuse from the *Electrical Service Panel.*

2. Disassemble the unit to access the motor (see above).

3. Remove the motor mounting bolts and the motor as needed. (Some models are easier to repair than others, so first refer to the owner's manual or a service manual.)

4. Remove the drive gear from the shaft.

5. Remove the chain from the drive gear's rear sprocket.

6. Remove the power screws from the frame without removing the power screw nuts.

7. Remove the chain from the sprockets.

8. Install the new chain around the sprockets and adjust the chain tension.

9. Reassemble the unit.

10. Plug the unit in, or turn on the circuit breaker or replace the circuit fuse.

**Fix-It Tip**

It's a good idea to check tension on the drive chain or belt once a year to make sure it isn't so loose that it damages gears and sprockets. If you're uncomfortable with this job, remove the unit and take it to a professional to save the price of a house call.

# Vacuum Cleaner, Corded

Tim the Toolman Taylor (from TV's *Home Improvement*) had the best idea: Hook up a 360 Ford engine to the vacuum and let it suck the dirt from crevices in the next room! His vacuum had enough suction to pull satellites out of the sky. Ahrr! Ahrr!

Seriously, it would be nice if home vacuums had more power. Actually, they can—by simply keeping them clear and in good repair. Most vacuums are working at well below capacity. You can fix them!

## How Does It Work?

A vacuum cleaner is an electrical appliance for cleaning surfaces by suction. It doesn't really produce a vacuum (absence of air), but a pressure differential (reduced air pressure in an enclosed chamber) that causes the suction. The air pressure outside of the chamber is greater than that inside. That difference in pressure causes the outside air to try to get into the machine, pulling any debris it picks up along the way. Once inside, the debris is trapped in a bag or container while the air passes through the container and back outside. Both upright and canister vacuums work about the same way. An electric motor drives a fan that draws the air—and dirt—into the chamber.

The primary difference between an upright and canister vacuum is what you have to push around. Uprights have everything (motor, controls, bag) in a single unit that is pushed and pulled over the surface to be cleaned. A canister vacuum cleaner places the most of its weight (vacuum motor, filters, bag, and cord winder) in a separate unit to make the power head lighter. With a long hose, the canister can be placed in the middle of the room and the power head moved around more easily. The advantage to this design is that larger and more powerful motors can be used. Both upright and canister vacuums typically have a spinning brush in the head that grabs debris and flings it toward the vacuum hose.

If you really need vacuuming horsepower—short of a 360 Ford engine—your home may have a built-in vacuum system with a wall-mounted unit in the garage and plastic pipes that run through interior walls. You simply plug in a special hose in the wall unit and start vacuuming. If the vacuum has a beater head, the connection must have electric power and wiring in the hose to get the power to the head or be powered by the suction produced by the unit with no extra wiring required.

**Fix-It Tip**

Vacuum bags aren't *dirt* cheap, but they are cheaper than taking a damaged vacuum to a service center. We recommend that you empty or change the vacuum bag when it is half to three-quarters full. Also, write the change date either on the bag or on a piece of masking tape fastened to the outside of the vacuum.

**Caution**

Don't try to vacuum up glass or other objects that can cut the bag. Instead, sweep them into a dust pan or use a shop vacuum that's designed to handle rough stuff.

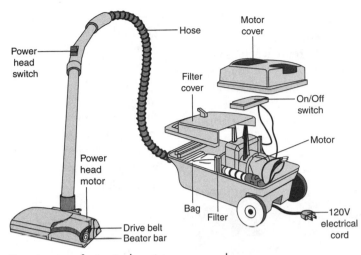

Components of a typical canister vacuum cleaner.

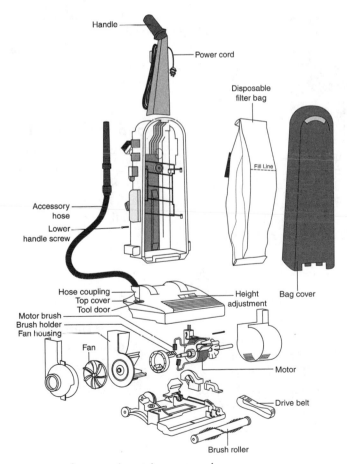

Components of a typical upright vacuum cleaner.

## What Can Go Wrong?

The most common problem with a vacuum cleaner is also the easiest to remedy: clogs in the hose, attachments, or filters. Also the electrical cord, motor, switch, fan, brushes, and motor bearings can all need repair or replacement. The drive belt may need replacing. Most of these problems you can fix yourself.

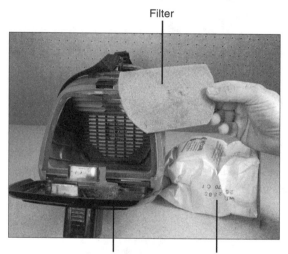

Filter

Access door    Bag

Replacing a filter on most vacuum cleaners is relatively easy. Open the access door or remove the cover and remove the filter. Also check for and replace secondary filters.

## How Can I Identify the Problem?

If the vacuum motor does not run, make sure power is on at the *Electrical Receptacle* and test the *Electrical Cord*; test the universal *Motor* and the switch (see *Appliance Controls*) and repair or replace any component that tests faulty.

If the motor seems sluggish, look for and remove debris, caked dirt, or other obstructions and replace the fan if damaged (see *Motor*); replace worn brushes and apply oil or light grease to dry motor bearings or replace worn bearings (see *Motor*).

If the motor stops and starts, test the *Electrical Cord*), the switch (see *Appliance Controls*), the *Motor*, and the *Motor* fan and service or replace as needed.

If the motor is noisy, open the vacuum housing and clean out dirt and debris from around the motor, and clean or replace filters; remove and replace a faulty drive belt (see below); inspect the *Motor* fan for damage and replace it if needed, and tighten the fan connection to the motor shaft.

If the vacuum suction is insufficient, empty or replace a full dust bag, look for and remove obstructions in attachments, clear a clogged hose (see below), clean or replace a clogged filter and check the *Motor* fan.

If the brush leaves lint on the carpet, check and replace a loose belt and inspect roller brushes and clean, adjust, or replace them (see below); clean air passages inside the cleaner and hoses (see below).

## What Parts, Materials, and Tools Do I Need?

You can find many replacement parts (hoses, filters, bags) at hardware stores and home centers. Replacement parts such as the motor, special hoses, seals, etc. are available from the manufacturer and aftermarket suppliers (see *Fix-It Resources*). The tools you will need to fix a vacuum cleaner include these:

- Screwdrivers
- Knife
- Pliers
- Wire cutter
- Garden hose
- Rubber cement

## What Are the Steps to Fixing It?

Disassemble an upright vacuum cleaner:

1. Unplug the vacuum. Remove the lower handle screw and the handle. Unscrew the accessory hose, if included, and remove it.
2. Turn the vacuum over and remove the top cover screws. Turn the unit right side up, move the height adjustment out of the way, and lift off the cover.
3. To remove the motor, first remove the brush roller (beater bar) and the drive belt (see below). Remove the screw securing the motor clamp. Be careful not to damage the gasket at the other end of the motor during reinstallation.

Disassemble a canister vacuum:

1. Unplug the vacuum. Remove hoses, dust bag, and filter. Remove cover screws and lift off the cover to access the motor and electrical components.
2. To service the *Motor* brushes or canister motor, remove any screws that secure the motor cover plate and lift out the motor. Make sure you find and replace sealing gaskets.
3. To service the brush roller (beater bar), turn the power nozzle over and clean out dust and debris. Remove screws securing the top cover. Turn the unit right side up and lift off the top cover.

Service a beater bar (upright or canister):

1. Turn the vacuum or vacuum head upside down to inspect the beater bar. It will be at the front edge of the housing.
2. Remove the clips at each end, remove the drive belt, and lift the beater bar from the housing.
3. Disassemble the beater bar, if necessary, by removing the end cap and flange, then pulling the brush from the casing.

4. If the brush is worn, replace it. As needed, replace a broken cap, flange, or case, or replace the entire beater bar.

Replace a drive belt:

1. Remove one end of the beater bar from the vacuum housing (see above).
2. Loosen the drive belt from the motor pulley and remove it from around the beater bar.
3. Slip the replacement drive belt over the beater bar and around the motor pulley. Note: The new belt will be smaller in circumference (but not wider or narrower) than the old one that has been stretched by use.
4. Reinstall the beater bar and adjust the drive belt as necessary.

Clear a clogged hose:

1. Attach the hose to the exhaust and attach the nozzle to the intake, using duct tape or a rag to seal around the intake.
2. Turn the vacuum on. If exhaust air doesn't force debris into the dust bag, disconnect the hose. Carefully feed a clean, dry garden hose or similar item through the hose to jar the clog loose.

Replace a vacuum hose:

**Caution**
If the vacuum hose has an electrical connection, check continuity with a multimeter (see *Fix Everything: Multimeter*). If it fails the test, replace the cord (if not built-in) or the entire powered hose. Don't cut into a powered hose.

1. If the hose is glued into its fitting, cut it near the fitting using a knife and wire cutter. Twist and pull out the remaining wire and hose and scrape out any glue.
2. Brush rubber cement onto the end of the hose and inside the fitting; then press the new hose into the fitting.

If the hose has a button collar, press the buttons and pull to release the hose from the fitting. Glue the hose to the insert, cover it with the collar, and slide it into the fitting to engage the buttons.

If you are replacing an entire hose, you can use a special reverse-threaded hose and a universal cuff that glues over the end fitting.

**Fix-It Tip**

Pet hair is the natural enemy of vacuum cleaners. It can easily wrap itself around the brush roller (beater bar) and clog the vacuum hose. If you have pets, be especially vigilant about keeping the brush roller and hose free of debris.

# Vacuum Cleaner, Cordless

Cleaning up a mess used to mean dragging out the big vacuum (or the broom and dustpan). Today, there are handy cordless vacuum cleaners to do the job. They are small, light, and handy to use—if they work. If they don't, it's time for another quick meeting of the Fix-It Club!

## How Does It Work?

A cordless vacuum cleaner is a hand-held, battery-operated small appliance designed to accomplish small cleaning tasks such as vacuuming up debris from floors, furniture, and other surfaces. They are sometimes referred to by the brand name DustBuster.

Cordless vacuum cleaners use a motorized fan to develop suction that pulls dirt into an internal bag that can be removed and dumped. In addition, cordless vacuums have an internal battery that stores electric power to run the DC (direct current) motor. An external battery charger (see *Battery Recharger*) and docking station is plugged into an AC (alternating current) electric outlet.

## What Can Go Wrong?

The most common problem faced by cordless vacuum cleaners is caused by dirt, the element it's supposed to be picking up. If the motor or collection bag isn't tightly mounted, dirt can enter through crevices and damage internal parts.

## How Can I Identify the Problem?

Besides getting jammed with dirt and debris, the major problem that cordless vacuums face is a weak battery or failing recharger. Some cordless vacuum batteries are easily replaced, while others are not and require that the entire unit be replaced (see *Battery Recharger*).

**Fix-It Tip**

You can clean the interior of a cordless vacuum with suction from a larger vacuum hose. Or you can use canned air to remove dust from internal surfaces. Make sure you wear goggles or other protection to keep dust from your eyes.

## What Parts, Materials, and Tools Do I Need?

Access to the filter and fan is relatively easy. Most cordless vacuums have clips that are pressed to open the unit. If you are in doubt, check the owner's manual. Replacement parts are available from the unit's manufacturer or aftermarket supplier (see *Fix-It Resources*). Tools you may need to remove and test components include these:

- Screwdrivers
- Pliers
- Multimeter

## What Are the Steps to Fixing It?

For most cleaning, maintenance, and trouble-shooting, refer to the unit's owner's manual. After each use, shake dust from the filter. Periodically wash a cloth filter in warm water and make sure the filter is dry before reinstallation. Replace a paper filter when it becomes dirty. Visually inspect the inside of the unit for obvious damage or sealing problems.

Disassemble the vacuum to find and replace the filter.

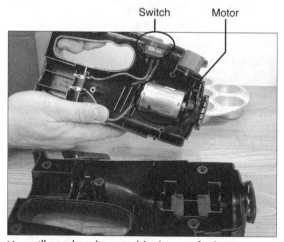

Switch     Motor

You will need to disassemble the unit further to access the vacuum motor and electrical switches.

Replace a faulty charger:

1. Unplug the cordless vacuum charger unit from the electric outlet.
2. Unscrew or unclip the wiring compartment cover located on the back side of the charger.
3. Disconnect wire harness clips as needed and unscrew or unclip the charger.
4. Use a multimeter (see *Fix Everything: Multimeter*) to test the battery. Replace a faulty battery with one of the same size and power (voltage and current) as the original, available from the manufacturer or an aftermarket parts supplier.

**Fix-It Tip**

If your cordless vacuum cleaner uses paper filters or collection bags, write the date of changing on it. Or you can affix a piece of masking tape on the outside of the unit and write the change date as a reminder.

# Videocassette Recorder (VCR)

VCRs are not leading-edge entertainment anymore. DVDs are taking over that slot. However, millions of us still have and use VCR tapes for playing back everything from family movies to this afternoon's soap opera. And these machines, some of them 10 years old and older, need fixing. Here's how.

## How Does It Work?

A videocassette recorder (VCR) is an electronic device for recording and playing back videocassette tapes. To record, the VCR takes the video signal from the television carrier signal and records it to magnetic tape. To play the signal back, the VCR reads from the tape and sends the signal to the television.

Most modern VCRs have four video heads (older ones may have two) and their own tuners. The tape is pulled across the heads using either a belt-, gear-, or direct-drive. Disassembly varies, but basic maintenance and repair procedures such as cleaning, lubrication, and belt changing are about the same for most models. The electrical components are generally quite reliable, but if they do fail, it may be more economical to replace the unit rather than to repair it.

**Fix-It Tip**

Don't toss that VCR until you've checked to make sure that it's not just the *Fuse* or the *Electrical Cord* that's the problem. If you want a new one anyway, fix the old one and donate it to a charity or a friend.

## What Can Go Wrong?

The power cord may fail. Internal parts may need cleaning. The idler wheel may become worn. The erase head may be faulty; tracking may need adjusting. Tracking may be off. The color board may be defective.

## How Can I Identify the Problem?

If the VCR won't operate at all, make sure power is on at the *Electrical Receptacle*, test the *Electrical Cord*, and check your owner's manual for proper connections to other home entertainment components; test the power switch (see *Appliance Controls*). Also check the internal *Fuse*.

Fuse

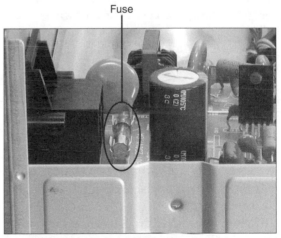

Most VCRs have an internal fuse on the power supply that can blow and stop electricity from flowing. Open the case to find and test.

If the VCR does not record or play back, clean or replace faulty belts (see below). Inspect and service the idler if faulty (see below).

If the VCR plays back but does not record, check for a faulty record safety switch (see *Appliance Controls*). Also try cleaning the heads (see below).

If playback does not work or a cassette won't load, clean and replace the belts as necessary (see below). Test and replace a playback switch if it tests faulty (see below). Clean a dirty logic switch or have a faulty one serviced (see *Appliance Controls*).

If the cassette is jammed or won't eject, remove and inspect the tape basket for jammed gears. Inspect and replace belts as needed. Remove and straighten a bent tape basket.

If a cassette binds when ejecting, test the eject *Motor* and have a faulty one serviced or replaced. Also clean or replace a dirty or faulty logic switch (see *Appliance Controls*).

If the VCR mangles tapes, clean the transport (see below) and check the idler wheel (see below).

If recordings are of poor quality, clean the video heads (see below).

If the picture quality is poor, clean the transport and adjust tracking according to your owner's manual (many units have automatic tracking adjustment).

If the picture is wiggly, adjust tracking and clean the heads and transport (see below).

If the picture is jumbled, clean the transport (see below).

If there is excessive dropout, clean the transport and adjust tracking.

If the picture bends at the top (flagging), have the unit serviced.

If the picture jumps, clean the video heads.

If there is no color, adjust tracking and clean the video heads.

## What Parts, Materials, and Tools Do I Need?

Replacement parts are available from the manufacturer and aftermarket suppliers (see *Fix-It Resources*) as well as from local electronics stores. The tools you will need to fix a VCR include these:

- Screwdrivers
- Small pliers or a pick
- Head-cleaning materials
- Denatured alcohol
- Canned air or vacuum cleaner
- Cotton or foam swabs
- Clean cloth
- Light machine oil
- Lubricating grease

## What Are the Steps to Fixing It?

Disassemble a VCR:

1. Unplug the VCR and remove any screws securing the top and bottom covers. To remove the face, take out the face latch screws from the bottom; then turn the VCR over and release the latches while tilting off the face. Align the slide switches with buttons to reinstall the face.
2. Tilt a circuit board away to access or test parts beneath it. Remove any mounting screws and latches.
3. Remove the tape basket and disconnect the power plug and grounding screw.
4. Remove the tape basket.

Clean the tape transport:

1. Remove general dirt and dust with canned air.
2. Clean the capstan and other tape loop components with cotton or foam swabs and denatured alcohol. Clean the video heads last to avoid recontamination.
3. Clean the video head and drum with a swab. Without touching the drum, hold a clean cloth flat against the head and slowly rotate the drum.

Service the idler assembly:

1. Remove the split ring holding the idler assembly on the shaft using small pliers or a pick.
2. Lift the idler assembly off the shaft. Remove the wheel to inspect and clean it as needed.
3. Clean the idler pulley and wheel with a foam-tipped swab dampened with denatured alcohol. Replace the pulley and wheel if they are damaged.

Lubricate a VCR (lubricate sparingly and only where original lubrication has failed or been cleaned off):

1. Lift up the capstan shaft washer and carefully add a drop of oil below it.
2. If the tape guide needs lubrication, first clean it with alcohol-soaked swabs. Apply a dab of lubricating grease on each track and turn on the VCR to spread the grease.

# Wallpaper

Have you discovered wallpaper at your home? It's a popular alternative to single-color walls, offering designs that set the room's mood. Of course, torn, dirty, or lumpy wallpaper breaks the mood. It's a good thing that you can fix it!

## How Does It Work?

Wallpaper is a special paper, plain or printed, adhered to a smooth interior wall surface as decoration. Wallpaper comes in several forms, thousands of designs, and a wide range of prices. The two most common types are standard wallpaper and solid sheet vinyl. Standard wallpaper is a paper backing with a decorative print directly applied to it. Solid sheet vinyl has a paper backing laminated to a solid vinyl decorative surface. Vinyl wallpaper is easier to clean and is especially popular in areas with moisture (kitchen, bath, etc.).

## What Can Go Wrong?

If wallpaper is so simple, what can go wrong? Wallpaper can become dirty and suffer tears. Seams and edges can come loose. Bubbles can appear. All are fixable problems.

## How Can I Identify the Problem?

If your wallpaper is dirty, try one of several cleaning methods (see below).

If there is a tear in the wallpaper, you can patch it (see below).

If a seam or edge comes loose, you can refasten it (see below).

If a bubble appears, you can easily flatten it (see below).

## What Parts, Materials, and Tools Do I Need?

The tools and materials needed for fixing wallpaper are available at wallcovering stores as well as larger hardware stores and home centers. Tools needed include these:

- Wallpaper (for patching)
- Scissors
- Wallpaper adhesive
- Utility knife
- Glue syringe
- Art-gum eraser
- Slice of rye bread (really!)
- Cleaning fluid
- Cornstarch
- Tape
- Sponge
- Seam roller

## What Are the Steps to Fixing It?

Clean nonwashable wallpaper:

1. Remove pencil marks and many other non-greasy spots from nonwashable papers by rubbing gently with an art-gum eraser or a slice of fresh rye bread.
2. Clean greasy spots, crayon marks, and food stains with a paste made of cleaning fluid and cornstarch. Let the solution dry and then brush it off. Repeat until the spot disappears.
3. Remove fingerprints with a damp cloth followed by a light dusting of cornstarch to absorb moisture. Let the cornstarch dry and brush it off.

Patch wallpaper:

1. Use scissors to cut a patch of new wallpaper larger than the area to be covered.
2. Carefully tear the edges of the patch wallpaper because it will be less noticeable than a straight-cut edge.
3. Remove any loose wallpaper from the area you are patching.
4. Align the patterns to make sure that the patch will work.
5. Clean and smooth the area to be patched with a damp sponge.
6. Apply wallpaper adhesive to the back of the patch, place it on the wall, and smooth it into place with a damp sponge.
7. Allow the patch to dry for 10 to 15 minutes, then lightly press the repaired seams with a seam roller.

### Match Your Patch

You can purchase replacement wallpaper for patching in wallpaper stores. However, even if you can find the correct pattern, how can you age the paper so it doesn't look like a patch? You can use a light bleach solution to age pieces. Or you can find a loose piece in the corner of a closet or other hidden location. The best option is to set aside unused wallpaper left over from a job, tacking it up on an attic or closet wall to age with the installed wallpaper. It will then be ready for quick fixes.

Refasten a seam or edge:

1. Carefully lift the edge of the seam.
2. Moisten the area to be refastened.
3. Use a glue syringe or glue that comes with a nozzle applicator to inject premixed wallpaper adhesive behind the seam.
4. Wait 10 to 15 minutes, then lightly roll the repaired seam with a seam roller.

Eliminate a bubble:

1. Carefully slit the bubble from edge to edge with a clean and sharp utility knife.

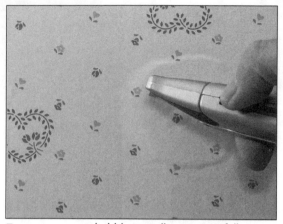

To remove an air bubble in wallpaper, carefully cut the surface with a utility knife, as shown, and press to allow air to escape, then rub the surface to flatten it.

2. Moisten the area that is bubbled.
3. Use a glue syringe or glue that comes with a nozzle applicator to inject premixed wallpaper adhesive into the slit.
4. Massage the glue in with your fingers, working excess adhesive out through the slit.
5. Use a clean, wet sponge to remove excess adhesive from the repaired area.

# Washer, Clothes

No one wants to go down to the (polluted) river and wash clothes on a rock! Instead, we stuff the clothes washer with everything wearable, dump some soap in, maybe add a glug of bleach, push a button or turn a knob, and don't give the washer another thought—unless we come back to wet and soapy clothes! It's a good thing that, for their size, clothes washers are relatively easy to work on. You just need to know how to fix them. A washer is a better option than a rock!

## How Does It Work?

A clothes washer is a major appliance designed for washing clothes, bedding, towels, and other linens. Knobs and buttons on the machine's control panel send instructions to a timer and electrically operated valves. The wash cycle begins by filling the washtub with hot, cold, or blended-temperature water. In a top-loading washer, the agitator in the middle of the tub churns back and forth or up and down to clean the clothes. In a front-loading washer, the drum tumbles the clothes clean. In all washers, the spin cycle extracts water from the clothes and a pump sends dirty water to the drain.

A direct-drive clothes washer uses gears on the motor to turn the agitator and spin the drum. A belt-drive washer transfers power from the motor to the agitator and drum using a belt-and-pulley system.

## What Can Go Wrong?

The electrical cord may be faulty. Switches can fail. The timer can be faulty. The motor, clutch, and transmission can malfunction. Hoses can become kinked or leak. Filters can become clogged. The pump can fail. The agitator can break.

**Fix-It Tip**

Modern major appliances, including clothes washers, use digital rather than mechanical timers and other controls. Some include diagnostic tests that report operating problems as trouble codes. Check your machine's owner's manual for information on how to activate and interpret diagnostic codes. You may be able to fix the problem yourself!

## How Can I Identify the Problem?

If the washer doesn't run at all, or if it hums, first make sure power is on at the *Electrical Receptacle* and test the *Electrical Cord*. Test the water level switch, the lid switch, the centrifugal switch, and the timer *Motor* (see *Appliance Controls* and *Fix Everything: Multimeter*). Test the clothes washer *Motor*. Replace any component that tests faulty or hire a service technician to do the repairs. Before doing so, inspect the pump for blockage (see below).

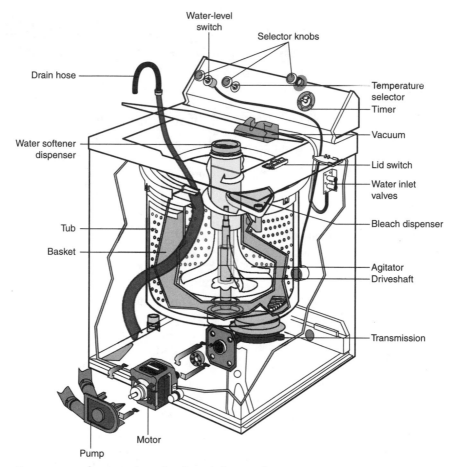

Components of a typical top-loading clothes washer.

If the washer doesn't fill, doesn't stop filling, or doesn't agitate, check the water-supply hoses for kinks. Also test the water-level switch assembly (see below), test the water inlet valve (see below), check the water temperature switch (see *Appliance Controls*), and test the timer *Motor*.

If the washer doesn't drain, test the water level switch assembly (see below). Test the water inlet valve (see below).

If the washer doesn't spin, test the water level switch assembly. If service is needed, consider calling a professional technician.

If the washer leaks, straighten or replace the drain hose and inspect the pump for blockage (see below).

If the washer is too noisy or vibrates too much, redistribute the load of laundry for better balance and adjust the leveling feet. If these efforts fail, clean the water supply screens. Next, test the timer *Motor*, inspect the pump for blockage (see below), test the machine *Motor*, and clean the water supply screens. If all else fails, call for professional service.

## What Parts, Materials, and Tools Do I Need?

Replacement parts are available from major appliance parts suppliers, larger plumbing and hardware stores and, of course, the manufacturer and aftermarket suppliers (see *Fix-It Resources*). The tools you will need to fix a clothes washer include these:

- Screwdrivers
- Pliers
- Wrenches
- Multimeter

## What Are the Steps to Fixing It?

Disassemble a direct-drive washer:

1. Unplug the washer from the *Electrical Receptacle* and turn off the water supply to the washer.
2. Remove the retaining screws from the bottom corners, top or back of the console.

3. Turn the console to expose the timer, timer motor, water level switch, water temperature switch, and cycle selector switch.
4. As needed, access the drum by pushing the blade of a putty knife between the washer's top and body to disengage attachment clips. Some units have clips near the console as well.
5. Disconnect the control housing from the washer housing, marking and disconnecting any electrical wiring harness plugs as needed.
6. As needed, remove the front panel by loosening screws at the panel corners to access the drum and motor.

You now can service the agitator and drum, and test the *Motor* and other components using a multimeter (see *Fix Everything: Multimeter*).

Disassemble a belt-drive washer:

1. Unplug the washer from the electrical receptacle and turn off the water supply to the washer.
2. Remove the retaining screws from the bottom corners, top or back of the console.
3. Turn the console to expose the timer, timer motor, water level switch, water temperature switch, and cycle selector switch.
4. As needed, access the drum by pushing the blade of a putty knife between the washer's top and body to disengage attachment clips. Some units have spring clips on the sides or front of the body.
5. As needed, access the motor, pump, water inlet valve, and drive belt through the back panel by removing screws around the perimeter.

You now can test the *Motor* and other components using a multimeter (see *Fix Everything: Multimeter*).

Service the pump:

1. Unplug the washer and turn off the water supply to the washer.
2. Remove the housing as needed to access the pump (see above).
3. Loosen the hose clamps and remove them from the pump inlet and outlet. Label the hoses for easier reinstallation.
4. Remove the clips securing the pump to the motor.
5. Remove the pump and inspect it for blockage or damage. Clean or replace it as needed.

Test the water level switch assembly:

1. Unplug the washer and access the control console (see above).
2. Mark and remove wires from the water-level switch.
3. Remove the air hose from the switch and gently blow into the switch, listening for a click as the switch moves to the *full* position.
4. While blowing into the switch, test all terminals with a Multimeter (see *Fix Everything: Multimeter*) set to R×1 (resistance times 1). For most switches, two pairs should indicate continuity and one pair should indicate resistance.
5. Stop blowing into the switch and retest the terminals. The pair that previously showed resistance should show continuity and the ones that showed continuity should show resistance.
6. If the test results are different from the description in step 5, replace the water level switch.

Service the water inlet valve:

1. Unplug the washer and shut off the water supply to the washer.

2. Loosen the water hose couplings and remove the hoses.
3. Inspect the filter screen inside each valve port. If it is clogged, replace the valve.

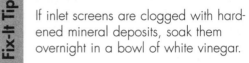

**Fix-It Tip**

If inlet screens are clogged with hardened mineral deposits, soak them overnight in a bowl of white vinegar.

4. As needed, remove the wires from the solenoid terminals and mark them for easier reassembly. Then set a multimeter (see *Fix Everything: Multimeter*) to R×1 (resistance times 1) and touch a probe to each pair of terminals in turn. The meter should indicate between 100 and 1,000 ohms of resistance on each pair. Replace the switch if the test results differ.

**Fix-It Tip**

If you need to adjust the machine's feet, it's better to make them end up shorter rather than longer. The closer the machine is to the floor, the less likely it is to vibrate.

# Water Heater, Electric

Who used up all the hot water?! Maybe nobody. Maybe your electric water heater needs fixing. Once you know how it works and how to diagnose it, *you* can fix it—and save some money. (If your home is not equipped with an electric water heater, see *Water Heater, Gas*.)

## How Does It Work?

A water heater is an apparatus for heating water and then storing it for later use. A residential water heater typically warms water to a temperature between 120° and 140°F. When a hot-water faucet is opened, hot water flows from the top of the tank toward the faucet, and cold water enters the tank to replace it. In an electric water heater, the thermostat senses a drop in the water's temperature and completes an electrical circuit to the heating elements. Electric water heaters usually have both an upper and a lower heating element; each is controlled by a separate thermostat. Once water in the tank reaches the set temperature, the thermostats stop the flow of electricity to the heating elements. In addition, an anode (magnesium) rod attracts impurities in the water that would otherwise attack the metal tank.

## What Can Go Wrong?

Because electric water heaters are simple in operation, few things can go wrong with them, and solutions are relatively easy to figure out. Heating elements and thermostats fail. The high-temperature cutoff may trip. The pressure relief valve may malfunction. Sediment can settle in the tank.

### Softening Hard Water

Many homes are located in areas with hard water. The contaminants in the water supply build up over time, creating a layer of sediment on the bottom of the water tank, hindering the heater's performance and shortening its life. You can slow this process by softening the hard water and by lowering the temperature to 130°F or less. Also, to minimize sediment, purge your tank every few months. Simply drain off 2 or 3 gallons of water from the tank, then let it refill.

## How Can I Identify the Problem?

If there is no hot water, first push the reset button on the high-temperature cutoff; test the thermostats and replace if faulty (see below and *Appliance Controls*). Test the *Heating Element*(s) and replace if faulty (see below).

If there is not enough hot water, adjust the thermostat settings. As needed, reset, test and replace thermostats and heating elements if faulty.

If the water is too hot, adjust the thermostat settings and reset. Test and replace the thermostat or high-limit cutoff (see below).

**Fix-It Tip**

How hot is "too hot" for your water heater? Homes with standard dishwashers typically require a setting of about 120°F, though energy-efficient models preheat incoming water. Homes with an energy-efficient model or without a dishwasher are typically set for about 110°F.

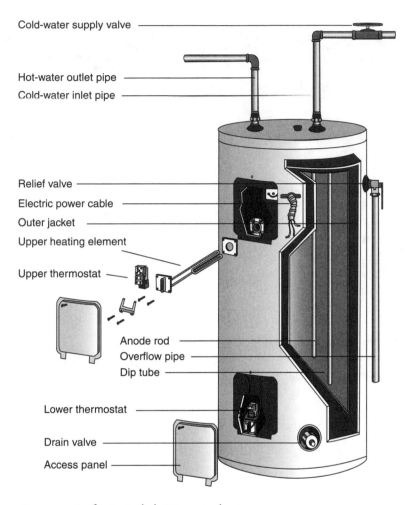

Cold-water supply valve

Hot-water outlet pipe
Cold-water inlet pipe

Relief valve
Electric power cable
Outer jacket
Upper heating element
Upper thermostat

Anode rod
Overflow pipe
Dip tube

Lower thermostat

Drain valve
Access panel

Components of a typical electric water heater.

If the heater leaks, check the pressure relief valve and if the leak persists, replace the valve (see below). Tighten mounting bolts on the heating element gasket and replace if needed.

If the tank is rusted, replace the water heater.

If the heater is noisy, drain and flush the tank (see below). Replace damaged or scale-encrusted elements.

If the hot water is dirty, drain and flush the tank. If the drain valve leaks, tighten or replace it (see below). Note: Regularly draining the tank will prolong the life of your electric water heater.

If your home has hard water, check the anode rod yearly (see below) and replace it if necessary.

## What Parts, Materials, and Tools Do I Need?

Replacement parts are available from local hardware and plumbing supply stores. The tools you will need to fix an electric water heater include these:

- Wrenches
- Screwdrivers
- Multimeter
- Hose
- Pipe tape
- Knife

## What Are the Steps to Fixing It?

Troubleshoot a thermostat:

1. Shut off power to the heater at the *Electrical Service Panel* and post a sign warning others not to turn it on.
2. Unscrew and remove the electric water heater access panel.
3. Using a small screwdriver, turn the thermostat dial counterclockwise to lower the temperature, or clockwise to raise it. If the water heater doesn't maintain the proper temperature, test the thermostat.

> **Caution**
>
> An electric water heater is a 240-volt appliance that can deliver a fatal shock. Always turn off power to the heater at the *Electrical Service Panel* before beginning work, and verify that power has been shut off. Make sure others in the house know not to restore electricity prematurely. If you have any doubt as to whether electricity has been turned off, seek professional assistance.

4. Disconnect one wire to the upper thermostat to test it. Set a multimeter (see *Fix Everything: Multimeter*) to R×1 (resistance times 1) and touch a probe to the thermostat terminals as indicated in the owner's manual. Depending on the model and the terminals tested, the tester should show infinity (*open*) or about 0 (*closed*).
5. Test the lower thermostat in the same manner.
6. If necessary, replace the thermostat. Unscrew it from its mounting and install one of the same model, size, and rating. Once you install it, adjust the thermostat following instructions in your owner's manual.

Test and replace a heating element:

1. Turn off power at the *Electrical Service Panel* and post a sign warning others not to turn it on.
2. Remove the access panel on the electric water heater.
3. Disconnect one of the element wires and set a multimeter (see *Fix Everything: Multimeter*) to R×1000 (resistance times 1,000). Touch one probe to an element mounting bolt and the other to each element terminal screw, in turn. If the tester displays anything but infinity (*open* circuit), replace the element.
4. If necessary, set the multimeter to R×1 and touch the probes to the terminal screws. If there is any resistance reading at all (*closed* circuit), then the element is good. If not, replace it. Both upper and lower elements are tested in the same manner.
5. To remove the element, first drain the heater.
6. Disconnect the remaining element wire. Remove the mounting bolts holding the element in place. Remove the element.
7. Replace the heating element with one of the same model, shape, and rating. Make sure you also replace any installation gaskets.

Test and replace a high-limit cutoff:

1. Disconnect power to the heater at the *Electrical Service Panel* and post a sign warning others not to turn it on.
2. Remove the upper access panel and push the reset button.
3. Replace the access panel and turn the power back on. If the water is hot, the reset was the problem. If not, you'll need to turn the power off again and reopen the access panel.
4. Use a multimeter (see *Fix Everything: Multimeter*) to test the cutoff terminals for continuity. If faulty, replace with an exact-replacement part.

Drain a tank:

1. Shut off power at the *Electrical Service Panel* and post a sign warning others not to turn it on.
2. Close the cold-water supply valve and open a hot-water faucet somewhere in the house (to speed draining).
3. Attach a garden hose to the drain valve and run it outside the house.
4. Open the drain valve and allow all water to drain out.
5. To refill the tank, close the drain valve tightly and open the cold-water supply valve. Also open a nearby hot-water faucet. When a steady stream of water flows from that faucet, the tank is full and the faucet can be closed.
6. Once the tank is full, turn the electrical power back on.

Test and replace a relief valve:

1. Lift the spring lever on the valve to fill a small cup. Check the cup for sediment.
2. If no water spurts out, or if water continues to drip after the valve is released, replace the valve.

3. Cut power at the *Electrical Service Panel* and post a sign warning others not to turn it on. Close the cold-water supply valve.
4. Drain a few gallons of water from the tank.
5. Unscrew and remove the discharge pipe if used.
6. Loosen the relief valve with a pipe wrench, then remove the valve by hand.
7. Apply pipe tape to the threads of the replacement valve and screw it into the tank by hand. Tighten it with a pipe wrench. Screw the discharge pipe (if any) into the valve outlet.
8. Refill the water heater and restore electrical power.

Replace a drain valve:

1. Shut off power at the *Electrical Service Panel* and post a sign warning others not to turn it on.
2. Close the cold-water supply valve and drain the water heater completely (see above).
3. Unscrew the drain valve with a pipe wrench.
4. Replace the drain valve with an identical unit, wrapping the end with pipe tape.
5. Refill the tank and restore electricity.

**Fix-It Tip**

Need to get replacement parts? Remember to take the old water-heater parts, the heater brand, and the model number with you when you buy replacements. It may save you a trip.

# Water Heater, Gas

Who used all the hot water?! Maybe your home's gas water heater just isn't keeping up with demand. Or maybe it has "issues," such as a pilot light that won't stay lit or a bunch of gunk that comes out with the hot water. No problem—because you are a member in good standing of the Fix-It Club!

## How Does It Work?

A water heater is an apparatus for heating and storing hot water. A water heater typically warms water to a temperature between 120° and 140°F. When a hot-water faucet is opened, hot water flows from the top of the tank toward the faucet, and cold water enters via the dip tube to replace it. The fuel for heating the water heater can be natural gas or propane, or it can be electricity (see *Water Heater, Electric*).

As the water temperature inside the tank drops below the setpoint, the thermostat opens a valve that sends gas to the burner, where it is ignited by a pilot flame or electric spark. Combustion gases are vented from the burner chamber through the flue and its heat-retaining baffle, then out the draft hood and vent. If the temperature or water pressure rises too high inside the water heater, a relief valve opens to prevent the tank from exploding.

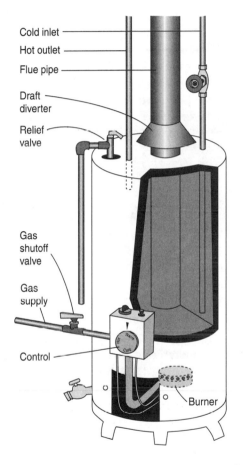

A natural or propane gas water heater uses a burner to heat water in the tank for distribution throughout the home.

## What Can Go Wrong?

The pilot light may be out or may not stay lit. There may not be enough hot water, or the water may be too hot. The water heater may leak or be noisy, or the hot water may be dirty.

> **Fix-It Tip**
>
> A problem with your water heater may be due to overwork, not mechanics. If your water heater holds less than 15 gallons per family member (tank volume is stamped on a metal plate affixed to most water heaters), consider a larger unit or staggering your use of hot water.

## How Can I Identify the Problem?

If there is no hot water, check to see if the pilot light is out and relight it if it is (see below).

If the pilot light won't stay lit, clean the pilot orifice (see below); tighten the thermocouple connections (see below), and replace a faulty thermocouple (see below).

If there is not enough hot water, check and reset the temperature control if necessary.

If the water is too hot, check and reset the temperature control. If it is set too high, have a faulty thermostat serviced professionally.

If the heater leaks, operate the pressure relief valve and if the leak persists and the temperature is okay, have the valve replaced.

If the tank is rusted, replace the water heater.

If the heater is noisy, drain and flush the tank (see below) and refill.

If the hot water is dirty, drain and flush the tank and refill (see below).

If the relief valve or the drain valve leaks, test and replace as needed (see below) Regular maintenance of the flue and vent (see below), and regular draining of the tank (see below) will prolong the life of your gas water heater.

If you have hard water, check the anode rod yearly (see below) and replace if necessary.

> **Fix-It Tip**
>
> Do you live in an area with hard water? If so, you know that minerals in the water supply can build up, creating a layer of sediment on the bottom of a water tank, hindering performance and shortening the system's life. Besides softening the water (see *Water Softener*) fed to the heater, you can minimize damage by lowering the temperature setpoint to 130°F or less.

## What Parts, Materials, and Tools Do I Need?

You can get replacement parts—and even a replacement gas water heater—from plumbing suppliers, large hardware stores, and home centers. The tools you'll need to fix your water heater include these:

- Pipe wrench
- Open-end wrenches
- Thin copper wire
- Plumber's pipe tape
- Soft brush
- Vacuum cleaner

## What Are the Steps to Fixing It?

Light a pilot light:

1. Remove the burner access panel. Read and follow lighting directions on or near the cover.
2. To light a pilot that has blown out, turn the temperature-control dial to its lowest setting and the gas-control knob to *off*. Wait at least five minutes for the gas to clear.

| | |
|---|---|
| **Caution** | If you smell a gas odor for more than a couple of minutes, close the gas-shutoff valve supplying the water heater, open a door or window to ventilate the room, and call the gas company for service. |

3. Tightly twist a piece of paper and light it. Turn the gas-control knob to *pilot*. Depress the reset button (or the gas-control knob if there is no reset button) while holding the burning paper near the pilot burner. The pilot may be hard to reach.
4. If the pilot fails to light after a few seconds, close the gas-shutoff valve and call the gas company. If it lights, continue pressing the reset button or knob for one minute, then release it.
5. If the pilot stays lit, turn the gas-control knob to *on*; the main burner should light when the temperature-control dial is set above 120°.
6. If the pilot does not stay lit, turn the gas-control knob to *off*. Check that the thermocouple's tip is positioned so the pilot's flame touches it, and tighten the nut holding it in place. Try lighting it once more. If the flame goes out again, replace the thermocouple.

Clean the pilot orifice:

1. Shut the gas cock (refer to the heater's owner's manual for specific instructions).
2. Disconnect the burner assembly lines at the gas control valve and remove the burner assembly.
3. Carefully probe the pilot light orifice with a thin wire; do not use a needle or paper clip, which can damage the orifice. Vacuum out any dislodged debris.

Service a thermocouple:

1. Check the thermocouple for loose connections at the control valve. The thermocouple is located near the pilot flame.
2. Make sure that the thermocouple's bulb tip is held in the pilot flame. If necessary, carefully tighten the nut, but don't overtighten it.

Replace a thermocouple:

1. Turn the gas-control knot to *off* and close the gas-shutoff valve.
2. Loosen the nut that secures the thermocouple lead to the control unit, then unscrew it by hand.
3. Remove the old thermocouple from the control unit.

| | |
|---|---|
| **Fix-It Tip** | When you buy replacements, take the old water-heater parts, as well as the brand and model number, with you. |

4. Push the tip of the new thermocouple into the pilot bracket clip as far as it will go and tighten the fitting.
5. Screw the nut at the end of the lead to the control unit.
6. Open the gas-shutoff valve and relight the pilot. If the pilot light goes out, close the gas-shutoff valve and call a professional.

Test and replace a relief valve:

> **Caution**
>
> The relief valve spews hot water. Make sure you use caution when working on this component. Before replacing it, turn off the hot water system and let it cool down.

1. Lift the spring lever on the valve for a few seconds to clear the valve of mineral scale.
2. If no water spurts out, or if water continues to drip after the valve is released, replace the valve.
3. Turn the gas-control knob to *off* and close the gas-shutoff valve. Close the cold-water supply valve.
4. Drain a gallon or more of water from the tank.
5. Unscrew and remove the discharge pipe if there is one.
6. Unscrew the relief valve from the tank with a pipe wrench.
7. Apply pipe tape to the threads of the new valve.
8. Screw the relief valve into the tank by hand, then tighten with a pipe wrench.
9. Screw the discharge pipe (if any) into the valve outlet.
10. Refill the water heater and light the pilot. If the valve leaks, have a plumber check for high water pressure in the house.

Replace a drain valve:

1. Turn the gas-control knob to *off* and close the gas-shutoff valve.
2. Close the cold-water supply valve and drain the water heater completely (see above).
3. Use a pipe wrench to unscrew the base of the drain valve.
4. Purchase an exact or better replacement drain valve.
5. Wrap pipe tape around the threaded end of the valve and screw it into the coupling.
6. Apply pipe tape to the pipe threads that emerge from the water heater.
7. Screw the coupling and valve onto the nipple and tighten.
8. Tighten the valve so that it faces down toward the floor.
9. Refill the tank and relight the pilot.

Test and maintain the flue and vent:

1. Set the water heater at a high temperature to light the burner and wait 10 minutes.
2. Hold a lighted match at the edge of the draft hood. A properly working vent will draw the flame under the edge of the hood. When you blow out the match, the hood should suck up the smoke. If the flame or smoke is blown away from the hood, the vent may be blocked.
3. To disassemble a blocked vent, first turn off the water heater and close the gas-shutoff valve; let the burner, draft hood, and vent cool.

4. Remove the burner access panels and cover the burner and floor with paper to catch soot and debris.

5. Mark the vent sections for reassembly.

6. Remove the draft hood from the top of the tank and carefully clean it with a wire brush.

7. Replace any rusted or damaged ductwork.

8. With the vent removed, lift the baffle from the flue and clean it of soot with a wire brush.

9. Reinstall the baffle, draft hood, and vent, then vacuum the inside of the combustion chamber.

10. Clean the burner and its ports with a small brush (such as an old toothbrush).

11. Relight the pilot. Test the vent with a match as in steps 1 and 2. If the flame or smoke is not drawn up, there may be a blockage in the main chimney; call for service.

Drain a hot water tank:

1. Turn the gas-control knob to *off* and close the gas-shutoff valve.

2. Close the cold-water supply valve and open a hot-water faucet in the house to speed draining.

3. Attach a garden hose to the drain valve and run it outside to a drain. If the heater is in the basement, you may need to run the hose to or through a sump pump.

4. Open the drain valve and allow the tank to drain.

5. Once done, close the drain valve, open the cold-water supply valve, and open any nearby hot-water faucet. When a steady stream of water flows from that faucet, the tank is full; close the hot-water faucet.

6. Once the tank is full, turn on the gas and relight the pilot.

# Water Softener

In many parts of the United States, a water softener isn't a luxury—it's a necessity. Water supplies (city and well) often include minerals and salts that not only taste bad, but also can damage pipes, plumbing fixtures, and other devices. If your home has a water softener, you know that they are virtually trouble-free. Here's how to fix their few quirks.

## How Does It Work?

A water softener is an appliance designed to remove minerals from water by means of an ion-exchange process. As water flows through a bed of sodium-impregnated resin beads, mineral ions are drawn from the water to the beads. The sodium ions are added to the water. The water softener unit recharges the beads with brine or a potassium chloride solution. Some water softeners have separate tanks for the sodium resin and the brine, while others have the resin tank *inside* the brine tank.

Full-home water softeners typically are installed right where the main water line enters the house. For economy, some systems bypass faucets and fixtures that don't need soft water, such as toilets and exterior water systems. Depending on what system you have and who owns it (you or a leasing company), your water softening system may be maintained by a service company. All you need to do to get soft water is turn on the tap—and pay the bill.

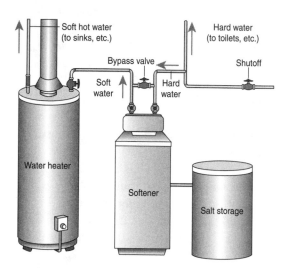

Components of a typical water softener system.

## What Can Go Wrong?

Most water softeners generally require little maintenance aside from periodic salt refill. If you have a water softener service, responsibility for the equipment is with the supplier. If you own the equipment, however, there are a few things you can do to maintain and repair it. The motor can break down, the water may not be softened, and the brine may not flow.

## How Can I Identify the Problem?

If the motor is not operating, make sure power is on at the *Electrical Receptacle*. If the unit is not under a service contract, test the *Motor*.

If the water is not softened, flush the tank (see below) and add salt. Reset the timer to increase regeneration frequency.

If the iron content of the water is too high, check and, if needed, replace the filter. On some models, purchase and use salt with iron-control agents. Make sure that the bypass valve is set to the *service* position and that water is not being lost to plumbing leaks.

If the brine is not flowing, flush out the brine line, then check and replace the injector and filter screen (see below). Check the brine line for kinks or damage. Make sure the brine line pressure is set according to the owner's manual.

## What Parts, Materials, and Tools Do I Need?

Replacement parts are available from the manufacturer and aftermarket suppliers (see *Fix-It Resources*), as well as from most plumbing supplies and larger hardware stores and home centers. The tools you will need to fix a water softener include these:

- Wrenches
- Shop vacuum
- Canned air
- Hose
- Syringe or turkey baster
- Paper clip or small wire
- Soapy water
- Small brush

## What Are the Steps to Fixing It?

Clean the injector:

1. Turn the water softener control to the bypass mode (so the main water line does not run through the softener). On some units, you also may need to disconnect the unit from the electrical source.

2. Unscrew the softener injector cap and remove the screen and injector nozzle. You may need the owner's manual to determine where these components are located on your model.

3. Remove and clean the screen with warm soapy water, then rinse in clear water. If it is damaged, replace the screen.

4. Clean the nozzle with canned air, a small wire, or a paper clip.

5. Reassemble and test the unit.

Flush the brine line:

1. Turn the water softener control to the bypass mode. On some units, you also may need to disconnect the unit from the electrical source.

2. Loosen the brine line fittings at the injector housing and salt tank with a wrench, then remove the brine line.

3. To clear a clog, use a large syringe or a turkey baster to inject warm water into the line.

Clean the brine compartment:

1. Turn the water softener control to the bypass mode. If suggested by the manufacturer, disconnect the unit from the electrical source.

2. Wash the brine intake with water and a small brush.

3. Remove the brine tank cover and dump out the brine with any salt residue. Alternatively, use a wet-dry or shop vacuum.

4. Flush the tank clean with clean water using a hose.

5. Refill with salt as recommended by the manufacturer.

# Whirlpool

There's nothing like a warm, relaxing whirlpool or spa bath at the end of a difficult day. It washes troubles away. The *last* thing you want is a whirlpool, spa, or hot tub that *doesn't* work. It's a good thing you can fix it!

## How Does It Work?

What's the difference between a whirlpool, a spa, and a hot tub? A whirlpool is a therapeutic bath tub, drained after every use, that uses water jets to soothe the body. A spa is a large soaking tub with water jets and a built-in heater; water stays in the tub between uses. A hot tub is like a spa except that it typically doesn't have water jets. Other than that, whirlpools are usually installed in an indoor bathroom while spas and hot tubs are either outside or in a special room because they are too large for most bathrooms.

Whirlpools and spas have adjustable water jets that massage the bather with streams of aerated water. A pump and a motor force water through the jet openings.

Because spas and hot tubs retain water between uses, the water is treated with chemicals to sanitize the water and maintain a comfortable pH level. Water treatment can be manual or automatic.

**Fix-It Tip**

Don't forget to clean and periodically replace a spa's inline filter. Check the owner's manual and/or your local spa shop for recommendations and replacement filters.

## What Can Go Wrong?

Whirlpools and spas may not start, jets may not work properly, and water may drain slowly. Spas and hot tubs may have faulty water chemistry. Any unit may leak.

## How Can I Identify the Problem?

If the unit won't start, make sure power is on at the *Electrical Receptacle* or the *Electrical Service Panel*. Then test the pump and motor (see *Swimming Pool* and *Motor*). Check for and repair broken wires or loose or corroded terminals. If necessary, have the pump switch control tested and serviced professionally.

If the jets do not work, clear a blocked water intake of hair and other particles (see below) or replace a broken jet (see below).

If the water in your spa or hot tub is too hot or too cold, check to see if the high-limit reset switch has been tripped and, if needed, reset it. Adjust the thermostat setting and have the thermostat serviced if the problem persists. If necessary, test and replace a faulty *Heating Element* (see below).

If the water level drops quickly or leakage appears under the unit, examine the pump and replace a leaking union gasket (see below) or seal (see *Swimming Pool*).

If the jets surge or emit water unevenly, check and replace a leaking pump union gasket.

If water drains slowly from the unit, check the drain for clogs and remove as needed.

If the water is cloudy or smells bad, or if there is green coloration on the spa, test and adjust the water chemistry (see *Swimming Pool*).

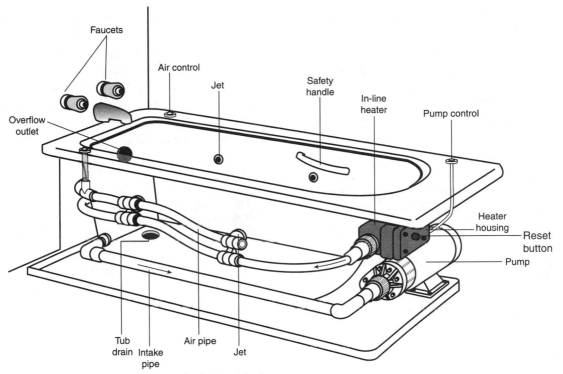

Faucets

Air control

Jet

Safety handle

In-line heater

Pump control

Overflow outlet

Heater housing

Reset button

Pump

Tub drain  Intake pipe  Air pipe  Jet

Components of a typical whirlpool bath.

If a wooden hot tub leaks between the staves, tighten the bands around the tub. If the tub still leaks, plug the leak with silicone caulk.

## What Parts, Materials, and Tools Do I Need?

Replacement parts are available from the manufacturer and aftermarket suppliers (see *Fix-It Resources*). Also check with local pool, spa, and tub suppliers. The tools you will need to fix a whirlpool, spa, or hot tub include these:

- Screwdrivers
- Wrenches
- Garden hose
- Toothbrush
- Laundry detergent

## What Are the Steps to Fixing It?

Clear a blocked water intake:

1. Twist-off or unscrew the intake cover.
2. Clean the intake cover with an old toothbrush and powdered laundry detergent. Rinse any soap residue from the cover before reinstalling.
3. Replace the cover.

Replace a jet:

1. Identify the damaged or inoperative jet and make sure it requires replacement.
2. Follow the owner's manual instructions for removing the old jet. Some twist out by hand, while others require a special wrench.
3. Find an exact replacement jet (through a pool or spa supplier) and install the new jet.

Test and replace a heating element (spas and hot tubs):

1. Unplug the unit from the electrical receptacle or shut it off at the *Electrical Service Panel.*
2. Remove the screws holding the heater housing cover in place.
3. Mark and disconnect the element leads.
4. Set a multimeter (see *Fix Everything: Multimeter*) to R×1 (resistance times 1) and clip the probes to the terminals. If the meter doesn't read low ohms (low, not infinite resistance), replace the element using the following instructions.
5. Drain all water from the unit and dry it out as well as possible. You may need a garden hose to drain water to the home's exterior.
6. Disconnect wires to the heating element and related sensors and switches as needed to remove the element.
7. Pull out the old element, the mounting plate, and mounting gaskets.
8. Attach the replacement element to the mounting plate.
9. Install the new element and remount all other parts.

Replace a pump union gasket:

1. Refer to the owner's manual for the location, size, and replacement part number for the pump union gasket. (Some units require that all water first be drained.)
2. Unscrew the fitting and remove the gasket.
3. Purchase and install the union gasket following the manufacturer's instructions.

**Fix-It Tip**

It's relatively easy to sanitize a whirlpool, a job that should be done monthly. Fill the unit and add a solution of 1 cup of bleach and 1/8 cup of liquid dishwashing soap to the water. Let the jets run for 5 to 10 minutes to circulate the solution and clean the jets and tub surface. Drain and rinse.

# Window

What can you do if your window to the world is broken? Yes, you can fix it! Most window problems, even broken glass, can easily be fixed—once you know how it works and the steps to making common window repairs. Let's get started.

## How Does It Work?

A window is an opening in a wall of a building for admission of light and air. A window typically has casements or sashes that contain transparent glass or plastic. Many newer windows are double paned, offering increased energy efficiency.

The main types of windows are double hung, casement, awning, sliding, and stationary. Double-hung windows are the most common in homes. A double-hung window is designed so that the lower portion of the window opens up in front of the upper portion. A casement window has hinges on one side that allow the window to swing out. An awning window is hinged hear the top and swings out at the bottom so it can be open even in rain. A louvered window is similar to an awning window except it has more panes and hinges. A sliding window slides from side to side on metal or plastic rollers that sit in channels along the top and bottom of the window frame. A stationary window does not open.

## What Can Go Wrong?

The two most common problems with windows are sticking casements and broken glass. Casement window mechanisms get dirty and sometimes break. Older windows often let in too much air from outside and need weatherstripping. The biggest problem with skylights is leaks.

## How Can I Identify the Problem?

If a window sticks, cleaning and lubricating (see below) may be all it needs, especially if it has an aluminum frame.

If a casement window or skylight opening mechanism does not operate easily or at all, you can replace it (see below).

If a window lets drafts in, you can add weatherstripping (see below).

If a window pane breaks, you can replace it (see below).

If a double-pane window is broken or the airtight seal between panes has moisture in it, the window will probably require professional repair, but it may still be under warranty.

If a skylight leaks, check for leaks around the flashing (see *Roof*) and use roofing cement to plug any cracks where the roof and skylight meet.

## What Parts, Materials, and Tools Do I Need?

Replacement parts are available from glass shops, hardware stores, home centers and other local retailers. The tools you will need to fix a window include these:

- Hammer
- Nail set
- Silicone lubricant
- Paraffin wax
- Mineral spirits
- Screwdrivers
- Roofing cement
- Weatherstripping
- Small wire brush

Awning window

Bow window

Sliding patio door

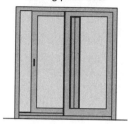

Double hung window

Bay window

Swinging patio door

Casement window

Gliding window

Popular types of windows.

- Screwdrivers
- Putty knife or chisel
- Vacuum
- Glazing points
- Glazing compound

## What Are the Steps to Fixing It?

Clean and lubricate a window:

1. Clean the bottom, side, and top tracks or channels with a rag, small wire brush, and/or vacuum.
2. If rollers, glides, and other small parts are dirty, clean them with mineral spirits.
3. Spray the tracks with a silicone lubricant or rub them with paraffin wax, cleaning up any excess.

Service a casement window or skylight opening mechanism:

1. Open the window halfway and remove the screws that hold the mechanism to the frame or the sill.
2. Remove the extension arm from the sash by sliding it along the sash until the tip reaches the access slot.
3. Push down the extension arm and pull the tip through the slot.
4. Pull the mechanism out of the slot, loosen the handle setscrew, and remove the handle.
5. Check the teeth under the handle and replace the operating mechanism if the teeth are stripped.
6. Reinstall and test the mechanism.

Weatherstrip a double-hung window:

1. Cut a length of weatherstripping equal to the width of the window sash.
2. Remove the backing and apply the weatherstripping to the bottom of the lower sash as directed by the manufacturer.
3. Cut two lengths of weatherstrip an inch longer than the height of the lower sash.
4. Apply those strips to the lower half of the interior side channels in the window frame as directed by the manufacturer.
5. Drop the sash halfway so its bottom rail is exposed.
6. Apply the weatherstrip to the inside edge of its bottom rail.
7. Lower both sashes and apply weatherstrip to the top of the sash.
8. Cut two lengths of weatherstripping an inch longer than the height of the upper sash, and apply the strips to the upper half of the exterior side channels in the frame.

**Fix-It Tip**

Weatherstripping requires a clean surface for it to adhere. Before applying self-stick weatherstripping, wash, rinse, and dry the surfaces to which it will be applied.

Replace a window pane:

1. Carefully remove the broken glass from the pane.
2. Use a putty knife or chisel to remove any putty left in the channel.
3. If you are installing glass in a wood window pane, first clean the channel and coat it with linseed oil. Apply a small amount of glazing compound to cushion the glass.
4. Place the new glass in the pane and carefully seal it into the glazing compound.

5. Place a glazier point every 3 inches along the pane to retain the glass.

6. Apply a small amount of glazing compound around the pane to hold the glass to the wood. If you are replacing glass in an aluminum frame, you will use a rubber gasket (available from hardware stores) to hold the glass in place.

7. Remove any excess compound with a putty knife. Allow the compound to dry for seven days and *Paint* as needed.

**Fix-It Tip**

Clean a glass skylight in the same way you clean any glass window. Clean a polycarbonate plastic skylight with a mild soap or detergent solution. Use a weak ammonia solution to clean an acrylic plastic skylight.

# Window Blind

A window treatment is a movable window covering that also serves a decorative function. Window treatments include blinds as well as *Window Shade* and *Window Curtain and Drape*. Here's how to fix window blinds.

## How Does It Work?

A window blind is a slatted window treatment that can be adjusted to admit varying amounts of light. Window blinds include venetian, mini, micro, and vertical blinds. They all work in about the same way. A tape or string ladder holds all the slats together. A cord or wand connects to a pulley in the headbox. The pulley uses a worm gear to rotate the tube and simultaneously change the angle of all slats. A lift cord threads through each slat and over a pulley at the end of the blind. Pulling on the lift cord raises the blind. The lift cord is adjustable so that the blind raises and lowers evenly. A vertical blind works in the same manner except that the blinds are vertical rather than horizontal.

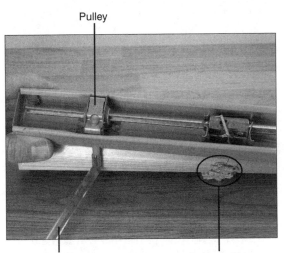

Pulley

Wand

String ladder

Components of a typical window blind operating system.

## What Can Go Wrong?

The tape or string ladders that hold a blind together can break. A blind can stick going up or down or may not go up evenly.

## How Can I Identify the Problem?

If the tape or string ladders on the blind wear thin or break, you can replace them (see below).

When buying a new window blind, purchase an extra set of tape or string ladders or cords for it at the same time. You'll eventually need them. To make sure they don't get lost or forgotten, you can tape the package to an unseen edge of the blind. Alternatively, have a replacement-part drawer or box where you keep such things.

If the tilting mechanism balks, look for cord threads or dirt in the worm gear and clean it out.

## What Parts, Materials, and Tools Do I Need?

Replacement parts are available from the manufacturer and aftermarket suppliers (see *Fix-It Resources*), and from local window treatment stores and larger home centers. You need only a few tools to work on window blinds, including these:

- Screwdrivers
- Wrenches
- Scissors

## What Are the Steps to Fixing It?

Replace a tape or string ladder (varies by model):

1. Remove the blind from the window and place it on a flat surface.
2. Remove the clips that hold the strings or tapes to the bottom bar.
3. Remove the end caps and slide apart the bottom bar to expose the ends of the lift cord and ladder tapes.
4. Remove the knots through the keyhole openings to free the lift cord. Undo or cut the knots to remove the bar.
5. Pull the adjustment loop until the ends of the tilt cord reach the headbox.
6. Make a knot in the lift-cord ends so they cannot pass through the headbox.
7. Pull the slats from the ladder tapes and undo the tapes. Fold over the ends of the new tape, and staple them to create a hem. Loop the hem over the bars or clips.
8. Remove the knots in the ends of the lift cord. Run the new lift cord through the headbox along the same path as the old cord.
9. Thread the tilt cord through the slats, feeding it along alternate sides of the tape rungs.
10. Attach the ladder tapes and lift cord to the bottom bar.
11. Install the equalizing buckle over the adjustment loop and adjust it for evenness.
12. Rehang the blind.

Venetian blind service can be very expensive, especially if you don't have an experienced service person nearby and must return the unit to the factory. A $1 cord may cost $75 to install—unless you do it yourself.

# Window Curtain and Drape

Curtains and drapes are multifunctional. They not only provide privacy, they also decorate the view. And they help to keep a home warm in cold weather and cool in hot weather. The wide variety of materials, colors, and designs available can serve all functions well—until they are damaged or fall from place. Here's how to quickly get them back to work without obvious damage.

## How Does It Work?

Curtains and drapes are fabric coverings for windows. Curtains are usually made of lightweight, sheer fabric and include a casing or pocket to insert the support rod across the top. Drapes are usually made of heavier fabric, often lined, have pleated tops, and are hung with hooks.

## What Can Go Wrong?

Curtain and drape fabric can be torn. Hems come undone. Fabric can become soiled. The hardware can pull out of the wall. Cords ravel and break.

## How Can I Identify the Problem?

If a curtain or drape has a minor tear or a hem comes unstitched, you can resew it (see *Fix Everything: Sewing*).

If a curtain becomes soiled, you can use spot remover or oxygen cleaner to wash it.

If a drape becomes soiled, you can spot clean it with an oxygen cleaner, take it to the dry cleaner, or try one of the home dry-cleaning solutions. Vacuuming drapes once a week with an upholstery brush will extend the time between dry cleanings.

If curtain or drape hardware comes loose from the wall, replace the small nails with longer nails or screws.

If the hardware is bent or otherwise damaged, replace it.

If a drape won't open when you pull the cord, check to see if it has slipped out of a pulley, and that the hangers or other components aren't dirty or bent.

If a cord ravels or breaks, you can replace it with new cord by using the old cord as a guide for installing the new one. You can purchase new cord at window treatment stores or from larger sewing and craft stores.

## What Parts, Materials, and Tools Do I Need?

Replacement parts are available at local hardware stores and home improvement centers. The tools you will need to fix curtains and drapes include:

- Screwdrivers
- Hammer
- Sewing supplies
- Oxygen cleaner (or whatever cleaning product or method is recommended on the care label)

# Window Shade

Window shades aren't as popular as they once were, but they still cover millions of windows—except when the shades are broken. Here's how to fix them.

## How Does It Work?

A window shade is a flexible covering attached to a roller mounted at the top of a window, designed to regulate the light or view. A window shade uses a hollow roller with a coiled spring inside. Pulling down on the shade puts more tension on the spring. Once you stop pulling, a ratchet and flat pin at one end of the roller holds the tension until you release it. The other end of the roller has a round stationary pin that turns freely in its bracket.

A roll-up blind is a combination of a venetian blind (see *Window Blind*) and a roller shade. A roll-up blind has slats and pulleys that move only up and down; there is no tilting mechanism.

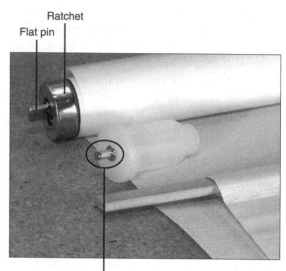

Ratchet
Flat pin

Stationary pin (at other end)

Components of a typical window shade mechanism.

## What Can Go Wrong?

Window shades are relatively simple in operation and easy to fix. The tension on the roller may be too loose or too tight. The shade may not stay down. The shade may be stuck all the way up or down. The shade may fall out of the bracket. The shade cloth may tear.

## How Can I Identify the Problem?

If the shade goes up too quickly or with a bang, the tension on the spring may be too tight (see below).

**Fix-It Tip**

When purchasing a new window shade, look for one that is made to last and won't require frequent service.

If the shade rolls up too slowly, the spring may be too loose (see below).

If the shade won't raise, you may need to adjust a fully uncoiled spring (see below).

If the shade won't pull down, the spring may be locked in the coil (see below).

If the shade doesn't stay down, the ratchet may not be locking (see below).

If the shade falls off the brackets, reposition the mounting brackets closer together.

If a shade tears, you can replace the cloth (see below) or patch it with a piece of clear tape.

If a roll-up blind cord fails, you can replace it (see below).

## What Parts, Materials, and Tools Do I Need?

Replacement parts are available from larger hardware stores and home centers as well as window treatment retailers. You also can buy replacement parts from the manufacturer and aftermarket suppliers (see *Fix-It Resources*). The tools you will need to fix a window shade include these:

- Screwdrivers
- Pliers
- T-square
- Scissors
- Staple gun
- Brush or canned air
- Penetrating oil

## What Are the Steps to Fixing It?

Loosen spring tension:

1. Roll up the shade and lift the roller out of the brackets.
2. Unroll the shade halfway by hand. Replace the roller in the brackets.
3. Repeat if necessary until the tension seems correct.

Tighten spring tension:

1. Pull the shade down halfway. Lift the roller out of the brackets.
2. Roll up the shade by hand. Replace the roller in the brackets.
3. Repeat if necessary until the tension seems correct.

Adjust a fully uncoiled spring:

1. Remove the roller from the brackets.
2. Unroll the shade halfway. Use pliers to turn the flat pin until you feel tension, then back off so the pawl (latch that allows movement in only one direction) hooks onto the ratchet.
3. Loosen or tighten spring tension as necessary using the directions above.

Release a spring that is locked in the coil:

1. Remove the roller from the brackets.
2. Use pliers to grip the pin and twist it clockwise to free the pawl. Release it quickly to unwind the coil.
3. Loosen or tighten the spring tension as necessary using the directions above.

Make the ratchet lock:

1. Remove the roller from the brackets.
2. Remove the metal end cap.
3. Use a brush or canned air to remove dust from the pawl and ratchet. Lubricate these parts with penetrating oil.

Replace roll-up shade fabric:

1. Remove the shade from its brackets and unroll it.
2. Remove the old fabric.
3. Use a T-square to align the fabric on the roller.
4. Staple or tape the new fabric to the roller.
5. Loosen or tighten the spring tension as necessary using the directions above.
6. Replace the shade in its brackets.

Replace a roll-up blind cord:

1. Cut the knots above the headbox and remove the old cord, saving the buckle.
2. Hang the blind to full length.
3. Feed the new cord through the headbox and knot it.
4. Drop the cord down behind the blind and pull it underneath to the front.
5. Feed the cord up through the blind, through the roller pulley, across the headbox, and through the locking pulley.
6. Bring the cord back through the pulley, down the front and up behind the blind. Knot the cord at the top.
7. Slide the adjustment buckle over the loop and adjust it.

**Fix-It Tip**

If you can't fix a window shade and need to replace it, remove any reusable parts for future repairs.

# Yard Trimmer

Call it a weed whacker, a weed eater, or a goat-on-a-stick, it's all the same: a yard trimmer. They are increasingly popular, especially with people who live in and daily battle nature. The better models require little maintenance, but the smaller ones can be sufficiently frustrating to make you trade them in for a scythe—almost. Here's how the Fix-It Club takes care of them.

## How Does It Work?

A yard trimmer is an electric- or gas engine-powered tool for cutting weeds and for trimming and edging grass. Yard trimmers come in a variety of sizes, designs, and power systems. String trimmers cut through vegetation with a short, rapidly spinning length of thick monofilament line. Heavy-duty trimmers use rotating plastic or metal blades. Power is provided by electrical cords, electric batteries, or small gas engines. The more power, the more it can cut.

---

**Fix-It Tip**

The first rule of using a yard trimmer is to use only monofilament line specified by the manufacturer of your trimmer. Make sure it is of the same size and stiffness.

---

## What Can Go Wrong?

The most common problem with a string trimmer is that the unit runs out of string. The string may also be twisted or loose on the spool. The cutting head may be dirty or the head outlet guide may be bent. An electric trimmer's power cord, switch, or motor may fail. A gas trimmer's engine may be faulty. The air filter or exhaust port may be blocked. The trimmer may need lubrication and cooling fins or air passages may be blocked. A cordless trimmer's battery or charger may be faulty.

## How Can I Identify the Problem?

If the trimmer doesn't cut, refill the monofilament line spool or replace the blades (see below). Inspect the cutting head and replace any damaged parts.

If the line doesn't advance or breaks during use, rewind loose line on the spool, clean a dirty cutting head, reshape a bent head outlet guide with pliers, and smooth the edges with sandpaper. As needed, replace a badly damaged head (see steps 1 through 3 of *Install monofilament line* below).

If an electric trimmer doesn't operate, make sure power is on at the *Electrical Receptacle*, and test the *Electrical Cord*, switch (see *Appliance Controls*), and *Motor*.

If an electric trimmer lacks power or overheats, make sure you are using an outdoor extension with the proper capacity for the trimmer (check your owner's manual). As needed, test the *Motor*.

If a gas trimmer doesn't work, first check the owner's manual to make sure all controls are set properly. Check the *Small Engine* that powers the unit.

If a gas trimmer stalls or runs intermittently, check the fuel lines for blockage and check the air filter or exhaust port for blockage. Check the *Small Engine* that powers the unit.

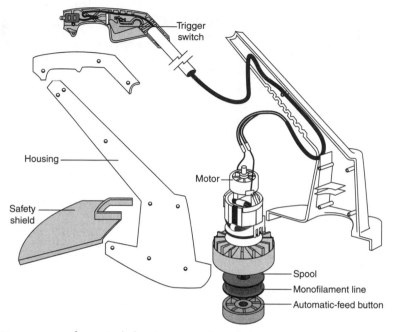

Components of a typical electric-powered yard trimmer.

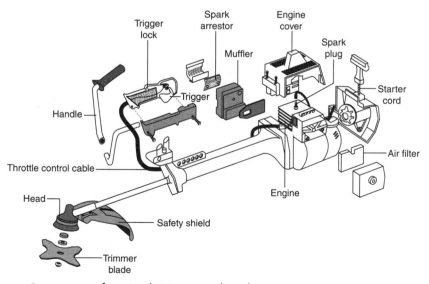

Components of a typical gas-powered yard trimmer.

If a gas trimmer overheats, check your owner's manual for lubrication points on the unit's *Small Engine* and remove any debris that may be blocking the cooling fins or air passages.

If a cordless trimmer doesn't work, check its battery and *Battery Recharger*.

> **Caution**
>
> Always inspect the yard trimmer before each use. Cracked or damaged parts can shatter and cause personal injury. And always wear eye goggles to protect your eyes.

## What Parts, Materials, and Tools Do I Need?

Replacement parts are available from lawn equipment suppliers and the manufacturer (see *Fix-It Resources*). Most hardware stores and home improvement centers have a supply of monofilament line and common replacement heads. The tools you will need to fix a yard trimmer include these:

- Screwdrivers
- Wrenches
- Multimeter

## What Are the Steps to Fixing It?

Access trimmer components:

1. Remove all housing screws and place them in a container for easier reinstallation.
2. Dismantle the housing, making sure you don't lose any parts.
3. Remove the trigger and other internal parts to check for wear and replace as needed. Heavy-duty trimmers will include a filter and other components.

Install monofilament line:

1. Press the locking tab on the side of the spool as you rotate the locking ring in the direction of marking arrows.
2. Remove the locking ring and inspect it, replacing it if damaged.
3. Remove the automatic-feed (or tap) button and inspect it for cracks or other damage, replacing as needed. Clean debris from around the button.
4. Remove the spool and slide it from the hub. Be careful, because some models include a spring underneath that can fly off and easily get lost.
5. Wind new monofilament line onto the old spool or replace with a prewound spool. If your yard trimmer has blades instead, check them for damage and replace as needed.
6. Insert the end of the line through the spool hole and wind the line in the direction of the arrow.
7. Reinstall the spool and test the unit.

> **Caution**
>
> Some yard trimmers come with or have been retrofitted by the owner with plastic blades replacing the monofilament line and heads. Make sure that the blades are firmly attached and in good condition before operation. Getting hit with a chunk of plastic will hurt more than with a mono line.

# Fix-It Resources

*Fix Everything!* showed you how to diagnose and fix every *thing* in your household. The *Fix-It Guides* offered step-by-step instructions for fixing and maintaining hundreds of the most common household items. This section offers additional resources—parts and service suppliers, books, magazines, manuals, and recycling info—to make sure you can fix what's broken and keep everything you own useful longer.

## Parts

You can find many parts for household things at your local hardware store or home center. If you haven't already done so, spend an hour wandering the aisles. You'll find replacement parts and useful tools for most repair jobs. In addition, you can contact the following sources of original, replacement, and used parts for virtually everything in your household.

### Original Part Sources

Need replacement parts? The original equipment manufacturer (OEM) probably has them. Here's where to start:

**Absocold Corporation**
P.O. Box 1545
Richmond, IN 47375
Phone: 1-800-843-3714
Fax: 765-935-3450
E-mail: absocold@absocold.com
Website: www.absocold.com

**Admiral**—see **Maytag**

**AGA Ranges**
100 Woodcrest Road
Cherry Hill, NJ 08003
Phone: 1-800-633-9200
E-mail: support@aga-ranges.com
Website: www.aga-ranges.com

**Amana (Maytag Brand)**
Maytag Appliances
One Dependability Square
Newton, IA 50208
Phone: 1-800-688-9900

**Anaheim Manufacturing Corporation**
P.O. Box 4146
Anaheim, CA 92803
Phone: 1-800-854-3229
Fax: 1-800-454-4406
E-mail: cs@anaheimmfg.com
Website: www.anaheimmfg.com

**Anolon**
Meyer Consumer Relations Department
One Meyer Plaza
Vallejo, CA 94590
Phone: 1-800-326-3933
Fax: 707-551-2953
E-mail: karen@anolon.com
Website: www.anolon.com

**Appliances International**
2807 Antigua Drive
Burbank, CA 91504
Phone: 1-888-423-6349
Fax: 1-800-953-9847
E-mail: info@appliancesint.com
Website: www.appliancesint.com

**Asko USA**
AM Appliance Group
P.O. Box 851805
Richardson, TX 75085
Phone: 1-800-898-1879
Website: www.askousa.com

**Bionaire**
The Holmes Group, Inc.
32B Spur Drive
El Paso, TX 79906
Phone: 1-800-253-2764
E-mail: bionaireservice@theholmesgroup.com
Website: www.bionaire.com

**Black and Decker**
Consumer Service Center
626 Hanover Pike
Hampstead, MD 21074
Phone: 1-800-544-6986
Website: www.blackanddecker.com

**Bosch Small Appliances**
5551 McFadden Avenue
Huntington Beach, CA 92649
Phone: 1-800-944-2904
Fax: 714-901-5360
Website: www.boschappliances.com

**Braun Consumer Service**
1 Gillette Park 4K-16
Boston, MA 02127-1096
Phone: 1-800-272-8611
Fax: 617-463-1625

**Broan-NuTone, LLC.**
P.O. Box 140
Hartford, WI 53027
Phone: 1-800-558-1711 (Customer Service)
Phone: 1-800-637-1453 (Technical Support)
Website: www.broan.com

**Brown Stove Works**
P.O. Box 2490
Cleveland, TN
Phone: 423-476-6544
Fax: 423-476-6599

**BSH Home Appliances Corporation**
Bosch Small Appliances
5551 McFadden Avenue
Huntington Beach, CA 92649
Phone: 1-866-44-BOSCH or 1-866-442-6724
Fax: 714-901-5360
Website: www.boschappliances.com

**Caldera Corporation**
93 Pilgrim Park
Waterbury, VT 05676
Phone: 1-800-725-7711
Fax: 1-800-962-3072
E-mail: caldera@calderacorp.com
Website: www.caldera.com

**Caloric**—see **Amana**

**Carrier Corporation Customer Relations**
P.O. Box 4808
Carrier Parkway
Syracuse, NY 13221
Phone: 1-800-227-7437
E-mail: 315-432-6620
Website: www.carrier.com

**Chambers USA**—see **Whirlpool Corporation**

**Circulon**
Meyer Consumer Relations Department
One Meyer Plaza
Vallejo, CA 94590
Phone: 1-800-326-3933
Fax: 707-551-2953
E-mail: dan@circulon.com
Website: www.circulon.com

**Compaq**
Hewlett-Packard Company
3000 Hanover Street
Palo Alto, CA 94304
See product for support telephone numbers
Website: www.compaq.com

**Conair**
150 Milford, Road
East Windsor, NJ 08520
Phone: 1-800-326-6247
E-mail: feedback@conair.com
Website: www.conair.com

## Crosley Corporation
675 North Main Street
P.O. Box 2111
Winston-Salem, NC 27102
Phone: 336-761-1212
Fax: 336-721-0685
Website: www.crosley.com

## Cuisinart
Conair Corporation
1 Cummings Point Road
Stamford, CT 06904
Phone: 1-800-726-0190
E-mail: cuisinart@conair.com
Website: www.cuisinart.com

## Dacor
1440 Bridge Gate Drive
Diamond Bar, CA 91765
Phone: 1-800-793-0093
Fax: 626-441-9632
Website: www.dacor.com

## Dell
Dell Computer Corporation
One Dell Way
Round Rock, Texas 78682
Phone: 1-800-WWW-DELL
Website: www.dell.com

## Dynamic Cooking System
5800 Skylab Road
Huntington Beach, CA 92647
Phone: 1-800-433-8466
E-mail: service@dcsappliances.com
Website: www.dcsappliances.com

## Dynasty Ranges (Maytag brand)
Jade Products Company
7355 E. Slauson Avenue
Commerce, CA 90040
Phone: 1-888-4MAYTAG
Website: www.dynastrange.com

## Electrolux
White Consolidated Industries, Inc.
P.O. Box 35920
Cleveland, OH 44135
Phone: 216-898-1800
Fax: 216-898-2366
Website: www.electrolux.com

## Elkay Sales, Inc.
2222 Camden Court
Oak Brook, IL 60523
Phone: 1-800-574-8484
Fax: 630-574-5012
Website: www.elkay.com

## Emerson Appliances
P.O. Box 4100
8000 West Florissant Avenue
St. Louis, Missouri 63136-8506
Phone: 314-553-2000
E-mail: contact@emersonhometechnologies.com
Website: www.emersonhometechnologies.com

## Emerson Quiet Kool (Fedders)
Fedders Corporate Center
505 Martinsville Road
P.O. Box 813
Liberty Corner, NJ 07938
Phone: 908-604-8686
Fax: 908-604-0715
E-mail: customerservice@fedders.com
Website: www.emersonquietkool.com

## Emjoi, Inc.
P.O. Box 7406
New York, NY 10150
Website: www.emjoi.com

## Equator Corporation
Equator Plaza
10067 Timber Oak Drive
Houston, TX 77080
Phone: 1-800-935-1955
Fax: 713-464-2151
E-mail: sales@equatorappl.com
Website: www.equatorappl.com

**Equator Products**
1300 White Oaks Road
Campbell, CA 95008
Phone: 408-369-5200
Fax: 408-371-9106
E-mail: support@equator.com
Website: www.equator.com

**Estate**—see **Whirlpool Corporation**

**Eureka Company**
807 N. Main Street
Bloomington, IL 61701
Phone: 1-800-282-2886 (Customer Service)
Phone: 1-800-438-7352 (Replacement parts)
Website: www.eureka.com

**Fedders Corporate Center**
505 Martinsville Road
P.O. Box 813
Liberty Corner, NJ 07938
Phone: 908-604-8686
Fax: 908-604-0715
E-mail: customerservice@fedders.com
Website: www.fedders.com

**Fisher and Paykel**
22982 Alcalde Drive, Suite 100
Laguna Hills, CA 92653
Phone: 1-888-9-FNPUSA
E-mail: fnpusa@fisherpaykel.com
Website: www.fisherpaykel.com

**Friedrich**
4200 N. Pan Am Expressway
P.O. Box 1540
San Antonio, TX 78295
Phone: 210-357-4400
Website: www.friedrich.com

**Frigidaire Company**
Phone: 1-800-FRIGIDAIRE
Customer Service: 706-860-4110
Website: www.frigidaire.com

**Gaffers and Sattler**—see **Maytag**

**Gateway Computers**
14303 Gateway Place
Poway, CA 92064
Phone: 1-800-369-1409
Website: www.gateway.com

**GE Appliances**
Headquarters
Appliance Park
Louisville, KY 40225
Phone: 1-800-626-2000
E-mail: GE_AnswerCenter@appl.ge.com

**GE Monogram**—see **GE Appliances**

**GE Profile**—see **GE Appliances**

**George Foreman**
E-mail: foremangrills@saltonusa.com
Website: www.biggeorge.com

**Gibson**—see **Frigidaire Company**

**Gillette Company**
Braun Consumer Service
1 Gillette Park 4K-16
Boston, MA 02127-1096
Phone: 1-800-272-8611
Fax: 617-463-1625
Website: www.braun.com

**Glenwood**—see **Amana**

**Hamilton Beach**
234 Springs Road
Washington, NC 27889
Phone: 1-800-851-8900
Website: www.hamiltonbeach.com

**Hardwick**—see **Maytag**

**Hearth Kitchen**
Customer Service
644 Danbury Road
Wilton, CT 06897
Phone: 1-800-383-7818
Fax: 203-834-9990
E-mail: support@hearthkitchen.com
Website: www.hearthkitchen.com

**Hitachi**
1855 Dornoch Court
San Diego, CA 92154
Phone: 1-800-HITACHI
Website: www.hitachi.com

**Holmes Electric**
P.O. Box 179
Renton, WA 98055
Phone: 425-235-8000
Fax: 425-255-5941
Website: www.holmes.com

**HoMedics Inc.**
Consumer Service
3000 Pontiac Trail
Commerce Township, MI 48390
Phone: 1-800-HOMEDICS
Website: www.homedics.com

**Hotpoint**—see **GE Appliances**

**IBM Corporation**
1133 Westchester Avenue
White Plains, New York 10604
Website: www.ibm.com

**Interactive Health**
3030 Walnut Avenue
Long Beach, CA 90807
Phone: 1-800-742-5493
Website: www.interactivehealth.com

**Interplak**—see **Conair**

**JennAir**
Maytag Customer Service
240 Edwards Street
Cleveland, TN 37311
Phone: 1-800-688-1100
Website: www.jennair.com

**Jiffy Steamer**
P.O. Box 869
Union City, TN 38261
Phone: 1-800-525-4339
Fax: 731-885-6692
Website: www.jiffysteamer.com

**JVC America**
Website: www.jvc.com

**Kelvinator**—see **Frigidaire Company**

**Kenmore** (Sears brand)
Phone: (Sears Parts) 1-800-366-part
Website: www.kenmore.com

**King Refrigerator Corporation**
76-02 Woodhaven Boulevard
Glendale, NY 11385
Phone: 1-800-845-KING
Fax: 718-830-9440

**Kitchen Aid Customer Satisfaction Center**
P.O. Box 218
St. Joseph, MI 49085
Phone: 1-800-422-1230
Website: www.kitchenaid.com

**Klondike Country Refrigerators**
Klondike Case Company
1610 Arbor Road
Paso Robles, CA 93446
Phone: 805-239-0222
Website: www.klondikerf.com

**Krups North America Inc.**
P.O. Box 3900
Peoria, IL 61614
Phone: 1-800-526-5377
Website: www.krups.com

**L'Equip**
555 Bosler Avenue
Lemoyne, PA 17043
Phone: 1-800-816-6811
Fax: 717-730-7200
E-mail: custserv@lequip.com
Website: www.lequip.com

**LiftMaster**
Phone: 1-800-528-5880
Website:www.liftmaster.com

**Mac-Gray**
22 Water Street
Cambridge, MA 02141
Phone: 1-800-MAC-Gray
Website: www.mac-gray.com

**Magic Chef**—see **Maytag**

**Malber USA**
64 Commercial Avenue
Garden City, NY 11530
Website: www.malberusa.com

**Manttra Inc.**
5721 Bayside Road, Suite J
Virginia Beach, VA 23455
Phone: 757-318-4603
Fax: 757-318-7604
Website: www.manttra.com

**Marvel Industries**
P.O. Box 997
Richmond, IN 47375
Phone: 1-800-962-2521
Fax: 765-962-2493
E-mail: marvel@marvelindustries.com
Website: www.marvelindustries.com

**Maytag Appliances**
One Dependability Square
Newton, IA 50208
Phone: 1-800-688-9900

**McClary**—see **Maytag**

**Miele, Inc.**
9 Independence Way
Princeton, NJ 08540
Phone: 1-800-843-7231
Fax: 609-419-9898
E-mail: moreinfo@mieleusa.com
Website: www.mieleusa.com

**Modern Maid**—see **Amana**

**Monogram**—see **GE Appliances**

**Mr. Coffee**
Sunbeam Products
P.O. Box 948389
Maitland, Florida 32794-8389
Phone: 1-800-MRCOFFEE
Website: www.mrcoffee.com

**Nesco/American Harvest**
P.O. Box 237
1700 Monroe Street
Two Rivers, WI 54241
Phone: 1-800-288-4545
Website: www.nesco.com

**Nintendo of America**
P.O. Box 957
Redmond, WA 98073
Phone: 1-800-255-3700
Website: www.nintendo.com

**Nokia**
Phone: 1-800-NOKIA-2U
Website: www.nokia.com

**Norcold**
7101 Jackson Road
Ann Arbor, MI 48103
Phone: 1-800-543-1219
Website: www.norcold.com

**Norelco Consumer Products Company**
1010 Washington Boulevard
P.O. Box 120015
Phone: 1-800-243-3050
Fax: 203-351-5717
Stamford, CT 06912
Website: www.norelco.com

**Norge**—see **Maytag**

**Northland Kitchen Appliance**
P.O. Box 400
Greenville, MI 48838
Phone: 1-800-223-3900
Fax: 616-754-0970
Website: www.northlandnka.com

**NuTone Inc.**
4820 Red Bank Road
Cincinnati, OH 45227
Phone: 1-888-336-3948 for Customer Service
Phone: 1-888-336-6151 for Technical Support
E-mail: www.webmaster@NuTone.com
Website: www.nutone.com

**OASIS Corporation**
265 North Hamilton Road
Columbus, Ohio 43213
Phone: 1-800-64-OASIS
Website: www.oasiswatercoolers.com

**O'Keefe and Merrit**—see **Frigidaire Company**

**Oster**
See Sunbeam Products
Website: www.oster.com

**Panasonic**
Phone: 1-800-211-7262
E-mail: consumerproducts@panasonic.com
Website: www.panasonic.com

**Peerless-Premier Appliance Company**
119 South 14th Street
P.O. Box 387
Belleville, IL 62222
Phone: 1-800-858-5844
Fax: 618-235-1771
E-mail: info@premierrange.com
Website: www.premierrange.com

**Pentax**
Website: www.pentax.com

**Proctor Silex**
234 Springs Road
Washington, NC 27889
Phone: 1-800-851-8900
Website: www.proctorsilex.com

**Quasar**
1911 Northfield Drive
Rochester Hills, MI 48309
Phone: 248-852-0300
Website: www.quasar.com

**Quietline Laundry System**
FJS Distributors, Inc.
1735 Miller Trunk Highway
Duluth, MN 55811
Phone: 218-727-1181
E-mail: quietline@quietline.com
Website: www.quietline.com

**Radio Shack**
300 West Third Street, Suite 1400
Fort Worth, Texas 76102
Website: www.radioshack.com

**RCA**—see **GE Appliances**

**Regina Vacuums**
21180 Johnson Road
Long Beach, MS 39560
Phone: 1-800-847-8336
Website: www.reginavac.com

**Roper**
See Whirlpool Corporation
Phone: 1-800-447-6737
E-mail: Whirlpool_CIC@email.whirlpool.com
Website: www.roperappliances.com

**Sanyo**
Phone: 1-800-421-5013
Website: www.sanyo.com

**Sharp Electronics Corporation**
Sharp Plaza
Mahwah, NJ 07430
Phone: 1-800-BE-SHARP
Website: www.sharp-usa.com

**Sinkmaster**—see **Anaheim Manufacturing Corporation**

**Sony**
Phone: 1-888-476-6972
Website: www.sony.com

**Staber Industries**
4800 Homer Ohio Lane
Groveport, OH 43125
Phone: 1-800-848-6200
E-mail: support@staber.com
Website: www.staber.com

**Steam Fast**
400 NW Platte Valley Drive
Riverside, MO 64150
Phone: 1-800-711-6617
Fax: 816-584-9066
Website: www.steamfast.com

**SubZero Freezer Company**
P.O. Box 44130
Phone: 1-800-222-7820
E-mail: customerservice@subzero.com
Website: www.subzero.com

**Summit**
770 Garrison Avenue
Bronx, NY 10474
Phone: 1-800-932-4267
Fax: 718-842-3093
Website: www.summitappliance.com

**Sunbeam Products**
P.O. Box 948389
Maitland, Florida 32794-8389
Website: www.sunbeam.com

**SunFrost**
P.O. Box 1101
Arcata, CA 95518
Phone: 707 822 9095
Fax: 707-822-6213
Website: www.sunfrost.com

**Tappan**—see **Frigidaire Company**

**Thermador**
5551 McFadden Avenue
Huntington Beach, CA 92649
Phone: 1-800-656-9226
Website: www.thermador.com

**Thetford**
7101 Jackson Road
Ann Arbor, MI 48103
Phone: 1-800-521-3032
Fax: 734-769-2023

**Thor Appliances**
268 Avenida Montalvo
San Clemente, CA 92672
Phone: 1-877-877-0540
Fax: 1-877-877-0530
E-mail: info@thorappliances.com
Website: www.thorappliances.com

**Tilia, Inc.**
P.O. Box 194530
San Francisco, CA 94119
Phone: 1-800-777-5452
Fax: 415-896-6469
E-mail: customerservice@tilia.com
Website: www.tilia.com

**Toshiba**
Phone: 1-800-631-3811
Website: www.toshiba.com

**Traulsen and Company, Inc.**
4401 Blue Mound Road
Fort Worth, TX 76106
Phone: 1-800-825-8220
Fax: 817-624-4302
E-mail: webmaster@traulsen.com
Website: www.traulsen.com

**U-line Corporation**
P.O. Box 245040
Milwaukee, WI 53224
Phone: 414-354-0300
Fax: 414-354-0349
E-mail: PatU@u-line.com
Website: www.u-line.com

**Vent a Hood**
P.O. Box 830426
Richardson, TX 75083
Phone: 972-235-5201
E-mail: customer_service@ventahood.com
Website: www.ventahood.com

**Vesta**—see **Frigidaire Company**

**Viking Range Corporation**
111 Front Street
Greenwood, MS 38930
Phone: 1-888-VIKING1, then press 1
Website: www.vikingrange.com

**VitaMix Corporation**
Household Division
8615 Usher Road
Cleveland, OH 44138
Phone: 1-800-848-2649
Fax: 440-235-3726
E-mail: household@vitamix.com, service@
vitamix.com
Website: www.vitamix.com

**Wahl Clipper Corporation**
2900 Locust Street
Sterling, IL 61081
Phone: 815-625-6525
Website: www.wahl.com

**Waste King**—see **Anaheim Manufacturing
Corporation**

**W.C. Wood Freezer Corporation**
677 Woodland Drive
P.O. Box 310
Ottawa, OH 45875
Phone: 1-800-523-0075
E-mail: usmarketing@wcwood.com
Website: www.wcwood.com

**Wearever**
Mirro Company
1512 Washington Street
Manitowoc, WI 54220
Phone: 1-800-527-7727
Website: www.wearever.com

**Weber**
200 East Daniels Road
Palatine, IL 60067
Phone: 1-800-446-1071
Fax: 847-407-8900
E-mail: support@weberstephen.com
Website: www.weber.com

**West Bend Company**
P.O. Box 2780
West Bend, WI 53095
Phone: 262-334-6949
Website: www.westbend.com

**Whirlaway**—see **Anaheim Manufacturing
Corporation**

**Whirlpool Corporation**
Benton Harbor Div.
151 N. Riverview Drive
Benton Harbor, MI 49002
Phone: 1-800-253-1301
E-mail: infor@whirlpool.com
Website: www.whirlpool.com

**White-Westinghouse**—see **Frigidaire
Company**

**Wolf Range**
19600 S. Alameda Street
Compton, CA 90221
Phone: 1-800-366-WOLF
Fax: 310-637-7931
Website: www.wolfrange.com

Do you need to find another home appliance manufacturer? Try:

**Association of Home Appliance
Manufacturers**
Suite 402
1111 19th Street, Northwest
Washington, DC 20036
Phone: 202-872-5955
Fax: 202-872-9354
Website: www.aham.org

## Replacement Part Sources

You can find numerous generic replacement parts at larger hardware stores and home centers. If you don't find what you need, try these resources:

**A-1 Appliance Repair**
2407 Triana Boulevard
Huntsville, AL 35805
Phone: 1-800-841-0312
E-mail: parts@a-1appliance.com
Website: www.a-1appliance.com

**Affordable Appliance Parts**
Phone: 570-622-6441
E-mail: sales@affordableappliance.com
Website: www.affordableappliance.com

**All Appliance Parts**
Phone: 972-241-9455
Website: www.allapplianceparts.com

**BestBuy**
Customer Care
P.O. Box 9312
Minneapolis, MN 55440
Phone: 1-888-BESTBUY (1-800-237-8289)
Website: www.bestbuy.com

**Factory Services, Inc.**
85 Willis Avenue
Mineola, NY 11501
Phone: 1-800-237-8699
Fax: 1-800-733-7838
E-mail: sales@factoryservices.com
Website: www.factoryservices.com

**Goodman's**
13130 SW 128 Street #3
Miami, FL 33186
Phone: 1-888-333-4660
Fax: 305-278-1884
E-mail: sales@goodmans.net
Website: www.goodmans.net

**Home Depot**
2455 Paces Ferry Road
Atlanta, GA 30339
Phone, Online: 1-800-430-3376
Phone, U.S.A: 1-800-553-3199
Phone, Canada: 1-800-668-2266
Website: www.homedepot.com

**Jewelry Service Centers, Inc.**
6719 Chesapeake Center Drive
Glen Burnie, MD 21060
Phone: 1-877-768-6400
Fax: 410-768-3967
E-mail: info@jewelryservice.com
Website: www.jewelryservice.com

**Jewels Express**
P.O. Box 1753
Spokane, WA 99210-1753
E-mail: staff@jewelsexpress.com
Website: www.jewelsexpress.com

**Mar-Beck Appliance Parts**
Phone: 1-800-959-5656
Website: www.marbeck.com

**Parts Depot Online, Inc.**
E-mail: orders@partsdepotonline.com
Website: www.partsdepotonline.com

**Partselect.com**
Phone: 1-888-895-1535
E-mail: customerservice@partselect.com
Website: www.partselect.com

**Partsolver.com**
Phone: 1-877-62-PARTS (1-877-627-2787)
E-mail: help@partsolver.com
Website: www.partsolver.com

**Point and Click Appliance Repair**
1305 SW 77th Terrace
Oklahoma City, Oklahoma 73159
Phone: 1-877-922-2880
E-mail: comments@pcappliancerepair.com
Website: www.pcappliancerepair.com

**Quality First Discount Appliance Center**
334 Oak Street
Buffalo, NY 14203
Phone: 716-847-9800
Fax: 716-847-9822
E-mail: sales@everythingappliance.com
Website: www.everythingappliance.com

**RepairClinic.com, Inc.**
47440 Michigan Avenue, Suite 100
Canton, MI 48188-2242
Phone: 1-800-269-2609
Fax: 734-495-3150
Website: www.repairclinic.com

**Sears**
Sears National Customer Relations
3333 Beverly Road
Hoffman Estates, IL 60179
Phone: 1-800-349-4358
Website: www.sears.com

**Turnpike Appliance Service**
3945A Lawson Boulevard
Oceanside, NY 11572
Phone: 1-888-277-5776
Website: www.smallappliance.com

**Wholesale Jewelry and Accessories**
72 Main Street
Sidney, NY 13838
Phone: 1-888-563-4411
Fax: 607-563-9485
E-mail: sales@wholesalejewelry.net
Website: www.wholesalejewelry.net

## Local Part Sources

Check your local phone book for a "Brand
Name Index" which is often located just before
the yellow pages index. Also look in the yellow
pages under categories such as:

Appliances-Major-Parts and Supplies

Appliances-Small-Service and Parts

Asphalt and Asphalt Products

Computer Supplies and Parts

Drywall Equipment and Supplies

Electronic Equipment and Supplies-Retail

Hardware-Retail

Lawn Mowers-Parts and Repair

Lumber-Retail

Plumbing Fixtures Parts and Supplies-Retail

Roofing Materials

Spas and Hot Tubs-Supplies and Parts

Swimming Pool Supplies and Accessories

# Tools and Materials

Besides replacement parts, you'll need the tools
and materials to install them. You can find
many of them at your local hardware store or
home center. In addition, you can contact manufacturers directly to find out more about their
products.

## Hardware Store Chains

**Kmart Corporation**
3100 West Big Beaver Road
Troy, MI 48084-3163
Phone: 1-800-63K-MART
Website: www.kmart.com

**Lowe's Companies, Inc.**
Customer Care
P.O. Box 1111
North Wilkesboro, NC 28656
Phone: 1-800-44LOWES
Website: www.lowes.com

**Orchard Supply Hardware**
6450 Via Del Oro
San Jose, CA 95119
Phone: 408-281-3500
Website: www.osh.com

**Sears National Customer Relations**
3333 Beverly Road
Hoffman Estates, IL 60179
Phone: 1-800-349-4358
Website: www.sears.com

**Target Corporation**
1000 Nicollet Mall
Minneapolis, MN 55403
Phone: (612) 304-6073
Website: www.target.com

**TrueValue Hardware**
8600 W. Bryn Mawr Avenue
Chicago, IL 60631-3505
Phone: 773-695-5000
Website: www.truevalue.com

**Wal-Mart Stores, Inc.**
Bentonville, Arkansas 72716-8611
Phone: 1-800-WAL-MART
Website: www.walmart.com

## Cleaners and Strippers

If you have product questions not answered by local retailers, contact these manufacturers of household cleaners and strippers:

Cuprinol   216-566-3131

DAP   1-800-543-3840

Dura Seal   1-800-526-0495

Flood Co.   1-800-321-3444

Fuller O'Brien Paints   415-871-3131

Glidden Co.   1-800-984-5444

Klean-Strip   1-800-238-2672

Kurfees Coatings   502-584-0151

Miracle Sealants   1-800-350-1901

Old Masters   1-800-747-3436

Plasti-Kote Co.   1-800-431-5928

Pratt and Lambert   716-873-6000

William Zinsser and Co.   908-469-4367

## Interior and Exterior Paint

If you have product questions not answered by local retailers, contact these manufacturers of interior and exterior house paints:

3E Group   1-800-800-2844

Ace Hardware Corporation   708-990-6751

Akzo Nobel Coatings   1-800-833-7288

Benjamin Moore and Co.   201-573-9600

DAP   1-800-543-3840

Dryvit Systems   1-800-556-7752

Dutch Boy   216-566-2929

Fuller O'Brien Paints   415-871-3131

Glidden Co.   1-800-984-5444

Kurfees Coatings   502-584-0151

Martin-Senour   1-800-542-8468

Olympic Paints and Stains   1-800-621-2024

Plasti-Kote Co.   1-800-431-5928

PPG Industries   1-800-243-8774

Pratt and Lambert   716-873-6000

Sherwin-Williams Co.   1-800-336-1110

William Zinsser and Co.   908-469-4367

## Finishes and Sealers

If you have product questions not answered by local retailers, contact these manufacturers of stains, varnishes, urethanes, and other finishing and sealing products:

3E Group   1-800-800-2844

Ace Hardware Corp.   708-990-6751

Basic Coatings   1-800-247-5471

Benjamin Moore   201-573-9600

Cuprinol   216-566-3131

DAP   1-800-543-3840

Dryvit Systems   1-800-556-7752

Dura Seal   1-800-526-0495

Dutch Boy   216-566-2929

Environmental Coatings   1-800-255-3325

Flood Co.   1-800-321-3444

Fuller O'Brien Paints   415-871-3131

Geocel Corp.   1-800-348-7615

Glidden Co.   1-800-984-5444

Klean-Strip   1-800-238-2672

Kurfees Coatings   502-584-0151

Macklanburg-Duncan   1-800-654-0007

Martin-Senour   1-800-542-8468

Minwax Co.    1-800-526-0495

Miracle Sealants
and Abrasives    1-800-350-1901

Old Masters    1-800-747-3436

Olympic Paints and Stains    1-800-621-2024

Penofin Performance
Coatings    1-800-736-6346

Plasti-Kote Co.    1-800-431-5928

PPG Industries    1-800-243-8774

Pratt and Lambert    716-873-6000

Saver Systems    1-800-860-6327

Sherwin-Williams Co.    1-800-336-1110

Thompson-Minwax    1-800-526-0495

Thoro Systems    1-800-327-1570

William Zinsser and Co.    908-469-4367

Wolman Wood Care
Products    602-460-5343

# Service

Is it defective? Is it under warranty? Would you prefer to take it to an authorized service center or a local repair shop than fix it yourself?

## Consumer Affairs

Having a problem with something you bought? Call the manufacturer's consumer affairs department directly to find out what options you have. If you don't see the number here, check the list under *Original Part Sources* (above).

Admiral    1-800-255-2370

Amana    1-800-843-0304

Caloric    1-800-843-0304

Chambers    1-800-445-8120

Frigidaire    1-800-451-7007

Gaffers and Sattler    1-800-255-2370

GE    1-800-626-2000

Gibson    1-800-458-1445

Hardwick    1-800-255-2370

Hotpoint    1-800-626-2000

KitchenAid    1-800-445-8120

Magic Chef    1-800-255-2370

Maytag    1-800-255-2370

Norge    1-800-255-2370

O'Keefe and Merritt    1-800-451-7007

RCA    1-800-626-2000

Roper    1-800-253-1301

Speed Queen    1-800-843-0304

Tappan    1-800-451-7007

Vesta    1-800-245-0600

Whirlpool    1-800-253-1301, 1-800-445-8120

White-Westinghouse    1-800-245-0600

## Authorized and Warranty Service

The first place to check for in-warranty service is with the manufacturer. Many websites have links to find a dealer or authorized service center wherever you live. Also contact the retailer that originally sold the item. If you don't get good results, go online to www.appliance411.com for information on warranty service companies in your area. In addition, you can contact the Consumer Product Safety Commission (CPSC) at 1-800-638-2772 or online at www.cpsc.gov.

## Independent Repair Shops

Need someone local to fix something for you? Fortunately, they may be as near as your telephone. Check your area phone book under categories like these:

Alterations-Clothing

Antiques-Repairing and Restoring

Appliances-Major-Dealers and Service

Appliances-Small-Service and Parts

Bathtub and Sinks-Repairing and Refinishing

Blinds-Repair and Cleaning

Boiler Repairing and Cleaning

Brick Cleaning

Building Contractors

Chimney and Fireplace Cleaning and Repairing

Clocks-Service and Repair

Computer Service and Repair

Dishwashing Machines-Dealers and Service

Doors-Repairing

Drapery Cleaners

Dry Wall Contractors

Electric Contractors

Electric Equipment-Service and Repair

Electric Motors-Repairing

Electronic Equipment and Supplies-Service and Repair

Engines-Gasoline

Engines-Rebuilding and Exchanging

Flooring and Floor Covering Contractors

Furnaces-Heating-Sales and Service

Furniture Repair and Refinishing

Garage Doors and Door Operating Devices

Gutters and Downspouts

Heaters-Sales and Service

Heating and Ventilating Contractors

Home Repair and Maintenance

Jewelry Repairing

Lawn Mowers-Parts and Repair

Masonry Contractors

Painting Contractors

Paving Contractors

Photographic Equipment-Repairing

Plastering Contractors

Plumbing Contractors

Plumbing Drains and Sewer Cleaning

Remodeling Contractors

Roofing Contractors

Roofing Maintenance

Shoe Repair

Software and CD-ROM Sales and Service

Spas and Hot Tubs-Service and Repair

Stereo-Dealers and Service

Stucco and Coating Contractors

Swimming Pool Service and Repair

Television Dealers and Service

Wall Covering-Contractors

Water Heaters-Repairing

## More Help

You have more options. There are thousands of additional resources available to you for fixing anything in your household. They include other books, magazines, repair manuals, owner's manuals, booklets, online resources, television programs, retailers, and numerous experts.

### Books

Hundreds of books have been published on various aspects of household repair. Check your local bookstore or online at www.FixItBookClub. com for these and other practical titles:

*101 Quick Fixes In and Around Your Home.* San Diego, Calif.: Thunder Bay Press, 2001.

*1001 Do-It-Yourself Hints and Tips.* Pleasantville, N.Y.: Reader's Digest Assoc., 1998.

*1001 Do-It-Yourself Tips.* Des Moines, Iowa.: Better Homes and Gardens Books, 1995.

*2500 Great Hints and Smart Tips from the Pros.* Pleasantville, N.Y.: Reader's Digest Assoc., 2000.

*Ask the Experts.* Pleasantville, N.Y.: Reader's Digest Assoc., 2000.

*Basic Home Repairs.* Menlo Park, Calif.: Sunset Publishing, 1995.

*Basic Wiring.* Menlo Park, Calif.: Sunset Publishing, 1995.

Becker, Norman. *The Complete Book of Home Inspection.* New York: McGraw-Hill, 2002.

*Best Buys for Your Home.* Yonkers, N.Y.: Consumers Union of United States, 2001.

Best, Don. *The Do-It-Yourself Guide to Home Emergencies.* Pleasantville, N.Y.: Reader's Digest Assoc., 1996.

Caprio, Dennis. *Appliance Repair.* Reston, Va.: Reston Publishing, 1980.

Ching, Francis D. K., and Cassandra Adams. *Building Construction Illustrated.* New York: John Wiley and Sons, 2001.

*Complete Fix-It.* Alexandria, Va.: Time-Life Books, 2000.

*The Complete Guide to Home Carpentry.* Minnetonka, Minn.: Creative Publishing International, 2000.

*The Complete Guide to Home Wiring.* Minnetonka, MN.: Creative Publishing International, 2001.

*Complete Home Wiring.* Menlo Park, Calif.: Sunset Books, 2000.

*The Complete Photo Guide to Home Improvement.* Minnetonka, Minn.: Creative Publishing International, 2001.

*Do-It-Yourself Flooring.* Menlo Park, Calif.: Lane Publishing, 1982.

*Floors and Stairways.* Alexandria, Va.: Time-Life Books, 1995.

*Home Improvement 1-2-3.* Des Moines, Iowa.: Homer TLC, 1995.

*Interior Home Improvement Costs.* Kingston, Mass.: RS Means, 2002.

*Kitchens.* Alexandria, Va.: Time-Life Books, 1994.

Lipinski, Edward R. *Home Repair Almanac.* New York.: Lebhar-Friedman Books, 1999.

Macaulay, David. *New Way Things Work.* Boston, Mass.: Houghton Mifflin, 1998.

Marken, Bill. *How to Fix Just About Everything.* San Francisco: Weldon Owen, 2002.

Miller, Mark R., Rex Miller, and Glen E. Baker. *Carpentry and Construction.* New York: McGraw-Hill, 1999.

*New Complete Guide to Home Repair and Improvement.* Des Moines, Iowa: Meredith, 1997.

*New Complete Home Repair Manual.* Lincolnwood, Ill.: Publications International, Ltd., 1996.

*New Fix-It-Yourself Manual.* Pleasantville, N.Y.: Reader's Digest Assoc., 1996.

Peterson, Franklynn. *How to Fix Damn Near Everything.* New York: Wings Books, 1977.

*Plumbing Essentials.* Minnetonka, Minn.: Creative Publishing, 1996.

*Popular Mechanic's Home How-to.* New York: Hearst, 1986.

Preston, Martin. *KISS Guide to Home Improvement.* New York: DK Publishing, 2001.

*Skills and Tools.* Pleasantville, N.Y.: Reader's Digest Assoc., 1993.

Ramsey, Dan. *The Complete Idiot's Guide to Building Your Own Home.* Indianapolis, Ind.: Alpha Books, 2002.

———. *The Complete Idiot's Guide to Car Care and Repair Illustrated.* Indianapolis, Ind.: Alpha Books, 2002.

———. *Small Appliance Repair Made Easy.* Lincolnwood, Ill.: Publications International, 1995.

———. *Small Engine Repair Made Easy.* Lincolnwood, Ill.: Publications International, 1995.

———. *Tile Floors.* Blue Ridge Summit, Pa.: Tab Books, 1991.

*Step-By-Step Wiring.* Des Moines, Iowa.: Better Homes and Gardens Books, 1997.

Tenenbaum, David J. *The Complete Idiot's Guide to Trouble-Free Home Repair.* Indianapolis, Ind.: Alpha Books, 1999.

*Tools and Techniques.* Minnetonka, Minn.: Handyman Club of America, 1998.

*The Ultimate Guide to Repairs, Improvements, and Maintenance.* Upper Saddle River, N.J.: Creative Homeowner, 2000.

Vandervort, Don. *How Your House Works.* New York: Gramercy Books, 1995.

Vila, Bob, and Howard, Hugh. *Bob Vila's Complete Guide to Remodeling Your Home.* New York: Avon, 1999.

Walker, Frank R. *F. R. Walker's Remodeling Reference Book.* Lisle, Ill.: Frank R. Walker, 1998.

Wing, Charlie. *The Big Book of Small Household Repairs.* Pleasantville, N.Y.: Reader's Digest Assoc., 1995.

———. *The Visual Handbook of Building and Remodeling.* Pleasantville, N.Y.: Reader's Digest Assoc., 1990.

*Wiring 1-2-3.* Des Moines, Iowa: Meredith Books, 2000.

*Wiring Basics.* Des Moines, Iowa: Meredith Books, 2000.

Woodbury, Raymond O. *Secrets of Appliance Repairmen.* Kearney, Nebr.: Morris Publishing, 2001.

*Working with Tile.* Menlo Park, Calif.: Sunset Publishing, 1995.

Young, Richard A., and Thomas J. Glover. *Handyman In-Your-Pocket.* Littleton, Colo.: Sequoia Publishing, 2002.

In addition, two complete series of books are available to the do-it-yourselfer:

Chilton Automotive Books. Available at www.chiltonsonline.com. Chilton publishes books for most makes, models, and years.

Home Repair and Improvement Series. Alexandria, Va.: Time-Life Books. Available at www.timelife.com. Time-Life publishes numerous sets of practical homeowner how-to books.

## Magazines

You can learn more about fixing things by subscribing to these and other periodicals aimed at the home do-it-yourselfer. Check your local newsstand for current copies and subscription cards.

*Better Homes and Gardens*
Website: www.bhg.com

*Family Handyman Magazine*
Website: www.familyhandyman.com

*Good Housekeeping*
Website: www.hearstmags.com/goodhouse.htm

*Old House Journal Magazine*
Website: www.oldhousejournal.com

*Popular Mechanics*
Website: www.popularmechanics.com

*This Old House* (combines *Today's Homeowner*)
Website: www.thisoldhouse.com

*Workbench Magazine*
Website: www.workbenchmagazine.com

## Owner's Manuals

You can check with any manufacturer to request and get a repair manual for your appliances, or other things. Many manufacturers offer copies of current product manuals online through their website. Refer to the *Original Part Sources* or *Consumer Affairs* listings.

## Repair Manuals

Need a general repair manual? Check with larger bookstores or contact one of these online resources:

www.appliancerepair.net

www.camerabooks.com

www.dreamscape.com

www.gearheadcafe.com

www.livemanuals.com

## How-to Booklets

Check your local home improvement center for a rack of informational pamphlets on do-it-yourself home repairs. One handy series is published by Creative Homeowner (www.ch-publisher.com) and includes nearly 100 pamphlets on specific jobs such as wiring three-way switches, repairing concrete, and hooking up video systems.

## Online Resources

Looking for a specific product's owner's manual or other technical information? Check online. Use one of the search larger engines (www.google.com, www.yahoo.com, etc.), entering the manufacturer's name and even a model number. In addition, try these online resources:

www.411homeimprovement.com

www.acmehowto.com

www.allabouthome.com

www.alude.com

www.amazon.com

www.appliance411.com

www.appliancestuff.com

www.b4ubuild.com

www.bobvila.com

www.buildfind.com

www.diynet.com

www.diynot.com

www.doityourself.com

www.ebay.com

www.fixer.com

www.fixitbookclub.com

www.fixitclub.com

www.friendlyplumber.com

www.growinglifestyle.com

www.handymanwire.com

www.hearth.com

www.hgtv.com

www.homecenter.com

www.homedepot.com

www.homeideas.com

www.homerepair.com

www.homeresearcher.com

www.hometime.com

www.howstuffworks.com

www.how-to-repair-clocks.com

www.insidespaces.com

www.momshelpmoms.com

www.msbuilder.com

www.naturalhandyman.com

www.remodelonline.com

www.repairfaq.org

www.repair-home.com

www.resourcecentral.com

www.thisoldappliance.com

www.toiletology.com

www.wrenchead.com

## Television Programs

Numerous television programs offer help to the do-it-yourselfer. In fact, whole networks of channels are dedicated to helping you fix things. Check local cable or your satellite guide for specific information. You also can check online:

www.diynet.com

www.hgtv.com

www.hometime.com

www.tlc.discovery.com

## Experts

Need an expert to help you troubleshoot and fix something? Besides the resources listed previously, check local newspaper classifieds, shopper publications, and bulletin boards for ads and business cards. You also can check online at www.ask.com.

# Recycling

If it's just plain broken, you still can find places that can use the parts for repairing other things, or people who will recycle them. Check your local phone book for recycling. Refer to *Fix Everything: What Can You Recycle?* for guidelines. Online, check www.recycle.net and www.geappliances.com/geac/donations.

## Charities

If you *can* fix it, but just don't want to keep it, consider donating it to a charity. Remember, don't give it something that you wouldn't give to a friend. Check Social Services Organizations in your local yellow pages. Here are a few:

**American Council for the Blind**
1-800-866-3242
Website: www.acb.org

**Deseret Industries**
Check local telephone listings in seven western states; affiliated with the Mormon Church.

**Dorcas Society**
Check local telephone listings; affiliated with the Seventh-Day Adventist Church.
Website: www.dorcas.net

**Goodwill**
Check local telephone listings.
Website: www.goodwill.org

**Salvation Army**
1-800-95-TRUCK
www1.salvationarmy.org

**St. Vincent de Paul**
Check local telephone listings; affiliated with the Roman Catholic Church.
Phone: 314-576-3993
Website: www.svdpusa.com

Your local church, synagogue, mosque, ashram, or other spiritual organization

Your local senior center, youth center, or other community organization

## Sharing Parts

Have some working parts left over that you don't need? Do a good turn by giving them to a repair shop. You won't get cash or a tax receipt, but you will know that it's in a better home than a landfill.

Also remember that you can set aside good motors and controls from otherwise bad appliances for future use in your new Fix-It Workshop. Old clothing can be reused as shop rags. Tired toothbrushes can be used for cleaning parts. You get the idea.

## Dust to Dust

If you still can't fix it—or it's not worth paying for repair—recycle it. Check your local phone book under "recycling" and "scrap metal" to see if anyplace local will take your unfixable appliances, furniture, clothing, electronics, and other household items. Also refer to *Fix Everything: How to Recycle Everything*.

# Fix-It Club Notebook

| Fix-It Job: | Shopping List |
|---|---|
| | **Shopping List** |
| | Parts: |
| What's wrong with it? | |
| About how much time will it take to fix it? | |
| On what pages are the Fix-It Steps? | Tools: |
| Disassembly/assembly notes and diagrams: | |

Fix-It Job:

What's wrong with it?

About how much time will it take to fix it?

On what pages are the Fix-It Steps?

Disassembly/assembly notes and diagrams:

**Shopping List**

Parts:

Tools:

| Fix-It Job: | **Shopping List** |
|---|---|
| | Parts: |
| What's wrong with it? | |
| About how much time will it take to fix it? | |
| On what pages are the Fix-It Steps? | |
| | Tools: |
| Disassembly/assembly notes and diagrams: | |

| Fix-It Job: | **Shopping List** |
|---|---|
| | Parts: |
| **What's wrong with it?** | |
| **About how much time will it take to fix it?** | |
| **On what pages are the Fix-It Steps?** | |
| | Tools: |
| **Disassembly/assembly notes and diagrams:** | |

| Fix-It Job: | **Shopping List** |
|---|---|
| | Parts: |
| What's wrong with it? | |
| About how much time will it take to fix it? | |
| On what pages are the Fix-It Steps? | Tools: |
| Disassembly/assembly notes and diagrams: | |

| Fix-It Job: | **Shopping List** |
|---|---|
| | Parts: |
| What's wrong with it? | |
| About how much time will it take to fix it? | |
| On what pages are the Fix-It Steps? | |
| Disassembly/assembly notes and diagrams: | Tools: |

| Fix-It Job: | **Shopping List** |
|---|---|
| | Parts: |
| What's wrong with it? | |
| About how much time will it take to fix it? | |
| On what pages are the Fix-It Steps? | Tools: |
| Disassembly/assembly notes and diagrams: | |

| Fix-It Job: | **Shopping List** |
| --- | --- |
| | Parts: |
| What's wrong with it? | |
| About how much time will it take to fix it? | |
| On what pages are the Fix-It Steps? | |
| | Tools: |
| Disassembly/assembly notes and diagrams: | |

| Fix-It Job: | **Shopping List** |
|---|---|
| | Parts: |
| What's wrong with it? | |
| About how much time will it take to fix it? | |
| On what pages are the Fix-It Steps? | Tools: |
| Disassembly/assembly notes and diagrams: | |

Fix-It Job:

What's wrong with it?

About how much time will it take to fix it?

On what pages are the Fix-It Steps?

Disassembly/assembly notes and diagrams:

**Shopping List**

Parts:

Tools:

| Fix-It Job: | **Shopping List** |
|---|---|
| | Parts: |
| What's wrong with it? | |
| About how much time will it take to fix it? | |
| On what pages are the Fix-It Steps? | Tools: |
| Disassembly/assembly notes and diagrams: | |

| Fix-It Job: | Shopping List |
|---|---|
| | Parts: |
| What's wrong with it? | |
| About how much time will it take to fix it? | |
| On what pages are the Fix-It Steps? | |
| | Tools: |
| Disassembly/assembly notes and diagrams: | |

Fix-It Job:

What's wrong with it?

About how much time will it take to fix it?

On what pages are the Fix-It Steps?

Disassembly/assembly notes and diagrams:

**Shopping List**

Parts:

Tools:

| Fix-It Job: | Shopping List |
| --- | --- |
| | Parts: |
| What's wrong with it? | |
| About how much time will it take to fix it? | |
| On what pages are the Fix-It Steps? | |
| Disassembly/assembly notes and diagrams: | Tools: |

Fix-It Job:

What's wrong with it?

About how much time will it take to fix it?

On what pages are the Fix-It Steps?

Disassembly/assembly notes and diagrams:

**Shopping List**

Parts:

Tools:

Fix-It Job:

What's wrong with it?

About how much time will it take to fix it?

On what pages are the Fix-It Steps?

Disassembly/assembly notes and diagrams:

**Shopping List**

Parts:

Tools:

| Fix-It Job: | **Shopping List** |
|---|---|
| | Parts: |
| **What's wrong with it?** | |
| **About how much time will it take to fix it?** | |
| **On what pages are the Fix-It Steps?** | Tools: |
| **Disassembly/assembly notes and diagrams:** | |

| Fix-It Job: | **Shopping List** |
|---|---|
| | Parts: |
| What's wrong with it? | |
| About how much time will it take to fix it? | |
| On what pages are the Fix-It Steps? | Tools: |
| Disassembly/assembly notes and diagrams: | |

# Index

## X–Y–Z